PHILIP W. LOWN INSTITUTE
OF ADVANCED JUDAIC STUDIES
BRANDEIS UNIVERSITY

Studies and Texts: Volume IV

JEWISH MEDIEVAL AND RENAISSANCE STUDIES

EDITED BY
Alexander Altmann

HARVARD UNIVERSITY PRESS
Cambridge, Massachusetts · 1967

Distributed in Great Britain
by Oxford University Press, London
Library of Congress Catalog Card Number 67-13250
Printed in the United States of America

Preface

The twelve studies collected in this volume represent, for the most part, papers read at the Research Colloquia of the Philip W. Lown Institute of Advanced Judaic Studies at Brandeis University during the academic year 1963–64. The general title of that year's sessions, "Jewish Medieval and Renaissance Studies," has been retained as the most fitting description of the book. Although of the twelve subjects published here only one deals with a Renaissance theme ("The Rise of Art Music in the Italian Ghetto"), the scale on which it is treated would seem to justify the *largesse* of the over-all title.

Starting from a study of the Jews in medieval Egypt and extending its vista to Jewish life in Renaissance Italy, the range of topics offered in this volume covers an important segment of Jewish history. The bulk of the papers is concerned with subjects touching the inner life of medieval Jewry. The study of "Esau as a Symbol"—a continuation, in a sense, of a series of papers contained in Volume III on the transformation of Biblical motifs—reflects the impact of the historical situation of the Jewish people upon eschatological concepts. All the remaining studies deal with topics of Jewish philosophy and mysticism, elucidating either the development of thought or the conflicts arising from the clash of ideas. The list of figures analyzed comprises Al-Muqammiṣ and Saᶜadya (representing Jewish Kalam); Isaac ibn Laṭif (who stands on the borderline of Neoplatonism and Kabbala); Maimonides (the chief spokesman of the first phase of Jewish Aristotelianism); his son Abraham and Yedaiah Bedershi (guarding the Maimonidean heritage); and, finally, Moses Narboni and Samuel ben Judah of Marseilles (who typify the advance toward radical Aristotelianism).

The reader will thus find a variety of phases of Jewish intellectual life portrayed in this volume. The transliteration of Hebrew and Arabic words, it will be noticed, does not follow one unified system. Each author was allowed the freedom of using his own.

Contents

Aspects of the Historical Background of Jewish Life in Medieval Egypt 1
NORMAN GOLB

Esau as Symbol in Early Medieval Thought 19
GERSON D. COHEN

Le Problème de l'Unité de Dieu d'après Dawūd Ibn Marwān al-Muqammiṣ 49
GEORGES VAJDA

Saadia's List of Theories of the Soul 75
HERBERT DAVIDSON

Some Non-Halakic Aspects of the *Mishneh Torah* 95
ISADORE TWERSKY

Maimonides' "Thirteen Principles" 119
ARTHUR HYMAN

Abraham Maimonides and his Pietist Circle 145
S. D. GOITEIN

Yedaiah Bedershi's *Apology* 165
A. S. HALKIN

Isaac Ibn Laṭif—Philosopher or Kabbalist? 185
SARA O. HELLER WILENSKY

Moses Narboni's "Epistle on *Shiʿur Qomā*" 225
ALEXANDER ALTMANN

Greek into Hebrew: Samuel ben Judah of Marseilles, Fourteenth-Century Philosopher and Translator 289
LAWRENCE V. BERMAN

The Rise of Art Music in the Italian Ghetto 321
ISRAEL ADLER

Indexes 367

Aspects of the Historical Background of Jewish Life in Medieval Egypt

By NORMAN GOLB

Even a cursory examination of the map of Egypt and Palestine reveals that these two countries have always had the closest topographical connection with each other and that no natural boundaries ever really divided them. Egypt itself is for the most part a long and very narrow belt of green bordering the Nile, a belt which widens in the Delta and extends, by way of the once not unfertile Sinai coast, into Palestine itself; it is as though the two countries were extensions of each other. The significance of this connection for Jewish history becomes meaningful in terms of the fact that already in Hellenistic and Roman times there were Jewish communities to be found from the very border of Palestine and thence far up the Nile. Either on the basis of archeological, literary, or papyrological evidence, the presence of Jewish communities is indicated: first, for Rafiaḥ, which was only several miles southwest of Gaza; then Ostrakine, farther westward along the coast; then Pelusium, where according to Josephus there was a garrison of Jewish soldiers; thence, proceeding south along the Pelusiac branch, perhaps Daphnae (=Tahpanhes), where Judeans were certainly settled in the time of Jeremiah (see Jeremiah 2:16 *passim*); thence, further up the Pelusiac branch (we omit here the mention of the two cities of Jewish settlement of the Phatnitic branch, Sebennytos and Athribis) and a little to the east of it, Tell el-Yahūd, near present-day el-Gheta (Ghaifah); then Tell el-Yahūdiyeh, probably the site of the temple of Onias, where numerous Jewish tombstones have been found; then, in quick succession, Heliopolis and Memphis; Arsinoë (Crocodilopolis) and numerous other settlements in the Fayyūm; Heracleopolis Magna, Oxyrhynchus, and Cynopolis; Antinoë and Hermopolis Magna; and finally, Lycopolis, Thebes, Apollinopolis Magna, and Elephantine-

Syne.[1] Insofar as most of the places above Memphis where Jewish settlements are indicated by the papyri are in almost every case also those places where other, non-Jewish, papyri have been found as well, and insofar as there are many Egyptian sites of antiquity where no papyri whatsoever have been found or which themselves have not been excavated, it is reasonable to conclude that there were Jewish communities in many cities and towns of Egypt besides the ones mentioned above. This dense Jewish settlement extending in an almost unbroken line from Gaza to Elephantine indicates not only the close connections of the Jewries of the two countries in ancient times but, more significantly, the continuous ability of the Jewish community of Palestine to replenish its sister community both demographically and spiritually as long as the Holy Land itself retained a creative Jewish population.

Contrary to the prevalent opinion of scholarship in the past century, it may now be maintained that there was just such a population in Palestine throughout the Byzantine period and up until the time of the first Crusade. This is indicated not only by the fact that the earliest documents from the Cairo Genizah (end of the tenth and beginning of the eleventh centuries) give evidence of a full communal and economic life for the Jews of Palestine and of their hegemony with respect to many Jewish communities in the Diaspora, but also by considerable earlier evidence of both a historical and literary nature. It is well known that, although suffering periods of intermittent persecution from the fourth through the sixth centuries, the Palestinian Jews were able to produce a Talmud of their own and much of the vast body of midrashic literature; furthermore, that it was they who were the chief composers of the early medieval liturgical poetry; and that the most widely accepted edition of the Hebrew text of the Bible was the work of their Masoretic scholars, who were extremely active at least between the eighth and the tenth centuries. The debates in the ninth and tenth centuries between the Babylonian and Palestinian leaders concerning the spiritual supremacy of their respective homelands were waged against the background of the genuine and often successful challenge of the Palestinian Jewry to the hegemony after which the Babylonians constantly strove. This

1. Cf. the list in V. A. Tcherikover, A. Fuks, and M. Stern, eds., *Corpus papyrorum judaicarum*, III (Cambridge, Mass., 1964), 197–209. This list, however, does not include places of settlement known from literary sources or from archeological evidence. See further J. Juster, *Les Juifs dans l'empire romain*, I (Paris, 1914), 204–207.

challenge, in turn, was the product of the continuing vitality of the Palestinian Jews over long periods of time, tempered by periodic hardships, and whetted by the consciousness of their historical priority over all the Jewries of the Diaspora.

If it is the case that Palestinian Jewry was active and populous during these periods of time, then it is most difficult to believe that—as is commonly claimed—the Jews of Egypt suffered a great decline during the Byzantine period. As in the case of Byzantine documents in general, so with documents concerning the Jews of Byzantine and early Islamic Egypt: they are extremely few in number. A paucity of documents, however, does not necessarily imply a paucity of population or of culture; it is a truism of archeological research that the better preservation of bottom layers of artifacts in no way indicates a superiority, numerical or otherwise, of the cultures they represent. Certainly in the case of the Jews of Byzantine Egypt, I do not see how it is possible to maintain that "the small number of documents . . . extending over 300 years, may serve as a good indication of the gradually declining importance of the Egyptian Jewry in . . . [this] period."[2] This interpretation, based only on papyrological evidence (or rather, the lack of it), is vitiated by a variety of important historical statements in literary and documentary sources. The most striking one, to be sure, is that which indicates that at the time of the Arab conquest of Alexandria in 641 C.E. the population of this city was six hundred thousand souls, of whom two hundred thousand were Greeks and forty thousand Jews, an additional seventy thousand Jews having fled before the arrival of the Arabs.[3] There is no reason to believe that these figures are exaggerated or distorted; the Jews living in Alexandria during the Byzantine period represented the continuation of the Jewish Diaspora in Egypt through and despite political upheavals, cultural decline and emergence, and the assimilation, both forced and voluntary, of a fair proportion of the people (compare, for example, the story of the conversion to Christianity of 375 Jews of the delta town of Tomei in 622 C.E.).[4] Were figures available for the size of the Jewish and non-Jewish populations of other cities and towns on the eve of the Arab conquest, they would probably be in consonance with those given for Alexandria.

2. *Corpus papyrorum judaicarum*, III, 88.

3. Cf. F. Wüstenfeld, *Die Statthalter von Ägypten zur Zeit der Chalifen* (Göttingen, 1875), p. 11.

4. Cf. Griveau in *Revue de l'Orient Chrétien*, 3(13):298ff. (1908).

The Hebraic and Palestinian orientation of these Egyptian Jews of the post-Roman period has already been suggested by V. A. Tcherikover,[5] who refers especially to a Hebrew letter on papyrus found in Oxyrhynchus and of undetermined date. The preserved portions of this letter read as follows "From the heads of the congregation . . . . [to] the sons of the congregation who are in M. . . . ., [to] Aginah [?] the head of the congregation . . . . and to the elders of the congregation and to . . . . the holy assembly who . . . . our prayers for your lives . . . . and for the peace of your sons and daughters [?] . . . . and . . . the commandments . . . ."[6] This and several other fragments discussed by Tcherikover all bespeak the renewed, perhaps even the heightened, interest of the Jews of Byzantine Egypt in their communal and religious life, as do additional Hebrew papyri of this kind published by M. Steinschneider.[7] A beautifully preserved Egyptian papyrus scroll (University Library, Cambridge: Taylor-Schechter 6), perhaps of the seventh century C.E., contains variegated selections of Hebrew liturgical poetry in the style of the Palestinian *piyyūṭīm*. Evidently, the Jews of Byzantine Egypt carried on the tradition of Jewish piety and Hebrew learning. It is also evident that this tradition extended far back in time.

A major piece of evidence for this contention is the presence in the Egyptian town of Dammūh of an ancient synagogue which was the object of a yearly pilgrimage on the part of the medieval Egyptian Jews. On the basis of scraps of evidence in Genizah documents and literary sources, it is possible to describe this synagogue and its significance in a rather clear way. According to Benjamin of Tudela and other writers, this synagogue was called the "Synagogue of Moses," while others called it simply the "synagogue of the Jews of Dammūh"; it was located several miles to the south of Fusṭāṭ-Miṣr, and on the *west* bank of the Nile. The yearly pilgrimage, in which Jews from all over Egypt were asked to participate, was one of great solemnity, and various rules were laid down by the communal leaders

5. Cf. V. A. Tcherikover and A. Fuks, eds., *Corpus papyrorum judaicarum*, I (Cambridge, Mass., 1957), 101–103.

6. This and several other fragments were first published by A. E. Cowley in the *Journal of Egyptian Archaeology*, 2:209–213 (1915). For additional bibliography on other Hebrew Oxyrhynchus papyri, see the discussions of H. Idris Bell in *JEA*, 9:105 (1923) and 10:160 (1924).

7. *Zeitschrift für ägyptische Sprache*, 17:93–96 (1879); see D. Chwolson, *Corpus inscriptionum hebraicarum*, cols. 120–125, for important additions and corrections to Steinschneider's article.

to be followed during the procession and upon arrival there. The people made monetary contributions in support of this synagogue, and donated Torah codices to its sanctuary; while some members of the community even owned land in its vicinity which they either leased out or donated, as late as the twelfth century, to the community as *waqf:* that is, *heqdesh* endowments. As I have pointed out elsewhere,[8] Dammūh, the name of the place where this synagogue was located, is probably a variant of Ṭammūh, an ancient town which was indeed several miles to the south of Fusṭāṭ-Miṣr and on the west bank of the Nile, and it is now possible to indicate why there was in this seemingly unlikely place an ancient synagogue which was venerated by the Jews of medieval Egypt.

A glance at a detailed map of Gizeh will show that the town of Ṭammūh lay among the ruins of ancient Memphis, which in ancient times was a huge city, extending north from the present el-Badrshein a distance of several miles to a position opposite Fusṭāṭ-Miṣr. (The city of Memphis was still heavily occupied during the Byzantine period, its real decline beginning only after the founding in the seventh century of Fusṭāṭ-Miṣr, for the construction of which stones of the buildings of Memphis were transported by the hundreds across the river.) In Coptic sources, Ṭammūh is called "Ṭammūh of Memphis," and it is known that the territory of Memphis was revered by the Jews as the scene of Moses' birth and mission. To be sure, the Synagogue of Dammūh was called by the name Kanīsat Mūsā because according to various traditions Moses was reputed either to have prayed there, to have prayed and slept there, or to have lived in Dammūh during his divine mission to Pharaoh, even at the very spot where the synagogue was later built.

This synagogue was evidently once an important house of prayer of the Jews of Memphis, who venerated this spot because of the associations with Moses. According to the Arabic historiographer Maqrīzī, the Jews contended that it was built "about forty years after the second destruction of the Temple by Titus—namely more than five hundred years before the appearance of Islam."[9] While it was undoubtedly used as a regular house of prayer in Roman and Byzantine times, it could not be so used after the decline and destruction of

8. "Topography of the Jews of Medieval Egypt," part 1, in *Journal of Near Eastern Studies*, vol. 24 (Summer 1965), where a full bibliography is given on the sources pertaining to this synagogue.

9. Maqrizi, *Khiṭaṭ*, II, 465.

Memphis and the gradual transfer of its population to the new metropolis across the river. After this happened, some remnants of the Jewish community continued to reside in a few of the villages of el-Gizeh, as in Dahshūr, Gizeh, and Ṭammūh itself, while the great majority took up residence at Fusṭāṭ-Miṣr. All of them, however, continued to remember the importance of the ancient synagogue of Moses at Dammūh, and persisted in venerating it in a variety of ways. In this they were joined by Jews from other parts of Egypt, who, to be sure, may even have been making this pilgrimage to the sacred synagogue of Moses in pre-Islamic times. Be this the case or not, the very continued existence and use of this Egyptian synagogue over a period of more than a thousand years and the perpetuation of sacred and ancient traditions concerning it well into the Fatimid period testify eloquently to the unbroken continuity of Jewish life in Egypt throughout this extensive period of history, and to the genuine pietistic character of the Egyptian Jewish community during this same period of time.

The power of survival of the Egyptian Jewry is lucidly illustrated by the example of the Jewish sect known as the Qarᶜiyah. According to the Ḳaraites Qirqisānī[10] and David ben Abraham al-Fāsi,[11] this sect traced its origin back to Joḥanan ben Kareaḥ (Jeremiah 42:5–7) and his flight to Egypt. While this may not have been its true origin, it is evident from the statements of the medieval writers about this sect that it originated in antiquity, certainly no later than the Hellenistic or at the latest the Roman period. Yet according to these same writers, the Qarᶜiyah, who practiced unusual rules of purity and abstention, were still in existence in the tenth century, living in their own communal settlement on the banks of the Nile, probably at a point about eighty miles above Fusṭāṭ, and therefore adjacent to the Fayyūm territory. By this time, however, they had taken on a quasi-Christian character, for they now observed Sunday as a day of rest along with the Sabbath. Such partial assimilation of a small and special Jewish group is not surprising, and the fact of it in no way detracts from the significance of the community's persistent survival as a Jewish sect for over ten centuries of time.

Given all these facts, it is not to be wondered at that immediately with the appearance of the earliest documents from the Genizah, the Egyptian-Jewish communal life is seen to have a full and wide-

10. *Kitāb al-anwār waʾl-marāqib*, ed. Nemoy, I (New York, 1939), 12, 47.
11. *Kitāb Jāmiᶜ al-alfāẓ*, II, 576.

spread development. There are established communal leaders; synagogues abound in cities great and small; the trades and professions are highly developed; international commerce is carried on intensively, and interurban commercial activities flourish. And as in antiquity, so once again the community is typified by settlements located throughout the delta and far up the Nile.

It is in the very character of the spread of these later settlements that the secret of the vitality and perseverance of the Jewry of this country is to be found. The most salient fact of this spread is that the very areas which sheltered Jewish communities in antiquity are often those which harbored them in the Middle Ages. This may be illustrated by the following comparative chart of Jewish settlements of Hellenistic and Medieval Egypt.

ANCIENT SETTLEMENTS	MEDIEVAL SETTLEMENTS
Canopic Region	
Alexandria } Schedia }	Alexandria
Xenephyris	Damanhūr
Phatnitic Region	
Athribis	Benhā
Pelusiac Region	
Pelusium	Al-Faramā (?)
Tell al-Yahūd	{ Ghaifah, Bilbeis
Middle Egypt	
Babylon	Fusṭāṭ-Miṣr
Memphis (incl. Σύρων κώμη)	{ Gizeh, Dammūh, Dahshūr
Fayyūm	
Psenyris	Sanhūr
Arsinoë	Madīnat al-Fayyūm
	Atfīh
Heracleopolite Nome	{ Būṣīr al-Malak, Dalāṣ, Būsh
Heracleopolis Magna	{ Ahnas al-Madīnah (?), Qalahā

Upper Egypt

Oxyrhynchus / Cynopolis	El-Bahnasah
Antinoë	Anṣinā
Hermopolis Magna	El Ashmūnein
Lycopolis	Asyūt
Thebes	Luxor
Apollinopolis Magna	Edfu
Syene-Elephantine	Aswān

In this comparative list, those Egyptian places settled by Jews during the Middle Ages (over one hundred places of settlement are now known)[12] have been omitted which cannot at the present time be related to settlements of antiquity, as have been settlements known to have been inhabited by Jews in antiquity but which show no evidence of occupation by Jews in the Middle Ages. Undoubtedly the comparative list of ancient and medieval Jewish settlements would grow were papyri for the other ancient sites extant, and were more Genizah fragments available. Nevertheless, the present list is sufficient to show a pattern of continuity, especially in the Fayyūm and upper Egypt, and therefore to allow the conclusion that the medieval Jews in many of these places were autochthonous residents whose forefathers had settled there in the distant past, and who perpetuated a long-established tradition of Jewish learning and piety. Undoubtedly one example of such a settlement was the town of Dalāṣ in the Fayyūm, which is located near several excavated sites whose papyri give evidence of Jewish settlement in antiquity (for example, Heracleopolis Magna and Tebtynis); Dalāṣ was the birthplace and early home of Saadia ben Joseph (born 892 C.E.), and it was here in this town that he gained the elements of his immense Jewish learning before setting forth on the journey which eventually led him to the gaonate of Sura. Other such settlements were Dammūh, where there were still Jews residing in the eleventh century, and the nearby town of el-Gizeh, which also nestled amongst the ruins of ancient Memphis. Still another town of this kind was Ghaifah, near Bilbeis, where a professionally executed Torah codex was written in the tenth century.[13] Until this period of time, Ghaifah was a town of considerable importance, being the last main station

12. See my "Topography of the Jews of Medieval Egypt," part 2, in *Journal of Near Eastern Studies*, vol. 26.

13. See M. Wallenstein in *Bulletin of the John Rylands Library*, 40:551–558 (1957–58).

on the road from Palestine to Fusṭāṭ-Miṣr; it is situated opposite a site known as Tell el-Yahūd, and is only about a dozen miles northeast of the more important Tell el-Yahūdiyeh. After its decline, the Jewish community of Ghaifah probably transferred to the nearby expanding city of Bilbeis or, in part, to the great metropolis some thirty-odd miles to the southwest.

A closer look at the map of this part of the Delta reveals another fact of salient interest. Beginning once again with the coastland near Gaza, we may count the following medieval settlements of Jews leading up to Fusṭāṭ: first, Rafaḥ, then al-ᶜArīsh and Qatia, then—proceeding along the old Pelusiac branch—al-Faramā, Fāqūs, Bilbeis and Ghaifah, perhaps al-Khankah (evidence only from the fifteenth century), and finally the metropolis. Along the busy Damietta arm (the Phatnitic branch of antiquity), there were many more Jewish settlements than these in the eleventh and twelfth centuries.[14] These two branches and the settlements along them, which together make up the *Sharqiyeh*, or eastern, province, together contained far more Jewish communities than the towns and cities of the *Gharbiyeh*, or western, province of the Delta. The heavy pattern of settlement here in the eastern province, and its continuation into upper Egypt (I refer to the six or seven known medieval Jewish communities of the Fayyūm and, above them, those in Bahnasah, Anṣinā, Ashmunain, Asyūt, Edfu, and Aswān as well as several others which are less certain) is strong evidence pointing to the steady connection of the Jewries of Palestine and Egypt into the Middle Ages. When it is remembered, furthermore, that the Jews of pre-Crusade Palestine were an active and creative community, settled in many towns and villages of the land as well as in the cities, then it is not difficult to assess the significance of this connection: namely, that as a result of their geographical relationship, the Jewish communities of Egypt and Palestine were mutual beneficiaries of each other's cultural and economic virtues; and that the Jews of Egypt were not only beneficiaries of spiritual and demographic renewal from their Palestinian brethren but also, because of the more favorable economic position of the former, they actively contributed to the perpetuation and enhancement of Jewish culture and learning in the land of Israel. Such is the picture which emerges full-blown from the study of the

14. See especially the map of D. Neustadt-Ayalon in *Zion*, 2 (1937): opp. p. 244, where, however, many changes and additions must now be made, for which see my "Topography of the Jews of Medieval Egypt."

pertinent Genizah documents of the first half of the eleventh century, and there is no reason on either historical or geomorphic grounds to believe that the situation was basically different in the Byzantine and early Arabic periods, when, as we have seen above, the Jews of Egypt had an awareness of their own communal and spiritual continuity and possessed a genuine tradition of Hebraic culture.

The fact that the Genizah documents emanate from the synagogue of the Palestinians in Fusṭāṭ-Miṣr necessarily obscures the true historical situation regarding the connection between the Jews of Egypt and their brethren in Iraq, the site of the foremost academies of Jewish learning in Sassanian and Abbasid times. Only a few dozens of letters of the Babylonian Geonim have been found in the Genizah, and there is a paucity of additional correspondence of a private and secular kind. However, the delineation of the evidence cited above makes it clear that the religious orientation of the Jews of Egypt as a whole was a decidedly Palestinian one, and that the Babylonian influence was of a more limited and special kind. (This influence perhaps developed as the Geonim—for example, Yehudai in the eighth century and Saadia in the tenth—sought to extend the hegemony of the Babylonian academies over the entire Diaspora, and as emigration from Iraq increased in the tenth century and thereafter, because of the worsening economic situation in the country.) The communal dignitaries in Egypt, on the other hand, had an intimate knowledge of the affairs of the Palestinian school and community, and engaged in voluminous correspondence with their leaders; they contributed heavily to the support of the latter and followed their political vicissitudes with keenest interest, also intervening in those vicissitudes when necessity demanded.[15] The spiritual highlight of the year was the annual pilgrimage at Tabernacles to Jerusalem and the Temple Mount, a ceremony which attracted many Jews from Egypt; undoubtedly this yearly ceremony helped to heighten and intensify their awareness of their close spiritual ties with the Holy land and with the Palestinian leadership.[16]

15. On this subject the Genizah contains many letters in Hebrew and Arabic, besides those published by Mann throughout his *The Jews in Egypt and Palestine under the Fatimids* and in his *Texts and Studies*. Several additional ones have been published by Goitein (see the pertinent items in the bibliography of S. Shaked, *A Tentative Bibliography of Geniza Documents* [The Hague, 1964], pp. 289–296); a number of others are still awaiting publication.

16. Cf. my remarks in *Ben-Zwi Memorial Volume*, I (Jerusalem, 1964), 89, n. 27, and also the text of the letter published by me there.

In Alexandria, probably in al-Maḥallah and some other communities of a comparable size and importance, and certainly in the metropolis of Fusṭāṭ-Miṣr, the Jews maintained separate synagogues for the Palestinians and Babylonians. Distinct and varying rites were followed in these synagogues, the most noteworthy being the different cycles for the completion of the reading of the Law. It is not without significance that the Synagogue of the Palestinians in Fusṭāṭ was called the "Great Synagogue,"[17] as opposed to the "Little Synagogue," evidently of the Babylonians.[18]

In most of the smaller towns of Egypt where Jews resided only one synagogue was to be found. There may be little doubt, in view of what has been said above, that as a rule the rite used in such synagogues was that of the Palestinian Jews. Mann has published fragments of an immense literature composed during the tenth and eleventh centuries on the subject of the Palestinian triennial cycle of the reading of the Law;[19] this literature was probably circulated widely among the Egyptian congregations, whose precentors and dignitaries had to make practical use of it while endeavoring to follow the accepted form of the ritual.

In view of what has been said, it would be an overstatement to characterize the Jewish community of medieval Egypt as a truly tripartite one, consisting of Palestinians, Babylonians, and Ḳaraites, each with its own separate and separative ethnic and religious character. While it is true that each of these groups had their own synagogues and ritual patterns in a number of Egyptian communities (the Ḳaraites had synagogues at least in Fusṭāṭ, Alexandria, Damietta, and Tinnīs), the factors which tended to draw them together and unify them far outweighed the divisive ritualistic factors, so that no distinction was ever made in legal documents between Palestinians and Babylonians, nor were marriages between Rabbanites and Ḳaraites disallowed.[20] On the social and economic level, all three of these groups mingled closely together, and had high esteem for one another; so that, for example, appeals for the ransom of both Rabbinic

17. T.-S. 13J-1, fol. 7; cf. T.-S. N.S. Box 323, no. 3.

18. T.-S. Misc. Box 36, no. 206; *ibid.*, no. 176.

19. J. Mann, *The Bible as Read and Preached in the Old Synagogue*, vol. I (Cincinnati, 1940). The second volume of this important work was prepared for publication by the late Isaiah Sonne.

20. See, e.g., T.-S. 8.223, an engagement contract between a Rabbanite and a Ḳaraite, in which each party agrees to respect the religious observances of the other. A number of such contracts have been found in the Genizah; see, e.g., Antonin no. 637.

and Ḳaraitic captives were sent to all sections of the community alike,[21] and the response was likewise on a communal rather than a sectarian basis.

Besides the obvious reasons for this feeling of unity and comradeship which tended to unite the various Jewish groups in medieval Egypt—the consciousness among the people of a common historical background, the sharing of the Biblical heritage and of the Hebrew language as the means of religious and even secular expression, and their common and more or less uniform treatment by the political authorities as *dhimmis* of the Jewish faith—other factors operated in both subtle and obvious fashion to impart this sense to them, especially to the common people who were not deeply influenced by religious and philosophical debate. Foremost among these was the practice of esoteric folk religion; it is important to pursue its description and the description of the fascination with it on the part of the Jews of Fatimid Egypt.

If the following discussion does not include the Muslims and Christians of medieval Egypt, it is primarily because the material on which it is based comes from a Jewish source. This is not to imply that the practices discussed here were not in vogue among residents of Egypt other than the Jews; on the contrary, we have every reason to suppose—and in most instances we are sure—that they were shared by the people regardless of their particular religions, and that what appears in the Genizah documents is a reflection of a general phenomenon of the age. At the same time we need to be reminded of the possibility that some of the practices may have been indulged in by Egyptian Jews in pre-Islamic times and that such practices as these may never have made their way to the population at large. This seems to be the case with certain of the formulas and incantations employed; besides occasional old Aramaic formulas which are like those employed on the Aramaic incantation bowls,[22] we find also certain Greek formulas such as סִיפּוֹן סִיפּוֹן בַּיוֹן בִּיוֹן מִיקוֹן אִיטוֹן אטימון,[23] and also the Abrasax formula (vocalized in one manuscript, T.-S. K-1, fol. 121, as אֲבַּרְסְכֵּס), which I am not familiar with from Muslim Arabic sources; these seem to indicate a continuity of tradition from earlier times, when, to be sure, Jews were residing in

21. See, e.g., T.-S. 12.283; cf. also the discussion in Mann, *Jews in Egypt*, I (Oxford, 1920), 88ff., and sources there cited.
22. See T.-S. Hebrew Boxes, K-1, fol. 121.
23. T.-S. Hebrew Box K-1, no. 58.

Egypt. Still, such peculiar and individual usages which were confined to the Jews seem to form an exception to the general rule regarding magical and esoteric practices.

We retain here a distinction employed by the inhabitants of Egypt themselves between *al-sīmīyā*—natural or deceptive magic—and *al-ruḥāniy* or *al-*^{c}*ilm al-ruḥāniy*—that is, the so-called "spiritual" magic. *Sīmīyā*, to be sure, is not absent from the Genizah documents; in one fragment,[24] for example, the practitioner is given explicit instructions for the performance of tricks of fire without harm, for making birds unable to fly and for restoring their flight, and other such performances (the fragment may be part of a treatise in which a number of such *sīmīyā* acts were described). There are other types of magic, namely the ^{c}*ilm al-nujūm* and its subsidiary the *ḍarb al-raml* or geomancy, as well as alchemy—examples of all of which are found in the Genizah, the former in some abundance, but these will not concern us here.

The ^{c}*ilm al-ruḥāniy*, examples of which are far more predominant in the Genizah than either *sīmīyā* or alchemy, was on the contrary formulated and designed with the idea of arousing wonder or surprise not in others, but in oneself; further, its goal was a genuinely spiritual one from the point of view of the people involved, to the extent that it consisted in arousing the angels, spirits, and jinn to the performance of acts on behalf of the practitioner. This "spiritual" magic was usually practiced in private; but at least in the case of the Jews of Egypt it was more than simply a private practice. Insofar as the official Judaism of the times, as personified in such Egyptian Jewish figures as Maimonides, was entirely opposed to practices of this sort, and insofar as we hardly ever find references to such practices in the social and business correspondence of the Jews of those times, we may feel justified in referring to such practices on the part of Jews as secret, or esoteric, practices, which out of personal considerations the practitioners did not wish to have divulged.

A most common type of secret practice, if we may judge from the Genizah, was that which was called "the swearing in of the angels." This is represented in numerous fragments. The practitioner, by making use of numerous oaths and magical sayings, would hope to win over to his side the angels or good spirits, so that they might work on his behalf in helping him to attain particular goals. The goals

24. T.-S. Ar. 44^{7}.

might be such as the implanting of love for the practitioner in the heart of a lady, the guarding of his dwelling from possible harm at the hands of thieves, ridding the house of lice, protection on a journey, and so on. Usually even such a process as this was accompanied by acts of purification and mortification, and by fumigatory incantations. A similar rite was the subjugation of evil spirits, the sense of which can perhaps be understood from the following passage taken from an old vellum fragment of the tenth or eleventh century, which reads: "If thou shouldst seek to rule over the demons and over all evil spirits and over the twelve families which descended from heaven in the days of Satan their father, learn first of all this book in its entirety, the names of those spirits and the names of their families and every one of their species; and when thou desirest to subdue them . . . . , go to a place where people do not dwell—a mountain, field, or an empty house; sweep the house well, make a circle before the door and make four openings therein, north, south, east and west . . ." This fragment seems to be from a magical treatise of Palestinian origin.

In an elaborate illustrated magical manuscript, fragments of which I have found in several places in the Genizah, the conjuring up of spirits and other processes receive their fullest elaboration. The conjuring up of spirits is initiated in our manuscript with incantations, but no doubt it was preceded by fumigations (as in another process described at the end of the manuscript, where filling the room with the smoke of citron and lemon is prescribed). After elaborate incantations, which are supposed to last much of the night, the hosts or "retinues" of spirits (singular, *mawkib*) begin to appear, until a total of twelve retinues has been reached. Each retinue bears its own name, and the practitioner is instructed in the manner of speaking to every one of them. First he must ask by what name they go, and if they answer as prescribed in the manuscript, he proceeds with a magical formula—a different one for each of them. Then a hundred and fifty golden lances are supposed to appear before the eyes of the incantator, another short formula is uttered, and the "Sheikh"—that is, a jinni—is supposed to appear at that moment. There follows a complete ritual of actions and speeches between the jinni and the incantator, an exchange of their magic rings, a sacrifice of an animal the following morning, further magical incantations when the jinni again appears; but we do not learn what the eventual outcome of this exchange is to be. There follow directions (with illustrations) for making certain charms, a description of a regimen of silence and fasting for five days, further recipes for fumigatory oblations, descriptions of particular jinn that will make their appearance upon the use of certain chants and magical practices, and the like. We have in these fragments the remnants of a complete regimen of the ᶜ*ilm al-ruḥāniy* as practiced by these residents of Egypt during the twelfth century.

There can be no doubt that the practitioners achieved a state of trance during the performance of some of these rituals. In the aforementioned manuscript, such a state is in fact alluded to, and it is specifically described in still another fragment from the Genizah.[25] After providing for the fervent utterance of a prayer, the writer says: "Behold and observe if thou hast recited until now and no [jinn or spirit] comes to thee, do not be ashamed because of those people in the room who are standing before thee. Repeat the prayer; before thou art half finished, they [the spirits] will come and take thee . . . [there is a break here in the document and then]: thou wilt be unable to stand upon thy feet; thou wilt see the world turning around before thee. Put thy face to the earth for one moment, and the dizziness and confusion will leave thee, and thy mind shall return to its former state . . ."

The most remarkable group of practices is undoubtedly that connected with the search for the treasures of the ancient Egyptians, which I have found represented in several variegated fragments from the Cambridge collection. It is now possible to say that various Jews of Fatimid Egypt, like their Muslim neighbors, did not refrain from seeking out the hidden wealth that was assumed to be buried within the pyramids, and which was occasionally uncovered. Aiding them in this search were secret manuals, written in Judaeo-Arabic—probably most of them copied from conventional Arabic books—that contained descriptions of towns and cities in both upper and lower Egypt and detailed directions for getting to monuments, pyramids, Coptic churches, and the like and for selecting the particular spots to begin the search. These descriptions, I may mention parenthetically, should prove to be of some interest to historians and geographers of medieval Egypt, for they include not only such well-known places as Fusṭāṭ and its environs, but also such locations as al-Qulzum and the vicinity, Girgeh and Antinoë in upper Egypt, the Jebel and Qaṣr

25. T.-S. Hebrew Box K-1, no. 2.

al-Muqawqaz, the Jebels al-Kubbah, al-Ṭabūnah, and al-Maṣlūb, names of streets in little-known villages of upper Egypt, wadis such as the Wadi al-Nu^{c}aim and al-Nağsa in upper Egypt and the Wadi Dhu Naw^{c}aḍ in the Muqattam range—and many other such places. But for the present moment our interest is in the magical and esoteric aspect of these documents. For the search for the treasures was, to people who practiced this "art," also a search for hidden "secrets" or hidden "knowledge." This theme of hidden knowledge runs like a scarlet thread through all of the treasure-hunting literature, and it is often intensified by the prescription to perform secret acts at certain of the tombs. In one notable description, the author of the treatise has copied down in what seems to be Coptic a five-word inscription, which, he says, is located on a rock at a certain place, the name of which is not legible in the document. Here are the instructions: "When thou hast found the inscription, copy it down on new parchment secretly [?] using rose water [and other substances] and hang the parchment on the breast of the statue [which is there]. When morning comes thou wilt find that the aforementioned statue is fallen upon the ground, and under the spot where it has fallen thou wilt find 20,000 good gold dinars. Here now is the inscription: learn the inscription well, beware lest thou skip so much as a single letter. Thereafter fumigate the parchment in the incense-vapors of sandrac."

From what has been said above, it may be seen that the Jews of Fatimid Egypt were not free of beliefs strongly at variance with the official belief and practice of the times; the reason for this must be quite in evidence, namely the dissatisfaction of numbers of people deriving from the inability of religion—that is, the formal, revealed religion—to secure many of their wants and needs and their difficulty in comprehending or their lack of desire to comprehend the ideas of the philosophers and the mystics. In the climate of Fatimid Egypt, with its wealth and bustling city life on the one hand and, on the other, its pyramids and tombs and monuments evoking the memory and mystery of Egypt's past, there was ample room for the secret doctrine to take root and grow. In view of the many fragments of an esoteric kind which have now been found in the Genizah, it is possible to conclude that the practices of secret religion, esotericism, and magic were much indulged in by the common people, and that the mutual fascination on the part of the formally separate religious communities with them tended to obscure and make less significant their outward differences.[26]

It was the Nile itself, however, which provided the greatest impetus for unity among the Jews of Egypt. Almost all of the Egyptian towns of Jewish settlement were located along its branches, and it is evident from a wide variety of Genizah papers that the Jews, especially those of the middle class, traveled freely up and down the river. Some of them were businessmen and traders, others physicians, still others religious dignitaries or simply pleasure-travellers bent on visiting friends and relatives in the towns of the Delta and Upper Egypt. The letters of these people reveal much by their silence: there is not to be found in them a single description of any of the monuments of ancient Egypt—no surprise, no wonder on the part of those sailing up to Ikhmīm and Quṣ, who surely must have noticed those monuments as they passed by. On the other hand, the human element is paramount; major parts of the letters are given over to descriptions of the hospitality extended to the writers by friends in the Delta towns or up the river. The dangers of the trip are usually dwelt upon; there is scarcely a letter in which mention is not made of seasickness or even of people dying from it while aboard. A common phrase of traveling merchants in describing their companions on these trips is "our brethren the Ḳaraites"[27] or "Jews, both Rabbanites and Ḳaraites." On such trips, it was not uncommon for Rabbanites and Ḳaraites to engage jointly in trade ventures, just as there was surely no distinction between the "Palestinians" and "Babylonians" on the waters of the Nile.

In other words, the correspondence of the Jews of Egypt during the Fatimid period makes it evident that on the social and economic levels the several groups had amicable and mutually beneficial relations with one another, and that the consciousness of their inner unity was heightened by the contiguous presence of Jewish communities, great and small, in every part of Egypt, where they knew they would be received as welcome guests and brethren and upon whom they depended for their economic well-being and success. Thus the geography of the Nile and the concomitant interurban economy conditioned the social character of the Jewish community itself. The eco-

26. To give a complete bibliography of Genizah manuscripts describing magical and esoteric practices would occupy several pages.

27. See, e.g., T.-S. 12.215.

nomic strength of this community, derived from the geography of the country and its mighty stream, and its spiritual resilience, nourished by the nearness of Egypt to the land of Israel and the essentially homogeneous quality of its membership, help to explain in goodly measure the process of continuity of Jewish life in Egypt for well over a millennium of time, and to account for some of its individual features.

Esau as Symbol in Early Medieval Thought

By GERSON D. COHEN

I. Edom—Rome

The affirmation of the sovereignty of God in the Rosh ha-Shanah liturgy comes to a climax with a series of verses from Scripture which makes the credo as much a view of history as a declaration of first principles, a preamble to eschatology no less than to theology:

Thus saith the Lord, the King of Israel,
And his Redeemer the Lord of hosts:
I am the first, and I am the last,
and beside Me there is no God (Isaiah 44:6).

And saviours shall come up on mount Zion
to judge the mount of Esau;
and the kingdom shall be the Lord's (Obadiah 1:21).

And the Lord shall be King over all the earth;
In that day shall the Lord be One, and His name one (Zechariah 14:9).

Hear O Israel, the Lord is our God, the Lord alone! (Deuteronomy 6:4).[1]

That the most diverse Jewish rites concur in the inclusion of the verse from Obadiah can hardly be a coincidence.[2] Hallowed throughout Jewry by the authority of Amoraic and perhaps even late Tannaitic usage,[3] they bespeak the antiquity of the Rabbinic view

1. On the *malkhuyot*, or proclamation of the sovereignty of God, see I. Elbogen, *Der jüdische Gottesdienst in seiner geschichtlichen Entwicklung* (Leipzig, 1913), pp. 141ff. On the date of the earliest form see L. Finkelstein, *Akiba* (New York, 1936), p. 312. For a representative text and translation, see *High Holyday Prayer Book*, trans. by P. Birnbaum (New York, 1951), pp. 377–384.

2. On the earlier variations in the structure of the *malkhuyot* see Elbogen, *Der jüdische Gottesdienst*, pp. 141ff., and especially S. Lieberman, *Tosefta Ki-Fshutah* (New York, 1955–62), V, 1053f.

3. The verse appears in the *malkhuyot* of Yose b. Yose (6th century) אהללה אלהי; see *Siddur R. Saadja Gaon*, ed. by I. Davidson *et al.* (Jerusalem, 1941), pp. 226f.

of universal monotheism as inseparably bound up with a conflict to the finish between the kingdom of God and the pretensions of human rulers.[4] In this liturgical passage and in the Rabbinic frame of reference as a whole, the war against the idols is synonymous with the conflict of Jacob with Esau, archetypal symbols of Jewry and Rome.

Ever since the destruction of the Temple, the Jews were obsessed with the blatant contrast between their election in Heaven and their subjection on earth. Since the rationale for collective survival precluded the possibility that God had rejected His people, the present state was inevitably construed as temporary. Indeed, Rome, the "wicked kingdom," would yet pay dearly, irrevocably, for its *hybris* and cruelty, for having afflicted Israel far beyond what God had decreed. Given such assumptions, sad reality generated comforting fantasy, and the despair of history was overcome by apocalyptic.[5]

Apocalyptic fantasy and literature is but one form of that genre of midrash characterized by Professor Wolfson as historical and eschatological predictive interpretations of Scripture. The historical interpretation attempts "to find in scriptural texts predictions of future events already known . . . to have taken place"; the eschatological interpretation attempts "to find in Scripture non-literal meanings referring to the events which are to take place in the end of days, such as the advent of the Messiah."[6] By such midrashic equation, Rome was identified with the Biblical Edom, and every name connected in Scripture with Esau was applied to the city of Romulus and the empire of the Caesars.

Although the Rabbinic identification of Rome with Esau and Edom is a commonplace and often cited, the exact origins of this identification have not yet been satisfactorily ascertained, and the question merits a fresh examination. The earliest known source

4. On the multifaceted character of the concept of the kingship of God in Rabbinic literature, see M. Kadushin, *The Rabbinic Mind* (New York, 1952), pp. 18f. On the insertion of passages bespeaking retribution to the Gentiles, see *Tos. R.H.* 2:12, p. 311 (ed. Lieberman) and Lieberman, *Tosefta Ki-Fshutah*, V, 1054. A specific example of such a verse, cited in *B.R.H.* 32 b, is Ps. 137:7: "Remember, O Lord, against the children of Edom the day of Jerusalem," etc.

5. Cf. G. D. Cohen, "Zion in Rabbinic Literature," *Zion in Jewish Literature*, ed. by A. S. Halkin (New York, 1961), pp. 56f.; A. Marmorstein, *Studies in Jewish Theology*, ed. by J. Rabbinowitz and M. S. Lew (Oxford, 1950), Hebrew section, pp. 1f.; J. Neusner, *A Life of Rabban Yohanan ben Zakkai* (Leiden, 1962), pp. 129f.; H. J. Schoeps, *Aus frühchristlicher Zeit* (Tübingen, 1950), pp. 144f.

6. H. A. Wolfson, *The Philosophy of the Church Fathers*, I (Cambridge, 1956), 27. See also I. Heinemann, *The Methods of the Aggadah* (in Hebrew; Jerusalem, 1949), chaps. iii–v.

often thought to make this identification dates from the latter part of the first or early part of the second century.[7] In an obscure passage in the Apocalypse of Ezra, the visionary implores God to reveal to him a sign by which the end of time will be recognizable. Although the heavenly response is both opaque and textually suspicious, the figures by which the present age and the one to come are characterized are quite clear: "From him sprang Jacob and Esau, but Jacob's hand held the heel of Esau from the beginnings. The heel of the first age is Esau; the hand of the second is Jacob." Latin and Arabic versions of the book render the answer even more pointedly: "For Esau is the end of this world, and Jacob is the beginning of the one which follows."[8] Since the Apocalypse of Ezra is one of the products of the despair and new eschatology born of the destruction of the Second Temple, the equation of the rulers of the present age with Esau, some scholars have felt, leaves no doubt as to the meaning of the reference.

Nevertheless, the passage in no way warrants the conclusion that the designation of Rome by Esau or Edom had been consciously made. In IV Ezra, Jacob and Esau clearly represent cycles of history as much as they do specific empires. They are archetypal symbols of the objects of God's love and God's hate and derive from the same bedrock of associations from which Paul of Tarsus had drawn his figures for "children of the promise" and children of rejection.[9]

Actually, it is only from the middle of the second century that we can discern the conversion of what may have been but one midrash

7. The widely entertained view that the name Edom was projected onto Rome from the Idumean origin of Herod was first suggested, I believe, by L. Zunz, *Zur Geschichte und Literatur* (Berlin, 1845), p. 483. However, as far as I can determine, this conjecture cannot be substantiated by any literary evidence, quite apart from the fact that the identification of Rome *through* Herod appears to be putting the cart before the horse. A. Schlatter, *The Church in the New Testament Period*, trans. by P. Levertoff (London, 1955), pp. 255f., subscribes to this view and adds an original twist. Recognizing that the identification of Edom with Rome is not discernible in the earliest strata of Rabbinic literature or in the Pauline epistles, he suggests that the midrash emerged as an anti-Herodian barb of the Zealots and was appropriated by the Rabbis only much latter. There is no more evidence for this view than for the more popular version of the Herodian *Sitz im Leben* of the equation. Even more farfetched is the suggestion that the name Edom derives from the Hebrew name for Mars; see A. Epstein, *Mi-Qadmoniot ha-Yehudim* (Jerusalem, 5717), p. 33.

8. IV Ezra 6:7–10 (trans. G. H. Box).

9. G. H. Box, *The Ezra Apocalypse* (London, 1912), p. 68. Cf. also Rom. 9:6–13 with IV Ezra 3:13–16. The use in Josephus, *Antiquitates*, I, 275, of IV Ezra 6:7–10 as proof that Esau represents Rome is unwarranted, particularly since Josephus merely paraphrases Gen. 27:39–40; see I. Heinemann, "Josephus' Method in the Presentation of Jewish Antiquities" (in Hebrew), *Zion*, 5:193 (1940).

among many—in any event, of a restricted apocalyptic circle—into a popular and explicit symbolism.

As far as I can determine, the first Rabbi to have clearly identified Rome with Esau and Edom was none other than Rabbi Akiba ben Joseph. He, it would appear, was the one who explained that the verse "The voice is the voice of Jacob, but the hands are the hands of Esau" (Genesis 27:22) was illustrated by the *anguished cry* of Jacob because of what the hands of Esau had done to him.[10] The meaning of Esau is here clear and unequivocal.

Moreover, as is a matter of common knowledge, at the time of the last great revolt against Rome, Rabbi Akiba pointed to Simeon bar Koseba and said: "This is the messianic king," and maintained that the verse "A star rises from Jacob" applied to the leader of the revolt.[11] The application of the verse to Ben Koseba clearly points to the bloody conflict that would usher in the end of days (compare Numbers 24:14, 19) and culminate with the defeat of Edom by Israel: "A star rises from Jacob; a meteor comes forth from Israel. It smashes the brow of Moab, the foundation of all children of Seth. *Edom becomes a possession, yea, Seᶜir a possession of its enemies; but Israel is triumphant. A victor issues from Jacob to wipe out what is left of ᶜIr*" (Numbers 24, 17–19). *ᶜIr* to the Rabbis was clearly "urbs," the city of Edom and the capital of the empire. Bar Koseba became Bar Kokhba (The Star), for he was locked in battle with the very nation whom Rabbi Akiba had identified with Edom.[12]

Once Rabbi Akiba had made the identification, his disciples could easily read Rome into other Scriptural passages where Edom was named. In a prophecy on the vengeance of the Lord against Edom, Isaiah says: "And the wild oxen (*reʾemim*) shall come down with them" (34:7). Rabbi Meir punned on the word *reʾemim* and read *Romiyyim*.[13] Furthermore, Isaiah's oracle on Dumah (21:11) was recorded in the scroll of the same Rabbi Meir as the oracle on *Rumi*.[14] This is a piquant play on words, since *Dumi* and *Romi* were

10. *Ber. R.* 65:21, p. 740 (ed. Theodor-Albeck). Cf. also W. Bacher, *Die Agada der Tannaiten*, 2nd ed. (Strassburg, 1903), I, 281, n. 2.

11. *Yer. Taᶜan.* 4:8, f. 68d; *Ekha R.* to 2:2 (and in ed. Buber, p. 101).

12. G. F. Moore, *Judaism* (Cambridge, Mass., 1927–30), II, 116. In Targum Pseudo-Jonathan to Num. 24:19, *ᶜIr* is rendered by Constantinople (i.e., Nova Roma), while Rashi and other medieval commentators identify *ᶜIr* with Rome itself.

13. *Pesiqta de Rav Kahana*, p. 134 (ed. Mandelbaum) and parallels.

14. *Yer. Taᶜan.* 1:1, f. 64a. On orthographic changes in R. Meir's texts, see Bacher, *Agada der Tannaiten*, II (1890), 10; S. Lieberman, *Hellenism in Jewish Palestine*, 2nd ed. (New York, 1962), pp. 24f.

written virtually identically in Hebrew script at that time, as noted already by Jerome.[15] Rabbi Simeon ben Yoḥai could speak of the exile of Edom as the last in the series of exiles endured by Israel.[16] Henceforth, the meaning of Edom would be well known, as attested by the countless passages in Rabbinic literature, where the name is clearly invoked with respect to the Roman empire and its way in the world.[17]

The real question that faces the student is why Edom of all Biblical figures should have become the stock one for Rome; or better still, given the homilies of apocalyptic writers and Rabbinic preachers, why should this one have seized the popular imagination and become part of the regular medieval vocabulary? That the identification is not an obvious one may be seen from the fact that the author of the Christian Apocalypse, who was no less midrashically oriented than any Rabbi of his day, invoked the more obvious figure of Babylon as a more appropriate designation, and from the fact that even Jews employed this figure for Rome.[18] Moreover, ancient Jewish exegetes had understood the Bible to have referred to the Romans by the name of *Kittim*,[19] whom the Bible had classified as the offspring of Japheth (Genesis 10:4), whereas Edom clearly was Semitic. Finally, of all the exiles described in Scripture, that of Edom was surely the

15. *Comment. in Isa.*, V, to Isa. 21:11 (Migne, *PL*, XXIV, 199), cited in part by N. Brüll, *Jahrbücher für jüdische Geschichte und Literatur*, 1:236 (1874); cf. L. Ginzberg, "Die Haggada bei den Kirchenvätern, VI," *Jewish Studies in Memory of George A. Kohut*, ed. by S. W. Baron and A. Marx (New York, 1935), p. 299, who cites Jerome and adduces further material on scribal changes in Rabbinic sources.

16. *Yer. Taᶜan.* 1:1. f. 64a; *B. Meg.* 29a. As to whether the citation in *Mekhilta de R. Ishmael*, Pisḥa 14 (ed. Lauterbach, I, 114), is to be credited to R. Akiba, see Bacher, *Agada der Tannaiten*, I, 281, n. 2; E. Z. Melamed, *Halachic Midrashim of the Tannaim in the Talmud Babli* (in Hebrew; Jerusalem, 1943), p. 102, notes to par. 50; A. J. Heschel, *Theology of Ancient Judaism*, I (in Hebrew; New York, 1962), 68, n. 1.

17. On Rabbinic attitudes toward Rome, see S. J. L. Rapoport, *ᶜErek Millin* (Prague, 5612), s.v. אדום and אדריינוס; M. Sachs, *Beiträge zur Sprach- undAlterthumsforschung* (Berlin, 1852–54), II, 134f.; M. Grünbaum, "Beiträge zur vergleichenden Mythologie aus der Hagada," *ZDMG*, 31:305–309 (1877); S. Krauss, "Griechen und Römer," *Monumenta Hebraica: Monumenta Talmudica*, V, part 1 (Vienna, 1914); *idem*, *Paras ve-Romi ba-Talmud u-ba-Midrashim* (Jerusalem, 5708); I. Heinemann, *The Methods of the Aggadah*, pp. 32f.; N. N. Glatzer, "The Attitude Toward Rome in Third-Century Judaism," *Politische Ordnung und menschliche Existenz: Festgabe für Eric Vögelin* (Munich, 1962), pp. 243–267.

18. H. L. Strack and P. Billerbeck, *Kommentar zum Neuen Testament*, 3rd ed. (Munich, 1961), III, 816, to Rev. 14:8 (cf. also I Peter 5:13); *Tanḥuma*, Tazriᶜa (ed. Buber), par. 16, II, 42; L. Ginzberg, *Geonica* (New York, 1909), I, 29; Y. Baer, *A History of the Jews in Christian Spain*, I (Philadelphia, 1961), 392, n. 49.

19. H. L. Ginsberg, *Studies in Daniel* (New York, 1948), p. 78, n. 21; Y. Yadin, *The Scroll of the War of the Sons of Light Against the Sons of Darkness* (in Hebrew; Jerusalem, 1955), pp. 22f.

least obvious, and it is odd that of all the dispersions and calamities suffered by Israel that of Edom should have been characterized as the most enduring and the most painful.

However, given the period in which the identification was made, it does not, after some reflection, appear strange at all. From the Rabbinic point of view, the situation of Palestinian Jewry and especially of Jerusalem in the years immediately following 70 C.E. corresponded perfectly to the state of affairs reflected in the Book of Lamentations: "How doth the city sit solitary, that was full of people! How is she become as a widow! . . . The ways of Zion do mourn, because none come to the solemn assembly . . . Her adversaries are become the head; her enemies are at ease . . . The adversary hath spread out his hand upon all her treasures; for she hath seen that the heathen are entered into her sanctuary" (1:4, 5, 10).[20] The accusing finger soon points at the guilty agent: "Rejoice and be glad, O daughter of Edom, that dwellest in the land of Uz; the cup shall pass over unto thee, also, thou shalt be drunken, and shalt make thyself naked . . . He will punish thine iniquity, O daughter of Edom; he will uncover thy sins" (4:21–22). Since it was Rome who had brought about the state of affairs reflected in Lamentations, was not Edom patently its Biblical name? Conversely, the book made no reference to Babylon or to the Chaldeans. Clearly, though Jeremiah had composed the work as a reaction to the calamities he had witnessed, he prophetically phrased the work in such a way that it would apply no less appropriately to the tragedy of the future.

There were other Scriptural considerations in support of this identification. The whole oracle of Obadiah is directed exclusively against Edom, and his characterization seemed to fit Rome to the last detail: "The pride of my heart beguiled thee, thou that dwellest in the clefts of the rocks, thy habitation on high; that sayest in thy heart: 'Who shall bring me down to the ground?' Though thou makest thy nest as high as the eagle, and though thou set it among the stars, I will bring thee down from thence, saith the Lord." Most important, it was with the downfall of Edom that Obadiah foresaw the final judgment, the restoration of dominion to God

20. That the Book of Lamentations was regarded even by the Tannaim as a prophetic description of the destruction of the Second Temple (and later of the fall of Bethar) is a commonplace. Cf. the revealing incident in *Sifre Deut.*, par. 43, pp. 94f. (ed. Finkelstein), where phrases from Lam. 2:1 and 5:17–18, among others, are quoted.

Himself. Who but a cosmocrator could have destroyed the Temple?[21] Who but a cosmocrator would serve a fitting adversary to usher in the day of fulfillment, the era of the Messiah? Scripture named Edom, and history pointed at Rome. By the most elementary syllogism, the two became one.

The facts of life made this midrashic identification far more apt than could be attributed by a Jew of the second century to mere coincidence. After all, there was a basic similarity between Rome and Judea in patterns of thought and expression. Neither of them could accept their existence as a mere fact. Each considered itself divinely chosen and destined for a unique history. Each was obsessed with its glorious antiquity. Each was convinced that heaven had selected it to rule the world. Neither could accept with equanimity any challenge to its claims.

This collective self-consciousness and obsession with past and future, with duty and destiny, came to its greatest expression in Rome in the Augustan age and most notably in the works of Livy and Virgil. Though shaken by civil wars and the decline of ideal Roman society, the average learned Roman echoed of his people what the Jew said of his own: "Thou didst choose us from among all peoples; thou didst love and favor us; thou didst exalt us above all tongues and sanctify us with thy commandments. Thou, our King, didst draw us nearer to Thy service and call us by Thy great and holy name."[22] As the Jews spoke of an eternal covenant between Israel and God, the Roman could quote the promise of Jove to Rome: "Imperium sine fine dedi."[23]

Although the Jewish feelings of election are clearly enunciated in, and derived from, Scripture, the doctrine of the election of Israel was accorded renewed emphasis in the generation following the Destruction. It was that generation which promulgated the allegorical interpretation of the Song of Songs as a record of the marital covenant between God and Israel at Sinai. It was the same Rabbi Akiba who approved of the revolt against Edom and who emphasized, "Beloved are Israel, for they were called children of God.

21. Ginsberg, *Studies in Daniel*, p. 5; *idem*, "Daniel" in *Encyclopedia Biblica* (in Hebrew), II, 689f. Cf. also *Mekhilta de R. Ishmael*, Beshallah 2 (ed. Lauterbach, I, 196f.); *B. Git.* 56b (beginning).

22. *Daily Prayer Book*, trans. by P. Birnbaum (New York, 1949), p. 589.

23. C. N. Cochrane, *Christianity and Classical Culture* (New York, 1957), pp. 16f., 63f.; R. Koebner, *Empire* (Cambridge, 1961), pp. 7f.; P. E. Schramm, *Kaiser, Rom und Renovatio* (Leipzig, 1929; I^2, Darmstadt, 1957), I^2, 29f., 340, where much further literature is cited.

Extraordinary is the love made known to them that they were called children of God . . . Beloved are Israel, for to them was given a precious implement with which the world was created, as it is said 'For I give you good doctrine, forsake ye not My Torah' (Prov. 4:2)."[24] The witty conversations between Rabbis and "philosophers," and between Rabbi Akiba and Tineius Rufus on the subject of Jewish faith and way of life are but homespun formulations of the conflict of two peoples (and their gods) wrestling for absolute dominion. Little wonder, therefore, that Jewish realists of the generation could lose heart and echo the Roman line by admitting that "this empire has been established by Heaven."[25] In that generation, the doctrine of election was no longer mere dogma. It had become a rallying cry.

Given two such mutually exclusive self-appraisals, and given the confrontation on the fields of battle, it was simple to make of Rome the archfoe of all times, far worse than Nebuchadnezzar. What more appropriate picture could come to mind than Jacob and Esau contending for the same blessing?

Such a conflict would inevitably be expressed by the Jews midrashically, by reading Rome into appropriate Scriptural passages. It cannot be overemphasized that verses were not just pulled out of the Scriptural hat and promiscuously associated with Rome. There is a method to this kind of homily that must be understood if we are to understand the Jewish—and for that matter, Christian—mentality. When the Aramaic Jewish translator of Isaiah 34:9 renders the verse: "And the streams of *Rome* shall be turned into pitch," and a midrash on the same verse identifies these streams with the Tiber and Mare Tyrrhenum,[26] they were merely spelling out what is clearly implied by that section, given the Jewish definition of Edom.

Once this identification had been made and accepted, all the classical associations, Biblical as well as Rabbinic, connected with the name of Esau and his descendents could come into play in connection with Rome. The dominant feeling in all of Hebrew literature is summed up in Rabbi Simeon ben Yoḥai's comment: "It is an

24. *Abot* 3:14; the translation is by J. Goldin, *The Living Talmud* (New York, 1957), p. 140. That the sentiment expresses the mood of the generation may be seen from the fact that the leader of the opposing school, R. Ishmael, uses a similar expression; noted by Bacher, *Agada der Tannaiten*, I, 280, n. 2.

25. Bacher, *Agada der Tannaiten*, I, 78f., 165f., 280f.

26. *The Bible in Aramaic*, ed. by A. Sperber (Leiden, 1959–62), III, 68; text and English translation in *The Targum of Isaiah*, ed. by J. F. Stenning (Oxford, 1949), pp. 112f.; M. Grünbaum, "Beiträge," p. 305.

axiom: Esau hates Jacob."[27] It was the same sentiment which provoked plays on words by later homilists on the name Edom as "bloodthirsty" and on the word "senator" as an abbreviation for three Hebrew words meaning hostile, vindictive, vengeful.[28]

To be sure, one can point to any number of counter-sentiments in Rabbinic literature expressing even appreciation, let alone acceptance of the positive values of the Roman imperial machine and of its contribution to civilization.[29] But at best these were *ad hoc* concessions made perforce. In the main, the more passive the Jews had become, the more graphic and extended became their exegetical fantasies on the prophetic oracles of doom for the enemy and of comfort and restoration for Israel. No possible hint in Scripture to the contemporary situation was left uninterpreted. The succession of empires enumerated by Daniel was now readjusted to reality and "Rome condemned" became the fourth kingdom.[30]

Thus it came about that more often than not Rome was referred to in medieval Hebrew literature not directly but by symbolic names and terms which had been drawn from the Bible and which carried with them a whole train of historic associations and emotional overtones. "Esau," "Edom," and "Seᶜir"—these are but the most common of a whole series of classical appellatives universally and unequivocally employed for imperial as well as medieval Rome, and in consequence for all of medieval Christendom.[31] The father of Spanish Hebrew poetry, Dunash ben Labrat (*circa* 950), was playing on time-worn motifs and allusions when he versified in his hymns:

The press of Bozrah do thou tread,
The vat in Edom of arrogant head.

* * *

27. *Sifre Num.* 69, p. 65 (ed. Horovitz); on the passage see Lieberman, *Hellenism in Jewish Palestine*, p. 45.

28. *Piyyute Yannai*, ed. by M. Zullay (Berlin, 1938), p. 45, line 13 (based on *Ber. R.* 63:8, p. 688); *Ber. R.* 67:8, p. 763 (ed. Theodor-Albeck).

29. See N. N. Glatzer, "The Attitude Toward Rome."

30. *Mekhilta de R. Ishmael*, Baḥodesh 9 (ed. Lauterbach, II, 268).

31. For lists of these usages see M. Steinschneider, *Polemische und apologetische Literatur* (Leipzig, 1877), pp. 266f., 278f.; L. Zunz, *Die Synagogale Poesie des Mittelalters*, ed. by A. Freimann (Frankfurt am Main, 1920), pp. 453f.; S. Krauss, "Die Hebräischen Benennungen moderner Völker," *Jewish Studies in Memory of George A. Kohut*, pp. 380f. Edom and Rome were so clearly synonymous in the Middle Ages that in a not uncommon error scribes substituted the name Rome for Palestinian Idumea! See F. Baer, "Eine jüdische Messiasprophetie," *MGWJ*, 70:16 (1926); Abraham ibn Daud, "Dibre Malkhe Yisrael be-Bayyit Sheni," *Seder ᶜOlam Rabbah* (Amsterdam, 5471), f. 52a (*bis!*), 54a, 57a. Cf. also Y. M. Grintz, *Sefer Yehudith* (Jerusalem, 1957), p. 14, where, however, the translation and emendations of "de Romanis" are by no means certain.

Destroy Alvan and Manahath . . .
Humble Shepho and seed of Nahath . . .
Restore the mount and Lebanon
Crush hastily the house of Pinon.

* * *

Uproot Edom for having sought
God's shoots to cut and turn to naught.[32]

We have here the old pleas for the destruction of Rome and medieval Christendom and for the redemption and restoration of Israel. Such hopes and prayers are a stock motif repeated in various forms by virtually all Hebrew poets of the Middle Ages in symbols and allusions which were perfectly clear to both Jew and Christian of the medieval world.

To the Jew of the high Middle Ages, even more than to his Christian contemporary, Rome was very much alive. If anything, the Jew required even less persuasion than his Christian neighbor that the ancient imperium had never disappeared but rather enjoyed an uninterrupted translation from one Caesar to another. Unlike Christian apologists, the Jews had to undergo no change of heart about Rome.[33] The Jew entered the medieval world with a fully developed view of Rome—and of her spiritual and political heirs—that had been crystallized in the course of five centuries when Roman rule over the Mediterranean world had altered the course of Jewish life forever. The official establishment of the Christian Church as the religion of the empire made no discernible impression on the Jews of the fourth century, for by that time the chasm between Judaism and Christianity had grown so deep and wide that the alignment of the machinery of state with the Church was of no greater moment than the succession of one emperor by another. To the Jew, it was a shift from one idolatry to another, one more aggressive and openly hostile, but not a change in kind.[34] Thus, it required no effort on

32. Dunash b. Labrat, *Shirim*, ed. by N. Allony (Jerusalem, 1947), p. 58, verse 5 (and see notes *ad loc.*, p. 117); pp. 56–57, verses 2 and 5; p. 59, verse 1. Even if, in the first citation, ונת באדום is not the original reading, the fact that it should have been substituted for וגם בבל is illuminating.

33. On Christian ambivalence toward Rome in the fifth century see T. H. Mommsen, *Medieval and Renaissance Studies*, ed. by E. F. Rice, Jr. (Ithaca, 1959), pp. 266f., 302f., 336f.

34. For a modern view that the early Christianized Roman aristocracy itself felt this way, see F. Schneider, *Rom und Romgedanke im Mittelalter* (Munich, 1926), pp. 17f., 21f.; Schramm, *Kaiser, Rom und Renovatio*, I, 30f. I do not mean to deny that much of Rabbinic polemic was anti-Christian, or that this polemic did not increase in volume as Christianity grew stronger. However, I am not aware that the official establishment of Christianity caused any basic reorientation on the part of the Rabbis either to Rome or to Christianity.

the part of Jewish homilists to extend the name of Edom to Christendom. Esau might exchange his eagle for a cross, but he was Esau nonetheless.[35]

Such are the foundations of Jewish feelings and symbolism for Rome and its successor nations. Medieval commentators and anthologists drew constantly on the rich fund of ancient exegesis on "the wicked empire" and unquestioningly applied it to the kingdoms and empires of their own later days. Nor was this merely idle rehashing of ancient dreams. It was the substance of the Jewish *raison d'être* in a hostile atmosphere in which they constantly heard the taunt that they had been rejected of God and displaced forever. To this the Jew had only one possible reply: If Scripture is revealed, then either God's prophecies had already been fulfilled, or they were as yet in the category of unfulfilled promise. If the latter, there was room for hope; indeed, the hope was a certainty. Accordingly, considerable energy was spent to prove by detailed references to historical facts that the prophecies of consolation had in no wise yet been fulfilled, that, in other words, the Christian claim was void and the Jewish hope well grounded.

The argument from history was of no little moment in the world of medieval polemic. Evidence is not lacking that Jews in alarming numbers on occasion did despair of a divine vindication of their people and even rationalized their despondency with the observation that the prophecies of consolation had long since been fulfilled. The Jews had been restored from Babylon; the Temple had been rebuilt, and the house of David restored in the person of Zerubbabel; a Jewish monarchy under the Hasmoneans had endured for a century and more. Clearly, the prophets had foretold correctly, but their predictions had already come to pass. Now that God had clearly rejected His people a second time, what hope was left? In reply Jewish theoreticians pointed out that the basic features of the prophecies had not been realized. In the first place, the truly cataclysmic changes foreseen by Isaiah, Micah, Ezekiel, and Zechariah had

35. On the identification of the Church with Rome, see R. Folz, *L'Idée de l'empire en Occident* (Paris, 1953), pp. 12f., 190f., and especially W. Ullmann, *The Growth of Papal Government in the Middle Ages*, 2nd ed. (London, 1962). See also the sources cited below, Note 71. Although the Church did not identify with "Romanitas" until the eighth century (Ullmann, pp. 61f, 120f.), the fact that imperial legislation against the Jews emanated from Nova Roma (Constantinople) was doubtless sufficient for the Jews to equate the two.

On medieval Jewish theory and practice with regard to Christians, see J. Katz, *Exclusiveness and Tolerance* (Oxford, 1961).

manifestly not yet come to pass. Not only was Israel physically dispersed but the miraculous changes in natural phenomena proclaimed by Scripture for the messianic age had not yet been witnessed. Moreover, even the history of the Jews proved that the prophecies of redemption could not possibly have been fulfilled in the days of the Second Temple. Zerubbabel had had no royal powers (*melukhah*) but merely *ad hoc* and interim authority (*serarah*); the Hasmonean dynasty was of no consequence in this respect, for it lacked the indispensable quality of Davidic lineage.[36]

Nevertheless, the increasing worldly success of Christendom ultimately did begin to have an effect. In the first place, Christians could point to the futility of Jewish tenacity to the ancient symbols of comfort in the face of divine rejection. Where was there a Jewish king or ruler anywhere on the face of the earth?[37] Was it not madness to equate the successful dominion of Christendom, the steady augmentation of which constituted proof of divine favor, with Edom? Nor did Christians remain silent about the Jewish symbols of hope. Christian typology had appropriated the very symbols that provided the substance of Jewish eschatological theory and had turned them against the Jews. If the character of Rome had not changed, as far as the Jew was concerned, the Jewish symbolism soon had to be defended, validated in ways that would seem cogent to a dispassionate observer. By the tenth century, no Jew could ignore the fact that Christian theory had clashed head-on with the Jewish view of Isaac's first-born son.

36. On Jews who felt that prophetic capital had run out, see A. H. Silver, *A History of Messianic Speculation in Israel* (Boston, 1959), pp. 209, 215ff.; B. M. Lewin, "Pirqe Peraqim mi-Milḥamot R. Saadiah Gaon," *Ginze Kedem*, 6:3–14 (1944). For the Jewish replies summarized here, see Saadiah, *The Book of Beliefs and Opinions*, trans. by S. Rosenblatt (New Haven, 1948), pp. 312ff.; Abraham ibn Daud, "Dibre Malkhe Yisrael," f. 50a, 79a–b; Judah Hadassi, *Eshkol ha-Kofer* (Eupatoria, 1836), Alphabet 377, f. 153c, and Z. Ankori, "Studies in the Messianic Doctrine of Yehuda Hadassi the Karaite," *Tarbiz*, 30:194 (1960–61); Moses Maimonides, *Mishneh Torah*, Melakhim 11:4 (ed. Rubinstein; Jerusalem, 1962), p. 415; *idem*, *Epistle to Yemen*, ed. by A. S. Halkin (New York, 1962), p. xv; *idem*, *Guide of the Perplexed* II:29; Abraham b. Moses Maimonides, *Perush ha-Torah* ed. by S. D. Sassoon (London, 1959), p. 204. Moses Nachmanides, *Sefer ha-Geʾulah*, ed. by I. M. Aronson (Jerusalem, 1959), pp. 12, 21f., 51; O. L. Rankin, *Jewish Religious Polemic* (Edinburgh, 1956), pp. 178ff., 200; Jacob b. Reuben, *Milḥamot ha-Shem*, ed. by J. Rosenthal (Jerusalem, 1963), pp. 157ff.; J. Rosenthal, "From 'Sefer Alfonso' [in Hebrew]," *Studies and Essays in Honor of Abraham A. Neuman*, ed. by M. Ben Horin *et al.* (Leiden, 1962), p. 589; Joseph Albo, *Sefer ha-ʿIkkarim*, ed. by I. Husik (Philadelphia, 1929–30), IV, 424ff.; Isaac Abravanel, *Comment. on Isa.* 35 (end).

37. See A. Poznánski, *Schiloh* (Leipzig, 1904), pp. 55f. (Origen), 61f. (Jerome), 71f. (Augustine), 206f., 288f.; for medieval Christian writers see also B. Blumenkranz, "Les Auteurs chrétiens latins du moyen âge sur les juifs et le judaisme," *REJ*, 111:12, 19, 38 (1951–52); 114:38f. (1955); 117:7f. (1958).

II. Esau the Jew

In his commentary on Isaiah, written toward the close of the fifteenth century, Don Isaac Abravanel included a long excursus in refutation of the "distortions" and "calumnies" spread by Paul of Burgos in identifying the Biblical Edom with the Jews.[38] The Christian typology, the bishop had argued, was appropriate inasmuch as the Jews live by the precepts of the Mishna, the present form of which derives from a recension redacted by Rabbi Meir, who, the Talmud proclaimed, was an Idumean convert.[39] What doubtless hurt Abravanel even more than the learned chicanery of Paul of Burgos was that an apostate quite well versed in Hebrew literature should have subscribed and lent his "Jewish" prestige to anti-Jewish homiletics. Paul's exegesis appeared like a gratuitous stab in the back, all the more unpardonable in that it seemed deliberately to turn Jewish exegesis on its head. Abravanel may well have judged Paul's motives correctly. What he did not appreciate or admit was that Paul of Burgos had turned up with nothing strikingly new, but had merely revived a classical Christian typology which had long since forced Jews to reappraise their own symbolic name for Rome.

Had the Romans of the second century known or cared about the stigma of Esau which the Jews had pinned on them, they might have been amused to learn that almost simultaneously the Gentile Christians of Egypt, Palestine, and Asia Minor had turned the very same epithet against the Jews. However, the new Christian usage of Esau did not originate as a retort to the Jews, but rather as a taunt inspired by the apostle Paul's Epistle to the Romans (9:6–13), quite without regard to—or, probably, even the vaguest knowledge of—what the Rabbis were saying about their pagan Roman overlords.

In arguing that not all born Jews were God's elect, Paul cited as evidence that only one of Abraham's sons was a child of God's promise. Moreover, of Isaac's two sons, Esau was hated by God and Jacob beloved; indeed, the former was doomed by divine decree to serve the younger. In other words, natural birth has nothing to do with whom God elects and whom He rejects. God had elected Israel.

38. Abravanel, *Comment. on Isa.*, 35; *idem*, *Mashmiʿa Yeshuʿah* III:7. On Paul of Burgos, see A. Lukyn Williams, *Adversus Judaeos* (Cambridge, 1935), pp. 267f.

39. *B. Erub.* 96b (and parallels). Cf. H. L. Strack, *Introduction to the Literature of the Talmud and Midrash* (Philadelphia, 1945), p. 22. According to *B. Git.* 56a it was Nero who was converted to Judaism and then begot R. Meir!

However, Jew and Israelite were not necessarily synonymous. The Jew who did not align himself with Paul's Israel[40] was as rejected as Paul himself conceded the seed of Esau to be.[41]

There is not the remotest suggestion in this argument that Paul considered the Jews to be the incarnation of Esau. However, it did not take too much effort for Gentile Christian typologists to convince themselves that that was precisely what he had meant. Paul had elsewhere explicitly designated Ishmael as a symbol of the covenant of Sinai, and Isaac as a symbol of the covenant of the Christ (Galatians 4:24–25). Clearly, these two sons must have represented the same values in the passage in Romans. Now, since Paul had there proceeded to give a second example of a disparate Biblical pair, the beloved and rejected of each pair clearly represented the same things. Ergo: Isaac = Jacob = the Church; Ishmael = Esau = the Jews.[42]

The steps by which this indigenous Christian exegesis came to full flower are fairly clear. First faintly echoed in the Epistle of Barnabas and in the Dialogue of Justin Martyr, the new midrash bears the stamp of the intensified allegorization of the Hebrew Bible of which pagan converts to Christianity were especially fond.[43] In expressing the encouragement derived by second-century Christians from the catastrophic blows suffered by the Jews between 67 and 136, this new typology reflects the ever-widening chasm between Jewish and Gentile Christians, as the number of the latter increased and their animus to Jews of any ilk attained greater intensity. Both circumstances provided the Gentile (= anti-Judaistic) wings of young Christendom with renewed vigor in their claim that the true Israel was destined to be essentially of Gentile stock.[44] It is no coincidence

40. Cf. Gal. 3:7f.; 6:16.

41. C. H. Dodd in *Moffatt Commentary* to Rom. 9:6f.

42. See below, Note 54.

43. See H. Wolfson, *The Philosophy of the Church Fathers*, chap. ii and especially pp. 43f. For this whole section I am particularly indebted to N. Bonwetsch, "Der Schriftbeweis für die Kirche aus den Heiden als das wahre Israel bis auf Hippolyt," *Theologische Studien: Theodor Zahn zum* 10 *Oktober* 1908 *dargebracht* (Leipzig, 1908), pp. 3–22, and to the superb study of B. Blumenkranz, *Die Judenpredigt Augustins* (Basel, 1946).

As examples of typology derived from etymology (a method employed by Philo as well as the Rabbis; see above, Note 28), note the Pseudo-Cyprian midrash on Sinai as signifying hate, and the explanation of Melito of Sardis that the Jews were called Edom, because they were red with the blood of Christ; Blumenkranz, p. 14; S. W. Baron, *A Social and Religious History of the Jews*, 2nd ed. (Philadelphia, 1952–58), V, 126.

44. Cf. Schlatter, *Church in the New Testament Period*, pp. 310f. For the most recent discussion see I. Baer, "Israel, the Christian Church, and the Roman Empire from the Days of Septimus Severus to the 'Edict of Toleration' " (in Hebrew), *Zion*, 21:3f. (1956).

that the unsuccessful Jewish wars for liberation from the Romans, culminating with the revolt of Bar Koseba, coincided with the emergence from the Christian community of a series of homilies which invoked the very terms which Jewish preachers had employed for different purposes. Jewish defeat on earth, to the Christians, was clear evidence of their rejection in heaven,[45] and many a Christian theoretician, in ancient times as well as modern, would claim that the downfall of Jewish self-government in the second century marks the end of the people of Israel; henceforth, Judaism would be carried by the Jews, who are to be distinguished from the true Israel. It is interesting to follow the steps by which the homilies become more explicit and increasingly pretentious. Thus, Barnabas invokes the promise of Genesis 25:23 that the older shall serve the younger fleetingly, and quickly passes to the case of Manasseh and Ephraim in support of the contention that the younger (the Church) is the favored one.[46] Justin harps on the new typology of Leah (the Synagogue) and Rachel (the Church), closing this particular homily, "Jacob was hated for all time by his brother; and we now, and our Lord himself, are hated by you and by all men . . . Jacob was called Israel; and Israel has been demonstrated to be the Christ."[47] If the Jews are Esau, they are still Esau only by implication, and only because they are now to be reckoned with mankind at large.

However, even this sufficed for Irenaeus in the latter part of the second century to take but one step further and spell out the implication that Jacob-Israel-Christendom had supplanted Esau-Jewry in birthright and blessing, the "younger" destined to freedom and victory, the "older" to eternal rejection and servitude.[48] Paul's example for the sake of argument had now become a *typos*, a theological term of reference. In the Pseudo-Cyprian polemic (*circa* 210–240), *De montibus Sina et Sion*, Esau and Jacob parallel Sinai (the Synagogue) and Zion (the Church) respectively.[49] In an allegorical interpretation (*mystica interpretatio*) of Hippolytus of Rome, cited by Jerome, Esau is represented as the incarnation of the devil, successor to Cain and prefigurative image of the Jews, Jacob as successor to

45. The argument goes back to Cicero, *Pro Flacco* xxviii:69 (Loeb Classics; trans. by L. E. Lord, p. 440/441); cf. J. H. Lewy, *ʿOlamot Nifgashim* (Jerusalem, 1960), pp. 86f.

46. *Epistle of Barnabas*, 13. For the dating of the Epistle of Barnabas around the time of the Bar Koseba revolt, see J. Quasten, *Patrology* (Utrecht, 1950–60), I, 90.

47. Justin, *Dialogue*, 134 (trans. by G. Reith in *The Ante-Nicene Fathers*, I, 267).

48. Irenaeus, *Against Heresies*, IV:21, 2–3.

49. Blumenkranz, *Judenpredigt*, p. 14; cf. also Williams, *Adversus Judaeos*, p. 14.

Abel and anticipatory of Christ and the Church.[50] Hence, Origen could speak of this exegesis as "common knowledge"—when he claims that "even the unbelieving Jews know [scilicet, that Christians say:] that one people has taken the place of another, i.e., that the Church has taken the place of the Synagogue, and that the elder is now the servant of the younger."[51] Indeed, the claim must have reached at least some Jewish ears, for it was being shouted far and wide, and in virtually identical terms, by these men as well as by their contemporaries Tertullian and Commodian, all of whom clearly drew on earlier funds for such interpretations.[52]

However, at this early stage of Christian history, the Christian midrash on Esau and Jacob bore no particular sting. After all, the Christians were at this point politically no better off—in many cases, far worse off—than the Jews. The Christian claim that the Synagogue was destined to serve the Church must have struck many Jews as downright ludicrous, particularly since the very same exegetes were shouting that the Jews were in league with Rome against the Church.[53] As for the specific midrash on Genesis 25:23, it was only one among many allegorical figures drawn from the Bible and applied to the Christian claim against the Jews. Cain and Abel, Hagar and Sarah, Ishmael and Isaac, Leah and Rachel, Manasseh and Ephraim, Eli and Samuel, Saul and David—all of these pairs, among many other figures, were regularly invoked as clear symbols of the old and the new covenants.[54] Even Christians were only too

50. Quoted by Jerome, Epist. 36, Migne, *PL*, 22:460 (Eng. trans., *Ante-Nicene Christian Library*, VI, 421f.); cf. Bonwetsch, *Theologische Studien*, p. 16.

51. Hom. in Gen. 12:3, cited by J. Daniélou, *Origen*, trans. by W. Mitchell (New York, 1955), p. 164. The theme occurs in Origen's commentaries repeatedly; see Baer, "Israel, the Christian Church . . .," pp. 18f.

52. Tertullian, *Adversus Judaeos*, I, Migne, *PL* 2:597f. (Eng. trans., *Ante-Nicene Christian Library*, XVIII, 202); Blumenkranz, *Judenpredigt*, pp. 9f., 23f.; Bonwetsch, *Theologische Studien*, p. 15.

53. Blumenkranz, *Judenpredigt*, p. 25; Baer, "Israel, the Christian Church . . .," p. 19, n. 83.

54. Blumenkranz, *Judenpredigt*, p. 170, n. 26. See also H. J. Schoeps, *Paul*, trans. by H. Knight (Philadelphia, 1961), pp. 141f., 229; J. Daniélou, *From Shadows to Reality* (London, 1960); *idem*, "La Typologie d'Isaac dans le christianisme primitive," *Biblica*, 28:363–393 (1947); E. E. Urbach, "Homilies of the Rabbis on the Prophets of the Nations and the Balaam Stories" (in Hebrew), *Tarbiz*, 25:276 (1955–56). Ironically enough, even the typology of antithetical pairs is probably a Christian midrash on a Jewish homily. The panegyric on Wisdom in Wisd. of Sol. 10 lists seven contrasts of righteous versus wicked who followed the Torah or spurned it, to their salvation and destruction respectively: Adam and Cain (verses 1, 3); Noah and the generation of the Flood (4); Abraham and the generation of dissension (5); Lot and the people of the Pentapolis as well as Lot's wife

well aware that these typologies—like midrashic etymologies[55]—were but allegorical interpretations, and Christians themselves laid greater stress on the new emotional overtones they sought to infuse into the distinction between "Jews" and "Israel."[56] To Christians as well as Jews, the latter were real and "objective" terms that had to be coped with, whereas Esau was a quasi-mythical figure, whose servitude to Jacob was as yet a dream, a wish by no means fulfilled. How could the oracles of the prophets on high-and-mighty Edom be applied to the lonely and defeated Jewry of the third century by a Church which, although on the increase, had as yet hardly achieved perfect security?

However, the events of the fourth century provided the Christian apologists with the necessary fuel with which to give their typology a grounding in real events. With the imperial enactments curbing former Jewish liberties and then increasingly imposing restrictions on the Jews, the allegory of the oracle of Genesis 25:23 suddenly became a fact.

The shift from theoretical exegesis to political theory is most dramatically represented in legislation outlawing Jewish ownership of Christian slaves, explained by Constantine's early biographer as having been enacted "in order that those who tormented the prophets and crucified the Christ may not have possession of those who were

---

(6, 7); Jacob versus Esau and Laban (8–12); Joseph and Potiphar's wife (13); Moses and Israel versus Pharaoh and Egypt (15–21). This list could easily have been construed as one of contrasting pairs. Furthermore, to philosophically oriented Christians, who in the wake of Philo would see in Biblical personalities ideal types, the pairing of Biblical personalities blended perfectly with the philosophical dualism which was so much a part of the Hellenic mode of thought; see F. M. Cornford, *From Religion to Philosophy* (New York, 1957), pp. 62f., 218f.

55. Cf. the difference between the allegorical meaning of Ishmael (=the Jews) and the literal meaning (=Saracens) in Bede, summarized by Southern, *Western Views of Islam in the Middle Ages*, pp. 16f.

56. On Christian claims to the title of "Israel" and the opprobrium attached to the word "Jew," see Blumenkranz, *Judenpredigt*, pp. 116f., 171f., 181f. On "Jews" as an epithet for a Christian heretic, see James Parkes, *The Conflict of the Church and the Synagogue* (London, 1934), pp. 300f.; H. A. Wolfson, *Religious Philosophy* (Cambridge, Mass., 1961), p. 169. Cf. also B. Blumenkranz, *Juifs et Chrétiens dans le monde occidental* (Paris, 1960), p. xvi. The conflict over the term *Israel* and its theological implications has been treated extensively; cf. W. D. Davies, *Paul and Rabbinic Judaism*, 2nd ed. (London, 1955), pp. 58f., Schoeps, *Aus Frühchristlicher Zeit*, pp. 153f.; M. Simon, *Versus Israel* (Paris, 1948). Although beginning with Cassiodorus (d. ca. 580) Christian writers would often claim even the title "Judei" for Christendom (cf. Romans 2:25f.), the term never lost its basically pejorative connotation; see Blumenkranz, "Les Auteurs chrétiens," *REJ*, 109:45f. (1948–49); 111:47, 58 (1951–52); 113:31 (1954); 114:56, 70, n. 1 (1955); 117:26 (1958).

saved by the Christ."[57] Although neither the Constantinian legislation nor the theological rationale of "Eusebius" makes reference to any specific Christian Scriptural foundation for the new restriction, the patristic exegesis of Genesis 25:23 clearly underlies the spirit and substance of the new enactments. If in the long and variegated history of Christian legislation with regard to Jewish ownership of Christian slaves, clear reference to the exegesis of Genesis 25:23 is not made explicit until much later, that is only because laws and legal decision were constantly harking back to the precedent of earlier formulations[58]—and in the earliest instance no reason had been inserted into the law itself—and because the impropriety of Christian subjection to the Jew, singly and collectively, had become accepted as basic. However, the underlying motive of separation from the Jews on the grounds of Christian superiority was soon made explicit. Repeated conciliar pronouncements, beginning with the Council of Vannes in 465, forbade Christian clerics to accept invitations to Jewish meals lest their acceptance be construed as a mark of Christian inferiority. Some forty years later the prohibition was extended to the laity. By 581 the prohibition against Jews' holding any public office was rationalized on the same grounds: "lest, Heaven forbid, Christians seem to be subject to the Jews."[59]

Once the Roman state itself had become officially Christian, it no longer could be the whore of Babylon; the Jewish identification of Rome with Edom could be dismissed as idle fantasy; the fate of the Jew vindicated the accuracy of Scripture: "The elder shall serve the younger." In the writings of Jerome[60] and more especially of

57. J. Juster, *Les Juifs dans l'empire romain* (Paris, 1914), II, 72. While it may be conceded to Simon, *Versus Israel*, p. 340, and Parkes, *Conflict of the Church and the Synagogue*, pp. 202f., that the limitations on Jewish rights in the slave market were partially motivated by the desire to prevent Jews from Judaizing, this will not explain the special formulation given to Jewish–Christian relations generally and specifically to Jewish disabilities in the case of Christian slaves, which were clearly in a *special* category; see Juster, II, 71, n. 3. On the doctrinal problem generated by Jewish ownership of Christian slaves, see also Blumenkranz, "Les Auteurs chrétiens," *REJ*, 109:60, n. 30 (1948–49).

58. Juster, *Les Juifs*, II, 72f.; Baron, *Social and Religious History*, III, 14, 30f.

59. J. Aronius, *Regesten zur Geschichte der Juden* (Berlin, 1902), pp. 5, no. 10; 7, no. 17; 15, no. 40. The papal chancellery represented these enactments of total separation from the Jews as part of a consistent policy inaugurated in the days of Constantine; see A. Erhardt, "Constantine, Rome and the Rabbis," *Bulletin of the John Rylands Library*, 42:288f., and especially 296f. (1960). I owe this reference to Professor E. J. Bickerman.

60. Jerome, *Comment. in Obad.*, Migne, *PL*, 25:1101f. For Jerome's heretical contemporaries, see *Pelagius' Exposition of Thirteen Epistles of St. Paul*, II (ed. by A. Souter; Cambridge, 1926 [= *Texts and Studies*, IX]), p. 74; Blumenkranz, "Les Auteurs," *REJ* 109:9 (Maximian the Arian).

Ambrose and Augustine,[61] of Gregory the Great[62] and Isidore of Seville,[63] the classical typology had become *political* theory.[64] Superficially one author parrots his predecessors, and there is little difference between the expositions of Genesis 25:23 by Tertullian and Isidore. However, what in the third century had been but an allegorical midrash provided the theory for the legal disabilities imposed on the Jews, which would later be justified by the theological doctrine aptly summarizing the situation: "servitudo Judaeorum." The oracle on Jacob and Esau now had to be and was increasingly implemented by law.[65] It was not any lack of tenderness that impelled Ambrose, for example, to protest against compelling Christians to restore a synagogue they had deliberately destroyed,[66] nor were the restrictions against Jewish rights to acquire slaves, the right to build new synagogues or hold public office arbitrary harassments. They grew out of the pious desire to translate a doctrine into a reality. This is particularly apparent in the case of ecclesiastical authorities, who refrained from, and even denounced, fanatical and arbitrary measures against the Jews. To moderates no less than to extremists it did not seem proper for the slave to exercise authority over the freeman, "Ne igitur per eos nomen Domini blasphemetur, *nec deterior sit Christianorum libertas, quam servitus Judaeorum*."[67] As a finishing touch,

61. Blumenkranz, *Judenpredigt*, pp. 42, 95f., 100f., 169f.; see also Augustine, *City of God* XVI, 35. On Eugarius (fifth century) see Blumenkranz, "Les Auteurs," *REJ*, 109:20, n. 17; on Pseudo-Augustine, *ibid.*, p. 31 and *passim*.

62. Baron, *Social and Religious History*, III, 29; see further, S. Katz, "Pope Gregory the Great and the Jews," *JQR*, N.S., 24:119 (1933–34).

63. *Allegoriae quaedam sacrae scripturae*, 25–26, Migne, *PL*, 83:105.

64. By the tenth century Remigius could argue that the prophecy of Gen. 25:23 had been fulfilled through the destruction of the House of David and through the dispersion of the Jews; Migne, *PL*, 131:101. Somewhat later, a bishop of Verceil contended that the fulfillment of this prophecy was so obvious as to require no explanation; Blumenkranz, "Les Auteurs," *REJ*, 114:79f. (1955). Thus, the interpretation of Gen. 25:23 was now brought into conjunction with medieval Christian exegesis of Gen. 49:10; see above, Note 37.

65. See Juster, *Les Juifs*, I, 226f., who stresses the theological motivation behind legislation against the Jews; Blumenkranz, *Judenpredigt*, pp. 66f.; Baron, *Social and Religious History*, III, 43; IV, chap. xx; V, 125f.; Parkes, *Conflict of the Church and the Synagogue*, pp. 179f., 326f.; S. Katz, *The Jews in the Visigothic and Frankish Kingdoms of Spain and Gaul* (Cambridge, 1937), chaps. vii–x. For the theory and practice in medieval times, see G. Kisch, *The Jews in Medieval Germany* (Chicago, 1949), pp. 145f.; S. W. Baron, "Plenitude of Apostolic Powers and Medieval 'Jewish Serfdom' " (in Hebrew), *Yiẓhak F. Baer Jubilee Volume*, ed. by S. W. Baron *et al.* (Jerusalem, 1960), pp. 102–124; S. Grayzel, *The Church and the Jews in the XIIIth Century* (Philadelphia, 1933).

66. Cf. Baron, *Social and Religious History*, II, 189; Blumenkranz, *Judenpredigt*, pp. 37f.; Parkes, *Conflict of the Church and the Synagogue*, pp. 166f.

67. Innocent III in Grayzel, *The Church and the Jews*, p. 108; see also *ibid.*, pp. 25f., 41f.

learned churchmen occasionally invoked the Philonic etymology which explained "Jacob" as meaning "the one who supplants" and Edom as mere "terrestrial" to further rationalize the pattern of thought permeating all Jewish–Christian relations in the Middle Ages. Jacob the spiritual Christian had supplanted and displaced Esau the carnal Jew.[68]

III. The Restoration of Edom

Christian exegetes were not content with advancing their own interpretation of the types of Esau and Jacob. By the fourth century, they had become aware of the Jewish translation of Edom and vigorously denied it.[69] This was one among the many Jewish in-

68. Blumenkranz, "Les Auteurs," *REJ*, 111:43 (1951–52); Migne, *PL*, 123:39; 131:102. For the pejorative overtones of "terrestrial" Edom, see H. A. Deane, *The Political and Social Ideas of St. Augustine* (New York, 1963), pp. 28f. As evidence of the great currency which the homily on Gen. 25:23 had gained we may note that early in the twelfth century Honorius of Canterbury invoked it, in connection with the struggle between royal and papal authority, as evidence of the superiority of the *sacerdotium* to *regnum*. Esau the elder son, he observed, typifies the king and the lay population, while Jacob the younger son typifies the Church. Honorius also traces the history of the relationship between Jacob and Esau back to Adam, Cain and Abel, etc., thus drawing a direct line from carnal Cain to Esau and from spiritual Abel to Jacob; cited by Ullmann, *Growth of Papal Government in the Middle Ages*, p. 415, n. 3. Needless to say, a homily with so long and venerable a history would make its way into the popular theater, where it would take on the rich and clear overtones of medieval symbolism. Thus Esau can symbolize not only the Jews and the synagogue but the Old Testament and the Law; cf. K. Young, *The Drama of the Medieval Church* (Oxford, 1954), II, 258f., 264f., 484f. (I owe this reference to Professor Norman Cantor.) Cf. also H. O. Taylor, *The Mediaeval Mind* (Cambridge, Mass., 1962), II, 67f.

69. While a number of modern scholars noted that Jerome was aware of the Jewish interpretation of Edom (see above, Note 15; M. Rahmer, *Hieronymus' Commentar zu den zwölf kleinen Propheten* [Berlin, 1902], I, 14; II, 4f.), it is no less important to indicate that each time Jerome cites this Jewish interpretation, he dubs it an *idle fantasy*. In this connection, note must be made of the effort by R. Duval, "Notes sur la Peschitto, I. Edom et Rome," *REJ*, 14:49–51 (1887), to interpret the Peschitta translation of Ps. 12:9 as "Like obscene Rome of the seed of Edom," a conjecture that has since made its way into other works as an established fact. Actually, the fact is far from established. A glance at R. Payne Smith, *Thesaurus Syriacus*, I, 34, s.v. ܐܕܘܡ; 1123, s.v. ܙܠܠܐ and II, 3860, s.v. ܪܘܡܐ will establish that Duval's suggestion is clever but fanciful. Duval himself had to emend the Peschitta reading from ܙܠܠܐ to ܙܠܠܬܐ. His contention that this interpretation was suppressed and accordingly not incorporated in the *Targum* because of fear is even more difficult. A more plausible explanation of the Peschitta rendering can be found in the similarity of the Syriac to the Hebrew. Not knowing what to make of the Hebrew of Ps. 9:12 b, the Syriac translator(s) took similar Syriac words, which were only a little less opaque than the original. The Peschitta passage in question is decidedly *not* proof of Christian acceptance of the Jewish interpretation of

terpretations of Scripture which ecclesiastical authorities denounced again and again.[70] Two circumstances which had become closely intertwined were at work. In the first place, the Jewish typology was an open challenge to the Church, which in the eighth century increasingly identified itself with the name and glory of ancient Rome.[71] With the growing influence of the Papacy, coupled with the fact that the never-ending conflicts over authority in the West always seemed to hinge on the question of authority over the city that had been mistress of the world, Jews had a new and added confirmation that Edom had never died. Accordingly, Christian exegetes had to prove that not their empire, but corporate Jewry was the Antichrist. Coupled with this was the desire to undermine Jewish exegesis wherever possible, and here Christian interpreters knew they were on surer footing. Christian apologists struck home when they pointed out that official Jewish sources themselves had identified the Romans with the Kittim of Scripture, and the Kittim were sons of Tubal the son of Japheth, not children of Esau the son of Isaac.[72] Here were "facts" that could not be dismissed.

From the Jewish point of view, once Jewish servitude had become an undeniable fact, the Christian exegesis of servitude could not long be ignored. Put otherwise, if Jewish exegesis was to be saved, the problems raised by the enemy camp could not be sidestepped.

It should, therefore, occasion no surprise that considerable Jewish effort was expended in the Middle Ages to vindicate the Rabbinic symbol without contradicting ethnological "facts." These solutions were not mere exegetical exercises. They sought to restore the bedrock of Jewish eschatology, the rationale for hope and survival.

As in so many other areas of medieval Jewish literature and tradition, two different sets of answers gained wide currency in the medieval

---

Edom. In conclusion, the early Christians are consistent: those who mention the Jewish interpretation do so out of a desire to be thorough and to refute it. Thus, the medieval Syriac lexicographers mention the Jewish interpretation of Edom as "some say"; see Smith, *Thesaurus Syriacus*, I, 34. For further Christian denials, see Rosenthal, "From 'Sefer Alfonso' " (cited above, Note 36).

70. Blumenkranz, *Judenpredigt*, pp. 162f.; *idem.*, "Les Auteurs," *REJ*, 109:22 (1948–49); 113:6 (1954).

71. Cf. D. Comparetti, *Vergil in the Middle Ages*, trans. by E. F. M. Benecke (New York, 1929), pp. 176f.; J. Bryce, *The Holy Roman Empire* (New York, 1961), *passim*, and especially pp. 8f., 13f.; Schramm, *Kaiser, Rom und Renovatio*, I, 31f., 46f., 225, who traces the coalescence of two originally discrete concepts, *Roma aeterna caput mundi* and *urbs sacra;* see also above, Note 35.

72. See above, Notes 19, 69.

world. The one was an Italian solution and the other a Babylonian-Spanish theory.[73]

The first medieval apologia for the Rabbinic theory of Edom-Rome comes from the work known as *Josippon*, a Hebrew abridgement and adaptation of Josephus composed by a Jew of southern Italy probably in 953.[74] Although the principal theme of this work is the history of the Jews from the rebuilding of the Second Temple until its destruction, after the fashion of many medieval chronicles the book opens with a brief introduction identifying the various nations of its own day with the peoples listed in the Noachian genealogy of Genesis 10. Having presented his classification of the nations at large, the author pauses to dwell in considerable detail on the origins of Rome and other Italian cities. This introduction on Italian antiquities is an interesting little document on several counts. In the first place, the essentials of Livy and Virgil are set forth in Hebrew for the first time from a Jewish point of view. Supernatural-mythological tales have been scrupulously omitted, while a number of details have been reworked so completely as almost to obscure their connections with well known stories of classical antiquity. Nor can Josippon's bizarre departure from standard mythology be dismissed as sheer ignorance. His accuracy in the genealogy of early Italic kings and his familiarity with the legends associated with local antiquities clearly indicate that he had access to good sources of information from which he departed on occasion quite deliberately.[75] Secondly, the excursus on Italy clearly shows Rome to be the real center of the author's interest. Josippon's concern with Rome and its antiquities reflects not only an interest in the power which more than any other affected Jewish destiny but also a sensitivity to the medieval ideal of *Renovatio* which was always focused on the eternal city and which took on new life after the ninth century.[76]

73. Cf. Baron, *Social and Religious History*, IV, 3; V, 61; H. J. Zimmels, *Ashkenazim and Sephardim* (London, 1958).

74. For the date see D. Flusser, "The Author of the Book of Josiphon: His Personality and his Age" (in Hebrew), *Zion*, 18:108 (1953).

75. See the useful Latin translation and commentary in the edition of J. F. Breithaupt, *Josephus Gorionides* (Gotha, 1707); Breithaupt gives full references to the classical sources underlying Josippon's mythology. For further observations on this section see Flusser, pp. 112f.; Y. Baer, "Sefer Yosifon ha-Ivri," *Sefer Dinaburg* (Jerusalem, 1949), pp. 180f.; Baron, *Social and Religious History*, VI, 188f.

76. On the resurgence of the ideal of Roman *Renovatio* in this period, which explains the *Sitz im Leben* of Josippon's Kittim theory, see Schramm, *Kaiser, Rom und Renovatio*, I, 44f. I owe the recognition of the connection between the ideal of *Renovatio* and Josippon's point of view to the study of I. F. Baer, mentioned in the previous note. However, the

To let Josippon speak for himself,[77] after the Lord dispersed the nations of the world, the Kittim settled in the plains of Campania on the banks of the Tiber, from which point they expanded and established a number of Italian cities. However, their way of life was destined to be radically reshaped from another quarter. According to a Talmudic legend, when Joseph and his brothers were conveying the remains of their father to Palestine for burial, the inhabitants of the country, the descendants of Esau, Ishmael and Qetura, attempted to block his entry.[78] At this point Josippon amplifies on his source and relates that in the course of the skirmish, Esau's grandson, Zepho, was taken captive by Joseph, and brought back to Egypt. Zepho managed to escape and make his way to Carthage, where he entered the service of Aeneas, who was ruler of that land.[79] Since Aeneas was engaged in constant war with the peoples of Italy, Zepho accompanied him on these expeditions until he finally defected and settled down to live with the native Kittim of Italy. Because of a heroic feat which he performed for the natives, Zepho was made king of the Kittim and his name was changed to Janus-Saturnus, after the name of the beast he had killed and after the star worshiped by the natives. Janus-Saturnus was succeeded by many kings of his line until finally one of his descendants, a certain Romulus, founded the city of Rome. (*Romulus was thus a direct descendant of Esau.*) During the reign of Romulus, some Arameans and Idumeans sought asylum in Rome, having fled from the arm of David, King of Judah and Israel. Although Romulus was most cordial to the new-

---

analysis offered here is in no way contingent on the date of the coronation scene, which, Flusser has shown, is a later interpolation found only in the recast of *Josippon* known from Spanish authors. On the two recensions of *Josippon* see Flusser, pp. 110f., 114, n. 24, 119; *idem.*, "An 'Alexander Geste' in a Parma MS," *Tarbiz*, 26:166 (1956–57); G. D. Cohen, "The Story of Hannah and Her Seven Sons in Hebrew Literature" (in Hebrew), *Mordecai M. Kaplan Jubilee Volume* (New York, 1953), Hebrew vol. pp. 118f. In presenting Josippon's views on Rome, I have deliberately referred to both recensions to indicate that which clearly represents the point of view of the original.

77. *Josippon* (ed. Hominer) chaps. i–iii, pp. 2f. (ed. Breithaupt, p. 9; ed. Mantua-Günzburg, col. 4f.).

78. *B. Sota* 13a. Cf. also Ginzberg, *Legends*, II, 153f., who has combined all of the legends into a running narrative; M. M. Kasher, *Torah Shelemah* VII, 1869f. (to Gen. 50:9), nos. 24, 28, 30.

79. "Agnios" of the Hebrew sources, as Breithaupt recognized, is clearly Aeneas. The enthronement of Aeneas over Carthage rather than Rome is part of Josippon's distortion (based on the stay of Aeneas with Dido) designed to make the foundation of Rome an Edomite achievement. The Arabic Pseudo-Orosius and, later on, Ibn Khaldun also regarded Dido as a lineal descendant of Esau; see G. Levi della Vida, "La Traduzione araba della storie di Orosio," *Al-Andalus*, 19:264f. (1954).

comers, he fortified Rome heavily for fear of King David and even signed a nonaggression pact with him.

Obviously, the long introduction is intended to alert the reader to the centrality of Rome in the story which follows. On the other hand, this is not its only aim, for it has gratuitously introduced a number of mythological elements that might easily have been omitted. Furthermore, this account of Roman origins is interesting not only for what it says but also for what it does not say. Not only does the author distort Roman mythology, but he also shuns some Jewish mythology as well. According to a story found in several versions in classical Rabbinic sources, Rome indeed had a supernatural origin. On the day that King Solomon wedded the daughter of Pharaoh, Michael or Gabriel descended from heaven, plunged a reed into the sea and there emerged an island which became a forest, which, in turn, later became the great city of Rome.[80] On the day that Jeroboam the son of Nebat set up the two calves in Bethel and in Dan, Romulus and Remus built two huts in Rome, thus initiating their dominion.[81] The Rabbinic story, adapted from ancient "foundation" motifs,[82] sets forth in legendary terms the view that the very existence of Rome was a divine punishment for Israel's sins. The rulers of Israel themselves sowed the seed for the destruction of their people, and the conflict between Rome and Judea is rooted in the decree of Heaven.

The author of *Josippon* is concerned no less than the Talmud to explain the enduring conflict between Rome and Israel. Although he will not break with basic religious vocabulary—Rome is to him "the fourth empire"[83]—he will have nothing to do with supernatural explanations, even Jewish ones, or purely homiletical plays on words, which one must take or leave by faith alone. He prefers an ethnological explanation, by going, after the fashion of the ancients, to a people's origins. In Josippon's view the Romans are indeed identical with the Biblical Kittim, but they became Edomites as well, once Zepho the Idumean and his lineal descendants had established their rule over them.[84] It was Zepho's grandson Latinus who gave the Kittim

80. On the reed and forest, see Grünbaum, *Beiträge*, p. 305.

81. Krauss, "Griechen und Römer," p. 9, n. 16; *idem.*, *Paras ve-Romi*, pp. 14f.

82. See R. Rieger, "The Foundation of Rome in the Talmud," *JQR*, N.S., 16: 227f. (1925–26).

83. *Josippon*, chap. xxiii (ed. Hominer, p. 90; ed. Breithaupt, p. 221; ed. Mantua-Günzburg, col. 148); see also Baer, "Sefer Yosifon," pp. 180f.

84. Ginzberg, *Legends* V, 372, n. 425.

their language and their alphabet. Thus, their very culture is an Edomite one. Since Zepho came to the West hostile to the descendants of Jacob, he doubtless imparted some of the hostility to his lineal and cultural heirs. This fear of and hostility to Israel was reinforced during the reign of David when Edomite refugees conveyed their enmity across the Mediterranean to the city of Romulus. Henceforth, the Romans would always keep a watchful eye on the deeds of their ancestral enemies.

The author of *Josippon*, a south-Italian who was much enamored of his country and its lore, had highly ambivalent feelings about the Roman–Jewish conflict. But his first loyalties were to his own ethnic group, and his ethnographic introduction was a tacit reply to the Christian polemic he heard round about him. Later readers, such as Abravanel,[85] understood his motives very well, and they gratefully invoked his evidence as proof of the authenticity of the Jewish identification of Edom.

It may be objected that Josippon merely replaced a beautiful Rabbinic allegory with a highly drab fabrication of his own or of some earlier source. Even more to the point, no polemical antagonist would readily accept this new explanation as more trustworthy than the Christian denial of the Jewish claim of the Edomite origins of Rome. To this the author would have replied that in reality he was merely providing the historical background for a "fact" accepted by *consensus omnium*. As already indicated, the author came from southern Italy, where Arabic and Byzantine influences were strongly felt. Now in Arabic, Greeks, Christians, and by extension the peoples of Europe generally, were called *Banu Aṣfar*, which means literally "yellow, or light colored, people," but which learned medieval Arabs claimed means "sons of the red one": that is, Edom or Esau. In modern days, Ignaz Goldziher showed that the latter explanation is indeed the correct one, although *aṣfar* does not mean "red" at all. Actually, the word in this connection is merely an Arabization of the Septuagintal rendition of Zepho, the grandson of Esau. *Banu Aṣfar* is thus a synonym for *Ahl al-Rum* ("the people of Rome").[86] In telling the story of Zepho's escape to the West, Josippon had merely invoked and doctored somewhat an old midrash that ex-

85. See above, Note 38.

86. I. Goldziher, "Aṣfar," *Encyclopedia of Islam*, I, 477 (rev. ed., I, 687); see also G. Levi della Vida, "The 'Bronze Era' in Moslem Spain," *JAOS*, 63:190 (1943).

plained quite plausibly an accepted linguistic usage, which he, like everyone else, regarded as quite valid.

Since Josippon soon gained a wide circulation and appeal, his theory made its way into a popular anthology of apocryphal stories on the Biblical period, *Sefer ha-Yashar*,[87] and in a somewhat "improved" form into exegetical works of a more traditional and respectable genre. This tailored version merits special notice in view of its potential consequences.

According to Scripture, after Jacob returned to Canaan from the home of Laban, Esau took his family "and went to another land because of his brother Jacob" (Genesis 36:6). Though earlier exegetes were at a loss to identify the place to which he repaired, those who had access to *Josippon* now knew very well. They explained that Esau went to Rome, for he had heard that his grandson Zepho, the founder of Rome, had been killed in battle with Turnus, King of Elishah. Accordingly, the old man came to avenge his grandson's death and remained there.[88] Later exegetes could not be satisfied with the flimsy explanations of *Josippon* invoking descendants of Esau but insisted that Rome had been taken over by Esau himself. Rome was New Edom, the second home of the father of all Edomites.

Once such theories became generally known, there was always the danger of their being taken seriously and made the basis of practical policy in the realm of *halakhah*. "You shall not abhor an Edomite," Deuteronomy enjoins, "for he is your brother" (Deuteronomy 24:8). The same collection of laws enjoins: "You shall not deduct interest from loans to your brother . . . you may deduct interest from loans to foreigners, but not from loans to your countryman" (Deuteronomy 24:20). Now, if Rome is the progeny of Esau, may one take interest from Christians or even more specifically from *an Italian of the vicinity of Rome*? Were they not brothers? Obviously,

87. *Sefer Ha-Yashar*, ed. by L. Goldschmidt (Berlin, 1923), pp. 202f. (The genealogical opening of *Josippon* is reproduced by *Sefer ha-Yashar*, pp. 31f.). On the work see L. Zunz, *Ha-Derashot be-Yisrael*, ed. by Ḥ. Albeck (Jerusalem, 5707), pp. 69f.

88. S. A. Wertheimer, *Bate Midrashot*, ed. by A. J. Wertheimer (Jerusalem, 1950–53), I, 160, par. 72; J. Mann, *The Bible as Read and Preached in the Old Synagogue* (Cincinnati, 1940), Hebrew section, p. 327; Samuel b. Nissim Masnuth, *Bereshit Zuta* (Jerusalem, 1962), p. 281.—No one of these texts is quite correct. Thus in Masnuth, read רבתא for ובתה; in the other texts, read לנקמו for לנחמו. Mann's dating of this version in n. 412 is unacceptable, since תורנוש מארץ אלישע obviously derives from *Josippon*, except that *Josippon's* details have been garbled somewhat. Moreover, the lateness of this version is evidenced by the fact that Rashi, Nachmanides, Kimḥi, and other medieval collections know nothing of it. Cf. further Ginzberg, *Legends*, V, 372, n. 424. Turnus, as noted by Breithaupt, p. 11, n. 10, is clearly Turnus, King of the Rutuli, of the *Aeneid* 7:56.

what was at stake here was the harmonization of law with the exigencies of life. It was at this point that jurists turned skeptics and categorically denied that the interdiction against usury applied to Christians. The latter were Edomites only theologically, not historically.[89] This was not a meretricious evasion. It was common-sense refusal to build law on polemical fantasy. Even Abraham ibn Ezra, who, as we shall see, vehemently denied the Edomite origin of Rome, had referred to Christendom in his poetry as Israel's "brother."[90] Poetry and myth were one matter, exegesis and law quite another.

To some, the issue was not so clear in matters of conversion, since the Bible by implication forbids marriage with Edomites until the third generation. Most authorities sanely followed Tannaitic precedent in regarding Biblical ethnic tabus void in this case as well as in those specifically nullified by the Talmud.[91] Abraham Maimuni insisted that the marital interdictions on Edomites applied only to those whose genealogy could be attested, and that, he stressed, was not the case with Italians of his day.[92] However, as late as the eighteenth century some jurists still felt that Roman stock had not been as tainted as that of other nations—since they had never been exiled by Sennacherib—and that since Romans may, therefore, be of pure stock the course of stringency should be followed.[93] The issue, to be sure, was raised only at rare intervals, and even then only in circles where *Josippon* had been taken seriously.

An entirely different approach to the problem of Edom-Rome was taken by Babylonian, Spanish, and Provençal Jewish scholars. Under the influence of Muslim genealogical science, they rejected out of hand the identification of Rome with Edom on the grounds that the Romans were clearly the Biblical Kittim, who, in turn, were of Ionian origin.[94] In the view of this school of thought, the

89. J. Rosenthal, "The Law of Usury Relating to Non-Jews" (in Hebrew), *Talpioth* 6, 1–2:143, 149 (1953); L. Stein, "The Development of the Jewish Law on Interest from the Biblical Period to the Expulsion of the Jews from England," *Historia Judaica*, 17:30f. (1955).

90. For reference to Christendom as "the brother" (i.e., Esau), see Zunz, *Synagogale Poesie*, p. 464.

91. *M. Yad.* 4:4. Cf. Jacob b. Asher, *Arbaᶜah Ṭurim*, Eben ha-ᶜEzer, 4.

92. Abraham Maimuni, *Perush, p. 126.*

93. Rosenthal, "The Law of Usury," pp. 139, n. 11; 152; *Encyclopedia Talmudit*, I, 71a.

94. See the material collected by Rosenthal, "The Law of Usury," pp. 141f. That the denial of the Edomite origin of Rome represented an effort to meet the challenge of Christian exegesis of Gen. 25:23 was noted by S. A. Wertheimer, *Geon ha-Geonim* (Jerusalem, 5685), pp. 56, n. 1; 57, n. 1.

name of Edom thus applied to Rome only secondarily. In the first instance the name Edom applied to the Christian Church, which became identified with the Roman empire in the days of Constantine. According to this view, Jesus was not the father of Christianity at all. Jesus had been just one more false Jewish prophet, who had come to an ignominious end. Long after his death, the pagan priests of Edom associated his name with their idolatrous religion, which they persuaded Constantine to adopt and impose on his empire. The books of the New Testament and the Christian claim to uninterrupted apostolic succession were among the fabrications of these Idumean priests or of Constantine himself.[95]

This solution actually reversed the process by which Rome and Edom had originally been made identical. In the Talmudic scheme—and for that matter, in Josippon's as well—the name of Edom had applied originally to Rome and by extension to Christendom. Now the situation was quite the reverse. In any event, the theory removed Christendom from an ethnic-political level to a strictly theological plane, for one obvious implication was that Edom was not a contemporary *empire* and could, therefore, not be identified with the fourth monarchy of Daniel's visions. Clearly this theory reflects the Judeo-Arabic milieu in which it originated, for to Jews of Muslim lands, especially of Muslim Spain, the fourth kingdom had to be that of Ishmael, and it was with the collapse of the Muslim empire that the messianic era would be inaugurated.[96]

95. See the copious references collected by A. S. Halkin in his edition of Maimonides, *Epistle to Yemen* (New York, 1952), p. 14, n. 15. Cf. also Abraham Maimuni, *Perush*, p. 64; Rosenthal, "From 'Sefer Alfonso,' " pp. 611, 593. So ingrained did this view become that some Jews credited Constantine with instituting the practice of having Christian males worship bareheaded; Leon Modena, *She᾿elot u-Teshuvot Ẓikne Yehudah* (Jerusalem, 5716), p. 34.

The theory that Constantine composed the New Testament is the Jewish counterpart of the medieval Christian theory (voiced by the Spaniard Petrus Alfonsi) that the Quran was composed after the death of Muhammad; N. Daniel, *Islam and the West* (Edinburgh, 1960), pp. 34f. On the other hand, it echoes the comparison of Constantine to Moses made in Christian circles; Schramm, *Kaiser, Rom und Renovatio*, I, 142f. Jews thus regarded him as the *nomothetes* of Christendom in every respect.

96. Ibn Ezra to Dan. 2:39 and especially "Abraham Ibn Ezra's Short Commentary on Daniel," ed. by H. J. Mathews, *Miscellany of Hebrew Literature*, 2:3 (1877), where Ishmael is explicitly called "the fourth kingdom." (Thus, the strictures of Steinschneider, *Polemische und apologetische Literatur*, p. 269, must be rejected.) Cf. further *Pirqe R. Eliezer* (ed. Higger) 27, *Horeb*, 10:187 (1948); *Midrash ha-Gadol*, Genesis (ed. Margulies) to Gen. 15:9, p. 254; *Ma᾿or ha-᾿afelah* (ed. Kafih), p. 87. These Yemenite anthologies also contain the Saadyanic tradition that Edom and Ishmael are "partners" in the fourth kingdom; however, the presence of traditions crediting Ishmael with exclusive dominion is undeniable. For parallel views of Christians living under Muslim domain, see R. W. Southern, *Western Views of Islam in the Middle Ages* (Cambridge, Mass., 1962), pp. 23f.

The motives for this new classification of empires are quite obvious, but the exegetes of the Judeo-Arabic milieu were not unanimous in the way they squared the Rabbinic traditions on Edom-Rome with the new needs of eschatological theory. Saadia and Ibn Aqnin maintained that the fourth kingdom consisted of a dominion shared by Edom and Ishmael—a common designation of Islam in Judeo-Arabic sources is "the partner"—while Ibn Ezra, adjusting exegesis to the facts of life, eliminated Rome completely from the fourth dominion and designated the latter as the exclusive legacy of Ishmael.[97] Rome, in Ibn Ezra's scheme, was identical with the Biblical Kittim and was but an offshoot of the third empire, which, he contended, was clearly that of Greece. Maintaining a rigid consistency, Ibn Ezra denied emphatically that Edom should in any way be implicated in the destruction of the Temple. That calamity was the work of the wicked Greek empire, which exists to this very day.[98] The subordination of Rome to Greece and its reclassification in the third empire did not necessarily lessen the role of Rome in the eschaton, for, Ibn Ezra noted, the third empire was destined to play a crucial role in ushering in the end of days. That end would be heralded by the mortal combat between the third and fourth empires: that is, between Rome, the Christian standard-bearer of Greece, and the eleven horns or petty kingdoms of Ishmael-Islam. Moreover, he pointed out, Daniel had not claimed that any but the fourth empire would be utterly destroyed. The others would survive, albeit denuded of their power.[99] Ibn Ezra's Spanish-Jewish orientation did not require that the Christian nations should be destroyed. It was enough that their power should be shattered in the fullness of time, and that Israel would then be redeemed. Now by making

97. Ibn Ezra's *Shorter Commentary to Daniel*, pp. 3, 7; Joseph b. Judah ibn Aqnin, *Divulgatio mysteriorum luminumque apparentia, commentarius in Canticum Canticorum*, ed. by A. S. Halkin (Jerusalem, 1964), pp. 414–415. I am indebted to Professor Halkin for making this information available to me prior to the appearance of his edition.

98. See Ibn Ezra to Gen. 27:40; Zech. 11:15, where the edition of Venice of 1524 and manuscripts of Ibn Ezra read:

כי יון הגלה ירושלם לא אדום

(courtesy of the collation of Mr. Melvin Libman).

99. Ibn Ezra to Dan. 7:14, *idem*, *Shorter Commentary*, p. 4. Exegetically, Ibn Ezra was on solid ground; see H. L. Ginsberg, *Studies in Daniel*, pp. 6f. The fact that Rome was really part of the Greek empire was information that was received with enthusiasm in Byzantium; see Z. Ankori, "Studies in the Messianic Doctrines of Yehuda Hadassi the Karaite," *Tarbiz*, 30:203, n. 51 (1960–61); *idem*, "The Correspondence of Tobias ben Moses, the Karaite, of Constantinople," *Essays on Jewish Life and Thought Presented in Honor of Salo Wittmayer Baron*, ed. by J. L. Blau *et al.* (New York, 1959), p. 5, n. 13.

the Roman Kittim a subcategory of the Greeks, Ibn Ezra had by implication clearly distinguished between the empire (*imperium*) and the specific monarchy (*regnum*) in control of it at any given moment. The Greek empire remained Greek whether its ruler was a Greek or a Roman.[100]

Ibn Ezra's solution represented the ultimate refinement of Danielian exegesis in accordance with the requirements of ethnology, exegesis, eschatology, and the facts of history, all of which had now been brought into perfect accord. To be sure, Israel was still at war with Edom, but that was a religious conflict. However, the Danielian eschatology foresaw a conflict of nations and empires, and in that regard Edom had no special function. Ibn Ezra's Edom was only a secondary characteristic of the essential enemies, Roman Greece and Ishmael.

When later, under the impact of the Reconquista, Ishmael's identity as the fourth monarchy had to be rejected, Edom regained its political connotation. Rome, the Jewish theoreticians explained, would suffer the fate of Edom, for the prophet had clearly foretold that Christianity and the Roman empire would become one. Ethnologically, the Romans might be Kittim. Religiously and eschatologically they were the seed of Esau.[101]

The Jewish–Christian polemic on Esau persisted to the end of the Middle Ages. However, the arguments that came from either side were essentially those formulated in the period we have surveyed. Speculation would continue on the date of the end and the identity of the actors in the final drama. But underlying the pursuit of that elusive day was the necessary theoretical foundation substantiating the reality of ancient Esau.

100. The same view underlies the fanciful account of the Sassanid call to arms in Abraham ibn Daud, *Sefer ha-Qabbalah* (ed. Neubauer, p. 60, lines 17f.; trans. G. D. Cohen, chap. iv, lines 131f.). The identity of the Greeks and Romans was a Sassanid conception, which probably came to Ibn Ezra and Ibn Daud by way of Arabic historiography; cf. T. Noeldeke, "Geschichte des Artaschir i Papakan," *Beiträge zur Kunde der indogermanischen Sprachen*, 4:36, n. 1; 54 (1878).

101. See Moses Nachmanides, *Commentary on the Torah* (in Hebrew), ed. by C. B. Chavel (Jerusalem, 1959–60), II, 302; *idem*, *Sefer ha-Geʾulah*, pp. 51f.

Le Problème de l'Unité de Dieu d'après Dāwūd ibn Marwān al-Muqammiṣ

By GEORGES VAJDA

Après les deux études que nous avons eu l'occasion de consacrer à celui qui fut très probablement le premier dans la longue série des théologiens juifs arabophones,[1] nous nous proposons d'analyser cette fois-ci l'enseignement des *ᶜIshrūn Maqālāt* sur l'unité de Dieu.

* * *

David Kaufmann a été le premier à signaler[2] qu'al-Muqammiṣ utilisait déjà dans son étude du problème de Dieu le schéma noétique des quatre questions: *an*, *quid*, *quale*, *cur*.[3] Connaissant aujourd'hui un peu mieux la structure des "Vingt Discours," nous pouvons préciser que cette étude y remplit quatre *maqālāt*, de VII à XI; de plus, nous savons qu'entre la première question, traitée dans le septième Discours, et la deuxième, qui forme l'objet du neuvième,[4] notre auteur a intercalé la question *quantum* (*kam huwa*). L'examen de cette question prend place dans la huitième *maqāla*, que nous tenterons d'analyser dans les pages qui suivent.

* * *

Après avoir démontré, dans le septième Discours, qu'il y a nécessairement, à l'origine de l'univers, un être (ou plusieurs, nous ne

1. G. Vajda, *A propos de la perpétuité de la rétribution d'outre-tombe en théologie musulmane* dans *Studia Islamica*, XI, 1959, pp. 29–38; *La finalité de la création de l'homme selon un théologien juif du IXᵉ siècle*, dans *Oriens*, XV, 1962, pp. 61–85. Dans ces articles, nous avons dit l'obligation que nous avons au Professeur A. S. Halkin de nous avoir communiqué une copie partielle de l'original arabe; nous y avons également exposé les raisons qui nous portent à fixer le *floruit* d'al-Muqammiṣ dans la seconde moitié du IXᵉ siècle, donc avant Saadia.

2. Dans un de ses premiers travaux, *Die Theologie des Bachja Ibn Pakuda* (1874): voir *Gesammelte Schriften*, II, 32, n. 1.

3. Voir A. Altmann et S. M. Stern; *Isaac Israeli* (Oxford, 1958), pp. 10–23, et G. Vajda, *Revue de l'Histoire des Religions*, 1959, p. 89.

4. Le mieux connu parce que conservé en version hébraïque dans le commentaire sur le *Séfer Yeṣīra* de Juda ben Barzilaï et édité dans l'original arabe par I. O. Ginzburg dans *Zapiski Kollegii Vostokovêdov*, V, 1930, pp. 481–507, avec introduction, traduction et notes en russe.

le savons pas encore) que n'affecte aucun des caractères impliquant *ḥudūth*, venue à l'être, "adventicité" (non pas "nouveauté," comme on dit assez improprement), al-Muqammiṣ passe, dans le huitième, à la question de savoir combien l'univers a de créateurs: un seul ou plusieurs?

Le Créateur de l'univers est *un*, non pas deux, ni trois, ni sept, ni douze.

De toute évidence, ces chiffres ne sont pas choisis au hasard. Le créateur n'est pas deux: ceci contre les dualistes; il n'est pas trois: refus de la doctrine trinitaire des Chrétiens; il n'est ni sept ni douze: erreur de ceux qui verraient dans les sept planètes ou les douze signes du zodiaque les suprêmes régulateurs du monde.

La démonstration de la thèse va être faite au moyen de divisions dialectiques: dilemmes dont chacun est à son tour divisé en deux branches.

Le Créateur, que peut-il être?
Substance ou accident
ou bien
ni substance ni accident
ou encore
soit corps ⟨ou non-corps⟩
soit ni corps ni non-corps.

Examinons successivement ces hypothèses.

Dieu est substance. La substance reçoit (nécessairement) des accidents; en faisant de Dieu une substance, nous le mettrions donc au nombre des substances non éternelles qui constituent le monde.

Dieu est accident. Si c'était vrai, il aurait eu éternellement besoin d'un autre être qui lui servît de substrat, ce qui est absurde.

De plus, substance porteuse d'accidents, Dieu ne saurait créer de telles substances (dont est pourtant constitué l'univers visible), car un agent (littéralement: "la chose") ne produit pas son semblable.

Mais, objectera-t-on, le Créateur ne pourrait-il pas être une substance non-porteuse d'accidents? La réponse à cette objection est malheureusement obscure et le texte paraît défectueux à cet endroit.

Passons au second dilemme: *le Créateur est-il corps ou non-corps?* S'il est corps au sens où nous entendons communément ce terme, il est non-éternel (car ce que nous appelons corps est inséparable des accidents, et ce qui est inséparable des accidents est, nous le savons aussi, non-éternel; or il a été établi dans le septième Discours que l'univers postule un créateur éternel). Dire qu'il est corps en un sens autre que celui que nous donnons à ce terme, revient à dire qu'il n'est appelé corps qu'au figuré, c'est à-dire qu'il n'est pas corps.

A ce stade de la discussion, il apparaît donc que l'auteur (*muḥdith*) du monde n'est ni substance, ni accident, ni corps; il est donc non-corps (c'est-à-dire être incorporel), puisqu'une chose (un "existant") est ou bien corps ou bien non corps. Il convient donc de poser ici la question: combien y a-t-il de tels êtres (l'arabe dit simplement *kam huwa*: "combien est-il"); c'est là l'objet de notre présente recherche.[5]

N'étant donc ni substance, ni accident, ni corps, le Créateur du monde est ou bien un ou bien deux.

La transition peut sembler ici manquer de clarté. L'on voit assez mal comment se lient les deux problèmes, celui de la corporéité ou incorporéité de l'être suprême et celui du nombre éventuel des êtres suprêmes au cas où il y en aurait plusieurs, du moins lorsque nous savons seulement que l'être suprême est incorporel. L'argumentation serait plus logique si l'on démontrait d'abord qu'il n'y a qu'un seul être suprême; c'est ce que faisaient, selon le texte cité de Maïmonide, les Mutakallimūn. Si notre auteur renverse l'ordre des questions, c'est, semble-t-il, qu'il n'a pu guère procéder autrement, puisque dans le discours précédent il avait prouvé que le monde suppose à son origine un ou plusieurs agents exempts de toutes les marques de "l'adventicité," ni substances, a-t-on vu au début du présent discours, ni accidents.

En revanche, on comprend aisément pourquoi la question de savoir si Dieu est trois, sept, ou douze n'intervient plus ici. La réfutation du dualisme, que nous entendrons développer maintenant, implique en fait celle de tout pluralisme. Si al-Muqammiṣ consacre

5. Notons ici que cet ordre de présentation des problèmes n'est pas celui qui, selon Maïmonide, est propre aux Mutakallimūn. Il écrit en effet, *Guide*, I, 71, (nous citons la traduction anglaise de S. Pines, dans S. Pines et L. Strauss, *The Guide of the Perplexed*, The University of Chicago Press, 1963, p. 179; dans la traduction française de S. Munk, le passage se trouve, t. I, p. 346): "Thus when they propound the premises that we will let you hear, they found by their demonstrations the [affirmative] judgment that the world is created in time. And when it is thus established that the world is created in time, it is likewise undoubtedly established that it has a maker who has created it in time. Then they adduced arguments in favor of the inference that this maker is one; whereupon, basing themselves upon his being one, that he is not a body. This is the way of every Mutakallim from among the Moslems in anything concerning this subject. Thus also do those belonging to our community who imitate them and follow their ways."

par la suite une réfutation spéciale au dogme chrétien de la Trinité, c'est qu'il s'agit là d'une doctrine qui se voulait elle-même unitaire.

Pourquoi nions-nous donc qu'il puisse y avoir deux créateurs?

S'il y avait deux créateurs, nous nous trouverions nécessairement en face d'une des trois possibilités suivantes.

1° Les deux créateurs concordent sous tous les rapports quant à leur essence, si bien qu'il n'y a aucune différence entre eux touchant leurs essences respectives.

2° Ils diffèrent sous tous les rapports, si bien qu'il n'y a aucune concordance entre eux quant à leurs essences respectives.

3° Ils concordent sous tel rapport, et diffèrent sous tel autre.

On attendrait, après cette position du problème, que ces trois possibilités soient examinées successivement afin de démontrer qu'aucune d'entre elles n'est compatible avec la thèse cardinale du dualisme, entendons le dualisme manichéen tel que ses adversaires se le représentaient ou voulaient se le représenter à l'époque. Le texte que nous avons ne répond pas à cette attente.

Nous y trouvons d'abord, il est vrai, l'amorce d'une discussion du premier point, mais cette discussion ne semble pas encore achevée que surgit un fragment, plus exactement la fin d'une argumentation dont le nerf est l'impossibilité de concevoir deux êtres primordiaux dont les domaines respectifs soient en contact mutuel, c'est-à-dire possèdent une frontière commune. Cette argumentation est bien connue dans la polémique anti-manichéenne des VIIIe–Xe siècles,[6] mais son insertion ici, sous une forme manifestement incomplète, porte à croire que notre texte est défectueux, peut-être parce que le copiste du manuscrit unique a travaillé sur un modèle lui-même lacuneux ou qu'il a sauté un ou deux feuillets.

Quoi qu'il en soit, le texte commence par affirmer que représenter les deux créateurs comme ne différant en leur essence sous aucun rapport, revient à abolir leur dualité. On peut demander, il est vrai, pour quelle raison on ne peut pas poser deux êtres tout en soutenant qu'il n'y a aucune différence entre eux, ou pour traduire aussi littéralement que possible l'objection: "Quel est l'indice qui

6. Voir Sa'dyāh, *K. al-amānāt wal-iʿtiqādāt*, éd. S. Landauer, pp. 48–55 (traduction anglaise, S. Rosenblatt, *The Book of Beliefs and Opinions*, pp. 58–66); M. Ventura, *La philosophie de Saadia Gaon* (Paris, 1934), pp. 127–133; P. J. de Menasce, *Shkand gumānīk vičār* (Fribourg, 1945), pp. 245, 255, 260; H.-Ch. Puech, *Le Prince des Ténèbres en son royaume* (dans *Satan*, Etudes Carmélitaines [Paris, 1948]), surtout p. 148 et suiv.; *Le Manichéisme* (Paris, 1949), pp. 75 suiv., 162 suiv.

t'amène à affirmer que lorsqu'il n'y a pas de différence entre eux, ils sont un [*wamā dalīluka ᶜalā annahu idhā lam yakun baynahumā farq fahumā wāḥid*]?"

La réponse à cette objection fait dépendre la dualité d'une différence qui intéresse soit l'essence soit les accidents des deux êtres envisagés, mais ensuite elle tourne court ou bien la fin de l'argumentation manque.

A ce développement incomplet fait suite la fin de l'argument tiré de la contiguïté des deux principes dont la conclusion est: "S'il est prouvé que la thèse est fausse qui soutient que l'auteur [*fāᶜil*] du monde est deux corps en contact ou séparés, une troisième possibilité étant exclue, l'auteur du monde ne peut être deux corps."

L'auteur passe ensuite à d'autres arguments (j'en compte quatre) contre le dualisme.

Premier argument.[7]

Si le monde avait deux auteurs, ou bien ils différeraient ou bien ils concorderaient.

Dans ce dernier cas, leur concordance concernerait
soit leur essence et leur action,
soit leur essence seule,
soit leur action seule.[8]

Le même trilemme serait à poser s'ils différaient.

On ne saurait soutenir que les deux auteurs présumés du monde concordent et quant à leur essence et quant à leur action, car, comme nous l'avons montré, il n'y a pas de dualité là où il y a concordance sous tous les rapports.

Nous avons montré d'autre part que pour être concordants sous tel rapport et différents sous tel autre, les choses envisagées doivent être porteuses d'accidents; or tout porteur d'accident est non-éternel, donc ne peut être le Créateur.

Dira-t-on que les deux auteurs concordent quant à leur essence, mais diffèrent quant à leur action? Voilà qui est absurde, car nous avons déjà démontré[9] que deux choses qui concordent quant à leur essence, concordent aussi quant à leur action.

7. Construit en dilemme dont chaque branche se subdivise en un trilemme.
8. La copie du texte arabe porte: *lā fi l-fiᶜl walā fi l-dhāt*, "ni quant à l'action ni quant à l'essence," mais je crois qu'il faut lire *fi l-fiᶜl lā fi l-dhāt*.
9. Cette démonstration ne se trouve pas dans le texte que nous avons pu consulter.

Troisième hypothèse: concordance quant à l'action, discordance quant à l'essence. Elle n'est pas moins fausse que la précédente. Notre proposition de tout à l'heure se convertit: deux choses qui concordent quant à leur action, concordent aussi quant à leur essence.

Examinons maintenant les trois subdivisions de la première branche du dilemme.

La première (les deux auteurs présumés du monde diffèrent quant à leur essence et quant à leur action) n'a de sens que si:

l'un des auteurs étant corps, l'autre est non corps;

l'un étant substance l'autre est accident

(ces deux conditions concernent la différence quant à l'essence);

l'un faisant les corps, l'autre ne les fait pas (différence quant à l'action).

Or cette hypothèse conduit à des contradictions inextricables (*khilāf*), car l'univers tel que nous l'appréhendons par la raison comporte des êtres corporels aussi bien qu'incorporels, des substances comme des accidents.

Il n'est pas clair à première vue de quelle manière cette considération affaiblit ou ruine la thèse combattue, mais ayant présentes à l'esprit les démonstrations antérieures, il est peut-être possible de comprendre le raisonnement ainsi (malgré les altérations qu'a subies le texte arabe):

Nous savons déjà que l'auteur du monde doit être non produit, donc ni corps (substance) ni accident, or la thèse combattue amène nécessairement à faire rentrer dans une de ces catégories l'un et l'autre des auteurs supposés, à moins de ne laisser subsister que le créateur non-corporel, ce qui ruine le système dualiste. Ceci sous le rapport de l'essence. D'autre part, sous le rapport de l'action, nous constatons que le monde tel qu'il est comprend des êtres corporels et des êtres incorporels. Un soi-disant créateur qui n'aurait produit que les uns ou les autres ne serait pas l'auteur universel des choses que l'hypothèse exige qu'il soit.

Dire, ajoute al-Muqammiṣ, que les deux auteurs diffèrent quant à leur essence, non quant à leur action, est absurde, car nous savons que la différence quant à celle-là a pour conséquence nécessaire la différence quant à celle-ci.

Non moins absurde est de soutenir la proposition inverse: les deux auteurs diffèrent sous le rapport de leur action non celui de leur essence, car la différence quant à l'action a aussi pour conséquence la différence quant à l'essence.

Il est ainsi prouvé que les six subdivisions sont toutes absurdes; la conclusion s'impose donc: l'auteur du monde est nécessairement unique.

Deuxième argument.

Si nous réfléchissons à la relation entre l'essence de l'auteur du monde et du monde qu'il a créé, nous nous trouvons devant un trilemme:

L'essence de l'auteur du monde est ou bien semblable à l'univers sous tous les rapports

ou bien

semblable sous tel rapport, différente sous tel autre,

ou encore

différente sous tous les rapports.

La thèse à retenir est la troisième; les deux autres sont fausses.

Contre la première thèse. Si l'auteur du monde est, quant à son essence, semblable au monde sous tous les rapports, il est composé; or tout être composé postule un agent qui réalise la composition; en admettant que cet agent soit semblable à ce dont il réalise la composition, il est lui-même composé, et ainsi de suite, d'où régression à l'infini, ce qui est absurde. Il faut dès lors aboutir à un agent qui ne soit pas lui-même l'œuvre d'un autre agent. Mais un tel agent n'est pas semblable au monde sous tous les rapports, car, contrairement au monde, il n'est pas l'œuvre d'un agent. S'il était semblable au monde sous tous les rapports, il n'y aurait pas plus de raison qu'il en soit l'auteur que le monde ne soit le sien. Or tous les gens sensés, à quelque dénomination qu'ils appartiennent, admettent que l'agent diffère de l'œuvre et réciproquement.

Admettre, et c'est la réfutation de la seconde thèse, qu'il est un rapport sous lequel l'auteur du monde est quant à son essence semblable au monde, n'est pas moins absurde. En effet, sous le rapport où l'auteur du monde serait semblable au monde, il serait non-éternel, composé et venu à l'être après n'avoir pas été.[10] Or pareille thèse

10. Al-Muqammiṣ ne dit pas pourquoi, mais il est facile de compléter son raisonnement: il n'y a rien dans le monde qui ne soit substance ou accident; de plus, la substance n'existe pas sans accident; l'accident est par définition ce qui n'a pas été puis est; mais nous savons aussi que ce qui n'est pas sans accident, et c'est précisément le cas de la substance, est lui-même affecté d'adventicité; rien de ce qui constitue le monde n'échappant à l'adventicité, il est clair que si l'auteur du monde ressemble au monde ne fût-ce que sous un seul aspect, il est, lui aussi, frappé d'adventicité, et nous retombons ainsi dans la première thèse, déjà réfutée.

n'est soutenue par personne à l'exception des Chrétiens qui enseignent que le Messie est Homme–Dieu; en tant qu'homme, il a, selon eux, le même statut que l'homme qui est un microcosme et il est affecté de la même adventicité que les hommes, tandis que, en tant que Dieu, il est éternel. Al-Muqammiṣ renvoie ici à un ouvrage antérieur qu'il a consacré à la réfutation du christianisme selon la méthode rationnelle[11] et annonce une critique de cette religion qui interviendra plus tard dans le présent ouvrage.

Sans procéder donc sur-le-champ à la réfutation de la doctrine chrétienne, al-Muqammiṣ se borne ici à souligner que l'éternité et l'adventicité sont deux notions contradictoires;[12] si donc l'auteur du monde ressemble par quelque côté au monde, il est à la fois éternel et non-éternel, ce qui est absurde.

Seule subsiste ainsi la troisième thèse:

> L'auteur du monde diffère du monde sous tous les rapports. Par conséquent, si le monde est composé, son auteur est incomposé; si le monde comporte diversité, il n'y a rien de tel en son auteur; si le monde est fini, son auteur est infini; si le monde est substance et accident, son auteur n'est ni l'un ni l'autre.

On peut illustrer cette argumentation, à titre, évidemment, d'analogie lointaine (*qiyās*) par un exemple comme le suivant.

Un livre, c'est du papier marqué de signes à l'encre; son scribe n'est dès lors pas tel, mais un être en chair et en os. Le livre n'est pas un être vivant doué de raison et mortel, son scribe possède dès lors ces attributs. Le livre étant un assemblage de lettres, son scribe n'est rien de tel. Le livre étant transposition[13] [écrite] de la parole (proférée), son scribe n'est pas cela.

Bref, l'auteur d'une chose diffère de cette chose, d'où l'on conclura nécessairement que l'auteur du monde est différent du monde. Ce raisonnement constitue, dit al-Muqammiṣ dont son lecteur ne partagera peut-être pas la satisfaction, une très forte preuve en faveur de l'unité du Créateur.[14]

11. *Al-radd ᶜalā l-Naṣārā ᶜalā⟨ṭarīq⟩al-qiyās; qiyās* désigne ici, croyons-nous, la méthode dialectique habituellement pratiquée par les Mutakallimūn plutôt que le syllogisme des philosophes.

12. Telle est bien l'idée qu'il veut exprimer, bien que son vocabulaire manque de rigueur, car il emploie le terme *khilāf* en plusieurs sens.

13. Littéralement: "narration" (*ḥikāya*, à prendre peut-être au sens qu'il a également d' "imitation").

14. L'insistance de l'auteur sur la différenciation radicale de Dieu par rapport à la totalité de l'être créaturel semble avoir une pointe antichrétienne. Ainsi Théodore Abū

Troisième argument.

Les deux auteurs du monde que postule la thèse adverse sont nécessairement soit opposés l'un à l'autre, soit d'accord entre eux. Opposés, ils sont soit de même force, soit l'un plus fort que l'autre. S'ils s'opposent étant de même force, chacun empêchera l'autre d'agir et l'œuvre ne sera pas réalisée.[15] L'un l'emportant en force anéantira l'autre qui, dès lors, n'existera pas.[16] S'ils s'accordent

---

Qurra, théologien chrétien arabophone si proche d'al-Muqammiṣ dans le temps (il vécut vers 740–820) et dans l'espace (il fut évêque de Harran), insiste précisément sur l'idée qu'on ne saurait récuser une certaine similitude (*shibh, shabah*) entre Dieu et l'homme, et il considère cette similitude comme l'une des "voies" qui mènent à la connaissance, quelque limitée qu'on la conçoive, que nous pouvons avoir de Dieu. L'une des voies, car elle doit être constamment corrigée par celle de la différence (*khilāf*): ainsi nous ressemblons à Dieu en tant que nous sommes vivants, mais la vie de Dieu est sans commencement ni fin ni soumise à aucune altération, tandis que la nôtre commence, finit et se trouve exposée aux contingences et aux accidents. Voir *Les œuvres arabes de Théodore Aboucara*, éd. Constantin Bacha (Beyrouth, 1904), IVe Mīmar, §§ 4–6, pp. 78–80, et la traduction allemande, souvent fautive, de Georg Graf, *Die arabischen Schriften des Theodor Abû Qurra . . .* (Paderborn, 1910), pp. 162–165. Cette méthode a dû paraître d'autant plus dangereuse à un théologien juif (ou musulman) qu'Abū Qurra s'en prévaut pour démontrer que Dieu a un Fils (voir le passage conservé en grec, *PG*, 97, 1497c, cité par Graf). Aussi comprend-on aisément qu'al-Muqammiṣ prenne exactement le contrepied de cette manière de voir. La polémique musulmane en faisait autant, à preuve que l'on a mis (peu importe ici que le trait soit historique ou non) dans la bouche du calife al-Mahdī (775–785), discutant avec le patriarche Timothée, cette mise en garde: "Il ne convient nullement de prendre les créatures comme exemples du Créateur"; voir A. Van Roey, *Nonnus de Nisibe, Traité Apologétique . . .* (Louvain, 1948), introduction p. 53, n. 132, citant A. Mingana, *Timothy's Apology for Christianity*, dans *Woodbrooke Studies*, t. II (Cambridge, 1928), p. 142.

Vers 820, l'apologiste chrétien Abū Rāʾiṭa (voir ci-après) voit dans l'idée de l'incomparabilité divine, résumée par l'expression coranique *laysa kamithlihi shayʾun* (XLII, 11[9]), un élément essentiel de la position théologique des Musulmans: voir *Risāla fi l-thālūth* (Epître sur la Trinité), éd. G. Graf, *Die Schriften des Jacobiten Ḥabīb Ibn Ḫidma Abū Rāʾiṭa*, CSCO, Script. Ar. tomes 14 (texte arabe), 15 (traduction allemande) (Louvain, 1951), p. 6, lig. 4 du texte, p. 7 de la traduction. Ceci n'est exact au sens plein qu'en parlant des Muʿtazilites, comme il ressort par exemple de ce que al-Khayyāṭ rapporte de l'enseignement d'Abū l-Hudhayl, contemporain d'Abū Rāʾiṭa et sans doute aussi contemporain plus âgé de notre auteur (il est mort très âgé vers 230/844): *Kitāb al-Intiṣār*, §§ 3 et 70, pp. 15 et 80 dans le texte arabe de Nyberg selon la réimpression d'A. Nader; pp. 7 et 98 de la traduction française de ce dernier. Cette même idée est très fortement mise en relief dans le résumé du *tawḥīd* par lequel al-Ashʿarī a jugé bon de commencer son exposé des thèses muʿtazilites: *Maqālāt al-islāmiyyīn*, ed. H. Ritter, pp. 155 suiv. (noter qu'elle est absente de la profession de foi orthodoxe; *ibid.*, pp. 290 suiv.; l'orthodoxie musulmane, on le sait, sauve la transcendance par le refus de qualification, *bilā kayfa*, des anthropomorphismes de la révélation coranique).—Voir aussi sur cette question, D. Kaufmann, *loc. laud.*, p. 56, n. 1, et *Geschichte der Attributenlehre*, aux endroits marqués à l'index, s.v. Gott, Unvergleichbarkeit; et H. A. Wolfson, *Philo* (Cambridge, Mass., 1947), II, 151–153. Voir aussi ci-après, Note 41.

15. Or le fait est que l'œuvre, c'est-à-dire le monde, existe.
16. Ce qui est contraire à la thèse.

entre eux, les mêmes deux possibilités se présentent: de même force, que feraient-ils sinon s'entre-aider, mais deux êtres qui s'entre-aident ne sont pas Dieu;[17] s'ils sont de force inégale, le plus faible n'est pas Dieu. Il reste donc que l'auteur du monde ne peut qu'être unique, non pas deux ni trois ni davantage.

Quatrième argument.

C'est un fait que le monde est un ensemble composite qui ne peut subsister en tant que tel que par la subsistance de chacun de ses composants. La terre ne subsiste pas sans l'eau, l'eau ne subsiste pas sans l'air, celui-ci postule le ciel, le règne végétal dépend de tout cela, le règne animal ne peut pas se passer du règne végétal; il n'est pas moins facile de constater de semblables interdépendances dans la structure de l'homme: chair et os, tête et cœur. Voilà donc un faisceau convergent de faits qui prouve que s'il y avait deux créateurs on se heurterait au dilemme suivant: ou bien chacun des deux créateurs est l'auteur d'une partie [déterminée] de la création, ou bien c'est un seul d'entre eux qui crée. Dans le premier cas, ils se trouvent coopérer à une œuvre unique, donc ni l'un ni l'autre n'est tout puissant. Dans le deuxième cas, nouveau dilemme: ou bien le seul créateur a inscrit dans son œuvre l'indice qu'il l'a créée seul et alors la prétention de l'autre à être créateur est réduite à néant, ou bien il y a inscrit l'indice prouvant qu'ils l'ont créée tous les deux, ce qui serait un mensonge; or l'être sage ne ment point et il ne fait pas passer l'indice qui le révèle pour un signe qui révélerait un autre. De cette manière encore, la thèse qui admet deux créateurs apparaît comme fausse et l'unité (ou plus exactement l'unicité) de l'auteur du monde se trouve solidement établie.

Des recherches poussées, auxquelles nous ne pouvons pas nous livrer ici, seraient nécessaires pour déterminer les sources immédiates de ces démonstrations, d'ailleurs assez sommaires dans le texte conservé de notre auteur. Il faut noter d'autre part que si elles coïncident en partie avec les développements sur le même thème que nous trouvons chez les théologiens juifs postérieurs, il ne semble pas qu'aucun d'entre eux se soit spécialement inspiré de notre texte.[18] Mais sur

17. Puisque Dieu, par définition, se suffit à lui-même.

18. Il est inutile de multiplier ici les renvois bibliographiques aux livres classiques de D. Kaufmann (*Attributenlehre*), de H. A. Wolfson (*Philo*), aux histoires générales de la philosophie juive du moyen âge (Husik, Jul. Guttmann, Vajda), aux monographies sur

ce point encore, il faut, pour l'heure, se garder d'émettre un jugement trop tranché.

* * *

Dieu est donc un. Mais comment faut-il entendre cet attribut?

"Un" ou "unité" se prend en effet en plusieurs significations. Al-Muqammiṣ en énumère six:

1° unité au sens de simplicité (= non-composition), comme l'âme simple;

2° unité du composé, par exemple l'unité psycho-somatique qui caractérise l'être vivant concret;

3° unité du genre, ainsi l'homme et le bœuf sont *un* quant à l'animalité;

4° unité de l'espèce, comme celle de Saʾīd et de Yazīd envisagés sous le rapport de l'humanité;

5° unité numérique, de Saʾīd et de Yazīd par exemple, lorsqu'ils sont considérés en tant qu'individus;

6° unité (unicité) de ce qui n'est à nul autre pareil (exemple: nul n'est pareil à un tel quant à la science; le texte est cependant altéré).[19]

Encore que nous sachions que Dieu n'est comparable à rien, il nous incombe d'examiner dans quel sens l'attribut "un" pourrait être prédiqué de Lui.

L'étude des six sortes concevables d'unité sera faite, comme on pouvait s'y attendre, moyennant force subdivisions.

1° L'unité au sens de simplicité comporte deux subdivisions:

(a) simplicité dans l'ordre corporel;

(b) simplicité dans l'ordre spirituel.

La simplicité dans l'ordre corporel se ramifie en trois branches:

(i) minéral, fusible, dont les parcelles sont homogènes (homéomères) comme l'or, et non fusible, telle la pierre (le texte n'est pas clair ici);

(ii) végétal, herbe constituée de parcelles homogènes, arbres qui sont faits de parties non homogènes;

Saadia, Baḥya, Joseph Ibn Ṣadīq, Maïmonide (qui met à nu les faiblesses de l'argumentation kalāmique au chapitre 75 de la première partie du *Guide*).

19. Voir ci-après, Note 57. Ces divers sens de l'unité étant rappelés au début du neuvième Discours conservé en version hébraïque; D. Kaufmann en fait déjà état dans *Attributenlehre*, p. 24, n. 51: le passage qu'l cite d'après *Halīkōt Qedem*, p. 73, et *Orient*, 1847, p. 620 se trouve dans le *Pērūsh Séfer Yeṣīra* de Juda ben Barzilaï, p. 78, et l'original arabe dans l'étude citée (notre Note 4) de Ginzburg, pp. 489 et suiv.

(iii) animal, espèces à parties homogènes et espèces à parties non-homogènes; à mentionner aussi les organes constitués de parcelles homogènes comme le foie ou le cœur.

Dans l'ordre incorporel, on distingue:

(i) les entités incorporelles qui, au dire des *ḥukamāʾ* (philosophes), subsistent par elles-mêmes: âme, esprits, anges;[20]

(ii) les entités qui subsistent en un substrat, au sein desquelles on distinguera encore deux sous-groupes: entités essentielles au substrat et accidentelles par rapport à celui-ci; les premières sont notamment les qualités élémentaires (chaleur du feu, et cetera); parmi les secondes on songera notamment aux couleurs (par exemple, la blancheur de l'argent; le texte est derechef altéré ici).

Ce qui est commun à toutes ces subdivisions et à leurs sous-groupes, c'est que chaque entité qui en fait partie est simple dans son ordre.[21]

2° Unité du composé: ici encore l'analyse découvre des subdivisions. Un composé de substance incorporelle et de substance corporelle peut constituer un tout unique: ainsi chaque homme, comme Moïse et Aaron, est composé d'âme spirituelle simple et de corps matériel hétérogène, mais n'en forme pas moins, à son plan, une unité. De même y a-t-il composition de substance corporelle avec substance corporelle, soit composé naturel, soit composé artificiel: la chair et l'os font corps, l'anneau et la pierre font bague.

3° Unité générique. Dans le règne minéral: l'or, l'argent, le plomb, et cetera. Dans le règne végétal: grenade, abricot, raisin . . . Dans le règne animal: homme, âne.

4° Unité spécifique: Moïse et Aaron sont "un" sous le rapport de leur appartenance à l'espèce humaine; Gabriel et Michel le sont en tant qu'inclus sous l'espèce angélique;[22] on raisonnera de même pour les espèces animales.

5° Unité numérique. Moïse et Aaron sont chacun, *un* homme.

20. On remarquera qu'al-Muqammiṣ cite cette opinion sans la prendre expressément à son compte.

21. Ici non plus, le texte n'est pas particulièrement clair, mais la difficulté vient plutôt de la gaucherie d'expression de l'auteur que de la transmission. Il semble vouloir exprimer cette idée que les êtres, incorporels et corporels, et les qualités qu'il qualifie de "simples," se comportent, dans leurs opérations respectives et en tant que phénomènes observables, avec une régularité et une constance qui témoignent de leur unité quelles que soient par ailleurs les différences dans leur structure interne ou leurs relations variées avec les autres êtres.

22. Noter qu'il n'y a pas encore trace ici de la spéculation plus récente qui fera de chaque ange-intellect séparé une espèce distincte.

6° Unité d'incomparabilité. Deux subdivisions:

(i) incomparabilité quant à l'essence; la terre (sans doute "le monde sublunaire") est unique en tant que contenant les quatre éléments, c'est-à-dire qu'il n'y a pas d'autre terre; le soleil est unique parmi les corps célestes, car il n'y a point d'autre soleil;

(ii) incomparabilité quant à l'action; le soleil est unique en tant qu'aucun autre corps céleste ne décrit autour de la terre la même trajectoire que lui; la terre est unique en tant que centre de gravité de la sphère.

Ces divisions précisées, il convient de demander en quel sens l'unité est prédiquée de Dieu.

Un docteur monothéiste (*baᶜḍ al-ᶜulamāᵓ al-muwaḥḥida*) a affirmé que "Dieu est un par simplicité"; c'est-à-dire qu'il est un non divers (hétérogène) d'essence sous quelque rapport que ce soit.

Selon un autre, Dieu est un en essence et en action, c'est-à-dire rien ne lui est semblable en ce qui regarde son essence, ni pareil en ce qui regarde son action.[23]

Al-Muqammiṣ juge recevable chacune de ces deux assertions.[24] Quant aux autres espèces d'unité, elles ne sauraient être prédiquées de Dieu.

L'unité générique n'entre pas en ligne de compte, car genre implique espèce et individu, donc composition.[25]

L'unité spécifique est également inapplicable parce qu'elle est prédiquée d'individus appartenant à la même espèce, or ces individus sont des substances non-éternelles.

Cela n'empêche pas les Chrétiens de prédiquer de Dieu l'unité spécifique; il convient donc de procéder ici à la réfutation de cette assertion: Dieu est un par unité spécifique, autrement dit de la doctrine trinitaire.[26]

* * *

23. Je n'ai pas su trouver les sources et les auteurs de ces formulations dont voici le texte arabe: *inna llāha wāḥid bil-basāṭa yaᶜnī annahū wāḥid ghayr mukhtalif al-dhāt biwajh min al-wujūh* et *inna llāha wāḥid fī l-dhāt wal-fiᶜil ay annahū lā naẓīra lahū fī dhātih walā mithla lahū fī fiᶜlih.*

24. La première correspond, on le voit sans peine, à la première sorte d'unité énumérée ci-dessus, la seconde, à la sixième.

25. Il va de soi que l'unité du composé est dès l'abord exclue de toute discussion sur le sens de l'unité divine.

26. Ici s'ouvre donc une digression dont la fin manque dans notre texte, ainsi qu'une partie de la discussion reprise ensuite sur d'autres définitions de l'unité de Dieu.

C'est une doctrine commune des Chrétiens qui professent la trinité, que Dieu, qui créa l'univers du néant, est "une seule substance en trois personnes" (*jawhar wāḥid* 3 *aqānīm*). Ces personnes sont trois de toute éternité; Dieu est cependant un, et il n'y a pas trois divinités.

Bien qu'il ait fait un exposé complet de cette question dans un autre ouvrage,[27] l'auteur juge utile d'avancer à cet endroit quelques arguments contre le dogme trinitaire puisqu'aussi bien cette controverse relève du thème ici traité: dans quel sens dit-on de Dieu qu'il est un?[28]

Formulé en termes de logique (*ᶜinda l-manṭiq*), le dogme trinitaire—Dieu est une seule substance en trois personnes—signifie: trois individus inclus dans une seule espèce; ainsi Saᵓīd, Yazīd, Khalaf rentrent sous l'espèce unique d'homme, trois monnaies d'or (*dīnār*) ne sont qu'une en tant que de même frappe, de même module et portant une inscription identique.

Voici alors comment on argumentera contre les Chrétiens.

Vous soutenez que Dieu est trois personnes, mais une seule substance. Vous vous trouvez dès lors devant un dilemme: ou bien ces trois personnes sont identiques à la substance unique qui les englobe ou bien elles ne le sont pas.[29]

Si elles sont identiques, ce que soutiennent les Jacobites,[30] on demandera: cette identité est-elle exclusive, les trois personnes étant substance unique et n'étant que cela, ou bien identiques quant à la substance, les trois personnes sont encore autre chose que celle-ci?

Dans le premier cas: trois personnes identiques, à la substance unique et dont l'être total ne consiste qu'en cette identité, la distinction des trois personnes se trouve abolie.

Là-contre, l'adversaire fait valoir ceci.

Considérons l'un des exemples choisis pour illustrer la doctrine trinitaire, celui des trois pièces de monnaie: elles peuvent être considérées comme identiques uniquement en tant que pièces de monnaie, ne constituer, pour parler le langage technique, qu'une seule "en-

27. Voir ci-dessus, Note 11.

28. Al-Muqammiṣ rappelle ici qu'il a inséré dans ce traité une réfutation des Sabéens et des dualistes en critiquant la doctrine de ceux qui distinguaient en l'Etre suprême des substances éternelles et des accidents adventices; ceci faisait probablement partie du VIIᵉ Discours dont seule la fin figure dans la copie mise à ma disposition par M. Halkin.

29. Le sens de ce passage est clair, mais le texte que nous avons eu sous les yeux nous est difficilement parvenu intact.

30. Les Monophysites, qui professent qu'il n'y a qu'une seule nature, la divine, au sein de la Trinité.

tité,"[31] abstraction faite de tout autre caractère qui peut leur appartenir. On peut aussi prendre trois couleurs quelconques, le blanc, le noir et le vert, par exemple, et affirmer leur identité en ne les considérant que comme des couleurs abstraction faite de tout le reste. Nous échappons ainsi, disent-ils, au dilemme dans lequel vous avez tenté de nous enfermer: à considérer les trois personnes de la Trinité sous le rapport entitatif exclusivement, nous ne sommes pas acculés à choisir entre une thèse qui, en maintenant l'unité de substance, supprime la distinction des trois personnes, et une autre qui pour sauvegarder cette distinction ferait bon marché de l'unité substantielle.

A cela al-Muqammiṣ réplique, non sans souligner l'importance qu'il attache à cet argument par un appel à l'attention et au sentiment d'équité du lecteur, que se rabattre, comme le fait son interlocuteur, sur la prise en considération exclusive de l'être commun auquel participent les individus (comme dans l'un de nos exemples les trois pièces de monnaie et l'or) ne répond que partiellement à la question qu'il s'était entendu poser. On lui avait demandé: ces trois pièces sont-elles seulement de l'or ou cela et autre chose; il a répondu qu'il était parfaitement concevable de ne considérer les trois pièces d'or qu'en tant qu'or, ce qui est évidemment éluder la question.[32] Nous sommes donc en droit de continuer à harceler l'adversaire en nous prévalant de l'exemple même qu'il s'est plu à choisir pour illustrer sa thèse.

Reposons donc la question: les pièces dont il s'agit sont-elles de l'or plus autre chose ou bien de l'or seulement et rien d'autre sous quelque rapport que ce soit? Le second terme de l'alternative est de toute évidence faux, puisque ces pièces ne sont ce qu'elles sont, c'est-à-dire monnaie ayant cours légal, qu'en vertu de la frappe et de l'inscription, ce qui est autre chose que l'or pris en lui-même. Ajoutons, et c'est encore plus grave, qu'il ne sert à rien de prétendre que les trois pièces de monnaie ne forment qu'une seule entité. Si l'exemple doit servir à illustrer le dogme de la Trinité pour lequel la distinction des trois personnes est aussi essentielle que l'affirmation

31. L'arabe emploie le mot *ʾūsiyā*, simple transcription d'un mot syriaque qui transcrit à son tour le terme grec *οὐσία*.

32. Il est à peine besoin de faire remarquer qu'une telle objection n'a de sens que dans la perspective de l'incroyant. Le théologien chrétien qui professe la Trinité en vertu d'une adhésion de foi ne prétend pas la démontrer rationnellement. Il a rempli son office de défenseur de la foi lorsqu'il a fait voir que tout en étant incompréhensible, le mystère n'était pas impensable, ou plus exactement qu'il y avait au moins un aspect sous lequel la contradiction logique qui scandalise l'incroyant pouvait être aplanie.

de leur unité, il ne faudra pas perdre de vue que la distinction ne s'établit pas en tant que les trois individus sont considérés sous le rapport entitatif exclusif de toute autre considération, qui les unifie en effet (comme dans notre exemple, l'or), mais eu égard à ce qui leur appartient en sus de cet être commun (la frappe et l'inscription).

L'exemple des trois couleurs n'est guère plus heureux. Certes, le nom générique de couleur convient au blanc, au noir et au vert, qui sont, si l'on veut, autant d'espèces du genre *couleur*. Mais justement il y a entre elles des différences spécifiques et ces différences font que telle couleur soit le contraire de telle autre: le blanc du noir notamment. Appliquer cet exemple aux personnes de la Trinité conduit à admettre[33] qu'il puisse y avoir contrariété entre elles comme entre le noir et le blanc, ce que les Trinitaires ne peuvent admettre, ôtant ainsi à leur argument toute valeur dialectique.

Ainsi donc, s'ils veulent que l'identité de substance soit exclusive de toute autre considération, les tenants de la Trinité ne peuvent échapper au dilemme: il faut renoncer ou bien à la substance unique ou bien à la distinction des trois personnes.

Diront-ils au contraire que les trois personnes sont substance unique plus autre chose?

Qu'est-ce que c'est, répliquerons-nous, que cette "autre chose"? S'ils répondent que ce sont les "propres" (*khawāṣṣ*) par lesquels les personnes se distinguent, tout en étant une seule substance, comme la frappe et l'inscription font que les pièces d'or soient une monnaie déterminée: des *dinars*, tout en étant le même, de l'or, nous les mettrons en face d'un nouveau dilemme: ces "propres" sont-ils substances ou accidents? S'ils répondent qu'ils sont substances, ils admettent autant de substances non-éternelles qu'il y a de propres.[34]

Si ces propres sont des accidents, ils affectent leur Dieu d'accidents, donc ils le font composé de substance et d'accident, par conséquent non-éternel.

Diront-ils que les propres dont il s'agit ne sont ni substances ni accidents?

La réponse est tout juste amorcée dans le texte conservé, mais avant qu'on en ait lu suffisamment pour en saisir la portée, survient

33. A la limite évidemment, mais nous sommes dans une controverse dialectique qui une fois engagée doit être poursuivie jusqu'à ce que l'un des deux adversaires rende les armes. Pour comprendre les attitudes mentales impliquées dans les discussions de cette sorte, on pourra utilement se reporter aux textes présentés par G. Vajda, *Etudes sur Qirqisānī*, V, Les règles de la controverse dialectique, *REJ*, CXXII, 1963, pp. 7–74.

34. Or le dogme trinitaire n'admet pour Dieu qu'une substance unique et éternelle.

une lacune qui nous prive de la fin de cette critique antitrinitaire. Les quelques lignes (une quinzaine environ) qui subsistent à la fin de ce Discours reprennent l'énumération des sens que divers docteurs ont donnés à l'unité de Dieu.

Nous avons d'abord la fin de l'appréciation portée par al-Muqammiṣ sur l'interprétation de l'unité de Dieu par l'infinitude: Dieu est un dans ce sens qu'il n'a ni commencement ni fin; en effet, dit al-Muqammiṣ, il est le seul être qui présente ces caractéristiques; est donc recevable la définition du savant qui attribue cette signification à l'unité.

Une autre définition de l'unité divine est: Dieu est un, en tant qu'incausé; cette formule est acceptable, mais elle rentre, comme d'ailleurs la précédente, sous celle déjà donnée: Dieu est un, en tant que rien ne lui ressemble.

Autre définition: Dieu est un, car il n'est ni substance ni accident, tout hormis lui étant l'un ou l'autre. Ceci encore, dit al-Muqammiṣ, rentre sous la rubrique de l'incomparabilité.

Dieu n'a donc, pour nous résumer, ni semblable ni pareil, ni équivalent ni contraire.[35]

* * *

Les pages d'al-Muqammiṣ que nous venons d'analyser mériteraient un commentaire approfondi que les limites de notre compétence et celles du présent article ne nous permettent pas de tenter. Nous nous bornerons donc à trois séries de remarques rapides dont l'insuffisance ne nous échappe point: en premier lieu, nous essaierons de situer les indications de l'auteur sur les divers sens de l'unité par

35. Il sera bon de reproduire ici la récapitulation des observations précédentes sur le sens de l'unité divine, telle qu'al-Muqammiṣ la présente au début du IXe Discours (cf. ci-dessus, Note 19): "Dieu est un [*wāḥid*]; non comme l'un dans le genre, non comme l'un dans l'espèce, non comme l'un dans le nombre, non comme l'un dans la composition. Au contraire, nous disons qu'Il est un dans la simplicité ou bien qu'il n'y a point de diversité dans son essence, Il n'a point de second. L'explication de ceci est qu'Il est le premier, qui n'a point de commencement, le dernier, qui n'a point de terme et qu'il est la cause non causée et la raison d'être qui n'a pas de raison d'être. [*inna llāha wāḥid lā kal-wāḥid fi l-jins walā kal-wāḥid fi l-nawᶜ walā kal-wāḥid fi l-ᶜadad walā kal-wāḥid fi l-tarkīb bal naqūl innahū wāḥid fi l-bisāṭa aw innahū lā ikhtilāfa fī dhātih lā thāniya lahū. tafsīr dhālika innahu l-awwal alladhī lā ibtidāᵓa lahū wal-ākhir alladhī lā ghāyata lahū waᵓinnahu l-ᶜilla al-ghayr maᶜlūla wal-sabab al-ghayr musabbab*]."

La réfutation du dogme chrétien se poursuivra dans le Xe Discours où al-Muqammiṣ consacrera plusieurs pages importantes à l'examen critique de la "génération" du Fils à partir du Père; pour ne pas dépasser les limites du présent article, nous réservons l'étude de ce texte pour une autre occasion.

rapport aux auteurs plus ancients et contemporains; puis nous rechercherons ce qui correspond, dans les textes théologiques chrétiens qu'il a pu connaître, aux arguments qu'il s'emploie à réfuter; enfin nous nous préoccuperons de préciser quelque peu dans quelle mesure son enseignement étudié ici a été connu et utilisé par les penseurs juifs postérieurs.

* * *

Les divers sens de l'unité.

En comparant le texte des "Vingt Discours" avec Aristote, qui a, le premier, essayé de systématiser les divers sens de l'un, et avec al-Kindī, contemporain de notre auteur, dont l'exposé, sans être d'une grande clarté, suit pas à pas les analyses du Stagirite, nous constatons que les distinctions proposées par notre auteur ne dérivent pas directement de l'enseignement d'école des Péripatéticiens.

En effet, mis à part l'un par accident, qui n'intéresse pas notre problème, Aristote propose tour à tour deux divisions des sens de l'un par essence, à quatre termes chacune: selon la première, l'unité signifie soit continuité, soit identité de substrat, soit identité de genre, soit enfin identité d'espèce; selon la deuxième, ce qui est un, l'est ou selon le nombre, ou selon l'espèce, ou selon le genre, ou par analogie.[36]

Je ne crois pas que la table des significations de l'un proposée par al-Muqammiṣ puisse être référée à l'un ou l'autre de ces classements; l'on pourrait à la rigueur, et avec quelque habileté dialectique, ramener les subdivisions qu'il énumère, au cadre du premier classement, mais celui-ci est trop général pour qu'une telle réduction soit probante; quant au deuxième, c'est précisément son terme le plus intéressant, "analogie" (en arabe *musāwāt*), qui est ignoré

36. Voir *Métaph.* Δ, 6, 1015 b 36–1016 b 17 et 1016 b 31–34. En arabe, dans Averroes, *Tafsīr mā baᶜd aṭ-ṭabīᶜa*, éd. M. Bouyges, pp. 527–537 (textes 8–11) et 544, lig. 11–545, lig. 1 (texte 12, o–r): al-Kindī, *Rasāᵓil Falsafiyya*, éd. Abū Rīdah, I, 159, et l'étude de M. E. Marmura et J. M. Rist: *al-Kindi's Discussion of Divine Existence and Oneness*, dans *Mediaeval Studies*, XXV, 1963, 338–354. Le chapitre d'Aristote (dont le thème est repris au début du livre I, 1052 a 15 sqq.) offre beaucoup de difficultés que l'auteur de ces lignes s'avoue tout à fait incapable de résoudre; il n'oserait donc contredire M. H. A. Wolfson qui voit dans le premier classement sémantique l'infrastructure rationnelle des discussions sur la nature de la Trinité chez les Pères grecs: *The Philosophy of the Church Fathers* (Cambridge, Mass., 1956), 314–317. Je remercie M. A. Altmann qui a bien voulu me renvoyer à ces pages (lettre du 1er juillet 1964); je ne puis cependant le suivre lorsqu'il écrit (*ibid.*), en parlant du premier classement: "This classification comes very close to al-Muqammiṣ' "; tel que j'ai pu comprendre l'un et l'autre texte, les divergences l'emportent nettement sur la similitude générale qu'il peut y avoir entre eux.

d'al-Muqammiṣ. D'autre part, la terminologie arabe de ce dernier rend *eïdos* par *nawᶜ*, non par *ṣūra* (qui, en arabe, signifie "forme" non "espèce"); elle échappe ainsi, contrairement à la version arabe qui est à la base des travaux des philosophes arabophones postérieurs, à une équivoque dont les effets se feront encore sentir dans le "Grand Commentaire" d'Ibn Rushd.

En revanche, al-Muqammiṣ est plus proche, malgré les apparences, de ses adversaires chrétiens qu'il critique en se prévalant, croyons-nous, d'une équivoque de leur terminologie. Nous ne pouvons pas les identifier d'une manière absolument certaine, puisque notre auteur ne les désigne pas nommément, mais il ne fait aucun doute qu'ils se situent dans le milieu jacobite avec lequel il avait été en contact pendant la période chrétienne de sa carrière; autrement dit, nous ne risquons pas de nous tromper trop grossièrement en prenant comme points de repère Abū Rāʾiṭa, évêque jacobite de Takrīt, qui florissait au premier tiers du IXᵉ siècle, et Nonnos (Nānā), que le texte bien connu et d'une incontestable valeur historique de Qirqisānī désigne comme le maître chrétien d'al-Muqammiṣ.[37]

Or dans les écrits conservés de ces deux théologiens, il est fait état des différentes significations de l'unité dont ils discutent aussi l'applicabilité à Dieu.[38] Ils en distinguent quatre, dont les trois premières sont à écarter de Dieu: l'unité numérique, celles du genre et de l'espèce, puis une quatrième qu'Abū Rāʾiṭa, qui écrit en arabe, appelle *wāḥid fi l-jawhar*, "un quant à [littéralement "dans"] la substance," tandis que Nonnos, qui s'exprime en syriaque, la désigne par le terme de *ʾadshānāyā*;[39] ce mot à la base duquel il y a le mot grec *eïdos* est traduit par "spécifique," mais il a aussi le sens de "ce

37. Voir G. Graf, *GCAL* II, 222–224, 226 suiv., et G. Vajda, *Oriens*, article cité (ci-dessus, Note 1), p. 61, n. 1.

38. Abū Rāʾiṭa, dans son opuscule sur la Trinité (voir ci-dessus, Note 14), pp. 6–7 du texte arabe, 6–9 de la traduction allemande; Nonnos, dans son *Traité Apologétique* (voir Note 14), texte p. 3, lig. 27–p. 4, lig. 2, traductions, p. 37, lig. 14–17.

39. Citons le passage dans la traduction latine de l'éditeur: "Si quidem in natura alia unitas, praeter unitatem secundum numerum, datur; scilicet unitas specifica, generica et communis, qua hypostases plures consubstantiales unum esse dicuntur, cum simul unaquaeque earum per se una est et particularis." Dans les pages de son introduction (pp. 56 suiv.) où il traite de cette question qui, en raison de son objet même, ne saurait être très claire, M. Van Roey écrit notamment: "L'unité spécifique suppose [. . .] dans sa conception la pleine subsistance des hypostases qu'elle unit." Que le Père, le Fils et le Saint Esprit, les trois personnes (*aqānīm*) de la Trinité soient "égaux en substance et en force" (*muttafiqūn fi l-jawhar wal-quwwa*) est pareillement affirmé dans la profession de foi de Théodore Abū Qurra; voir I. Dick, *Deux écrits inédits de Théodore Abuqurra*, *Le Muséon*, 72, 1959, pp. 56 et 60.

qui est par soi, non par accident."[40] Le terme syriaque de Nonnos équivaut dès lors, en fait, au terme arabe d'Abū Rāʾiṭa. Ce que les Chrétiens professent lorsqu'ils disent que Dieu est un d'unité *fi l-jawhar* ou d'unité *ʾadshānāyā*, c'est qu'il est un par soi, sans que son unité soit altérée par aucun accident. En cherchant à ramener cette formule à l'unité "spécifique" *fi l-nawʿ* (cependant explicitement récusée par Abū Rāʾiṭa) pour la réduire ensuite dialectiquement à l'absurde, al-Muqammiṣ joue sur l'ambiguïté que le terme *ʾadshānāyā* ne laisse pas d'offrir. En réalité l'incompréhension vient, et il n'en peut être autrement, de l'inadéquation de toute formule philosophique (servant surtout à l'usage externe chez les apologistes chrétiens s'affrontant avec l'Islam) à une vérité de foi aussi évidente pour le croyant que dépourvue de justification rationnelle aux yeux de l'incroyant.

Ceci dit, il n'y a pas de divergence fondamentale entre les sens différents de l'unité selon al-Muqammiṣ et selon les théologiens chrétiens qu'il a certainement connus. Il énumère en somme six unités. En réalité, la simplicité et l'incomparabilité coïncident et l'unité du composé n'entre pas en ligne de compte, cela va de soi et nul ne le conteste, en parlant de Dieu. L'unité numérique, générique et spécifique étant éliminées à leur tour (malgré l'équivoque exploitée par le polémiste juif), il reste que la simplicité–incomparabilité d'al-Muqammiṣ correspond à l'unité substantielle d'Abū Rāʾīṭa et de Nonnos, compte tenu, certes, de la croyance trinitaire des auteurs chrétiens et des réserves qu'en vertu même de cette croyance, ils ont pu faire valoir contre une conception trop rigide de l'incomparabilité.[41]

40. Cette définition, "per se non per accidens," est de I. Brun, *Dictionarium syriaco-latinum*, éd. altera (Beyrouth, 1911), p. 5; les grands lexiques de Payne-Smith et de Brockelmann ne la donnent pas. Mais elle est confirmée, comme me l'apprend mon collègue Antoine Guillaumont, par le *Livre de définitions* de Michel l'Interprète (vers 600), où le substantif correspondant *ʾādshā* est défini comme "ce qui est contraire au genre, à la variation, à la propriété et à l'accident"; Payne-Smith donne aussi, comme me le rapelle également M. Guillaumont, *ʾādshānāyā* comme opposé à *gedshânâyâ* (accidentel) dans un texte de Barhebraeus dont il ne précise pas la référence. Quant à Bar Bahlūl, *Lexicon syriacum*, éd. R. Duval, I, col. 43–45, il rend *ʾadshā* par les mots arabes *nawʿ* et *ṣūra*.

41. Voir ci-dessus, Note 14. Abū Rāʾiṭa déclare expressément que l'unité substantielle de Dieu en trois personnes signifie sa transcendance absolue et son incomparabilité: "Epître sur la Trinité," texte arabe, p. 7, lig. 7–10, traductions, p. 8.

La profession de foi musulmane *Fiqh al-Akbar* II (texte arabe dans *al-Rasāʾil al-sabʿa fi l-ʿaqāʾd* [Hyderabad, 1367/1948], p. 33, traduction anglaise A. J. Wensinck, *The Muslim Creed* [Cambridge, 1932], p. 188), qui semble cependant être postérieure à al-Muqammiṣ, s'exprime ainsi: "Allah the exalted is one, not in the sense of number but in the sense that He has no partner [. . .] he resembles none of the created things, nor do any created things resemble him." Voir les observations de Wensinck, pp. 205 suiv. Ce texte condense certes, avec la concision exigée par le genre des brèves professions de foi, des discussions

Une meilleure connaissance des spéculations théologiques au IXe siècle dans la sphère de civilisation musulmane apporterait certainement d'autres données propres à éclairer la pensée d'al-Muqammiṣ. Nous nous bornerons ici à nous arrêter en passant aux indications fournies par le *K. al-Zīna fi l-kalimāt al-islāmiyya al-ᶜarabiyya*, du théologien ismāʿīlien Abū Ḥātim al-Rāzī (mort en 322 / 934).[42]

En parlant des significations du mot "un," cet auteur commence par citer "un savant" (philosophe? *baᶜḍ al-ḥukamāʾ*) dont il ne précise pas l'identité, selon qui "Dieu est unique [*wāḥid*] parce qu'il n'a pas cessé d'être solitaire dans la prééternité avant les créatures, sans second ni création qui lui fussent simultanés; puis il produisit la création."[43]

La suite développe cette conception de l'unité divine comprise comme antériorité ontologique par rapport à tout l'ensemble de l'extradivin. Assez logiquement, cette façon d'entendre l'unité divine va de pair avec la notion, bien connue par ailleurs, de "l'un" antérieur à la série des nombres dont il ne fait pas partie;[44] aussi les êtres créaturels ne sont-ils jamais "un" que sous tel ou tel aspect alors qu'ils ne le sont pas sous tel autre.[45] Bref, le créé est "un" au sens figuré, multiple quant au sens réel.[46]

* * *

---

théologiques plus prolixes; il en ressort toutefois qu'il ne considère pas non plus l'unicité (*wāḥid*, non *ʾaḥad*, est le terme qu'il emploie) comme étant d'ordre arithmétique, mais la définit par la négation de tout être de même rang que Dieu et par l'incomparabilité mitigée (la formule *laysa kamithlihi shayʾ* n'y figure pas) par la position dogmatique de l'auteur inconnu, orthodoxe modéré, peut-être influencé, comme le pensait Wensinck, par les idées d'al-Ashᶜarī.

42. *Al-Zinat on Arabic and Islamic Nomenclature . . .*, edited by M. Ḥusayn . . . al-Hamdāni [Cairo, 1957/8], II, 32–35; sur l'intérêt que ce livre peut avoir pour l'histoire de la pensée juive, voir notre article dans *Arabica* 1961, pp. 113–130.

43. *lam yazal qabla l-khalāʾiq mutawaḥḥidan bil-azal lā thāniya maᶜahū walā khalq thumma abdaᶜa l-khalq*. La préposition arabe *bi-* signifiant "dans" et "par," *bil-azal* possède un double sens que la traduction en une langue occidentale ne peut guère rendre: dans la pensée de l'auteur, il ne s'agit pas seulement d'une constatation de l'antériorité de Dieu par rapport à la création, mais de l'affirmation d'un lien ontologique indissoluble entre l'unité et l'éternité de Dieu; en d'autres termes, Dieu n'est pas seulement unique *et* éternel, unique parce qu'il s'était trouvé seul dans la prééternité avant de créer, antérieur à sa création d'une durée sans commencement; il est unique *parce que* éternel, du fait de son existence dans la prééternité, aucun être ne partageant cette prééternité avec lui.

44. *qabla kull ᶜadad wahuwa khārij min al-ᶜadad:* voir à ce sujet *REJ*, 107, 1946/7, 131 suiv., et A. J. Festugière, *La révélation d'Hermès Trismégiste*, IV (Paris, 1954), pp. 18–31. Al-Muqammiṣ ne fait point état de cette notion; sur ce point aussi, il s'écarte d'Al-Kindī, *Rasāʾil* I, 146–151.

45. *wal-khalq* [. . .] *waʾin kāna yusammā bil-wāḥid wakānat hādhihi l-ṣifa qad lazimat jamīᶜa l-ashyāʾ fi wajh faʾinnahā tazūl ᶜanhā fi l-wajh.*

46. *fal-makhlūq wāḥid bitaʾwīl ᶜadad fil-maᶜnā.*

L'or divisé ne laisse pas d'être de l'or.

L'illustration de l'unité au sein de la Trinité par l'or qui divisé ne cesse pas d'être de l'or se trouve chez Théodore Abū Qurra[47] comme chez Abū Rāʾiṭa.

Ce dernier, supérieur de Nonnos, lui-même maître d'al-Muqammiṣ durant la période chrétienne du théologien juif, écrit dans son "Epître sur la Trinité":[48]

> Si le nom *Dieu* est un nom de substance, c'est-à dire le nom des trois [personnes], l'appellation par le nom général revient à chacune d'elles puisque aucune d'elles n'est contraire par son essence à celle des autres qui forment avec elle une substance générale. C'est ainsi que le nom général d'or appartient à la totalité de l'or, une partie [quelconque] de l'or étant complète et non partielle en tant qu'or.[49]

On aura noté qu'al-Muqammiṣ (ou sa source directe) a élaboré la comparaison: il s'agit chez lui non pas de morceaux quelconques en lesquels un lingot d'or aurait été divisé, mais de pièces de monnaie dont la matière (le métal précieux) et la façon (frappe, inscription, et cetera) sont les mêmes. Cette complexité prête, il faut en convenir, le flanc à la critique que l'auteur juif soulève à l'endroit de la comparaison, tandis que l'image plus simple utilisée par les deux écrivains chrétiens y échappe, sans être pour cela plus convaincante aux yeux de l'incroyant.

* * *

Traces laissées de l'étude de l'unité divine par al-Muqammiṣ chez les auteurs postérieurs.

Les pages des *ʿIshrūn Maqālāt* que nous avons analysées n'ont pas laissé beaucoup de traces chez les théologiens juifs des siècles suivants, même parmi ceux, et ils ne semblent pas être fort nombreux, qui ont connu son œuvre. Ainsi Baḥya Ibn Paqūda, qui est pourtant l'un des rares à nommer "le livre d'al-Muqammiṣ,"[50] ne les a pas particulièrement utilisées lorsqu'il traite à son tour du problème de

47. IIIe Mīmar, 16, éd. Bacha, p. 37, trad. Graf, pp. 148 suiv.
48. Ed. Graf, p. 24, 18–25, 1, trad., pp. 28 suiv.
49. *kaʾism al-dhahab al-ʿāmm likull al-dhahab wabaʿḍ al-dhahab kāmil lā baʿḍ al-dhahabiyya.* Je ne pense pas que Graf a bien traduit cette phrase en écrivant: "Gleichwie der Name Gesamtgold sowohl für alles Gold als auch für einen Teil des Goldes vollauf gilt, nicht nur für etwas Goldähnliches."
50. *Hidāya* (*Ḥōbōt ha-lebābōt*), introduction, éd. A. S. Yahuda, p. 8.

l'unité divine au premier chapitre des "Devoirs des Cœurs." Juda ben Barzilaï n'a retenu, on le sait, que les Discours IX et X du traité, si bien que seule la récapitulation des divers sens de l'unité apparaît dans la version hébraïque qu'il en a insérée dans son commentaire sur le "Livre de la Création."[51]

Il se peut, en revanche, que Moïse Maïmonide se soit souvenu, dans une de ses premières œuvres, des définitions de l'un rassemblées et discutées jadis par al-Muqammiṣ. En effet, dans le second de ses treize articles de foi,[52] il énumère cinq sens du terme *wāḥid*: l'unité du genre (*wāḥid al-jins*), l'unité de l'espèce (*wāḥid al-nawᶜ*), l'unité de l'individu en tant que tel, mais cependant composé quant à sa structure (*al-shakhṣ al-wāḥid al-murakkab*), l'unité numérique du corps indéfiniment divisible (*al-jism al-basīṭ al-wāḥid bil-ᶜadad*), alors que Dieu est unique d'une unité à laquelle nulle autre unité n'est semblable (*wāḥid biwaḥda laysa kamithlihā waḥda biwajh*).

Maïmonide conserve donc, sans trop la préciser dans cette brève profession de foi, la notion d'incomparabilité divine; quant à l'unité de "simplicité," elle semble être absorbée en tant qu'elle concerne les créatures, par la troisème et la quatrième sorte de l'unité dans l'énumération de Maïmonide; la simplicité divine, elle, s'identifie avec l'incomparabilité puisqu'il s'agit précisément d'une simplicité par rapport à laquelle tout ce qui est "simple" dans l'ordre créaturel ne l'est que, pour nous servir de la terminologie du moyen âge, par homonymie.

Le seul auteur chez qui nous constatons une utilisation massive sinon peut-être exclusive de l'exposé d'al-Muqammiṣ sur l'unité de Dieu est le Karaïte Qirqisānī.

Bien que le chapitre où il expose, très brièvement d'ailleurs, la signification de l'unicité divine soit un des plus fragmentaires et des plus lacuneux de sa vaste encyclopédie théologique telle que nous la possédons actuellement,[53] sa dépendance, dans ce morceau, du VIIIᵉ Discours de *ᶜIshrūn Maqālāt* est évidente; il ne s'est pas contenté, toutefois, de copier le texte de son modèle; il l'a adapté à la contexture de son propre ouvrage et il s'est peut-être servi en plus (mais vu l'état du texte, ce n'est qu'une hypothèse que j'avance avec hésitation) d'une autre source.

51. Voir ci-dessus, Note 19.

52. Texte arabe dans I. Friedländer, *Selections from the Arabic Writings of Maimonides* (Leyde, 1909), p. 28.

53. *Kitāb al-Anwār wal-Marāqib*, éd. L. Nemoy, VI, 4 (III, 569–570).

Voici un essai de traduction de la page de Qirqisānī. "Sur *Ecoute Israël, le Seigneur notre Dieu* [est] *Seigneur unique* (Deutéronome VI, 4). Qu'est-ce que l'unité (*waḥda*)? Les opinions émises au sujet de l'unicité (*waḥdāniyya*) du Créateur glorieux et sur la signification de ce terme. Explication du passage qui suit l'*Ecoute Israël*.

[1] Nous parlerons d'abord de l'unicité et du sens du mot ᵓ*eḥad* employé par l'Ecriture.

Les philosophes (*ḥukamā*ᵓ) enseignent que le terme *wāḥid* s'emploie de six manières:[54]

(a) un quant à la simplicité; ainsi, l'âme [est] simple, contrairement[55] au corps, composé et formé de parties;
(b) un quant à la composition, comme l'âme et le corps qui, dans leur composition, forment une unité;
(c) un quant au genre: l'homme et le bœuf forment un seul genre sous le rapport de l'animalité;
(d) un numérique, comme des deux dont chacun est un quant au nombre;[56]
(e) un quant à l'espèce, comme "homme" qui est prédiqué de chacun [des individus appartenant à l'espèce humaine];
(f) sans pareil, comme nous disons unique . . . sa signification.[57]

[2] Un savant enseigne: Dieu est un quant à la simplicité ⟨c'est-à-dire un sans aucune diversité en son⟩ essence sous quelque aspect que ce soit.[58] Selon *un* autre ⟨Dieu est unique quant à son essence et son action, c'est-à-dire qu'il n'a pas son semblable quant à son essence⟩ et n'a pas son pareil quant ⟨à son action⟩.[59] Ces deux opinions sont vraies, l'une et l'autre ⟨. . . lacune⟩

54. Littéralement: "le nom de l'unique advient selon six aspects" (*ism al-wāḥid yaqa*ᶜ ᶜ*alā sittat awjuh*, le texte correspondant d'al-Muqammiṣ porte *al-aḥad yuqāl* ᶜ*alā sittat awjuh*); il s'agit plus précisément de prédication logique: quels sont les sens en lesquels l'attribut "un" est susceptible d'être prédiqué du sujet de la proposition?

55. *Laysat,* que l'éditeur aurait préféré (p. 569, n. 1), se lit effectivement dans le text d'al-Muqammiṣ.

56. Le texte est probablement altéré; M. Nemoy a affecté avec raison le mot *kal-ithnayn* d'un point d'interrogation. Dans le texte d'al-Muqammiṣ (où l'un numérique est en cinquième place), nous avons simplement: "un quant au nombre, comme Saᵓīd et Yazīd quant au nombre." Cette proposition y est construite exactement comme la quatrième, qui formule l'unité spécifique: "un quant à l'espèce, comme Saᵓīd et Yazīd quant à l'humanité."

57. Dans son état actuel cette phrase n'est que partiellement intelligible. Le texte correspondant d'al-Muqammiṣ est, lui aussi, gravement altéré, mais je crois qu'il peut être corrigé ainsi: *fulān wāḥid walā thāniya* ⟨*lahū*⟩ *fī* ᶜ*ilmih* (texte WLTHNY FY ᶜLMH) *alladhī innamā na*ᶜ*nī bih innahū lā mithla* ⟨*lahū*⟩ *fi* ᶜ*ilmih* (texte ᶜ ᵓLMH) עאלמה, confusion également possible en écriture arabe et en écriture hébraïque et dont on a d'autres exemples). La phrase signifie donc: "Comme nous disons qu'un tel est unique et n'a pas de second quant à sa science, ce qui revient à dire: il n'a pas son pareil quant à sa science." Il est tout à fait vraisemblable que la ligne conservée de Qirqisāni représente un débris de cette phrase.

58. La lacune peut être exactement comblée ici par le texte d'al-Muqammiṣ: *ya*ᶜ*nī innahū wāḥid ghayr mukhtalif al-dhāt*.

59. Ici encore la restitution est sûre. Al-Muqammiṣ avait écrit: *inna llāha wāḥid fī l-dhāt wal-fi*ᶜ*il ay innahū lā naẓīra lahū fī dhātih walā mithla lahū fī fi*ᶜ*lih.*

Dire que Dieu est un numériquement ne signifie point qu'il rentre sous la catégorie de la quantité ⟨. . . lacune⟩ le premier et que la création[60] n'est pas ⟨. . . lacune⟩ seconde parce que (?) ⟨. . . lacune⟩ il est l'éternel, qui n'a pas de second ni de troisième autre que (?) l'éternel qui n'a pas cessé ⟨. . . lacune⟩.[61] Selon un autre [encore], Dieu est un quant *au* nombre parce que ⟨. . . lacune⟩ l'existence du premier parce que l'un est un nom indépendant (??*munqaṭiᶜ*), il n'y a pas ⟨. . . lacune⟩ après lui de troisième,[62] de quatrième et les autres nombres.

Autre opinion: Dieu est un, en ce sens qu'il n'a ni commencement ni fin, alors que tout, hormis Lui, commence et finit. Enfin: Dieu est un, en ce sens que sans cause lui-même, il est cause de tout causé et tout, hormis Lui, est causé.

Ce sont là les opinions exprimées au sujet de l'unicité, du sens de "l'un" et de l'énoncé scripturaire "Seigneur un."

Qirqisānī a donc, sans aucun doute, exploité l'exposé d'al-Muqammiṣ sur les divers sens de l'un, en joignant les deux parties du développement séparées dans les *ᶜIshrūn Maqālāt* par la digression polémique contre la Trinité. Il s'est peut-être servi d'une autre source qui lui a fourni l'interprétation de l'unité numérique au sens de l'antériorité ontologique; mais ce n'est qu'une hypothèse non entièrement dépourvue de vraisemblance, et nous ne pouvons pas non plus affirmer avec une pleine assurance qu'al-Muqammiṣ n'ait pas fait état d'une telle thèse dans son livre.[63]

60. *Al-khalīqa:* l'ensemble de l'être créaturel, tout ce qui n'est pas Dieu.

61. Les débris qui subsistent de cette phrase n'en permettent pas une interprétation tant soit peu sûre. On peut conjecturer que Qirqisānī a rapporté ici l'interprétation de l'unicité comme antériorité ontologique de Dieu par rapport à l'ensemble de la création, qui a été retenue, nous l'avons vu, par le *kitāb al-Ẕīna*. Il y a quelque vraisemblance qu'al-Muqammiṣ lui-même ait développé cette idée dans un passage dont nous n'avons plus que la fin: . . . *jawhar ayḍan kamā ᵓanna hādhā lā yaḍurruh (?) bimaᶜnā mā lā mithla lahū wa-dhālika innahū lammā kāna kull mā huwa ghayr Allah muḥdath munqaḍī wakāna llāh waḥdahu lā ibtidā lahū walā inqiḍā kāna man zaᶜama annahū wāḥid min hādhihi l-jiha qad atā bifarq(in) ṣaḥīḥ.*

62. On complèterait volontiers: il n'y a pas ⟨après lui de second⟩ qui serait suivi d'un troisième, etc., et l'on aurait alors une allusion à la théorie de l'un qui n'est pas nombre. Mais le fragment tel qu'il présenté dans l'édition Nemoy n'est pas favorable à cette façon de voir; il est donc plus prudent de suspendre, sur ce point aussi, notre jugement.

63. Nous avouons ignorer si Qirqisānī a été utilisé à son tour sur ce point par des auteurs karaïtes postérieurs. Comme on sait, les dix-huit premiers alphabets du *ᵓEshkōl ha-kōfer* de Juda Hadassi n'ont pas été imprimés; nous ne savons donc pas si cet auteur qui a sûrement puisé des renseignements chez al-Muqammiṣ, notamment dans son aperçu sur les sectes, alphabet 96, lui a emprunté ou non des considérations sur l'unité divine. Dans le *ᶜEṣ Ḥayyim* d'Aaron b. Elie, éd. F. Delitsch (Leipzig, 1841), qui traite spécialement, au chapitre 64, de l'unité divine, nous n'avons rien trouvé qui rappelle al-Muqammiṣ ou Qirqisānī.

Saadia's List of Theories of the Soul

By HERBERT DAVIDSON

Saadia had a penchant for enumeration. Some of his writings consist of nothing more than a list of one sort or another,[1] and in *Emunot we-Deᶜot*, his main philosophic work, almost every chapter contains a list, generally not even of a philosophic character. One of the lists in *Emunot we-Deᶜot* which is philosophic in content appears at the beginning of section six, the section where Saadia discusses the essence of the human soul and related questions. Before presenting his own position on the essence of the human soul, Saadia discusses some opposing theories. As is his wont, he does not name the authors of the different theories,[2] and his statements have been studied by several scholars with progressively greater success in identifying the sources. The first important attempt was made by Jakob Guttmann, who tried to trace the various theories by means of the reports which Aristotle gives of earlier philosophers in the *De anima*.[3] S. Horovitz continued on the same lines but consulted additional ancient works including, most importantly, the Greek doxographies.[4] The doxographies are lists of the views of the ancient philosophers on various questions, stemming from an original list drawn up by Theophrastus, the student of Aristotle. The most important remains of the doxographic tradition are two closely related lists, one in Stobaeus' *Eclogae*, and a second entitled *De placitis philosophorum* and attributed to Plutarch.[5] For the present question, material from the doxographic tradition

1. See H. Malter, *Saadia Gaon, His Life and Works* (Philadelphia, 1921), pp. 306–308, 330–331, 335.
2. For this characteristic of Saadia, see Malter, *Saadia Gaon*, p. 180, and n. 412a.
3. Jakob Guttmann, *Die Religionsphilosophie des Saadia* (Göttingen, 1882), pp. 194–197, esp. p. 195, n. 2.
4. S. Horovitz, *Die Psychologie bei den jüdischen Religions-Philosophen* (Breslau, 1898–1912), pp. 12–21.
5. See J. Burnet, *Early Greek Philosophy*, 4th ed. (London, 1930), pp. 34–35. *De placitis philosophorum* and the relevant sections of the *Eclogae* were edited, together with other remains of the doxographic tradition, by H. Diels, *Doxographi graeci* (Berlin, 1879), pp. 273–444. Diels, pp. 47–48, traces both of these works to a work also entitled *De placitis philosophorum*, written by a certain Aetius.

is also preserved in a work on the "nature of man" written by one Nemesius, bishop of Emesa.[6] Horovitz found the doxographies, and particularly Nemesius, useful for identifying many of the theories listed by Saadia but he did not attach any particular significance to that fact. More recently, Julius Guttmann, building on the work of Horovitz, raised a new question:[7] Granted that the ancient authors of the various theories discussed by Saadia had already more or less been identified, what was Saadia's immediate source?[8] Julius Guttmann points out, to a greater extent than Horovitz, that almost all of the theories listed by Saadia have their parallel in one or another of the aforementioned three Greek doxographic works. But he also points out certain differences between Saadia's list and each of the other three. To Guttmann this proved that Saadia had drawn from the doxographic tradition without using any of those three books, and his conclusion is that Saadia used a "similar" work[9] which is no longer extant. At the end of his analysis Guttmann notes that one of the three doxographies, the *De placitis philosophorum*, had been translated into Arabic during the Middle Ages.[10]

The object of the present paper is to carry the analyses of the two Guttmanns and Horovitz a step further. Considering the fact that the *De placitis philosophorum* was available to Saadia in Arabic, there is a very strong a priori presumption that Saadia drew from the doxographic tradition precisely through that book rather than through a "similar" work, which is not known to have existed and must be assumed to have been lost. And when, in fact, one actually does compare Saadia's list with the relevant sections in *De placitis*, considering content rather than expecting word-for-word parallels, the correspondence is so great that it is difficult to understand how Horovitz and Julius Guttmann could have failed to see that it was just the *De placitis* which underlies Saadia's list. Since Julius Gutt-

6. See A. Pauly and G. Wissowa, *Real-Encyclopädie*, supplement, vol. VII, cols. 562ff.

7. Julius Guttmann, "The Soul According to Rav Saadya Gaon" (Hebrew), *Magnes Anniversary Book* (Jerusalem, 1938), pp. 80–88.

8. *Ibid.*, p. 80.

9. *Ibid.*, pp. 81, 88.

10. *Ibid.*, p. 88. The medieval Arabic bibliographers report that the translator was Costa ben Luca; see M. Steinschneider, *Die Arabischen Übersetzungen aus dem Griechischem* (Graz, 1960), p. 141. There are no exact dates for Costa ben Luca's life. *Encyclopaedia of Islam*, *s.v.*, gives ca. 820–912; i.e., one generation before Saadia.

Information on Arabic writers who used the *De placitis philosophorum* in their works is given by S. Pines, *Beiträge zur islamischen Atomenlehre* (Berlin, 1936), p. 93, n. 2, and P. Kraus, *Jābir ibn Ḥayyān, Contribution à l'histoire des idées scientifiques dans l'Islam* (Cairo, 1942–43), II, 337–338.

mann's time, it happens that the Arabic translation of the *De placitis* has been published,[11] so that we are now also provided with the means for studying the manner in which Saadia made use of his source.[12]

The most convincing method of demonstrating that the *De placitis philosophorum* underlies Saadia's list is simply to tabulate the items in Saadia's list and in the relevant sections of *De placitis* and then compare the two.

Saadia prefaces his review of theories of the essence of the human soul with the warning that he is "leaving aside most"[13] of the theories on the question. He is going to consider only "seven theories, apart from the four listed previously, giving a total of eleven."[14] This rather awkward way of enumerating indicates that the "seven" theories to which Saadia refers have a different status from the "four"; and in fact the "four" theories are simply corollaries, almost surely derived by Saadia himself from theories of creation which had been discussed in an earlier section of *Emunot we-Deᶜot*.[15] We are interested only in the seven new theories.

The first of the seven theories, writes Saadia, is that the human soul is not a substance but just an "accident."[16] And here again there is something awkward in Saadia's enumeration, for we are presented not with a single such theory but with a total of five. They are the theories that the soul is:

(1a) "a self-moving number";[17]
(1b) the "entelechy of a natural body";

11. Published together with the medieval Arabic translation of Aristotle's *De anima* by A. Badawi (Cairo, 1954).

12. M. Schreiner, *Der Kalam in der jüdischen Literatur* (Berlin, 1895), p. 17, quotes the testimony of Ibn Hazm concerning various Moslem writers who held views similar to those listed by Saadia. Saadia's discussion of the soul is also treated by H. Malter, "Ha-deᶜot bemahut ha-nefesh lefi R. Saadia Gaon," *Ha-Shiloaḥ*, 26:128–137 (1912), and M. Ventura, *La Philosophie de Saadia Gaon* (Paris, 1934), pp. 228–231.

13. *Kitab al-Amānāt wal-Iᶜtiqādāt*, ed. S. Landauer (Leiden, 1880), p. 188, last line. Hebrew translation, *Sefer ha-Emunot we-ha-Deᶜot* (Jozefow, 1885), p. 149. These two works will be cited subsequently as "Saadia, *Arabic*" and "Saadia, *Hebrew*" respectively.

14. *Arabic*, pp. 188–189; *Hebrew*, pp. 149–150.

15. *Arabic*, p. 189, referring back to pp. 41ff.; *Hebrew*, p. 149, referring back to pp. 63ff.

16. *Arabic*, p. 189; *Hebrew*, p. 149.

17. This is the reading of a gloss in the St. Petersburg manuscript of the Arabic, and it is also the reading of the medieval Hebrew paraphrase; cf. Saadia, *Arabic*, p. 189, n. 2. Landauer's edition of the Arabic and Judah Ibn Tibbon's Hebrew translation have "a self-moving accident." Horovitz, *Die Psychologie*, p. 13, n. 19, presents the arguments in favor of the former reading, and I have preferred it mainly because it appears in Saadia's source, the *De placitis;* see below, Page 79. On the possible significance of the second reading, see below, Note 76.

(1c) the "combination of the four natures" (that is, of the four elements);

(1d) "the tying together of the senses";

(1e) an "accident which is generated from the blood."

After listing these five theories, or subdivisions of a single theory, Saadia summarizes by describing them as all having "in common the position that the soul is an accident—for number,[18] entelechy, combination, being tied together, and being generated are accidents"; then Saadia proceeds to refute all five subdivisions by means of common arguments.[19]

The other theories that Saadia enumerates are that the soul is:

(2) "wind," according to "some";

(3) "fire," according to "some";

(4) "two parts, one of which is intellectual, rational, does not perish, and is located in the heart; the other is animal, diffused [منبث] through the rest of the body, and does perish";

(5) "two kinds of air [literally: two airs], one internal and the other external";

(6) "pure blood"; this is identified by Saadia as the view of the Karaite Anan;[20]

18. Here too an alternate reading is "accident." See the previous note.

19. *Arabic*, pp. 189–190; *Hebrew*, p. 150. There are two arguments, both of which appear in Ikhwān al-Ṣafāʾ. The first is that if the soul were an accident, it could not be the source of such extensive knowledge as is possessed by man. See F. Dieterici, *Die Abhandlungen der Ichwān es-Safā in Auswahl* (Leipzig, 1886), p. 569; German translation in F. Dieterici, *Die Lehre von der Weltseele* (Leipzig, 1872), p. 167; Horovitz, *Die Psychologie*, p. 16, n. 26. The second argument is that the soul is subject to accidents, while one accident cannot be the subject of other accidents. In Ikhwān al-Ṣafāʾ this second argument is given in a slightly different form. It is argued there that if the soul were an accident it could not act; for action is an accident, and if an accident could act, one accident would be the subject of another accident, which is impossible. Cf. Dieterici, *Die Abhandlungen der Ichwān es-Safā*, p. 569; German translation in Dieterici, *Die Lehre von der Weltseele*, pp. 166–167; Jakob Guttmann, *Die Religionsphilosophie des Saadia*, p. 196, n. 3. Two other important features of Saadia's discussion that also appear in the Ikhwān al-Ṣafāʾ are the grouping of a number of theories as theories of the soul as an accident, and the acceptance of the theory that the soul is a created substance similar in nature to the spheres; see below, Notes 44, 51, and also Note 40 for an additional possible point of contact. The writings of Ikhwān al-Ṣafāʾ were not edited until after Saadia's death but the contents go back before that time. See *Encyclopaedia of Islam*, *s.v.* "Ikhwān al-Ṣafāʾ."

For a further analysis of Saadia's argument against construing the soul as an accident, see Horovitz, *Die Psychologie*, p. 16, n. 27.

20. *Arabic*, p. 190; *Hebrew*, pp. 150–151.

(7) a created substance, "pure like the celestial spheres . . . It receives light as the sphere does . . . but becomes finer than the spheres"; this is Saadia's own view.[21]

The most relevant sections in the *De placitis philosophorum* are sections two, three, and four of Book Four.[22] These sections are conveniently divided into a total of sixteen paragraphs in Diels' edition.[23] Section two is entitled "Concerning soul" and it contains the following paragraphs.

(A) "Thales was the first to assert that the soul is ever-moving and self-moving."

(B) "Pythagoras [said that it is] a self-moving number . . ."

(C) "Plato, an intellectual substance . . ."

(D) "Aristotle, the first entelechy of a natural, organic body, potentially possessing life . . ."

(E) "Dicaearchus, the harmony of the four elements."

(F) "Asclepiades . . . the training together of the senses."

Section three is entitled "Whether the soul is a body and what its substance is." It contains the following.

(G) "All the preceding assume that the soul is not a body [Greek: is incorporeal], saying that it is a self-moving number, an intellectual substance, and the entelechy of a natural organic [body] possessing life."

(H) "The followers of Anaxagoras [said that it is] airlike . . ."

(I) "The Stoics, a warm *pneuma*."

(J) "Democritus, a fiery mixture of things . . . possessing spherical shapes [that is, of spherical atoms] and a firelike power . . ."[24]

(K) "Epicurus, a mixture of four things: a fiery quality, an airlike quality, a *pneuma*-like quality, and a fourth unnamed quality . . ."

21. *Arabic*, p. 193; *Hebrew*, p. 152.

22. The Greek will be cited from Diels, *Doxographi graeci*, pp. 386ff., and the Arabic translation will be cited from Badawi's edition (see above, Note 11), pp. 156ff. They will be cited as "*Greek*" and "*Arabic*" respectively.

23. Diels, *Greek*, pp. 386–390. I have added the alphabetized notation.

24. The Arabic text, p. 158, omits the word "fiery" at the beginning of this statement.

(L) "Heraclitus [held that] the soul of the universe is an exhalation from the damp [elements] in the universe, while the soul of animals is [formed] from the exhalation without and the related exhalation within" (Arabic text).[25]

Section four is entitled "Concerning the parts of the soul," and contains the following.

(M) "Pythagoras and Plato [said that] in the most general sense the soul is twofold, one part having the rational [faculty], and the other, the irrational; in a more precise sense it is threefold . . ."

(N) "The Stoics say that it is composed of eight parts: the five senses . . ., the vocal . . ., the *spermatikos* . . ., and the governing . . ."

(O) "Democritus and Epicurus [said] that the soul is twofold, having its rational part located in the chest and its irrational part diffused [منبث] throughout . . . the body . . ."

(P) "Democritus said that everything partakes of soul . . ."

When we compare Saadia's list with the *De placitis* we get the following correlation:

Saadia's Theories	Equivalent in *De placitis*
1a	B
1b	D
1c	E
1d	F, (N)
1e	see below, Page 83
Summarizing statement	G
2	H, I, K (parts 2 and 3)
3	J, K (part 1)
4	M, O, (C)
5	L
6	
7	

At four points in this comparison, it will be noted, we have matched more than one theory in the *De placitis* with a single theory in Saadia.

25. In the Greek original, p. 389, the second half of this statement reads: ". . . while the soul of animals is related, [formed] from the exhalation without and the exhalation within themselves." For Heraclitus' conception, see Burnet, *Early Greek Philosophy*, pp. 151–154.

We have done this on the basis of Saadia's own introduction to his discussion. Saadia warned that he was going to omit "most" of what had been said on the question of the soul.[26] This presumably indicates both that he did not do extensive research on the subject, limiting himself to the use of a single source, and also that he intended to restate the theories from his source in summary fashion without entering into all the nuances and details, the result being that several theories in the *De placitis* sometimes appear as a single theory in Saadia. That several theories have been combined is explicitly stated in the case of theories 2 and 3 in Saadia's list, where he writes that the positions in question were held not by a single philosopher, but by "some" (قوم).

With Saadia's theory (1d) that the human soul is the "tying together" of the senses, we have matched two theories in the *De placitis*: that same theory as reported in the name of Asclepiades (F) and also the Stoic division of the soul into eight parts (N). Our assumption is that after he had recorded the theory once, Saadia assumed that the Stoics had merely given another variation of it. It is also possible, though, that Saadia disregarded the Stoic position, since it is not really a theory of the essence of the soul at all, but rather of the division of the soul.[27]

Again, with Saadia's theory (2) that the soul is "wind" (ريح) we have matched the reported view of the followers of Anaxagoras (H), that the soul is airlike (ἀεροειδής, هوائية); the theory of the Stoics (I), that the soul is *pneuma* (روح); and those parts of the theory of Epicurus (K) according to which the soul contains an "airlike [هوائية] quality" and a "*pneuma*-like [روحية] quality." With Saadia's theory (3) that the soul is fire (نار), we have matched the report of Democritus (J) that the soul is a "fiery mixture" of spherical atoms having "firelike power," as well as that part of Epicurus' theory (K) which says that one quality of the soul is "fiery."[28] In both of these cases (2 and 3) Saadia presumably decided to ignore minor nuances and group a number of theories under general headings that would cover them all. It should be added that in the

26. See above, Note 13.
27. Also see below, Page 92.
28. The Arabic text of Epicurus' position (*Arabic*, pp. 158–159) is corrupt. The Arabic text of Democritus' theory omits the term "fiery" at the beginning (see above, Note 24), but this would not affect our identification.

former case he could hardly have been able to understand the difference between a theory that the soul is airlike (هوائية) and a theory that it is *pneuma* or spirit (روح).[29]

What Saadia enumerates as his fourth theory is slightly more complicated. It consists of a conflation of two theories in the *De placitis*, with additions from the present sections and also from later sections of that book. Still, almost every word in Saadia's statement can be accounted for from the *De placitis*. As a theory of the *division* of the soul, the *De placitis* reports the position of Pythagoras and Plato (M) that "the soul is twofold, one part having the rational [λογικόν, منطقى] [faculty], and the other part, the irrational [faculty] . . ." To the term "rational" Saadia adds the term "intellectual" either on the basis of the earlier report of Plato (C) that the soul is an "intellectual substance," or on the basis of a later reference in the *De placitis* to Pythagoras' views concerning the "faculty of reason and intellect."[30] Saadia describes the irrational part of the soul as the "animal" (حيوانى) part, probably on the basis of a later reference to the "vital" power (*τὸ ζωτικόν*, قوة الحياة); and he writes that the rational part "does not perish," while the irrational part "does perish"—again on the basis of later statements in the *De placitis* reporting the position of Pythagoras and Plato.[31] And then for some reason[32] he conflates the position of Pythagoras and Plato with that of Democritus and Epicurus (O) which located the rational part of the soul in the chest[33] and the irrational part "diffused" throughout the body. The result is Saadia's statement (4) that the soul "is two parts, one of which is intellectual, rational,

29. On air and *pneuma* in Epicurus, see C. Bailey, *The Greek Atomists and Epicurus* (Oxford, 1928), pp. 389–390.

The fourth quality in Epicurus' theory is omitted, but Saadia could hardly be expected to take account of an "unnamed quality."

30. In section five, entitled "Concerning the governing part"; *Greek*, p. 392, lines 1–2; *Arabic*, p. 161, line 2.

31. In the report of Pythagoras' position "concerning the governing part," the "vital" part of the soul (*τὸ ζωτικόν*, قوة الحياة) is contrasted with the rational and intellectual part; *Greek*, pp. 391–392; *Arabic*, p. 161, line 2. See below, Note 76. In the section entitled "Concerning the survival of the soul," it is reported that Pythagoras and Plato held the rational part to be incorruptible and the irrational part corruptible; *Greek*, p. 393; *Arabic*, p. 162.

32. See below, Page 91.

33. Pythagoras is reported to have located this faculty in the "head" (Arabic: *brain*) and Plato to have located it "in the entire head." See below, Notes 81, 82.

does not perish and is located in the heart;[34] the other is animal, diffused through the rest of the body and does perish."

The theory (1e) that the soul is an accident generated from the blood has not yet been accounted for.[35] It seems to be based on reports of the views of Empedocles, which are given in later sections of the *De placitis*. According to the *De placitis*, Empedocles held that the "governing" part of the soul is "in the blood."[36] Saadia could have understood this as meaning that it is an *accident* of the blood, for according to Aristotle, the accident is what is *in* a subject.[37] Another later section of the *De placitis*, which by a corruption our Arabic text entitles "Concerning soul,"[38] discusses the origin in animals not of soul, but of respiration. Whether or not this section was entitled "Concerning soul" in Saadia's manuscript, he could have understood it as a description of the origin of the soul both because it appears in *De placitis* as part of the general discussion of soul, and also because in Arabic the term soul (نفس) is derived from the same root as the term respiration (تنفس). It is reported there that according to Empedocles respiration originates in a process, the climax of which is the movement of the blood toward the surface of the body and then its return.[39] Understanding this as referring to the origin of the soul, and taking it together with Empedocles' position that the governing part of the soul is *in* the blood, Saadia could have come to his statement (1e) that the soul is an "accident which is generated from the blood."[40]

34. Saadia's change of "chest" to "heart" is unaccounted for. However, the location of this faculty in the heart is reported by the *De placitis* in the name of several writers; cf. *Greek*, p. 391, lines 13, 16, 19; *Arabic*, p. 160, lines 7, 8, 9.

35. Jakob Guttmann, *Die Religionsphilosophie des Saadia*, p. 196, n. 1, suggests as the source both a report according to which the Stoics held that the *pneuma* which constitutes the soul is attached to the blood, and also the report that Critas held that the soul is blood. Horovitz, *Die Psychologie*, p. 15, n. 23, prefers the former suggestion, and Julius Guttmann, "The Soul According to Rav Saadya Gaon," *Magnes Anniversary Book*, pp. 82–83, prefers the latter (adding that the reading must have been corrupt in the version that Saadia saw). Horovitz and Julius Guttmann each rejects the alternative suggestion on the grounds that it construes the soul not as an accident but as a substance.

36. *Greek*, p. 391, line 17: ἐν τῇ τοῦ αἵματος συστάσει; *Arabic*, p. 160, line 9: في الدم.

37. *Categories* 2, 1a, 23–26.

38. *Greek*, p. 411, line 25: περὶ ἀναπνοῆς (concerning respiration); *Arabic*, p. 170, line 6: في النفس.

39. *Greek*, pp. 411–412; *Arabic*, p. 170 (partially corrupt). The Greek is paraphrased by K. Freeman, *Companion to the Pre-Socratic Philosophers* (Oxford, 1946), p. 195.

40. عرض يتولّد من الدم. It may be significant that Ikhwān al-Ṣafāʾ also use the expression "generated from" in explaining the general theory that the soul is an

It may be asked why from all of the later material in the *De placitis* Saadia chose only the view of Empedocles to add to his list of theories, and why he chose to take the soul's being *in* the blood as meaning that it is in the blood as an accident.[41] The answer probably is that of all the theories which Saadia reviews here, the only one which he would have considered to be a living danger to rabbinic Judaism was the Karaite view that the human soul is blood. Saadia records and rejects that theory in the form which he understood to be accepted among the Karaites, when he lists and rejects Anan's theory (6) that the soul is identical with the substance of the blood. Very likely he wished to consider the Karaite theory in every possible version. Since it might be possible to understand the Karaite theory as meaning that the soul is not the substance of the blood, but an accident in it, Saadia records and rejects that possibility as well.

The parallel between Saadia's list and that of the *De placitis* is so great that even a summarizing statement in the *De placitis* has its reflex in a summarizing statement in Saadia. In the *De placitis* we have the statement (G) that the theories in the first group were theories that the soul is not a body, and this statement is followed by a recapitulation of those theories; in Saadia we similarly find a summarizing statement, here to the effect that the theories in the first group have "in common that the soul is an accident," also followed by a recapitulation.[42]

The comparison of Saadia's list with sections two, three, and four of Book Four of the *De placitis* shows that, except for the first and last paragraphs (A and P) in the *De placitis*, everything there has something corresponding in Saadia. However, the first and last items in the *De placitis* are not really theories of the essence of the human soul at all,[43] so that everything relevant in these sections of the *De placitis* is reflected in Saadia.

In Saadia's own list, on the other hand, there are two theories

---

accident. They explain that this theory means that the soul is "generated from [متولّد من] the mixture of the body." See Dieterici, *Die Abhandlungen der Ichwān es-Safā*, p. 567, line 11; p. 568, line 18.

41. Other meanings of being "in" are given by Aristotle; see *Physics*, IV, 3, 210a, 14–24.

42. See above, Page 78.

43. The first is the statement that the soul is self-moving, and the last is the statement that everything participates in soul; see above, Pages 79–80. Neither says anything of the essence of soul.

which could not have been taken from these sections in the *De placitis*. They are the theory of Anan that the soul is pure blood (6), and Saadia's own position (7) that the soul is of a substance similar to the spheres. But both of these theories clearly have a status of their own. Saadia's own position, however he may have developed or found it,[44] surely does not belong with the others, since the others form a review of incorrect theories. That Anan's theory does not belong with the rest is indicated simply by the fact that the proponent is named. This means that the heart of Saadia's review comprehends ancient, and for him incorrect, theories of the essence of the human soul, beginning with the theory that the human soul is an accident (1) and ending with the theory that the soul is "two kinds of air" (5). As an appendix to this enumeration Saadia added the recent view of the Karaite Anan, since that view was an all too living possibility in Saadia's time, and finally his own view. Not only does Saadia's enumeration of ancient theories contain a parallel to everything relevant in the *De placitis*, but with one exception it preserves the order in which the items appear there.[45] Moreover, Saadia's use of the *De placitis* is confirmed even by the awkwardness in his method of enumeration.[46] What Saadia calls the theory that the human soul is an accident is really five separate theories, and it would be expected that each of them should be enumerated in its own right. By grouping them, Saadia indicates that he found them

44. Saadia's position is that the soul is "created" and that its substance is "pure like the celestial spheres . . . It receives light . . . [and] becomes finer than the spheres"; see above, Page 79; Saadia, *Arabic*, p. 193; *Hebrew*, p. 152. Schreiner, *Der Kalam in der jüdischen Literatur*, p. 17, n. 3, points out a certain resemblance between Saadia's position and that of al-Naẓẓām. Horovitz, *Die Psychologie*, pp. 24–30, describes Saadia's theory as lying between the Platonic and Aristotelian positions. Julius Guttmann, "The Soul According to Rav Saadya Gaon," *Magnes Anniversary Book*, pp. 85 and 87, finds resemblance to Neo-Platonic and Christian theological thought and particularly to John Philoponus. Perhaps most striking, however, is the resemblance of Saadia's statement to that of Ikhwān al-Ṣafāʾ, who describe the soul as created and as of a "celestial, spiritual" character; cf. Dieterici, *Die Abhandlungen der Ichwān es-Safā*, p. 568, lines 9–11; German translation in Dieterici, *Die Lehre von der Weltseele*, p. 165. Horovitz, p. 27, n. 47, discounts the resemblance of Saadia's statement to Ikhwān al-Ṣafāʾ because the latter's emanationist views would be unacceptable to Saadia (cf. Saadia, *Arabic*, p. 46; *Hebrew*, p. 66); but Horovitz's objection does not do full justice to Saadia's eclecticism.

The "light" which the soul receives is the actualization of its intellect. The metaphor goes back to Plato, *Republic*, VI, 508, and Aristotle, *De Anima*, III, 5, 430a, 15–17. Also cf. Alfarabi, *Kitāb al-Siyāsāt al-Madaniyyah* (Hyderabad, A.H. 1346), p. 7; Hebrew translation: *Sefer ha-Hatḥalot*, ed. Z. Filipowski, in *Sefer ha-Asif* (Leipzig, 1849), p. 5.

45. Saadia puts Heraclitus' theory (5) after the Pythagorean-Platonic division of the soul (4), while in the *De placitis*, Heraclitus' theory (L) precedes it (M).

46. See above, Page 77.

grouped in his source, and they are in fact a restatement of the theories[47] which appear grouped in section two of the *De placitis*.

Julius Guttmann presented a number of arguments intended to show how Saadia's list differed from, and therefore could not have been derived from, Nemesius, Stobaeus, or *De placitis*. For our purposes we need be concerned only with the difficulties that Guttmann raised against identifying the *De placitis* as Saadia's source, and we believe that there is an obvious explanation for all of them.

First, Guttmann noted that that there is nothing in the doxographies to justify Saadia's description of the first group as theories that the soul is an accident.[48] In the course of his article, though, Guttmann concludes, on the contrary, that whatever Saadia's source may have been, it must have been Saadia himself who introduced that designation of these theories as theories of the soul as an accident.[49] Since Guttmann is almost surely correct in this conclusion, it is not a consideration against identifying the *De placitis* as Saadia's source. Just why Saadia described the first group as theories that the soul is an accident can only be surmised. One possibility is that Saadia was reasoning in the Kalam terms which categorize everything apart from the atoms as accidents.[50] Another possibility is that Saadia is following the scheme found in Ikhwān al-Ṣafā᾽ which states that all theories of the essence of the soul can be divided into those which construe the soul as an accident, those which construe it as a corporeal substance, and those which construe it as a celestial substance.[51] Saadia's enumeration parallels this scheme in a striking fashion, for the first theory that it gives is, together with its subdivisions, a theory that the soul is an accident; the following theories (2–6, with the exception of 4) are theories that the soul is a corporeal substance, and Saadia's own theory (7) is the theory that the soul is a celestial substance. A further possibility is that Saadia reasoned from the fact that of the six theories in the first group in *De placitis*, only one—the Platonic (C)—describes the soul as an incorporeal substance. If only Plato held the soul to be an incorporeal substance, the others held

47. With the exception of Plato's theory (C); see below, Page 87.

48. Julius Guttmann, "The Soul According to Rav Saadya Gaon," *Magnes Anniversary Volume*, p. 81.

49. *Ibid.*, pp. 84, 88.

50. Cf. Horovitz, *Die Psychologie*, p. 12, n. 18. Horovitz suggested but did not accept this explanation.

51. Cf. Dieterici, *Die Abhandlungen der Ichwān es-Safā*, p. 567; German translation in Dieterici, *Die Lehre von der Weltseele*, p. 164. For other similarities between Saadia's treatment and that of Ikhwān al-Ṣafā᾽, see above, Notes 19, 40, and 44.

it to be something else. It is explicitly stated in the *De placitis* that the first group is not a group of theories that the soul is a *corporeal* substance.[52] Saadia, we may suppose, inferred then that according to all of the theories in the first group, except for Plato's, the soul is not a substance at all but an accident. Since Saadia has omitted Plato's theory from his own first group,[53] he described that group as theories of the soul as an accident.[54]

Second, Guttmann pointed out that Plato's theory (C) of the essence of the soul does not appear in Saadia's list.[55] Actually, as was shown earlier, Saadia seems to have made incidental use of Plato's theory of the essence of the soul when stating the Platonic division of the soul.[56] Saadia's reason for not listing the Platonic theory in its own right seems perfectly clear. His intention was to review only incorrect theories of the soul. Whatever he meant precisely by his own position (7) that the soul is a substance similar to the spheres,[57] this position is not sufficiently different from the Platonic theory for Saadia to brand the latter as incorrect. Therefore the Platonic view had no place in his list.

Third, Guttmann stated that it could not have been from the *De placitis* that Saadia derived the theory (1e) that the soul is an accident generated from the blood.[58] We have tried to show that Saadia could in fact have derived that theory from the *De placitis*.[59]

Fourth, Guttmann pointed out that the theory (6) that the soul is blood—that is, Anan's theory—does not appear in the *De placitis*.[60] This is hardly a relevant argument, for whatever we should assume Saadia's source to have been, he clearly added Anan's theory himself.[61]

52. See above, Page 79, G.
53. See immediately below.
54. One of the theories in this group is Aristotle's definition of the soul (D), and this raises a difficulty since we know that the "first entelechy of a natural organic body . . ." is not an accident but a substance in one of the Aristotelian senses of that term; cf. *De anima* II, 1, 412a, 19–21. Jakob Guttmann, p. 195, n. 3, Horovitz, p. 13, n. 20, and Julius Guttmann, p. 84, suggest solutions to the difficulty by seeking sources for Saadia's interpretation. But perhaps those solutions are superfluous since there is nothing to indicate that Saadia knew all of the Aristotelian senses of substance or that he would have accepted them all if he had known them.
55. Julius Guttmann, "The Soul According to Rav Saadya Gaon," pp. 81–82.
56. See above, Page 82.
57. See above, Note 44.
58. Julius Guttmann, "The Soul According to Rav Saadya Gaon," p. 81.
59. See above, Page 83.
60. Julius Guttmann, "The Soul According to Rav Saadya Gaon," p. 82.
61. See above, Page 85.

Fifth, Guttmann pointed out that the *De placitis* does not contain a theory (4) that the human soul has a rational part which does not perish, located in the heart, and an irrational part, distributed throughout the body, which does perish.[62] We have seen, however, that virtually everything in this theory, including even the different adjectives that Saadia uses to describe the two parts of the soul, can be explained from the *De placitis*.[63]

The evidence seems overwhelming that it is just the *De placitis* which lies behind Saadia's list of theories of the soul.

It may still be asked, however, in what form Saadia used his source. While we have seen that in a general way everything in the *De placitis* is reflected in Saadia, there are numerous small differences between the two, and some of them are instructive.

Most obvious perhaps is that Saadia's list is briefer. All explanatory material in the *De placitis* is eliminated by Saadia, and he gives only the barest statement, in each case shorter than the original form in the *De placitis*. An aspect of this is the combination of several theories into one, which was noted earlier.[64] As a result of abbreviating and combining Saadia loses some of the distinctions which were present in his source. Earlier it was seen how, by combining several theories, Saadia loses the distinction between "airlike," "airlike quality," or "pneuma," on the one hand, and "wind," on the other;[65] and between "fiery quality," "fiery mixture," or "firelike power," on the one hand, and "fire," on the other.[66]

Sometimes even material which is essential to understanding the theory is omitted by Saadia. The key to Democritus' theory (J) is not the fiery mixture or the firelike power, but the spherical atoms which constitute the substance of the soul. They are not mentioned in Saadia's bare statement (3) that "some" hold the soul to be "fire." Again, the report given by *De placitis* of Heraclitus' theory (D)

62. Julius Guttmann, "The Soul According to Rav Saadya Gaon," p. 82.

63. See above, Page 82. After having raised the objection, Guttmann, p. 83, also concluded that Saadia's statement is a conflation of the position of Pythagoras and Plato with the position of Democritus and Epicurus. Guttmann did not observe that the other elements in Saadia's statement are paralleled in the later sections of the *De placitis*.

64. See above, Pages 81–82.

65. See above, Page 81.

66. See above, Page 81, and Note 28. We assumed that just these theories from the *De placitis* were combined by Saadia into his own theories 2 and 3 ("wind" and "fire") because of the striking correspondence in the order of the theories in the two lists, and Saadia's explicit statement that theories 2 and 3 were held by "some" philosophers.

places individual souls into a wider framework, explaining that the "soul of the universe is an exhalation from the damp [elements] in the universe," while the souls of animals are a combination of the exhalation from without and the exhalation within the animal itself. This statement, as it stands, is difficult enough to understand unless one has some notion of what Heraclitus meant by these "exhalations."[67] But Saadia, who was not interested here in the soul of the universe, omits reference to that soul and writes only (5) that the human soul is "two kinds of air, one internal and the other external."[68] This could hardly be meaningful to an uninformed reader. Once again, Saadia's restatement (1b) of Aristotle's definition of the soul as the "entelechy of a natural body" is so incomplete that it is not correct; for not every natural body has a soul, but only those "organic" bodies which "potentially possess life." The positions of Democritus, Heraclitus, and Aristotle are not easy to understand without a commentary, and Saadia's omissions may partially be due to his own difficulty in understanding them.

Saadia's terminology also differs from that of *De placitis* and generally it is less precise and less technical.[69] The Arabic translation of the *De placitis*, like the Greek, speaks of the "four elements" (E) using a transliteration of the Greek word for element (στοιχεῖα, اسطقسات). This technical term does not appear in Saadia. Saadia speaks instead (1c) of the "four natures," which could mean not the physical elements at all, but rather the four humours in the body.[70] In the theory (F) that the soul is the "training together [συγγυμνασία] of the senses," the Arabic uses two words, both of

67. Cf. Burnet, *Early Greek Philosophy*, pp. 151–154.

68. Saadia, *Arabic*, p. 190, *Hebrew*, pp. 150–151, adds the explanation that what led to this theory was the observation that the soul can be "maintained only by inhaling air from without," while the theory is erroneous since inhaling air serves only to "fan the natural heat [الحرارة الغريزية] in which the soul is situated." This explanation cannot be connected to Heraclitus' theory in the form transmitted by *De placitis* and it apparently was added by Saadia himself. Conceivably it was suggested in part by the fact that Empedocles' theory relates the soul to the process of respiration (above, Page 83), and also, although in a completely different way, assigns to natural heat (ἔμφυτον θερμόν, الحرارة الغريزية) a function in respiration; cf. *Greek*, p. 412, lines 4–5; *Arabic*, p. 170, line 8.

69. Before preparing these observations on Saadia's language I was fortunate in being able to consult with Professor David Baneth.

70. See E. W. Lane, *Arabic-English Lexicon* (London-Edinburgh, 1863–93), *s.v.* مزاج; طبيعة.

which represent the notion of training.[71] Saadia, however, writes less precisely (1d) of the "tying together" (ارطبات) of the senses.[72] The theories that (H) the soul is "airlike" (هوائية) and that (I) it is spirit or "pneuma" (روح) is represented in Saadia by the theory (2) that the soul is "wind."[73] Instead of the technical, philosophic description of the parts of the soul as "corruptible" (φθαρτόν, فاسد) and "incorruptible" (ἄφθαρτον, غير فاسد),[74] Saadia writes (4) that one part of the soul "perishes" (يفنى), while the other "does not perish" (ليس يفنى).[75] And finally, Heraclitus' "exhalation" or giving off of vapor (ἀναθυμίασις) is more or less represented in translation (L) by an Arabic term for "vapor" (بخار). In Saadia's statement of the theory (5) it becomes simply "air" (هواء). This use of less technical language is to be considered as one aspect of Saadia's simplification of the presentation in the *De placitis*.[76]

71. The Arabic translation of *De placitis*, p. 157, lines 5–6 (see n. 4), has: شيء مع تدرب الحواس وارتياضها. The terms تدرب and ارتياض are closer translations of the Greek συγγυμνασία than Saadia's loose ارتباط. On the other hand, the first three words in the Arabic are such a strange overliteral attempt to capture the Greek prefix συν that from the point of view of sense, Saadia's simplified version is preferable.

72. Professor Baneth has suggested that ارتباط may simply be a corruption of ارتياض.

73. Again Professor Baneth has suggested that in a text written in Hebrew characters the ريح which we have in our texts of Saadia could be an easy corruption of روح.

74. Cf. *Greek*, p. 393, lines 11 and 13; *Arabic*, p. 162, lines 7–8.

75. Saadia, *Arabic*, p. 190.

76. In restating Pythagoras' theory (1a) that the soul is "a self-moving number" Saadia, *Arabic*, p. 189, writes محركا نفسه in place of the phrase يحرك ذاته in *De placitis*, *Arabic*, p. 156. Here too the term ذات perhaps should be considered a more technical term that Saadia has changed.

In stating the position of Democritus and Epicurus (O), the Arabic *De placitis*, p. 159, line 12, states literally that the rational part of the soul is "driven in" (مركوز) to the chest. Saadia (4), *Arabic*, p. 190, writes that this faculty "resides" (يسكن) in the heart. Saadia has here given a simpler term than the Arabic *De placitis*, but the result is that he has returned closer to the Greek, p. 390, line 16, καθιδρυμένον.

Above, Note 31, it was seen that Saadia speaks of the "animal" (حيوانى) part of the soul instead of the "vital" faculty (قوة الحياة). This may also be considered a substitution of a less, for a more technical term.

In Saadia's restatement of Pythagoras' theory that the soul is a "self-moving number" it was seen above, Note 17, that an alternate reading gives "a self-moving accident." If by chance that alternate reading is correct, this would be yet another example of simplification by Saadia.

Virtually all the changes which have been pointed out could be explained by supposing that Saadia wrote this section of *Emunot we-De^cot* with the *De placitis* before him, condensing and simplifying as he worked. However, the form in which Saadia presents the Pythagorean-Platonic division of the soul (4) shows that he could not, after all, have had the *De placitis* before him in its entirety. It has been seen that Saadia's statement of this theory is a conflation of two positions reported in section four of *De placitis*, that of Pythagoras and Plato (M), and that of Democritus and Epicurus (O).[77] The later sections in the *De placitis*, of which Saadia made only slight use,[78] state how the two positions which he combined actually differ from one another. In the earlier section it is reported that Democritus and Epicurus (O) located the rational part of the soul in the chest,[79] and this reappears in Saadia's conflation as the location of the rational part of the soul in the heart.[80] But Pythagoras and Plato, according to the later sections of the Arabic translation, located the rational part of the soul in the brain,[81] or in the entire head.[82] Again, as was seen earlier, Saadia's conflation repeats a later statement in the *De placitis* according to which Pythagoras and Plato held the rational part of the soul to be incorruptible.[83] However, in that same section of the *De placitis*, it is reported that the materialists Democritus and Epicurus hold the entire soul to be "corruptible, being destroyed along with the body."[84] Thus two positions from the early sections of *De placitis* have been combined by Saadia, although they are clearly distinguished in the later sections. This means that at the time when Saadia was writing either he was unable to consult all of the later sections, or else he did not know the names of the authors of the various theories and was therefore unable to match the positions in the earlier sections with those in the later.

Even without considering the later sections there is evidence for supposing that Saadia worked without having all the material in

77. See above, Page 82.
78. See above, Pages 82–83.
79. Later, *Greek*, p. 391, it is stated that "Plato and Democritus" located this part of the soul "in the whole head." C. Bailey, *The Greek Atomists*, p. 161, n. 1, discounts the later statement of Democritus' position in favor of the former.
80. See above, Page 83.
81. This is reported of Pythagoras in the Arabic, p. 161, line 2. The Greek, p. 392, lines 1–2, has "around the head."
82. This is reported of Plato; *Greek*, p. 391, lines 3–4; *Arabic*, p. 160, lines 1–2.
83. *Greek*, p. 393, lines 10–11; *Arabic*, p. 162, lines 6–7. See above, Page 82.
84. *Greek*, p. 393, lines 8–9; *Arabic*, p. 162, lines 5–6.

the *De placitis* before him, and without knowing the names of the authors of the various positions. In *De placitis* the two positions on the division of the soul (M and O) that Saadia combined do not immediately follow one another, but are separated by the Stoic eightfold division of the soul (N). It seems probable that the Stoic position was not there at the time when Saadia was working on *Emunot we-Deᶜot*;[85] for he would be more likely to combine two anonymous twofold divisons of the soul that followed one another directly than to combine two such theories between which a different theory intervened. Further, the very fact that he combined differing statements of Pythagoras and Plato, and of Democritus and Epicurus, indicates that the statements were not labeled as having been maintained by different philosophers. The absence of names is also indicated by the fact that he places Pythagoras' position on the *essence* of the soul (1a) with theories of the soul as an accident, and Pythagoras' *division* of the soul (4) with theories of the soul as a substance. He would hardly consciously have classified the same philosopher's position as a theory that the soul is an accident and as a theory that it is not.

While it has been seen to be Book Four of the *De placitis* which underlies Saadia's list, from his statement of the Pythagorean-Platonic division of the soul the following can be inferred: he apparently used *De placitis* in a form which omitted some material from sections two, three, and four, which contained only selected material from the later sections, and which presented the statements of *De placitis* without naming the proponents.

We can only conjecture what this form of the *De placitis* was. One possibility is that Saadia never actually saw the book itself but used a condensation that had been made from it. If this condensation be conceived of as an actual literary work, its existence should be questioned—if for no other reason—because of the principle *libri non sunt multiplicandi*. Besides, there would be no explanation why an Arabic epitomizer, while simplifying and combining various other theories in the *De placitis*, should record just Empedocles' difficult theory of respiration.[86]

However, on the assumption that Saadia had prepared the mate-

85. In terms of the analysis given above, Page 81, this means that if the Stoic division of the soul is to be understood as grouped with the position of Asclepiades (F), the grouping had been made before Saadia took up the material to work on *Emunot we-Deᶜot*.

86. See above, Page 83.

rial for himself, we have seen why Empedocles' theory was important enough to be included.[87] That assumption is also suggested by the absence of the names of the authors in the material that Saadia was using, for the omission of names is typical of his method.[88] The reason that Saadia did not work directly from a manuscript of *De placitis* was probably simply the fact that one was not always available to him. It is virtually inconceivable that he owned one.[89] He could at best have used a copy from one of the public libraries that existed in Iraq at the time,[90] or else have borrowed a copy from a private party. It is possible that when he did have the use of a manuscript he excerpted whatever he thought he might wish to use when dealing with the problem of the human soul. The material from which he wrote the present section of *Emunot we-Deᶜot* would, on this hypothesis, have been reading notes that he made some time earlier. The character of the material—abbreviated and simplified, yet preserving the structure of the original—fits in well with the hypothesis that Saadia was using notes.

Another possibility is more intriguing. The accepted date for the composition of *Emunot we-Deᶜot* is ca. 933,[91] and that falls within the period when Saadia was deposed from the Gaonate following his quarrel with the Exilarch.[92] The evidence is that he spent this period in Baghdad.[93] Reports from the time describe the existence of groups in Baghdad which met to discuss philosophic and semiphilosophic subjects.[94] Non-Moslems as well as Moslems are known to have

87. See above, Page 84.

88. See Malter, *Saadia Gaon*, p. 180, n. 412a.

89. On the extremely high price of manuscripts, see O. Pinto, "Le biblioteche degli Arabi nell' età degli Abbassidi," *Bibliofilia*, 30:143 (1928).

90. In Baghdad at this time there was a large public library attached to Dār al-ᶜIlm; see Pinto, "Le biblioteche degli Arabi," p. 150. According to Pinto, public libraries were generally open to all, paper, pen, and ink were supplied without charge to those using the library, and frequently books could be borrowed for outside use (Pinto, p. 158). Also see *Encyclopaedia of Islam, s.v. Kitābkhāna.*

Saadia, sitting and working in a public library, would present a rather unexpected picture.

91. A passage in one of the early sections suggests that this was the time when Saadia was writing. Cf. Saadia, *Arabic*, p. 72, lines 5–6; *Hebrew*, p. 81; Malter, *Saadia Gaon*, p. 193. Malter, p. 194, presents evidence that the book was not originally written as a single whole, so that this date can only be taken as an approximate date for the other sections.

92. See Malter, *Saadia Gaon*, p. 117.

93. *Ibid.*, p. 118 and n. 257.

94. Circles of this type are described by Tauḥīdī in *K. al-Muqābasāt* and *K. al-Imtāᶜ*, and by Masᶜūdī, *Les Prairies d'or* (Paris, 1861–77), VI, 368–376; on the last, see G. E. von Grunebaum, "Avicenna's Risāla fi ᵓl-ᶜišq and Courtly Love," *Journal of Near Eastern Studies*, 11:235–236 (1952). R. Dozy, *Journal Asiatique*, 5th series, 2:93 (1853), quotes the

participated in these meetings, and there are reports of the presence of Jews.[95] If it were possible for a person of Saadia's standing to allow himself to participate in meetings of this type, it is conceivable that he heard a reading of the sections on the soul from the *De placitis*, made notes, and later used them when writing *Emunot we-De*ᶜ*ot*, so that conceivably he worked not from reading notes but from lecture notes.

These last suggestions must remain in the realm of conjecture until and unless we have more information concerning the manner in which Saadia and the other Jewish philosophers acquired their philosophic knowledge.[96] What may be taken as established is that Saadia's list of theories of the soul is based upon the *De placitis philosophorum*, and that when Saadia actually wrote *Emunot we-De*ᶜ*ot* he did not work directly from the *De placitis* but from material prepared from it, apparently by himself.[97]

---

report of a Spanish Moslem visitor to Baghdad at the end of the tenth century who was shocked at such meetings, in which atheists and Jews participated and complete freedom of speech reigned. For references to debates, see G. E. von Grunebaum, *Der Islam im Mittelalter* (Zürich, 1963), p. 553, n. 67. There apparently were no formal schools; see M. Meyerhof, "Von Alexandrien nach Baghdad," *Sitzungsberichte der preussischen Akademie, Phil.-Hist. Klasse*, 23:413 (1930), who states that he was unable to discover any mention of the existence of either a public or a private school of philosophy in Baghdad at this time. (For most of the references in this note I am indebted to Professor von Grunebaum.)

95. See the reference to Dozy in the previous note. I. Goldziher, "Mélanges judéo-arabes, XVI," *REJ*, 47:42–43 (1903), and S. Goitein, "Yediᶜot Ḥadashot ᶜal Pilosophim Yehudim mi-Tequfat Rabbenu Saadia," *Rab Saadia Gaon* (Jerusalem, 1943), pp. 567–570, identify two of the participants referred to by Tauḥīdī in *K. al-Muqābasāt* as Jews. Goldziher, "Mélanges," p. 45, also gives a report according to which a son of one of the Exilarchs in the eighth century belonged to a group of intellectuals that included representatives of different religions. (For the reference to Goldziher I am indebted to Professor Moshe Perlmann.)

96. There is a report that a Jewish contemporary of Saadia studied philosophy with Thābit b. Qurra. See Masᶜūdī, *K. al-Tanbīh* (Leiden, 1894), p. 113; trans. Carra de Vaux, *Le Livre de L'Avertissement* (Paris, 1896), pp. 160–161.

97. Saadia also provides reviews of rejected philosophic theories in his two discussions of creation: Commentary on *S. Yeṣirah*; and *Emunot we-Deᶜot*, section 1. While some of those theories can be correlated with statements in Books 1 and 2 of *De placitis*, there is not sufficient ground for supposing that *De placitis* was Saadia's source for those two lists.

Some Non-Halakic Aspects of the *Mishneh Torah*

By ISADORE TWERSKY

I

This paper seeks to call attention to some motifs of Maimonidean rationalism explicitly or allusively incorporated into the *Mishneh Torah*—motifs by no means concentrated exclusively in the overtly philosophic sections of the *Sefer ha-Madda*ᶜ but deftly sprinkled throughout the entire work. By noting certain emphases underscored time and again, some of them in midrashic-exegetic garb, we obtain additional insight into the conceptions which predominated in Maimonides' mind when he was writing the *Mishneh Torah.* Brief philosophic comments and rationalistic directives, effectively inserted here and there, reveal in the code a vigorous intellectualistic posture usually associated exclusively with the *Guide.*

The image of Maimonides as a philosopher insisting upon the superiority of the theoretical life, questing for a rationale of the law and intimating what are its postulates, is, in fact, fully developed in the pre-*Guide* writings. Maimonides consistently espoused a sensitized view of religion and morality, demanding a full and uncompromising but inspired and sensitive observance of the law, openly disdaining the perfunctory, vulgar view of the masses (*hammon ha*ᶜ*am*), searching for the ultimate religious significance of every human action, indicting literalism and equating it with ignorance (*siklut*), and urging a commitment to and quest for wisdom (*ḥokmah*).[1] The latter is

1. See, e.g., *Mishnah Commentary* on *Berakot*, end (Kapaḥ translation, pp. 91–92); *Rosh ha-Shanah*, 2:6; *Abot*, 4:5; introduction to *Ḥeleḳ*; *Iggeret Teman*, ed. A. Halkin (New York, 1952), p. 39; *Mishneh Torah, De*ᶜ*ot*, V, 11; *Teshubah*, V, 1; ᶜ*Edut*, II, 1–3; *Melakim*, XI, 3. *Moreh Nebukim*, II, 29; III, 11, 13; *Teshubot ha-Rambam*, ed. A. Freimann (Jerusalem, 1934), 5, 345, 370; *Iggerot ha-Rambam*, ed. D. Baneth (Jerusalem, 1946), p. 63, and many others. See also the letter published by A. Scheiber, in *Sefunot*, 8:137–144 (1964). For the phrase רוב גלמי בני ישראל in *Teshubah*, V, 1, see D. Rosin, *Die Ethik des Maimonides* (Breslau, 1876), p. 70, n. 2. This phrase will be fully explicated in Professor Wolfson's forthcoming *The Philosophy of Kalam*. It is noteworthy that the term "fools" (טפשים), found in many of these passages, is used also to designate Karaites—another type of literalist; see, e.g., *Mishneh Torah, Temidim u-Musafim* VII:11.

absolutely indispensable for religious perfection—is indeed the crowning achievement. This thread—the process of intellectualization—is woven uninterruptedly and unabashedly from his earliest writings through the *Moreh Nebukim* and on through all his responsa. It is especially discernible in the texture of the *Mishneh Torah.*

Furthermore, if we add historical-biographical information to textual investigation, it becomes clear that Maimonides' reputation as creative religious philosopher and enthusiastic propagator of philosophy and his identification with a lofty rationalism were widespread long before the circulation of the *Guide.* As early as in the first letter of Joseph ben Judah (Ibn Aḳnin) to Maimonides—a flowery, artistically constructed epistle—the latter is extolled as enlightener of the bewildered, purifier of religious belief, and philosophic pedagogue par excellence.[2] Professor Baneth[3] noted in passing that we may infer from this that Maimonides' fame as philosopher was firmly entrenched relatively early in his public career. I would suggest that this reputation could have been based not only on hearsay but on thoughtful reading of "our Talmudic works," as he usually designates them. Such a reading of the *Commentary on the Mishnah* and the *Mishneh Torah* would reveal these characteristics, general definitions of purpose and tendencies of thought. The significance of such an early statement as "expounding a single principle of religion is dearer to me than anything else that I might teach" is transparent and sheds its light on the entire Maimonidean corpus. We may now combine this reference of Ibn Aḳnin with the suggestive statement of another contemporary (also named Joseph ibn Aḳnin), who, at a rather early date, described Maimonides in similar vein, as battling for the Torah with the "swords of syllogistic demonstration."[4] On the other hand, it is equally clear that not only did Maimonides' luster as halakic authority not dim while he was preoccupied with his philosophic opus but that he continued to write commentaries and novellae, let alone responsa, even after the *Mishneh*

2. *Iggerot ha-Rambam*, ed. D. Baneth, 5–6.

3. *Ibid.*, 4. In light of the references in this epistle we may with greater certitude disregard the ascription to Ibn Aḳnin of the poem in *Diwan* of Judah ha-Levi, ed. H. Brody, p. 105, n. 72. See Brody's comments *ad loc.;* also J. Mann, *The Jews in Egypt and in Palestine under the Fatimid Caliphs* (London, 1920), I, 234, n. 3. J. Toledano has published a poem of Ibn Aḳnin in praise of Maimonides; see *Oẓar Genazim* (Jerusalem, 1960), pp. 29–31.

4. See *Hitgalut ha-Sodot we-Hofaᶜat ha-Meᵓorot: Perush Shir ha-Shirim*, ed. A. Halkin (Jerusalem, 1964), p. 431: מופת הזמן הנלחם מלחמתה של תורה בחרבות המופת. On the identity of this Ibn Aḳnin see the review article by D. Baneth, *Oẓar Yehude Sefarad*, 7:11–21 (1964). See also *Essays on Maimonides*, ed. S. Baron (New York, 1941), p. 269.

Torah was in circulation and the *Guide* was in various stages of preparation.[5] The two preoccupations—not without some tension, even friction—coexisted and both were operative in all his writings. There is a beginning and an end and in between there are unified, if multidimensional, themes of development.

It is hoped that this study will therefore have some bearing also upon the more general, complicated question of the unity of Maimonides' writing and especially the intrinsic relationship between his two major works, the *Mishneh Torah* and the *Guide for the Perplexed*. The relationship between these two monumental works, one juridical and the other philosophical, is obvious and straightforward to some, obscure and problematic for others. Some detect harmony and find deliberate progression in his writings while others hear only cacophony and see intentional disjunction. The recognition of such a problem is a commonplace of Jewish historiography.[6] However, not only is there no scholarly consensus concerning its solution but the very nature of the problem is conceived in a variety of different ways. *Quot homines, tot sententiae.* Some boldly bifurcate the Maimonidean corpus: (a) by disestablishing the *Guide* and dismissing it as the pseudepigraphic composition of one "who hanged himself on a mighty oak-tree";[7] or (b) by identifying two antithetical, unintegrated doctrines of Maimonides: an inner, traditional, authentic one articulated in the *Mishneh Torah* vis-à-vis an extraneous, foreign, spurious one borrowed from alien neighbors and formulated in the *Guide*.[8] Some see these two works on entirely different levels (Talmudic versus philosophic or exoteric versus esoteric), with the implication that the *Mishneh Torah* can suggest nothing of the typically intellectualistic stance of Maimonides inasmuch as it "deals with beliefs

5. See Note 70, below.

6. See R. J. Z. Werblowsky, *Joseph Karo* (Oxford, 1962), p. 8: "The problems posed by the necessity of determining the relationship between Maimonides' code and his philosophy are still far from being solved, but Jewish historiography has at least had time to get used to them."

7. This is the view formulated very bluntly, for example, by the seventeenth-century Yavetz, R. Jacob Emden; see his *Siddur*, *Ḥallon Shebiᶜi:*

ספר מורה נבוכים אינו מעשה ידי אומן המחבר הגדול הר"מ ז"ל אלא מאחד שרצה ליחנק תלה עצמו באילן גדול.

See A. Shoḥet, *ᶜIm Ḥilufe Teḳufot* (Jerusalem, 1960), p. 207. This view has been revived in many different forms and for disparate reasons. A partial adumbration of this approach is to be found in the commentary of Shem Tob, *Moreh Nebukim*, III, 51.

8. Z. Yavetz, *Toledot ᶜAm Yisrael*, V. X, pp. 41, 42, 47 and *passim*. Note ᶜAzariah de Rossi, *Maẓref le-Kesef*, II:9 (p. 34):

בספרו הנכבד מו"נ אשר בו אמנם דבר כאיש יהודי מחוכם אך לא כרבן תלמודי.

and opinions only insofar as they are implied in prohibitions and commands,"[9] or that it actually conceals the author's true convictions. Some posit an irreducible tension or congenital incompatibility between law and philosophy—or between law and any metajuridical system; that is, between the temporal and the spiritual, the contingent and the eternal—and therefore any attempted combination must be discordant or incongruous.[10] Many scholars, of course, assume that Maimonides' writings are structured and informed by an integrated community of interests embracing theology and law.[11]

I would submit that the uncovering of certain nonhalakic emphases in the *Mishneh Torah* as well as in other popular, mass-directed writings—emphases which are indeed undocumented but also uncamouflaged—will contribute to a more balanced approach to this problem of unity.

II

The *Mishneh Torah*, on many occasions, renders homage to the supremacy of the intellect and intellectual pursuits. This is, of course, the general thrust of book one, the *Sefer ha-Madda*ᶜ.[12] One can find explicit statements to this effect in such places as *Hilkot Yesode ha-Torah* 4:13 or *Hilkot Teshubah* 9:1 and 10:6. The conclusion of the last book (*Hilkot Melakim*), with its political conception of the messianic period as an instrument of intellectual achievement and the completely incorporeal view of the future life, is another obvious case in

9. E.g., Leo Strauss, "The Literary Character of the Guide for the Perplexed," *Essays on Maimonides*, ed. S. Baron, p. 38 and *passim*. See L. Ginzberg, "Caro, Joseph," *Jewish Encyclopedia*, III, 584.

10. See, e.g., the analogy between Maimonides and R. Eleᶜazar of Worms drawn by G. Scholem, *Major Trends in Jewish Mysticism*, p. 95. Also S. Pines, introduction to the French translation of the *Mishneh Torah*, tr. V. Nikiprowetzky and A. Zaoui (Paris, 1961), especially p. 5. Cf., however, G. Scholem, *Jewish Gnosticism* (New York, 1960), pp. 9–13. On the prevalent but often avoidable antagonism between canon law and theology, see Stephan Kuttner, *Harmony from Dissonance: An Interpretation of Medieval Canon Law* (Latrobe, Pa., 1960), especially pp. 1–4 and 50.

11. E.g., S. Baron, *Social and Religious History of the Jews*, VI, 101–102 and VIII, 63; J. Guttmann, *Philosophies of Judaism* (New York, 1964), p. 154. A notable example of the integrative-wholistic approach to the entire Maimonidean corpus is I. Goldziher, *Pseudo-Baḥya: Kitāb maᶜāni al-nafs* (Berlin, 1907), pp. 58ff. (One might add *Abot*, 3:9 to his references.) See also Aḥad Ha-ᶜAm, *Shilṭon ha-Sekel*.

12. See Maimonides' own statement in *Iggeret Teḥiyyat ha-Metim* (Tel-Aviv, 1951), p. 345; my *Rabad of Posquières* (Cambridge, Mass., 1962), p. 285.

point.[13] There are, however, more subtle and therefore more suggestive and meaningful indications of this emphasis, many of them in overtly halakic contexts. Here are a few illustrations.

First,

> The words of the Torah do not abide with one who studies listlessly, nor with those who learn amidst luxury, and high living, but only with one who mortifies himself for the sake of the Torah, constantly enduring physical discomfort, and not permitting sleep to his eyes nor slumber to his eyelids. "This is the law, when a man dieth in a tent" (Numbers 19:14). The sages explained the text metaphorically thus: "The Torah abides only with him who mortifies himself in the tents of wisdom."[14]

This is, in essence, a quotation of the well-known rabbinic aphorism, expressing the idea that study requires commitment unto exhaustion and death.[15] The underlying Talmudic statement concludes

אין התורה מתקיימת אלא במי שממית עצמו עליה

and it appears so, verbatim, in most later sources up to the *Shulḥan Aruk.*[16] In an adjacent passage on the Talmud,[17] Rashi paraphrases the ending and inserts "in the tents of Torah" (**באהלי התורה**) while in a Geonic fragment we find the ending "in the house of study" (**בבית המדרש**),[18] but there does not seem to be any antecedent or parallel for Maimonides' interpretive paraphrase, which allows his emphasis on *ḥokmah* to emerge forcefully and distinctly.[19]

13. *Kesef Mishneh, Melakim*, XI, 1, noted the essentially nonhalakic character of these two chapters:

הפרק הזה ושאחריו א מ ו נ ו ת טובות בביאת משיחנו

See, generally, J. Finkel, "Maimonides' Treatise on Resurrection: A Comparative Study," *Essays on Maimonides*, ed. S. Baron (New York, 1941), pp. 93–123; S. Schwarzfuchs, "Les Lois royales de Maimonides," *REJ* (N.S.), 11:63–86 (1951), and the latter's reference to G. Vajda, *La Théologie ascétique de Baḥya* (Paris, 1947), p. 105, n. 2; A. Freimann, *Teshubot ha-Rambam*, p. xlv.

14. *Talmud Torah*, III, 12. The ending reads באהלי החכמה or החכמים. See all the variations in the new edition of *Sefer ha-Madda*ᶜ (Jerusalem, 1964), editor-in-chief S. Lieberman.

15. *Berakot*, 63a; *Shabbat*, 83b; *Zohar*, *Terumah*, 158b.

16. *Yoreh De*ᶜ*ah*, 246:21.

17. *Berakot*, 63a. Similarly, *Hukke ha-Torah* in S. Assaf, *Meḳorot le-Toledot ha-Ḥinnuk* (Tel Aviv, 1925–26), I, 10.

18. L. Ginzberg, *Ginze Schechter* (New York, 1928–29) II, 639.

19. Menaḥem b. Zeraḥ, *Zedah la-Derek* (Warsaw, 1880), I:4, 21 (p. 82), reads: מי שממית עצמו . . . באהלי התורה והחכמה, apparently a conflation of Rashi and Maimonides. The phrase אהלי חכמה is found in the midrash to Exodus 33:11 and is quoted by Rashi, *Pirḳe Abot*, 1:1. For *Torah* and *ḥokmah*, see also *Abot*, 1:17.

It is, of course, either foolhardy or presumptuous to contend unqualifiedly that a given Maimonidean statement has no source, for new sources or antecedents are constantly being discovered and a contention *ex silentio* can never be too persuasive. However, even in such cases, Maimondies' choice of a particular, not too popular formulation, would remain noteworthy.

Second, the incorrigible, professional dice thrower (משחק בקוביה) is decried and his "profession" discountenanced in the Talmud. Two explanations are offered for the strong disapproval: (a) gambling approximates robbery (גזל מדבריהם), inasmuch as the high odds are unjust and indefensible; (b) the gamblers themselves are not engaged in constructive work beneficial for humanity or in professions which further the welfare of society.[20] In Maimonides' formulation of this law—which happens to be studded with difficulties—we need only note again the casual insertion and implicit exaltation of *ḥokmah*: "Playing dice . . . entails the prohibition of wasting time on useless pursuits, for it is not fitting for a person to spend any part of his life other than on studying wisdom and furthering civilization."[21]

Third, Maimonides' description of the procedure of conversion vividly reflects his uniform insistence upon the indispensability of knowledge of the theoretical bases and theological premises of religion. A potential convert must be carefully informed about Judaism and instructed in its ritualistic patterns and, most emphatically, its metaphysics, its dogmatic principles. Maimonides emphasizes that the latter must be presented at great length.[22] Now, the need to expatiate concerning the theological foundations, in contradistinction to ritual commandments, is not mentioned in the Talmud.[23] Some scholars were inclined to assume that Maimonides found these details in his text of *Masseket Gerim*, inasmuch as a few other variants can be traced to this source, but this seems to be a gratuitous assumption.[24] Given the Maimonidean stance, this emphasis is a logical corollary or even a self-evident component of the underlying text which stipulates that the convert be informed about "some [מקצת] command-

20. *Sanhedrin*, 24b.

21. *Gezelah wa-Abedah*, VI, 11.

אין ראוי לאדם שיעסוק כל ימיו אלא בדברי חכמה וביישובו של עולם.

See J. Anatoli, *Malmad ha-Talmidim* (Lyck, 1866), p. 173; ᶜ*Edut*, X, 4, where Maimonides has only יישובו של עולם and commentaries *ad loc.* for the difficulties.

22. *Issure Biᵓah*, XIV, 2:

ומודיעין אותו עיקרי הדת שהוא ייחוד השם ואיסור עכו"ם ומאריכין בדבר הזה.

23. *Yebamot*, 47a; *Masseket Gerim*.

24. See S. Rappaport, *Oẓar Neḥmad*, 1:30 (1856); F. Baer, *Toledot ha-Yehudim Bi-Sefarad ha-Noẓrit* (Tel Aviv, 1945), p. 482. In *Ẓion*, 15:5 (1950), Baer has noted a striking parallel with Philo. The *Migdal ᶜOz, ad loc.*, offers no corroborative evidence for Rappaport, whose methodological assumption—that every phrase and nuance of the *Mishneh Torah* is explicit in some source—is misleading. It fails to acknowledge the interpretive-derivative aspects of the *Mishneh Torah*. See next note.

ments."[25] Selective instruction concerning Judaism and its commandments would be ludicrously inadequate or warped if it omitted the first and most important commandment of all: a true conception of the unity of God. That this is a sustained emphasis is corroborated further in the same chapter where Maimonides defines a truly righteous person, the person for whom the world to come was prepared, as the wise man (בעל החכמה) who practices and understands these commandments. This is also Maimonides' expository interpolation.[26] As a matter of fact, the entire presentation bristles with suggestive Maimonidean novelties which should not be glossed over and obscured.[27]

Fourth, the Talmud states that the unintentional killer who flees to a city of refuge should be provided with all the necessities and amenities of life. This statement is based on the verse "that fleeing unto one of these cities he might live [וחי]", which is interpreted to mean "see to it that he lives properly."[28] The halakah subsumes under this the provision that when a student flees to a city of refuge

25. See *Maggid Mishneh, ad loc.:*

אינו מבואר בגמ' רק שפשוט הוא מעצמו

This is not in the category of a Maimonidean novelty, usually heralded by the formula "it seems to me," but an interpretive elaboration which, in Maimonides' opinion, is implicit in the text; see my article in *Biblical and Other Studies*, ed. A. Altmann (Cambridge, 1963), p. 164. See also Radbaz, *Shemiṭah we-Yobel*, XIII, 13; *Maggid Mishneh*, *Mekirah*, XIV, 14; *Leḥem Mishneh*, *Sanhedrin*, II:7. The *Mishneh Torah* clearly does not efface Maimonides' personality. It should be noted here that when Maimonides says in his responsum (Freimann, 152, p. 147)

לא נניח תלמוד ערוך ונפסוק הלכה ממשא ומתן של גמרא

this does not eliminate or minimize the role of his interpretive elaborations. See also responsum 89.

26. *Yebamot*, 47a, reads:

אומרים לו הוי יודע שהעולם הבא אינו עשוי אלא לצדיקים.

Issure Bi'ah, XIV, 3 reads:

ומודיעין אותו שבעשית מצות אלו יזכה לחיי העולם הבא. ושאין שום צדיק גמור אלא בעל החכמה שעושה מצות אלו ויודען.

See also *Teshubah*, IX, 1:1

העושה כל הכתוב בה ויודעו דעה גמורה.

27. E.g., the application and interpretation of Hosea 11:4 in *Issure Bi'ah*, XIV, 2. (See the Talmudic use of this verse in *Shabbat*, 89b.) It is noteworthy that these interpretive additions and philosophic amplifications were omitted by medieval writers, even those who lean heavily on Maimonides and often quote him verbatim. See ha-Me'iri, *Bet ha-Beḥirah on Yebamot* (Jerusalem, 1962), p. 189; *Sefer Mizwot Gadol, lo ta'aseh*, 115; *Ṭur* and *Shulḥan 'Aruk*, *Yoreh De'ah*, 268.

28. *Makkot*, 10a; *Deut.* 4:42.

his master is exiled with him. At this point Maimonides sounds his bell. Whereas the Talmud derives from this the admonition to teachers to screen their students,[29] Maimonides underscored that the seekers of wisdom cannot live without study, inasmuch as such an unintellectual existence is tantamount to death.[30]

There are many other instances where Maimonides demonstratively interpolates *ḥokmah* or an equivalent emphasis into his formulations. Let me cite a few, without any additional comment.

> One should always cultivate the habit of silence and only converse on words of wisdom . . . So too in discussing Torah and wisdom.[31]
>
> In short, he will limit his speech to topics of wisdom or lovingkindness.[32]
>
> He will realize that nothing endures to all eternity except knowledge of the Ruler of the Universe.[33]
>
> But the conversation of the worthy ones of Israel is none other than words of Torah and wisdom.[34]

To these instances of interpolation may be added the consistent juxtaposition of Torah and *ḥokmah* either as sources of his teaching, objects of his attention, or just as natural companions.[35] Already in the introductory poem which he wrote for his commentary on the Mishnah, this parallelism is present.[36]

29. *Ḥullin*, 133a.
30. *Roẓeaḥ*, VII, 1:

וחיי בעלי חכמה ומבקשיה בלא תלמוד תורה כמיתה חשובין.

By leaving the rest of the Talmudic inferences for *Roẓeaḥ*, VIII, 8, this one is made even more emphatic. Cf. *Sefer Miẓwot Gadol*, *ᶜaseh*, 76:

וחיי בעלי החכם (חכמה) הוא התלמוד.

Another interesting interpolation is found in *Mekirah*, XIV, 14. See also *Sanhedrin*, II, 1; III, 7; *Genebah*, VIII, 1.

31. *Deᶜot*, II, 4, 5.
32. *Deᶜot*, V, 7. See also *Deᶜot*, V, 5; my *Rabad of Posquières*, p. 272.
33. *Mezuzah*, VI, 13.
34. *Ṭumeᵓat Ẓaraᶜat*, XVI, 10. See M. Berlin, *Sefer ha-Rambam*, ed. J. L. Fishman (Jerusalem, n.d.), II, 247ff. These endings, however, are not merely haggadic perorations.
35. E.g., *Shemonah Peraḳim*, introduction (Gorfinkle, p. 6);

ענינים לקטתים מדברי החכמים . . . ומדברי הפילוסופים גם כן הקדומים והחדשים . . . ושמע האמת ממי שאמרו

Ḳobeẓ Teshubot ha-Rambam (Leipzig, 1859), II, 37b:

ולולי התורה שהיא שעשועי ודברי החכמות שאשכח בהם יגוני

36. See the edition by A. Marx, *JQR*, 25:389 (1935):

לשום בתורתו לבד חשקו. לאכול פרי חכמה לבד חוקו.

In the introduction to the Commentary, Maimonides includes among his sources and resources: *ḥokmah* (*ilm*). Kapaḥ's translation (p. 47) ומה שהשגתי מן ה ל מ ו ד י ם is an evasive circumlocution. Note also that in the characterization of R. Ashi, Kapaḥ (p. 34) translates למוד instead of חכמה.

In addition to this deft projection of *ḥokmah*, the *Mishneh Torah* has visible traces of philosophic ideas and even the philosophic exegesis needed to sustain them. For example, the interpretation of the Song of Songs as an allegory of the soul's relation to or communion with God—introduced into Hebrew literature for the first time by Maimonides[37]—is found clearly and explicitly in the *Mishneh Torah*: "This Solomon expressed allegorically in the sentence, 'for I am sick with love' (Song of Songs 2:5). The entire Song of Songs is indeed an allegory descriptive of this love."[38] Or, Maimonides interprets Leviticus 26:27–28 "But walk contrary (*ḳeri*) to me; then I will walk contrary unto you in fury" as emphasizing the providential design in all events and rejecting the theory of chance (*miḳreh*). Adversity is not to be looked upon as merely accidental, and therefore the only proper response is to "cry out in prayer and sound an alarm." This idea and its exegesis are also found in the *Mishneh Torah*.[39] Likewise, Maimonides presents in the *Guide* one general "obvious reason" for all the commandments (prayer and benedictions) enumerated in book two of the *Mishneh Torah*: "the end of these actions . . . is the constant commemoration of God . . . the love of Him and the fear of Him." I find this explanation, in elliptical form, in the *Mishneh Torah* itself: "The sages have instituted many blessings . . . in order that we should constantly commemorate God . . . blessings . . . the purpose of which is that we should always commemorate the Creator and fear Him."[40] There are also suggestive statements in the *Mishneh Torah* which are fully elucidated only in the *Guide*.[41] His frank avowal of the relevance of non-Jewish sources of wisdom is notable.[42] Finally, we may note that Maimonides not only insisted upon the total rejection of astrology and other superstitious practices or beliefs but demanded that this rejection be

37. *Moreh Nebukim*, III, 51. See A. S. Halkin, "Ibn Aḳnin's Commentary on the Song of Songs," *Alexander Marx Jubilee Volume* (New York, 1950), pp. 396–398; A. Altmann, "The Delphic Maxim," *Biblical and Other Studies* (Cambridge, Mass., 1963), pp. 230–231; Werblowsky, *Joseph Karo*, p. 57, n. 1. See now Ibn Aḳnin's commentary, edited and translated by Halkin (Jerusalem, 1964).

38. *Teshubah*, X, 3, 10. It is not mentioned in *Yesode ha-Torah*, II, 2.

39. *Moreh Nebukim*, III, 36; *Taᶜaniyot*, I, 3. See also *Iggeret Teman*, ed. A. S. Halkin (New York, 1952), 77 and introduction, p. 25.

40. *Moreh Nebukim*, III, 44; *Berakot*, I, 3.

41. E.g., *ᶜAbodah Zarah*, IV, 6 and *Moreh Nebukim*, I, 54; *ᶜAbodah Zarah*, XII, 1 and *Moreh Nebukim*, III, 37; *Teshubah*, III, 4, and *Moreh Nebukim*, III, 43. I hope to treat the discrepancies between the *Mishneh Torah* and *Guide* concerning *ṭaᶜame miẓwot* separately.

42. *Ḳiddush ha-Ḥodesh*, XVII, 24. See *Shemonah Peraḳim*, introduction, cited above, Note 35.

motivated by rational conviction. One who believes these "false and deceptive" practices to have been arbitrarily forbidden by the Torah is "a fool, deficient in understanding." Routine conformity without rational conviction is inadequate.[43] Any form of belief in magic or superstition, even without practice, is damnable. This statement is so sharp and unequivocal that many medieval writers found it offensive and took exception to it. People like Ibn Adret[44] and Simon ben Ẓemaḥ Duran[45] could and did, in other words, take the full measure of Maimonides' rationalism even without reference to the *Guide*.

Perhaps the single most significant illustration of the presence in the *Mishneh Torah* both of basic philosophic ideas and their concomitant exegesis concerns Maimonides' rationale of the commandments. It is well known that Maimonides was as articulate in the *Mishneh Torah* about the permissibility, indeed the desirability, of a sustained inquiry into the reasons for the ceremonial and moral law as he was in the *Guide*.[46] However, I would suggest that the *Mishneh Torah* not only issues a general mandate for such speculation but intimates the specific guidelines or coordinates along which this goal is to be pursued. It sketches a framework into which all details are to be fitted, and this framework is identical with the one erected more laboriously and solidly in the *Guide*, where Maimonides submits a threefold classification of the laws, corresponding to a similar classification of the philosophic virtues: intellectual, moral and practical.[47] All laws teach true beliefs, inculcate moral virtues, or else themselves constitute actions which train one in the acquisition of intellectual and moral virtues. The practical commandments also have an outer-directed, social motive: to help establish a society in which "wronging each other" has been abolished and in which the individual can, therefore, flourish and devote himself to the attainment

43. ᶜ*Abodah Ẓarah*, XI, 9.

44. *Teshubot* (Venice, 1546), 414 (pp. 63a–65b, esp. p. 63a):

אבל הרב ז"ל כתב בהלכות ע"ז... וכפל עוד זה בפרק ל"ז בספר המורה... עוד חזר וחזק דברים אלה בספר המורה.

45. *Magen Abot* (Leghorn, 1785), part III, p. 73b:

ונראה שהרב ז"ל הפריז על מדותיו שכתב בס' המדע...

See also *Ẓedah la-Derek*, p. 34; R. Elijah Gaon, *Yoreh De*ᶜ*ah*, 179:13. For an appreciative reaction, see the comment of the fifteenth-century Saadya b. David, published by S. Assaf in *Ḳiryat Sefer*, 22:242 (1946).

46. *Me*ᶜ*ilah*, VIII, 8; *Temurah*, IV, 13; *Miḳwa*ᵓ*ot*, XI, 12. See C. Neuburger, *Das Wesen des Gesetzes in der Philosophie des Maimonides* (Danzig, 1933); I. Heinemann, *Ṭa*ᶜ*ame ha-Miẓwot* (Jerusalem, 1954), esp. pp. 66–78.

47. *Moreh Nebukim*, III, 27, 31, 35; see H. A. Wolfson, *Philo*, II, 208, 305, and esp. 312.

of intellectual perfection. The moral virtues are also propaedeutic: they bring about the proper social relations necessary for mankind—"moral qualities useful for life in society."[48] In essence, therefore, the intention of the law is a twofold one: "the welfare [*tikkun*] of the soul" (which consists of the acquisition of true beliefs) and "the welfare of the body" (which is achieved by practical and moral virtues).[49] This entire provocative rationale seems to have been artfully compressed by Maimonides into the following summary statement: "The majority of the commandments of the Torah are but *counsels from of old* (Isa. 25:1), from Him who is *great in counsel* (Jer. 32:19), to improve (*le-taken*) our knowledge of religious beliefs and to make straight all our doings."[50] And Maimonides adds a proof-text, apparently never before quoted in this context: "Have not I written unto thee excellent things of counsels and knowledge, that I might make thee know the certainty of the words of truth that thou mightest bring back words of truth to them that sent thee."[51]

This view, then, concerning the instrumental or teleological role of *mizvot* is a completely exoteric doctrine. As a matter of fact, Maimonides alludes to or operates with it a number of times *in the Mishneh Torah.* (a) "For the knowledge of these things [Talmudic law] gives preliminary composure to the mind. They are the precious boon bestowed by God to promote social well-being on earth [יישוב העולם] . . ."[52] (b) "Honor is due not to the commandments themselves but to Him who ordained them . . . and therewith saved us from groping in the dark. He prepared for us a candle to make straight the perversities and a light to teach us the paths of righteousness. As it is said 'Thy word is a lamp unto my feet and a light unto my path' (Ps. 119:105)."[53] (c) "This is the right moral principle.

48. *Moreh Nebukim*, III, 35. Note also III, 43.

49. *Ibid.*, III, 27.

50. *Temurah*, IV, 13. (Danby's translation in the Yale Judaica Series [IV, 188] misses the point.) See also Maimonides' commentary on *Abot*, I, 18, where this view is clearly formulated.

The "exoteric potential" of *ṭaᶜame mizwot* is perhaps indicated also by the fact that he freely refers his inquirers to it; see *Kobez*, I, 14 (n. 61).

51. Prov. 22:20. For rabbinic citation of this verse, see A. Hyman, *Torah ha-Ketubah we-ha-Mesurah*. J. Schachter, *Sefer Mishle be-dibre Ḥazal* (Jerusalem, 1963), cites only *Megillah* 7a. Maimonides apparently interprets counsels (מועצות) as practical and "knowledge" (דעת) as intellectual.

52. *Yesode ha-Torah*, IV, 13. See *ᶜAbodat ha-Melek*, *ad loc.*, who submits that it was this statement rather than the designation of Talmud as a "small matter" which provoked his critics.

53. *Sheḥiṭah*, XIV, 15. E. Askari, *Sefer Ḥaredim*, introduction, cites *Midrash Tanḥuma* as the source of this—without mentioning Maimonides.

It alone makes civilized life [יישוב הארץ] and social intercourse possible."[54] (d) The words of the Torah should not be used to "cure the body for they are only medicine for the soul [רפואת הנפש], as it is said, 'they shall be life unto the soul' (Prov. 3:22)." Indeed, people who use the Torah so improperly are not only in "the category of sorcerers and soothsayers but they are included among those who deny the Torah."[55]

III

The legitimacy and inner consistency of these assorted references, explanations, and emphases—apparently beyond the scope of the Oral Law—can perhaps be clarified in light of one axial statement in the *Mishneh Torah*, a statement which was capable of working a silent revolution in Jewish intellectual history.

> The time allotted to study should be divided into three parts. A third should be devoted to the Written Law; a third to the Oral Law; and the last third should be spent in reflection, deducing conclusions from premises, developing implications of statements, comparing dicta, studying the hermeneutical principles by which the Torah is interpreted, till one knows the essence of these principles, and how to deduce what is permitted and what is forbidden from what one has learnt traditionally. This is termed Talmud.
>
> For example, if one is an artisan who works at his trade three hours daily and devotes nine hours to the study of the Torah, he should spend three of these nine hours in the study of the Written Law, three in the study of the Oral Law, and the remaining three in reflecting on how to deduce one rule from another. The words of the Prophets are comprised in the Written Law, while their exposition falls within the category of the Oral Law. The subjects styled *Pardes* (Esoteric Studies), are included in *Talmud*. This plan applies to the period when one begins learning. But after one has become proficient and no longer needs to learn the Written Law, or continually be occupied with the Oral Law, he should, at fixed times, read the Written Law and the traditional dicta, so as not to forget any of the rules of the Torah, and should devote all his days exclusively to the study of Talmud, according to his breadth of mind and maturity of intellect.[56]

54. *Deᶜot*, VII, 8. This is an exact parallel to *Moreh Nebukim*, III, 27 and 35(3).

55. ᶜ*Abodah Zarah*, XI, 12. The Maimonidean emphasis is sharpened when compared with the underlying passage in *Shebuᶜot*, 15b and commentaries *ad loc.* See also R. Jonathan ha-Kohen of Lunel on Alfasi, *Berakot*, 5a (ed. J. Blau [New York, 1957], p. 6). See also *Tefillin*, V, 4, and cf. A. Hilbitz, *Lileshonot ha-Rambam* (Jerusalem, 1950), p. 64. Note the commentary of R. Abraham Maimonides on Exod. 15:26 (כי אני . . . רופאך). ed S. Sassoon and E. Wiesenberg (London, 1959), p. 278. Maimonides' רפואת הנפש is obviously reminiscent of תקון הנפש. Note also *Ḳobeẓ*, II, 23 (נימוסין ומשמרות לנפש); II, 24: תקון הנפש; *Shemonah Peraḳim*, chap. 4; and *Iggeret Teman*, ed. Halkin, pp. 17–19.

56. *Talmud Torah*, I, 11, 12.

This unusually expansive, almost prolix, formulation is based on the following concise, almost epigrammatic, saying in the Talmud: "One should always divide his years into three: [devoting] a third to Miḳra, a third to Mishnah, and a third to Talmud."[57]

The Maimonidean paraphrase is highly problematic and the following items require explication: (a) the nonchalant substitution of what appears to be the genus for a species, in other words "Oral Law" for "Mishnah"; (b) the designation of "Gemara" or "Talmud"[58] as an independent unit of study, distinct from the "Oral Law," and the inclusion of metaphysics and the natural sciences in this third unit of study. A precise definition of the terms *Mishnah* and *Gemara* according to Maimonides, determination of their scope, and definition of their relations will help resolve these difficulties. It would be helpful perhaps to indicate the conclusions and then provide the documentation.

(a) *Mishnah* and *Gemara* are exactly coterminous in scope—complete, unabridged summaries of Oral Law.

(b) They differ in method and form, *Mishnah* being apodictic and popular while *Gemara* is analytic and technical, but they are alike in purpose and actual achievement. *Gemara* is to *Mishnah* what rational demonstration (מופת) is to traditional belief (קבלה).

(c) Philosophy is an integral, even paramount component of this oral law and, like *halakah* proper, can be presented either in apodictic, catechetic summary or in analytic, demonstrative elaboration.

That Maimonides equates *Mishnah* with the *Oral Law* in his paraphrase of *Ḳiddushin* 30, interpreting it to mean the authoritative corpus of the entire Oral Law, is not really perplexing upon closer scrutiny. The basic text of the Oral Law *in toto* is the work redacted by Rabbi Judah ha-Nasi: the Mishnah. *Every other work*—Tannaitic or Amoraic—stands in interpretive-commentatorial, but not actually innovating, relation to the Mishnah. Maimonides repeats this assertion, carefully and consistently, in his introductions to the *Commentary on the Mishnah* and the *Mishneh Torah*. The purpose of the *Sifra* and *Sifre* is to explain the principles of the Mishnah (לבאר עיקרי המשנה) while the function of the Tosefta is to explain the subject matter of the Mishnah (לבאר עניני המשנה). The same is true for the *Baraita*, whose purpose is to elucidate the words of the Mishnah

57. *Ḳiddushin*, 30a.

58. The terms are interchangeable; see variants *ad loc.* in new edition referred to in Note 14 above.

(לבאר דברי המשנה). This interpretive relation characterizes also the Talmud, the Palestinian as well as the Babylonian; both continue the task of explanation (פירוש דברי המשניות וביאור עמקותי). One of the four goals that R. Ashi set for himself in the compilation of the Talmud was to reveal the principles, methods, and proofs utilized in the Mishnah.[59] In light of this we may perhaps explain the fact that Maimonides frequently uses the term *Talmud* when he is actually quoting the Tosefta,[60] for they are generically identical. *Mishnah*, in brief, represents the entire Oral Law.

Mishnah differs from *Gemara* only in that its contents are cast in an apodictic mold—and this is the second characteristic or connotation of the term. *Mishnah* includes the normative conclusion, the obligatory *mizvah*, without excessive explanation or review of the process of exegesis and inference. It is for this reason that in many different contexts the terms *mishnah*, *mizvah* and *halakah* (or *hilkata*) are interchangeable and used freely as equivalents.[61] The following instance is especially significant. The introduction to the *Mishneh Torah* begins as follows:

> All the precepts which Moses received on Sinai were given together with their interpretation, as it is said "And I will give unto thee the tables of

59. *Commentary on the Mishnah*, introduction (ed. Kapaḥ, pp. 34–5):

החדושים שחדשו מן המשנה חכמי כל דור וביאור הכללים והראיות שלמדו מהם.

In his letter, *Ḳobeẓ*, I, 25b, Maimonides speaks of התלמוד שהוא פירוש המשנה. The phrase is found in Abraham ibn Ezra, *Yesod Mora* (Prague, 1833), p. 12.

60. For examples, see S. Lieberman, *Tosefta Ki-Feshuṭah*, *Zeraᶜim*, 637, n. 1; 642, n. 25; 645, n. 38, and others.

61. E.g., *Ḳiddushin*, 49b, reads:

עד דתני ה ל כ ת א ספרא וספרי ותוספתא.

Maimonides, *Ishut*, VIII, 4 reads:

צריך להיות יודע לקרות ה מ ש נ ה וספרא וספרי ותוספתא.

Note also *Tefillah*, VII, 10–11. See Responsum of R. Hai Gaon, ed. Harkavy, *Teshubot ha-Geonim*, 262 (p. 135):

אבל הילכאתא היא משנתנו;

Assaf, *Teshubot ha-Geonim* (Jerusalem, 1927), 58 (p. 68):

ויש צורך לכם לדעת שעיקר כל חכמתם של רבותינו בכל מאמריהם בברייתא ובגמרא הוא המשנה;

Mebo ha-Talmud, attributed to R. Samuel ha-Nagid:

המשנה היא הנקראת תורה בעל פה;

R. Nissim, *Sefer ha-Mafteaḥ:*

כל מה ששנה ר' חייא . . . בתוספתא רמזו רבנו הקדוש במשנה.

stone, and the law [*torah*], and the commandment [*mizvah*]." "The law" refers to the Written Law, "and the commandment" to its interpretation. God bade us fulfil the Law in accordance with "the commandment." This commandment refers to that which is called the Oral Law.[62]

Here the equation of *mishnah*, *mizvah* and *torah she-be*ᶜ*al peh* is sharply delineated. That this is a conscious equation, carefully reasoned and consistently maintained, is clear from the cross reference to it in a subsequent book of the *Mishneh Torah*.[63] The Talmudic source (*Berakot* 5a) for this was noted for the first time apparently by Rabbi Elijah Gaon of Vilna.[64] Happily, we now have the explicit testimony of Rabbi Abraham Maimonides to the effect that this "explanation of the *tradentes*" (פירוש המעתיקים [אלנאקלין]) indeed underlies the opening statement of the *Mishneh Torah*. What is more, our general thesis which has Maimonides equating *Mishnah* with the Oral Law as a whole (or *mishnah* and *mizvah*) is fully corroborated by Rabbi Abraham, who asserts very forcefully, almost dramatically, that *mishnah* refers not to a given text but to the "principles [sources] of tradition" (אבות הקבלה [אלנקל]).[65] *Mishnah* refers to the traditional corpus of the oral law and *Talmud* is its ever-expanding commentary.

As a final illustration we turn to the passage in the oft-quoted letter of Maimonides to Rabbi Phineḥas the judge of Alexandria.[66] In defending the purpose and nature of the *Mishneh Torah*, Maimonides defined the structural and stylistic differences between *perush* and *ḥibbur*, monolithic code and discursive commentary, justifying his own opus by characterizing it as *ḥibbur*. What has not been stressed in this passage is the telling equation of *ḥibbur* with the "way of the Mishnah" (דרך המשנה) and *perush* with the "way of the Talmud"; in other words, two approaches to or two presentations of the same material. Maimonides then proceeds to equate his own work not only with the Mishnah but with the "way of the Mishnah," which can now be paraphrased as follows: the *Mishneh Torah*, a complete summary of Oral Law, is equal to the Mishnah in its com-

62. ומצוה זו היא הנקראת תורה שבעל פה.

63. *Sheḥiṭah*, I, 4. This is, I think, the only cross-reference to the introduction.

64. See ᶜ*Abodat ha-Melek*, *ad loc.* Cf. W. Bacher, "Die Agada in Maimunis Werken," *Moses ben Maimon*, ed. Bacher *et al.* (Leipzig, 1908), II, 145, n. 1, who says that this is Maimonides' own formulation.

65. *Perush R. Abraham Maimonides*, ed. Sassoon and Wiesenberg, pp. 382–384.

66. *Ḳobeẓ*, I, 25b.

prehensive scope and apodictic method. This is further substantiated by all Maimonidean descriptions of his code. I have collated six substantive statements.[67] If one were to conflate them, the following characterization would emerge: an authoritative summary and guide for the entire Oral Law, practical and nonpractical, modeled upon the genre as well as the style of the Mishnah and obviating the need for exacting analysis of Talmudic demonstration and argumentation, and on the basis of which one will be able to know in capsule form the contents of *torah she-beʿal peh*. Especially significant is the elimination of Talmudic "depth study."

I would now venture to submit that we should perhaps be able to terminate the debate as to the meaning of the term *Mishneh Torah* and its alleged aim of superseding the Talmud. This is how Maimonides describes its aim: ". . . a person who first reads the Written Law and then this compilation will know from it the whole of the *Oral Law*." If we rephrase this in light of the three units or categories defined in *Hilkot Talmud Torah* it means that Maimonides has provided a new text for the study of *mishnah-torah she-beʿal peh*.[68] He has dealt with unit two of the three units of study, but has not trespassed on the grounds of unit three, *gemara*. When, therefore, he says with considerable pathos that he has never urged the abandonment of *gemara*,[69] we have no reason to impugn this declaration. We may rather vindicate this contention and amplify it as follows: I composed a text for what I designated as *torah she-beʿal peh*—that is, the *mishnah*, unit two—but unit three remains: *gemara*. This consists of the expansive-analytic study and conceptual analysis of what has been

67. *Sefer ha-Mizwot*, introduction; *Mishneh Torah*, introduction; letter to Jonathan of Lunel (ed. Freimann, *Teshubot ha-Rambam*, p. xliv); letter to Phinehas of Alexandria (*Kobez*, I, 25b); letter to Ibn Aknin (ed. Baneth, *Iggerot ha-Rambam*, I, 50ff.); *Iggeret Tehiyyat ha-Metim*. There are significant statements, some of them in the form of direct quotations, also in the anonymous defense of the *Mishneh Torah* edited in *Tarbiz*, 25:413–28 (1956).

68. On the phrase *Mishneh Torah* as "a presentation (or formulation) of the Torah," see the brief comment of S. Duran, *Milhemet Mizwah* (1869), end. I am planning to treat this more fully elsewhere.

69. *Kobez*, I, 25b. The fact is that the *Mishneh Torah* immediately achieved wide popularity as an admirably comprehensive textbook and independent juridical guide; see, e.g., the letter of R. Sheshet, ed. A. Marx, *JQR*, 25:427 (1935); the statement of Isaac ibn Latif referred to in Note 101, and references in S. Assaf, *Mekorot le-Toledot Ha-Hinnuk* (Tel Aviv, 1925–26), vol. II, *passim;* also Maimonides' comment in *Teshubot ha-Rambam*, ed. Freimann, 69:

ושמענו שבהם פוסקים רובי הישיבות . . .

Opponents could therefore impute to Maimonides the design to have the *Mishneh Torah* supersede the Talmud.

summarized first in the Mishnah and then in the *Mishneh Torah.*[70] Its essence is independent reflection, conceptualization, and interpretive innovation.

IV

A component of Gemara, which deserved special mention alongside of that "which is forbidden or permitted, clean or unclean," is philosophy, or *pardes.* Let us note immediately a formal resemblance between these two parts of Gemara: both are uniformly described as demanding "a broad mind, a wise soul, and prolonged study." The same qualities of mind and prerequisites of knowledge are prescribed for both branches of Gemara study.[71]

Now, the inclusion of philosophy in the Oral Law had already been established by Maimonides in an earlier chapter of the *Sefer ha-Madda*ᶜ where—following what he elaborated in his *Commentary on the Mishnah*[72]—he reiterated the identification of *ma*ᶜ*ase bereshit* with physics and *ma*ᶜ*ase merkabah* with metaphysics: "The topics connected with these five precepts, treated in the above four chapters, are what our wise men called *Pardes.*"[73]

70. The above conclusion stems primarily from an analysis of the passages in the *Mishneh Torah.* To this should be added other pertinent historical-biographical data. It would appear that there was considerable tension, perhaps even vacillation, in Maimonides' attitude toward study of the Talmud itself—unit three: see especially the letter to Ibn Aḳnin, *Iggerot ha-Rambam,* ed. Baneth, 68–69; A. Halkin, "Sanegoriyah ᶜal Sefer *Mishneh Torah,*" *Tarbiz,* 25:413–428 (1956), esp. 414–416. Maimonides is quoted as saying:

ותעשהו ספרך המובהק ותורהו בכל מקום.

Some of his partisans seem to be almost contemptuous of "full-time" Talmudists; see my article in *Biblical and Other Studies,* p. 172, n. 51. On the other hand, Maimonides himself displayed an abiding devotion to "pure" Talmudic exposition divorced from any practical consequences. Note the example discussed by S. H. Kook, *ᶜIyyunim U-Meḥḳarim* (Jerusalem, 1963), I, 304: a problem concerning the Temple ceremonial on the Day of Atonement was treated in his *Mishnah Commentary* (*Yomah,* 2:1), was resumed in *Hilkot Jerushalmi* (see p. 11), and was still under discussion in his responsa (Freimann, pp. 313–314). Furthermore, Maimonides continued to write commentaries and *novellae* even after the *Mishneh Torah,* which should allegedly have acquitted him of his Talmudic obligations. See the very important *Ḥiddushe Ha-Rambam la-Talmud,* ed. J. L. Sacks (Jerusalem, 1963). It is noteworthy that his son R. Abraham also engaged in both kinds of literary activity simultaneously; study of the code and explanation of the Talmud

דקדוק פירוש התלמוד וספר הביאור לעקרי החבור.

See *Perush R. Abraham Maimonides,* 22, n. 99.

71. *Sefer ha-Mizwot,* introduction; *Mishneh Torah,* introduction; *Yesode ha-Torah,* IV, 13; *Talmud Torah,* I, 13 and see the references in my Note 67.

72. *Ḥagigah,* 2:1.

73. *Yesode ha-Torah,* IV, 13.

I would call attention, however, to a new proof-text which Maimonides introduces here for the first time and whose relevance is established by his interpreting it with a crushing literalism. The Talmud reports in praise of Rabbi Joḥanan ben Zakkai that he studied everything: "He did not leave [unstudied] Scripture, Mishnah, Gemara, Halakah, Haggada, details of the Torah, details of the Scribes, inferences *a minori ad majus*, analogies, calendrical computations, gematriot, the speech of the Ministering Angels, the speech of spirits, and the speech of palm-trees, fullers' parables and fox fables, great matters or small matters." "Great matters' mean the *maᶜaseh merkabah*, 'small matters' the discussions of Abbaye and Rabba."[74] The consensual explanation of this concluding passage, which describes the Talmudic deliberations (Abbaye and Rabba symbolizing all the Amoraim) as a "small matter," is that all the future queries of the Amoraim were crystal clear to Rabbi Joḥanan ben Zakkai and his Tannaitic colleagues. They did not have to struggle with these questions because they had all the answers and the subject matter was smooth and unproblematic. Later generations, further removed from the original teachings, were marked by a decline in knowledge and insight and therefore had many sharp questions. This explanation is found in the *Iggeret R. Sherira Gaon*,[75] the commentaries of Rabbi Ḥananel,[76] Rabbi Gershom,[77] and Rashi,[78] and *Perush Sefer Yeẓirah* of Rabbi Judah of Barcelona,[79] and continues to prevail in post-Maimonidean writing. It should be noted that Judah ha-Levi[80] also quotes this passage but—fortuitously or prudentially—cites a shorter version[81] omitting the crucial conclusion and thereby evades the interpretive issue. Maimonides, realizing that this passage provided him with a powerful prop for his position, takes the phrases "great matter" and "small matter" at face value, thereby buttressing his argument concerning the nobility and superiority of metaphysics. As in the famous palace metaphor of the *Guide*,[82] *maᶜase merkabah* emerges as the summit of *torah she-beᶜal peh*.

74. *Sukkah*, 28a; *Baba Batra*, 134b.
75. Ed. B. M. Lewin (Haifa, 1921), pp. 8–9.
76. *Oẓar ha-Geonim* on *Sukkah*, *Perushim ad loc.* (p. 95).
77. *Baba Batra*, 134b.
78. *Sukkah*, 28a.
79. Ed. S. J. Halberstam (Berlin, 1885), pp. 101–102.
80. *Kuzari*, III, 65.
81. See *Abot de R. Natan*, chap. 14; *Masseket Soferim*, chap. 16.
82. *Moreh Nebukim*, III, 51.

The need for arduous preparation for the ascent—a pervasive theme of Maimonides—is also stressed in passing.[83] That Maimonides maintained this unprecedented explanation of the Talmudic passage is seen from his repetition of it in one of his letters to Ibn Aḳnin.[84] His ardent protagonist Jacob Anatoli also repeats this literal explanation as if it were routine.[85] The mainstream of Talmudic exegesis, however, continues to carry the standard Geonic explanation.[86] One writer, in obvious deprecation of the Maimonidean view, even adds that the Geonic explanation is "true and correct for every believer, and not as others have explained":[87]

וזה הפירוש אמת ונכון לכל המאמין ולא כמו שפירשו אחרים. הא—לקים יכפר בעד.

Rabbi Joseph Karo bemoans the fact that Maimonides wrote what he did.[88]

This conviction that *pardes* is an integral, indispensable part of Oral Law led Maimonides to frequent tours de force in interpreting Talmudic maxims. In his commentary on *Pirḳe Abot*—a rich hunting ground not yet explored systematically—Torah is regularly interchanged with *ḥokmah*. Maimonides introduces *ḥokmah* into the opening statement of Simeon the Just and notes curtly: "this is what he meant by Torah."[89] When only "Torah" appears in the underlying passage, Maimonides interprets it to include *ḥokmah* as well. When "Torah"

83. See, of course, *Moreh Nebukim*, I, 31–34, but note also *Commentary on the Mishnah*, introduction (*Kapah*, p. 38), which seems to compress this entire teaching:

חולשת שכל, והתגברות התאוות. והעצלות מללמוד והחריצות לרדיפת עניני העולם הזה . . . ;

also the peculiar explanation of לא חס על כבוד קונו in Mishnah, *Ḥagigah*, 2:1. Also, *Abot*, 2:15.

84. *Iggerot ha-Rambam*, ed. Baneth, I, 57.

85. *Malmad ha-Talmidim*, 11. P. Duran, *Maʿaseh Efod*, 7, alludes to it. See the apologetic treatment of Z. H. Chajes, *Tifʾeret le-Mosheh* (Zolkiew, 1840), 7b.

86. E.g., ha-Meʾiri, *Bet ha-Beḥirah* on *Abot*, 59.

87. *Ḥiddushe ha-Riṭba* on *Sukkah*, *ad loc.* See *Ḥiddushim* of R. Aaron ha-Levi (who was the teacher of Riṭba) in *Ginze Rishonim*, ed. M. Hershler (Jerusalem, 1962), p. 95. On Riṭba and Maimonides, see *Sefer ha-Zikkaron*, ed. K. Kahana (Jerusalem, 1957), pp. 27–30.

88. *Kesef Mishneh*, *Yesode ha-Torah*, IV, 13.

89. *Abot*, 1:2. See the significant observation of S. Duran, *Magen Abot ad loc.*:

וזה אמת הוא אבל אינו כוונת המאמר.

Medieval writers were often cognizant of the fact that Maimonides introduced strained interpretations in order to reinforce his theses. See also the statement of D. Kimḥi printed in *Kerem Ḥemed*, 5:31 (on Ps. 4:5):

והרב מורה צדק פירש . . . מצוה למשכילים החשובים שיכירו האמת . . . ואין זה מענין המזמור.

R. Baḥya b. Asher, *Perush ha-Torah*, beginning of *Nizavim* (New York, 1945, V, p. 81):

והפירוש הזה בעצמו . . . יקר וספיר אבל אינו בענין הפרשה.

and "ḥokmah" both appear, their separate identity or autonomy is maintained.[90] The rabbinic description of Moses as "a father in Torah, a father in wisdom [*ḥokmah*] and a father in prophecy"[91] is a favorite theme for Maimonides because, as he says, it vigorously differentiates between Torah and *ḥokmah* while establishing their precise relation.[92] All this interpretive energy, skill and pressure are compressed in Maimonides' adaptation of the following Talmudic maxim: "The Holy One, blessed be He, has nothing in His world but the four cubits of Halakah alone."[93] "Halakah" is, of course, metamorphosed by Maimonides so that it emerges several pages later as including not only positive law but all other sciences as well.[94] No comprehensive description of the components of Torah will be allowed to omit *ḥokmah*.[95]

Furthermore, Maimonides' halakic formulation, which grafts philosophy on to the substance of the Oral Law, dovetails perfectly with his view on the history of philosophy. In common with many medieval writers, Jewish, Christian, and Muslim, Maimonides is of the opinion that Jews in antiquity once cultivated the science of physics and metaphysics, which they later neglected for a medley of reasons, historical and theological.[96] He does not, however, repeat the widespread view, as does Halevi, that all sciences originated in Judaism and were borrowed or plagiarized by the ancient philosophers. Halevi, echoing a Philonic view, states: ". . . The roots and principles of all sciences were handed down from us first to the Chaldeans, then to the Persians and Medes, then to Greece, and finally to the Romans."[97] That Maimonides does not subscribe to this view of the Jewish origin of all wisdom has been inferred—a kind of argument *ex silentio*—from his formulation in the *Guide*, where he merely establishes the antiquity of philosophy per se. It

90. See again S. Duran, *Magen Abot* on *Abot*, 3:13:

ורבינו משה ז"ל פירש . . . התורה בביאור מצוותיה וחכמה מעשה בראשית ומעשה מרכבה.

91. *Megillah*, 13a.

92. *Moreh Nebukim*, III, 54; *Abot*. 4:4. See also Isaac Abravanel, *Naḥalat Abot* (New York, 1953), p. 205 (on *Abot* 3:22).

93. *Berakot*, 8a.

94. *Commentary on the Mishnah*, introduction (Ḳapah, p. 39).

95. For *ḥokmah* in Talmudic sources, see L. Ginzberg, *Perushim we-Ḥiddushim*, IV, 19–31; S. Lieberman, in *Biblical and Other Studies*, p. 132; also the review of Ginzberg's volume by A. Goldberg, *Ḳiryat Sefer*, 38:197 (1963). It is obvious that Maimonides could have read his meaning of *ḥokmah* into a good number of the original sources.

96. *Moreh Nebukim*, I, 71. See Wolfson, *Philo*, I, 163.

97. *Kuzari*, II, 66.

seems to me that this is clearly noted by Maimonides in the introduction to his *Commentary on the Mishnah* where, in buttressing an argument, he says that this matter is known to us not only from the prophets but from the wise men of the ancient nations "even though they did not see the prophets or hear their words."[98] Maimonides does not care to trace all philosophic wisdom back to an ancient Jewish matrix. His sole concern is to establish *ḥokmah* as an original part of the Oral Law, from which it follows that study of the latter in its encyclopedic totality—that is, *gemara*—includes philosophy. This is the position—a harmonistic position unifying the practical, theoretical and theological parts of the Law—which Maimonides codified in the *Mishneh Torah*.

On a number of subsequent occasions, Maimonides seems to be reflecting upon or justifying this inclusive concept of *gemara*. In the *Guide* he refers to the fact that the "foundations of religion" were reviewed in his Talmudic works.[99] Elsewhere he explains why he was compelled to begin the *Mishneh Torah* with the *Sefer ha-Maddaᶜ*[100] and in the same vein some of his immediate successors called attention to the twofold but unified objective of the Maimonidean code: halakic and philosophic.[101] As a matter of fact, both goals are depicted in the letter to Ibn Aḳnin where Maimonides uses the term *diwan* to describe the *Mishneh Torah*, asserting that the Jewish people lacked such an authoritative compilation, and then he adds that the people also lacked "true exact beliefs."[102] The implication is that these beliefs can be presented in the same summary fashion as the details of law. Indeed, the Talmudists (people of the *fiḳh*,

98. *Kapaḥ*, p. 42. See *Teshubah*, V, 5.
99. I, introduction; 71, and others.
100. See my Note 11.
101. Isaac ibn Laṭif, introduction to *Shaᶜar ha-Shamayim*, quoted in *He-Ḥaluẓ*, 7:91 (1865):

ושם כונתו הראשונה לבאר בו עקרי היחוד ושרשי האמונה... והכונה השנית היתה לברר הדברים המתבררים מכל אלו הענינים ר"ל התלמוד.

Levi b. Abraham, *Sefer Pardes ha-Ḥokmah* in *Oẓar ha-Sifrut*, 3:19 (1890), in the section *Orot Me-Ofel:* חבר במשפטי התורה ורזיה. Inasmuch as the author later singles out the *Moreh Nebukim* for individual consideration, this reference must apply exclusively to Maimonides' Talmudic works. See also *Iggeret of* R. Sheshet ha-Nasi in *JQR*, 25:417 (1935).

102. *Iggerot ha-Rambam*, p. 50:

אין לה ספר כולל לאמתו של דבר ואין לה ד ע ו ת א מ ת י ו ת ומדויקות

and subsequently, p. 51, the reference to י ס ו ד י ה א מ ו נ ה הכלולים בו. See B. Cohen in *JQR*, 25:519–520 (1935). Such a reference is missing from Maimonides' definition of *mishnah*, in *Talmud Torah*, I, 12.

the third group in the palace metaphor) are not without true beliefs; rather they possess true beliefs by means of tradition.[103] In other words, the *fikh*, the Oral Law, contains philosophic truths presented descriptively or apodictically as articles of tradition instead of being elaborated demonstratively as syllogistic premises and conclusions.[104] These articles of tradition may ultimately be rationalized, just as the judicial part of *torah she-beᶜal peh* is subject to amplification. Both expansive processes take place in the domain of *gemara*, which had been explicitly defined as consisting of (a) the study and application of hermeneutic principles and (b) the subject matter of *pardes*. In this respect the *Moreh Nebukim* may be described as part of the *gemara* of the *Mishneh Torah* just as the actual Talmud and its commentaries are the other part.

V

Two pointed questions remain. We should inquire first whether Maimonides could have derived this understanding of *mishnah* and *gemara* from antecedent sources or at least found implicit support for it in earlier writings.[105] Then we should seek to determine whether

103. *Moreh Nebukim*, III, 51:

התלמודיים אשר הם מאמינים ד ע ו ת א מ ת י ו ת מצד הקבלה.

104. *Iggeret Teḥiyyat ha-Metim*, 346:

ראינו שצריך לנו לבאר בחבורנו התלמודיים ע ק ר י ם ת ו ר י י ם על צד הספור לא על צד הביא ראיה.

In the introduction to *Moreh Nebukim*, he speaks of the *Mishneh Torah* containing כללים מזה הענין. Y. Bedershi, in his letter to S. ibn Adret (*Teshubot*, n. 419; p. 72a), echoes this note:

והנה היום ת״ל נעקרה אותה האמונה הרעה מעקרה מכל כחותינו, לא שמענו מי שהחזיק בה כלל או שיתבלבל, וזה אם ב י ד י ע ה מ ו פ ת י ת א ו ב י ד י ע ה (ע פ ״ י) ק ב ל ה.

Generally, Maimonides realized that the *Mishneh Torah* was an exoteric work and therefore could not be unreasonably rigorous or excessively exacting; see *Ḳiddush ha-Ḥodesh*, XI, 5–6. This fact does not mean, however, that he altered or compromised or censored the subject matter—whether abstruse halakic material or technical scientific material. This fact is relevant rather to the expository method used by Maimonides. For some discussion of this, see J. Levinger, "ᶜAl ha-ᶜIyyun we-ha-Diḳduḳ be-dibre ha-Rambam," *Bar-Ilan Annual*, 1:246–269 (1963); B. Benedikt, "Le-Darko shel ha-Rambam," *Torah She-beᶜal Peh* (Jerusalem, 1964), pp. 97–98.

It seems that what Isaac Abravanel says about the motivation of Maimonides in his formulation of the thirteen principles of faith in the *Mishnah Commentary* is applicable to the *Sefer ha-Maddaᶜ* and other philosophic fragments of the *Mishneh Torah*. See *Rosh Amanah* (Venice, 1505), chap. 23 (p. 31a):

בחר הרב . . . ללמד אותם דרך קצרה אותם הדברים שיש בהם מהחכמות . . . באופן שישתלמו כל בני אדם ואפי׳ עמי הארץ בקבלת אותם האמונות . . .

105. For *mishnah*, see the references in my Note 61. *Maᶜaseh Efod*, 15.

or not the revolutionary impact of this halakic formulation was felt and how it was received by successors. By thus approaching the Maimonidean formulation from upstream and following it downstream, we shall be in a better position to assess its originality and significance.

The idea that *gemara* stood in an interpretive, amplificatory relation to *mishnah* could be found in many places, even though not distinctly or precisely articulated. The closest approximation of the first part of the Maimonidean definition seems to be in the *Iggeret R. Sherira Gaon*, which describes *gemara* as the "true investigation" of the Divine Commandments and adds specifically: "to deduce conclusions from premises and to study the thirteen hermeneutical principles by which the Torah is interpreted . . ."[106]

For the second part—the inclusion of *pardes*—two possible sources suggest themselves. Rabbi Judah of Barcelona says parenthetically that the Talmud (*gemara*) contains the "explanations of the Torah and the *mizwah* [*torah she-be*ᶜ*al peh*]" and that it provides "the key of *ḥokmah*"—a statement which is as suggestive as it is cryptic.[107] We may assume that Judah of Barcelona was no stranger to Maimonides.[108]

A more intriguing antecedent is to be found in the statement of Rabbi Joseph Rosh ha-Seder, an older contemporary of Maimonides, who apparently undertook to produce an abridgement of the Talmud.[109] In the introduction to this work, he describes five goals which Rabbi Ashi set for himself in the redaction of the Talmud, and in this context refers briefly to "secular sciences" (*ḥokmot ḥizoniot*) contained in some sections of the Mishnah.[110] Inasmuch as this description has many affinities with Maimonides' well-known de-

106. *Iggeret*, p. 8:

המכוון בתלמוד הוא החקירה האמתית במשפטי המצות... מכח השכל להוציא דבר מתוך דבר ולהבין בי"ג מדות שהתורה נדרשת בהם . . .

See the reference to Profiat Duran, *Ma*ᶜ*ase Efod*, cited in *Iggeret* by B. M. Lewin.

107. *Perush Sefer Yezirah*, p. 5:

ובתוך התלמוד בלול ושקוע פירושי התורה, והמצוה. והוא מפתח החכמה . . .

See also p. 276.

108. See E. Urbach, "Halakah u-Nebuʾah," *Tarbiz*, 18:20–22 (1947).

109. L. Ginzberg, *Ginze Schechter*, II, 403–407; J. Mann, *The Jews in Egypt and Palestine under the Fatimids* (London, 1922), II, 312–313; S. D. Goitein, *Sidre Ḥinnuk* (Jerusalem, 1962), 148–149.

110. *Ginze Schechter*, II, 407: חכמות חיצוניות הנחקקין על מקצת משניות. This line is missing in the fragment published by Mann. Maimonides apparently combined the philosophic interpretation of *derashot* and the allusions to *ḥokmot* into one unit.

scription—and may well be the immediate source or impetus for the latter—this reference is of obvious relevance.

If we follow this formulation downstream, we notice a striking phenomenon: the post-Maimonidean writers either ignore this formulation, camouflage it or blunt its edges.[111] Ha-Meᵓiri provides a pointed illustration of conscious compromise: he seems to be in a dilemma of "woe to me if I speak and woe to me if I am silent."[112] Turning to the *Shulḥan ᶜAruk* we see how Rabbi Joseph Karo quotes both long paragraphs of *Hilkot Talmud Torah* verbatim with the single flagrant deletion of the sentence, which obviously caused him more than a twinge of discomfiture, about *pardes*. Rabbi Moses Isserles, author of the *Torat ha-ᶜOlah* and moderate protagonist of philosophic study, reinserts this reference less conspicuously and more restrainedly toward the end of his gloss.[113]

The significance of the treatment—either a conspiracy of silence or various shades of qualification—accorded Maimonides actually in this instance transcends this case and is indicative of the general reaction by medieval writers to the markedly Maimonidean emphases in the *Mishneh Torah*. They took a rather accurate measure of the Maimonidean temper (sometimes correlating it with the *Guide*, sometimes considering it in isolation) and acclaimed it, condemned it, or ignored it.[114] In any event, they had an ear for the characteristic phrase as well as an eye for the novel, nonhalakic features of the *Mishneh Torah*.

111. See, e.g., *Sefer Miẓwot Gadol*, ᶜ*aseh*, 12; *Orḥot Ḥayyim*, I, 28b (n. 10); *Toledot Adam we-Ḥawah, netiv sheni; Ṭur Yoreh Deᶜah*, 246; *Ẓedah la-Derek*, I:4:7 (p. 81).

112. *Bet ha-Beḥirah* on *Ḳiddushin*, 30 (p. 177):

שליש בתורה ושליש במשנה ושליש בתלמוד ושאר מיני מחקר הראויים במה שהוא לומד.

Cf. *Sefer ha-Ḥinnuk*, *miẓwah* 419:

שליש בעסק תורה שבכתב ושליש בעסק תורה שבעל פה ושליש להבין הענינים משורש.

113. *Yoreh Deᶜah*, 246:4. Note the comment of R. Elijah Gaon *ad loc.*

114. See also my Notes 27, 30, 44, 45, 87–89.

Maimonides' "Thirteen Principles"

By ARTHUR HYMAN

Introduction

"The Law[1] as a whole," writes Maimonides in his *Guide of the Perplexed*,[2] "aims at two things: the welfare of the soul[3] and the welfare of the body."[4] The welfare of the soul, for Maimonides, consists in the development of the human intellect, the welfare of the body in the improvement of men's political relations with one another. To improve men's political relations the Law sets down norms for the regulation of human conduct; to develop man's intellect true opinions,[5] which are communicated to men in accordance with their different intellectual capacities.[6] Of the two aims of the Law, the development of the intellect through the acquisition of true opinions is the final goal, while the improvement of men's political relations serves a preparatory purpose.

In the light of the primary importance he assigns, in his *Guide*, to the acquisition of true opinions, it is not surprising that Maimonides discusses these opinions in the majority of his works. The true opinions propagated by the Law are discussed by him in his three major legal works—the *Commentary on the Mishnah*, the *Sefer ha-Miẓvot*, and the *Mishneh Torah*—they provide him with some of the basic themes of his *Guide of the Perplexed*, and individual opinions form the subject matter of a number of responsa and independent treatises.

1. אלשריעה̈: התורה.
2. III, 27. The remainder of this paragraph is based on the same chapter. The following texts of the *Guide of the Perplexed* (cited hereafter as *Guide*) were used: Arabic, ed. S. Munk with additions by I. Joel (Jerusalem, 1931); Hebrew, reprint of the Warsaw text of 1872 (New York, 1946); English, translation by Shlomo Pines (Chicago, 1963).
3. צלאח אלנפס: תקון הנפש.
4. צלאח אלבדן: תקון הגוף.
5. ארא צחיחה̈: דעות אמתיות. Cf. below, Notes 9 and 106.
6. See also *Guide*, I, 31.

Maimonides, as is well known, presents his primary account of the basic opinions of the Law in his so-called "thirteen principles," which are set down in the *Introduction to Pereḳ Ḥeleḳ* of his *Commentary on the Mishnah*.[7] Though this *Commentary* is an early work, Maimonides states explicitly that the *Introduction* and, with it, the "thirteen principles" are the product of his mature reflection. Thus he writes in his conclusion of the *Introduction*:[8] ". . . I did not set it [the *Introduction*] down as it happened [to come to mind], but after reflection and deliberation and [after] the careful examination of true opinions as well as untrue ones . . ."[9] Moreover, it seems that Maimonides considered the "thirteen principles" definitive throughout his life. He lists them with only a slight modification in the *Mishneh Torah*,[10] and in his *Treatise Concerning the Resurrection of the Dead*,[11] a work postdating his *Guide of the Perplexed*, he indicates that he had worked out his earlier enumeration of the principles with great care and that he considered this enumeration still definitive.

That the "thirteen principles" contain the definitive statement of

---

7. References to the *Introduction to Pereḳ Ḥeleḳ* are to the Arabic text found in J. Holzer, *Moses Maimûnis Einleitung zu Chelek* (Berlin, 1901), and the Hebrew translation of Solomon ben Joseph ibn Jacob appearing in the same work. Holzer's edition of the texts is cited hereafter as *Ḥeleḳ*, his Introduction and German notes as Holzer, German section. In addition the following texts were consulted: the text of the *Introduction* appearing in the standard editions of the Babylonian Talmud; the modern Hebrew translation and notes of M. Gottlieb in *Perush ha-Mishnah la-Rambam, Masseket Sanhedrin* (Hannover, 1906) (cited hereafter as Gottlieb); the text and notes in *Haḳdamot le-Perush ha-Mishnah*, ed. M. D. Rabinowitz (Jerusalem, 1961) (cited hereafter as *Haḳdamot*); the text of the "thirteen principles" in Isaac Abrabanel's *Rosh Amanah* (Tel Aviv, 1958). Abrabanel (*Rosh Amanah*, chap. i, p. 14) attributes to Samuel ibn Tibbon, the well-known translator of the *Guide*, the translation of the principles used by Abrabanel. On stylistic grounds, M. Gottlieb (pp. 82–84) expresses the opinion that the translation used by Abrabanel is a composite of two earlier translations, one by Samuel ibn Tibbon, the other by Judah al-Ḥarizi. For another discussion of the Hebrew translations, see Holzer, German section, pp. 19–22. The Arabic text of the *Introduction* is also found in *Selections from the Arabic Writings of Maimonides*, ed. Israel Friedlaender, reprint of 1909 ed. (Leiden, 1951).

The most thorough analytic study of the "thirteen principles" is that of Abrabanel in his *Rosh Amanah*, the most extensive modern study that of David Neumark in his *Toledot ha-Iḳḳarim be-Yisrael* (Odessa, 1919), II, 127–161. In addition, the following discussions were found to be helpful in the preparation of this paper: S. Schechter, "The Dogmas of Judaism," *Studies in Judaism*, first series (New York, 1896), pp. 147–181; "Articles of Faith," *JE*, II, 148–152; "Dogmen," *EJ*, V, 1167–1175; H. A. Wolfson, *Philo* (Cambridge, Mass., 1947), I, 164–199.

Professor Saul Lieberman directed my attention to the Gottlieb translation and kindly made his copy of this rare work available to me.

8. *Ḥeleḳ*, pp. 29–30.

9. דעות ברורות אמיתיות וזולתי אמיתיות: ארא צחיחה וזיר צחיחה. Cf. above, Note 5.

10. See below, Pages 131ff.

11. See "Treatise Concerning the Resurrection of the Dead," ed. J. Finkel, *PAAJR*, 9:4–6 (1939). This *Treatise* was written in 1191–92 after the completion of the *Guide*.

Maimonides' view was also the judgment of posterity. These principles became the possession of the masses by being incorporated into the liturgy as the poem "Yigdal"[12] and the doxology, " ʾAni maʾamin,"[13] while for philosophers and theologians, they became the subject of a lively debate concerning the fundamental principles of Jewish tradition. Those who agreed with Maimonides that Jewish tradition contains distinguishable principles of belief inquired whether their number was indeed thirteen, and whether Maimonides' list was correct,[14] while those who disagreed with him set out to show that Jewish tradition knows of no separate principles of belief, but only of the totality of the Commandments of the Law.[15]

It is the purpose of this paper to examine and interpret a number of Maimonidean texts devoted to an account of the fundamental principles of the Law. To that end I shall (1) analyze the *Introduction to Pereḳ Ḥeleḳ*, in which the "thirteen principles" are first set down, (2) compare the *Introduction* with a number of parallel texts in Maimonides' other legal writings, and (3) compare the discussions in the legal writings with that contained in a chapter of his speculative work, the *Guide of the Perplexed*. In the fourth and final section of this paper I shall attempt to interpret the "thirteen principles" in the light of Maimonides' general views.

I

The *Introduction to Pereḳ Ḥeleḳ* takes the form of a commentary on the first mishnah of the tenth chapter of the tractate *Sanhedrin*.[16] This mishnah begins: "All Israelites [*kol yisraʾel*] have a share in the World to Come [*ʿolam ha-baʾ*][17] as it is said (Isaiah 60:21): 'and Thy

---

12. *The Authorized Daily Prayerbook*, trans. S. Singer, pp. 2–3. Israel Davidson, *Oẓar ha-Shirah ve-ha-Piyyut*, IV (New York, 1933), 493, lists ninety-four medieval poems which have the "thirteen principles" as their subject. Cf. A. Marx, "A List of Poems on the Articles of the Creed," *JQR*, n.s., 9:305–336 (1918–19).

13. *Daily Prayer Book*, pp. 89–90.

14. For example, Ḥasdai Crescas in his *Or Adonai* and Joseph Albo in his *Iḳḳarim*. Cf. Schechter, "Dogmas."

15. See Abrabanel, *Rosh Amanah*, chaps. xxiii–xxiv. Cf. Schechter, "Dogmas."

16. Though in our editions of the Talmud this chapter appears as the eleventh chapter of the tractate *Sanhedrin*, this is its correct position. See *Tosafot Yom Tob* on Mishnah, *Sanhedrin*, X, 1; Holzer, German section, p. 23, n. 1; The Mishnah, *Seder Nezikin*, explained by Ḥ. Albeck (Tel Aviv, 1953), p. 168; *Haḳdamot*, p. 109, n. 1.

17. For a ready reference to the rabbinic notion of "the World to Come," see G. F. Moore, *Judaism in the First Centuries of the Christian Era* (Cambridge, Mass., 1927), II, 377ff.

people shall all be righteous, they shall inherit the land forever . . .' "[18] The mishnah then continues: "The following are those who have no share in the World to Come: he who says 'there is no resurrection of the dead,'[19] and 'the Law is not from God,'[20] and the ᵓ*apikoros* . . ."[21]

In the tractate *Sanhedrin* this mishnah appears within a set of chapters devoted to the four kinds of capital punishment imposed upon certain criminals by Biblical and rabbinic law.[22] Within this legal context our mishnah comes to emphasize that, though these criminals are judged and executed by human agency, they are not deprived thereby of having a share in the World to Come. Having affirmed this presumption in its opening statement, the mishnah—in its second section—lists three exceptions to this rule.

Since the second part of this mishnah lists three beliefs the denial of which excludes someone from the World to Come, it may be asked whether the affirmation of these beliefs is required in order to have a part in it. More generally, it may be asked whether this mishnah can be used as a source for determining the fundamental beliefs of Jewish tradition. Upon the simplest interpretation the answer to these questions seems to be: no.[23] The mishnah, according to this interpretation, opens by affirming that all Israelites have a share in the World to Come, without specifying any conditions—be they of practice or belief—which are required for being considered an Israelite and, hence, for having a share in the World to Come. The three beliefs listed in the second section are of importance only for clarifying who will be excluded from the World to Come, but from this listing it can not be inferred that an affirmation of these beliefs is required to gain a share in it. In short, it can not be

18. The righteous of the nations of the world also have a share in the World to Come. Cf. Tosefta, *Sanhedrin*, XIII, 2; BT, *Sanhedrin*, 105a; *Commentary on the Mishnah*, *Sanhedrin*, X, 2; *Mishneh Torah*, *Teshubah*, III, 5; *Melakim*, VIII, 11.

19. The printed editions of the Talmud and Rashi have the reading, "The resurrection of the dead is not derived from the Law" (אין תחיית המתים מן התורה). Maimonides' text does not seem to have had the additional phrase מן התורה. Cf. *Mishneh Torah*, *Teshubah*, III, 6; Holzer, German section, p. 23, n. 3. For the opposite view, see Gottlieb, p. 84, bottom.

20. מן השמים. Literally, "from heaven."

21. In its concluding section this mishnah lists the opinions of Rabbi Akiba and Abba Saul concerning additional categories of those excluded from the World to Come. Since this concluding statement has no direct bearing on the subject of this paper it was omitted. For a discussion of the origin of this mishnah, see Louis Finkelstein, *Maboᵓ le-Massektot Abot ve-Abot d'Rabbi Natan* (New York, 1950), pp. 212–238.

22. Mishnah, *Sanhedrin*, VII–XI.

23. See Commentary of Obadyah Bertinoro on Mishnah, *Sanhedrin*, X, 1.

shown from our mishnah that Jewish tradition demands of its adherents the explicit affirmation of certain principles of belief.

According to a second interpretation, which is that accepted by Maimonides,[24] the enumeration of those excluded from the World to Come can be used to derive from it a list of basic principles the affirmation of which is required in order to be considered an Israelite and, hence, for having a share in the World to Come. For if the denial of certain principles, so the argument goes, excludes someone from the World to Come, the affirmation of these principles is required in order for him to have a share in it. To have a part in the World to Come requires, then, the affirmation of beliefs related to the resurrection of the dead and to the divine origin of the Law, as well as the affirmation of beliefs denied by the *ᵓapiḳoros.*

Having interpreted the mishnah in this manner, Maimonides could proceed to an explanation of its parts. For him this meant to explain the two basic phrases "all Israelites" (*kol yisraᵓel*) and "the World to Come" (*ᶜolam ha-baᵓ*), as well as certain other terms occurring in the mishnah. These exegetical requirements determined the structure of the *Introduction to Pereḳ Ḥeleḳ*. Of the three sections into which this *Introduction* may be divided, the first is devoted to a discussion of the World to Come, the second to a variety of terms occurring in the mishnah (among them *ᵓapiḳoros*), and the third to a clarification of the phrase "all Israelites." It is in this latter section that the "thirteen principles" are set down. It should be noted, in addition, that the section devoted to the World to Come contains an excursus describing him who serves God out of love (*ᶜobed me-ᵓahabah*).[25] The significance of this excursus will be seen later on.[26]

Of the three categories of unbelievers enumerated in the second part of our mishnah, those of the denier of the resurrection of the dead and of the denier of the divine origin of the Law are clear enough. But who is the *ᵓapiḳoros*?[27] Our mishnah does not provide a description of this term nor do other passages in the Tannaitic literature in which the *ᵓapiḳoros* is mentioned. It is clear that the *ᵓapiḳoros* is the "Epicurean," who in the rabbinic literature becomes

24. *Ḥeleḳ*, pp. 29–30. For the same interpretation, see Joseph Albo, *Iḳḳarim*, ed. and trans. by Isaac Husik (Philadelphia, 1946), I, 10, pp. 96–100.

25. *Ḥeleḳ*, pp. 3–7. Cf. *Commentary on Mishnah, Abot*, I, 3; *Mishneh Torah, Teshubah*, X.

26. See below, Pages 125–126.

27. See Samuel Krauss, *Griechische und lateinische Lehnwörter in Talmud, Midrasch und Targum*, I (Berlin, 1898), 211; II (Berlin, 1899), 107.

the archetype of the "heretic," but in what the "heresy" of the ʾ*apiḳoros* consists is not explained in the Tannaitic sources.[28] The Gemara[29] which comments on our mishnah offers two descriptions of the term. According to Rab and Rabbi Ḥanina, the ʾ*apiḳoros* is someone who "reviles a Sage,"[30] while, according to Rabbi Yoḥanan and Rabbi Joshua ben Levi, he is someone who "reviles his fellow before a Sage."[31]

Though the reviling of a Sage or of one's fellow before a Sage may have been principle "heresies" at the time[32] of the authorities who described the ʾ*apiḳoros* in this manner, these descriptions seem hardly adequate for determining the original meaning of this term in our mishnah. For, if the second section of this mishnah, as seems likely, is devoted to beliefs, one would expect that, just as the first two categories of those excluded from the World to Come refer to persons denying certain beliefs, so the ʾ*apiḳoros* is someone who denies certain beliefs, not someone committing a certain action—that of reviling. Moreover, should it be true that our mishnah is not simply a random collection of beliefs, one would expect the ʾ*apiḳoros* to be someone who denies some propositions about God. Reflections such as these seem to have been in Maimonides' mind when he undertook to interpret the term ʾ*apiḳoros* in the *Introduction to Pereḳ Ḥeleḳ*.

In Maimonides' writings the term ʾ*apiḳoros* is used in a variety of ways.[33] Commenting on the term in the *Introduction to Pereḳ Ḥeleḳ*,[34] Maimonides seems to have followed the lead of the Gemara in defining the ʾ*apiḳoros* as someone "who makes light of and reviles the Law or the bearers of the Law."[35] Apparently aware, however, of the difficulty of this interpretation, Maimonides adds as a further

28. Krauss, *Lehnwörter*, I, 207, writes: ". . . der religiöse Jude versteht unter . . . אפיקורוס, 'Επίκουρος . . . etwas Anderes als der Grieche und Römer . . ." For a discussion of Epicurus and Epicureanism in rabbinic literature, see Saul Lieberman, "How Much Greek in Jewish Palestine?" *Biblical and Other Studies*, ed. A. Altmann (Cambridge, Mass., 1963), pp. 129–130.

29. BT, *Sanhedrin*, 99b.

30. המבזה תלמיד חכם.

31. המבזה חברו בפני תלמיד חכם.

32. Third century C.E.

33. To the descriptions of the ʾ*apiḳoros* which will be discussed presently, that in *Mishneh Torah*, *Teshubah*, III, 8, should be added. In this passage Maimonides describes him as someone who denies prophecy, the prophecy of Moses, and Divine knowledge of human deeds. For still other uses of the term, particularly in legal contexts, see *Leḥem Mishneh* on *Teshubah*, III, 8.

34. *Ḥeleḳ*, pp. 19–20.

35. מי שמפקיר ומבזה את התורה או לומדיה: אלאסתכ̇פאף ואלתהאון באלשריע אן בחמלה̈ אלשריע.

characteristic of the *ʾapiḳoros* that he is someone "who does not believe in the principles of the Law."[36] Yet Maimonides does not specify in this passage the principles which the *ʾapiḳoros* does not believe.

In his *Guide of the Perplexed* Maimonides discusses the *ʾapiḳoros* in two passages, in each of which he identifies him with someone who agrees with the opinions of Epicurus and his followers. In a chapter devoted to various cosmogonic theories,[37] Maimonides describes Epicurus and his followers as persons who, not knowing the existence of God, attribute changes in the world to chance and who deny that God governs and orders the world. Similarly, in an enumeration and description of various theories of providence,[38] Maimonides describes Epicurus as a philosopher who denies Divine providence and attributes everything to chance. In the latter passage he adds significantly: "Those in Israel who were unbelievers also professed this opinion; they are those of whom it is said (Jeremiah 5:12) 'They have belied the Lord, and said: It is not He.' " From these two passages it becomes clear that in the *Guide* Maimonides identifies the *ʾapiḳoros* with the Jewish follower of Epicurus whose unbelief consists in the denial of propositions about God—in particular, in the denial of Divine providence. Since in Maimonides' enumeration of the "thirteen principles" propositions about God are the counterpart of principles denied by the *ʾapiḳoros*,[39] it seems fair to say that the unspecified principles denied by the *ʾapiḳoros* are propositions about God.

Having seen how Maimonides understood the term *ʾapiḳoros*, we are now in a position to turn to the first section of the *Introduction to Pereḳ Ḥeleḳ*—his account of the World to Come. Maimonides begins by examining five opinions, current among his contemporaries, concerning the World to Come. In spite of certain differences among them, the proponents of these opinions agree in that they identify the afterlife with some sort of earthly reward—be it food or drink, an easy life, being with one's family, the attainment of one's desires, or a mixture of these.[40] In contrast to these popular views, Mai-

36. מי שאינו מאמין ביסודי התורה: מן לא יעתקד קואעד אלשרע.

37. *Guide*, II, 13, end.

38. *Guide* III, 17, first opinion. The opinion of Epicurus is also mentioned in passing in the discussion of prophecy in *Guide*, II, 32.

39. See below, Page 128.

40. *Ḥeleḳ*, pp. 1–3.

monides holds that man's ultimate happiness—that is, the World to Come—consists in the immortal existence of the human intellect apart from any body—this intellect being engaged in the contemplation of God.

In support of his opinion Maimonides cites the saying of Rab that "in the World to Come there is no eating, no drinking, no bathing, no annointing, no cohabitation, but the righteous sit, their crowns on their heads, and enjoy the radiance of the *shekinah*."[41] In his *Introduction to Perek Ḥelek*, Maimonides comments on this rabbinic saying as follows:[42]

And when saying[43] 'and their crowns on their heads,' he [Rab, the author of the statement] has in mind the continuous existence of the soul[44] through the continuous existence of that which is known by it[45] and the soul's being the same thing as that which is known by it,[46] as the skilled ones among the philosophers have mentioned on the basis of methods the explanation of which would be too lengthy in this place. And when saying 'and they enjoy the radiance of the *shekinah*' he has in mind that those souls rejoice in that which they understand of the Creator . . . And the continuous existence of the soul—as we have explained—without end is like the continuous existence of the Creator, great be His praise, who is the cause of its [the soul's] continuous existence in accordance with its understanding of Him, as has been explained in 'first philosophy.'[47]

41. BT, *Berakot*, 17a, where the text is somewhat different. Maimonides quotes Rab's saying anonymously as אמרו ע"ה: קאלוא ע'אס. Cf. *Teshubah*, VIII, 2, where he quotes the same saying in the name of חכמים ראשונים.

42. *Ḥelek*, pp. 13–14. Cf. *Mishneh Torah*, *Teshubah*, VIII, 2–3; *Resurrection*, pp. 6–7.

43. יריד בקולה. Literally, "he intends by his saying."

44. השארת הנפש: בקא אלנפס. This is Maimonides' term for the immortality of the soul, which, according to him, is the same as the immortality of the intellect. He writes in *Guide*, I, 41: "Soul [*nefesh*] . . . is also a term denoting the rational soul [אלנפס אלנטקה: הנפש המדברת], I mean the form of man . . . And it is a term denoting the thing that remains of man after death [הדבר הנשאר מן האדם אחר המות: אלשי אלבאקי מן אלאנסאן בעד אלמות] . . . ." Cf. *Mishneh Torah*, *Teshubah*, VIII, 2; *Guide*, III, 27, end (Arabic, p. 373, line 2: אלבקא אלדאים, Hebrew, p. 41b, line 8: העמדה המתמדת); III, 54 (Arabic, p. 469, line 4: אלבקא אלדאים, Hebrew, p. 70b, line 4: [ה]קיימות הנצחי).

45. The Hebrew text has the additional phrase "namely, the Creator, blessed be He" (והוא הבורא יתברך).

46. Arabic: וכונהא הי והו שי ואחד. The Hebrew text has: והיותה היא והוא (רוצה לומר המושכל והוא). That the intellect and the intelligible are one in the act of knowing is stated by Maimonides in *Guide*, I, 68. Cf. S. B. Scheyer, *Das psychologische System des Maimonides* (Frankfurt, 1845), pp. 72–73; and Holzer, German section, p. 30, n. 75.

47. That the "future life" of the soul is studied by metaphysics is also the view of Avicenna. He writes in *Al-Shifāʾ*, *De Anima*, ed. F. Rahman (London, 1959), V, 5, p. 238, lines 3–7: "But since our discourse in this place is only about the nature of the soul insofar as it is soul, that is, insofar as it is conjoined to this matter, it is not necessary for us to speak about the future life of the soul [*maʿād al-nafs*] (for we are speaking about nature) until we have passed on to the art of wisdom [metaphysics] [*al-sinaʿah al-ḥikmiyyah*], in which we shall speculate about separate [immaterial] substances."

How did Maimonides derive this conception of human immortality, that is, of the World to Come? In spite of the rabbinic origin of the term "the World to Come" and in spite of the mishnah's reference to a Biblical proof-text, Maimonides derived his definition from philosophical considerations alone. Man is a rational animal, his argument proceeds, whose intellect can survive death, provided it has become actualized through the acquisition of knowledge in this life. Maimonides' references to the "skilled ones among the philosophers" as those who have developed a correct understanding of immortality and to "first philosophy"—that is, metaphysics—as the science which demonstrates the survival of the soul, provide sufficient evidence for the philosophical origin of his view. For Maimonides, we may conclude, the philosophical account of human immortality is identical with the religious notion of the World to Come.

Having clarified his understanding of the World to Come, it remained for Maimonides to explain the phrase "all Israelites," which occurs at the beginning of the mishnah on which he comments. His interpretation of this phrase becomes clear from a statement with which he concludes his discussion of the "thirteen principles." Toward the end of his *Introduction to Pereḳ Ḥeleḳ* Maimonides writes:[48] ". . . and when all these [thirteen] principles have been accepted by someone and his belief in them has become clear,[49] then he enters the community of Israel . . ."[50] This conclusion shows that, for Maimonides, the affirmation of the "thirteen principles" is a necessary, if not a sufficient, condition[51] for being considered an Israelite and subsequently, according to the mishnah, for having a share in World to Come.

The principles[52] which, according to Maimonides, must be affirmed by every Israelite may be divided into three general classes: propositions about God, about the Law, and about reward and punishment. In selecting this threefold division Maimonides was guided by his

---

48. *Ḥeleḳ*, p. 29.

49. Arabic: וצה אעתקאדה להא, Hebrew: ונתבררה אמונתו בהם. Friedlaender: צח—to be firm.

50. The Arabic text (like the Hebrew) reads בכלל ישראל. This is an obvious allusion to the term כל ישראל with which the mishnah begins.

51. The good life, according to Maimonides, also requires moral perfection (see, for example, above, Page 120). However, since he limits himself to principles of belief in the *Introduction to Pereḳ Ḥeleḳ*, there exists no need for him to discuss the moral prerequisites of the good life.

52. For a review and critique of various interpretations of Maimonides' use of the term "principle," see Abrabanel, *Rosh Amanah*, chaps ii and vi.

previously mentioned interpretation of the mishnah. Propositions about God contain affirmations of principles denied by the ᵓ*apiḳoros*, propositions about the Law correspond to the Mishnaic principle of its Divine origin, and propositions about reward and punishment are counterparts to the principle of the resurrection of the dead.

The section containing statements about God[53] consists of the following five principles: first, the existence of God; second, the unity of God; third, the incorporeality of God; fourth, the eternity of God, and a fifth principle, the content of which is not completely clear. Maimonides begins the statement of this principle by affirming that God is to be worshiped and concludes with the prohibition of idol worship. Though most interpreters take this principle to state that God is to be worshiped, the conclusion "and this fifth principle is the prohibition of idolatry"[54] makes it seem correct that the prohibition of the worship of beings other than God is its subject.[55]

The second group of principles—that dealing with the Law—[56] consists of the following four propositions:[57] sixth, the existence of prophecy; seventh, the prophecy of Moses and its superiority to that of the other prophets; eighth, the divine origin of the Law, written as well as oral; ninth, the eternity of the Law.[58]

The third class of principles—that dealing with reward and punishment—[59] contains the following four propositions: tenth, God's knowledge of human deeds; eleventh, reward and punishment; twelfth, the days of the Messiah; thirteenth, the resurrection of the dead.

An examination of Maimonides' "thirteen principles" permits the following observations. (1) Each principle is composed of an expression or phrase setting down the principle and of explanatory com-

53. *Ḥeleḳ*, pp. 20–23.

54. והדׄה אלקאעדׄה אלכׄאמסהׄ פי אלנהי ען עבודה זרה: וזה היסוד החמישי הוא שהזהיר על עבודת אלילים. Cf. Gottlieb, pp. 94–95.

55. This interpretation is supported by the parallelism between Maimonides' enumeration of beings whose worship is prohibited which is set down in the present passage and that which is set down in *Hilkot ᶜAbodah Ẓarah*, II, 1. See below, Note 78. Cf. *Mishneh Torah*, *Teshubah*, III, 7, and *Guide*, I, 35.

56. *Ḥeleḳ*, pp. 23–27.

57. The numbering of the principles is that of Maimonides.

58. Arabic: אלנסךׄ. The ninth principle denies the abrogation of the Mosaic Law. The Arabic term נסךׄ has two meanings: abrogation (Hebrew: בטול), and transmission (Hebrew: העתק). The Hebrew translator mistakenly took the Arabic term in its second sense. Cf. Holzer, German section, p. 40, n. 190; Gottlieb, pp. 52, 99, n. 77; Neumark, *Toledot*, II, p. 129.

59. *Ḥeleḳ*, pp. 27–29.

ments of various length.[60] These comments vary from a full discussion of four differences between the prophecy of Moses and that of other prophets to the brief phrase "and we have already explained it," referring for the explanation of the principle of the resurrection of the dead to an earlier passage in the *Introduction* in which this principle is discussed.[61] (2) The explanation of each principle is philosophically rather complex. To know, for instance, that God's unity differs from the unity of genus, species, aggregate, and magnitude,[62] or to know that in prophecy an emanation proceeds from the Active Intellect to the human intellect[63] requires at least a rudimentary philosophical sophistication of the reader. (3) In the text contained in our editions of the Talmud, as well as in the "ʾAni ma-ʾamin" of the liturgy, the term "to believe" and its derivatives occur with great frequency.[64] By contrast, these cognitive terms are almost completely lacking in the Arabic original. In this text the "thirteen principles" are set down didactically as declarative statements with hardly any reference to their cognitive status. The term "to believe" and its derivatives are mentioned only in connection with four principles: the prophecy of Moses (principle 7), the Divine origin of the Law (principle 8), the days of the Messiah (principle 12), and the resurrection of the dead (principle 13).[65] (4) The language of the principles suggests that they have a certain internal structure. One gains the impression that certain principles are independent, others derivative. For example, of the five principles concerning God, three—His existence, His unity, and the prohibition of idol worship—appear to be independent principles, while two—God's incorporeality and His eternity—seem to be derivatives of the principle of Divine unity.[66]

60. Gottlieb goes too far in adding an expression to those principles (5, 10, 11) which, in fact, begin with a descriptive phrase. Gottlieb's additions are: p. 50, היסוד החמישי [רוממותו משישתתף אחר בכבודו]; p. 52, היסוד העשירי [השגחת הבורא בתחתונים]; p. 53, היסוד האחד עשר [שכרם וענשם].

61. This reference is found in *Ḥeleḳ*, pp. 15–16.

62. Second principle.

63. Sixth principle.

64. In the version contained in the editions of the Talmud the term "to believe" and its derivatives occur at the beginning of principles 1, 2, 3, 4, 7, 8, 12. In the "ʾAni maʾamin" each principle begins with the phrase "I believe with perfect faith that . . ."

65. See Neumark, *Toledot*, II, 151.

66. That the third and fourth principles are derivatives of the second is indicated by their beginning. The third principle begins: ". . . the denial of corporeality of Him, and it is that this unitary being [האחד: אלואחד] is not a body nor a power in a body . . ." The

II

Having set down the "thirteen principles" in the *Introduction to Pereḳ Ḥeleḳ*, Maimonides discusses them once again in his two other legal works, the *Sefer ha-Miẓvot* and the *Mishneh Torah*. But, whereas in the former work Maimonides is interested primarily in the enumeration of these principles and the explanation of their content, he discusses them in the latter works to investigate their legal backgrounds: that is to say, Maimonides inquires how the principles are related to the commandments and prohibitions of Biblical law.

The discussion in the *Sefer ha-Miẓvot*[67] is brief. Maimonides composed this work as a preliminary study for his *Mishneh Torah*. Since the *Mishneh Torah* was to be a compendium of the totality of Biblical law and its interpretation, he had to establish first which were the six hundred and thirteen Biblical commandments and prohibitions of which Jewish tradition spoke, but which it had neglected to list in definitive fashion.[68] To find a method for determining which laws are Biblically commanded and to formulate the content of each law became Maimonides' twofold task in the *Sefer ha-Miẓvot*.

In accordance with the purpose of the work, Maimonides discusses in the *Sefer ha-Miẓvot* only those principles which, in his view, are explicitly commanded or prohibited by the Bible. Of the "thirteen principles" only three can be classified in this manner with certainty, but it seems safe to add a fourth principle to this list.

Of the principles concerning God, that affirming His existence (principle 1) appears in the *Sefer ha-Miẓvot* as the first of the positive commandments,[69] that affirming His unity (principle 2) as the second of the positive commandments.[70] As in the *Introduction to Pereḳ Ḥeleḳ*, the first of the Ten Commandments[71] is offered as the Biblical text requiring the affirmation of God's existence, the verse "Hear, O

---

fourth principle begins: ". . . eternity, and this is that this unitary being [האחד: אלואחד] who has been described is eternal in an absolute sense . . ."

The three principles dealing with the Law of Moses depend on the principles of prophecy, though they are not derived from this principle as are the third and fourth principle from the principle of Divine unity. The principles devoted to reward and punishment do not seem to have any particular internal structure.

67. References to the *Sefer ha-Miẓvot* are to the Hebrew translation of that work edited by Chaim Heller (Jerusalem–New York, 1936).

68. *Sefer ha-Miẓvot*, Introduction, p. 4.

69. *Sefer ha-Miẓvot*, p. 35.

70. *Ibid.*

71. Exodus 20:2.

Israel, the Lord our God, the Lord is One"[72] as the text requiring the affirmation of the unity of God. In the *Sefer ha-Mizvot* the principle of God's existence has as its correlative the prohibition against affirming the existence of other gods. This correlative principle, which appears as the first of the negative commandments, has as its Biblical source the second of the Ten Commandments.[73] Of the remaining principles concerning God, the prohibition against worshiping other gods (principle 5) is the only other one considered as Biblically commanded. It is listed in the *Sefer ha-Mizvot* as the tenth of the negative commandments.[74]

To these principles which are listed as Biblical commandments or prohibitions in the *Sefer ha-Mizvot*, the principle of prophecy (principle 6) may be added. For though this principle is not explicitly set down as Biblically commanded, it is a prerequisite for the Biblical command to obey any prophet whom God may send (Deut. 18:15). In the *Sefer ha-Mizvot* this is the one hundred and seventy-second of the positive commandments.[75]

From the brief discussion of the principles appropriate to the *Sefer ha-Mizvot*, Maimonides proceeds once again to a full discussion of all thirteen in the *Mishneh Torah*.[76] In this work the principles appear twice. They are listed in summary fashion in *Hilkot Teshubah*, III, 6–8, and they are discussed at length in a variety of halakot dispersed through *Hilkot Yesodei ha-Torah*, *Teshubah*, and *ᶜAbodah Zarah*.

The summary listing in *Hilkot Teshubah*, III, 6–8, is almost identical with that in the *Introduction to Perek Ḥelek*. Citing the original mishnah on which his discussion of the "thirteen principles" is based, Maimonides begins: "The following are those who have no share in the World to Come," proceeding in the halakot mentioned to list thirteen principles, the denial of which excludes one from the World to Come. Though the arrangement of the thirteen principles in

72. Deuteronomy 6:4.

73. It is rather striking that there is no reference to the second of the Ten Commandments in the enumeration of the principles in the *Introduction to Perek Ḥelek*, inasmuch as Maimonides mentions the first two of the Ten Commandments together in his other writings. Cf. also *Mishneh Torah*, *Yesodei ha-Torah*, I, 6; *Guide*, II, 33. It is to be noted that the prohibition against affirming the existence of other gods differs from the prohibition against worshiping them (principle 5).

74. *Sefer ha-Mizvot*, pp. 98–100.

75. *Sefer ha-Mizvot*, p. 78. For a cogent remark concerning the position of this commandment in Maimonides' enumeration, see Leo Strauss, *Persecution and the Art of Writing* (Glencoe, 1952), p. 91, n. 156.

76. In addition to the Warsaw edition, Moses Hyamson's edition of *Sefer ha-Maddaᶜ* (Jerusalem, 1962) was consulted.

Hilkot Teshubah differs from that in the *Introduction to Perek Ḥelek*,[77] the two listings differ basically in only one respect. The belief in the divine origin of the Law (principle 8), which in the *Introduction* is set down as one principle referring both to the written and the oral Law, is divided in *Hilkot Teshubah* into two separate principles—one affirming the Divine origin of the written Law, the other affirming the Divine origin of the oral Law. To retain thirteen as the number of the principles, Maimonides omits the principle of reward and punishment (principle 11) from the enumeration in *Hilkot Teshubah.* However, this modification does not indicate a fundamental revision of his views, since the principle of the Divine knowledge of human deeds (principle 10), which he retains, is a kind of equivalent to the omitted principle.

In the other account in the *Mishneh Torah* Maimonides returns to a full discussion of the principles. Of the five principles concerning God, the first four are discussed at length in the first chapter of *Hilkot Yesodei ha-Torah.* As in the *Sefer ha-Mizvot*, the principles of God's existence (principle 1) and His unity (principle 2) are listed as direct Biblical commandments and the same Scriptural verses are offered as their basis. In addition, again as in the *Sefer ha-Mizvot*, the prohibition against having other gods is considered as a correlative to the belief in God's existence. The principles of the incorporeality of God (principle 3) and His eternity (principle 4), which are not listed in the *Sefer ha-Mizvot*, appear in the *Mishneh Torah* as derivatives of the principle of Divine unity. God's eternity, it should be noted, receives bare mention. The prohibition against worshiping other beings (principle 5) finds its parallel in the first halakah of the second chapter of *Hilkot ᶜAbodah Zarah.*[78]

The second group of principles, that dealing with the origin of the Law and with its nature, is discussed in chapters seven through

77. The present listing of the principles forms part of an enumeration of twenty-four categories of those who have no share in the World to Come. This more elaborate enumeration—as Hyamson points out in a note—seems to have been influenced by the statement in *Tosefta*, *Sanhedrin*, XIII, 5. This source probably determined Maimonides' rearrangement of the principles.

78. See above, Note 55. The parallel passages read:

Ḥelek, pp. 22–23: ... שהוא יתברך הוא ראוי לעבדו ... ולא יעשו כזה למי שהוא תחתיו במציאות מן המלאכים (והכוכבים) והגלגלים והיסודות ומה שהורכב מהם ...

Mishneh Torah, ᶜ*Abodah Zarah*, II, 1: עקר הצווי בעבודה זרה שלא לעבוד אחד מכל הברואים לא מלאך ולא גלגל ולא כוכב ולא אחד מארבע היסודות ולא אחד מכל הנבראים מהם ...

nine of *Hilkot Yesodei ha-Torah.* Of these principles only the belief in prophecy (principle 6) can possibly be considered as Biblically commanded. As in the *Sefer ha-Mizvot,* its Biblical root is the commandment to obey any prophet whom God may send. In the *Mishneh Torah* the other principles referring to the Law—the prophecy of Moses (principle 7), the Divine origin of the Law (principle 8) and its eternity (principle 9)—are considered as principles which are subsidiary to that of prophecy but not derived from it directly. The similarity between the discussion in the *Mishneh Torah* and that in the *Introduction to Perek Ḥelek* is illustrated once again by the fact that the four differences between the prophecy of Moses and that of other prophets are repeated in the *Mishneh Torah.*[79]

The principles concerning reward and punishment are discussed in *Hilkot Teshubah,* chapters seven through nine. In these chapters Maimonides speaks of God's knowledge of human acts (principle 10), reward and punishment (principle 11), and the days of the Messiah (principle 12). In addition, a full discussion of the World to Come is included in this section.[80] It should be noted that, though Scriptural verses are cited in support of all these principles, none is considered as Biblically commanded. The principle of the resurrection of the dead (principle 13) is missing from this discussion. Because of the omission some of Maimonides' contemporaries (as well as later scholars) questioned Maimonides' belief in this principle. Aware, however, of the furor caused by this omission, Maimonides, in his later years, wrote the *Treatise Concerning the Resurrection of the Dead*[81] to fill this gap. This *Treatise,* it is permissible to state, can be considered as a kind of appendix to the *Mishneh Torah,* designed to complete the full discussion of the "thirteen principles."

An analysis of the discussion of the principles in the *Sefer ha-Mizvot* and in the *Mishneh Torah* yields these additional observations. (1) The "thirteen principles" set down first in the *Introduction to Perek Ḥelek* are retained with barely a modification in the *Mishneh Torah.* This shows Maimonides' commitment to his original listing. (2) The use of cognitive terms becomes somewhat more frequent in the *Sefer ha-Mizvot* and in the *Mishneh Torah.* Thus, in the former work, the existence of God and His unity are described as Biblical command-

79. *Yesodei ha-Torah,* VII, 6.
80. Cf. *Mishneh Torah, Teshubah,* VIII.
81. *Resurrection,* pp. 10–15.

ments the "belief" in which is required by the Law.[82] Similarly, in the *Mishneh Torah*, God's existence and the existence of prophecy are listed as principles which are "to be known."[83] If, as the editor of the Hebrew text of the *Sefer ha-Mizvot* suggests,[84] the term "to believe" used in this work has the same meaning as the term "to know" in the *Mishneh Torah*, it would follow that the Law, according to Maimonides' interpretation, requires that at least some of the principles *be known*. (3) The legal structure of the principles is clarified in these works. Of the "thirteen principles," three—the existence of God, His unity, and the prohibition against worshiping other beings—are considered as direct commandments of the Bible. To this list, as has been seen, the principle of prophecy may be added. Two principles concerning God—His incorporeality and eternity—and three principles related to prophecy—the prophecy of Moses, the Divine origin of the Law, and its eternity—are considered as derivatives of Biblical commandments or as dependent on them. The four principles concerning reward and punishment are considered as independent of any Biblical law, though Biblical verses are cited in their support.

III

Maimonides discusses the principles once again in chapter thirty-five of the first part of his *Guide of the Perplexed*. This chapter forms the conclusion of a section in which Maimonides discusses the study of metaphysics,[85] showing, as part of his discussion, the dangers and difficulties encountered in teaching metaphysics to the masses. Yet in this chapter Maimonides emphasizes that, in spite of these dangers

82. *Sefer ha-Mizvot*, p. 35:

מצוה א׳ היא הצווי אשר צונו להאמין (נ"א: בהאמנת, באמונת) האלהות והוא שנאמין שיש שם עלה וסבה הוא פועל לכל הנמצאות . . .

מצוה ב׳ היא הצווי שצונו באמונת היחוד והוא שנאמין כי פועל המציאות וסבתו הראשונה אחד . . .

83. *Mishneh Torah, Yesodei ha-Torah*, I, 1:

יסוד היסודות ועמוד החכמות לידע שיש שם מצוי ראשון . . . וידיעת דבר זה מצות עשה . . .

Mishneh Torah, Yesodei ha-Torah, VII, 1:

מיסוד הדת לידע שהאל מנבא את בני אדם . . .

It is to be noted that in the *Mishneh Torah* the term דעה is also used in the sense of "intellect." See *Teshubah*, VIII, 3.

84. *Sefer ha-Mizvot*, p. 35, n. 1.

85. *Guide*, I, 31–35, esp. 33–34.

and difficulties, some metaphysical propositions must be communicated to the masses in a literal fashion. The primary proposition of this sort is that of the incorporeality of God. Maimonides writes:

> For just as it is fitting[86] to bring children up in the belief and to proclaim to the multitude that God, may He be magnified and honored, is one and that none but He ought to be worshiped, so it is fitting that they should be made to accept on traditional authority the belief that God is not a body and that there is no likeness in any respect whatever between Him and the things created by Him . . .

A study of this chapter discloses further that to the principles that God is one and incorporeal and that no other being should be worshiped, principles which must be affirmed in a literal manner by masses and philosophers alike, there should be added His existence and eternity. Beyond that Maimonides considers it an obligation to present these principles to the masses in as philosophic a manner as possible.[87]

In contrast to those principles which are to be made intelligible to all, Maimonides lists in our chapter principles which he describes as "the hidden teachings of the Law" (*sitrei torah*) or its "secrets" (*al-sodot*).[88] Their correct meaning is to be communicated only to those chosen few who possess the right kind of intellectual ability and training. Of the "thirteen principles," prophecy, Divine knowledge, and providence are listed as "secrets of the Law" in the present chapter.[89] Five of the "thirteen principles"—the prophecy of Moses, the Divine origin of the Law, its eternity, the days of the Messiah, and the resurrection of the dead—are not mentioned in this chapter at all. These same five principles are either completely missing from the *Guide*, or, if they are discussed, they are discussed only in an incidental fashion.[90]

This chapter of the *Guide* provides another classification of the "thirteen principles." According to this classification, the principles may be divided into three kinds: (1) those principles (the five concerning God) which are to be accepted literally by masses and philosophers alike; (2) those described as "secrets of the Law"

86. Arabic: ינבגי; Hebrew: צריך.

87. *Guide*, I, 35, second part of the chapter. Cf. Isaak Heinemann, "Maimuni und die arabischen Einheitslehrer," *MGWJ*, 79:102–148 (1935), esp. pp. 126–142.

88. The Hebrew terms סתרי תורה and אלסודות appear in the Arabic text.

89. In addition, the following topics are listed as "secrets of the Law": Divine attributes, creation, God's governance of the world, His will, His knowledge, and His names.

90. Cf. Neumark, *Toledot*, II, pp. 131–132.

(prophecy, Divine knowledge, and providence), which, lending themselves to philosophic interpretation, are to be understood in one way by the masses, in another by the philosophers, and (3) those principles (prophecy of Moses, Divine origin of the Law, its eternity, the days of the Messiah, and the resurrection of the dead) which, nonphilosophic in their nature, lie outside the strict subject matter of the *Guide*.

IV

Scholars have suggested three theories concerning the nature and function of the "thirteen principles." The first of these may be described as their historical interpretation. Among others, Schechter[91] and Neumark[92] defended it. According to this interpretation, Maimonides set down his principles under the influence and, possibly, pressure of his times. Maimonides noted that Muslims had a confession of faith and Christians dogmas. In order to show that Judaism was not inferior to the other religions and in order to polemicize against them, Maimonides composed his list of principles as a kind of Jewish catechism or doxology. Now, it can not be denied that the affirmation of such principles as the supremacy of the prophecy of Moses and the eternity of the Law had a certain urgency in Maimonides' times in the face of Christian and Muslim claims that their revelations had superseded that of Moses.[93] But a careful study of the passages analyzed discloses no evidence that the "thirteen principles" were formulated primarily because of the influence of the times or for polemical reasons. Students of Maimonides are well aware of his general lack of interest in historical matters[94] and of the scant mention that Christianity and Islam receive in his speculative writings.[95] The historical interpretation, it seems, can safely be ruled out.

A second interpretation of the principles has come to the fore in recent years. It may be characterized as their political interpreta-

91. Schechter, "Dogmas," pp. 176–179.

92. Neumark, *Toledot*, II, p. 130 bottom. Among the late medieval philosophers, Abrabanel already gave a "historical" explanation of the principles. He writes in *Rosh Amanah*, chap. xxiii, pp. 136–137, that Maimonides in setting down his principles imitated the methods of Gentile scholars.

93. See *Mishneh Torah*, *Hilkot Teshubah*, III, 8. (See text in Hyamson ed.)

94. For a discussion of Maimonides' interest in history, see S. W. Baron, "The Historical Outlook of Maimonides," *PAAJR*, 6:5–113 (1934–35), esp. 7–12.

95. In all the texts discussed in this paper Christians and Muslims are mentioned only in that cited in Note 93, above.

tion. Though scholars favoring this view have not yet provided us with a detailed analysis of the principles, the trend of this interpretation is clear enough. In a dissertation entitled *Ibn Bājjah and Maimonides*[96] Professor Lawrence Berman takes occasion to discuss some of these principles, among them those describing God. Commenting in this connection on Maimonides' demand that even the masses must be taught correct opinions about God, in particular that He is incorporeal, Professor Berman states that there is no cognitive significance in this demand. According to him, the knowledge required by Maimonides of the masses possesses no intrinsic intellectual value.[97] Professor Berman suggests three reasons for Maimonides' demand that even the masses must be taught an enlightened concept of God, and all these reasons are political. For (1) a belief in God and in a certain order in the world influences people to mold their political actions in accordance with the cosmic order. Thus the city (state) remains stable. (2) If the opinions of the masses are close to the opinions of the philosophers, the philosopher will find it easier to live within the state and guide it without friction. (3) If the opinions of the masses are close to philosophic truth, individuals of a philosophical nature will find it easier to achieve true philosophical knowledge. They can attain such knowledge without having first to free themselves of the habits of faith which may oppose philosophical truths.[98]

It is the merit of this interpretation to have called attention to the political dimension of Maimonides' principles, but, to my mind, it has gone too far in making all of them political. It is well known that Maimonides' contemporary Averroes was of the opinion that it was dangerous to require of the masses philosophically correct notions about God.[99] When, then, Maimonides demands that even the masses

96. L. V. Berman, "Ibn Bājjah and Maimonides" (unpub. diss., Hebrew University, May 1959—mimeographed), *passim*. Cf. S. Pines' "Translator's Introduction" to his translation of the *Guide*, pp. cxviii ff.

97. Berman, chap. iii, esp. pp. 139–144. Berman's thesis emerges from the following passage (p. 140, lines 19–23):

אם כן הדעות האמתיות שיש להמון אינן יכולות להשתייך לסוג השלמות העליונה אלא לסוג השלמויות האחרות. הסוג היחידי של השלמויות המתאים לדעותיהם הוא השלמות השלישית, כלומר שלמות המדות הנתפסות מבחינה מדינית. ולכן הדעות ההמוניות כלן הן צורך מדיני.

98. *Ibid.*, pp. xvii–xviii; pp. 137–138. This is Berman's interpretation of al-Fārābi's views, but he goes on to argue that Maimonides' position is close to that of al-Fārābi.

99. Averroes, *Kitāb Fāṣl al-Maqāl*, ed. G. F. Hourani (Leiden, 1959), pp. 24–25. For a note on a difficult passage in this text, see N. Golb's edition of the Hebrew translation of the work in *PAAJR*, 26:47 (1957), n. 3. English translation: *Averroes on the Harmony of*

must be taught correct opinions about God, in particular His incorporeality, it seems that he moves away from the realm of political expediency. The purely political interpretation of the "thirteen principles" seems to neglect their metaphysical dimension.

The interpretation followed in this paper takes the metaphysical character of at least some of the principles seriously and, for that reason, it may be called their metaphysical interpretation. This interpretation was proposed by Julius Guttmann in his history of Jewish philosophy,[100] but Guttmann did not develop it in any detail.

Our interpretation begins with a question that many of the commentators have raised: how did Maimonides derive his "thirteen principles" and why did he list these and no other?[101] The answer to this question becomes clear once it is recalled that in the *Commentary on the Mishnah* Maimonides serves primarily as a commentator on a given work, not as an independent author presenting his own views. Thus the general framework of his enumeration is determined by the three categories of beliefs (or more correctly unbeliefs) which he finds in the second section of the mishnah on which he comments. Beyond that, Maimonides derives the specific principles contained within each section by examining carefully the teachings of the Bible concerning these matters. It can then be said that the "thirteen principles" contain Maimonides' account of basic Jewish beliefs *set down according to the structure of the mishnah on which he comments.*[102]

The principles omitted from the list in the *Introduction to Perek Ḥelek* but discussed by him in other works provide further evidence that the structure of the mishnah on which he comments determined Maimonides' enumeration. Thus, in *Hilkot Teshubah*, Maimonides, in language reminiscent of his discussion of the existence of God, describes the principle of human freedom as one of the "pillars of the Law,"[103] and in the *Guide* the creation of the world is said to

---

Religion and Philosophy, trans. G. F. Hourani (London, 1961), pp. 59–60, and p. 105, n. 135. Note the reference to al-Fārābi appearing in the latter note. Cf. commentaries of Falaḳera, Ibn Kaspi, and Narboni on *Guide*, I, 35.

100. Julius Guttmann, *Philosophies of Judaism* (New York, 1964), pp. 178–179 (German: pp. 201–203; Hebrew: pp. 165–166).

101. Cf. Abrabanel, *Rosh Amanah*, *passim.*

102. This was already seen by Abrabanel, who writes (*Rosh Amanah*, chap. vi, p. 40): "... but it was his [Maimonides'] intention to explain that mishnah which states, 'All Israelites have a share in the World to Come.' " Cf. *Resurrection*, p. 4 (Arabic: lines 8–10; Hebrew: lines 7–8).

103. *Mishneh Torah*, *Teshubah*, V, 3:

ועיקר זה [הבחירה] עיקר גדול הוא והוא עמוד התורה והמצוה . . .

be a principle second only to that of the unity of God.[104] Had it been Maimonides' purpose to present an exhaustive enumeration of the principles of Jewish belief, there would have existed no reason for omitting these two principles from the list. Even more striking is Maimonides' omission of the World to Come from the "thirteen principles." But the World to Come, as has been seen, appears as a separate term in the mishnah and, hence, Maimonides devotes a separate section of the *Introduction* to it.[105]

In discussing the purpose of the "thirteen principles" it should be recalled that Maimonides followed the philosophical tradition of his day in distinguishing sharply between an elite which possesses intellectual ability and training and the masses, who function primarily through their imagination. In our context this distinction comes to the fore in a chapter of the *Guide* in which Maimonides discusses the categories into which the opinions of the Law may be divided. In chapter twenty-eight of the third part—a chapter which follows that with which this paper started—Maimonides divides the opinions of the Law into two kinds: true opinions,[106] and opinions necessary for the well-being of the state.[107] As examples of true opinions he lists a number of attributes describing God,[108] as an example of necessary opinions the proposition that God becomes angry with those who disobey His will. The true opinions of the Law have as their purpose to impart correct knowledge concerning God to the intellectual elite and the masses alike. The necessary opinions have as their purpose to move the masses to obey the Divine Law.

In an essay appearing in an earlier volume of the *Texts and Studies*[109] I had occasion to show that Maimonides' division of the opinions of the Law into true and necessary ones is based on the medieval distinction between apodictic and persuasive propositions.

104. *Guide*, II, 13:
והו קאעדה̈ שריעה̈ משה רבנו ע"אס בלא שך והי ת̇אניה̈ קאעדה̈ אלתוחיד: והוא יסוד תורת משה רבנו בלי ספק, והוא שנית ליסוד היחוד.

105. It is to be noted that in *Hilkot Teshubah*, VIII, where no such methodological consideration exists, the World to Come forms a part of the discussion of reward and punishment.

106. אלארא אלצחיחה̈: הדעות האמתיות. Cf. above, Note 5.

107. אעתקאדאת מא אעתקאדהא צ̇רורי פי צלאח אלאחואל אלמדניה̈: אמונות שאמונתם הכרחית בתקון ענייני המדינה.

108. In this chapter Maimonides lists the following Divine attributes: existence, unity, knowledge, power, will, eternity, and incorporeality.

109. "Spinoza's Dogmas of Universal Faith in the Light of their Medieval Background," *Biblical and Other Studies*, ed. A. Altmann (Cambridge, Mass., 1963), pp. 188–190.

Apodictic propositions have as their purpose to convey certain truths, persuasive propositions to induce certain actions. Persuasive propositions, I showed, may be true in some respect, false in another. Persuasive propositions are important for philosophers for the truth that can be discovered by correct interpretation, while, for the masses, they are important for the actions they induce.

This twofold division was sufficient for the *Guide*, since in this work Maimonides primarily discusses topics which lend themselves to philosophical clarification. However, for a study which includes his legal writings, the category of historical propositions must be added to this classification.[110] It is true that such historical events as the revelation at Sinai may hold slight interest for the philosopher, but for the student of the Law they are of great importance.

With this classification in mind, it can be said that the first group of the "thirteen principles," that containing propositions about God, is speculative in intent. Addresses to philosophers and masses alike, these principles have as their function to convey true knowledge about God. This knowledge, to be sure, is set down only in the form of final conclusions and philosophers can find demonstrations for its truth,[111] but the masses, no less than the philosophers, are expected to know the content of these propositions.

That Maimonides considers these propositions as speculative can be argued first from the language in which they are set down. In the *Introduction to Pereḳ Ḥeleḳ* all five propositions are set down didactically without any reference to their cognitive status. This suggests that the principles are to be known rather than to be believed.[112] According to the *Sefer ha-Miẓvot*, to be sure, propositions about God must be "believed," but it appears that in this work "to believe" is equivalent to "to know." In the *Mishneh Torah* Maimonides states explicitly that the first commandment is *to know* that a first being exists.

Further evidence for the speculative nature of the principles concerning God is provided by chapter thirty-five of the first part of the *Guide* on which we commented. If it were the function of these

110. Cf. Neumark, *Toledot*, II, 151ff.

111. *Guide*, III, 28.

112. In his listing of the "thirteen principles" Maimonides sets down some of them didactically, while he affirms of others that they are to be "believed" (see above, Page 129). It appears to be the purpose of this linguistic usage to distinguish between those principles which are philosophical or subject to philosophical interpretation and those which contain historical statements. This seems to be a rather special use of the term "to believe," since generally Maimonides does not use the term in this restricted sense. See his definition of "belief" in *Guide*, I, 50, beginning.

principles to motivate human action, Maimonides' insistence that the masses must be taught the incorporeality of God is difficult to understand. To move the masses to obedience it would have been sufficient to teach them that God exists, is one, eternal and solely to be worshiped. Maimonides' contemporary, Averroes, who was more concerned with the political implications of beliefs concerning God, proscribed the teaching of His incorporeality to the masses.[113]

Moreover, Maimonides' division of the opinions of the Law into those which are true and those which are necessary indicates that the five propositions about God are speculative in intent. For, were they meant only to persuade men to obey the Law, no distinction between true and necessary opinions would have to be made.

Maimonides' insistence that Divine incorporeality must be taught to all helps to clarify further the purpose of the first five principles. Maimonides himself states that the unity of God can only be correctly understood if it is known that God is incorporeal.[114] But further reflection shows that of the five principles concerning God, that of Divine incorporeality is the only one which guarantees *conceptual* knowledge of Him for all. For the masses might well affirm that God exists, is one, eternal, and solely to be worshiped and yet picture Him through categories of the imagination. But once God is to be known as incorporeal, this knowledge can only be conceptual.[115]

Once it has been seen that it is the function of the first five principles to convey correct conceptual knowledge about God, their purpose becomes clear. It is to make immortality possible for all. Maimonides, it will be recalled, identifies the World to Come with the philosophical notion of the incorporeal existence of the human intellect, which takes place only when this intellect becomes actualized through the understanding of true opinions, primarily those about God. The Law, then, by commanding that all Israelites, the masses no less than the intellectual elite, must know certain true propositions about God, provides the possibility of immortality for all.[116] The

113. Cf. above, Note 97.

114. *Guide*, I, 35.

115. This observation, together with the observation that immortality depends on the acquisition of conceptual knowledge (see next paragraph), explains Maimonides' stringency in excluding someone who affirms the corporeality of God from the World to Come. Cf. *Ḥeleḳ*, pp. 21–22, together with p. 29; *Mishneh Torah*, *Teshubah*, III, 7.

116. Cf. *Ḥeleḳ*, p. 29. Arabic: פכן בהא סעידא Hebrew: (לכן דע אותם) והצלח בהם. Gottlieb, p. 53, translates the Arabic phrase: [ואתה עמוד עליהן] והיה בהן לבן ישע [לעולם הבא]. See also, Gottlieb, p. 88, n. 21.

Abrabanel, *Rosh Amanah*, chap. vi, p. 39, writes: ". . . and it is as if he [Maimonides]

first five principles make it possible for Maimonides to embrace a philosophical understanding of human immortality without restricting immortality to a small philosophical elite.

Maimonides' second group of principles is meant to guarantee the validity of the Law, for man's well-being in this world and his immortality in the next require, according to Maimonides, a Divine Law. Left to themselves, few men could discover the required truths concerning God,[117] nor could men agree on the norms required for human conduct.[118]

The propositions about the Law are divisible into two kinds: the principle of prophecy and the principles describing the Law of Moses. For Maimonides, the prophet plays a twofold role. He is philosopher and legislator in one.[119] As philosopher, the prophet understands truths that the unaided human intellect is unable to discover,[120] while as legislator he brings the Divine Law.[121] Though Maimonides in his "thirteen principles" describes prophecy in general terms, the context suggests that he has primarily legislative prophecy in mind.[122]

With the principle of prophecy the intellectual elite and the masses begin to diverge in their understanding of Maimonides' principles and their interpretation. While both accept the principle of prophecy as a requisite guaranteeing the existence of the Law, for the philosopher this principle is also one of the "secrets of the Law." Besides being interested in the legislative function of prophecy, the philosopher inquires into its nature and into the psychological processes productive of it.

Sufficient to guarantee the existence of a Divine Law, the principle of prophecy is not sufficient to guarantee the existence of a particular historical law. For this, historical principles are required.

---

had said that these principles are those upon which there is based and established the inheriting of the spiritual World to Come for everyone who is called by the name 'Israelite' . . . And without these beliefs and principles a man can not inherit the World to Come." Cf. also "Spinoza's Dogmas," pp. 188–189.

117. *Guide*, I, 34. Cf. Harry A. Wolfson, "The Double Faith Theory in Clement . . .," *JQR*, 32:229–230, 240–243, 249–250, 261–262 (1942–43).

118. *Guide*, II, 40.

119. See Leo Strauss, *Philosophie und Gesetz* (Berlin, 1935), pp. 87–122.

120. *Ibid.*, pp. 76–79, esp. p. 78; pp. 92, 93–96.

121. *Ibid.*, pp. 108–122.

122. The validation of the Law is the main topic of the section. It should be noted, however, that the description of prophecy can also be applied to the cognitive aspects of prophecy and that the cognitive aspect of Moses' prophecy is emphasized by Maimonides.

Thus, to guarantee the validity of the Law of Moses and to argue for its supremacy is the purpose of the remaining three principles devoted to the Law. Maimonides, as an adherent of the Law, accepts these principles on historical grounds, though, as philosopher, he finds little in them that lends itself to philosophical explication.

That Maimonides distinguishes between the principle of prophecy and the principles guaranteeing the Law of Moses is indicated by his use of language in the "thirteen principles." The principle of prophecy is set down didactically, without any reference to its cognitive status, while the prophecy of Moses and the Divine origin of the Law are said to be principles which are "to be believed." Moreover, this distinction is indicated in the *Sefer ha-Miẓvot* and in the *Mishneh Torah*, where the principle of prophecy is the only one that can possibly be considered as a direct commandment of the Bible.[123] Again, the prophecy of Moses, the Divine origin of the Law, and its eternity are discussed only incidentally in the *Guide of the Perplexed*, while a complete section of the work is devoted to the nature and psychology of prophecy.[124]

Having listed the principles which guarantee the existence of Divine law in general and the Law of Moses in particular, Maimonides turns, in the third section, to principles required for instilling obedience to the Law. In the understanding and interpretation of this group of principles the difference between the intellectual elite and the masses is most marked. The intellectual elite obeys the Law because it understands that to obey the Law is good, while the masses obey because of the fear of punishment or the expectation of reward.[125]

As has been noted earlier,[126] Maimonides' discussions of the World to Come contains an excursus describing him who worships God out of love (*ᶜobed me-ᵓahabah*). To worship God without the expectation of reward is, for Maimonides, the highest form of worship, yet at the same time he is aware that such unselfish service can be expected only of the few. For that reason the majority of men to whom the Law is addressed require principles promising reward

123. There appears to be a gradation of the principles based on their relation to Biblical commandments. See above, Page 134.

124. The major portion of *Guide*, II, 32–48, is devoted to an analysis of the nature and processes of prophecy. *Guide*, II, 35, discusses the prophecy of Moses; II, 32, the assembly at Sinai; II, 39, the eternity of the Law.

125. *Guide*, III, 28.

126. See above, Pages 125–126.

or threatening punishment, for it is only under these conditions that they will obey the Law. However, the third group of Maimonides' principles is not without importance for the intellectual elite, since philosophically gifted men will accept these principles for the truths they teach and the historical statements they contain.

Like the principles relating to the Law, those concerning reward and punishment are divisible into two sections. The first of these consists of the principles of God's knowledge of human deeds and reward and punishment. Though Maimonides lists these two principles among the "thirteen" in the *Introduction to Perek Ḥelek*, it seems that in his later works his interest shifts to their more general equivalents, Divine knowledge and Divine providence. This shift seems already to be indicated in the omission of reward and punishment from the listing in *Mishneh Torah, Hilkot Teshubah*, III, 8 and it becomes still clearer in *Guide*, I, 35, where of the principles referring to reward and punishment only Divine knowledge and providence are listed among the "secrets of the Law."[127]

The second section of the principles dealing with reward and punishment is once again devoted to historical propositions: namely, the days of the Messiah and the resurrection of the dead. For Maimonides, the coming of the Messiah initiates a period of peace in this world and no miraculous occurrences are expected by him.[128] In view of this, the days of the Messiah still fit into Maimonides' general scheme. By contrast, the resurrection of the dead is somewhat more difficult to harmonize with his general views. Maimonides himself writes in the *Treatise Concerning the Resurrection of the Dead*[129] that he accepts the principle on traditional authority alone and that it is a miracle like other miracles recorded in the Law. It seems that Maimonides, in spite of the generally rationalistic character of his views, accepts the principle of resurrection as a believing Jew, just as he accepts at least some of the Biblical miracles in a literal fashion.

127. For Maimonides' discussion of Divine providence and knowledge, see *Guide*, III, 17–21.

128. See *Ḥelek*, pp. 16–18; *Mishneh Torah, Teshubah*, IX, 2; *Melakim*, XI; *Resurrection*, pp. 20–21.

129. *Resurrection*, p. 25.

Abraham Maimonides and his Pietist Circle*

By S. D. GOITEIN

Abraham, the son of Moses Maimonides, represents a unique phenomenon in the history of Jewish religious thought.[1] There have been in Israel other great men than Moses Maimonides who were succeeded by worthy descendants. The work of Rashi, the immortal commentator on the Bible and the Talmud, was continued by his two grandsons, Rashbam (Rabbi Samuel ben Meir) and Rabbenu Tam (Jacob ben Meir), who in their generation shared between them the crowns of being the foremost expounders of the two main sources of the Jewish faith. The Rosh, Rabbi Asher ben Yeḥiel, the last great author of a digest of the Talmud arranged in the same order as its source, was followed by his son Jacob, Baᶜal ha-Ṭūrim, whose code of Jewish law, divided into sections according to subject matter, became authoritative for all Israel.

Abraham Maimonides, however, was a special case. On the one hand, one cannot imagine a spiritual heir more dedicated to his predecessor than he was. He devoted three separate treatises and a great number of shorter responsa and letters to the defense of his father's philosophical and halakhic writings.[2] His first literary attempt was a book on the principles of the *Mishneh Torah*. In all his extant writings he copiously quoted the elder Maimonides wherever an opportunity offered itself. Even more significant is the fact that he

* This paper is based on materials from the Cairo Geniza. The author wishes to express his gratitude to the directors of the libraries the manuscripts of which have been used in this study.

1. The basic studies about Abraham Maimonides are: S. Eppenstein, "Abraham Maimuni, sein Leben und seine Schriften," *Jahresbericht des Rabbinerseminars* (Berlin, 1912–13); Samuel Rosenblatt, ed., *The High Ways to Perfection of Abraham Maimonides*, I (New York, 1927), introduction, pp. 1–128; A. H. Freimann, ed., *Abraham Maimuni Responsa* (Jerusalem, 1937), pp. ix–xxii; N. Wieder, *Islamic Influences on the Jewish Worship*, East and West Library (Oxford, 1957; in Hebrew), see index, pp. 95–96; E. Wiesenberg in *Pērūsh Rabbēnū Avrāhām* . . . ed. S. D. Sassoon (London, 1959), pp. 11–63. Further literature is listed in the last-cited, p. 12.

2. According to Abraham Maimonides' letter from the year 1231/2, republished by Samuel Rosenblatt in *The High Ways*, I, 125: *bēʾūr leᶜiqqārē ha-ḥibbūr*.

emphasized again and again that he lived according to the principles of conduct adopted by his father.[3] On the other hand we see Abraham working out a complete system of his own of religious thought and practice—a procedure which certainly would not have been necessary had the son found full satisfaction in the religious practice and literary creations of his father. It seems that the import of Abraham's magnum opus has not yet been fully appreciated. In view of this, before we submit and evaluate the new material from the Cairo Geniza, a few words about that book may not be out of place.

The title of the book, *Kifāyat al-ᶜābidīn*, may be translated approximately as "Complete [Guide] for the Pious." A Muslim contemporary and compatriot of Abraham Maimonides, ᶜAbd al-ᶜAẓīm al Mundhirī, who was born in Egypt in November 1185, six months before Abraham, and who died in 1258, surviving him by twenty years, wrote a book with an almost identical title: *Kifāyat al-mutaᶜabbid wa-tuḥfat al-matazahhid* "Complete [Guide] for the Pietist and a Present for the Ascetic." This book is extant in manuscript, but, as far as our present information goes, it has not yet been published.[4] As is well known, Abraham Maimonides greatly admired the Muslim mystics, the Sufis, and went so far as to state that they were worthier disciples of the prophets of Israel than were the Jews of his time.[5] It is obvious that he was much influenced by Sufi doctrines, and those who have written about him have adduced parallels from the classics of Sufism in order to illustrate this fact. However, Sufism was an extremely ramified movement, and, as the present writer has already pointed out in his review of the second volume of the *High Ways to Perfection*, the task at hand is to find out which particular school of Islamic mysticism served Abraham Maimuni as model.[6] An answer to this question is possible because of the specific terminology and also some specific teachings appearing in the *Kifāya*. Such an inquiry is also absolutely imperative, for the book has been preserved only in part, and we are not able to reconstruct Abraham's thought without finding out first which Sufi school attracted him the most.

Abraham refers to his chef d'œuvre as *ḥibbūrī*, "my book," although

3. *Responsa*, ed. Freimann, p. 18.
4. See C. Brockelmann, *Geschichte der arabischen Litteratur*, I (Weimar, 1898), 367, Supplementband I (Leiden, 1937), 627.
5. Rosenblatt, *The High Ways*, I, 50.
6. *Kiryath Sepher*, 15:442–444 (Jerusalem, 1938/9).

he wrote quite a number of other books.[7] At the same time he constantly called the *Mishneh Torah* of his father *al-ḥibbūr*, "the book."[8] The scope of the *Kifāya* was very wide. Its original size can be gauged from the parts still extant. The text published by Samuel Rosenblatt represents the second section of the fourth part and formed volume nine of the manuscript. Rosenblatt's edition comprises 248 pages of Arabic text. Since the second section of the fourth part was followed by a third, which, as we shall presently see, must have been rather extensive, the whole manuscript consisted originally of at least ten volumes. On the assumption that the various volumes were approximately equal in size, we arrive at a total of about 2500 pages of 21 lines each, a text nearly three times as large as *The Guide of the Perplexed* of the elder Maimonides.

This discrepancy in size finds its explanation in the fact that the *Kifāya* is, so to speak, a combination of the subject matter of both the *Mishneh Torah* and the *Guide of the Perplexed*. The first three parts of Abraham's *ḥibbūr* dealt with the religious injunctions incumbent on all members of the community, and only the fourth and last part was devoted to the "special way" or "the high paths" (in the plural) of the pietists. Why, then, did the son find it necessary to recapitulate the religious duties, after the father had expounded them so completely and so lucidly in his code of law? Fortunately there is no need to guess the answer to this question. The second section of the second part of the book, containing fourteen chapters (as against thirteen chapters that form the second section of the fourth part referred to before), is preserved in a manuscript in the Bodleian Library, and parts of it have been published by various scholars. Moreover, there are in other writings of our author copious references to the lost sections. From all this it becomes evident that the younger Maimonides had to recapitulate the institutions of the Jewish religion first and foremost, for the plain reason that he intended to reform them. The section preserved deals mainly with prayer, and in this field far-reaching changes were suggested by him. Prayer should be accompanied by a great number of prostrations. The Biblical gesture of raising the hands in supplication should be observed, wherever a benediction contained a request. The con-

7. *Responsa*, ed. Freimann, pp. 19 and 62. In his *Pērūsh* (see Note 1) Abraham always calls his book *al-Kifāya*, see, for example, *Pērūsh*, p. 539.

8. *Responsa*, ed. Freimann, pp. 123, 131, 133, 146, etc. Until recently the *Mishneh Torah* used to be referred to by Oriental Jews as *al-ḥibbūr*.

gregation should be seated and should stand in prayer, not along the four walls, as was, and still is, usual in Oriental synagogues, but in rows facing the Holy Ark. While seated, members of the congregation should sit upright and not recline comfortably, as was and still is usual. The feet should be washed before every prayer, as was done at the sacrifices in the Temple of Jerusalem. And so forth.[9]

Second, it was necessary to restate the laws of Jewish religion and ethics, because they were now reinterpreted, deepened, and broadened in the new spirit of pietism. The very names of the various sections of the book point in this direction. Thus, the third part, which deals with the duties toward our fellow men, *miṣvōth she-bēn ādām laḥavērō*, is called "Rules of Behavior for Companions" ("companion" having the connotation of "fellow traveler on the way to God"), *ādāb al-ṣuḥba*. *Ādāb al-ṣuḥba* is the title of a treatise (which, by the way, was published by the Israel Oriental Society)[10] by the famous Muslim mystic of the tenth century, Sulami. We have to keep in mind that Abraham Maimonides, although he stresses so often the contrast between the masses and the elect few, conceives of the Torah as given to guide all Israel to the "high paths" for perfection.[11] Accordingly, the words of the Bible have to be interpreted with a view to this aim, and where they seem to oppose it—for example, when they stress so much material prosperity as a sign of God's grace—they have to be reinterpreted. All in all, we understand now why Abraham saw fit, in the first three parts of his magnum opus, before he embarked on the discussion of the specific aspects of pietism in the fourth, to recapitulate the content of Jewish religion and ethics.

The great size of the *Kifāya* is also the result of its literary character. According to Abraham Maimonides, pietism, *ḥasīdūt*, is not only a way of life, it is a branch of knowledge, a science (a concept in vogue also in Sufi circles). The definition of its "place within religion" (*maḥalluhā fi ʾl-sharīʿa*, which means: its derivation from the established sources of Judaism) was the master's main concern. Consequently, the *Kifāya*, like the *Guide of the Perplexed*, is largely a book of exegesis. Moreover, Abraham Maimonides was a passionate *darshān*, an exegete and preacher by natural inclination. His explications of the Bible and the Talmud are so graceful, so lucid, so persuasive that one is almost convinced that his *derāsh* is *peshāṭ*, that his moralistic

9. See Wieder, *Islamic Influences* . . ., passim.
10. Ed. M. J. Kister (Jerusalem, 1954).
11. See, e.g., *The High Ways*, II (Baltimore, 1938), 276–277.

and pietist interpretation constitutes the literal meaning of the text. Be that as it may, the expository character of the *Kifāya* is largely responsible for its comprehensive size.

Any attempt at an evaluation of Abraham Maimuni's lifework must take into account that most of his chef d'oeuvre has not come down to us. It seems that modern treatments of our author have not exercised this necessary precaution. The first part of the *Kifāya*, which contained his theology, is entirely lost. This is perhaps not too grave a damage, since here he probably more or less followed his father, although this is by no means certain. However the lack of the tenth and concluding volume, which dealt with the *wuṣūl*, the attainment of the goal of the mystic—in other words, Abraham Maimuni's esoteric philosophy—is an irreparable loss. According to all we know from Sufi parallels, this section (the third and last of the fourth part) must have been very extensive. I still hope that fractions of this section may turn up one day among the many thousands of Arabic Genizah papers of literary character which have not yet been systematically scrutinized.[12]

I am encouraged in this hope by a little find I made while preparing this paper. This is a draft of a short treatise written in Abraham Maimonides' characteristic and elusive hand, and it once may well have belonged to one of the lost sections. It bears a separate title page, but our master used to publish parts of his great book as separate publications. He says so expressly in his letter of 1231/2 in which he speaks about his writings,[13] and one section, that about prayer, which we mentioned above, is repeatedly referred to in his responsa as "The Book on Prayer."[14]

The title page of the treatise clearly gives Abraham ben Moses as its author, but the catalogue of the Hebrew manuscripts in the Bodleian Library, where it is preserved, did not list the work under Abraham Maimonides. This fact, together with the very difficult handwriting, may have prevented the numerous scholars devoting attention to our master from using this manuscript, despite its great interest.[15] It is a treatise in defense of the *ḥasīdīm*, the pietists and

12. The present writer has not examined the Bodleian MS. Heb. d 23 (Catalogue Neubauer-Cowley, 2752), which contains eleven much damaged and obliterated leaves from the *Kifāya*.

13. Referred to above, Note 2.

14. *Responsa*, ed. Freimann, pp. 124, 126, 133: *al-maqāla al-ṣalawiyya*.

15. The Bodleian Library, Oxford, MS. Heb. c 28, ff. 45 and 46 (Catalogue Neubauer-Cowley, 2876, nos. 45 and 46).

ascetics. Three groups are opposed to them. First, the judges, *dayyānīm*—we would say: the rabbis—and the experts in rabbinical law. These are not competent, he says, to pass judgment on the pietists, for *ḥasīdūt* is a science by itself, and just as an expert on civil law would not dream of making decisions with regard to *qodāshīm*, or the rites connected with the Temple, so these experts should refrain from dealing with matters of *ḥasīdūt*, of which they are ignorant. Besides, the Talmud clearly indicates that the *ḥasīdīm* rank higher than the students of religious law. Second, there are people who strive with all their might for communal leadership and public office. A person of this description by his very nature hates the ascetics and is therefore disqualified to judge them, even if he should have theoretical knowledge of *ḥasīdūt*. While writing this, I believe, the author had a particular person in mind. Finally, there are the great masses, who abhor the pietists because their whole way of life is so different from their own. Therefore any testimony of the common people about the sayings or deeds of the pietists is suspect and should be subjected to most careful scrutiny.

What, then, were the accusations hurled against the *ḥasīdīm*? A *ḥāsīd* may use strange expressions, appearing to those hearing them to be blasphemous. If such an accusation were substantiated, the person concerned should be made to be more careful with his utterings about his religious experience. Another charge, echoed in the *Kifāya*,[16] was laxity in the observance of the details of the ritual. In our treatise, Abraham Maimonides deals with this aspect only in passing. His main concern here was a third accusation: heretical beliefs and doctrines. If such a charge were found to be true, the convicted was a *mēsīt umaddīaḥ*, a false prophet, who, we remember, is according to the Torah liable to be punished with death.

On analysis, the treatise, taken together with some passages in the *Kifāya*, gives the impression that the pietist movement among the Jews of the Muslim East was not confined to the circle of Abraham Maimonides and of his elder companion and perhaps guide, Abraham ibn Abu ʾl-Rabīʿ—that is, Solomon, *he-ḥāsīd*.[17] In any case, the

16. *The High Ways*, I, 146–147. See also Wieder, *Islamic Influences . . .*, pp. 39–40.

17. The *kunya Abu ʾl-Rabīʿ* is invariably connected with the name Solomon. The manuscript quoting Abraham ibn Abu ʾl-Rabīʿ he-ḥāsīd (Bodleian MS. Heb. e 74, Catalogue Neubauer-Cowley 2862, no. 7) (see Wieder, *Islamic Influences . . .*, p. 34) was perhaps written during his lifetime, since the eulogy for the dead is attached only to the name of his father. According to the catalogue, the manuscript bears the date "14 Tammuz . . . 93 Sel.," which thus would correspond to 1182: i.e., four years before Abraham Maimonides

movement embodied in Abraham Maimonides was very remarkable and deserves a special place in the history of religion at large. For Abraham united in one person three spiritual trends which were mostly opposed to each other: strict legalistic orthodoxy, ecstatic pietism, and Greek science—sober, secular humanism. He represented all the best found in medieval Judaism, as it developed within Islamic civilization.

On top of all this, Abraham served as *Rayyis al-Yahūd*, as spiritual and secular head of the Jews of Egypt, throughout his adult life from the spring of 1205, when he was only nineteen, to his death in December 1237.[18] In this capacity, he had to deal with countless religious and legal questions, with time-absorbing communal and other public affairs, and with the continuous care of the poor, the sick, orphans and widows, foreigners, and other persons in need of help. Naturally, these extended and variegated activities left their traces in the Cairo Geniza. I tried, during the years of my research into that ancient hoard of manuscripts, to collect all the evidence related to him. I did so first because of the great importance of the man, which has just been pointed out. Second, beginning in the year 1936–37, when I translated his Arabic responsa into Hebrew, I have developed a quite personal affection for him. For those responsa, as well his letters found later in the Geniza, show that he lived up to the standard which he had set in his writings: he was *nāʾe dōrēsh we-nāe meqayyēm*. Abraham Maimonides was possessed with a most lovable personality. He combined the humility and meekness to be expected in an ascetic with the firmness and determination required in a communal leader. His fervent religiosity and his strictness in the enforcement of the law were paired with common sense and humane consideration for special circumstances, while the lucidity and grace of his exposition betrayed the disciple of the Greeks.

The material thus assembled is rather extensive. There are about seventy-five autographs. Most of them are short, but some are of

---

was born. Abraham he-ḥāsīd died at the beginning of 1223, or at least his library was auctioned after his death in February and March of that year (see MS. Taylor-Schechter 20.44, *Jewish Quarterly Review*, 20:460–463) [1929/30]: i.e., approximately fourteen years before Abraham Maimuni's death.

18. He is already referred to as *Rayyis* in the month of Nisan 1205; see MS. TS 16.187 published by S. D. Goitein, *Ignace Goldziher Memorial Volume*, II, ed. S. Löwinger, A. Scheiber, J. Somogyi (Jerusalem, 1958), 52–53. However, the title *Nagid* was assumed by him a number of years later, apparently in 1213.

considerable length and interest, such as the treatise in defense of the pietists analyzed above. Quite a number of letters addressed to the *Nagid* have also been preserved, and in many documents and letters he is referred to. We shall now try to survey this material with special emphasis on Abraham Maimonides as leader of a pietist movement.

First, there is a strange document, a genealogical list of our master's ancestors on his mother's side.[19] A similar list has been already published by Jacob Mann,[20] but that does not contain the particular feature which makes our document so interesting. In it, through nine generations, most members of the family bear honorific titles in which the word *ḥāsīd* (pietist) occurs. Yeshaᶜayāhū Rōsh ha-Seder, Isaiah "The Head of the School," who opens our list as in Jacob Mann's text, is called *pᵓēr ha-ḥasīdīm we-anshē ha-maᶜase*, "The Pride of the Pious and Saintly Men." The title *pᵓēr ha-ḥasīdīm* is attached to the names of three other members of that family; a fifth one is called *segullat ha-ḥasīdīm* ("the elect one among the pious"); six others are labelled briefly *he-ḥāsīd*. Since nine generations comprise about three hundred years, it is very unlikely, although not entirely impossible, that all these titles were actually borne by the persons concerned, which would mean in practice that they were called up to the reading of the Torah with these epithets. On the other hand, in none of the many published and unpublished memorial lists from the Geniza studied by the present writer has anything comparable been found. Therefore it is reasonable to assume that the family of Abraham Maimonides' mother adopted at some time the hasidic way of life and then attributed these pious epithets to its ancestors. Abraham Maimonides himself, at the end of his life, in a letter addressed to him,[21] bears among many other well known official epithets the very appropriate title *rōsh kol ha-ḥasīdīm*, ("the head of all the pietists"), and I have no doubt that at that time this title was mentioned in every public announcement in which his name occurred.

It is a pity that we do not know a thing about the pietist activities

19. MS. TS Box K 15, f. 68. This document has been published and discussed by the present writer in *D. Z. Baneth Jubilee Volume, Tarbiz* 33, no. 2 (1963/64).

20. *The Jews in Egypt and in Palestine* . . . , II (Oxford, 1922), 319 (MS. TS 8 K22). Through an oversight the name of the fifth brother of Abraham's mother was omitted. It was (Abu ᵓl-) Makārim Jekuthiel. The *kunya* of the fourth brother was Abu ᵓl-Ṭāhir, not Abu ᵓl-Ṭār.

21. University Library, Cambridge, Or 1080 J 281.

of the family of our master's mother. It should be noted also that (as far as I know), Abraham does not quote any of his five uncles or any other member of his mother's family in his extant writings. However, the very existence of such a tradition is highly significant and it is possible that we shall learn more about it at some later date.

A number of Geniza texts deal expressly with disciples of our master. Of particular interest is a letter from Alexandria in which Abraham Maimuni's followers complain to him of persecutions by their coreligionists, who prevented them from practicing their pietist prayer rites. Even more deplorable was the fact that the antihasidic propaganda was instigated by a *nāsī*, or member of the Davidic family of the Exilarch, who acted in this way out of a personal grudge against the *Nagid*. On the other hand, the letter itself is a fine testimony to the spirit of its writer. For it does not curse or even blame the persecutors, but describes their behavior as a sign that Israel was not yet ripe for redemption—a state of affairs which could be changed only by repentance and prayer.[22]

Another Geniza fragment reveals the remarkable fact that Abraham Maimonides' circle of pietists attracted novices from distant countries and that among these was also a fellow traveler who wore the cloak of the ascetic, but gave himself up to worldly pleasures. The writer of the fragment dissociates himself from the addressee in the strongest terms and admonishes him to rejoin the master's team in study and practice: namely, fasting during the daytime and standing up in prayer during the night. He also advises him to take up a profession, a principle of conduct for which the master himself gave a shining example. He also refers to a letter to him from Abraham, in which the latter had invited him to come and in which he had described to him briefly the addressee's state.[23]

The model pietist is introduced to us in a fully preserved letter of recommendation, in which the bearer is described as a disciple of the *Nagid* and as one "who had pushed the world of existence out of his heart and was seeking God alone." The young man had some experience in the art of silkweaving, but lacked the equipment and the necessary means for exercising his craft. Thus far, the *Nagid* and the writer himself had assisted the bearer of the letter. Now it was up to the addressee to show his munificence, but, as the writer

22. TS 10 J 13, f. 14, published in *Tarbiz*, 33, no. 2 (1963/64).
23. TS 10 J 13, f. 8, published in *Tarbiz*, 33, no. 2 (1963/64).

emphasizes: *be-derekh kāvōd*, "in a dignified way." A full translation in English of this letter is given in the present writer's forthcoming volume, *Mediterranean People*,[24] to be published by the University of California Press.

A *dayyān*, or judge, in a provincial town, before addressing the *Nagid* in a legal matter, expresses his grief at being separated from his company, which led men to the blessings of the world to come, and at being concerned with the opposite sort of occupation. In taking up public office he was not aware of what he was doing, but he hoped to be able to resign and to join again the master's Yeshiva, this time for good.[25]

The Geniza has preserved two letters of recommendation for disciples of his, written in his own hand, by Abraham Maimonides. Although they do not refer to the young scholars as being members of his pietist circle, they are not without interest in our context. The first letter, dated October 1235, is addressed to a *dayyān* in a provincial town. The latter was piqued because the young man had held his wedding according to a custom not approved by the *dayyān*, who imagined that Abraham had not attended the wedding because of this deviation. On this the *Nagid* retorts that such insistence on customs not warranted by religion was unhealthy and that the *dayyān* himself should give up his idiosyncrasies in this matter. He, Abraham, had been unable to attend the wedding, because on that particular night it was his turn at the government hospital and for certain reasons he did not want to defer it. The *dayyān* was obliged to help the newcomer in his town, because the latter had had trouble with the police (he had left the capital city without the required permit) and, second, because he had married an orphan, who deserved consideration according to Jewish law. On the other hand, if it was true that "the beloved son," as Abraham calls his disciple, had tried to encroach on the addressee's right to lead the community in prayer and on his other privileges, he would have to face retribution.[26]

The same consideration for the two parties concerned is displayed in another letter by Abraham to a local *dayyān*, in which he asked him and his sons to grant the bearer's request to marry the *dayyān's* daughter. The young man was persistent in his love—love, of course,

24. The text, TS 12.289, is published in *Tarbiz*, 33 (1963/64).
25. University Library, Cambridge, Or 1080 J 281.
26. TS 10 J 14, f. 5, published in *Tarbiz*, 33 (1963/64).

not for the young lady, whom he probably did not even know, but for a family of *ḥākhamīm wa-ḥasīdīm*, scholars and pious men—and was prepared to make all the financial sacrifices required. Abraham understands, however, that the family might have reasons for refusing this request. In this case he asks them not to put the suitor off but to give him a clear-cut and definite reply.[27]

The five examples summarized aptly show how troublesome and time-consuming Abraham Maimuni's care for his disciples must have been, but this was nothing when compared with his duties as *Rayyis al-Yahūd*, the spiritual and secular head of the Jews in the Ayyubid Kingdom. The printed responsa vividly illustrate the long-drawn-out lawsuits and intricate ritualistic controversies which were submitted to him. In addition, however, he was asked many questions to which the writers would have found ready answers in Maimonides' code. Why then, did they apply for information to the *Nagid*? The reason for this course of action was mostly not ignorance, but the technique of legal procedure prevailing at that time among Jews and Muslims alike. The local judge was but a *nāʾib*, a deputy, of the chief justice in the capital. Whenever there was even the slightest doubt about a case, the deputy wrote to the chief, in order to be backed up in his judgment by a rescript from his superior. The Geniza contains quite a number of examples of this procedure, even on the Muslim side.

The Geniza shows us also how Abraham Maimuni's book of responsa, as we hold it now in our hands, came into being. Those who submitted a query left below it sufficient space for a reply. The *Nagid* wrote his decision with his own hand in the free space. The decision was copied by a scribe and sent back to the person concerned. The original questions, together with the *Nagid's* autographic rulings, were preserved in the synagogue archives and finally used for preparing a complete copy of his responsa. The claim of the medieval scribe of the manuscript of Abraham Maimuni's *Teshūvōt* (which is now in Copenhagen), that he had copied from the originals, is fully borne out by the procedure just described. It is finally proven by the fact that a decision given by Abraham and preserved in the Geniza coincides word for word with the text of that manuscript. This was not known at the time of the publication of the manuscript, because the difficult handwriting of our master had precluded the identification of the relevant Geniza text. In the catalogue of the

27. TS 10 J 30, f. 11, published in *Tarbiz*, 33 (1963/64).

Bodleian Library, the piece is described as follows: "Two forms of affidavit in Arabic; the first much injured."[28] In fact, it is a query submitted to the master, with his reply. It is reasonably certain that the text was already in this unsatisfactory state at the time when it was copied by the medieval scribe. For he copied only the answer, while he contented himself with summarizing the question, a procedure he did not normally follow.

In order to facilitate the *Nagid's* heavy task, the local judges and scholars used to assemble a number of problems arising from their legal and religious practice before addressing their superior, and the latter answered them all at once. Some such collected responsa are contained in the printed edition of Abraham Maimuni's decisions, and one, still unpublished, comprising seven responsa has been found in the Geniza. At the end of the query—only the end is preserved—Abraham is asked to write his reply in nontechnical language, intelligible to persons untrained in Talmudic studies. This indicates again that the local scholar wanted to show the answers to the parties and persons concerned, and there is little doubt that the *Nagid's* letter, as we know from many other instances, was read out *in toto* in the synagogue. Its content is a typical example of the variety of topics handled by the master day in and day out. The first two responsa dealt with cases of civil law, the third with a similar case also involving the rights of a first-born, the fourth with the position of slaves and Karaites with regard to ritual matters, the fifth with a detail concerning the circumcision ceremony, the sixth with the ritual bath obligatory for married women, and the seventh with the question of the extent to which an unscholarly person was allowed to serve as a ritual slaughterer. An average of five lines, couched in simple, straightforward language, sufficed the master to provide the desired information concerning each item.[29] Another unpublished responsum, the answer to a long query concerning the inheritance of a freed woman who died without heirs, consists in a marginal note

28. MS. Heb. d 66, f. 85 (Catalogue Neubauer-Cowley 2878, no. 84). When I discovered this item, I was not aware that it was included in the published responsa and that I had translated it into Hebrew twenty-seven years before. Therefore, I translated it again, but was disappointed when I found that I had already translated it once and that my Hebrew style of 1936 was definitely superior to that of 1963. This reminds me of an answer given to me by an old teacher of Arabic in Safed, Israel, whom I asked why he did not speak a single sentence of Arabic in his lesson: "Does your honor, the inspector" (I was then senior education officer to the Mandatory Government of Palestine) "not know that speaking a language means spoiling it?"

29. University Library, Cambridge, Or 1080 J 110.

of three and a half lines.[30] Such brevity, so uncommon among Ashkenazi scholars, was a mere means of survival.

In this connection attention is drawn to the facsimile of two queries written on one page, published by Simḥa Assaf in his *Texts and Studies in Jewish History* (Jerusalem, 1946), page 169. The writer, knowing Abraham Maimonides' habits, left room for an answer of about six lines before he began with his second query. Abraham actually needed only four lines.

The unpleasant subject matter of that query recurs again in three other queries, still unpublished, addressed to our master, the answers to which, however, have not been preserved or have never been given. They all deal with Jewish men who lived with slave girls, mostly of European extraction, either while unmarried or to the neglect of their wives or fiancées. As is well known, this was a social evil rampant among the Jews of Spain of the thirteenth century. Our Geniza finds seem to indicate that it was not unknown at that time in Egypt, either.[31] According to Muslim law the female slave is at the disposal of her master. In Jewish and Christian laws the use of a slave as a concubine was a grave sin, and it is out of the question that the writers of those queries were ignorant of this fact. But again, they wanted to have a rescript from the *Nagid* before proceeding against the transgressors. Abraham's responsum also states that a Jewish man is not allowed to pass a night under the same roof with a maidservant, if there is no female relative in the house.

The Geniza has preserved other queries addressed to our master to which no answers have come down to us. Two concern milking sheep on the Sabbath Day. Cheese was the main protein food of the poorer population in those times, and strict *kashrūt* was required in this matter. Therefore, sheepbreeding and the manufacture of cheese were favored Jewish occupations.[32] Two other questions to which the answers have not been preserved referred to Jews traveling to India and the Far East. One mentions a trader who had been away for fifteen years and who died in Fanjūr on Sumatra, Indonesia,

30. TS 8 J 16, f. 4. *Mediterranean People.*

31. British Museum Or 10.652, translated in my *Readings*; Budapest, David Kaufmann Collection, XXV; University Library, Cambridge, Or 1080 J 281. In my article "Slave and Slavegirls in the Cairo Geniza Records," *Arabica*, 9:1–20 (1962), I assumed that the two later queries referred to the same cases as those dealt with in the queries published by S. Assaf. A closer examination revealed that this assumption was not correct.

32. TS 13 J 9, f. 10, translated in my *Mediterranean People.*

the farthest point East reached by a Jew, according to the Geniza documents.[33]

An interesting question with regard to the synagogue liturgy was never completed, as the manuscript indicates, and therefore cannot have reached the master.[34]

In addition to giving decisions in writing, Abraham Maimonides acted as judge in the capital. There was of course a rabbinical court in Old Cairo at that time. Through the Geniza we know the names of its members and many of their activities. But the Geniza proves also that the *Nagid* dealt with much of the regular business of the court. A note in his handwriting, from December 1210, states that the parties had reached a settlement and one would pay to the other twenty dirhems every month.[35] Another fragment shows him signing a *qiyyūm bēth dīn*, or validation of the signatures of a legal document.[36] In a third, Abraham instructs a scribe how to make out a declaration that the court of Old Cairo had acceded to a ban pronounced against a certain person by a court in another country.[37]

The scribes of the eleventh and twelfth centuries were scholarly persons with excellent command of legal parlance and they always displayed beautiful handwriting. The general decline of the Jews of Egypt in the thirteenth century is evident also in the poor script and sloppy formulation of their legal documents (with the exception of some written by expert judges). Our master must have been plagued by the inefficiency of his clerks, for in June 1218 we see him again correcting a document dealing with a simple matter, the case of a widow acting as a guardian for her children, and adding to it four lines in his own hand.[38]

The incompetence of community officials even of good social standing is evident from the draft of a *ketubba* (marriage contract), from Bilbēs, a town on the highway between Cairo and Palestine. It was written in 1221 and submitted to the *Nagid* with the request to correct any mistakes which it might contain. A *ketubba* in those days was not a mere formulary, as it is today, but a real contract,

33. Nos. 169 and 233 of the collection of Geniza documents related to the India trade, prepared by the present writer.

34. MS. David Kaufmann, published by A. Scheiber, *Sinai*, 46:268–270 (1960).

35. TS 13 J 3, f. 21, verso.

36. TS 10 J 4, f. 4.

37. TS 8 J 10, f. 19. The person was called Ebyatar ha-Kohen al-Āmidī (from Āmid; i.e., Diyārbakr, now in southeastern Turkey).

38. TS 13 J 3, f. 27, verso.

and its drafting at times required a legal expert. However, the *ketubba* in question contained no particular conditions, and it is hard to imagine why the Nagid should have been troubled with such a trifle. Still, the official concerned must have had some status, because in the accompanying letter he asks whether the wedding could be held in Old Cairo in the *Nagid's* residence with the *Nagid* officiating, while he, the writer, would recite the *shevaᶜ berakhōt*, the wedding benedictions, and hand over his masterpiece, the *ketubba*, to the bride. We see here, by the way, that in addition to all his other occupations Abraham Maimonides occasionally fulfilled the regular functions of a rabbi.[39]

While the threefold task of jurisconsult, judge, and rabbi might have been frequently troublesome, it was the administrative aspect of the office of *Nagid* which was most time-consuming and exasperating. The *Nagid* had to appoint, or to confirm the appointment of, all the Jewish community officials and to define and to redefine again and again their duties and privileges. In case of insubordination he had to reprove and, if necessary, to punish the incalcitrants. He was responsible before the government for all affairs of Jewish marriages and divorces. And above all, he was in charge of the Jewish social service. In better times, as the documents of the tenth through the twelfth centuries show, the latter was the domain of the *parnāsīm*, the social officers, some of whom were honorary functionaries and some of whom were paid. However, with the decline of Egyptian Jewry, the old Jewish democratic *kehilla* gave way to the Muslim autocratic order of things, where the cadi, or judge, united in his hands all civil authority, including the social services, insofar as they existed.[40]

The Geniza material about Abraham Maimuni's administrative activities is very rich and reveals the appalling fact that he attended to all these variegated duties in person. He had under him *dayyānīm*, specializing more or less in the duties of judge, overseer of the poor, and teacher. Likewise, the institution of the *parnāsīm* was not yet entirely extinct. However, the amount of work done by him personally, as we can judge from the papers written by him and still

39. University Library, Cambridge, Or 1080 J 287, published by Israel Abrahams, *Jews' College Jubilee Volume* (London, 1906), pp. 101–108. At the time of publication the document did not yet have a shelf mark.

40. See the present writer's "The Title and Office of the Nagid: A Re-examination," *JQR*, 53:93–119 (1962).

preserved, was incredible. This copious material needs to be treated in a separate paper. I would like, however, to illustrate each of the three main branches of the *Nagid's* administrative duties with one example.

Here is a letter written in Abraham's own hand to a *muqaddam* of the Jewish communities in two small towns situated on the eastern and western banks of the Nile respectively. The *muqaddam* was the spiritual and communal leader, whose exact functions varied from place to place and from person to person and had to be fixed or approved by the *Nagid*. The letter is self-explanatory. After referring to previous correspondence in the matter, the *Nagid* continues:[41]

After the sending of that letter the aforementioned Sheikh al-Muhadhdhab, [may his] R[ock] p[reserve him], came and registered a complaint with me contending that you and he had reached an agreement concerning his rights and responsibilities, and that you demanded his due from him, but did not undertake what was coming to him.

To make a long story short, the upshot of his words was the following: You are the *muqaddam* of Minyat Ghamr and Minyat Zifta. The man has no desire to encroach on your position of *muqaddam*. He does not arrange marriages or divorces and does not act as judge or administer inheritances. This is because of his feeling of what is just and proper. But as for leading communal prayers and ritual slaughtering and the like, which he used to undertake in the days of the *Ḥāvēr*, our Master Moses ha-Kohen, m[ay his Rock] p[reserve him], you should certainly have him as substitute in one of the towns, since it is not possible for you to be in two places at once on a holiday or Sabbath; on the other hand, if you appoint someone else and reject him—there is no justification for this! He has more right than another since he is your relative, your cousin, and "one does not change over from one house in which the ʾ*Erūv* is placed to another for the sake of peace."

These feelings of jealousy are not worthy of you. If you led the congregation in prayer on the first day of a holiday and he on the second day, as your substitute, it would surely not involve any weakening of your honored position. Or, if you led the prayers in one town and he in another as your substitute, what harm would it do? None at all! Whoever hears that you are behaving grudgingly in this, will attribute to you something which is [not] befitting of you. A statement signed by you regulating these matters would be useful. Do not think, God forbid, that he goes around gossiping about you. Finally, be on good terms for the purpose of the welfare of Israel and peace. If I had said less in this matter it would have been enough.

May your prosperity increase!

The letter shows the impatience of Abraham Maimonides with the petty jealousies of those narrow-minded so-called communal leaders.

41. Oxford, Bodleian Library, MS. Hebr. a 3, fol. 15 (Catalogue 2873, no. 15). Translated into English in my *Readings*.

One of them, submitting a complaint in a similar matter, excuses himself indeed for troubling the master, "whose pure soul, benevolent constitution, and noble mind are repelled by hearing such affairs."[42]

As to family laws, one single case, when Abraham issued an order that a man was not allowed to remarry before he had indemnified his former wife in full, is represented in the Geniza by three items and, in one, reference is made to a personal letter sent by him in this matter. The secretary who wrote the main document is superior to the two mentioned before, but he still falls short of the standards of the previous centuries.[43]

The *Nagid's* perpetual preoccupation with social service is best illustrated by over fifty orders of payment written in his own hand in the course of about two months (spring 1218). They concern dues to the government, salaries to officials and teachers, subventions to a traveler from Spain, a *nazīr* from Persia, and many other needy persons, payment to a mason for work on a house dedicated to the poor of Jerusalem, and sundry additional items.[44]

One of the official duties of the *Nagid* was the preservation of peace within the community. This involved dealings not only with the community officials and their supporters and opponents, but also with the contending members and factions of the more prominent families. Thus Abraham Maimonides succeeded in restoring peace in the great ᶜAmmānī family of Alexandria: specifically, between the grandsons and great-grandsons of Aaron ᶜAmmānī, the Jewish judge of Alexandria, who became famous through the poems dedicated to him by the poet Judah ha-Levi. In a detailed letter of thanks about this affair, written in March 1217, a member of this family has the following to say: "Everything has been settled through you, my lord, and all we have attained is from God and through your merit, my lord, for everything crooked and difficult becomes straightened out in your days, may God crown us all with your life."[45]

42. TS 13 J 21, f. 11, verso, lines 6–12.

43. TS 18 J 3, f. 12, the main document, written by Abu ʾl-Barakāt Solomon, son of the judge Elijah. At least sixty items have come down to us in the unpleasant hand of this scribe, who served also as schoolteacher, bookseller, and wine merchant. TS 8 J 22, f. 22, contains the eloquent complaint of the divorced woman, who, by the way, was eager to give her younger son a good education, while she was afraid that her former husband would take him away from her and then neglect him. University Library, Cambridge, Or 1080 J 285 is a ruling in this matter by Abraham Maimonides.

44. TS Box K 25, no. 240.

45. TS 16.305, verso, lines 20–23.

As the most prominent personality in Egyptian Jewry, Abraham Maimonides had also to waste much time with a social duty incumbent on all notables: writing letters of recommendation or otherwise acting in favor of persons approaching him. A Davidic *nāsī* who wishes to be honored while visiting a provincial town turns to the *Nagid*, and the latter instructs the local *dayyān* in person and, in addition, writes a letter in his own hand to the community.[46] A physician and colleague asks him rather impertinently to help him in a matter of inheritance.[47] A gentleman from Alexandria intends to travel to Damascus, so a friend of his asks Abraham to write for him a letter of recommendation to the head of the Palestinian Yeshiva, which at that time had its seat in the capital of Syria.[48] And there are letters of thanks making mention of recommendations granted.[49]

The office of the *Nagid* was political by nature, and as always in politics, there was rivalry and opposition. Very soon after his arrival in Egypt, Moses Maimonides found himself in opposition to the family of Nathaniel ha-Levi ha-Shishshi, which provided Egypt with two *Rayyis al-Yahūd* in the time of the Fatimids and one in that of the Ayyubids. In the fall of 1171—exactly at the time when Saladin abolished the Fatimid caliphate—Moses Maimonides replaced Sar Shalom, a scion of this ha-Levi family, as head of the Jews, but in, or slightly before 1177, Sar Shalom regained his position and held it until at least 1195. At the end of his life, Moses was again appointed *Rayyis al-Yahūd* and was followed in this office by his son Abraham. However, his opponents were not idle, and as early as Nisan 1205 a *taqqāna*, or statute, was made that the *reshūt* (authority) of the *Rayyis* should no longer be mentioned during the synagogue service.[50]

The *taqqāna* was to be valid for thirty years, but it must have been abrogated after a comparatively short period, for from Av 1213 we find documents all over Egypt bearing Abraham Maimonides' authorization.[51]

In their attempt to undermine Abraham's position, the opposition, centering around the Nathaniel family, used an even more poisonous and dangerous weapon. They denounced Abraham's pietist reforms to the Sultan as a *bid*ᶜ*a*, or an unwarranted innovation, which was

46. TS 18 J 3, f. 11.
47. Oxford, Bodleian Library, MS. Heb. f 56, fol. 126.
48. TS 10 J 12, f. 27.
49. E. g., TS 8 J 9, f. 16.
50. TS 16.187, in *Goldziher Volume*, II, 52–53.
51. See Mann, *The Jews in Egypt* . . . , II, 327 (b).

anathema according to Muslim concepts. The Ayyubids were simple-minded Kurds and very orthodox, and al-Malik al-ᶜĀdil especially, to whom this complaint was submitted, was extremely conservative. Abraham realized the full impact of such an accusation and retorted by a memorandum saying that the new religious practices were confined to his private synagogue and that no one was coerced to follow them. How seriously he took this threat may be seen from the fact that he had about two hundred persons sign the memorandum. Our report about these happenings, which comes from one of his opponents, states bluntly that the memorandum was a lie, for everyone knew that the *Nagid* had made changes in the synagogue service everywhere.[52]

Thus we see that political rivalry combined with opposition to the pietist reforms of the son and the philosophical teachings of the father to make Abraham Maimonides' life not too easy. There was also discontent with the new style of rabbinical study, inaugurated by Moses Maimonides' *Mishneh Torah* and perpetuated by the use made of that great code. It is interesting that it was a Yemenite rabbi sojourning in Egypt who used very strong language against Abraham because in his halakhic expositions he allegedly failed to refer to the Talmudic sources, confining himself, we may assume, to the text of his father's code, wherever there was no reason to go beyond it.[53]

Finally we should not forget that Abraham's profession and main occupation was that of a physician to the court, including work in the government hospital. As such, Abraham had to ride every day from Fustat, or Old Cairo, where he lived,[54] to New Cairo, the seat of the government, a distance of about two miles. How time-devouring and exhausting this occupation was and how much it interfered with his literary activities, he himself described in the letter of 1231/2, referred to above.

When we look back on this long, long list of impediments to Abraham Maimuni's noble endeavors to sanctify Jewish religious thought

52. See S. D. Goitein, "New Documents from the Cairo Geniza," *Homenaje a Millás-Vallicrosa*, I (Barcelona, 1954), 707–719. (The manuscript published there, p. 717, should now be quoted as Arabic Box 51, f. 111.) The manuscript published by Richard Gottheil, *Mélanges H. Derenbourg* (Paris, 1909), p. 98, refers to the same affair.

53. See "Yemenites in Jerusalem and Egypt at the time of Maimonides and his son Abraham," *Harel, Refāᵓēl al-Shaykh Memorial Volume* (Tel Aviv, 1962), p. 142 (in Hebrew).

54. That Abraham Maimonides lived in Fustat and not in Cairo is proved by MS. Bodl. b 3, f. 6 (Catalogue Neubauer-Cowley 2806, no. 6), dated Teveth 1213/4, which deals with his domicile there, and by TS NS J 59, where he is asked when he could come to Cairo and spend a week end there.

and life, we feel what he himself has written about the detrimental effect on piety of communal leadership. Quoting the Proverbs of Solomon, he says: "Can a man take fire in his bosom and his clothes not be burnt? Or can one walk upon hot coals and his feet not be scorched?"[55] Abraham tried the impossible. He took too much upon himself. Therefore his influence was not as lasting as the nobility of his mind and the excellence of his spiritual gifts had warranted. He also died too young: he lived only fifty-one years, while his father Moses had been almost seventy when he died.

Moreover, Judaism in the East was in full decline, but it was still strong enough to repudiate pietism, which Abraham tried to inject into it. This negative victory of conservatism was a great calamity. For pietism and asceticism were in the air. Those religious minds who did not find satisfaction within Judaism sought God outside its precincts and adopted Islam. The mass conversions of the late Middle Ages were mainly due to social and economic pressure, but as a document published by the present writer proves, and as we learn also from Muslim sources, Jews were also attracted by the teachings and the example of the great masters of the Sufi movement.[56]

As we know from the highly interesting mystical treatise published by Franz Rosenthal, Abraham Maimonides did not remain entirely without a successor.[57] However, that great reform of Jewish life about which he dreamt never took place. Our presentation of the Geniza material illustrating his life explains, at least partly, why this had happened. On the other hand, our analysis of his life work has shown, I hope, that his personality is worthy of our affection and his writings deserve and demand renewed study.

The impression made by Abraham Maimonides' saintly personality on his own contemporaries is best rendered by a phrase found in an unfortunately incomplete query addressed to him. Here he is described, among other things, as "the Presence of God dwelling amongst us."[58]

55. *High Ways to Perfection*, II, 263.

56. See "A Jewish Addict to Sufism," *JQR* 44:37–49 (July 1953).

57. "A Judaeo-Arabic Work under Sūfic Influence," *Hebrew Union College Annual*, 15:433–484 (1940).

58. TS 8 J 20, fol. 20, line 3: *shekhīnā sherūyā bēnēnū*. While it was not uncommon in the Talmud to *compare* a scholar or one's master with the Presence of God (cf. *Berakhot* 64a and *Sanhedrin* 110a), I do not remember another instance in the Geniza of a person *addressed* thus as in this letter.

Yedaiah Bedershi's Apology

By A. S. HALKIN

On Saturday, July 31, 1305, which fell on the ninth of Ab,[1] a number of rabbis, headed by no less a figure than Rabbi Solomon ben Adret, gathered in the synagogue of Barcelona to pronounce a ban.[2] It consisted of three statements.[3] The first, addressed to the city and its environs (presumably Aragon), forbids the Jews to study philosophy or science, except medicine, before having reached the age of twenty-five. In the second, the ban is extended to all other communities, and is justified by a recital of the excesses committed by the Jews of Provence in the interpretation of the Bible and in the practice of Judaism. The third contains a call to respect and accept the unchallengeable truths expounded by the Rabbis, and it proclaims anathema on those who fail to do so.[4]

The reason offered for the publication of the ban was the contention that there were Jews in Provence who unhesitatingly annihilated the teachings of the Torah by treating the entire account of events from the creation of the world to the revelation on Mount Sinai not as fact but as allegory. In their view, Sarah and Abraham represented matter and form; the twelve tribes designated the signs of the zodiac; the four kings who made war on the five represented the four elements and the five senses respectively. The Urim and Tummim on the breastplate of the high priest stood for the astrolabe.

1. The *Ḥerem* (see next note) gives the date:

ביום השבת בפרשת אלה הדברים שנת ששים וחמש לפרט האלף הששי.

See Edward Mahler, *Handbuch der jüdischen Chronologie* (Leipzig, 1916), p. 569.

2. It is printed in *She᾿elot u-Teshubot . . . Rabbenu Shelomo ben Adret* (Venice, 1545), 65d–67a, and numbered 416–418.

3. It is doubtful that all the three were prepared simultaneously. Of the thirty-eight signatures on the *Ḥerem*, twenty-seven appear on the other two documents, nine on only one of the two, and two on neither. Three additional names each appear on the second and third, one of them on both. The order of the signatures also varies from one declaration to the other. But it is possible that they were all read at one gathering.

4. 67a: . . . והנה אנחנו מסכימין ובגזרת עירין ובמאמר קדישין מנדין האנשים הפושעים שהם כאלה באחת מאלה ומחרימים בבית דין של מעלה ובבית דין של מטה . . .

They make it plain that they do not believe in the literal meaning of the Commandments.[5] Their guilt was increased by their reckless preaching of these heresies in synagogues and schoolhouses.[6] It was their zealous pursuit of foreign (that is, Greek) culture which had resulted in these outrages. To them Aristotle was a virtual oracle, while Jewish learning unaffected by Greek wisdom was held to be a mark of ignorance.[7]

Ben Adret's accusation against Provence, and his argument that these aberrations were the reason for proclaiming the ban, provoked Yedaiah ben Abraham of Beziers[8] to address an epistle to the learned Rabbi.[9] Composed in the florid style current at the time, the letter opens with a lengthy encomium of Ben Adret as the leading Jewish personality of his time. This is followed by an expression of amazement at the fact that this outstanding scholar should have been ready to condemn a community of the renown of Provence, and should have employed phrases which could not possibly be true. It was astonishing to find a land that enjoyed an enviable reputation for piety and devotion to the study of Torah indiscriminately stigmatized as one of sinful people.[10]

As for the charges themselves, Yedaiah disposed of them one by one. The identification of Abraham and Sarah with form and matter respectively sought to explain not the Biblical record of these figures but the Talmudic legend according to which Abraham was seen in

5. 66: ... ואשר אלה לו וללא תועלת ממשל משלים במקרא כלו באמת יקלו ויהפכו במצות כלם להקל מעליהם את עול סבלם . . . ובאמת מראים עצמם שאין להם בפשטי המצות שום אמונה . . .

6. ... ודורשין בבתי כנסיות ובבתי מדרשות משתיהן (כלו׳ דברי תורה ודברי חכמים) דברים לא יחיו בהן ולמרות עיני כבוד כל ישראל פורצים לעיני הכל כל גדרי התורה.

In confirmation of this complaint the following autobiographical item from Jacob Anatoli's introduction to his *Malmad ha-Talmidim* may be quoted:

... ובהרגילי בענין ההוא (כלו׳ בלמוד החכמות) הסכמתי לדרוש מעט ברבים בכל שבת ושבת עוד מעט ושבתי מן הדרך ההיא כי לא ישרה בעיני קצת חברי ואם היתה כונתי ואלהים יודע כי עשיתי זה להועיל לעצמי ולאחרים עמי.

7. 66b: ... והנער היולד על ברכי חכמת הטבע ויראה ראיות אריסטו עליו שבע באמת יאמין בו ויכפור בעקר ואם נשיב אליו כל שכן דפקר רק שלומדים התורה ולבם לא נכון לפנים ויהפכוה לשבעים פנים. כי כה אמר אחד מחכמיהם אשר יחשב ראש לראשי מטותיהם לימוד התורה טוב להתערב בה בינות אנשים וטוב הדבר אך בלא חכמת היונים ההיא יקרא פרא למוד מדבר. לומדי התורה חכמת מה להם שהם בהמה המה להם . . .

8. I. Zinberg, *Toldot Sifrut Yisraʾel* (Tel Aviv, 1955), II, 84–89.

9. It is called *Ketav Ha-Hitnaẓlut* and published in Ibn Adret's responsa (see Note 2), 67a–75b. It also appeared in a separate edition by Shimshon Bloch (Lvov, 1809; reprinted Warsaw, 1882). The celebrated Talmudist Menaḥem ben Shelomo ha-Meʾiri (E. Renan, *Les Rabbins français*, pp. 528–546) also took exception to the ban, as can be learned from the reply made to it by En Duran Shimʿon ben Yosef, which includes excerpts from it (see below, Note 107); the tract itself is not extant.

10. *Responsa*, 68b–c.

the Cave of Machpela resting in Sarah's lap.[11] Obviously, this legend called for an allegorical interpretation. Had not Maimonides laid down the principle that respect for our sages obliges us to apply the method of allegory to statements which, if taken literally, may lead either to unqualified belief in absurdities or to disdain for the author of such statements?[12] The individual who presented this interpretation[13] was guilty of only one mistake: that of discussing it at a public lecture.[14]

Yedaiah vigorously denied the allegation that the twelve sons of Jacob had been converted into the twelve signs of the zodiac.[15] He surmised that Ben Adret and his companions were actually referring to a heretic (*Epiḳoros*), who had argued that Jews, like all other groups, were subject to the influence of the stars and planets, and had sought to prove this by equating the twelve sons of the Patriarch with the twelve signs.[16] Yet even this heretic, Bedershi added, had not dismissed the historicity of the sons of Jacob. Moreover, it was libelous to suggest that anyone, "even the least qualified," had ever identified the Urim and Tummim with the astrolabe.[17] Nor had anyone ever so misunderstood the story of the war between the four kings and the five as to find in it allusions to the four elements and the five senses.[18] It was a sad thing to be charged with the allegorization of the Biblical accounts and with disdain for the fulfillment of the precepts. This charge was tantamount to branding his countrymen as atheists and rebels.[19]

11. *Bava Bathra* 58a.

12. *Sefer Ha-Maʾor*, introduction to *Pereḳ Ḥeleḳ* (ed. I. Friedlaender, *Selections from the Arabic Writings of Maimonides* [Semitic Study Series, no. XII], 10–13). See also A. S. Halkin, *Tarbiz*, 25:413–428 (1956), esp. pp. 419, 425–426.

13. He calls him אחד מחשובי החברים בארץ ההיא (69a). It cannot be determined whether האומר in Abba Mari's statement כי באו אלי קרובי האומר אברהם ושרה חומר וצורה is the same individual, although he also names him מגדולי הארץ (*Minḥat Ḳenāʾot*, 69).

14. See Pages 166, 173.

15. 69b: זה לא שמענוהו מעולם ולא הוגד לנו בו דבר.

16. See below, Page 170. The epithet "Epiḳoros," by which our author identifies him, suggests that Yedaiah did not feel kindly disposed towards him.

17. . . . אבל שהתפקד ואפי' אחד מקטני מתחילי העיון . . . לדבר התועה ההיא על כלי בית האלהים מימינו לא שמענו כך . . . ומה יעשו העשוקים האלה בקום כל לשון מהולכי ארח עליהם להרשיעם לפני אדוננו בסתר כנושאי מנחה להסביר להם אדוננו . . . וכמה הפליגה מליצת תפואיהם שהגיעה לשעור זה בדברים שלא ישאר בהם חולק בשום צד בתורת משה . . . אומ' אני עלינו לשבח אל מגידי התלונות אשר כאלה המביאות לצחוק הטיבו אשר דברו.

18. 70a: גם בספור מלחמת ארבעה מלכים את החמשה אין פוצה פה ומצפצף שומו שמים על זאת ועל יתר הדברים מבטן מי יצאו איפה היינו אנחנו כלנו בקום המתפקרים האלה מאמיני דעות כאלה ביסדם הבליהם כי לא שמענו בלתי היום.

19. ארץ ארץ אל תכסי דמנו ואל יהי מקום לזעקתנו . . . בני פרובינצה היקרים איכה נחשבו לנבלי חרש . . . המסלאים בעדיי המצוות והמדות והתורה והחכמה זוכים לכל הכתרים איך נפלה תפארתם . . . פה קדוש יאמר דבר זה פה קדוש יתן חיתנו לקדשים שלם בתורתו שלם במדותיו יאמין לשמועת חסרונות

Yedaiah also reacted to Ben Adret's resentment over the mounting interest in foreign studies and its effect on the attitude toward religion. In the author's view, Greek wisdom[20] had made a tremendous contribution to the strengthening, purifying, and ennobling of the faith. It had provided the scientific foundation for belief in God's unity and incorporeality.[21] It had established the truth of man's free will; it had clarified the notion of the soul; it had demonstrated the truth of prophecy and the uniqueness of Moses' rank.[22] This list of the merits of philosophy is oriented toward Maimonides' *Guide*, whose teachings were undoubted truths to Yedaiah. That the philosophers did not reject miracles was evident from the distinction they drew between two classes of the impossible: that is, that which man is unable to alter but God can, and that which is simply absurd.[23] All miracles recorded in the Bible could therefore be considered literally true.[24]

כאלה על ארץ קדושה . . . אוי לדור שראה כבודו בכך ואין לאל ידו להראות תמתו כי רבו החושדים עליהם חשדים . . . שמעוני כל עוברי דרך מאשימי הארץ . . . לא תשבעו עד ראות בעיניכם הכרת שמנו מעל פני האדמה . . . אז תשקוט רתיחת הלבבות אז תשמחו לראות כי תביטו נקמת אלהים באויביו . . .

20. He calls it החכמה without the adjective יוונית (70d). Ibn ᶜAknin also says

לא תטלק אל חכמה סתם אלא עלי מערפה הד̈א אלעלם

(Wisdom undefined refers to the noble knowledge [metaphysics]). See my article in the H. A. Wolfson Jubilee Volume, Heb. section, p. 232.

21. 70d. He comes back to the achievement of removing the belief in anthropomorphism, contending that before this it spread very widely (71d–72b) but that at present, thanks to philosophy, it has been extirpated. Cf. S. Ravidowicz, *Beᶜayat ha-hagshama* . . . in *Kenesset* (1938), pp. 324–328.

22. 70d–71a.

23. Unlike the other benefits from philosophy listed by our author, with which the orthodox also agreed (see *Minḥat Ḳenāʾot*, 7, end of chap. 5), the issue of the "impossible" was thorny. In the second of the three statements of the ban, one of the sins of Provence is their assertion:

שאי אפשר לשנות את הטבע ובזה יודיעו לכל שאינם מאמינים בחדוש העולם ולא במופתים שבאו בתורה

(66b; cf. also *Minḥat Ḳenāʾot*, p. 12). Yedaiah traces his exposition of the impossible to Maimonides (*Guide*, II, 15:

לנמנע טבע קיים קיום עומד . . . אי אפשר השתנותו כלל ומפני זה לא יתואר השם ביכלת עליו)

In reality the class of impossibles which God cannot alter is evidently recognized by Ibn Adret; see Pages 176–179 of this essay. However, the distinction between two kinds of impossibles refutes the accusation of the orthodox; our author lists in detail all the miracles of the Bible (73rd) which he accepts as literally true. This is also the position of Joseph Kaspi (*Mishne Kesef*, ed. Last, chap. 11). So also Ibn Falaḳera, *Iggeret Ha-Wikuaḥ*, 16, and Narboni in his *Biʾur . . . le-Sefer More Nevukim*, 53a.

24. Our author takes greater liberty with Rabbinic aggadic lore. Although he applies the distinction between the two kinds of impossibles to these as well, he divides the *aggadot* into four groups: (1) unusual but clearly possible incidents which should be accepted on the authority of their source; (2) impossibles of the first class which also teach a precept, unless they are refuted by another statement (e.g., he would recommend belief in the

As one reads Yedaiah's defense two problems arise. The first concerns the facts of the matter. Between the accusations hurled against Provence and the refutation by our author where does the truth lie? Yedaiah dismissed two of the charges as outright slander. On the other hand, the letters in *Minḥat Ḳenāʾot*[25] mention the allegorization of the twelve sons of Jacob several times,[26] and Shimᶜon ben Yosef, in his reply to Rabbi Menaḥem ben Shelomo ha-Meiri,[27] details the significance assigned to the name of each of the sons, although not as zodiacal signs,[28] in accordance with the explanation offered by Levi ben Abraham ben Ḥayyim.[29] The equation of the Urim and Tummim with the astrolabe, also found in Levi's book,[30] is credited by him and others to Abraham ibn Ezra.[31]

---

hyperboles of the Messianic age if not for the statement אין בין העולם הזה לימות המשיח אלא שעבוד מלכיות בלבד.)

These are also to be taken literally; (3) impossibles of the first class which offer nothing instructive. They are to be interpreted even though God could have effected them, for the following reasons: (a) concern for the honor of the Rabbis; (b) defense of the faith, by not multiplying miracles and thus weakening their impact (so also Kaspi, *Mishne Kesef*, 12–13); (c) recognition of the truth that miracles serve a purpose; (4) impossibles of the second class which must be denied reality, 73d–74b.

25. Referred to hereafter as *M. Ḳ.* This is the primary source for the entire controversy. It was compiled by Abba Mari Moshe ben Yosef of Lunel, known as Don Astruc. It is made up of letters written by the various individuals involved in the conflict. In addition it includes a theological introduction by the editor and also a tract called *Sefer Ha-Yareaḥ*, detailing his point of view on the issue, which he forwarded to Ibn Adret (122–130). It was published by M. Bisliches (Pressburg, 1833).

26. It is noted by Ibn Adret, pp. 41, 54, 72, and in his letters to the scholars of Montpellier, *Teshuvot*, 65b.

27. *Zunz Jubelschrift*, Hebrew section, pp. 142–174.

28. *Ibid.*, pp. 158–159. Each of the twelve sons, as well as their mothers, represents a virtue or a vice.

29. His relative Samuel ben Reuben of Beziers defends him (*M. Ḳ.*, 92):

גם מי"ב שבטים שהעמיד כנגד י"ב מזלות אמר הקב"ה ליעקב מאשר יקרת בעיני נכבדת קבעתי איקונין שלך בכסא כבודי העליון והנורא; והם י"ב מזלות כנגד י"ב שבטים שהעמדתי ממך וסמך מן המקרא יצב גבולות עמים למספר בני ישראל.

For the equation *mazalot*=*shevatim* see *Midrash Ha-Gadol*, *Bereshit*, ed. Margaliot, 865. Presumably their identification was made in the longer recension of his *Livyat Ḥen* (see C. Sirat in *REJ*, 122:175 [June 1963]), where a chapter is entitled "Be-sippurey Yaᶜḳov Avinu" (f. 178a). The manuscript was completed in 1295.

30. Microfilm, Jewish Theological Seminary Library, of Oxford MS. 1285, 68a.

31. ולפי דעת אבן עזרא היה ענינו כענין כלי ההבטה ולזה נקרא חשן המשפט.

Ramban reacts to this view of Ibn Ezra very sharply:

סבר ר"א להתחכם בעניו האורים והתמים ואמר כי הם מעשה אומן כסף וזהב והאריך בענינם כי חשב שהם על הצורות שיעשו בעלי הכוכבים לדעת מחשבת השואל ולא אמר כלום.

(*Commentary*, Exod. 28:30). Abba Mari relates an interesting incident (*M. Ḳ.*, 106), which occurred when he explained that the Ḳesamim brought by the Moabite emissaries (Num. 22:7) were the astrolabe. A distinguished member of the community challenged this as deprecating an instrument which the Rabbis utilized in determining the new moon (*Ḳid-*

The meaning of the four kings and the five is likewise recorded in Levi's work.[32] In view of this evidence it cannot be maintained that the charges were leveled on the basis of mere hearsay. Nor can it be reasonably contended that Yedaiah stated what he knew to be untrue. What probably accounts for the disagreement between him and the rabbis is his refusal to regard Levi ben Abraham, who was labeled an *Epiḳoros*, as a representative Provençal Jew.

The second and far more important problem is to discover the fundamental reason for the divergent views of accusers and defendant. It can be plausibly argued that the terms of the ban as such did not carry any serious threat to the pursuit of philosophic study. Not unlike the stipulation in the ban, the philosophers visualized the age of thirty, if not later, as the time appropriate for training in Greek wisdom. Shemtob Falaḳera deemed forty the age proper for delving into the *Guide*.[33] In the curricular programs prepared by several scholars of the period concerned, the student is not expected to turn to philosophy before about the age of thirty.[34] Quite irrespective of the ban, a person would hardly commence the study of philosophy before the time specified in the ban. The conclusion is forced upon us that an issue larger than the time limit divided the men involved in the conflict.

In his commentary on the Song of Songs,[35] Maimonides' contemporary, Joseph ibn ᶜAḳnin, digresses from his subject to offer an interpretation of the story of Jacob's wrestling with the angel.[36] He depicts it as an account of a struggle within Jacob's mind between the active intellect and the maturing individual. In the course of

---

dush ha-ḥodesh). For Ibn Ezra's view see S. Gandz, "The Astrolabe in Jewish Literature," *HUCA*, 4:480 (1927).

32. Oxford MS. 1285, 72b–73a:

מלחמת המלכים הנזכרת בפרשת לך לך הוא משל על כוחות האדם. הארבעה מלכים הם ד' ליחות . . .
והנכון כי הם ד' כחות גשמיים המולכים בגוף . . . והחמשה מלכים אשר לא עמדו כנגדם הם חמשה כחות
הנפש הזוכר והמתעורר ושלשת חלקי שני חלקי'.

33. *More ha-More*, 6. In addition to the age requirement, Falaḳera also lists sound knowledge of the Jewish tradition and a lengthy period of training in the propaedeutica.

34. See *Yaʾir Netiv* by Judah b. Samuel ibn Abbas (in Moritz Güdemann, *Das jüdische Unterrichtswesen während der spanisch-arabischen Periode* (1873), p. 60; Ibn ᶜAḳnin sets the age at thirty (see *Wolfson Jubilee Volume*, Hebrew section, p. 233), and the subjects of logic, mathematics, physics, and medicine will require several years before the student is ready to turn his attention to philosophy. Ibn Abbas reckons that these studies will take twenty-two years (*ib.* 61), so that only at forty will he be able to begin his study of philosophy.

35. *Hitgalut ha-Sodot we-Hofaᶜat ha-Meʾorot* (Jerusalem, 1964), pp. 130–143.

36. Gen. 32:25–33.

this allegorical exegesis Ibn ᶜAḳnin discovers also a symbolic meaning in the concluding verse, which relates that in consequence of the incident the children of Israel do not eat the thigh muscle. In the end he mentions[37] that on completing this particular analysis he happened to receive a copy of Maimonides' *Mishneh Torah*, in which the ruling appears that "he who misinterprets the Torah or discards the simple meaning of the precepts is a liar, and perpetrator of evil, and a heretic."[38] Ibn ᶜAḳnin realized that at the first blush Maimonides' statement sounded like a condemnation of what he had just done to the story of Jacob. On closer examination, however, he contended there was no difference of opinion between him and Maimonides. Both equally condemned the method of the Batiniyya[39] and of the Christians, who rejected the literal meaning in favor of the spiritual.[40] They also agreed in disparaging the literalists, who frowned on any departure from the plain sense.[41] They confirmed the method, approved by Jewish tradition and illustrated by numerous examples from Rabbinic literature, which was to recognize the literal meaning of the precepts and of the historical accounts, and to grant at the same time that the Bible has many facets, and that it is therefore altogether proper to indulge in nonliteral interpretations.[42]

The position taken by Ibn ᶜAḳnin is essentially the one maintained by the disciples of Maimonides in Provence and elsewhere. Samuel ibn Tibbon declared: "All we have said concerning the Tower of Babel is with the understanding that the text does not thereby lose its literal sense, because the interior deeper meanings of the Torah do not, Heaven forbid, eliminate the simple meaning of the words. Were it not so [that is, to presume this kind of understanding], the Sages would not have discarded the plain meaning of the Torah and of those [that is, the prophets] who spoke in a state of inspiration.[43] The 'seventy aspects' which the Torah possesses[44] do not

37. Ibn ᶜAḳnin, pp. 142–146.

38. P. 142, line 9, and the note.

39. A party within Islam which was accused of allegorization and implicit denial of the literal meaning of the Koran (*Encyclopedia of Islam*, vol. II, *s.v.* "Batiniyya"; see I. Goldziher, *Streitschrift des Gazali gegen die Batiniyya Sekte*, introduction, especially pp. 3ff.

40. Smalley, *The Study of the Bible in the Middle Ages*, pp. 1–26.

41. *Encyclopedia of Islam*, *s.v.* "Hashwiyya"; A. S. Halkin, "The Hashwiyya," *JAOS*, 54:1–28.

42. Ibn ᶜAḳnin, pp. 144–147.

43. He refers to the Midrashim, which abound in homiletic exposition, but do not lead us to the conclusion that their authors consequently disregarded the literal sense.

44. *Num. R.*, 13, 15.

contradict one another.[45] Joseph Kaspi adhered to the principle that it was improper to discard the simple meaning of a story unless we were compelled to do so."[46]

The philosophers' readiness to accept Biblical narratives at their face value, unless there were compelling reasons to do otherwise, is more than matched by their attitude toward the precepts. They point out that the study of the Torah in depth makes the fulfillment of the *Miẓvot* inevitable. Joseph Kaspi divided the commandments into those of the heart, the word, and the deed, and described the duties of the heart as the most important, those of the word and the deed being subservient and preparatory to them. According to him, "the perfect ones[47] will therefore be more punctilious about the precepts of deed and word than others." He continues: "The multitude of the ignorant say that the philosophers do not pray. This is contrary to the truth . . . The philosophers appreciate the virtues of prayer . . . Indeed, they alone understand the words of our liturgy that were composed by great philosophers, the men of the Great Synagogue . . . In general I declare: No one is as punctilious about precepts of word and deed as the philosophers in our nation if there be such. By my word, I am not speaking rhetorically or from partiality for the Jewish religion. I am prompted only by my desire to state a truth because it is the truth. The masses, however, mistakenly consider as philosophers those who have nothing to do with

45. *Ma᾽amar Yiḳḳawu Ha-Mayim*, p. 174. He continues:

והנה קצת החכמי׳ שם פסוקי הפרשה הראשונה בדורות:

(he probably has Abraham bar Ḥiyya's *Megillat ha-Megalle* in mind.)

ואילו היה מפני זה מוציא הפסוקים מפשוטיה(ן) לא היה אצלו בתורה חידוש העולם וזה מה שאין ראוי להעלות על לב.

46. *Mishne Kesef*, chap. 15 (p. 20). He explains that the stories of the Bible, if our reason does not rule out their plausibility, have to be accepted literally unless we are informed that a vision is the source of any of them. He repeats it in his *Commentary* on Proverbs [ed. Last, 83]:

וכבר הודעתיך בס׳ הסוד כי כל דברי התורה והמקרא הם אצלי כפשוטם כספרי ההגיון והטבע לאריסטו זולת מה שהפשט נמנע היותו.

Jacob b. Makir, an opponent of the ban, writes in a letter to Ibn Adret (*M. Ḳ.*, 85):

ואיש אין בארץ יעשה מספורי התורה משלים שלא יהיה באחד ממנו מאמין בפשטים: לבל יהיה עוקר הגבולים. ואם ח״ו ימצא איש כזה יאספו עליו כל ישראל יסחבו אותו בחבלים.

Indeed, "the archfiend" himself (see below) teaches the duty of believing the actual incident in the story.

47. I.e., the philosophers, because they recognize the relation among the three. For while the heart is king, it requires the services of the ministering limbs and organs (*Mishne Kesef*, chap. 5, pp. 6–7).

it."[48] Jacob Anatoli's preface to his collection of sermons presents one continuous argument stressing the fundamental importance of *Mizvot.*[49] Yedaiah feels particularly pained by Ibn Adret's apparent ignorance of the steadfastness displayed by virtually everyone in Provence in the observance of the Law.[50]

In his insistence that the number of transgressors was negligible, Yedaiah added the further point that even those few were guilty not so much of heresy as of discussing mysteries publicly. He reiterates this point several times.[51] He expostulates with Ibn Adret that the allegorical interpretation of the *aggadot* was of old standing, and that Maimonides instructed his disciples to keep it concealed.[52] There was general agreement among the philosophers concerning the advisability to treat the "secrets of the Torah" in esoteric fashion, although both Maimonides and his followers often honored the injunction in the breach.[53] Joseph Kaspi likewise felt that the right

48. The "would-be philosophers" are the whipping boy of many of the philosophically-minded. Averroes argues in his *Fasl-al-makāl* for a clear division between the masses, whose duty it is to accept the Koran literally, and the philosophers, who comprehend its real meaning. The dangerous group is made up of the Kalamists (the Muᶜtazila and the Ashᶜariyya) who do not have the proper understanding of problem and method and only succeed in confusing the masses and opening the road to heresy (see pp. 26ff.). Cf. Falaḳera, *Iggeret ha-Wikuaḥ*, pp. 15–16, and *More ha-More*, p. 15; Kaspi warns his son against the company of two groups: the would-be philosophers and those who disdain Greek wisdom (*Sefer ha-Musar*, pp. 67–68, and his *Commentary* on Proverbs, 3, p. 19.)

49. See, e.g., pp. 1ff.

50. 68a–d. It may in fact be questioned how much substance there is to the complaint that the Jews of Provence have become neglectful of observance, in spite of the readiness of some scholars to treat it seriously. (Cf. I. Heinemann, *HUCA*, vol. 23, Part 1, p. 635: "Liegt gewiss ein berechtigter Kern.") Yedaiah is not the only one to defend the steadfastness of Provençal Jewry. Don Crescas, who minimizes the danger of heresy, asks: "If a few in the land are challengers, they live in academies and set time aside for Bible and Mishna. I wonder what impelled them to stir up matters, what innovation exists in the land now which was not there before, that this case has to be brought to judgment?" (*M. Ḳ.*, 47). Rabbi Shelomo ben Adret himself has the highest praise for the communities of Provence, with the exception of "two or three" (*M. Ḳ.*, 50, 95, 105, *et passim*). Indeed, he at first thought that silence would be the wiser treatment of these isolated sinners, but they have become aggressive and impudent. Even the observation of Moses de Leon, the probable compiler of the Zohar (G. Scholem, *Major Trends in Jewish Mysticism* [New York, 1946], p. 203 and note 154, pp. 397–398) or of the anonymous Kabbalist quoted by A. Jellinck (see Falaḳera, *Iggeret ha-Wikuaḥ*, p. 19) do not establish the case for the charge of impiety beyond a numbered few. It is only the zeal of a neophyte (he was first a rationalist) which leads Moses de Leon to assert that "the students of Torah hid themselves, and did not have the courage to utter a single word [of protest] . . ." (Scholem, *Major Trends*, p. 398).

51. 68c, 69a, 72d.

52. See the beginning of the Introduction to the *Guide*.

53. E.g., his analysis of the *Maᶜase Merkava* in Ezekiel and his opening remarks in part 3, up to chap. 7. Ḳalonymus b. Ḳalonymus criticizes Kaspi for his publication of the inner meanings (*Teshuva*, ed. Perles, 4), yet he expresses amazement (p. 6) that Maimonides

course was to confine such knowledge to the few.[54] Reference was made above to the criticism offered by Ḳalonymus ben Ḳalonymus.[55] It contended that Muslim thinkers like Ibn Aflaḥ, Ibn Tayyib al-Baghdādi and Ibn Rushd all supported this kind of position.[56] Incidental to the recognition of a hidden content to Scripture alongside the exoteric, a difference of opinion existed regarding the audience for whom the Torah was primarily intended.[57]

In view of the protestations by the philosophers that they were not pursuing heretical objectives in their exegesis, and that they were urging scrupulous observance of the commandments, it is necessary to look further in order to discover the true causes of the controversy which culminated in the ban. It appears that the factual basis of the dispute concerned the indigent scholar Levi ben Abraham ben Ḥayyim of Villefranche de Confluent, near Perpignan.[58] A respected resident of Perpignan, Samuel Sulami,[59] who was host to Levi, was urged by Ibn Adret not to give him shelter because of the heresies which he was spreading.[60] In a reply which Don Crescas Vidal, of the same city[61] made to an admonition by ibn Adret to exert himself in behalf of religion in its challenge from philosophy,

---

could not offer an explanation of the cleansing effect of the ashes of the heifer (*Guide*, III, 47) or of the table and the candelabra in the Tabernacle (*Guide*, 45).

54. *Mishne Kesef*, 2, 8–9. So also in his super-commentary on Ibn Ezra (Ms. Munich 239, 143; Cambridge 47.2).

55. See Note 53.

56. For Averroes' view see Note 48. He reports that Ibn Allah in his *Sefer Ha-Tamar* admonished his disciple to keep the mysteries hidden from the masses:

ואל ידיח עלינו הבן תרבות לשונם ויזיק אותנו הפך כוונתינו להועילנו . . . ומה נעשה לאנשים שהחכמים יראים מסכלותם.

57. To Samuel ibn Tibbon (*Yiḳḳawu Ha-Mayim*, p. 132) it appears that the entire Torah or its main purpose was concerned with its secret lore, but he himself insists that the main purpose was to benefit the masses. This is also the position of the thirteenth-century philosophers (Ḳalonymus, p. 3; Falaḳera, *Iggeret ha-Wikuaḥ*, p. 14; Kaspi, *Mishneh Kesef*, pp. 16–17). While Maimonides also recognized that the forms in which the secrets of the Torah are taught were meant for the uninformed and the immature (see the introduction to the *Guide*), it was his view that it was God's purpose to keep the secrets from the masses (cf. also Kaspi, *Mishneh Kesef*, chap. 8), whereas ibn Tibbon maintained that it was given to all people, but God included in it the mysteries which only the select few would understand.

58. See his biography in Renan, *Les Rabbins français*, p. 628; for a bibliography of studies on him see Davidson in *Scripta Mathematica* (Jan. 1936), pp. 58–59.

59. His surname, a translation of *l'échelle* or *L'escalette*, suggested that he or his family, came from l'Escalette, a locality in the Département de l'Hérault; see Gross, *Gallia judaica*, 431.

60. *M. Ḳ.*, letter 15 (p. 53, 10 lines from the bottom); letter 16, esp. on p. 55, line 2.

61. He was evidently an influential personality, since both his brother Bonafus and Ibn Adret ask for his help in checking the heresy (*M. Ḳ.*, letters 10, 11, 13, 14).

he agreed with him in principle.[62] But he was nevertheless eager to give an honest estimate of both Samuel Sulami and his guest. According to him they were both observant and careful about details of the Law, and followed the words of the wise.[63] At the same time he writes with reserve, and perhaps even disapproval, of some of the other information which has reached him about Levi. He teaches foreign learning to every seeker, he consistently refuses to let people see the book which he has written. Don Vidal was further told by Ṭodros of Beaucaire[64] in Montpellier "that one of the would-be philosophers wrote a commentary à la Greek to the Torah."[65] The Rabbi of Barcelona did not relent. In a second letter to Don Vidal he reproaches him for his reluctance to start action, and rejects his defense of Samuel Sulami, although Ibn Adret himself knows his virtues.[66] He also addresses a letter to Samuel,[67] remonstrating with him against his interest in philosophy and preaching the self-sufficiency of Torah.[68] When Samuel's daughter died, the father saw in it God's punishment, and he sent Levi away. He then went to live with a relative, Samuel ben Reuben of Béziers.[69]

62. Letter 12, p. 47 top.

63. He is witness for Sulami, and the latter for Levi:

או אלו מדברים בשנאתם באיש השלם במעשיו החכם הסלמי כי מאז קנאוהו וישטמוהו ועתה מצאו מקום להבאישו בעיני העדה על האיש הלוי אשר הכניס בביתו כי שנאוהו . . . אני היום על גלילות הארץ ידעתי [עברתי?] ומעירנו עיר הקדש מארסילייה העיר הגדולה בדקתי ולא מצאתי דרך כל איש כמוהו גדול בתורה ובמעשים גדול בחסידות גם תמצאוהו שפל רוח ועניו מאריך בתפלתו . . . ואם היום הכניס האיש אשר נקרא בשם לוי בביתו אמת כי בשמעי דאגתי מאד . . . כי יראתי פן ח"ו רוח אחרת תהיה אתו וחקרתי אחריו ומצאתיו כבראשונה שלם בתורתו שלם במשנתו.

Of Levi's behavior he has this to say:

ואין אדם אשר כגילו כי ידבר כאיש אשר ידע כי תורת אלהיו בקרבו ובדברי רז"ל חזק ואמיץ לבבו . . . והרבה טרחתי להראות לי את ספריו והיה דוחה אותי לאמר כי לא היה עמו בעירו אך אחרים אמרו לי כי הוא הלוי שחת ברית . . . וכשהרצתי הדברים לפני החכם הסלמי אמר אין זה כי אם לזות שפתים כי ראיתיו מדקדק כל דקדוקי סופרים ומעריב ומשכים והולך בארחות טובים ודרך צדיקים ואם אולי אמצאהו באחד מן הדברים פושע ואשם לא היה לו בביתי ובחומותי יד ושם.

64. The text in *M. Ḳ.*, p. 48 reads אנטידוס, but see *M. Ḳ.*, p. 61 (beginning of letter 21). Renan, *Les Rabbins français*, p. 763 seems to distinguish between this person and Ṭodros (Sire de Beaucaire), to whom Abraham Bedershi addressed a poem. Yet the title in the poem is הקצין as in *M. Ḳ.*, p. 48.

65. .כי אחד מן המתחכמים עשה לו לתורה פי' ע"ד היונית ולא הניח בפירושו זכר לפשטי התורה

66. Letter 14, pp. 50–51.

67. Letters 15, 16 (pp. 52–55).

68. He asks him whether he would not emulate Rashi or Rabbi Yiẓhaḳ (Alfasi?), or whether he should not follow Rabbi Eleazar ben Pedat, who refused to study *Maᶜase Merkava* with Rabbi Yoḥanan (*Ḥagiga* 13a).

69. Samuel wrote a letter to Ibn Adret in which he apologized for having mistakenly signed the protest against the projected ban, lent his support to the position taken by the Rabbi, and included a defense of his cousin Levi as a pious individual whose allegoric interpretations follow the practice of the Rabbis, who indulged in the same pursuit (let-

In a communication despatched by Ibn Adret to the new host of Levi, in which he welcomes the change of mind reported in Samuel's letter,[70] he insists that it is sinful to house an individual who outrages God by dispensing his knowledge to the mature and immature alike.[71] Some modern scholars are persuaded that actually Levi was neither more extreme nor less pious than his colleagues.[72] The late Leo Baeck suggests that Levi served as the butt of the attacks of the orthodox not because he was the most extreme, but because he possessed neither wealth nor protection nor influence.[73]

In a penetrating study,[74] the late Yiẓḥak Heinemann clarifies the difference between the metaphorical and the allegorical interpretation of a Biblical verse. A metaphorical explanation is the only rendering of a verse acceptable to its sponsor, so that the literal meaning is necessarily ruled out. The allegorical, on the other hand, is the understanding of a verse or a passage which is forwarded in addition to its simple sense, not in place of it. When Saᶜadia Gaon demands acceptance of the literal meaning of Scripture except in four types of difficulty which require reinterpretation,[75] he is arguing for the employment of metaphor. This is also the view of Ibn Adret, who rules that when the literal meaning would outrage our faith or our sense, it must be treated as a metaphor.[76] It cannot be admitted that God possesses olfactory organs or a respiratory organ, so Genesis 8:21 must be denied its literal meaning. So must also Isaiah 55:12 and Zechariah 14:4. But the allegoristic method, which the Aggada pursues very liberally, is not intended to replace the simple sense. It is rather the application, as Ibn ᶜAknin points out,[77] of the rab-

---

ter 41, pp. 89–93, esp. 91–92). Reuben, Samuel's father, ranks as a great scholar; see A. Geiger in *He-Ḥaluẓ*, 2:13–17 (1853).

70. See preceding note.

71. Letter 42, esp. p. 95, bottom. It is not known whether Levi had to leave this home. Gross, *Gallia judaica*, pp. 83, 200, writes that he lived in Arles towards the end of his life.

72. Renan, *Les Rabbins français*, pp. 639, 642; Leo Baeck (*MGWJ*, 44:28, N.F. 8 [1900]) concludes: "*Seine* [*scil. Levi's*] Allegoristik . . . ist gemässigt . . . gemässigter z. B. als die des Jakob Anatoli. Seine Rationalisierung biblischer Wunder, um deren willen er verketzert wurde, ist im grossen und ganzen unschuldig und geht in nichts über das damals gewohnte Maass hinaus." It should be mentioned that the Talmudist Isaac ben Judah de Lattes (Gross, *Gallia judaica*, pp. 265f.) speaks of the *Liwyat Ḥen* as "le précieux livre" (Renan, *Les Rabbins français*, p. 647).

73. Renan, *Les Rabbins français*, p. 647.

74. *HUCA*, vol. 23, part 1, pp. 611–643.

75. *Emunot We-Deᶜot*, chap. 7 (ed. Yusefov), p. 83a.

76. *Perushe Aggadot la-Rashba*ᵓ (in F. Perles, *R. Salomo ben Adereth*, pp. 24–56), pp. 28–29.

77. *Perush Shir Ha-Shirim*, pp. 142–143.

binic principle that "one verse is capable of several meanings,"[78] or of the accepted truth that "Torah has seventy faces."[79]

However, it is important to reckon with a difference in degree between the views of Ibn Adret and those of the more philosophically-minded. The Rabbi of Barcelona will grant that there is nothing wrong in a homiletic exposition of a statement or a precept if its simple truth or validity are not impugned.[80] Yet his personal preference, which is clearly stated, is that "in the case of both the promises and the stories, whatever can be explained literally, reason[81] dictates that we must not alter the plain meaning. Why should we? Indeed, whoever alters the plain meaning on his own is acting foolishly."[82] The conclusion to be drawn from this statement is that while at first blush he seems to agree with the philosophers—he recognizes human reason and experience as qualified judges—he sets limits to their right to judge which fall far short of the needs required by the reason and experience of the philosophers.

But where does one draw the line? Samuel ben Ḥofni Gaon understood the story of the witch of Endor as a piece of chicanery by the woman, without a kernel of truth, while Saᶜadia Gaon and Hai Gaon assumed that Samuel did speak to Saul.[83] Similarly there was a considerable division of opinion on the nature of the miracle which occurred at Gibeon and Ayyalon,[84] from the unqualified acceptance of the plain meaning to the efforts to explain it.[85] Many other examples may be cited. It is clear that in this area it is impossible to determine unequivocally which is necessarily metaphorical and which may be utilized for allegoric interpretation.

But this raises the question of the moral right which was evidently claimed by the leaders in this conflict. One could legitimately attack the trend of philosophic exegesis from the position of Rabbi Mosheh Taku.[86] In his work *Ketab Tamim*,[87] he rejects unexceptionally any

78. *Sanhedrin*, 34a. 79. *Num. R.* 13, 15–16.

80. *Perushe Aggadot la-Rashba*ʾ, 27: ואלו היה המשל והנמשל נכנס בתוך גדר הצואה זה אפשר ונכון.

81. *Or* the proper course (הדין).

82. *Loc. cit.*, 28–29: גם ביעדים או בספורים כל שאנו יכולים לפרשם על פשוטיהם כך הדין שאין לנו להוציאם מן משמעות הפשט ולמה? כי באמת מי שמוציא דבר מפשוטו מדעת עצמו הוא אולת לו . . . ואם כן נשאיר כל המצות על פשטיהן והיעודים והספורים על מה שיאות לכל אחד ואחד מהם

83. See Kimḥi's commentary on I Samuel 28:24; its author seems to agree with Samuel ben Ḥofni's view.

84. Joshua 10:12–14.

85. See the various comments *ad loc. Guide*, II, 35, beginning: ואל יטיעך מה שבא מעמידת השמש and the remarks of Crescas and, esp., Abravanel.

86. E. E. Urbach, *Baᶜalē Ha-Tosafot* (Jerusalem, 1955), pp. 348–352.

87. *Oẓar Neḥmad*, 3:58–99; only a part of the work is extant.

and all reinterpretation or speculation, no matter what the verse or the Rabbinic statement asserts.[88] He limits himself to the literal meaning, and, like his counterparts within Islam,[89] he denies anybody's right to explain.[90] He consequently attacks Saᶜadia, Maimonides, and even the Karaites as blasphemers of one kind.[91] The divergence between his position and that of the philosophers is so clear that the assault from that quarter could be expected. But when the opponents, who are themselves affected by the rational conclusions, raise their voices in protest against those with whom they disagree and accuse them of heresy, one is justified in questioning the validity of the grounds for these charges. Abba Mari Mosheh ben Yosef, the chief instigator of the quarrel under discussion, and the compiler of the correspondence bearing on it,[92] opens the compilation with a short tract on the three cardinal fundamentals of Judaism: the acknowledgement of God, creation, and providence.[93] In this brief composition he derives from the plural **של נעליך** as addressed to Moses,[94] compared to the singular in the command to Joshua,[95] that Moses was completely stripped of matter when he confronted God, whereas Joshua was not.[96] Is not this allegory? Like the philosophers, he also argues that miracles were set in the world order at the time of creation.[97] Ibn Adret's admission of the

88. He quotes this statement from R. Saᶜadia's commentary on *Sefer Yeẓira*, and then reacts:
ומי שאמר י״ח אלף עולמות ברא הקב״ה סומך על פסוק זה סביב שמנה עשר אלף ולא נועדו כל ישראל על זה . . . עני בדעת! על דברי האמורא שהוא דורש ברוח הקדש ומקבלה נאמר לא נועדו כל ישראל על זה ועל שיחה בטלה שלו מי נועד עליה . . . (69–70).

89. Cf. L. Gardet and M.-M. Anawati, *Introduction à la théologie musulmane* (Paris, 1948), pp. 66, 398.

90. *Ketab Tamim*, p. 63, bottom, and so on; the large number of statements by Rabbinic and post-Rabbinic writers serve him as strong arguments.

91. See, e.g., pp. 75–79, 80–84.

92. He is the compiler of the collection *Minḥat Ḳenaᵓot*. See the first letter, pp. 20–21.

93. It is interesting that these articles of faith are also listed by Naḥmanides (*Torat Ad. Temima*), Shimᶜon Duran, and Joseph Albo (see Guttmann, *Ha-Dat we-ha-Madaᶜ* [Jerusalem, 1955], p. 6, n. 7; pp. 169ff.)

94. Exod. 3:5.

95. Joshua 5:15.

96. ואל זה רמז הכתוב למשה של נעליך מעל רגליך שהיה מופשט מן החומר לגמרי ולא היה לכח המדמה מבוא בנבואת משה כאלו הוא כלו שכל נבדל דבק בעליונים . . . אבל יהושע היה במדרגת שאר הנביאים אשר נבואתם על ידי מלאך ולא היתה לו הפשטה גמורה מן החומר ע״כ נאמר בו של נעלך לשון יחיד.
Kaspi, *Adne Kesef*, 5, dismisses the distinction.

97. . . . כן יתחדשו האותות והמופתים כולם ברצון הקדמון הפועל על הזמן שגזרה חכמתי ולא בהשתנות הפעולות נשתנה רצון הפועל, כי המשתנה צריך אל המשנה בהכרח והוא ית׳ סבת כל הסבות ועילת כל העילות ואין זולתו עושה בו ואין דבר שיגרום לו שנוי.
For the vigorous strictures of Naḥmanides on this approach see *Torat Ad. Temima*, 13–15.

legitimacy of allegory was noted above.[98] It is hardly likely that these leaders failed to realize that the line of demarcation between the proper and the improper was hard to draw.

Nor was it only rationalistic allegorization which might come up with some unwelcome suggestions. Literal exegesis may also provide cause for alarm. The celebrated halakhist Rabbi Samuel ben Meir, the author of an extremely literal commentary on the Torah, declares that Exodus 13:9, which is the Biblical verse for Tephillin, literally means merely remembrance.[99] At the other, allegorical, extreme, we read, in the *Zohar's* homily on Genesis 2:8, the following introduction: Woe to the man who says that this Torah came simply to tell stories or common talk. If it were so, it would be possible even in our day to produce a Torah of common talk superior to all of them.[100] This is no doubt a dangerous doctrine, in that it condemns any but the esoteric rendering which it offers. Yet Isaac ᶜArama, the fifteenth-century Rabbi who witnessed the expulsion from Spain, not only builds his sermon on it,[101] but also devotes a good part of his remarks to establishing the factual truth of the account along with the deeper content. No alarm was raised against the *Zohar* that it was threatening Judaism. On the contrary, it became incomparably more authoritative to incomparably more people than rationalism ever was.[102]

These men whom Yedaiah undertook to defend were all loyal disciples of Maimonides.[103] They drew their inspiration from him and followed the example he had set. He not only laid down the general principle that the Torah and the other books of Scripture were all depositories of secret lore,[104] but also provided illustrations

98. See above, Page 168.

99. לפי עומק פשוטו יהיה לזכרון תמיד כאילו כתוב על ידיך כעין שימני כחותם על לבך (ed. D. Rosin, 98). Ibn Ezra's *Iggeret ha-Shabbat*, which criticizes Rashbam's explanation of the order of day and night is well known.

100. ווי להוא ברנש דאמר דהא' אוריתא אתיא לאחואה ספורין לעלמא ומילין דהדיוטי דאי הכי אפילו בזמנא דא יכלין אינון למעבד אוריתא במלין דהדיוטי בשבחא יתיר מכולהו (*Zohar*, III [Warsaw, 1867], 152a).

101. ᶜ*Akedat Yizhak* (Lemberg ed.), 16d–17b.

102. Much can be concluded from the fact that Rabbi Isaac ᶜArama is the author of *Hazut Kasha*, which contains a bitter diatribe against philosophy blaming it for the expulsion.

103. The reverence with which they regard him is evident in almost every reference to him in their writings.

104. *Moreh Nevukim* (Warsaw ed.), 4bff.; W. Bacher, *Die Bibelexegese Moses Maimunis* (Budapest, 1896), pp. 8–19.

of it.[105] Now, when, despite this, leaders in the movement to enact the ban took great pains to differentiate between the master and their contemporaries and to speak of him with the greatest reverence, it can be explained by the tremendous reputation as halakhist which he enjoyed and the increasing awe which he commanded.[106] But, surprisingly, modern scholars also, evidently for similar reasons, make an effort to distinguish between the master's approach and the practice of the disciples. The eminent David Kaufmann states in his introduction to an antiphilosophical tract composed at the time of the controversy[107] that Maimonides "only perforce allowed himself in certain points [to say] that which was now regarded, following Christian models, as unconditionally applicable."[108] He confidently presents his thesis that the philosophers adopted the Christian method of Bible study.[109] Similarly, Heinemann,[110] who concedes that the defendants received their impetus from Maimonides, is inclined to the view that they were influenced by Christian exegesis, and went much further than their master. This reasoning does not carry conviction.[111] In the first place, the spiritual (that is, allegorical) rendering of Bible by Christian exegetes was so imbued with their specific religious doctrine that it is very unlikely that Jews could have been attracted by it.[112] Moreover, Christian allegorical interpretation has

105. *Moreh Nevukim*, I, chap. 4 (19b) and elsewhere; *Hilḳot Teshuva*, 7.2; Bacher, *Die Bibelexegese*, pp. 106ff.

106. Ibn Adret sets Maimonides as an example (*M. Ḳ.*, p. 40):

כהרב ז"ל שאמר על עצמו שלא לקחם רק לרקחות ולטבחות ולאופות ומעידין ספריו על דבריו ואשר לא ירחק כמוהו לא יוכל עשוהו.

Cf. also his rejection of the charge that he maligned Maimonides, *M. Ḳ.*, p. 166.

107. "Simeon b. Josefs Sendschreiben . . . ," in *Zunz Jubelschrift*, pp. 143–153 (German), pp. 142–174 (Hebrew); see Note 9.

108. *Ibid.*, p. 145 (German); one is really surprised to read this judgment in the face of Maimonides' addiction to allegory. Cf. Bacher, *Die Bibelexegese*, esp. pp. 1–17.

109. Kaufmann, "Simeon b. Josefs Sendschreiben," p. 145; on Christian Bible study at this time see Smalley, *The Study of Bible in the Middle Ages*, chap. v, esp. pp. 242ff.

110. *HUCA*, vol. 23, part 1, pp. 635–637. Zinberg also believes that it was Christian influence, *Toldot*, II, 62, and 350, n. 18.

111. Since these men correctly identify Maimonides as their master, any suggestion of Christian influence would have to apply to him. See below.

112. Following their master (*Moreh*, I, 70), Samuel ibn Tibbon and his son-in-law Jacob Anatoli also speak of philosophy as ancient Jewish lore which was lost (*Yiḳḳawu ha-Mayim*, 173, *Malmad*, 9), and is now in the possession of the Gentiles. (Ibn Tibbon asserts (*Yiḳḳawu*, 175) that the Christians are more adept in it than the Muslims). The Jews are now objects of derision (Ibn Tibbon:

. . . אומרים עלינו . . . שאין בידינו מדברי הנביאים רק הקלפות והכופרים . . . אומרים שאנו אוכלין הקלפות והם אוכלים הפרי.)

Anatoli frequently credits Michael Scotus (החכם שהתחברתי עמו) but the explanations which the critics single out are not among his suggestions.

a tradition going back to the beginning of its history, and Jewish students were acquainted with it and their attitude to it had long been defined.[113] Finally it must not be forgotten that early in the thirteenth century a fight was waged against Maimonides in which charges were leveled against him similar to those hurled at the beginning of the fourteenth century.[114] Not only did he suggest numerous allegorical explanations,[115] but he also identified them with the *sitrē Torah* of which the Rabbis spoke.[116] It can hardly be argued that he was exposed to the influence of Christian Biblical interpretation.[117]

The preceding examination and analysis of the background of the ban and the reaction to it lead to the conclusion that the presence in Provence of "two or three" individuals who angered Abba Mari and Ibn Adret, and the possible discovery of a certain laxity in the practice of Judaism, may have been the immediate cause of the conflict but not the true reason. To understand the excitement it must be realized that the dispute was another stage, perhaps the last in the Middle Ages, in the effort of the religious tradition to disembarrass itself of the discipline imposed upon it by the trend of rationalism. It was an undertaking which paralleled a similar phenomenon in the other monotheistic faiths. History knows of the striking decline of secular studies, notably philosophy, in the Islamic world from the end of the twelfth century.[118] It is true that by the time the decline set in, the orthodox system had absorbed views and attitudes from the liberal school,[119] but inasmuch as such views were now held to be religious truths, the recognition of the decline is not thereby contradicted.[120]

113. Smalley, *Study of the Bible*, pp. 149ff.

114. J. Sarachek, *Faith and Reason* (Williamsport, Pa., 1935), pp. 17ff.

115. Bacher, *Die Bibelexegese*, p. 12 and elsewhere.

116. *Ibid.*

117. Or of Philo. Cf. Kaufmann's inclusion of Philo in his discussion of the alleged Christian influence, "Simeon b. Josefs Sendschreiben," p. 145, and the introductory paragraph of S. A. Poznânski's study, "Philon dans l'ancienne littérature judéo-arabe," *REJ*, 50:10–31 (1905).

118. The decline was the theme of a conference reported in *Classicisme et déclin culturel dans l'histoire de l'Islam*, organized by Braunschwig and von Grunebaum (Paris, 1957). Gardet ("Ankylose de la pensée religieuse," *Classicisme et déclin*, pp. 93–105) dates the decline of the religious sciences, viz. exegesis, law, Kalam in the fifteenth century, but he looks upon the last preceding centuries as a time of "fixation" and systematization, whereas real originality ceased much earlier. Among other causes, orthodoxy can be counted (Ritter, "L'Orthodoxie a-t-elle une part dans la décadence?" *Classicisme et déclin*, pp. 167–183).

119. Gardet, "Ankylose," p. 102.

120. Cf. Ritter, "L'Orthodoxie." In discussing Ghazali's conflict with various dissident groups, including the philosophers, he summarizes: "Au cours de cette lutte, des œuvres

In Europe the fourth Lateran Council met in 1215 after a bloody and victorious fight on heresy within its ranks.[121] It adopted measures and established procedure for preventing recurrence of heresy in the future and securing complete triumph for the Church.[122] Although the apparent achievement and the program eventually proved quite costly and even inflicted defeats on it, the immediate results were undoubtedly gratifying to those within it who had feared for its future while heresy was rampant.

Owing to the radical differences between Christian authorities and Jewish leaders in their attitudes to the challenge, the objectives sought, and the means at their disposal, the vigor and the course of the conflict within Jewry were much milder and much less spectacular than the Christian offensive on heresy. Nevertheless, it was serious and fateful. The climax of the first stage, which was reached when Maimonides' books were burned about 1232, called a temporary halt to the quarrel, but did not resolve it,[123] although efforts were made to vindicate and to conciliate.[124] Toward the end of the same century, attacks on Maimonides were resumed. But his reputation was so renowned and firm by that time that the defenders had little difficulty in quelling them and even threatening punishment.[125]

By 1305 conditions were changed. The triumph of orthodoxy within Christianity and Islam created a favorable climate for a similar success within Judaism. Some of the teachings of the ra-

---

très importantes out vu le jour; on a utilizé dans la lutte des arguments philosophiques rationnels, mais le but était fixé d'avance. C'est un combat lié intimement à la théologie, et non une activité autonome de la raison dans le sens de la construction d'une image du monde uniquement par des moyens rationnels. De cette lutte, malgré l'utilization de moyens de pensée rationnels, aucune impulsion n'est venue tendant vers une libre activité de la raison. Mais il y a encore un autre combat bien plus primitif, et cependent plus éfficace, de l'orthodoxie contre la philosophie dont nous allons parler tout à l'heure," p. 170. It is the religious conception of God, His power and control, man's role vis-à-vis God. As he summarizes it: "Un dogme basé sur l'autorité de la parole divine et la tradition du Prophète devait nécessairement trouver plus d'audience auspès de la masse que les raisonnements compliqués des Muᶜtazilites, pour ne pas parler des philosophes," p. 175.

121. Hayward, *Histoire des Papes*, pp. 256–257; *Catholic Enyclopedia*, VIII, 16; *Encyclopedia of Religion and Ethics*, I, 282ff.

122. Hayward, *Histoire des Papes*, p. 260; *Cambridge Medieval History*, V, 697; *Catholic Encyclopedia*, IX, 18a–b; *Encyclopaedia Britannica*, XIII, 40.

123. Sarachek, *Faith and Reason*, pp. 73–88. For reactions to this action see Sarachek, pp. 89–113, and *Ḳobez ᶜal-Yad*, I, 1–20.

124. Sarachek, *Faith and Reason*, pp. 116–127; *Teshuvot Ha-Rambam* (Leipzig, 1859), III, 8aff.

125. A. Strauss, *Toldot ha-Yehudim be-Mizrayim u-be-Suria* (Jerusalem, 1944), 131–141; *Teshuvot ha-Rambam*, 21c–22d.

tionalists were adopted,[126] but the toleration of rationalism lost ground. The essentially negative attitude toward philosophy, characteristic of the rabbis of the Franco-German tradition, penetrated Provence and Spain during the thirteenth century, together with their method of Talmudic study, which was being adopted, and their views on that study.[127] The role of Rabbi Asher ben Yeḥiel, a German Tosaphist, who was making his way to Spain at this time to become the Rabbi of Toledo, was significant in galvanizing the energy of the leaders to act, as it was in creating an atmosphere of piety in Spain.[128] His feelings about philosophy were decidedly hostile, and he disliked secular studies, of which he admitted he knew nothing, as intensely as philosophy.[129]

The growing strength of the antirationalist trend was augmented by the new development of mysticism in the same district in which the quarrel was going on.[130] The recent evolution of the phase known as Kabbala marks a departure in the history of that lore in that it presented itself as a tradition going back to the ancients.[131] Its concern with fundamental problems, and its incorporation of philosophical concepts into a system which vaunted a purely Jewish ancestry and claimed that it represented the deepest understanding of the revealed books, qualified it both to satisfy the curiosity of those who sought answers to theological and cosmological questions and to challenge Aristotelianism and its Jewish exponents as alien plants within Jewry.

No later conflict between rationalists and their opponents broke

126. E.g., the thirteen articles of faith.

127. Scholem, *Major Trends in Jewish Mysticism*, pp. 80f.; Urbach, *Baʿale ha-Tosafot*, pp. 523ff.

128. Alfred Freimann, "Ascher ben Jechiel," *Jahrbuch der Jüdisch-Literarischen Gesellschaft*, 12:237–317, 250–255, 260–264 (1918).

129. תשובות, נה, (90b–91a): ועל שכתבת מגזרת השכל וגזרת הדת מה אשיב על זה לא תהא תורה שלנו כשיחה בטלה שלכם חכמת הגיונכם אשר הרחיקו כל חכמי הדת נביא ממנה אות או מופת לחייב ולזכות ולאסור ולהתיר והלא חובבי מקורה לא האמינו במשה ובמשפטים ובחוקים צדיקים אשר נתנו על ידו בכתב ובקבלה ואיך שואבי מימיה יביאו ראיה מכם לחוקים ומשפטים של מרע"ה ולפסוק דינין במשלים שהורגלו בהם בחכמת הגיונם. האף אין זאת וכי בימי ובמקומי יפסקו הדינין על פי המשלים ת"ל בעודי חי עוד יש תורה בישראל להביא משלים לפסקי הדינים כי חכמת הפילוסופיא וחכמת התורה אינן על דרך אחת כי חכמת התורה היא קבלה למשה מסיני . . . אעפ"י שאין הדברים נמשכים אחר חכמת הטבע אנו הולכין על פי הקבלה. אבל חכמת הפילוסופיא היא טבעית וחכמים גדולים היו והעמידו כל דבר על טבעו ומרוב חכמתם העמיקו שחתו והוצרכו לכפור בתורת משה לפי שאין כל התורה טבעית אלא קבלה . . . כל הבא ונכנס מתחלה בחכמה זו לא יוכל לצאת ממנה להרוס בלבו חכמת התורה כי לא יוכל לשוב מחכמה טבעית שהורגל בה כי לבו תמיד נמשך אחריה.

130. Scholem, *Reshit Ha-Kabbala*, pp. 12–22.

131. Scholem, *Major Trends in Jewish Mysticism*, pp. 20–22. The belief was much older, but the new name marked its formal profession.

out until modern times. The philosophers aligned themselves with Orthodoxy, either by attacking Aristotle on philosophic grounds,[132] or by identifying fully with the orthodox position.[133] Within Spain, the last century or two of Jewish life hardly boasts scientists in any field. The Jewish culture in Italy under the impact of the Renaissance was of no mind to stimulate a renewed rational activity.[134] The only notice taken of rationalists in the period from 1400 is in the attacks on them by those who blamed them for the calamities which overwhelmed Spanish Jewry.[135]

To sum up, the ban itself was not a decisive act with immediately fateful consequences. Its importance lies in the attention it calls to the triumph of the antirationalist group over the forces which it designated as alien and hostile to the faith and the tradition. It marks the self-assertion of that trend within Judaism which, believing that it was thus faithful to the ideals of its tradition, preferred living within its own world to adopting influences from without. Indeed, in view of this triumph, it is appropriate to conclude with a statement taken from a discussion of the decline of rationalism within Islam:[136]

> Truth to tell, the Caliphs and the leading personalities are not altogether responsible for the situation; the bright light shed by the Arabs during the golden age of their borrowed culture had been only an accident in their history, and it was natural for an equilibrium to be attained at a lower level, better suited to their aptitudes. The predominance of religious interests does not thereby become a less essential factor of their decline.

132. Ḥasdai Crescas, whose work *Or Adonai* has been closely studied by H. A. Wolfson, *Crescas' Critique of Aristotle* (Cambridge, Mass., 1929).

133. Works like Albo's *Sefer Ha-ᶜIkkarim*, or Duran's Introduction to his Commentary on Job.

134. Burckhardt, *The Civilization of the Renaissance in Italy*, pp. 309–311.

135. Shelomo Alᶜami, *Iggeret Musar* (ed. Habermann), pp. 41–43; Yiẓḥaḳ ᶜArama, *Ḥazut Ḳasha*, chaps., 8, 9; Yosef Yabeẓ, *Or ha-Ḥayyim*, introd. and chaps. 3–10.

136. Charles Pellat, "Les Etapes de la décadence culturelle dans les pays arabes d'orient" (in *Classicisme et déclin dans l'histoire de l'Islam*, p. 85).

Isaac Ibn Laṭif — Philosopher or Kabbalist?

To Gershom G. Scholem

By SARA O. HELLER WILENSKY

Isaac ibn Laṭif—a paradoxical, multifaceted personality who lived in Spain during the thirteenth century[1]—occupies a unique position in the history of medieval Jewish thought.

To Kabbalists, Laṭif was a gifted philosopher on whose Kabbalistic theories, however, they reserved judgment; to philosophers, on the other hand, Laṭif was primarily a Kabbalist whose philosophical doctrines they criticized. Isaac Albalag,[2] for example, takes Laṭif to task for his critical attitude toward Aristotelian philosophy, while Isaac Abravanel[3] includes Laṭif in the company of such radical disciples of Maimonides as Samuel ibn Tibbon, Joseph Kaspi, Moses Narboni, and Albalag himself. In contrast to Abravanel, Isaac ben Sheshet, who regards Laṭif very highly as a philosopher (even comparing him favorably to Maimonides),[4] nevertheless maintains that although Laṭif "perceived much in the study of philosophy, he was nevertheless a traditionalist and a *ḥasid*."[5] On the other hand, Sheshet questions Laṭif's authority as a Kabbalist, arguing that Laṭif's mystical speculations were "concocted out of his own heart and mind, not from true Kabbala."[6] Still another contrary view is

1. For chronological data that are not repeated here I refer the reader to my "The Problem of the Authorship of the Book *Sha*ᶜ*ar ha-Shamayim* Ascribed to Abraham ibn Ezra" (Hebrew), *Tarbiz*, vol. 32, no. 3, p. 293 (1963).

2. Cf. J. H. Schorr, "Isaac Albalag," *He-Ḥaluẓ*, 4:88–89 (Breslau, 1859); 7:168 (Frankfurt am Main, 1865).

3. See Commentary on Genesis 1:6 (Hanover, 1710), p. 10a. Cf. also S. Sachs in *Ha-Teḥiyya*, 2:63–64 (1857).

4. *Responsa* (Vilna, 1878), no. 157:

הספר הגדול והנאה שבספריו קראו שער השמים והוא כעין מורה הנבוכים.

5. *Ibid.*

6. *Ibid.* On the other hand, Ẓemaḥ ben Solomon Duran, when asked to explain Laṭif's Kabbalistic doctrines, answered rather humbly that he was not able to understand them

found in the Vatican manuscript of Laṭif's hitherto unpublished chief work, *Shaᶜar ha-Shamayim*[7] (*The Gate of Heaven*), in which we find the following inscription on the title page: "This book presents a synthesis between Kabbala and philosophy."[8]

Yehuda Ḥayyat, a Spanish Kabbalist at the time of the Expulsion, evaluates Isaac ibn Laṭif as follows: "that godly sage . . . who composed the books of [*Shaᶜar*] *ha-Shamayim* and [*Ẓurat*] *ha-ᶜOlam*,[9] as well as *Ẓeror ha-Mor*[10] and *Ginzē ha-Melek.*[11] Now his words in these books are more valuable than pearls, but as for matters which touch upon Kabbala, he stands with one foot outside, one foot inside."[12] Ḥayyat thus describes Laṭif as being perched at the crossroads of medieval Jewish thought, one foot "outside"—in philosophy, and one foot "inside"—in Kabbala.

"because of his own shortage of understanding and the depth of [the latter's] theories." Cf. *Yakin u-Boaz* (Leghorn, 1782), I, 135.

7. It should be noted, however, that some parts of it have been published. The introduction to *Shaᶜar ha-Shamayim* was published by A. Jellinek in *Ha-Shaḥar*, vol. 2, no. 2, pp. 81–88 (1871), and again by O. H. Schorr in *He-Ḥaluẓ*, 12:114–124 (1881). Jellinek had also published chapters 23–26 of part I and chapters 2–3 of part II in *Ha-Shaḥar*, vol. 2, part 3, pp. 97–104; part 4, pp. 129–132.

I am preparing a critical edition of *Shaᶜar ha-Shamayim* which will include a critical text based upon ten manuscripts, a critical apparatus (which contains the variations, additions, and marginal corrections of the ten manuscripts collated), explanatory notes, and a comprehensive introduction.

8. MS. Vatican 335: ספר זה מחבר חכמת הקבלה עם חכמ' הפילוסופיאה. All references to *Shaᶜar ha-Shamayim*, unless otherwise stated, are based on the Vatican manuscript, hereafter referred to as *SH.*

9. Ed. Z. Stern (Vienna, 1860); hereafter referred to as *ẒH.*

10. Ed. A. Jellinek, in *Kerem Ḥemed*, 9:154–159 (1856), subsequently referred to as *ẒM.*

11. Published by A. Jellinek in *Kokbe Yiẓḥaḳ* (Vienna, 1862–67), hereafter referred to as *GH.*

His other works include:

(a) An early and incomplete (anonymous) version of *Shaᶜar ha-Shamayim* ascribed to Abraham ibn Ezra and published by S. Gerondi and S. D. Luzzatto in *Kerem Ḥemed*, 4:5–9 (1839); *Virgo Filia Jehudae* (Prague, 1840), pp. v–xii; *Ha-Teḥiyya* (Berlin, 1850), pp. 63–65. Cf. my "The Problem of the Authorship of the book *Shaᶜar ha-Shamayim* Ascribed to Abraham ibn Ezra," pp. 277–295, in which I have established Laṭif's authorship of this much-discussed work. This work will be cited as *Short SH.*

(b) A commentary on Kohelet n.p., n.d.

(c) *Rab Peᶜalim*, ed. A. Jellinek, in *Kokbe Yiẓḥaḳ*, 25:7–14 (1860), and also by S. Schoenblum (Lemberg, 1885).

(d) *ʾIggeret Teshuba*, ed. A. Berliner, *Ḳobeẓ ᶜal-Yad* (Berlin, 1885), pp. 46–70. Parts of it have also been published in *Ha-Teḥiyya*, 2:50–64 (1857).

Laṭif mentions in his writings the following works which, apparently, have been lost: *Sefer Toledot Adam;* a commentary on the Book of Job; and a commentary on *Sefer Yeẓira.* Two alleged passages from Laṭif's commentary on *Sefer Yeẓira* are cited by Moses Boṭarel. Cf. Boṭarel's commentary on *Sefer Yeẓira* (Mantua, 1568), pp. 71a, 82b.

12. Cf. his introduction to *Minḥat Yehuda*, a commentary on *Maᶜareket ha-Elohut* (Ferrara, 1558), p. 4b.

The fact that Laṭif takes an intermediate stand between philosophy and Kabbala, and tries to formulate his own unique synthesis of the two, at a time when Kabbala was taking its first halting steps in Spain, obviously holds great interest for the historian. Yet to this day no serious attempt has been made to clarify Laṭif's theories or to determine his position in medieval Jewish thought, with the sole exception of David Neumark's treatment of Laṭif in his *History of Jewish Philosophy.*[13]

Neumark, however, had a unique theory of the history of Jewish mysticism. Unlike Graetz, who viewed Spanish Kabbala as a reaction to the radical rationalism fostered by Maimonides and his disciples, Neumark held Kabbala to be the product of a certain dialectical tension, fomented by an inner struggle, that had developed between the various elements of Judaism itself. The general medieval aim of interpreting the fundamental concepts of Judaism had led, on the one hand, to rationalism, as crystallized in the schools of Jewish philosophy, and, on the other hand, through an inner dialectic, to an opposite trend, which instead emphasized the mythic elements. In other words, the same developments that had given birth to Jewish philosophy also engendered, by a concomitant process, Jewish mysticism.[14] Spanish Kabbala, then, a "secret parallel" to philosophy, was, according to Neumark, a "latter-day return to *Merkabah* mysticism,"[15] involving the translation of philosophical terminology to the realm of myth. Neumark was convinced that he had succeeded in exposing the details of the stratification of this process, through his analysis of certain literary documents, which, in his opinion, clearly revealed the transition from philosophical to Kabbalistic perceptions.[16] He accordingly conceived of Isaac Ibn Laṭif as being one of the mainstays of the Spanish Kabbala.[17]

However, the specific Kabbalistic doctrines with which Neumark invests Ibn Laṭif are not to be found in the latter's writings. According

13. Cf. *Toledot ha-Pilosofia be-Yisrael*, I (New York, 1921), 186–192, 288–300. See also S. Sachs' remarks in *Ha-Teḥiyya*, 1:63–65; 2:50–64.

14. Cf. *Toledot ha-Pilosofia be-Yisrael*, I, 166–354.

15. *Ibid.*, pp. ix, 167.

16. *Ibid.*, pp. 166–354. Even though Neumark's conclusions from his analysis of the literary documents do not bear historical investigation—as was demonstrated by Gershom G. Scholem—and his rather rationalistic approach to Jewish mysticism cannot explain the development of some of the basic concepts of Kabbala, one should not underestimate the depth of his perception, as indeed Scholem himself points out in his *Reshit ha-Kabbala* (Jerusalem, 1948), pp. 9–11.

17. *Toledot ha-Pilosofia be-Yisrael*, I, 186–192.

to Neumark, Spanish Kabbala is based upon four fundamental doctrines—the theory of the primordial point, the science of the combination of letters, the doctrine of primordial man, and the principle of sexual union in creation.[18] These four doctrines, according to Neumark, are clearly evident in Laṭif's writings.[19] In fact, however, Laṭif ignores altogether the doctrine of primordial man, practically never makes use of the science of the combination of letters, and utterly rejects sexual symbolism. Neumark's contention, finally, that Laṭif's *Ginzē ha-Melek* is "in literary form the closest signpost to the *Zohar*"[20] is completely groundless.

What were in fact Isaac ibn Laṭif's Kabbalistic and philosophical doctrines? Where does he take his place in the history of medieval Jewish thought? These are the questions we shall attempt to answer in the present paper.

We think it best for this purpose to analyze Laṭif's literary sources, both philosophical and mystic.

Philosophical Sources

Greek Sources

Isaac ibn Laṭif mentions the names of two Greek philosophers, Plato and Aristotle. In contrast to Maimonides[21]—who had little use for Plato but held Aristotle in high esteem—Laṭif's attitude toward Plato is, to a certain extent, favorable, while toward Aristotle he is openly and sharply critical.

Laṭif refers to a Platonic doctrine according to which "God looks at the world of the intellects and thus causes existence [the universe] to emanate therefrom."[22] This is probably a reference to the dictum in the *Timaeus* concerning the model imitated by the demiurge.[23] Laṭif notes the resemblance of this Platonic idea to a dictum of the

18. *Ibid.*, p. 182.
19. *Ibid.*, pp. 186–192.
20. *Ibid.*, p. 299.
21. Cf. Maimonides' letter to Samuel ibn Tibbon, ed. A. Marx, *JQR*, N.S., 25:378–380 (1935). See also S. Pines' introduction to *The Guide of the Perplexed* (Chicago, 1963), pp. lix-lxi, lxxv.
22. *ZH*, chap. 14:

אלא שמצינו מאמר לאפלטון להשיג אל מה שלמעלה מעיונו והוא אמר שהאל ית' יעיין בעולם השכלים וישפיע ממנו המציאות.

23. Cf. 28a ff.

Jewish rabbis, "The Holy One, blessed be He, does nothing without first contemplating the *Pamalya* [Host] above."[24]

Now, this analogic relationship between the words of Plato and this particular rabbinic dictum had already been noticed by Maimonides,[25] and one may well assume that the *Guide* was Laṭif's immediate source. Laṭif—who goes on to interpret this, as well as similar rabbinic dicta,[26] in the light of the theory of emanation—contends that Plato and the Greek philosophers following him had in fact borrowed the doctrine of emanation from Jewish secret lore.[27] But, Laṭif maintains, Plato did not realize the full significance of his own perceptions, as he posited matter to be pre-existent;[28] whereas other Greek philosophers were misled into believing that the process of emanation is a necessary, rather than a voluntary, activity.[29] Laṭif puts in Plato's mouth a statement confessing his inability to understand the Torah: "Said Plato: 'We are unable to understand the words of the Torah, we know but little, while much is misapprehended.'"[30] As the close similarity of the text clearly indicates,

24. *SH*, *Shaᶜar*, I, folio 21a:

וכענין זה עצמו מצינו מאמר לחכמים ז"ל מוסכם עם דברי קצת הפילוסופים הידועים ממקומותיהם שהאל מסתכל בעולם השכלים שהם המלאכים והוא אמרם אין הב"ה עושה דבר עד שמסתכל בפמליא של מעלה.

It should be noted that the origin of this Talmudic quotation is unknown. A similar dictum, however, is to be found in *Sanhedrin* (BT 38b, JT 80a): "The holy one, blessed be He, does nothing without first consulting the Pamalya above."

25. Cf. *Guide*, II, 6.

26. He quotes in this context *Tanḥuma* on Gen. 1:1 (ed. Buber, p. 4), and *Pirke de-Rabbi Eliezer*, 3. He does not, however, quote the famous dictum in *Gen. Rabba* 1:1. Cf. *SH*, I, f. 21a–22b. As to the parallels to be found between these midrashim and Plato's thought, see Theodor on *Gen. R.* 1:1 (Berlin, 1913), p. 2. Cf. also H. A. Wolfson, *Philo*, I (Cambridge, Mass., 1948), pp. 243, 268; F. Baer, "Ha-Yesodot ha-historiyim shel ha-Halaka," *Ẓion*, 17:1–55 (1952); *Idem*, "Ha-Hasidim ha-rishonim be-kitbe Philon u-ba-masoret ha-ᶜibrit," *Ẓion*, 18:91–108 (1953).

27. *ẒH*, 14:

מכלל מה שאנו צריכין להתבונן בו הוא במקצת דברים מוגנבים אצל קצת מן הפילוסופים היחידים לומדי העיון ומכללם אפלטון ולאיזה מקום הגיעם עיונם אלא שרואים ואינם יודעים מה הם רואים.

As to the spiritual kinship between Plato's thought and Kabbala compare also Joseph del Medigo's statement in his *Maẓref le-Ḥokma* (Odessa, 1865), p. 84:

ובפרט אפלטון רבו של ארסטוט' שדעותיו כמעט הן דעות חכמי ישראל ובכמה דברים נראה שדבר כפי המקובלים ובלשונם.

28. *ẒH*, 14:

אלא שמצינו מאמר לאפלטון כנוגע ואינו נוגע להשיג אל מה שלמעלה מעיונו והוא אמר שהאל ית' יעיין בעולם השכלים וישפיע ממנו המציאות. וכמה סתרי סתרים גנוזים במאמר זה אילו יבין ואחר ידבר וכבר נתפרסם דעתו ג"כ במציאות חמר קדמון.

29. *SH*, III, f. 55b:

אלא שמשכם הטועה בקבלתו או המוטעה להבינו על דרך החיוב.

30. *Ibid.*, f. 62a:

אמר אפלטון אין בנו יכולת להבין דברי התורה ואין אנו יודעים מהם אלא מעט ונסכל הרבה.

Laṭif borrowed Plato's alleged statement from the *Kitāb al-Ḥadāʾiḳ*[31] by the Andalusian philosopher Abu Muhamad ibn al-Sīd al-Baṭalyawsi (1052–1127). Laṭif must, however, have made his own translation of the text, as indeed was his practice in all Arabic texts which he cited.[32] It may be added that both Simeon Duran and Joḥanan Alemanno quote this very statement, the latter explicitly ascribing it to al-Baṭalyawsi.[33]

In speaking of the goals of philosophy, Laṭif approvingly adduces the following definition attributed to Plato: "The aim of philosophy is assimilation to the works of God according to human capacity."[34] This ideal of the *imitatio Dei*, which goes back to a passage in Plato's *Theatetus*,[35] and which was used for a definition of philosophy in the Neoplatonic commentaries on Aristotle, was well known to the Arabs.[36] As is indicated by A. Altmann, one meets this definition in the writings of al-Kindī, al-Fārābī, al-Baṭalyawsi, in the Epistles of the Ikhwān, and other Islamic authors.[37] Among Jewish authors, it occurs in the writings of Philo,[38] Isaac Israeli,[39] Moses ibn Ezra,[40]

31. Hebrew version by Moses ibn Tibbon, *Sefer ha-ᶜAgulot ha-Raᶜayoniyot*, ed. D. Kaufmann (Budapest, 1880), p. 16:
אמר אפלטון אנחנו לואים להבין מה שבא בתורות על ידי הנביאים ואמנם נדע ממנו מעט ונסכל הרבה.
The Arabic original was published by M. Asín Palacios in *Al-Andalus*, 5:63–68 (1940); Spanish translation: *ibid.*, pp. 99–154.

32. See, e.g., below, Page 195, where Laṭif admittedly offers his own translation of Moses ibn Ezra's *Kitāb al-Ḥadīḳa*. See also below, Pages 195–200 (Arabic Sources), Page 191, Note 43.

33. Cf. *Magen Abot* (Leghorn, 1785), p. 26; *Shaᶜar ha-Ḥesheḳ* (Leghorn, 1717), p. 51a:
כמו טולמיוס בשם אפלטון באמרו אנחנו לואים מהבין מה שבא בתורות על ידי הנביאים ואמנם נדע ממנו מעט ונסכל הרבה.
Cf. D. Kaufmann, *Die Spuren al-Baṭlajusis in der jüdischen Religionsphilosophie* (Budapest, 1880), pp. 55, 57.

34. *SH*, f. 62a:

גדר הפילוסופיה הדמות פעולות האל ית' בהשגת האדם.

In another context (*ibid.*, f. 69b) Laṭif quotes this definition in the name of the early philosophers:

שהקדמונים מהם שמו גדר הפילוסופיאה ההדמות בפעולות השם ית'.

35. Cf. 176b.

36. See F. Rosenthal, "On the Knowledge of Plato's Philosophy in the Islamic World," *Islamic Culture* (1940) pp. 387–422; A. Altmann and S. Stern, *Isaac Israeli* (Oxford, 1958), p. 197. See also J. Guttmann, *Die philosophischen Lehren des Isaak ben Salomon Israeli* (Münster, 1911), p. 21, n. 1.

37. See Altmann-Stern, *Isaac Israeli*, p. 197, notes 2–5.

38. Cf. H. A. Wolfson, *Philo*, II, 195–196.

39. Cf. *Book of Definitions*, § 2, lines 15–16; published in Altmann-Stern, *Isaac Israeli*, p. 24; *Sefer ha-Ḥibbur*, ed. H. Hirschfeld, in *Festschrift zum 80. Geburtstag M. Steinschneiders* (Leipzig, 1896), p. 132, line 16. The text of the anonymous Hebrew translation of the *Book of Definitions*, found in the Leningrad MS. and published by A. Altmann, is very similar to that of Laṭif. Cf. A. Altmann, "Isaac Israeli: Some Fragments of a Second Hebrew Translation," *JJS*, 2:237 (1957).

40. *ᶜArugat ha-Bosem*, *Ẓion*, 2:121 (Frankfurt am Main, 1842–43).

and Joseph ibn Ṣaddiḳ.[41] Hence, Laṭif may have known of this definition from a variety of sources. However, in view of the similarity of Laṭif's text to that of Israeli,[42] and of Laṭif's explicit dependence of Israeli's *Book of Definitions* in another case—that is, in the definition of nonexistence[43]—it is very likely that Israeli's *Book of Definitions* was his immediate source. Laṭif goes on to explain that this ideal of the *imitatio Dei* is in fact the command of Jewish religion as well.[44]

Plato comes up again in Laṭif's treatment of the role of moral perfection in philosophy. Thus he ascribes to Plato the statement, which he clearly borrowed from al-Baṭalyawsi, that whoever wishes to become a philosopher should first achieve moral perfection: "Said Plato, 'The impure man is not able to acquire pure philosophy, just as a man can not see his face in a rusty mirror or muddied water.' "[45]

In his treatment, however, of the problem of creation, Laṭif rejects the theory attributed to Plato, according to which the world was created in time, out of pre-existent matter, and insists rather on creation *ex nihilo*.[46]

Laṭif, then, knew Plato at second hand, through the medieval Neoplatonists; Aristotle, however, he cites directly from Arabic versions.

Laṭif maintains a critical attitude toward Aristotle. He declares

41. *Sefer ᶜOlam Ḳaṭan* (Breslau, 1903), p. 68.

42. See above, Note 39. Laṭif must have made, however, his own translation of the Arabic text. See below, Note 43.

43. Cf. *SH*, I, f. 27a; *Book of Definitions*, § 43, lines 5–7, 10–11; *Sefer ha-Ḥibbur*, p. 140, lines 31–34; Cf. also the passage quoted by S. Fried in his introduction to Israeli's *Sefer ha-Yesodot* (Drohobycz, 1900), p. 47. Altmann had noted that Laṭif quoted § 43 of the *Book of Definitions* in a form which followed neither the first nor the second Hebrew translation and surmised that Laṭif must have made "an ad hoc translation of the passage quoted." See his article "Isaac Israeli's Book of Definitions: Some Fragments," pp. 235–236. This conclusion is reinforced by our analysis of Laṭif's treatment of his Arabic sources. Thus, his quotations from Maimonides' *Guide* follow neither Ibn Tibbon's nor al-Ḥarizi's translations. Cf., e.g., his quotation from the *Guide* in IT, 20, *Ḳobeẓ al-Yad* (Berlin, 1885), p. 55, and of the last paragraph of the introduction to the *Guide*. Similarly, Laṭif's quotations from Ibn Ṣaddiḳ's *ᶜOlam Ḳatan* and Halevi's *Kuzari* do not correspond to the Hebrew translations of these works. See also above, Note 32; below, Notes 99, 100.

44. On the principle of *imitatio Dei* in Judaism see S. Schechter, *Some Aspects of Rabbinic Theology*, pp. 199ff.; G. F. Moore, *Judaism*, I, 441; II, 110ff, 172ff.; A. Marmorstein, *Studies in Jewish Theology* (London, 1950), pp. 106ff.; Wolfson, *Philo*, II, 195; Altmann-Stern, *Isaac Israeli*, pp. 197–198.

45. *SH*, f. 62a:
אפלטון אמר לא יוכל הרוצה לקנות הפילוסופיה הטהורה איש אשר הוא טמא כאשר לא יוכל האדם לראות פניו במראה שהעלתה חלודה ולא במים עכורים.
Cf. *Sefer Ha-ᶜAgulot ha-Raᶜayoniyot*, p. 15.

46. Cf. *SH*, I, f. 18b.

it is his duty to remove the "veil" before the eyes of the "multitude of philosophers" who follow Aristotle to the point of claiming that his theories are infallible.[47] Laṭif thus devotes a large number of chapters in his *Shaᶜar ha-Shamayim* to a refutation of Aristotelian physics and metaphysics, attacking both Aristotle and his followers with the philosophical means at his disposal.

We do not intend at this time to go into the details of Laṭif's rather involved critique of Aristotle.[48] But it might be noted here that Laṭif to a certain degree marks the beginning of the anti-Aristotelian trend which culminates in the philosophy of Ḥasdai Crescas.[49] Particularly interesting in this connection is the criticism leveled by Laṭif against the doctrine of the motion of the spheres, entertained by medieval Aristotelian philosophers. It is scarcely necessary here to give the history of this doctrine or of those who opposed it.[50] Let us merely point out Laṭif's general stand on this question.

According to the view that Laṭif ascribes to Aristotle, the spheres are beings endowed with soul and intellect.[51] As in all animate beings, the principle of their motion is their soul, and their motion is therefore to be called "voluntary," differing from the motion of sublunar elements, which is called "natural" motion. Now Laṭif contends that this opinion of Aristotle is merely an "unproved assertion."[52] As against Aristotle, Laṭif argues in favor of the view which maintains that the motion of the spheres is natural motion.[53]

47. Cf. *SH*, I, chaps. 3, 5–6, 12–13. See also introduction to *ZH*, p. 3.

48. We propose to offer a detailed analysis of it in our forthcoming book on Laṭif.

49. As to Crescas' refutation of Aristotelian philosophy, see H. A. Wolfson, *Crescas' Critique of Aristotle* (Cambridge, Mass., 1929). This work will be cited as *Crescas*.

50. As to the various opinions on the motion of the spheres in Greek and medieval philosophy, see Guthrie's introduction to Aristotle's *On the Heavens*, The Loeb Classical Library (Cambridge, Mass., 1939), pp. xxix–xxxvi; Werner Jaeger, *Aristotle* (Oxford, 1934), pp. 148ff., 345ff.; Wolfson, *Philo*, I, 336–338, 417–418; *Crescas*, pp. 77–78, 236, 273, 535–538.

51. Cf. *SH*, I, chaps. 3, 12. See *De caelo*, II, 2, 285a, 29; II, 12, 292b, 29. Aristotle, however (as noted by many scholars), speaks also of the heavenly bodies as being moved naturally, without a soul. See *De caelo*, I, 2, 269a, 5–7. On the development of this view in Aristotle see Jaeger, *Aristotle*, pp. 153ff., 346ff.; Guthrie, *On the Heavens*, pp. xxix-xxxvi.

52. *SH*, I, 12, f. 26a.

53. Needless to say, this view was not original with Laṭif. Al-Ghazālī, as is well known, devoted an entire chapter to it in his *Tahāfut al Falāsifa* (ed. M. Bouyges, Beirut, 1927, chap. xiv, pp. 239–246). Laṭif does not mention al-Ghazālī's work, and the question may be raised as to whether he was acquainted with it. No certain answer can be given to it, but the possibilities are that he must have read it. Among medieval Jewish philosophers the view that the motion of the spheres is natural was held by Saᶜadia (*Emunot we-Deᶜot*, I, 5 (8); Halevi (*Kuzari*, IV, 1); Crescas (*Or Adonai*, I, 1:6; IV, 3); Isaac ᶜArama (see my *Issac ᶜArama u-Mishnato ha-Pilosofit*, Jerusalem, 1956, pp. 113–116), and Isaac Abravanel

Laṭif contends that there is no need to explain the motion of the spheres by a psychic principle, or soul. He argues that one may explain the motion of the spheres purely in terms of a physical force, the principles of which are similar to those of "magnetic attraction."[54] A magnet possesses a certain "power" which "attracts" iron and "causes it to move without the magnet itself being moved."[55] Similarly, the spheres may be described as naturally moving in a given direction as if pulled by the force of "magnetic attraction."[56]

Indeed, one cannot help noticing in this context the striking parallel between Laṭif's contentions that the motion of the spheres is natural and should be included in the category of magnetic attraction, and Crescas' similar contentions in his *Or Adonai*.[57] Whether there is any literary connection between Laṭif and Crescas, or whether they both followed a common source, we are not in a position to say. In any case, if Laṭif did not influence Crescas, he certainly anticipated him here. Laṭif's theory on the motion of the spheres had evidently influenced Isaac ᶜArama and Isaac Abravanel. They both quote approvingly Laṭif's arguments, whereas ᶜArama complains (incorrectly) that he found no support for this view among Jewish philosophers.[58] It may be added that Laṭif's interpretation of the nature of magnetic attraction itself as a "certain force communicated to the air which is in contact with the iron" is evidently based directly on the *Guide*[59] and represents the general view of the Atomists.[60]

In his criticism of Aristotle's theory of the eternity of the world, Laṭif contends, in agreement with Maimonides, that Aristotle's proof does not have a force of a demonstration.[61] In refutation of

---

(*Mifᶜalot Elohim*, III, 3), whereas the view that the motion of the spheres is voluntary was held by Ibn Daud (*Emuna Rama*, I, 8); Maimonides (*More Nebukim*, II, 5), and Gersonides (*Milḥamot Adonai*, V, 3, 6). Cf. also *Crescas*, p. 538.

54. *SH*, I, 12, f. 25b:
שתהיה תנועת עצמו טבע ולא ציור ולא חשק. ויביא זה החולק ראיה ויקיש מהנמצא אצלנו בזה החמר ההיולי והיא האבן המושכת הנקראת מגניטוס.

55. *Ibid.*

56. Laṭif adds, however, his own explanation for the continuous circular motion of the spheres (*SH*, I, 12, f. 25b). This explanation is quoted verbatim by both Isaac ᶜArama and Abravenal. See my *Isaac ᶜArama*, pp. 54, 114–115.

57. Cf. *Crescas*, pp. 77–92; see also below, Page 194.

58. On account of which he was criticized by J. Moscato in his commentary on the *Kuzari* (*Kol Yehuda ad Kuzari*, IV, 2). See my *Isaac ᶜArama*, pp. 54–55, 114–116. Cf. also *Crescas*, p. 538.

59. See *SH*, I, f. 25b; cf. *Guide*, II, 12.

60. Cf. *Crescas*, p. 563. As to the different views on magnetic attraction found in Greek and medieval philosophy, see *Crescas*, pp. 90–92, 121–122, 255, 257, 565–568.

61. *SH*, I, f. 19a; cf. *Guide*, II, 19, 22.

Aristotle Laṭif reproduces Maimonides' argument from determination,[62] which is based upon the fact of deviations from order and regularity observed in the translunar world. Following Maimonides, Laṭif contends that these deviations could not be satisfactorily explained by a system of necessary causality, but only by the assumption of a free will in God.[63]

However, unlike Maimonides, Laṭif argues against Aristotle's theory of the eternity of the world from the finitude of the universe. Laṭif contends that if the world were indeed eternal, it would also—like God—have to be infinite. Furthermore, there should have been in the universe "an infinite number of worlds, each of them infinite in magnitude."[64] Aristotle, therefore, contradicts himself when he says, on the one hand, that the world is eternal, and on the other hand, that it is finite in magnitude. In this context it is interesting to compare Laṭif's critique of Aristotle to that of Crescas. Whereas Crescas concludes, in contradistinction to Aristotle, that the universe is indeed "an infinite space within which are floating an infinite number of worlds,"[65] the purpose of this argument in Laṭif is to establish the creation of the world on the basis of Aristotle's own principle of the finitude of the universe. Laṭif uses it rather as an argument to prove that God acts by free will, which ultimately leads him to disprove the eternity of the world. Laṭif notes that although this argument is not original with him, yet he claims to have given it a "deeper meaning" and a "somewhat different formulation."[66] Indeed, in a different (somewhat simplified) version, the argument from the finitude of the universe occurs in Saᶜadia, who in turn borrowed it from the Kalam.[67]

Only once does Laṭif mention Aristotle favorably. In a letter ascribed to Aristotle, Laṭif finds the philosopher expressing a belief in the Messianic Age, when war will cease, and an ideal society will arise, based on righteousness and the love of wisdom. Laṭif quotes the letter from Moses ibn Ezra's *Kitāb al-Ḥadīḳa*, translating it from Arabic into Hebrew. It reads as follows:

62. Cf. *SH*, I, f. 19a; *Guide*, II, 19. For a detailed analysis and history of the argument from determination see H. A. Wolfson, "The Kalam Arguments for Creation," *PAAJR*, pp. 197–244 (1943); "Halevi and Maimonides on Design, Chance and Necessity," *PAAJR*, pp. 105–163 (1941); S. Pines' introduction to the *Guide*, pp. cxxix–cxxx.

63. Cf. *SH*, I, 6; *Guide*, II, 19.

64. *SH*, I, 6, f. 19b.

65. See *Crescas*, p. 118.

66. Cf. *SH*, f. 19b.

67. Cf. Wolfson, "The Kalam Arguments for Creation," pp. 199–203.

I have found an important statement by Rabbi Moses Ibn Ezra, of blessed memory, which he attributes to Aristotle and maintains that he took it from a letter sent to his student Alexander. In the letter, though not in these precise words—I do not presume to claim absolute fidelity to the text since I have it second-hand in any case—the philosopher foresees a great new world composed of one society, with one king and one [social] contract. "In this world, [he says] men will gather together in one accord, war and banishment will cease, and all will agree on pursuing that which is useful for their state and land. Peace and security will encompass mankind. Each day will be divided into two periods, one for the benefit and enjoyment of the body, one for the higher pursuit of wisdom. He who has attained wisdom will continue to pursue it; he who has not, will seek it. My only wish is that I might live to see that day, if not all of it, then at least some of it; but if because of the length of my years it does not prove possible for me to see it, then may it be possible for my loved ones and friends, and if not for them, then for those like them in future times." This is the essence of the letter. Would that I knew how some spirit of God passed from us to speak to him. For he himself testifies in several places that he had not attained the rank of prophecy.[68]

Arabic Sources

Laṭif explicitly refers in his writings to Abū Naṣr al-Fārābī,[69] whom he held in the highest esteem. Laṭif follows al-Fārābī in his theories on the nature and function of prophecy and the purpose of the Ideal (Virtuous) City. It is interesting to note in this connection that, unlike Maimonides, Laṭif most often cites al-Fārābī's political writings: namely, those very works which are not cited explicitly in the *Guide* by Maimonides, although it is quite evident that they had influenced him.[70] Laṭif's quotations from al-Fārābī come principally from the *Al-Madina al-Faḍila* (*The Virtuous City*).[71]

68. *SH*, III, f. 61a. This passage is not included in the Hebrew selections of Moses ibn Ezra's *ʿArugat ha-Bosem*, published in *Ẓion*, 2:117–123, 157–159, 175 (Frankfurt am Main, 1842–43). However, another reference to the same passage occurs in Menaḥem ben Zeraḥ's *Ẓeda la-Derek* (Lemberg, 1859), p. 144a. It may be added that L. Dukes (*Literaturblatt des Orient*, 8:406–407 [1847] quotes few lines of this letter and ascribes it (incorrectly) to Laṭif's *Rab Peʿalim.*

69. At times he is referred to explicitly as החכם הפילוסוף אבונצר and otherwise as החכם הפילוסוף הישמעאלי. Although it seems quite certain that Laṭif was also well acquainted with al-Baṭalyawsi's *Kitāb al-Ḥadāʾiḳ*, he nowhere refers to this author's name. As to the question whether he was acquainted with al-Ghazālī's *Tahāfut al Falāsifa*, see, above, Note 53. Avicenna is referred to in Laṭif's *ʾIggeret Teshuba* (*Kobez ʿal-Yad*, I, 48). However, Avicenna's name (Hebrew: Ben Sina) is misprinted as Ben Sira. As was noted by G. Scholem, this typographical error led to the association of Avicenna with the Golem of Ben Sira. Cf. *Ẓur Kabbala und ihrer Symbolik* (Zurich, 1960), p. 288, n. 77.

70. See L. Strauss, "Quelques remarques sur la science politique de Maïmonide et de Fārābī," *REJ* (1936), pp. 1–37; S. Pines' introduction to the *Guide*, p. lxxxvi.

71. Ed. F. Dieterici (Leiden, 1895).

Indeed, two whole chapters of Laṭif's *Shaᶜar ha-Shamayim* consist of his translation of selected passages from that work.[72] In these chapters Laṭif presents al-Fārābī's views on the "Virtuous City" and its opposites; "Said he: the virtuous city has its opposites and these are the ignorant city and the unrighteous city. Indeed he mentioned as opposites other cities which we need not refer to here."[73]

In al-Fārābī's *The Virtuous City* the main types of divergence from the "Virtuous City" are the "Ignorant City," the "Unrighteous City," the "Misguided City," and the "Altered City."[74] The last two, then, are the "other cities" referred to by Laṭif in the paragraph quoted above. The "Ignorant City" does not know the true good, and so puts false goods in its place; the "Unrighteous City" knows the true good but refuses to follow it; the "Misguided City" has a distorted view of the good, and the "Altered City" formerly held a true view of the good but abandoned it.[75] Indeed al-Fārābī records these four types consistently as the opposites of his "Virtuous City,"[76] although his conception of the "Virtuous City" itself is given to changes and variations.

Laṭif cites in al-Fārābī's name the following concept of the "Virtuous [Ideal] City":

> Let me return now to the statement of the wise philosopher as I promised. I state that man's perception of axiomatic truths constitutes his first [stage of intellectual] perfection. These axiomatic truths were given to him to use in order that he shall attain final perfection. Namely, [at that state] man's soul would be so perfect that it would no longer have need of its attachment to the body, but would belong to that class of beings which is separate from matter, and would remain so, a degree below the active intellect . . . And the city which strives to attain this end, and is familiar with the means of achieving it, is what this philosopher has called the Virtuous City.[77]

This is a rather interesting passage in view of the contention made by Averroes and Ibn Bājja that according to al-Fārābī man cannot

72. Cf. *Shaᶜar*, I, chaps. 27–28.
73. *SH*, I, f. 31b.
74. Cf. *Al-Madina al-Faḍila*, ed. Dieterici, pp. 61–63.
75. Cf. *SH*, I, f. 37b–38a.
76. Cf. *Al-Madina*, pp. 61–63.
77. *SH*, I, f. 37b. I was not able to find the precise reference for this quotation in the extant text of al-Fārābī's *Al-Madina*. However, in the *Risala fil-ᶜaql* (ed. M. Bouyges, Beirut, 1938, p. 31, lines 11–12), al-Fārābī states that when man reaches the highest perfection his soul becomes "one of the things separate from bodies and one of immaterial substances" and that at that state the acquired intellect does not need the bodily organs for its operation.

be united with the active intellect.[78] On the other hand, this passage seems to be opposed to the view attributed to al-Fārābī by Ibn Ṭufayl that the highest perfection possible to man is to be found in the life of practical action, rather than in the life of thought.[79] According to Laṭif, however, al-Fārābī considers the purpose of the "Ideal City" as perfecting the intellect of its members and guiding them toward intellectual perfection.

Al-Fārābī, as had already been said by many scholars, chose Plato's *Republic*, instead of Aristotle's *Ethics*, as a textbook of political theory—a deliberate choice which was of "crucial importance for the whole course of medieval Arabic and Jewish philosophy."[80] Thus he introduced Plato's idea that organized society must be governed by philosopher-kings. Laṭif reproduces al-Fārābī's conception of the "perfect man," the philosopher-prophet, who ought to be the ideal ruler of the ideal state. Laṭif also quotes, almost verbatim, the twelve innate physical, moral and intellectual qualities, which, according to al-Fārābī, the ideal ruler, the philosopher-prophet, must possess.[81] These twelve qualities, according to Laṭif, are physical perfection, courage, intellectual perception, superior memory, superior imagination, love of wisdom, excellence in persuasion, humility, rejection of bodily pleasures, love of justice, knowledge of the art of ruling, ability to guide men to happiness.[82] Following al-Fārābī,

78. See Averroes, *Commentarium Magnum in Aristotleis "De Anima Libros"* (Cambridge, Mass., 1953), pp. 433, 481, 485, 502. Cf. also S. Pines' introduction to the *Guide*, p. lxxx. Pines notes that Ibn Bājja attacked al-Fārābī for his refusal to admit the possibility of man's union with the active intellect. As to the stand on this question, taken by al-Fārābī, who seemed to have expressed various contradictory views on this problem, see the passage quoted by S. Munk, *Mélanges de philosophie juive et arabe* (Paris, 1859), p. 348, n. 3, and by M. Steinschneider, *Al-Farabi* (St. Petersburg, 1869), p. 102. See also F. Rahman, *Prophecy in Islam* (London, 1958), p. 24; R. Walzer, "Al-Farabi's Theory of Prophecy and Divination," *Greek into Arabic* (Cambridge, Mass., 1962), pp. 206ff.; S. Pines' introduction to the *Guide*, pp. lxxx–lxxxii. Pines concludes that there is no valid answer to this problem and suggests that the contradictions may be due to an evolution in al-Fārābī's thought.

79. According to Ibn Ṭufayl (*Ḥayy ibn Yaḳẓan* [Beirut, 1936], p. 14) al-Fārābī declared that happiness exists in this life and made the statement that "everything else that is spoken of is [nothing but] drivel and old-wives' tales." Laṭif makes a similar statement in answer to a question pertaining to the immortality of the soul:

וכמה נתבלבלו הפילוסופים בענינו עד שאבונצר אלפארבי גזר אומר שהוא כהבלי הטפשות.

Cf. ᵓ*Iggeret Teshuba*, *Ḳobeẓ ᶜal-Yad*, p. 51.

80. See S. Pines' introduction to the *Guide*, p. lxxxvii.

81. *SH*, I, f. 32b–33a. Cf. *al-Madina*, 59–60. R. Walzer notes that al-Fārābī actually borrowed his twelve qualities, as he himself reports, from Plato's *Republic* (vi, 1) and merely arranged them in a more systematic manner. See Walzer's "Platonism in Islamic Philosophy," *Greek into Arabic*, p. 245.

82. Cf. *SH*, I, f. 32b–33a. Laṭif notes that these twelve qualities are actually included in the three conditions of prophecy stated by the rabbis (BT *Shabbath* 92a; *Nedarim*, 38a):

Laṭif does not distinguish between the innate qualities and the conditions for prophecy.

In his treatment of the nature and function of prophecy Laṭif follows al-Fārābī,[83] with a certain modification introduced by al-Baṭalyawsi on one hand and Maimonides on the other. Thus he maintains that "every prophet is also a philosopher, but no philosopher is a prophet."[84] The essential difference between the two is to be found in the fact that the prophet, unlike the philosopher, is endowed with a powerful imagination. The faculty of imagination is intermediate between perception and reason, and enables the prophet to "see" metaphysical truths in a visible form, translating, as it were, metaphysical truths into symbols. With the help of the faculty of imagination, the prophet is able to see the future.[85] When the imagination reaches its peak, there is a further flow from the rational faculty to the imaginative faculty, and that faculty is connected with the active intellect as well. Hence, Laṭif states that "the more one's faculty of imagination is perfected, provided one reaches the highest intellectual perfection as well, the more one is able to divine the future."[86] The activity of the imagination comes into play mostly in sleep and dreams, but also in waking life. Laṭif quotes al-Fārābī's classification of the three classes of prophecy.[87] The first class divine in waking, the second, partly in sleep and partly in waking. The lowest class divine in sleep and communicate their experience in symbolic and allegorical expressions.

Laṭif, however, introduces another essential distinction between the philosopher and the prophet. Drawing upon al-Baṭalyawsi's *Kitāb al Ḥadāʾiḳ*, Laṭif reproduces the following classification of the five faculties of the soul—"vegetative," "animate," "rational,"

"prophecy rests only upon a wise, strong and rich man." Cf. *Guide*, II, 32. It may be added that in his *Fuṣul al-Madanī* (ed. Dunlop, Cambridge, 1962, p. 54) al-Fārābī speaks only of six conditions which must be fulfilled in the ideal ruler. They differ somewhat from the twelve qualities of the ideal ruler given in the *Al-Madina* (59–60) and quoted by Laṭif.

83. As to al-Fārābī's theory of prophecy, see Walzer, "Al-Farabi's Theory of Prophecy and Divination," *Greek into Arabic*, pp. 206–220; Rahman, *Prophecy in Islam;* S. Pines' introduction to the *Guide*, pp. lxxviii–scii.

84. *SH*, I, f. 33a.

85. *Ibid.*, f. 32b–33a. A similar conception of the relationship between the prophetic faculty and that of imagination occurs in Isaac Israeli. See Altmann-Stern, *Isaac Israeli*, pp. 135ff.

86. *SH*, I, f. 33b.

87. *Ibid.*

"philosophical," and "prophetic."[88] Following al-Baṭalyawsi, Laṭif explains the difference between the "philosophical" and the "rational" soul as the difference between the intellectual, or speculative, part of the soul: that is, theoretical reason, and the practical.[89] Attempting to define the nature of the last two souls, Laṭif differentiates between two kinds of knowledge—intellectual knowledge derived by cogitation and investigation, and intuitive knowledge, which knows without cogitation and investigation. Drawing upon al-Baṭalyawsi, Laṭif further defines intuitive knowledge as the knowledge of the soul, which "contains the truth within itself,"[90] whereas the knowledge of the philosophical soul is discursive. Hence, he maintains that the difference between philosophical and prophetic knowledge is like the one between acquired and intuitive knowledge.[91] However, Laṭif seems to deem it necessary that prophetic illumination

88. *Ibid.*, f. 32a:
הפילוסופים... אמרו כי הם חמשה קראום נפש צומחת ונפש חיה ונפש מדברת ונפש פילוסופית ונפש נבואית.
Cf. *Sefer ha-ᶜAgulot ha-Raᶜayoniyot*, ed. D. Kaufmann (Budapest, 1880), p. 8. Professor A. Berman mentioned to me that a similar classification occurs in the *Epistles* of the *Ikhwān al-Ṣafāᶜ*; see Dieterici, *Die Abhandlungen der Ichwan Es-Safa in Auswahl* (Leipzig, 1886), pp. 406ff., 413–414. One meets a five-fold classification of the soul, albeit a different one, in the writings of al-Fārābī: "The main parts and faculties of the soul are five: the nutritive, sensory, imaginative, appetitive, and rational." (See *The Aphorisms of the Statesman*, trans. D. M. Dunlop, p. 29). In the Hebrew version of al-Fārābī's *Siyasa al-Madaniya* the following five-fold classification of the soul is found:
וזה כי כחות הנפש האנושית חמש המדברת העיונית והמדברת המעשית המתעוררת המדמה והמרגשת.
Cf. *Sefer ha-Hateḥalot: Sefer ha-Asif* (Leipzig, 1849), p. 35. It is noteworthy that a five-fold classification of the soul occurs also in the writings of the Kabbalists of Gerona (see *Perush ha-Agadot le Rabbi ᶜAzriel*, ed. J. Tishby, Jerusalem, 1945, p. 19; *Perush ha-Agadot le-R. ᶜEzra*, MS. Vatican 441, 34a).

89. See *SH*, I, f. 32a: *Sefer ha-ᶜAgulot*, p. 12. Another term used by Laṭif for the "philosophical soul" is *ha-nefesh ha-ḥakama*. The distinction between the rational and the intellectual soul occurs also in the *Zohar*. See Tishby, *Mishnat ha-Zohar*, II (Jerusalem, 1963), p. 33.

90. *SH*, I, f. 32b:
כי השלם בשלמות זו מוצא הדברים השכליים חקוקים בנפשו ואינו צריך לקנות החכמות על ידי הקדמות והיקשים.
Cf. *Sefer ha-ᶜAgulot*, pp. 16–17:
והנפש הזאת לא תצטרך לקנות הידיעות בהיקשים והקדמות... וימצא הדברים השכליים כאלו הם מצויירים בנפשו.
A similar distinction occurs in Gabirol's *Fons Vitae* (ed. C. L. Bäumker, Münster, 1895), III:48; II:3.

91. *SH*, I, f. 32b; cf. *Sefer ha-ᶜAgulot*, p. 17. A. Altmann points out that although Isaac Israeli, too, makes a distinction between two kinds of knowledge—discursive and intuitive—yet "nowhere" does he describe the "difference between philosophy and prophecy as one between acquired and revealed (or intuitive) knowledge." See *Isaac Israeli*, pp. 210–211. According to S. Pines, al-Fārābī denied the possibility of intuitive theoretical knowledge other than knowledge of axiomatic truths. See Pines' introduction to the *Guide*, p. cvi.

be preceded by philosophical speculation. By virtue, then, of his "prophetic soul" the prophet is said to stand on the shoulders of the philosopher and starts where the latter leaves off.

In agreement with al-Fārābī, Laṭif maintains that the prophet is, unlike the philosopher, also a lawgiver, and, for that reason as well, he stands higher than the philosopher.[92] However, following Maimonides, Laṭif insists that although prophecy is a "natural," universal process, depending upon certain human perfections, "God may prevent one from becoming a prophet."[93] Thus, in agreement with Maimonides, he introduces God's Will indirectly into prophecy.

Jewish Sources

Laṭif refers, implicitly and explicitly, to virtually every work written by the Jewish Neoplatonists who preceded him: Isaac Israeli's *Book of Definitions*;[94] Solomon ibn Gabirol's *Fons Vitae*;[95] Moses ibn Ezra's *The Book of the Garden;*[96] Abraham ibn Ezra's commentaries to the Pentateuch;[97] Abraham bar Ḥiyya's *Scroll of the Revealer*;[98] Joseph ibn Ṣaddiḳ's *Microcosm*;[99] and Judah Halevi's *Kuzari.*[100]

Laṭif cites Maimonides quite frequently, referring most often to the *Guide* and the *Mishneh Torah.*[101] He regards Maimonides with the highest esteem and declares himself a faithful disciple of the great philosopher.[102] Nevertheless, Laṭif cannot be regarded as a

92. Cf. *SH*, I, f. 32b; *Al-Madina al-Faḍila*, p. 52.
93. Cf. *SH*, I, f. 33a; *Guide*, II, 32.
94. See *SH*, I, 14, f. 27a. Cf. above, Page 190.
95. See below, Pages 201ff.
96. See above, Pages 194–195.
97. See, e.g., *SH*, f. 47a; commentary on Kohelet, p. 18a.
98. See below, Page 218.
99. Laṭif quotes rather extensively from Ibn Ṣaddiḳ's *ᶜOlam Ḳatan*, without, however, referring to its author by name. Cf. S. Sachs, *Ha-Teḥiyya*, 1:64; A. Jellinek's introduction to *ᶜOlam Ḳatan* (Leipzig, 1854); S. Horovitz, *ᶜOlam Ḳaṭan* (Breslau, 1903), p. 2. I have indicated some of the parallel passages (which deal with the difficulties presented by Gabirol's theory of the will) in my "The Problem of the Authorship . . .," *Tarbiz*, pp. 285–286, nn. 46–50.
100. *ᵓIggeret ha-Teshuba*, 25 (*Ḳobeẓ ᶜal-Yad*, p. 57). Laṭif disapprovingly quotes the *Kuzari* (I, 109) in answer to the question as to why belief in the immortality of the soul was not mentioned in Scripture. S. Sachs has pointed out the discrepancy between Laṭif's quotation of the *Kuzari* and Ibn Tibbon's version. Cf. *Ha-Teḥiyya*, 2:63–64. Laṭif's own answer to this problem is:

ובעבור זה לא הזכירה התורה ענין נפלא לפי שידעה שאין כח המון לקבלה.

Joseph Albo refers to this answer in his *ᶜIḳḳarim*, iv, 39.
101. It should be noted that Laṭif refers to Maimonides' Code by the title *Mishneh Torah.* See, e.g., *SH*, f. 54a.
102. See his introduction to *SH*, f. 14b.

disciple of Maimonides, nor does he belong to the general Aristotelian trend. We may perhaps state here, at the risk of oversimplification, that Laṭif follows Maimonides whenever the latter, knowingly or not, takes a Platonic or Neoplatonic stand.[103]

Of the Jewish philosophers after Maimonides, Laṭif refers to Samuel ibn Tibbon as a contemporary[104] and takes issue with the latter's theory of creation.[105] As his philosophic terminology would indicate, Laṭif was familiar with the Hebrew translations of the *Guide* made by Samuel ibn Tibbon and Judah al-Ḥarizi, in many instances preferring the latter to the former.[106]

We wish to analyze here Isaac ibn Laṭif's relationship to one of the above-mentioned sources: namely, to Solomon ibn Gabirol.

Solomon ibn Gabirol, who exerted a decisive influence on Laṭif,[107] particularly in his doctrine of the Will, is explicitly mentioned by Laṭif.[108] Although it seems quite certain that Laṭif knew the *Fons Vitae* in its Arabic original, and borrowed from it not only Gabirol's theory of the Will, but also many of his philosophical doctrines, as

103. Laṭif was influenced by Maimonides in his theories of Divine attributes, providence, and prophecy.

104. Cf. *SH*, I, f. 18b, 27b. It is noteworthy that R. Ezra of Gerona also refers to Ibn Tibbon as a contemporary. Cf. G. Scholem, *Reshit ha-Kabbala*, p. 153, n. 2. It should be added, however, that in Laṭif's commentary on *Kohelet*, which was written after the *SH*, he adds ז"ל after Tibbon's name. Hence, one may assume one of two possibilities: either that Ibn Tibbon had died in the meantime, or that ז"ל is a later addition. Laṭif also quotes Ibn Tibbon's interpretation of the Beloved in the Song of Songs as the active intellect, as does R. Ezra of Gerona. Cf. *Reshit ha-Kabbala*, p. 153, n. 2.

105. See *SH*, I, f. 18b–19a. For Ibn Tibbon's theory of Creation, see G. Vajda, *Recherches sur la philosophie et la Kabbale* (Paris, 1962), pp. 13–31. For Jacob ben Sheshet's critique of Ibn Tibbon's theory of creation see Vajda, pp. 45–55.

106. The following terms, for example, occur in *SH:*
מחויב המציאות, אפשר המציאות, שמות משותפים, שמות מסופקים, גשמות, מופת נחתך, תשומה, שכל קנוי.
The last three terms are peculiar to al-Ḥarīzī, whereas Ibn Tibbon translates them by:
מופת חותך, הנחה, שכל נקנה.
Cf. Ibn Tibbon, *Perush ha-milot ha-zarot;* I. Efros, *The Philosophical Terms of the Moreh Nebukim*, index to Ḥarīzī terms (New York, 1924), pp. 145–149.

107. Although this influence has been pointed out by many scholars (e.g., S. Sachs, *Ha-Teḥiyya*, 2:56, *Kerem Ḥemed*, 9:155; J. Guttmann, *Die Philosophie des Salomon ibn Gabirol* [Göttingen, 1889], p. 46, n. 4; M. Steinschneider, in N. Brill's *Jahrbücher*, IX, 72ff.; D. Kaufmann, *Studien über Salomon ibn Gabirol* [Budapest, 1889], p. 110), no serious attempt has been made to analyze its precise scope and character.

108. He is referred to explicitly as שלמה בעל השירים in *ʾIggeret ha-Teshuba*, 36 (*Ḳobeẓ ʿal-Yad*, I, 64). See also D. Kaufmann, *Studien über Salomon ibn Gabirol*, p. 110, n. 3. Also, implicitly in *Ẓurat ha-ʿOlam*, 6, p. 11:
ואולי סוד זה השם המתואר גם כן בחפץ אל אצל הקדמונים החריפים לוטשי העיון ההקשי החוקרים אל חפץ אמצעי בין החמר והצורה ובין הישות הראשונה.
Cf. also Jacob Guttmann, *Die Philosophie des Salomon ibn Gabirol*, p. 46, n. 4.

well as his analogies, methods of exposition, and usage of language, yet not once does he refer to it by name.

In discussing the influence upon Laṭif of Gabirol's theory of the Will, we must first state a methodological reservation. Gershom Scholem[109] has rightly pointed out that not all doctrines that deal with the Divine Will are evidence of Gabirol's influence. Such influence can be posited only if one succeeds in tracing the specific aspects of this theory from Gabirol to another philosopher. In our case, an analysis of Laṭif's doctrine of the Will does indeed reveal a precise one-to-one correspondence to the specific aspects of this theory as they are found in Gabirol.

Like Gabirol before him, Laṭif introduces the Divine Will as a mediating link between God and the world. The cosmic process, Laṭif contends, is not a necessary and impersonal flow or radiation, but a voluntary activity. Furthermore, like Gabirol, Laṭif identifies the Divine Will with the Divine Word: "The Word with which the world was created was none other than pure Will."[110] Indeed, Laṭif's frequent identification of the Will with the Word of God places his doctrine of the Will in the broad stream of the history of the Philonic *Logos*.[111] Moreover, like Gabirol, Laṭif claims that the Will is the source of all reality, and refers to it as the "fountain of life."[112] In describing the Will Laṭif uses certain pantheistic phrases, which recall the language of *Fons Vitae*. He says, for example, that the Will is the source of all beings, exists in, and pervades all things: "From the will everything emanated . . . for he is everywhere and everything is in him, as written (Isa. 6:3) the whole earth is full of his glory. And all beings emanate from him and exist through him by means of emanation and evolvement and nothing exists outside of him."[113]

It is by virtue of the Will, then, that God is said to be in everything.

109. In his article "ᶜIḳbotav shel Gabirol be-Kabbala," *Meᵓassef Sofre Ereẓ Yisrael* (Tel Aviv, 1940), p. 161.

110. *SH*, f. 4b; *ẒH*, 21, 24. See also *SH*, f. 54b; *GH*, 14; *Fons Vitae*, ed. Bäumker, V, 36, 43. Cf. Shemtob ibn Falaqera's *Liḳḳutim mi-Sefer Meḳor Ḥayyim* (in S. Munk, *Mélanges*, Paris, 1857), V, 56 and 57.

111. On Philo's *Logos* theory and its subsequent influence, cf. H. A. Wolfson, *Philo* (Cambridge, Mass., 1948), I, 200–293.

112. *GH*, 13:

שהוא המתואר במקור חיים כאמרו כי עמך מקור חיים וכו' והבן כונתו באמרו עמך.

Laṭif seems to imply here that the will is eternal, like God.

113. *GH*, 5. See also *GH*, 3: היותו נמצא בכל והכל בו and *Ẓeror ha-Mor*, 6: היותו בכל והכל בו בהכרח. Cf. *Fons Vitae*, V, 38, 39, 43. In *Liḳḳutim* (V, 18) this reads: אשר הוא בכל והכל בו. See also *Liḳḳutim*, V, 62.

Laṭif accepts completely the Gabirolean system of pantheistic emanation. God is the source of all reality, and all reality is in God. Pantheism, however, identifies God with the world, and thus tends to eliminate the personal God. Attempting to synthesize the theistic and the pantheistic tendencies, Laṭif maintains that all reality is in God, not that reality and God are identical.[114]

Laṭif also turns to the problems inherent in this theory of the Will when it is confronted with the concept of Divine Unity.[115] It would seem that the concept of Divine Unity demands an identification of the Will with the Divine Essence, but to be able to perform its function, the Will must also be separate from God. In answer to this problem, Laṭif maintains that the Will conceived of as inactive is identical with God; conceived of as active, it is different from the Divine Essence. The Will is thus identical with God, but also, with regard to its activity, the first emanation from God. On the one hand, then, the Will is a hypostasis, a subsistent essence; on the other hand, Laṭif, like Gabirol, considers it, to a certain extent, an "attribute" of God.[116] The unification of these two principles in Gabirol's philosophy is quite involved, and this is not the place to enter into its pitfalls, since we are interested here merely in demonstrating the influence of Gabirol's theory of the Will upon Laṭif. And, "in fine," Laṭif—like Gabirol—states that one of the functions of the Will is to "unify" and "bind" together the two first elements, universal matter and universal form.[117]

In Gabirolean philosophy it is unclear how universal form and matter emanated, whether both came from the Will, or whether matter alone came from the Divine Essence and form from His Will.[118] Again, it is not our task here to go into this question, which remains a point of debate among scholars of Gabirol.[119] But we should

114. Three centuries later Cordovero would sum up this system in his well-known formula, "God is all reality but not all reality is God." See G. Scholem, *Major Trends in Jewish Mysticism* (Jerusalem, 1941), p. 249.

115. See *SH*, f. 6a. In similar language argues Joseph ibn Ṣaddiḳ. See ᶜ*Olam Ḳatan* (Breslau, 1903), p. 53. Cf. my "The Problem of the Authorship," *Tarbiz*, p. 285, n. 47, where the parallel passages are quoted. Cf. also Cordovero, *Shi*ᶜ*ur Ḳoma* (Warsaw, 1883), p. 115.

116. *SH*, f. 5b:

שחפץ הבורא ית׳ הוא קדמון בעצמו לפי שאינו דבר חוץ ממנו כי אם מדה דבקה בו.

117. *ZH*, 24, 26, 27; *ZM*, 6. Cf. *Fons Vitae*, V, 38; *Liḳḳutim*, V, 60.

118. Cf. *Fons Vitae*, V, 25, 36, 37.

119. A. Heschel resolves some of these difficulties in his analysis of these concepts in the *Fons Vitae*. See his articles "Der Begriff der Einheit in der Philosophie Gabirols," *MGWJ*, 82:89–111 (1938); "Der Begriff des Seins in der Philosophie Gabirols," *Festschrift*

note here that a somewhat similar ambiguity is found in Laṭif's writings as well. Whereas in one passage he claims that both matter and form emanated from the essence of God, who is the "root of existence" (*Shoresh yesh*), and both were united by the will,[120] in another passage he seems to identify the will with the Divine intellect,[121] and in still another passage he argues that both matter and form stem from the will.[122] Again, in a fashion similar to Gabirol's, Laṭif insists that matter and form exist separately only in our mind, whereas in reality matter does not exist without form.[123] Furthermore, like Gabirol, Laṭif contends that universal form has no form of its own and while it includes all "colors," it has no color of its own.[124] We shall also point out here that whereas in his *Shaᶜar ha-Shamayim* Laṭif follows Maimonides' view that the angels are "pure forms,"[125] he seems later to have changed his mind. Thus we find that in his later works he accepts the well-known principle (of Gabirol) that the spiritual substances are composed of both matter and form.[126]

Following Abraham ibn Ezra, Laṭif considers the universe to be composed of three gradually descending "worlds"—an "upper," immaterial, intelligible world, an "intermediate" world of the heavenly spheres, and a "lower," sublunar world.[127] In a fashion similar to Gabirol's, Laṭif contends that the material worlds emanate from the immaterial, "upper" one, "radiating" or flowing out of the superabundant light of the "upper world."[128] The "upper," imma-

---

Jacob Freimann (Berlin, 1937), pp. 68–77; "Das Wesen der Dinge nach der Lehre Gabirols," *HUCA*, 14:359–385 (1939).

120. *ZH*, 6.

121. *ZH*, 26, 27.

122. *Ibid.*, 6, 22.

123. *ZH*, 24:

והרי נמצאו החמר והצורה פשוטים ואין הפרש ביניהם כלל מחוץ לשכל אלא בשכל.

This was already noted by J. Guttmann, *Studien*, p. 46, n. 4.

124. Cf. *Fons Vitae*, II, 8.

125. *SH*, f. 5b; cf. *Guide*, II, 6; I, 59.

126. *ZH*, 24. It should be noted that one meets a similar change in attitude toward Gabirol's theory in the writings of the Kabbalist Joseph Gikatilla. Whereas in his *Ginnat Egoz* he follows Maimonides' view, he seems to accept Gabirol's theory in his *Shaᶜare Ora*. Cf. G. Scholem, *ᶜIkbotav shel Gabirol be-Kabbala*, p. 175.

127. *SH*, f. 5a; 22a. Cf. Abraham ibn Ezra's commentary on Exod. 3:15. See also Maimonides, *Guide*, II, 10; *Hilkot Yesode ha-Tora*, 2:3. As to the doctrine of the three worlds in Kabbala, cf. G. Scholem, "Hitpatḥut Torat ha-ᶜOlamot be-Kabbalat ha-Rishonim," *Tarbiz*, 2, no. 4 (1931); 415–492. Laṭif identifies the "upper world" with the world of the *Sefirot*.

128. See *Short SH* (*Kerem Ḥemed*, IV), p. 9; *SH*, I, f. 27a–b, II, 43b. Cf. *Fons Vitae*, III, 15, 45. Moses ben Solomon of Salerno, who quotes this passage from the *Short SH*, ascribes it to Ibn Gabirol. Cf. my "The Problem of the Authorship," *Tarbiz*, p. 280.

terial world is conceived of as the cause of the being of the corporeal world, as well as the cause of the dynamic forces immanent in it.

Following Gabirol, Laṭif takes great pains to prove the existence of an immaterial, intelligible world as an intermediate link between God and the material world. To this end he reproduces Gabirol's argument that the concept of unity requires that there should be an intermediate world between the absolute unity of God and the multiplicity of the material world.[129] Furthermore, while rejecting the Aristotelian proofs of the existence of immaterial substances, Laṭif reproduces, in a modified form, Gabirol's argument that the activity of thought within ourselves must have its origin in cosmic immaterial substances.[130]

In accordance with the Neoplatonic tradition, and in agreement with Maimonides, Laṭif emphasizes the principle of the unknowability of God. Thus he argues that God is ineffable, that He has no name, that He cannot be grasped by thought nor described in human language. Following Maimonides, Laṭif insists, that the only way in which we are allowed to speak of God is by negation.[131] However, whereas Maimonides' objection to describing God in human language is based on the contention that any sentence about God necessarily introduces the plurality of subject and predicate, thus endangering the unity of God,[132] Laṭif reproduces Gabirol's argument, which goes back to Plotinus and is based on the concept of God's infinity, which cannot be limited by any attribute.[133]

Now, Gabirol's influence upon Laṭif is not limited to the substantive theory of the Will alone, nor to his general Neoplatonic outlook, but it is also evident in Laṭif's choice of analogies, turns of phrase, and usage of language. We shall restrict ourselves to a few examples by way of illustration.[134]

(1) When Laṭif speaks of the aim of human life he states that the

129. *SH*, I, 13; *Fons Vitae*, III, 2; *Likkutim*, III, 4.
130. *SH*, I, chaps. 12–13; *Fons Vitae*, III, 45, 46.
131. *SH*, I, chaps. 1–4; *Guide*, I, 57, 58.
132. Cf. *Guide*, I, 52.
133. *SH*, I, 4 (MS. Florence 487, f. 17b):
ואומר כי גבול ההשגה הוא להקיף היודע את הידוע ומי שאין לו בעצמו קץ ותכלית אין השכל יכול להקיפו.
Cf. *Fons Vitae*, I, 5; *Likkutim*, I, 5. See also Moses ibn Ezra, ᶜ*Arugat ha-Bosem*, in *Ẓion*, 2:123.

134. A methodological reservation has to be stated. Since many of these analogies are commonplace in Neoplatonic literature, it is often difficult to determine whether or not it was in fact the *Fons Vitae* which provided Laṭif's immediate source. They could have been available to Laṭif from a variety of sources. Hence a direct influence of the *Fons Vitae* upon Laṭif may be suggested only in cases wherein the similarity of the texts is close enough to lead to such a conclusion.

ultimate aim of man is the attachment of his soul to the "upper world," and achievement brought about with the aid of both knowledge and practice. Thus he contends that "the righteous, continuous actions separate the soul from its contrary elements (הפכיה) and cause it to reach its final perfection. Hence, said the philosopher, with knowledge and practice will the soul cleave to the upper world."[135] This seems, in all probability, to be a direct quotation from the *Fons Vitae* (I, 2): "Scientia et opere, quia per scientiam et operationem coniungitur anima saeculo altiori. Scientia etenim ducit ad opus, et opus separat animam a suis contrariis quae laedunt eam, et reducit eam ad suam naturam et suam substantiam."[136]

Indeed, one may argue that this motif of *ᶜilm* and *ᶜamal*, which became a commonplace in Islamic and Jewish Neoplatonism,[137] might have been available to Laṭif from a variety of sources. It appears, in a somewhat different formulation, in Isaac Israeli,[138] in al-Baṭalyawsi,[139] Abraham bar-Ḥiyya,[140] and Joseph ibn Ṣaddiḳ.[141] The close similarity, however, of Laṭif's text to that of Gabirol seems to lead to the conclusion that here the *Fons Vitae* was Laṭif's immediate source. Among later Jewish authors, this motif is quoted by Isaac Albalag,[142] Moses ibn Ḥabib,[143] Samuel Ẓaraẓa,[144] Abraham Shalom,[145] Isaac Aboᵓab,[146] and in the book *Menorat ha-Maᵓor*.[147]

135. *SH*, f. 10b:
כי המעשים הנכוחים המתמידים ממלטים את הנפש מהפכיה ומגיעים אותה לשלימותה האחרונה. וכן אמר הפילוסוף כי בדעת ובמעשה תדבק הנפש בעולם העליון.
See also *SH*, f. 62a; commentary on Kohelet, p. 10; *Rab Peᶜalim*, 31; *GH*, 33, quoted in part by D. Kaufmann, *Studien*, p. 73, n. 1.

136. *Fons Vitae*, I, 2, ed. Bäumker, pp. 4–5; *Liḳḳutim*, I, 2.

137. This motif is discussed by D. Kaufmann, *Die Spuren al-Bataljusis in der jüdischen Religionsphilosophie* (Leipzig, 1880), p. 27, n. 2; *Studien über Salomon ibn Gabirol* (Budapest, 1899), p. 73, n. 1; S. Horovitz, *Die Psychologie bei den jüdischen Religions-Philosophen des Mittelalters von Saadia bis Maimuni* (Breslau, 1898), p. 145, n. 174; see also Horovitz's introduction to *ᶜOlam Ḳaṭan* (Breslau, 1903), p. x, n. 40; J. Guttmann, *Die Philosophie des Salomon ibn Gabirol* (Göttingen, 1889), p. 68, n. 1; I. Heinemann, *Die Lehre von der Zweckbestimmung des Menschen im griechisch-römischen Altertum und im jüdischen Mittelalter* (Breslau, 1926), p. 60, n. 4. I wish to thank Professor Altmann for referring me to the above literature on the subject.

138. Cf. *Book of Definitions*, § 2, lines 18–19; *Sefer ha-Ḥibbur*, p. 132.

139. *Sefer ha-ᶜAgulot*, p. 15.

140. *Hegyon ha-Nefesh* (Leipzig, 1860), p. 5.

141. *ᶜOlam Ḳaṭan*, ed. Horovitz (Breslau, 1903), p. 66.

142. *He-Ḥaluẓ*, 7:168.

143. Commentary on *Beḥinat ha-ᶜOlam* (Ferrara, 1551), p. 37b. It is noteworthy that Ibn Habib quotes this from al-Baṭalyawsi.

144. *Meḳor Ḥayyim*, p. 43d.

145. *Neweh Shalom*, VII, 1, 1.

146. *Nehar Pishon*, p. 115.

147. P. 46b. The passages referred to in Notes 144–147 are quoted in Kaufmann, *Studien*, p. 73, n. 1.

(2) In his *Fons Vitae*, Gabirol attempts to explain the derivation of quantity from unity, thereby bridging the gap between the multiplicity of the material world and absolute unity by means of an analogy with the mathematical point, from whose motion there develops first a line, then a surface, and finally a volume.[148] Laṭif is quite fond of this analogy, and quotes it a number of times as a "deep mystery": "A deep mystery is posited in the point, the line, the surface, and the volume."[149] This analogy, which goes back to Neoplatonic literature (it appears, as noted by H. A. Wolfson,[150] in the writings of Albinus, Plotinus, Simplicius, and in al-Nairizi's Arabic commentary on Euclid's *Elements*), is also found in al-Baṭalyawsi's *Kitāb al Ḥadāʾiḳ*.[151] Hence it is difficult to determine whether in fact it was the *Fons Vitae* or the *Kitāb al Ḥadāʾiḳ* which provided Laṭif's immediate source. It is quite possible to assume that here Laṭif has followed both. It is noteworthy that one finds this analogy used by many thirteenth-century Kabbalists as well. It appears in the writings of Jacob ben Sheshet, Naḥmanides, Isaac ha-Kohen of Castile, and the *Zohar*.[152] Likewise, Moses de Leon, in his Hebrew writings, speaks of the "mystery of the point."[153]

(3) In reply to the question of the development of the many from the One, Laṭif cites the well-known analogy of a numerical series. The process of creation resembles the process of the multiplication of numbers from the numeral one. Laṭif contends that we must differentiate between the number one as the starting point of a series and the Absolute One. "The Lord is One" means something other than the beginning of a series. To the number one of a series are counterposed its multiples: 2, 3, 4, etcetera, but no multiplicity whatsoever can be opposed to the Divine One. Absolute One, then, is the basis of all numbers, but it is not itself a member of any numerical series: "The One is the primary cause of all numbers, but is not itself a number."[154] This analogy, common in Neoplatonic

148. See *Fons Vitae*, II, 22.

149. *GH*, 5; 13; *Rab Peʿalim*, 45, 58; *ZH*, 26.

150. See H. A. Wolfson, "Albinus and Plotinus on Divine Attributes," *The Harvard Theological Review*, 45, no. 2 (1952): 118–119.

151. *Sefer ha-ʿAgulot*, p. 19.

152. Cf. G. Scholem, *Major Trends*, pp. 241, 394–395, nn. 42–43.

153. *Sheḳel ha-Ḳodesh* (London, 1911), p. 25. Cf. G. Scholem, *Major Trends*, p. 394, n. 42.

154. *SH*, II, f. 40a; *Short SH* (*Kerem Ḥemed*, IV), p. 7; *GH*, 15.

literature,[155] is found in both the *Fons Vitae*[156] and the *Keter Malkhut*.[157] However, it might have been available to Laṭif from a variety of sources: for example, al-Baṭalyawsi,[158] Baḥya ibn Paḳudah,[159] Joseph ibn Ṣaddiḳ,[160] and Moses and Abraham ibn Ezra.[161]

(4) Another analogy dear to Laṭif is the one that is well known in Neoplatonic literature, comparing the process of emanation to the radiation of light: "All beings flow from Him and exist through Him in the manner of emanation and evolvement, and nothing is outside Him, as the light emanates from the sun and yet the light is nothing but the sun."[162] Laṭif's particular analogy, however, comparing the process of emanation to the light of the sun which penetrates through different colored glasses yet remains unchanged, is very similar to the one found in the *Fons Vitae*.[163] The process of emanation is also compared by Laṭif to putting on garments of light.[164] Laṭif's image of lower beings providing garments of light for higher ones is also to be found in the *Fons Vitae*: "The humble lower beings dress the higher in garments of light and all dress the Prime Mover in light."[165]

(5) The process of emanation is at times compared by Laṭif to a linguistic process, the world emanating from God like speech from a speaker: "For the existence of the world coming from God is like the

155. See D. Kaufmann, *Geschichte der Attributenlehre in der jüdischen Religionsphilosophie* (Gotha, 1887), pp. 287ff.; S. H. Bermann, "The Philosophy of Nicholas Cusanus," *ᶜIyyun*, 12:6–7 (Jerusalem, 1961).

156. *Fons Vitae*, IV, 11; *Liḳḳutim*, IV, 20.

157. Ed. Zeidman (Jerusalem, 1950), p. 9:

אתה אחד ולא כאחד הקנוי והמנוי

Likewise, Laṭif states in his poem introducing *SH:*

אתה אחד ולא כשאר האחדים ולא כאחד ראש המנויים והנפרדים.

158. *Sefer ha-ᶜAgulot*, pp. 3, 28, 33.

159. *Ḥobot ha-Lebabot*, I, 7.

160. *ᶜOlam Ḳaṭan*, p. 5.

161. *ᶜArugat ha-Bosem*, *Ẓion*, 2:122 (1842), and Abraham ibn Ezra's commentary on Exod. 3:10, 15; 33:22; Dan. 10:21, Job 23:3. See also Baḥya ben Asher, *Kad ha-Kemaḥ* (Constantinople, 1515), pp. 44a–b.

162. *GH*, 5. Cf. *Liḳḳutim*, III, 10, 11; *Sefer ha-ᶜAgulot*, p. 45. Cf. also Isaac Israeli's frequent metaphors of the sun (see Altmann-Stern, *Isaac Israeli*, p. 176).

163. *ẒH*, 26:

כדמיון ניצוצי השמש הפוגשים בעששיות הזכוכיות ונראה האור כמשתנה בהשתנות גווניהן וצבעוניהן לא שהאור משתנה בעצמו.

Cf. *Fons Vitae*, IV, 14; *Liḳḳutim*, IV, 22. The very same analogy is employed by Cordovero. See *Pardes Rimonim* (Krakow, 1592), p. 74.

164. See *Short SH* (*Kerem Ḥemed*, IV), p. 9; *SH*, I, f. 27a–b, II, 43b.

165. *Liḳḳutim*, III, 27.

existence of speech coming from a speaker."[166] We find the same analogy made in the *Fons Vitae*.[167] This analogy, prominent in the writings of the Ikhwān,[168] appears also in al-Baṭalyawsi.[169] It is noteworthy that it is rather common in the writings of many thirteenth century Kabbalists.[170] Indeed, Laṭif at one point notes that this idea is common to both Kabbalists and philosophers and suggests that the latter had borrowed it from the former.[171]

(6) The process of emanation is also compared by Laṭif to the reflection by a mirror of the form of its beholder.[172] This analogy, which goes back to Plotinus,[173] is also found in the *Fons Vitae* (V, 41): "Sigillatio autem formae in materia, quando aduenit ei a uoluntate, est tamquam resultatio formae in speculo quando resultat in eo ex inspectore."[174] G. Scholem had noted that one meets this analogy in Kabbalistic writings of the Gerona circle.[175]

(7) A further parallel between Gabirol and Laṭif is the latter's allegorical interpretation of the story of the Garden of Eden[176] which is very similar to that of Gabirol as transmitted to us by Abraham ibn Ezra.[177] Thus we are told that Eden presents the world of the "heavenly spheres"; the Garden—the "sublunar world"; the river which flows out of Eden is the "prime matter"; the four divisions of the river are the "four elements." Adam is the "rational soul," Eve—the "animate soul," and the serpent—the "vegetative soul and the faculty of the imagination." The tree of life is the "active intellect." The serpent persuades Adam to eat of the forbidden tree; that is, when the lower soul—imagination—succeeds

166. *SH*, III, f. 55b:
כי מציאות העולם מהאל ית' כמציאות הדבור מן המדבר.
167. *Fons Vitae*, V, 43; *Likkutim*, V, 71.
168. See Dieterici, *Weltseele*, p. 130; Guttmann, *Die Philosophie des Salomon ibn Gabirol*, p. 254, n. 3.
169. *Sefer ha-ᶜAgulot*, p. 45.
170. See G. Scholem, *Reshit ha-Kabbala*, p. 109.
171. *SH*, f. 55b.
172. See *SH*, I, f. 34b. Cf. *Likkutim*, IV, 22, V, 35.
173. See Guttmann, *Die Philosophie des Salomon ibn Gabirol*, p. 257, n. 1.
174. See *Fons Vitae*, p. 330, lines 22–25; *Likkutim*, V, 64.
175. Cf. G. Scholem, *ᶜIkbotav shel Gabirol*, p. 173.
176. See *SH*, II, chaps. 14–18 (f. 47a–49b); see also *GH*, chaps. 22–25.
177. See Ibn Ezra's commentary on Gen. 3:21; *Ozar Neḥmad*, II, 218; M. Friedländer, *Essays on the Writings of Ibn Ezra* (London, 1877), p. 40; Jellinek, *Beiträge zur Geschichte der Kabbala*, 2, p. 30; Steinschneider in Berliner's *Peletat Sofrim*, pp. 45–49; Munk, *Mélanges*, pp. 166ff.; Kaufmann, *Studien*, pp. 63ff.; W. Bacher, *Die Bibelexegese der jüdischen Religionsphilosophen des Mittelalters vor Maimuni*, pp. 46–49; J. Guttmann, "Zu Gabirols allegorischer Deutung der Erzählung vom Paradies," *MGWJ*, 80:180–184 (1936).

in controlling reason, the result is sin and loss of immortality.[178] The cherubim which were placed in the Garden are the angels, and the flaming sword which turned every way to keep the way to the tree of life is the sun.[179]

One might continue and note additional parallels[180] between Gabirol and Laṭif, but these should suffice to indicate the great influence exerted by the former upon the latter.

We may conclude, then, that as a philosopher, Laṭif belongs to the Neoplatonic trend in general, and to Gabirol's school of thought in particular. In fact, Laṭif should be considered, along with Abraham ibn Ezra and Joseph ibn Ṣaddiḳ, as one of the main continuers of Gabirol's school in medieval Jewish philosophy.

However, Laṭif's relationship to philosophy was a dialectical one. In his later writings Laṭif confesses his deep personal disappointment in philosophy. The philosophers, he complains, seem to go around in circles, searching in vain for the key to the mysteries of true reality. He concludes with a plea that mysticism, a stage beyond intellect, unlock for him the door to a domain of reality, to which philosophy had not provided the key.[181]

Mystical Sources

It is no easy task to trace Laṭif's mystical background, since Laṭif himself chose not to reveal his Kabbalist sources. Aside from the *Sefer Yeẓirah*, from which he quotes extensively, Laṭif does not refer by name to any source of Kabbalist literature. We do know, however, that he had personal connections with the Kabbalist Ṭodros ben Joseph Abulafia of Toledo—to whom Laṭif dedicated his *Ẓeror ha-Mor*[182]—and also, one may safely assume, with the Kabbalist

178. *SH*, II, f. 47a–49b.

179. *GH*, 25. See Altmann-Stern, *Isaac Israeli*, p. 194, on Isaac Israeli's concept of hell and on the influence of this concept on Gabirol and other Jewish Neoplatonists.

180. E.g., Laṭif's theory on the nature of the soul, which has a strong Neoplatonic flavor, resembles, to a large extent, Gabirol's theory, as was noted by S. Sachs, *Iggeret ha-Teshuba*, VII, *Ḳobeẓ al-Yad*, pp. 46, 49, n. 32; cf. *Fons Vitae*, V. 35. Likewise J. Guttmann, *Die Philosophie des S. Ibn Gabirol*, p. 234, n. 1, noted that Laṭif's comparison of the earth to a "point" in its relation to the universe at large (*ẒH*, p. 4) is similar to that of the *Fons Vitae*. Cf. also *Iggeret Teshuba*, 36, *Ḳobeẓ al-Yad*, p. 63.

181. *ẒH*, 5, p. 9; *GH*, 41–42.

182. See introduction to *Ẓeror ha-Mor*, *Kerem Ḥemed* (Berlin, 1856), IX, 154. According to S. Schoenblum, Ṭodros Abulafia dedicated his *Shaʿar ha-Razim* to Laṭif (see *Rab Peʿalim*, p. x). It is impossible, however, to determine on the basis of Abulafia's ambiguous remarks

circle of his native city, Toledo. In his writings he frequently alludes to a living Kabbalist tradition, to secrets transmitted from mouth to mouth "in a whisper," and he speaks of a circle of admirers, or "comrades," whom he instructed in "mysteries"; as well as of "visions" and "revelations."[183]

In his *Iggeret Teshuba* Laṭif quotes the following question pertaining to the inner meaning of the sacrificial laws, posed by one of his admirers: "Are you following the *Moreh Ẓedek* [Maimonides] or the interpretation of the *baᶜalē sod* [Kabbalists]?"[184] Laṭif replies that he is not pleased with Maimonides' attitude, and states: "I relied on the secret [knowledge] of R[abbi] A., hear it and know it for yourself."[185] Senior Sachs opined that the Rabbi A. referred to here was Rabbi Abraham ibn Ezra.[186] But we think it is clear that Laṭif did not mean Abraham ibn Ezra, to whom he regularly refers by his full name.[187] We would suggest rather that he refers to Rabbi Abraham ben Isaac, *Ḥazan* of Gerona, who was known as a Kabbalist in the Gerona circle, and to whom Rabbi Ezra of Gerona addressed two letters,[188] signed with the phrase, "Hear it and know it for yourself."[189] These are the same words used by Laṭif in his reference to the name of Rabbi Abraham; we may thus conclude that it was an expression common among Kabbalists of the time in alluding to mysteries of the Kabbala.[190] Moreover, Rabbi Ezra's letter to Rabbi Abraham apparently did come to Laṭif's attention, for he takes issue with the view put forward therein by Rabbi Ezra, that the seven things which, according to the rabbis, pre-existed prior to the creation of the world[191] were actually the seven *sefirot*.[192]

---

the identity of the "friend" to whom his book is dedicated. See Abulafia's introduction to *Shaᶜar ha-Razim*, MS. Munich 209, f. 40a ff.

183. See his respective introductions to *SH*, f. 11a, 15a; *Iggeret Teshuba*, pp. 46–47; *Rab Peᶜalim*, 83; *GH*, 42.

184. *Iggeret Teshuba*, q. 23, *Ḳobeẓ al-Yad*, p. 56. I am quoting MS. Vatican 335.

185. *Ibid.*: על סוד ר"א נסמכתי שמענה ואתה דע לך.

186. *Iggeret Teshuba*, p. 70; *Ha-Teḥiyya*, 1:34, n. 2.

187. See, e.g., *SH*, f. 47a; commentary on Kohelet, p. 18a.

188. See G. Scholem, "Teᶜuda Ḥadasha le-Toledot Reshit ha-Kabbala," *Sefer Bialik* (Tel Aviv, 1934), pp. 155–162.

189. *Ibid.*, p. 160.

190. This, at any rate, is its meaning throughout Laṭif's writings. Other expressions used by Laṭif in alluding to the mysteries of the Kabbala are as follows:
והשומע ישמע, החי יתן אל לבו, קחנו ועינך שים עליו, לטוש מחשבותיך לזה, שים לבך בזה, הישר דעתך לזה, איש תבונות ידלנה, אצל אנשי לבב, והמשכילים יבינו, ומבקשי ה' יבינו כל.

191. See *Pesaḥim*, 54a; *Pirḳe R. Eliᶜezer*, 3.

192. See Scholem, *Teᶜuda Ḥadasha*, p. 159, q. 7; *SH*, I, f. 20a–b; cf. my "The Problem of the Authorship," *Tarbiz*, pp. 283–284, nn. 39, 40, 41.

If this conjecture has merit, it offers us a clue to Laṭif's mystical sources.

An analysis of Laṭif's Kabbalist ideas reveals a surprising degree of closeness to the mystics of Gerona. Aside from the currency of Gabirol's theory of the Will among this group,[193] we find other important doctrines which they held in common with Laṭif, as well as interpretations of rabbinic legends, choices of analogies, and use of language.

Laṭif discloses his mystic doctrines in the second and third sections of his *Shaᶜar ha-Shamayim*. Introducing these sections, he expresses much doubt and hesitation as to the danger of revealing these mystic secrets.[194] He announces his intention to "scatter" the "mysteries" throughout the section (as Maimonides did in his *Guide*) so as to conceal his true meaning from the uninitiated and unworthy reader.[195] Indeed, he implies that his book is intended to serve as a mystical guide of the perplexed. After this somewhat tantalizing introduction, one is thoroughly astonished when the "mystery" revealed in this chapter turns out to be none other than "the mystery of the Will by which the world was created."[196] Laṭif seems to regard Gabirol's theory of the Will as an esoteric, mystic doctrine[197] (and perhaps this is one reason that he does not mention the *Fons Vitae* by name). Indeed, commenting upon Ecclesiastes 12:10, "Kohelet sought to find words of delight [*dibre ḥefeẓ*]," Laṭif states: "In his search to find *dibre ḥefeẓ* (taken here to mean words concerning [the doctrine of] the will) he found the wisdom of Kabbala."[198] He goes on to explain, "Words of delight" are those "which lead to the doctrine of the Will; that is, that the world was created by Will."[199]

Laṭif goes on to unite Gabirol's theory of the Will with the Kabbalist doctrine of the ten *sefirot*.[200] From the Will emanated the ten

193. See Scholem, *Reshit ha-Kabbala*, pp. 140–141, 149.

194. *SH*, II, f. 53b.

195. *SH*, II, f. 39b; cf. Maimonides' introduction to the *Guide*.

196. *SH*, III, f. 54b–55a; *Short SH* (*Kerem Ḥemed*, IV), p. 8.

197. See, e.g., *ibid.*: והחפץ כבר ידוע סוד ענינו. It is noteworthy that Gabirol, too, speaks of the "mystery of the will" (*Fons Vitae*, II, 20).

198. Commentary on Kohelet, p. 56a:

כי בבקשו דברי חפץ מצא דברי חכמת הקבלה.

Cf. Ibn Ezra's commentary on Eccles. 12:10:

דברי החפץ היא החכמה העליונה.

Maimonides quotes Eccles. 12:10 in his "Epistle Dedicatory" to the *Guide*.

199. See commentary on Kohelet, *loc. cit.*

200. See *SH*, f. 4a–5b, 20a–b, 27a–b.

sefirot in which the "upper," intelligible world is comprehended. Laṭif places the Will above the process of emanation. The Will is the primary source from which the rest of the *sefirot* emanate, and "Will is eternal," while the rest of the *sefirot* are created in time.[201] The act of creation is therefore contingent upon the emanation of the ten *sefirot* from the Will. In one place, however, Laṭif maintains that the *sefirot* existed as potential within the Will before the act of emanation, so that emanation only caused them to move from potentiality to actuality.[202]

We should point out here the parallels that we observe between these ideas of Laṭif, and the doctrines of the Gerona mystics. One of the major innovations of this "circle," according to Gershom Scholem, was that in their system "Will took the place of *Maḥashabah* [Thought],"[203] that is, whereas pure thought counted as the first *sefirah* for their master, Rabbi Isaac the Blind, Will became the first *sefirah* for his disciples. Laṭif's theory that the first *sefirah*—Will—was pre-existent to creation, is a view also held by the Kabbalists of Gerona. The Kabbalists of Gerona, like Laṭif, place Will above the process of emanation. Rabbi Azriel and Naḥmanides, as one, state that the first *sefirah*—Will—is pre-existent and is the source of all being. Rabbi Azriel says that the Divine Will includes all things and pre-exists prior to all things: "The Will which nothing has preceded"; "The Will from which nothing is excluded."[204] Naḥmanides holds that the first *sefirah*—Will—is the "source of all being" and exists eternally.[205] And just as Laṭif maintains that the *sefirot* existed *in potentia* before the act of emanation, so we find Rabbi Ezra stating in his above-mentioned letter to Rabbi Abraham: "The truth is that the essences [*hawwayot*] had been in existence before, whereas the emanation was innovated."[206]

As one reads Laṭif's discussion of the ten *sefirot*, the ten "spiritual forms" that emanated from the Will, one is struck with the problem

201. *Ibid.*; *Short SH*, *ha-Teḥiyya*, 1:63–65.

202. See *SH*, f. 20a–b; *Short SH* (*Kerem Ḥemed*), p. 6. Cf. *Megillat ha-Megalle* (Berlin, 1924), pp. 8, 10. See my "The Problem of the Authorship," *Tarbiz*, p. 284, n. 40.

203. See *Reshit ha-Kabbala*, p. 140.

204. See *Perush ha-Agadot*, ed. Tishby, p. 55a; G. Scholem, *Kitbe Yad be-Kabbala* (Jerusalem, 1930), p. 5; *Reshit ha-Kabbala*, p. 141.

205. See Naḥmanides, commentary on *Sefer Yeẓira*, published by G. Scholem in *Kiryat Sefer*, 6:401–410 (1930); *Reshit ha-Kabbala*, p. 149.

206. See Scholem, "Teᶜuda Ḥadasha le-Toledot ha-Kabbala," p. 158. Cf. A. Altmann's English translation of R. Ezra's letter, "A Note on the Rabbinic Doctrine of Creation," *JJS*, 7:205 (1956), p. 205.

of defining their precise character. Are these ten "spiritual forms" intermediate worlds outside the Divinity, as in the Neoplatonic system of emanation, or are they included within the Divinity itself, as in the Gnostic version of the Kabbala? It appears at first as if Laṭif himself were unclear on this point. He identifies the ten *sefirot* first with the ten *maʾamarot* with which the world was created, according to the rabbis,[207] then with the ten pre-existent numbers of the *Sefer Yeẓirah*,[208] later, with the ten ranks of angelology that Maimonides delineates in his *Mishneh Torah*,[209] and finally with the ten separate intellects of the medieval-Aristotelian philosophy.[210] Do we have here a confusion of Neoplatonic and mystic concepts, a failure to distinguish between the Neoplatonic idea of God and the Kabbalist-theosophical concept of God, between the world of separate intellects and the world of *sefirot*? These questions are difficult to answer. I think we must be guided in this by Gershom Scholem, who dealt with the same questions in discussing the early Kabbalists, and who concluded that we have here a "double standard and double usage of terms, one for those initiated into the mysteries, and another for those who stand without."[211] Indeed, Laṭif speaks explicitly in his *Shaʿar ha-Shamayim* of the "two roads"[212] through which he has chosen to speak of "these matters." And whereas he discusses the ten separate intellects of the philosophers quite openly, when speaking of the ten *sefirot* he becomes very cautious and abstruse, reminding us from time to time that the matter is a "deep mystery" far from the understanding of the "multitude."[213] And the expression "multitude" (*hamon*) in this connection, however paradoxical it might seem to us today, means none other than the philosophers. Therefore, what the philosophers call the ten separate intellects is actually, for those initiated into the mysteries of the Kabbala, the ten *sefirot*.

Laṭif draws a distinction between the first three *sefirot* and the other seven, relying upon a remark of Rabbi Eliezer the Great:

207. See *SH*, I, f. 20a–b; *Short SH* (*Kerem Ḥemed*), p. 7. Cf. *Abot* 1:5.
208. See *SH*, *loc. cit.*
209. See *SH*, I, 9, f. 22a; *Short SH* (*ha-Teḥiyya*), p. 63; cf. *Hilkot Yesode ha-Tora*, chap. 2:7.
210. See, e.g., *SH*, I, 8, f. 22a; *Short SH* (*Kerem Ḥemed*), p. 7.
211. See *Hatḥalot ha-Kabbala*, *Keneset*, 10 (Tel Aviv, 1946): 215.
212. *SH*, I, 9, f. 22a–b:
והוא דרך אחת משתי הדרכים שיעדתי לדבר בהם באלו הענינים . . . והיא דרך שלא דרכו בה הפילוסופים.
Laṭif repeatedly refers to the "two roads." See, e.g., *SH*, I, 8, f. 22a; I, 10, f. 22b, 23a; I, 13, f. 26a–b; cf. also his introduction to *SH*, f. 10b.
213. See *SH*, f. 22a, 39b; *ẒH*, p. 3.

"With ten *maʾamarot* was the world created and in three included."[214] Laṭif confines his discussion to the three first *sefirot*, and hardly speaks of the other seven at all. We should perhaps point out here that for Laṭif the number of *sefirot* is given to some variation;[215] sometimes he speaks of ten, sometimes of twelve (following the twelve diagonals of the *Sefer Yeẓirah*), sometimes he divides the *sefirot* into triads, each group containing three *sefirot* and the Will above all as the first *sefirah*. Moreover, the term *sefirot* does not appear in the *Shaᶜar ha-Shamayim*, but only in his later works.[216]

Laṭif identifies the first three *sefirot*, on the one hand, with Gabirol's three first elements—Will, Universal Matter, and Universal form—and, like Gabirol, states that the three are the root of all reality.[217] Incidentally, we find the same correspondence drawn by Rabbi Azriel.[218] On the other hand, Laṭif also identifies the three first *sefirot* with the three cosmic elements found in the *Sefer Yeẓirah:* אש (fire), רוח (spirit), and מים (water).[219] Then, using this symbology, Laṭif suggests a daring interpretation of the first verse of Genesis, "Bereshit baraʾ Elohim": *Bereshit* = the first *sefirah*, or the Will, called *esh*, *bara* = caused to emanate, *Elohim*; that is to say, the emanation of the Will is *Elohim*, that is, the world of the *sefirot*.[220] It is interesting to compare Laṭif's interpretation of this verse with that of the *Zohar*:[221] The *Eyn-Sof*, the hidden nothing, emanated through the medium of the "beginning," that is, of *Ḥokmah*, = *Elohim*. For both Laṭif and the *Zohar*, *Elohim* is the object, not the subject, of the sentence. Both interpret *Elohim* here not as the creator, but as that which is created; and for both, creation means emanation. Indeed, Gershom Scholem has already noted that the same inter-

214. See *SH*, I, 8, f. 22a; *Pirḳe de-Rabbi Eliᶜezer*, 3. This distinction, which goes back to the *Sefer ha-Bahir*, was accepted by all Kabbalists. Cf. Scholem, *Hatḥalot ha-Kabbala*, pp. 204–205.

215. For this he was criticized by R. Isaac ben Sheshet. See *Responsa*, 157.

216. See, e.g., *ZH*, 15, 20. In *SH*, he uses instead the following terms:
מעלות, מדות, מאמרות, צורות, דבורים, לבושים, שכלים נפרדים, קצוות, קולות, שרים, אראלים, חשמלים, מלאכים, שרפים, אלהים, בני־אלהים, כרובים, אישים, חיות הקדש, אופנים, מים עליונים, ימים, קוים.
Cf. the terms used by R. Azriel, *Perush ha-Agadot*, ed. Tishby, *Shaᶜar ha-Kinnuyim*, pp. 129ff.

217. See *SH*, III, f. 45a; cf. *Liḳḳutim*, IV, 18; *RP*, 59.

218. See G. Scholem, "ᶜIḳbotav shel Gabirol be-Kabbala," pp. 160–178.

219. See *SH*, III, chaps. 3–8. Similar terms occur in the writings of Gikatila; see, e.g., *Shaᶜare Ora* (Lemberg, 1858), p. 57b.

220. *SH*, II, 10, f. 45a–b.

221. See *Zohar*, I, 15b. Cf. G. Scholem, *Major Trends in Jewish Mysticism*, p. 217. Laṭif, however, goes on to explain that the words *Elohim*, *Shamayim*, and *Areẓ* in Gen. 1:1 refer to the "upper," "intermediate," and "lower" worlds, respectively.

pretation is given by all the disciples of Rabbi Isaac the Blind.[222] Laṭif also discusses the mystery of the letters of the word *bereshit*, which to his mind allude, in anagram, to *esh* (fire)—*rosh* (first)—*bayit* (palace),[223] an explanation which, to a certain degree, parallels that of the *Zohar*: "The letters of *bereshit* mean *bayit rosh*."[224] Laṭif goes on to explain the rest of the verse in Genesis 1:1 as follows: *et ha-shamayim we-et ha-areẓ*—with the heavens and the earth.[225] One meets a similar interpretation in Naḥmanides[226] and the *Zohar*.[227]

Laṭif is fond of taking Midrashic texts, especially those which were rejected by the philosophers, and interpreting them according to his Kabbalistic doctrines.[228] Thus, for example, Laṭif quotes the Midrash of Rabbi Eliezer the Great: "Whence were the heavens created? From the light of the garment with which He was robed; He took it and stretched it like a garment."[229] Laṭif interprets it in the light of the theory of emanation,[230] as do Rabbi Ezra and Rabbi Azriel of Gerona, who, in turn, borrowed this interpretation from Rabbi Isaac the Blind.[231] Furthermore, like Rabbi Ezra, Laṭif defends Rabbi Eliezer's dictum against the criticism of Maimonides, who regarded it as an expression of the Platonic doctrine of creation.[232] One should point out, however, the discrepancy between

222. See Scholem, *Major Trends in Jewish Mysticism*, p. 395, n. 55. See also *Sefer Maᶜareket ha-Elohut*, 7.

223. *SH*, II, 3, f. 41a.

224. See *Zohar*, I, 15b.

225. See *SH*, II, 10, f. 45b.

226. See *Beᵓur Maᶜase Bereshit*, pub. by G. Scholem, *Kiryat Sefer*, 6:109 (1928–29):
ואמר כי החכמה האצילה אלקים עם השמים.

227. Cf. *Zohar*, I, 15b.

228. See *SH*, II, chap. 10.

229. *Pirḳe de-Rabbi Eliᶜezer*, 3 (ed. Friedländer), p. 15. Cf. also *Bereshit Rabba*, ed. Theodor, pp. 19–20, and the numerous parallel passages noted by the editor. As to the sources of this haggadic motif of the garment of God, see V. Aptowitzer, *Licht als Urstoff* (1910), pp. 224–227; Altmann, "A Note on the Rabbinic Doctrine of Creation," pp. 195–206; G. Scholem, *Jewish Gnosticism, Merkabah Mysticism and Talmudic Tradition* (New York, 1960), pp. 57–64. Cf. also the Greek material assembled by R. Eisler in *Weltenmantel und Himmelszelt*, pp. 49–112, and the Iranian material to be found in R. C. Zaehner, *Zurvan, a Zoroastrian Dilemma* (1955).

230. See *SH*, I, 14, 27a–b; *Short SH* (*Kerem Ḥemed*), p. 9. See also the passage quoted in my "The Problem of the Authorship," *Tarbiz*, p. 288.

231. See R. Ezra's *Perush ᶜal Shir ha-Shirim* (Altona), pp. 5b–6a; R. Ezra's letter to R. Abraham, published by G. Scholem in *Sefer Bialik*, pp. 157–158; R. Azriel's *Perush ha-Agadot*, ed. Tishby, pp. 110–111; Altmann, "On the Rabbinic Doctrine of Creation," pp. 203–206. As to Isaac Israeli's concept of emanation and metaphor of "radiance," and their influence on the Gerona mystics, see Altmann, *Isaac Israeli*, pp. 119, 132.

232. See *SH*, I, f. 27a–b; *Guide*, II, 26. Cf. Scholem, "Teᶜuda Ḥadasha," *Sefer Bialik*, pp. 157–158; Altmann, "The Rabbinic Doctrine of Creation," pp. 203–206. It may be added

the interpretation of this rabbinic dictum as it appears in Rabbi Ezra and Rabbi Azriel, on the one hand, and as it appears in Laṭif, on the other. For both Rabbi Ezra and Rabbi Azriel the "garment" of light in which God is wrapped symbolizes *Ḥokmah*, from which emanated all the other *sefirot*.[233] For Laṭif, this "garment" meant the totality of the *sefirot*, from which emanated all other beings.[234] Moses ben Solomon of Salerno points out that one finds an interpretation similar to Laṭif's in Jacob Anatoli's *Malmad ha-Talmidim*. In the opinion of Moses ben Solomon of Salerno, Anatoli borrowed this interpretation from the (short early version of) *Shaᶜar ha-Shamayim*.[235] (It is rather significant that the work of [the Short] *Shaᶜar ha-Shamayim* itself, which came to Moses ben Solomon in the form of an anonymous treatise, is attributed by him to Solomon ibn Gabirol). However, whereas Anatoli, like Laṭif, interprets the "garment" of light of Rabbi Eliezer the Great as the "upper world" from which the heavens emanated, he does not identify this "upper world" with the world of the *sefirot*, but with the world of the separate intellects.[236] Indeed, we find an interpretation similar to Laṭif's in the writings of Kabbalistic authors of the thirteenth and fourteenth century, as for example in Rabbi Isaac ben Jacob ha-Kohen's *Commentary on the Chariot of Ezekiel*[237] and in the book *Maᶜarekhet ha-Elohut*.[238]

Laṭif also interpreted the three *hafṭarot*[239]—that is, the chariot of Isaiah, the chariot of Ezekiel, and the *menorah* of Zekhariah—three subjects which attracted many thirteenth-century Kabbalists: for example, R. Jacob ben Sheshet, R. Isaac ha-Kohen, R. Moses of Burgos, and R. Todros Abulafia.[240] There, however, we find allegorical and mystical interpretations side by side.

---

that both J. Anatoli and Moses ben Solomon of Salerno quote Friedrich II in defense of R. Eliᶜezer's dictum against Maimonides' criticism. See *Malmad ha-Talmidim* (Lyck, 1866), p. 53b; Moses ben Solomon's commentary on the *Guide*, MS. Bodleian, Op. 576, f. 263a.

233. See above, Note 231.

234. See *SH*, I, 14, f. 27a–b; *Short SH* (*Kerem Ḥemed*), p. 9. Cf. my "The Problem of the Authorship," pp. 280, 288–289.

235. See commentary on the *Guide*, MS. Bodleian, Op. 576, f. 262a–b; cf. *Malmad ha-Talmidim*, p. 53a.

236. See *Malmad ha-Talmidim*, p. 53a.

237. See *Perush R. Isaac Hakohen le-Mirkebet Yeḥezkel*, pub. by G. Scholem, *Tarbiz*, 2:194 (1930).

238. Ed. of Ferrara, 1558, p. 68b. Cf. Scholem, *Perush R. Isaac*. As to the authorship of the book, see G. Scholem, "Le-Beᶜayot Sefer Maᶜareket ha-Elohut," *Kiryat Sefer*, vol. 4 (Jerusalem, 1945). D. Neumark suggested that the R. Isaac mentioned frequently in the book is none other than R. Isaac Laṭif. See *Toledot ha-Pilosofia be-Yisrael*, I, 196.

239. See *SH*, I, chaps. 22–24; III, 9.

240. See, e.g., Jacob ben Sheshet, *Meshib Debarim Nekoḥim* (cf. G. Vajda, *Recherches sur*

In addition to the doctrine of the Will, and the doctrine of the ten *sefirot*, Laṭif also develops, in this esoteric section of *Shaʿar ha-Shamayim*, the theory which is known in thirteenth-century Kabbala as the doctrine of the *shemiṭṭot*.[241] Laṭif draws a parallel between the specific content of each of the six days of creation and its corresponding millennium in world history,[242] an idea borrowed from Abraham bar Ḥiyya's *Megillat ha-Megalleh*.[243] Within this structural framework, in which the history of the world takes place in accordance with the cosmic week, Laṭif attempts to understand the history of the Jewish people. Since every day of the creation was a "Day of the Lord," that is, a thousand years, at the end of the sixth millennium there should arrive a *shemiṭṭah* (that is, a new aeon), in which Utopia will, at last, be established.[244] Laṭif also relies on the well-known Talmudic phrase, "The world lasts six thousand years, and one thousand years it is a waste."[245] The "waste" is interpreted by Laṭif to mean the end of the cosmic order of this world—as symbolized under the aspect of stern judgment—and the beginning of a new order—the age of grace and the days of the Messiah. Accordingly, Laṭif hints that the date for this "end of days" will occur at the end of the sixth millennium, starting from the creation of the world. With the beginning of the seventh millennium the Messianic Age will commence.[246] With great caution and many arcane allusions,[247] Laṭif presents this theory, which was developed by the Kabbalists of Gerona (upon it Naḥmanides constructed his interpretations of the commandments of *shemiṭṭah* and Jubilee)[248] and achieved its classic expression in the *Sefer Temunah*.[249]

---

la philosophie et la kabbalah, "Jacob ben Šešet: Les visions d'Ezéchiel et d'Isaïe," pp. 92–104); *Perush R. Isaac Hakohen le-Mirkebet Yeḥezkel*, pub. by G. Scholem, *Tarbiz*, 2:188–217; G. Scholem, "R. Moses of Burgos," *Tarbiz* 3:61. G. Scholem notes (in the latter, p. 64) that Ṭodros Abulafia, too, had written a commentary (which has been lost) on the Chariot of Ezekiel.

241. As to the doctrine of the *shemittot* and its sources, see G. Scholem, *Reshit ha-Kabbala*, chap. 7: "Sefer ha-Temuna we-Torat ha-Shemiṭṭot."

242. *SH*, III, 4, f. 57a.

243. See *Megillat ha-Megalleh* (Berlin, 1924), pp. 10–11. Cf. G. Scholem, *Reshit ha-Kabbala*, pp. 176ff.

244. *SH*, III, 4, f. 57a.

245. See *Sanhedrin* 97a; *Rosh ha-Shana* 31a; *Aboda Zara* 9a; *SH*, III, 7, f. 58b.

246. Laṭif claims that the above date is original with him. See *SH*, III, 10, f. 61a.

247. N. Krochmal attempted to decipher some of these allusions in his *More Nebuke ha-Zeman*, chap. xvii (Warsaw, 1894), pp. 300–301. See also below, Page 222.

248. See Scholem, *Reshit ha-Kabbala*, pp. 176–193.

249. *Ibid.*, pp. 176ff.

Throughout his interpretation of Scripture Laṭif stresses the principle of the manifold meanings of the Torah and the different levels of meaning within the Torah. He adopts the philosophical terminology of the two levels of meaning in Scripture—the "outward," "exoteric" and the "inner," "esoteric"—and, as noted by G. Scholem,[250] identifies the "inner" meaning with the mystical interpretation of the text. Indeed, in his introduction to the early version of *Shaᶜar ha-Shamayim* (presumably written before 1238),[251] Laṭif explicitly speaks of "four methods" of interpretation of Scripture: the literal—that is, strictly grammatical—(*dikduk ha-milot*), aggadic (*peshaṭ*), philosophical-allegorical (*mashal*), and mystical (*derash*).[252] This fourfold aspect of the Torah bears a marked similarity to the well-known concept of the "four levels of meaning of the Torah," which made its appearance, as noted by G. Scholem,[253] toward the end of the thirteenth century in the *Zohar* and in the Kabbalistic (Hebrew) works of Moses de Leon, Baḥya ben Asher, and Joseph Gikatila (or Pseudo-Gikatila),[254] although Laṭif's definition of the four levels differs somewhat, and the term *PaRDeS* as a cipher for the four levels—*peshaṭ*, *remez*, *derash*, *sod*—employed by Moses de Leon[255] was not known to him.

These, in brief outline, are Laṭif's principal Kabbalistic ideas.[256] They correspond in great measure to those of the thirteenth-century Spanish Kabbala, in general, and to those of the Gerona mystics, in particular. Of special significance to the historian, who is faced with the riddle of the influence of Gabirol on thirteenth-century Spanish Kabbala,[257] is the fact that most of the ideas of the Gerona mystics which exhibit traces of a Gabirolean influence are to be found in Laṭif.

However, if we wish to place Laṭif in the framework of Spanish

250. See *On the Kabbala and its Symbolism* (New York, 1965), p. 51; see also *Virgo Filia Jehudae*, p. viii.

251. Laṭif explicitly states (*SH*, f, 14b) that he had composed his *Shaᶜar ha-Shamayim* "sixty years" after Maimonides had completed his *Mishneh Torah*, dating the latter work in the year 1178. According to his own testimony, however, his (short) *Shaᶜar ha-Shamayim* had been in circulation before then.

252. Cf. *Virgo Filia Jehudae*, pp. vii–ix.

253. See *On the Kabbala*, pp. 54ff.

254. *Ibid.*, p. 59.

255. *Ibid.*, p. 57.

256. Another major idea frequently referred to in Laṭif's writings is the concept of *ha-nibra ha-rishon*. The meaning and sources of this peculiar term will be discussed, however, elsewhere.

257. On this problem, see G. Scholem, "ᶜIkbotav shel Gabirol be-Kabbala," *Meʾassef Sofre Ereẓ Yisrael* (Tel Aviv, 1940), pp. 160–178.

Kabbala, we must remember that his relationship to it was a dialectical one, that he was at once drawn to it and repulsed by it.[258] We would say that Laṭif's individuality as a Kabbalist is, perhaps, expressed most in what he did not accept, what he omits or rejects from Kabbala. He omits or rejects its mythology, much of its Gnostic element, and what we call today "practical Kabbala."[259] He explicitly rejects the doctrine of the transmigration of the soul,[260] Kabbalistic demonology, and sexual and anthropomorphic symbolism. He sought to dress Kabbala in philosophical garb, to invest it with philosophical form and language. And though he was primarily a Kabbalist—and wished to regard himself as such—in language and external appearance he in fact belonged to the very camp of philosophers whom he openly criticized. Indeed, in the great debate which raged over the philosophy of Maimonides at the beginning of the thirteenth century, we find Laṭif defending the philosopher with great zeal.[261] Furthermore, in his allegorical interpretation of the Commandments, and in his theories of Providence and prayer, Laṭif stands not with the Kabbalists, but with the philosophers.

Rabbi Jacob ben Sheshet, in his polemic against the Jewish philosophers, challenges their stand on the question of Providence and prayer. Thus he contends that, according to the philosophers, Divine Providence does not mean God's interference with the external course of nature, but is instead interpreted by them as a natural connection between the human intellect and the active intellect. Hence, according to them, the strength of this connection is dependent on the individual's level of knowledge. Thus intellectual, and not ethical, factors are decisive for the rule of Divine Providence.[262] A similar theory of Providence occurs in Laṭif, who, following Maimonides, states that "the human individual's share in

258. See, e.g., *ZH*, chap. 5, in which Laṭif expresses his disappointment in contemporary Kabbalists, as a result of which he decided to compose his own system.

259. See, e.g., *SH*, III, 1, f. 54a–b, where Laṭif warns against those Kabbalists who use the names of God in order to perform miracles.

260. See *Rab Peʿalim*, 21, p. 9. As noted by G. Scholem, Laṭif here uses the Hebrew term *gilgul*. Scholem contends that the term *gilgul* is of relatively late origin and appears first in the *Sefer Temuna* (around 1250), whereas the term *ʿibbur* is used in the writings of the mystics of Gerona. See G. Scholem, "Le-Ḥeker Torat ha-Gilgul ba-Kabbala ba-Meʾa ha-13," *Tarbiz*, 17:135–150 (1945). Scholem had also noted that Laṭif's rejection of the theory of *gilgul* had influenced R. David ben Abraham ha-Laban (end of the thirteenth century). See Scholem's introduction to *Sefer Masoret ha-Berit*, *Ḳobeẓ al-Yad* (Jerusalem, 1936), p. 27.

261. See, e.g., his introduction to *SH*, f. 14b.

262. See Vajda, *Recherches sur la philosophie et la kabbale*, pp. 105–109.

Divine Providence is in proportion to his intellectual powers."[263] In his criticism of the Jewish philosophers' theory of prayer, R. Jacob ben Sheshet argues that the philosophers maintain that whoever had attained that degree of spirituality in which his soul adhered to the Active Intellect was exempt from praying aloud.[264] A concept of prayer, similar to a certain extent, is found in Laṭif, who states that "the intention required [in prayer] is not movement of the lips but the contemplation of the Divine only,"[265] and "the pure and holy form of prayer is in the adhesion of the human intellect . . . to the Active Intellect, in the manner, as it were, of a kiss."[266]

Nevertheless, one is tempted to agree with Laṭif that essentially he was a Kabbalist. In his *Rab Peᶜalim* (39) Laṭif defines with subtlety the difference between the philosopher and the Kabbalist as follows: whereas the philosopher is engaged in the pursuit of "timeless wisdom," the dimension of "time" is peculiar to the mystical thought (experience) of the Kabbalist.

The peculiar contribution of Isaac ibn Laṭif to the development of speculative Kabbala is in the ontological, rather than the anthropological, aspect of mysticism. In his interesting and unique attempt to strike a synthesis between Neoplatonic philosophy and Kabbala, we observe the influence of the former upon the latter. We see rather clearly the process of transition from philosophic to Kabbalistic concepts, the intricate process of recasting philosophic doctrines as Kabbalistic perceptions, and we note how mystic symbols are born out of philosophical terms. When we come, therefore, to place the name of Laṭif in the history of Kabbala, we must see him in the perspective of the four streams into which Spanish Kabbala divided in the thirteenth century:[267] (1) the stream of Gnostic Kabbala, whose chief proponents were the Kabbalists of Castile: the brothers Rabbi Isaac and Rabbi Jacob ha-Kohen, Rabbi Moses of Burgos, and Rabbi Todros Abulafiah; (2) the theosophical stream, whose representatives were Rabbi Isaac the Blind and his disciples—the mystics of Gerona—Rabbi Ezra, Rabbi Azriel, Rabbi Jacob ben Sheshet, and Naḥmanides; (3) the ecstatic-visionary

263. *SH*, I, f. 35a. Cf. *Guide*, III, 17–18, 51.
264. See *Shaᶜar ha-Shamayim*, *Oẓar Neḥmad*, 3:165 (1860).
265. *Iggeret Teshuba*, 36, p. 64.
266. See *Ẓeror ha-Mor*, 6.
267. This four-fold division was mentioned to me by Professor G. Scholem in a seminar, held at the Hebrew University, Jerusalem, 1941–42, on the beginning of the Spanish Kabbala.

stream, led by Abraham Abulafiah; (4) the philosophic-mystical stream, in which speculative philosophy joined Kabbala, whose principal representatives were Isaac ibn Laṭif and his disciple, David ben Abraham ha-Laban. The *Zohar*, as is well known, embraced the first and second of these streams, but rejected or suppressed the third and fourth. Hence, the influence of these last two over the later development of Spanish Kabbala was greatly diminished. A new attempt, however, at the reconciliation of philosophy and Kabbala would be made three centuries later by Moses Cordovero.[268]

But who can foretell where repercussions cease? Laṭif's work influenced two nineteenth-century thinkers who were as far apart as east and west. On the one hand, Laṭif's mark is to be seen in the work of the Yemenite Kabbalist and poet Salam Shabazi[269] and, on the other hand, Laṭif exerted an unwitting influence on Nachman Krochmal's *The Guide of the Perplexed of Our Time*. Krochmal, in fact, was of the opinion that Laṭif's earlier version of *Shaᶜar ha-Shamayim* was the work of Abraham ibn Ezra.[270] In chapter seventeen of his *Moreh Nebukē ha-Zeman*, Krochmal does his interpretation of Ibn Ezra's philosophy on this work.[271] Julius Guttmann has rightly pointed out that this very chapter, in which Krochmal interprets the philosophy of Ibn Ezra in light of the idealistic thought of Schelling and Hegel, also forms the principal source of our understanding of Krochmal's own metaphysical system.[272] Guttmann notes that Krochmal, in describing the philosophy of Abraham ibn Ezra, time after time interweaves the language of the historian, who merely explains the ideas of others, with that of the philosopher, who speaks for himself. Thus, for example, the opinion which Krochmal attributes to Ibn Ezra,[273] namely, that God created the world out of His own Essence, rather than out of pre-existent matter, is actually his own opinion as well—one which he shared with the Kabbalists. One wonders whether Krochmal, in ascribing to Abraham ibn Ezra

268. Another attempt at the reconciliation of philosophy and Kabbala was to be made by Joseph ibn Waḳār. See Vajda, *Recherches sur la philosophie et la kabbale*, pp. 115–297; G. Scholem, "Sifro ha-ᶜArabi shel Joseph ibn Waḳār," *Kiryat Sefer*, 20:153–162.

269. See *Ḥemdat Yamim* (Jerusalem, 1883–1885); cf. G. Scholem, "Sefer Ḥemdat Yamim le-R. Salam Shabazi," *Kiryat Sefer*, 5:272.

270. Cf. my "The Problem of the Authorship," p. 277.

271. See, e.g., *More Nebuke ha-Zeman* (Warsaw, 1894), pp. 288–300. It does not surprise us, therefore, that this chapter of his book reads like Kabbala.

272. See "Yesodot ha-Maḥashaba shel R. Naḥman Krochmal," *Kenesset*, 6:269–276 (1940).

273. See *More Nebuke ha-Zeman*, XVII, 299–300.

Isaac ibn Laṭif's *Shaᶜar ha-Shamayim*, was not motivated by the desire to see in the former a forerunner of German idealistic philosophy. For indeed the Kabbalists, to a certain extent, arrived at Hegelian conclusions six hundred years before Hegel. Now, as for the extent of Laṭif's influence on Krochmal, that is another problem, to be dealt with elsewhere.[274]

274. Laṭif's influence on subsequent Jewish thought will be analyzed in detail in the forthcoming edition of his *Shaᶜar ha-Shamayim.*

Moses Narboni's "Epistle on *Shi'ur Qomā*"

A Critical Edition of the Hebrew Text with an Introduction and an Annotated English Translation

By ALEXANDER ALTMANN

1. Introduction

Among the documents of anthropomorphism in religion the *Shiᶜur Qomā*[1] ("The Measure of the [Divine] Body") may certainly claim pride of place. Drawing on the rapturous descriptions of the body of the beloved in the Song of Songs and assuming this poem to be an allegory of the love between God and Israel, the *Shiᶜur Qomā* unashamedly portrays the limbs of the Creator in terms of gigantic measurements and secret names. Yet if, in Edmund Burke's phrase, "greatness of dimension is a powerful cause of the sublime,"[2] this attribute hardly applies in this case. The impression created by the fantastic numbers and *nomina barbara* is one of stupefaction rather than elevation, relieved only by the hymns of the *Hekalot* type thrown in at the end. Still, there can be no doubt that the vision of the *shiᶜur qomā* stems from the same mental climate which produced the *Hekalot* and their hymnody: that of Merkabā mysticism.[3] The vision is associated with the Creator's appearance on the throne,[4] and the angel Meṭaṭron plays a notable part in it.[5] What lends a color of

1. See Gershom G. Scholem, *Major Trends in Jewish Mysticism* (New York, 1946), pp. 63–67; *Idem, Jewish Gnosticism, Merkabah Mysticism, and Talmudic Tradition* (New York, 1960), pp. 36–42.
2. Edmund Burke, *A Philosophical Inquiry into the Origin of our Ideas of the Sublime and Beautiful*, 6th ed. (London, 1770), p. 127.
3. This has been conclusively proved by Scholem, *Jewish Gnosticism*, pp. 36–42, and corroborated by Saul Lieberman in Appendix D of the same work, pp. 118–126. Scholem follows Moses Gaster, "Das Schiur Komah," *Monatsschrift für Geschichte und Wissenschaft des Judentums*, N.F., 1: 179–188, 213–230 (1893), reprinted in Gaster, *Studies and Texts*, II, 1330–1353. Both Gaster and Scholem rejected Heinrich Graetz's assumption that the book originated in the Geonic period under the influence of Islamic anthropomorphism.
4. See the text (opening of the second version) in *Merkabā Shelemā*, ed. Shelomo Mussajov (Jerusalem, 1921), 36a.
5. See *Merkabā Shelemā*, 32a; 34a; 36a; 39b–40a.

its own to this bizarre tract is the use it makes of Canticles rather than of Ezekiel's theophany. The very term *qomā* (meaning here "body," not "stature") is taken from Canticles (7:8).[6] Hence some of the sanctity attached, according to Rabbi ᶜAqiba's famous *dictum*,[7] to the canonical text of that book was claimed for this esoteric *midrash* on its descriptions of the body of the beloved: "Rabbi Yishmael said: 'When I recited this before Rabbi ᶜAqiba, he said to me: Every one who knows this measure of our Creator [*yoẓerenu*] and the glory of the Holy One, blessed be He, Who is hidden from the creatures, is assured to be a son of the world-to-come.' "[8] It is, perhaps, this emphatic promise, more than anything else, which secured the hold of this strange text on the imagination and loyalty of posterior generations.

That the crude anthropomorphism of the *Shiᶜur Qomā* proved a severe stumbling block to its acceptance can, however, scarcely be in doubt. The Targum on Canticles may indeed contain "rejoinders" to some of the passages in *Shiᶜur Qomā*, as has recently been argued.[9] The history of the reactions evoked by this tract from the tenth century onward is one of disquiet—even where belief in its authenticity prevailed—alternating with open rejection. The Geonim Sherira and Hai (tenth century) sought to allay the misgivings of certain Jews of Fez who wanted to know whether Rabbi Yishmael, the presumed author of the book, was supported by an accredited tradition or had written it "out of his own head," in which latter case he had obviously violated the Mishnaic injunction against discoursing on esoteric matters in a manner irreconcilable with the honor of God (*Ḥagigā* II, 1). They explained that far from expressing a merely personal view, Rabbi Yishmael had written down profound mysteries the meaning of which could be revealed only to the select

6. This was noted by the Kabbalists. See below, Page 236. The statement by Raphael Loewe, "The Divine Garment and Shiᶜur Qomah," *The Harvard Theological Review*, vol. 58, number 1, p. 153 (1965), that "the term *qomah* does not occur in the original text itself" seems to admit only Canticles 5:10–16 as the basic text for *Shiᶜur Qomah* mysticism.

7. *Mishnā Yadayim*, III, 5.

8. *Merkabā Shelemā*, 38b. This statement is immediately followed by another one to his disciples, which is the one most frequently cited in kabbalistic and other medieval works: "I and Rabbi ᶜAqiba pledge our word that everyone who knows this measure of our Creator and the glory of the Holy One, blessed be He, will be a son of the world-to-come, provided he studies this mishnā every day." Both statements occur also in the version contained in *Sefer Raziᵓel* (Amsterdam, 1701), fol. 38a. The first version in *Merkabā Shelemā* (34b) has simply: "Every one who knows this mystery [*raz zē*] is assured that he will be a son of the world-to-come and will be saved from the punishment of hell . . ."

9. By Raphael Loewe, "The Divine Garment and Shiᶜur Qomah," p. 155.

few possessed of the requisite qualifications; the questioners, though held in high esteem, did not belong to that group; at any rate, the literal meaning of the anthropomorphic terms was out of question, since God had no limbs nor measures, and "what likeness will ye compare unto Him" (Isaiah 40:18).[10] In contrast to Sherira and Hai, Saᶜadya Gaon admitted the possibility of the spuriousness of the *Shiᶜur Qomā*. There was, he pointed out, no agreement among scholars as to its origin, and hence no compelling need to refute the objections raised against it. He remarked, however, that "were we to attribute the book *Shiᶜur Qomā* to Rabbi Yishmael, we could find in his words many aspects [that is, of an acceptable character] and could explain that they do amount to the way of the Faith and the Unity, namely, that . . . the Creator creates a splendid light for all his prophets to serve as a sign and proof and testimony of His Glory and Divinity so that they may know that the word which is audible to them comes at the command and behest of God."[11] In other words, Saᶜadya applied to the vision of the Divine Body reported in the *Shiᶜur Qomā* his well-known theory of the "created glory" (*kabod nibraʾ*), which explains the prophetic theophanies as visions not of God Himself but of a luminous substance created by God. According to his theory, God creates this light (*kabod; shekinā; ruaḥ ha-qodesh*) in order to assure the prophet of the Divine origin of the verbal revelation which he receives.[12] It should be noted that Saᶜadya makes no attempt to read into the *Shiᶜur Qomā* an allegorical meaning which would make its descriptions symbolic of Divinity itself. It is also significant that he offers his interpretation only on the hypothetical assumption that the book is authentic. He would, however, rather disclaim any concern with this text "since it is not found in either Mishna or Talmud, and since we have no way of establishing whether or not it represents the words of Rabbi Yishmael; perhaps someone else pretended to speak in his name."[13]

Saᶜadya's embarrassment was all the more acute because the Karaites had fastened upon the *Shiᶜur Qomā* as evidence of the theo-

10. *Oẓar Ha-Geʾonim*, ed. B. M. Lewin, *Ḥagigā*, pp. 10–12.

11. Quoted by Jehuda b. Barzilay of Barcelona in his *Perush Sefer Yeẓirā*, ed. Solomon Zalman Ḥayyim Halberstam, with additional notes by David Kaufmann (Berlin, 1885), pp. 20–21, from "one of the books of our teacher Saᶜadya, of blessed memory, in refutation of the claims of a certain heretic [*mīn*] . . ." (reproduced in *Oẓar Ha-Geʾonim*, *Berakot*, responsa section, 17).

12. See my article, "Saadya's Theory of Revelation," *Saadya Studies*, ed. Erwin I. J. Rosenthal (Manchester, 1943), pp. 4–25.

13. See Jehuda b. Barzilay, *Perush Sefer Yeẓirā*, p. 21.

logical backwardness of the Rabbanites. The *Sefer Milḥamot Adonai*, by the Karaite Salmon ben Yeruḥim, contains in its last three chapters (15–17) lengthy quotations from the *Shiᶜur Qomā* interspersed with violent attacks upon Rabbis Yishmael and ᶜAqiba.[14] Saᶜadya's statement on the *Shiᶜur Qomā* cited above is probably a direct answer to this particular Karaite assault. The work embodying his reply seems to be his *Kitāb al-radd ᶜalā Ibn Sāqawaihi*, of which only fragments have survived,[15] and Ibn Sāqawaihi, against whom it is directed, may be identical with Salmon ben Yeruḥim, as Abraham Geiger and Israel Davidson maintained.[16] The Muslims, likewise, charged the Rabbanites with anthropomorphism (*tashbih*: literally "likening," specifically, of God to man) on account of the *Shiᶜur Qomā*, and this may have lent a special urgency to Saᶜadya's rebuttal of the Karaite attack. There is an explicit reference by Ibn Ḥazm (944–1063/4) to the *Shiᶜur Qomā* in the chapter on the Jews in his *Kitāb al-milal wa ᶜl-niḥal*:[17]

> In one of their books called *Shiᶜr Toma* [sic][18] which forms part of the Talmud (the Talmud being their trusted foundation in their jurisprudence and in the minutiae of their religion and revealed Law) and which in their unanimous view forms part of the dicta of their rabbis,[19] [it is said] that the extension of the face of their Creator (Who is exalted above their speech) from its extreme altitude down to his nose amounts to 5,000 ells. There be far from God any shape, measure, limits and extreme points.

Ibn Ḥazm obviously quoted only from hearsay, since this particular measure does not occur in the text, but he certainly caught the gist of the book and correctly reproduced the term "Creator" which is characteristic of it.[20] In the twelfth century, al-Shahrastānī repeated

14. See *Sefer Milḥamot Adonay*, ed. Israel Davidson (New York, 1934), pp. 114–132.

15. See Henry Malter, *Saadia Gaon, His Life and Works* (Philadelphia, 1942), pp. 265, 382–384.

16. See Davidson's introduction to *Sefer Milḥamot Adonay*, pp. 21–28.

17. The chapter is reproduced in both the original text and in a German translation by Ignaz Goldziher, "Proben muhammedanischer Polemik gegen den Talmud," *Jeschurun*, ed. Joseph Kobak, VIII, 4 (Bamberg, 1872), pp. 76–104. The passage quoted here is found on p. 87/98. See also Miguel Asín Palacios, *Abenházam de Córdoba y su Historia Critica de las Ideas Religiosas*, II (Madrid, 1928), 385–386.

18. M. Asín suggests that *shiᶜr* for *shiᶜur* may be a deliberate arabism by the editor so as to give the title of the book the meaning: "Poem of Toma." Goldziher, "Proben muhammedanischer Polemik," p. 87, n. 28, records the reading found in the manuscripts.

19. M. Asín's Spanish translation obscures the point made here that the *Shiᶜur Qomā* forms part of the dicta of the rabbis. Goldziher's German translation, though clear on this point, does not cover the parenthetical clause.

20. Ibn Ḥazm was in personal contact with Samuel ha-Naggid, who was his compatriot, and may have derived some of his knowledge of *Judaica* directly from him. Cf. Goldziher, "Proben muhammedanischer Polemik," pp. 76–77.

the charge of crude anthropomorphism against the Jews in general, without, however, referring specifically to the *Shiᶜur Qomā*.[21] Al-Maqrīzī (fifteenth century) still maintained the well-worn accusation but differentiated between various Jewish groups. The relevant passage in his *Khiṭaṭ* reads: "The *ᶜAnaniyya* upholds the unity and justice [that is, of God] and rejects anthropomorphism [*tashbih*]; the *Ashmaᶜath* admit *tashbih*; the *Djālūtiyya* carries *tashbih* to excess."[22] From the motley list of Jewish sects offered by al-Maqrīzī in the same context it is clear that by *ᶜAnaniyya* he designates not the Karaites in general (to whom he refers as *al-Qarā* in contradistinction to the Rabbanites, *al-Rabbaniyya*),[23] but merely one of the many Karaite groups.[24] The *Ashmaᶜath*, who are said to admit *tashbih*, denote most probably the Talmudists or adherents of tradition (*shemuᶜā; shemuᶜatha*), as has been plausibly suggested by de Sacy.[25] Finally, the *Djālūtiyya*, who are described as radical anthropomorphists, are probably the Babylonian Jewish mystics who adhered to the *Shiᶜur Qomā*.[26] At any rate, the reference to anthropomorphism carried to excess can apply only to the *Shiᶜur Qomā*. To these Muslim condemnations of the book may be added an instance of Christian polemics. In his letter to the Emperor Ludwig the Pious, Bishop Agobard launched an attack against Jewish anthropomorphism. The letter (*De judaicis superstitionibus*, *circa* 829) was based either on the *Shiᶜur Qomā*, as was suggested by Graetz,[27] or on an Anglo-Saxon writing of the eighth century, which had drawn on the book, as Gaster proposed.[28]

21. *Kitāb al-milal wa l-niḥal*, ed. Curton, pp. 164, 169–171. Al-Shahrastānī contrasts the allegorism of certain sects with the anthropomorphism of the Jews in general.

22. Quoted from Antoine-Isaac Silvestre de Sacy, *Chrestomathie arabe*, I, 1826, text, p. 116; French translation, p. 307. The full title of the work is *Al-Mawāᶜiẓ wa l-Iᶜtibār fī Dhikr al-Khiṭaṭ wa l-Āthār*, paraphrased in the title of the French translation by U. Bouriout and P. Casanova (in six volumes, 1893–1920): "Description topographique et historique de l'Egypte."

23. See de Sacy, *Chrestomathie*, text, pp. 90f. On p. 106 Rabbanites and Karaites are referred to as *banū mishnō* and *banū miqrā* respectively.

24. De Sacy, *Chrestomathie*, pp. 116–117.

25. *Ibid.*, pp. 313, 351, 356. Al-Maqrīzī cites a passage from al-Masᶜūdī, *Kitāb al-tanbīh wa l-ishrāf*, in which the Ashmaᶜath are said to comprise the majority of the Jewish nation, and Saᶜadya, among others, is called an Ashmaᶜathī. The passage mentions Abū Kathīr as Saᶜadya's teacher, and is referred to by Malter, *Saadia Gaon*, p. 32.

26. See de Sacy, *Chrestomathie*, text, p. 90: *al-djālia bi-bābil;* p. 91: *ᶜAnan rās al-djālūt.* For the term *rās al-djālūt* (*resh galuta*) see also al-Shahrastānī, *Kitāb al-milal*, p. 167; Goldziher, "Proben muhammedanischer Polemik," p. 77. Graetz (*Monatsschrift*, 8:117–118 [1895]), derives the term *Djālūtiyya* from the "Chaldaic" *galiyyata* in the sense of "revelation of mysteries," which is hardly plausible.

27. *Monatsschrift*, 8:110ff. (1859).

28. *Monatsschrift*, N.F., 1:226ff. (1893).

Sa^cadya's tentative interpretation of the *Shi^cur Qomā* along the lines of his theory of "created glory" was not followed up by subsequent Jewish philosophers. (As we shall note, it played an important role in the mystics' treatment of the theme.) Abraham ibn Ezra dealt with the subject briefly in his *Yesod Mora*ᵓ and at some length in an excursus on the passage in his Long (Standard) Commentary on Exodus explaining Exodus 33:21. In *Yesod Mora*ᵓ he says: "Our ancients, of blessed memory, knew the mystery of the *Merkabā* and of *Shi*ᶜ*ur Qomā*, and God forbid that they compared a likeness unto Him; but their words are in need of interpretation, as are the words of the Tora, 'Let us make man in our image after our likeness,' and as [the words] in Ezekiel's prophecy (1:26–27), 'a likeness as the appearance of a man upon it above' and 'from the appearance of his loins and downward.' "[29] These hints are elaborated in the final chapter of the work:

> Now consider that One is the foundation [*yesod*] of all number, while itself no number; it subsists in itself, and has no need for what follows it. Every number too is composed of ones . . . Hence it is written in the *Shi*ᶜ*ur Qomā:* "Rabbi Yishmael said: Every one who knows the measure of the Creator (*yozer be-re*ᵓ*shit*) is sure to be a son of the world-to-come, and I and ᶜAqiba vouch for this." In this way the intelligent will be able to know the One in so far as the All is attached to it, whereas to know it in so far as its total good is concerned is beyond the power of a created being . . . Being attached to the total good is like [the vision of] the face; and being attached to the created [things] is like [the vision of] the back. This is meant by "And thou shalt see My back" . . .[30]

It would appear from these cryptic remarks that Ibn Ezra saw in the *Shi*ᶜ*ur Qomā* an allegory of the macrocosm. He distinctly mentions in this context the notion of man as a microcosm (identified by him with the "mystery" of Meṭaṭron, the Prince of the Presence). The created beings are attached to God in a way analogous to the presence of the root number One in all numbers. The measures listed in the book *Shi*ᶜ*ur Qomā* would, therefore, seem to signify to Ibn Ezra the dimensions of the created world. The limbs of the figure described in the book are, no doubt, the parts constituting the universe. This interpretation of Ibn Ezra's view of the book is borne out by the more explicit (though far from plain) remarks offered in his Commentary on Exodus (see below, Pages 268–269). The reverence in

29. *Yesod Mora*ᵓ, ed. M. Creizenach (Frankfurt a.M.-Leipzig, 1840), pp. 10–11 (Hebrew section).
30. *Ibid.*, pp. 50–51.

which Ibn Ezra clearly holds the book reflects a tradition which, in spite of an undercurrent of misgivings, surrounded it with the halo of a deep mystery.[31]

Maimonides, too, was in his youth affected by the same outlook, as is attested to by his reference to the *Shiᶜur Qomā* in the Introduction to *Sanhedrin* XI (*Pereq Ḥeleq*) of his *Commentary on the Mishna*. Speaking about the difficulty of doing justice, in the present context, to such subtle subject matters as Moses' prophecy, the existence and hierarchical order of the angels, and the faculties of the soul, he adds:

> The circle would have to be extended to include a discourse on the forms (*fī al-ṣuwar; ba-ẓurot*) which the prophets mentioned in connection with the the Creator and the angels; into this there enters the *Shiᶜur Qomā* and its subject-matter. For [a treatment of] this subject alone, even if shortened to the utmost degree, a hundred pages would be insufficient . . .[32]

The authenticity of the brief sentence referring to the *Shiᶜur Qomā* cannot be doubted.[33] Nor is there any doubt that Maimonides subsequently deleted this sentence. The Manuscript (295) of the Edward Pococke Collection in the Bodleian Library (Neubauer 404), which is Maimonides' autograph[34] of the Commentary on the Mishna Order *Neziqin*, carries both the sentence and the bold stroke of deletion.[35] As in many other instances, Maimonides changed his mind on the subject.[36] Strangely enough, he even went so far as to deny that he had ever considered the *Shiᶜur Qomā* as an authentic work, and he used the harshest language possible in its condemnation:

> I never thought [*lam arā qaṭṭ; lo ḥashabti me-ᶜolam*] that it was one of the works of the Sages [*ḥakamim*], of blessed memory, and far be it from them

31. On this tradition see Lieberman, Appendix D to Scholem's *Jewish Gnosticism*, p. 124, particularly the references given in nn. 29–30.

32. *Maboᵓ le-Pereq Ḥeleq*, ed. J. Holzer (Berlin, 1901), p. 24 (Arabic–Hebrew section).

33. Such a doubt was expressed by M. Gottlieb in his edition of Maimonides' Commentary on *Mishnā Sanhedrin* (Hanover, 1906), pp. 97–98. Lieberman, Appendix D to Scholem, *Jewish Gnosticism*, p. 124, n. 32, lists four manuscripts which contain the sentence. He takes the authenticity of the entire passage for granted.

34. See the careful weighing up of all the evidence to this effect in Solomon D. Sassoon's introduction to *Maimonidis Commentarius in Mischnam* (Copenhagen, 1956), vol. I, chaps. ii–vi.

35. See the facsimile of Maimonides' autograph in Sassoon's edition referred to in the preceding note, vol. II, which reproduces the Commentary on *Seder Neziqin* from MS. 295 of the Edward Pococke Collection.

36. Sassoon, introduction to *Maimonidis Commentarius*, I, 33, n. 4, thinks that the deletion of the passage by Maimonides need not be taken as evidence for a change of mind but merely as an indication of anxiety lest the anthropomorphic language should occasion misunderstanding. This interpretation is, however, untenable since it ignores the complete disavowal of the *Shiᶜur Qomā* in the *responsum* (see next note).

that this [book] should have come from them. It is but a work of one of the Byzantine preachers, and nothing else. Altogether, it is a great *miẓwā* to delete this book and to eradicate the mention of its subject matter; "and make no mention of the name of other gods" (Exodus 23:13), etc., since he who has a body [*qomā*] undoubtedly is [to be classed among] "other gods."[37]

The severity of Maimonides' attack accords with his well-known stand against anthropomorphism in religion, and chimes also with his known attitude to mysticism.[38] His earlier approval of the *Shiᶜur Qomā* was probably facilitated by Ibn Ezra's allegorical interpretation of the work. Since Maimonides used the allegorical method in his treatment of Biblical and Midrashic anthropomorphism, he might have found it possible to adhere to his original approach to the book. It seems, however, certain that he was repelled by its basic features (measurements, *nomina barbara*) and was forced to the conclusion that it was a spurious work. To what extent his repudiation of the *Shiᶜur Qomā* became known in wider circles and in later periods is a matter still to be determined. We note a certain disdain for the work among some of the rationalists of the thirteenth century.[39] Interestingly enough, Moses ben Ḥasday Taku (1250–1290), though a strict literalist and fierce opponent of philosophy, also cast serious doubts on the authenticity of the book.[40]

Ibn Ezra's positive evaluation of the *Shiᶜur Qomā* was shared by his contemporary, Jehuda Ha-Levi, although perhaps to a smaller degree and on different grounds. "One should not reject," he said in his *Kuzari* (IV, 3, end), "what has been said about 'And the image of God did he behold' (Numbers 12:8) and 'They saw the God of Israel' (Exodus 24:10) and the *maᶜasē merkabā*, and [one should not reject] even the *Shiᶜur Qomā* since it helps to produce the fear of Him in the souls, even as it is said, 'And that His fear may be

37. *R. Moses b. Maimon Responsa*, ed. Jehoshuᶜa Blau (Jerusalem, 1957), I, 200–201. Lieberman's interpretation (Appendix D . . . , p. 124) of Maimonides' reply is based on Freimann's translation and cannot be maintained in the light of the Arabic text and Blau's more exact rendering of it. Maimonides' words *lam ʾarā qaṭṭ* (Blau: *lo ḥashabti me-ᶜolam*) clearly indicate a denial of ever having attributed the work to the *ḥakamim*. This is a statement difficult to explain, but it has to be accepted as textually incontrovertible.

38. See my article, "Das Verhältnis Maimunis zur jüdischen Mystik," *Monatsschrift*, 80, N.F., 44 (1936), 305–330.

39. See the reference to the book *Shiᶜur Qomā* in one of Zeraḥya Gracian's letters to Hillel b. Samuel of Verona, published in *Oẓar Neḥmad*, 2:142 (1857).

40. See the passage in his *Ketab Tamim*, published in *Oẓar Neḥmad*, 3:61–62 (1860).

before you' (Exodus 20:17)." The possible effect of the vision of God described in the *Shiᶜur Qomā* is here considered a sufficient reason not to reject "even" this strange book. Jehuda Ha-Levi need not, of course, have expressed here his entire view of the work. Close as he was to Jewish mysticism, he might have regarded it as a repository of profound mysteries.

Ibn Ezra's approach to the *Shiᶜur Qomā* will, as we shall see, reassert its influence in the fourteenth century. Before, however, proceeding with our account of the reaction to this book among the philosophers, we might glance at the way in which the mystics related themselves to it. It may be noted at the outset that there is no trace to be found, among this group, of the critical attitude that had led others to doubt or deny the authenticity of the work. Yet is is obvious that there was considerable concern among the members of this group too about the description of the *qomā* in terms at variance with the notion of God's unity and incorporeality. Eleazar of Worms (*circa* 1160–*circa* 1230), the theologian of German Hasidism, took issue with this problem in his *Shaᶜarē ha-Sod we-ha-Yiḥud we-ha-ᵓEmuna.*[41] What he did in order to remove any flaw from the concept of God was to separate the notion of *shiᶜur qomā* from that of the Creator. He resorted to this radical step in spite of the fact that it contradicted the very text of the *Shiᶜur Qomā*, which distinctly portrays the figure and its measures as belonging to the Creator (*yoẓer be-reᵓshit*). According to Eleazar's theory, the vision described refers not to the Creator but to something created: the "visible glory" (*kabod nirᵓē*), also called the "special cherub" (*kerub meyuḥad*), which is created by way of emanation from the invisible "inner glory" (*kabod penīmī*) representing the Creator. Eleazar applies to both the visible and inner glory the term *shekinā*, calling the former *shekinā of His greatness* and the latter *shekinā of His holiness*. The *Shiᶜur Qomā* does indeed speak about the *shekinā*, but only in the qualified sense of the lower, created *shekinā*. One will notice that this doctrine is a revival, albeit in a more complicated fashion, of Saᶜadya's tentative interpretation of the *shiᶜur qomā* as a vision of the "created glory" or *shekinā* (see above, Page 227).[42] Eleazar takes the text much more seriously than Saᶜadya did, seeing that its authenticity was for him undisputed. Yet just because of

41. Ed. A. Jellinek, *Kokebe Yiẓḥaq*, 27:7–15 (1862).

42. See particularly pp. 10, 13–14. On Eleazar's concept of the *merkabā* see Gershom G. Scholem, *Major Trends in Jewish Mysticism*, pp. 111–116, and my article "Eleazar of Worms' Ḥokhmath Ha-ᵓEgoz," *Journal of Jewish Studies*, 11:101–113 (1960).

this he had to render it theologically innocuous. The context in which he explains the *Shiᶜur Qomā* is an eloquent and moving plea for faith in the infinite Creator who "fills all worlds and yet transcends them," and to whom no measure or similitude may be applied. Rabbi Yishmael's statement promising the bliss of the next world to everyone who "knows the measure of the Creator" is given a meaning opposite to what it originally implied: only he who has faith in the infinity of God will inherit the world-to-come.[43]

Eleazar's view of the *Shiᶜur Qomā* was challenged by Menaḥem Recanati (*circa* 1300)[44] on the ground of its incompatibility with the text. According to Recanati, the "Measure of the Body" is to be identified with the *Sefirot* spoken of by the Kabbalists. Yet there is a rider to this statement. Recanati is careful to point out that in his view (which, he knows, is not shared by his fellow Kabbalists) the *Sefirot* are not of the same nature as the Divine essence but distinct from it: they are but the organs or instruments (*kelim*) thereof.[45] Hence, the descriptions of the measures found in the *Shiᶜur Qomā* have no bearing on the essence of Divinity. They relate merely to its *modus operandi*, and even so must be understood in a figurative, non-quantitative sense. Recanati suggests that the *parsaʾot* (parasangs) mentioned in the book are not to be taken in their literal meaning but stand for articulations, in the form of letters, of the Divine power or "divisions" (as in Daniel 5:28: *peres perisat malkutek*) defining its various operations.[46] He lays down the following canon of interpretation:[47]

Know thou that whenever the Sages, of blessed memory, speak about the *Sefirot* and say something that is fit to be said only about the Creator, blessed be He, they do, in fact, speak about the Creator Who dwells in them . . . Finally, whenever you find them saying about the *Sefirot* things which are not

43. Jellinek, *Kokebe Yiẓḥaq*, p. 10. Eleazar's interpretation of the *Shiᶜur Qomā* is quoted by Naḥmanides in his letter to the French rabbis (see *Qobeẓ Teshubot ha-Rambam we-Iggerotav* (Leipzig, 1859), section *Iggerot Qanaʾut*, 10a; for a critical text see F. Perles' article in *Monatsschrift*, 9:192 (1860).

44. In a passage said to be taken from Recanati's *Sefer Taᶜamē ha-Miẓwot* by Jehuda Ḥayyat in his commentary (written ca. 1494–1500) on the *Sefer Maᶜareket ha-Elohut* (Ferrara, 1557), fols. 33b–34a. The printed editions of Recanati's *Taᶜamē ha-Miẓwot* do not contain the lengthy quotation (fols. 33a–41b) offered by Ḥayyat.

45. *Maᶜareket ha-Elohut*, 34a ff. In taking this view of the *Sefirot*, Recanati followed Azriel of Gerona. See A. Jellinek, *Beiträge zur Geschichte der Kabbala*, II (Leipzig, 1852), 38–40.

46. *Maᶜareket ha-Elohut*, 41b–42a.

47. *Ibid.*, 39b.

fit to be said about the Creator, blessed be He, as, for example, "the measure of the body" [*shiᶜur qomā*] and suchlike matters, it all refers to the *Sefirot* . . . [48]

The sense of uneasiness about the *Shiᶜur Qomā* felt by Recanati is only too plain from this passage. He admitted, indeed, openly that he had to draw a line between the *Sefirot* and the Creator in order to accommodate the *shiᶜur qomā* in a de-Divinized realm, as it were.[49] He was conscious of thereby violating the concept of Sefirotic Divinity as firmly held by other Kabbalists but saw no other way of safeguarding the notion of the unity of God.[50] His way of dealing with the problem follows the earlier pattern of Eleazar's. While the latter assigned the *shiᶜur qomā* to the "visible glory" as distinct from the Creator, he related it to the *Sefirot* as distinct from the essence of God. He, therefore, hardly improved on Eleazar in so far as adherence to the text was concerned.

Later Kabbalists seem to have taken a more relaxed view of the *Shiᶜur Qomā*. Since the very concept of the *Sefirot*, in whatever way interpreted, already amounted to a kind of fragmentization of the absolute unity of God, the ice had been broken or, to use the Talmudic phrase adduced in this connection by Jehuda Ḥayyat at the end of the fifteenth century: "the strap was untied" (*hutera ha-reẓuᶜā*): that is, there really was no further reason for excessive restraint, provided one took great care to shun all literalness and, in particular, to interpret the quantitative measures of the *Shiᶜur Qomā* along the lines suggested by Recanati.[51] Viewed in this light, Recanati's separation of the essence of God from the *Sefirot* no longer seemed necessary. Jehuda Ḥayyat, who considered the emanation (*aẓilut*) of the *Sefirot* as a process within Divinity, could say: "If we ascribe a measure [*shiᶜur*] to them, this refers to their power; for He [sc. God] set an end and limit to their power in order that the emanation should not expand in its operations beyond the pre-established plan."[52] In other words, the measure and limitation of the *Sefirot* or *shiᶜur qomā* do not indicate any finitude in the Divine world per se but

48. This passage and the subsequent statement about the meaning of the measurements are reproduced as a gloss by the editor in the printed text of *Tiqqunē ha-Zohar*, no. 70, fol. 121b, in the name of Jehuda Ḥayyat. The editor had obviously failed to notice that Ḥayyat was quoting Recanati. A printed marginal gloss (*ibid.*) laconically states: "This text is not by Rabbi Jehuda Ḥayyat, of blessed memory," without referring to Recanati.

49. *Maᶜareket ha-Elohut*, 40a.

50. *Ibid.*

51. *Maᶜareket ha-Elohut*, 108b.

52. *Ibid.*, 160b.

express a Divinely imposed finitude of operations of the *Sefirot*. "What emerges from this is [the realization] that there is a necessity on high for a distinction between the Divine powers operating upon the created beings in order that one should not intrude into the domain of the other; and this is indicated by the letters [viz., each having its clearly defined articulation]; and the parasangs [*parsaʾot*] which are mentioned are Divine powers."[53] Once this position is reached, the *Shiʿur Qomā* no longer presents a serious problem. Jehuda Ḥayyat is able to refer to various interpretations of the book conceived on this level. What is common to them is the duplication of the *shiʿur qomā* into a male and female aspect or figure. This new departure is not a capricious overloading of an already highly charged concept but the logical conclusion of the step taken in identifying it with the *Sefirot*. The bisexual character of the Sefirotic system was now transferred to the *shiʿur qomā*. This procedure had also the advantage of making complete the correspondence of this ancient midrash on Canticles to the text. Since Canticles contains descriptions of the bodies of the lover and the beloved, it was natural to think in terms of a two-fold or two-faced (*du-parẓufim*) *shiʿur qomā*. The very name of the book borrows the term *qomā* from the verse *zoʾt qomatek* . . . (7:8), where the reference is to the female partner. Ḥayyat speaks, accordingly, of a *shiʿur* of the *arik anpin* or male aspect, and of a *shiʿur* of the *zeʿir anpin* or female aspect of the *Sefirot*.[54] According to the *Tiqqunē Ẓohar*, the male *Sefirā Ẓaddiq* is called "measure" (*shiʿur*) and the female *Sefirā Binā* is termed *qomā*.[55]

Of particular interest is the link established by the Kabbalists between the *shiʿur qomā* concept and the Biblical story of the Tower of Babel. It is not clear to which original source this connection is to be assigned. From Naḥmanides' guarded remarks in his *Commentary on the Tora* (Genesis 11:2) it would appear that he was alluding to a mystical interpretation well understood by the Kabbalists. It involved the secret meaning of the word *shem* (name) in the verse, "Let us make ourselves a name" (Genesis 11:4), the "measure" (*shiʿur*) of the tower designed, and the sin of "cutting off the plants," or heresy. Naḥmanides' remarks were explained by Isaac of Acco in his *Meʾirat ʿEnayim*,[56] and by Recanati in his *Com-*

53. *Ibid.*, 161a.
54. *Ibid.*
55. *Ibid.*, 160a.
56. Quoted by Jehuda Ḥayyat in his commentary. See *Maʿareket ha-Elohut*, 158a.

mentary on the Tora, where the language is rather terse and obscure.[57] A reference to this theme occurs also in the *Sefer Ma^{c}areket ha-Elohut* (circa 1300) on which Jehuda Ḥayyat in his commentary on this work based his interpretation.[58] According to his explanation, the heresy of the generation of the Tower consisted in their attempt to build a miniature image of the *shi^{c}ur qomā*—that is, of the *Sefirot*—by employing the gigantic measurements of the *qomā* on a proportionate small human scale. This way of using inadequate substitutes is said to be alluded to in the words, "And they had brick for stone, and slime had they for mortar" (Genesis 11:3). They tried to imitate the structure (*binyan*) of the *Sefirot* by building a "city" (a kabbalistic synonym for the last *Sefirā ^{c}Atarā* or *Malkut*) and a "tower" (synonymous with the *Sefirā Tif$^{\supset}$eret*). In this way they sought to procure the influx upon them of the Divine Power so as to be unified and safe against dispersal and separation. Their intention was good in so far as it was directed against succumbing to the power of the stars which threatened to disperse them all over the earth. It was, however, evil in that their secret aim was to break away from the worship of the *Sefirot* as a whole and to seek their unity under the aegis as it were of the last *Sefirā* alone. Hence they said, "Let us make ourselves a name": that is, let us make the *Sefirā ^{c}Atara* (which is called "name") our only object of worship.[59] This act constituted heresy.[60]

The ingenious interpretation of the Biblical story just mentioned obviously rests on the assumption that the *shi^{c}ur qomā* has to be identified with the *Sefirot*. As we have noted, the *Sefer Ma^{c}areket ha-Elohut* subscribes to this interpretation. There is, therefore, every reason to believe that the author of this work shared also the view of the identity of *qomā* and *Sefirot*. He does not make an explicit statement to this effect, and from his various utterances on the subject of *shi^{c}ur qomā* Jehuda Ḥayyat drew the inference that the other author's view

57. See the text in *Lebushē Or Yeqarot* (Jerusalem, 1960/61), fol. 20a, and the slightly different recension quoted by Ḥayyat, *Ma^{c}areket ha-Elohut*, 158a–b. Ḥayyat assumed that Recanati had plagiarized from some kabbalistic scholar (158b).

58. *Ma^{c}areket ha-Elohut*, 158b–159a. On the question of the authorship of the *Ma^{c}areket ha-Elohut*, see Scholem, *Kiryat Sefer*, 21:248ff. (1944–45).

59. Cf. Mordecai Jaffe's commentary *Eben Yeqarā* in *Lebushē Or Yeqarot*, 20a.

60. The designation of the exclusive worship of the tenth *sefirā* as idolatry (*^{c}abodā zarā*) par excellence is a widespread kabbalistic motif. It is pronounced in the *Sefer Ta^{c}amē ha-Miẓwot* attributed to Isaac ibn Farḥi, a work which was, however, written toward the end of the thirteenth or at the beginning of the fourteenth century. (On its authorship see my article in *Kiryat Sefer*, XL, no. 2 [1965], 256–276). The term *harisā* used in *Ma^{c}areket ha-Elohut* (see *sha^{c}ar ha-harisā*, fols. 138a–177b) for "heresy" is probably a deliberate coinage in imitation of the Latin *heresia*.

approximated that of Eleazar of Worms. One will remember that the latter saw in the "measure of the body" the prophetic vision of the created "visible glory." The author of *Maᶜareket ha-Elohut* also repeatedly identifies the *shiᶜur qomā* with "prophetic vision,"[61] but he makes it clear at the same time that the prophetic vision—of a human figure on high—finds its true explanation in the light of what he had pointed out as to the structure (*binyan*) of man.[62] The reference is to his treatment of the theme in the chapter on man,[63] where it is stated, and elaborated in great detail, that man is created in the image of the *Sefirot*. The prophetic vision can, therefore, only refer to the *Sefirot*, in whose image man is made. According to Ḥayyat, the author saw in the *shiᶜur qomā* not the *Sefirot* but Meṭaṭron.[64] He based his view undoubtedly on a statement in the chapter on man[65] in which the author pronounces his agreement with Rabad's notion of Meṭaṭron as a power emanated from God ("the first cause") in whose image man was created and who appeared unto Moses and Ezekiel in the form of a man; and with regard to whom it was said, "He who knows the measure of the Creator . . ." The author admits that at first blush he had considered this view of Rabad's contrary to his own (which we take to mean the view of the identity of *qomā* and *Sefirot*). "And he who understands the prophetic vision to which I have alluded [*videlicet*, that of *shiᶜur qomā*] will be able to understand that his words are like mine, something profound and true." This can only mean that the author regards the supernal Meṭaṭron spoken of by Rabad as identical with the *Sefirot*, and not merely as "the body of the *shekinā*," as Ḥayyat suggested. According to him, Rabad and the author of *Maᶜareket ha-Elohut* assumed the existence of the "great Meṭaṭron" or "Meṭaṭron of the [world of] emanation" (*aẓilut*), also called "body of the *shekinā*," who is of a Divine nature, in contradistinction to the "small Meṭaṭron," who is created. There is, however, no warrant in the text to confine the concept of the supernal Meṭaṭron according to the *Sefer Maᶜareket ha-Elohut* to the "body of the *shekinā*." It would rather seem that there was unanimity among the Kabbalists of the thirteenth and fourteenth centuries that the *shiᶜur qomā* referred to the *Sefirot*.

61. *Maᶜareket ha-Elohut*, 157b; 191b.
62. *Ibid.*, 190a; 191b.
63. *Ibid.*, 178a; 180b ff.
64. *Ibid.*, 159a.
65. *Ibid.*, 213a.

The account we have given of the various ways in which the *Shiᶜur Qomā* was received and interpreted will serve to place in its proper setting a fourteenth century *opusculum* on this theme by an eminent Jewish philosopher. We are referring to the *Iggeret ᶜal Shiᶜur Qomā* ("Epistle on the Measure of the Body") by Moses ben Joshua ben Mar David of Narbonne (Moses Narboni), also called Maestre Vidal Bellsom Narboni.[66] The work, which we present below in a critical edition accompanied by an annotated English translation, was completed in Perpignan on the Eve of Sukkot, 5103 (September 15, 1342),[67] when the author had already composed his commentary on al-Ghazālī's *Maqāṣid al-Falāsifa* ("The Intentions of the Philosophers" [to be cited in Notes as CIP])[68] and a commentary on Lamentations.[69] The great bulk of his literary production then still lay ahead. His commentary on Averroes' treatise on *The Possibility of Conjunction with the Agent Intellect* [cited as CPC] was written in 1344, when he was still in Perpignan.[70] Most of his works, however—and they number twenty, according to Steinschneider's list[71]—were produced in Spain. His magnum opus, the commentary (*biᵓur*) on Maimonides' *Guide of the Perplexed* [cited as CG], was commenced in Toledo and finished, after seven years of labor, at Soria in 1362, the year in which he probably died.[72]

What moved Narboni, who is known as a radical Averroist and who on this account incurred the opprobrium of many orthodox thinkers,[73] to concern himself with the *Shiᶜur Qomā*, the most obnoxious document of Jewish mysticism? Was he unaware of Maimonides' stern repudiation of this text? The answer to the last question is definitely: yes. In his view Maimonides himself had offered a kind of commentary on the subject of *shiᶜur qomā* (more precisely, he had

66. For biographical details see S. Munk, *Mélanges de philosophie juive et arabe* (Paris, 1859), pp. 502–506; M. Steinschneider, *Catalogus Libr. Hebr. in Bibliotheca Bodleiana*, cols. 1967–1977; *idem*, *Die Hebr. Übersetzungen des Mittelalters*, pp. 311–319; Ernest Renan and A. Neubauer, *Les Ecrivains juifs français du XIVᵉ siècle* (Paris, 1893), pp. 320–355.

67. See the *explicit* of the text, where, however, the place is not given. It is certain that Narboni was in Perpignan (his native town) at the time, since he did not emigrate to Spain until 1344.

68. It is referred to in our text, line 62.

69. See Steinschneider, *Cat. Bodl.*, col. 1975.

70. *Ibid.*, col. 1971.

71. *Ibid.*, col. 1969ff.

72. *Ibid.*, cols. 1967, 1977.

73. See Joseph Solomon Delmedigo's letter to Zeraḥ b. Nathan in: Abraham Geiger, *Melo Chofnajim* (Berlin, 1840), Hebr. section, p. 18; German section, pp. 65–68, n. 70; Steinschneider, *Hebr. Übersetzungen*, p. 313.

"alluded" to it) in his description of the universe as a *makroanthropos* and of man as a microcosm in the *Guide* (I, 72).[74] He obviously had not heard of Maimonides' responsum (see above, Pages 231f.) nor of his deletion of the passage in the Introduction to *Pereq Ḥeleq.*[75] He shared, moreover, the prevalent view that the *Shiᶜur Qomā* was an authentic work. He states in two places in our text (lines 13, 160) that it was written by "the Sages of Israel" and makes the specific point (not made before him) that the Sages found it necessary to write the book in order to elucidate, at a time of diminishing understanding, the prophetic visions of God in human form (lines 12–13). His acceptance of the *Shiᶜur Qomā* as authentic does not yet, however, explain his motivation in offering an elaborate commentary on it. Two factors have to be taken into account in answering the question we have posed. The first concerns Narboni's relation to Ibn Ezra, the second his interest in Kabbala. We shall elaborate these two points.

(1) Narboni's *Epistle* takes the form of commentary on Ibn Ezra's excursus in the *Long Commentary on Exodus* (33:21), which deals with the *Shiᶜur Qomā* (see above, Page 230). He quotes most of the Ibn Ezra passage verbatim (lines 16–38) and interprets it word by word in two large sections (lines 39–55; 186–226), separated by a relevant metaphysical disquisition (lines 55–95), a quotation from Averroes (95–109) on which he amplifies (110–134), another quotation from Averroes (135–156), and his comments (157–185). There follows a reference to the final part of Ibn Ezra's excursus with his comments (227–249) and a concluding paragraph (250–265) with the *explicit* (266–268). The *Epistle* is thus clearly structured around the Ibn Ezra text. Ibn Ezra is presented as having explained the *Shiᶜur Qomā* more fully than Maimonides did in his allusions to the subject in *Guide*, I, 72 (13–14), but not as fully as required: "[His words] are . . . in need of elucidation if his intention is to be perfectly understood" (line 40). Here, then, is a clear statement explaining the motivation of the *Epistle*. "I, Moses son of Joshua son of Mar David of Narbonne, therefore decided to comment on this subject and enlarge on its presentation" (40–42).

What enabled Narboni to make Ibn Ezra's rather cryptic remarks the basis of his interpretation of *Shiᶜur Qomā* was his view that they

74. See lines 13–14 of our text. The reference to chapter 70, instead of 72, is obviously due to a slip of the pen.

75. The unexpurgated version is still extant in a number of manuscripts. See Lieberman, Appendix D . . . , p. 124, n. 32.

are the words of a man "who faithfully reflects the metaphysical science" (line 39). In other words, Narboni believed that Ibn Ezra, the "perfect scholar" (*ibid.*), expressed in his allusive way notions that accord with the truths of metaphysics—that is, of Averroes' metaphysics—and that a proper exegesis of his comments will show the very text of *Shiᶜur Qomā* to represent "the fruit of metaphysics" (line 56). Unfortunately, the text of the sentence in which this rather startling pronouncement occurs is somewhat corrupt, but the essential meaning seems clear. In what way the claim is made good will be seen later. At this stage we may simply note the fact that Narboni holds Ibn Ezra in high veneration as a spokesman for metaphysics, and that he feels justified in projecting his own Averroist concepts upon the twelfth-century Neoplatonist. This attitude fits very well into what one might call the fourteenth-century Ibn Ezra renaissance. Leon Jehuda Mosconi, a contemporary of Narboni's, who wrote (between 1362 and 1370) a supercommentary on Ibn Ezra's commentary on the Tora,[76] reports having seen nearly thirty supercommentaries on Ibn Ezra's works on his extensive journeys.[77] Joseph Solomon Delmedigo of Kandia (Crete) (1591–1655) was shown twenty-four such supercommentaries in Constantinople.[78] As Steinschneider observed, "none of the authors [of supercommentaries on Ibn Ezra] known to us goes as far back as the thirteenth century, while in the fourteenth one follows upon the heels of the other."[79] The fascination which Ibn Ezra held for the fourteenth century may have been partly due to the rising interest in astrology.[80] It may also reflect the then growing impact of Kabbala, since Ibn Ezra appeared to be closer to the mystical approach than any other Jewish philosopher. Yet there were also those who regarded Ibn Ezra simply as a profound metaphysician. Joseph ibn Waqār, who was the outstanding representative of the fourteenth-century attempt at reconciling philosophy and Kabbala,[81] recommended Ibn Ezra and

76. See Steinschneider, *Hebr. Übersetzungen*, pp. 313–314; and *Magazin für die Wissenschaft des Judentums*, ed. A. Berliner and D. Hoffmann, III (Berlin, 1876), pp. 94–100; 140–153; 190–205; Hebr. section, 24–25, contains Mosconi's supercommentary on the Ibn Ezra passage treated by Narboni in our text.

77. See Berliner, *Magazin*, III, 44–45; Hebr. section, 7.

78. See Geiger, *Melo Chofnajim*, Hebr. section, p. 20.

79. See Steinschneider, "Supercommentare zu Ibn Esra," *Jüdische Zeitschrift für Wissenschaft und Leben*, ed. A. Geiger, VI (Breslau, 1868), p. 123.

80. See Steinschneider, *Hebr. Übersetzungen*, p. 318.

81. See Steinschneider, *Gesammelte Schriften*, ed. H. Malter and A. Marx (Berlin, 1925), I, 171ff.; G. Vajda, *Recherches sur la philosophie et la kabbale dans la pensée juive du moyen âge* (Paris–La Haye, 1962), pp. 115–297.

Maimonides as the two philosophers to be studied.[82] Joseph Kaspi (1279–*circa* 1340), who was perhaps closest in spirit to Narboni, wrote a commentary on the obscure passages in Ibn Ezra's commentary on the Tora.[83] It contains an interpretation of the excursus on Exodus 33:21 treated in Narboni's *Epistle*,[84] and has certain points of contact with the latter. How much Narboni himself was attracted by Ibn Ezra may be gauged also from the fact that he wrote yet another Epistle (which, unfortunately, is lost) commenting this time on Ibn Ezra's allegorical interpretation of the Genesis account of paradise.[85] From the references to this work in the Commentary on the *Guide*[86] it appears that he interpreted the "garden" (*gan*) as a symbol of man or microcosm, and the "tree of life" as man's intellectual conception of all beings in the sublunar sphere. In this context too the term *shiᶜur* occurs, denoting here the "measure" of the tree of life which equals the measure of Jacob's ladder, and being tantamount to the measure of man's intellect.

(2) Narboni's second motivation in writing the *Epistle* on the theme of *shiᶜur qomā* was his interest in Kabbala. Although a staunch Averroist, he was, at least in his younger years, captivated by the then somewhat fashionable tendency to bring about a reconciliation between philosophy and Kabbala. His commentary on Ibn Ṭufayl's *Ḥayy ibn Yaqẓān*, written in 1349 (only seven years after he had written the *Epistle*) contains an elaborate passage on the *Sefirot*, the separate intellects, and the spheres[87] which clearly shows the extent to which he had become a follower of Joseph ibn Waqār's effort of harmonization. We do not know in which year Ibn Waqār's great work *Al-Maqāla al-jamīᶜa bayna l-falsafa wal-sharīᶜa* was completed. It would appear that it was already known by the time when Narboni wrote his *Epistle* (1342).[88] When he met him personally in Toledo many years later (1355 or 1358),[89] Ibn Waqār was already a very

82. See the text published by G. Scholem in *Kiryat Sefer*, 20:155 (1943).
83. Edited by Isaac Last in *Zehn Schriften des R. Josef Ibn Kaspi*, II (Pressburg, 1903), 145–196.
84. Last, *Zehn Schriften*, II, 160-162.
85. Listed as no. 20 in Steinschneider, *Cat. Bodl.*, col. 1975.
86. Ed. Jacob Goldenthal (Vienna, 1853), 41a.
87. Quoted and analyzed by Vajda, *Recherches*, pp. 396–403.
88. According to Vajda, *Recherches*, p. 118, Ibn Waqār approached his task circa 1340. In fact, Narboni's commentary on the *Maqāṣid al-falāsifa* (written prior to the *Epistle*) already shows the influence of Ibn Waqār (see below in the text and Note 97.)
89. See CG (ed. Goldenthal), 4a. On Narboni's stay in Toledo see *Cat. Bodl.*, cols. 1967, 1975.

old man.[90] At any rate, his outline of the reconciliation of the Sefirotic system with the philosophical bears, for all its oddities, unmistakable traces of Ibn Waqār's influence. The important thing is that this harmonized system is presented not on behalf of either the Kabbalists or any other group[91] but as his own view: "I shall reveal to you a wonderful mystery . . ."[92] When, toward the end of his life, in the commentary on the *Guide* he refers to certain of these very same matters, he does so by quoting them in the name of the Kabbalists,[93] which seems to indicate that he had moved away from his earlier position. In fact, the commentary on the *Guide* abounds in open or veiled criticisms of the Kabbalists. Thus, under the cloak of rigid objectivism befitting a mere commentator, Narboni refuses to be drawn into the controversy about Maimonides' theory of the purpose of the sacrificial cult but clearly dissociates himself from the kabbalistic notion that it was meant to bring about the unification of the *Sefirot*.[94] He openly rejects the kabbalistic view, which regards the *shekinā* as "being not outside the essence of the Creator." In his opinion, the *shekinā* is identical with the *Merkabā* and as such created.[95] He ironically calls the Kabbalists, who allegedly interpret the rabbinic reference to God as the "Place" of the world in a semiliteral sense, "the Kabbalists who dwell in the light," which obviously is intended as a euphemism for darkness.[96] There is, then, sufficient warrant for assuming that some change of heart had taken place.

What was Narboni's harmonistic view at the earlier stage, and how is it reflected in the *Epistle*? Broadly speaking, Narboni adopted Ibn Waqār's principle of coordination between the *Sefirot*, the separate intellects of the philosophers, and the spheres, or celestial souls, of the astronomers and astrologers. In his commentary on al-Ghazālī's *Maqāṣid*, which precedes the *Epistle*, he relates the special attributes (*middot*) of each of the *Sefirot* to the corresponding qualities of the celestial souls. "For it is in accordance with the action that comes

90. Narboni calls him (CG, 4a) *ha-ḥakam ha-zaqen*.

91. As is the case at the beginning of the passage (Vajda, *Recherches*, p. 396), when Narboni refers to a view held by some "adepts of the Law" (*toriyyim*): viz., the Kabbalists (designated by him also as *toraniyim* or *ha-mequbbalim min ha-toraniyim* or *baᶜale ha-qabbala*). For his use of *toriy* in the general sense of "religious" see Vajda, *Revue des Etudes Juives*, 3(120):391 (1961); Charles Touati, "Dieu et le monde selon Moïse Narboni," *Archives d'Histoire Doctrinale et Littéraire*, 21:194 (1954).

92. Vajda, *Recherches*, p. 399.

93. CG, 62a.

94. *Ibid.*; similarly in the case of the kabbalistic interpretation of *teqiᶜat shofar*, CG, 63b.

95. CG, 49a; see also 62a.

96. *Ibid.*, 14b.

from the sphere that the power and quality of the soul of the sphere and of the *Sefirā* is specified."[97] In the commentary on Ibn Ṭufayl's *Ḥayy ibn Yaqẓān* he offers a full list of correspondences. It starts with the first three *Sefirot*—*Keter* (also named *reʾshit*, *rom*, *ʾayin*), *Ḥokmā*, and *Binā*—which are correlated with the all-encompassing, starless sphere, the sphere of the stars, and Saturn respectively.[98] Exactly the same coordination was offered in one of Ibn Waqār's tentative proposals, the assumption being that this scheme implies also the correlation of the separate intellects or movers of the spheres. The assignment of the first *Sefirā* (*Keter*) to the outermost sphere presupposes the non-identity of *Keter* and *En-Sof*, or, in philosophical terms, of the prime mover and the First Cause.[99] Ibn Waqār discusses also an alternative scheme based on the notion of the identity of *Keter* and *En-Sof*,[100] and it seems that in the *Epistle* Narboni takes this view when referring to God as being called *Keter*.[101] It accords with his philosophical position in the great controversy about the identity or non-identity of God and first mover.[102] As far as the remaining seven *Sefirot* are concerned, Narboni's scheme deviates from Ibn Waqār's outline of alternative possibilities.[103] It does not adopt even the standard denominations and order of the *Sefirot* (which are accepted by Ibn Waqār). He has the following list of *Sefirot* 4–10: (4) *Tifʾeret* or *Ḥesed*, corresponding to Jupiter, (5) *Neẓaḥ*, corresponding to Mars, (6) *Hod*, corresponding to the sun, (7) *Malkut*, corresponding to Venus, (8) *Meʿon Ẓedeq*, corresponding to Mercury, (9) *Yesod*, corresponding to the moon, (10) *Kallā* or *Keneset Yisraʾel*. There is nothing in Ibn Waqār resembling this strange assortment, except that he too, in his first scheme, has a *Sefirā* (in his case, *Yesod*) which is unrelated to any specific sphere, and which (as in the case of Narboni's last) has the function of transmitting the influx from above to the sublunar world. Ibn Waqār identifies it with the agent intellect, the last of the separate intellects.[104] Narboni does not

97. CIP, Vatican MS. 260, fol. 54*r*. In this connection Narboni identifies Samaʾel (to whom the scapegoat is offered) with the soul of Mars.

98. See Vajda, *Recherches*, pp. 399–401.

99. *Ibid.*, pp. 400, 265.

100. *Ibid.*, pp. 266ff.

101. Line 161 of our text.

102. On this controversy see Vajda, "Un Champion de l'avicennisme," *Revue Thomiste*, XLVIII, No. 3 (1948), 480–508. Narboni clearly sides with Averroes. See CPC, Bodleian MS. Michael 119, fol. 139(i)*v*.

103. See Vajda, *Recherches*, p. 266.

104. *Ibid.*, p. 265.

mention the agent intellect in this context but he does so in the *Epistle*, where he approvingly mentions the kabbalistic designation *Keneset Yisraʾel* for the agent intellect.[105] Whatever Narboni's source for the compilation of his list of *Sefirot* 4–10, his basic concept of co-ordination could only have been Ibn Waqār's treatise. For while he may have adopted the identification of the *Sefirot* with the separate intellects from other Kabbalists,[106] their correlation with the astrologically conceived souls of the spheres or stars could only have come from Ibn Waqār.

Since by the time of Narboni's literary activity all Kabbalists were practically agreed in identifying the *shiᶜur qomā* with the *Sefirot*, it is not difficult to see why he was attracted to this theme. It held out the prospect of a philosophical treatment once the *Sefirot* were correlated or equated with the separate intellects, a position which Narboni had already embraced in his commentary on the *Maqāṣid*. The sophisticated manner in which the Kabbalists themselves had dealt with the *Shiᶜur Qomā* must have heightened the respectability of this previously embattled tract and may have served as a challenge to a philosopher like Narboni to try his hand at commenting on it. This and the fact that in Ibn Ezra's exposition he found a precedent combined to arouse his desire to write on the subject. The way he tackled it, however, owed its inspiration to Averroes.

In the *Epistle*, he quotes two passages from Averroes[107] which are taken from the Long Commentary on *Metaphysics* and from the *Tahāfut al-Tahāfut* respectively.[108] The first of these makes the point that each of the separate intellects recognizes the First Cause (God) under different aspects and that the totality of motions of the spheres forms a harmonious whole owing to the unifying principle provided by God as the common object of the intellects' cognition. The second enlarges on this theme by showing God to be the principle and cause of the hierarchy of existents. The key notion of the entire passage is

105. Lines 88–89 in our text.

106. Thus Jacob b. Sheshet and Abraham of Cologne identified the *sefirā ḥokmā* with the agent intellect (cf. Scholem, *Tarbiz*, 2:215, n. 96 [1930–31]); Abraham Abulafia equated the latter with the *sefirā malkut* (Scholem, *Major Trends*, p. 143), Jacob Ha-Kohen, in a text representing a late recension, with the *sefirā reshit*: viz., *keter* (Scholem, *Madaᶜē Ha-Yahadut*, II, 227, text b, lines 4–13). See also Scholem, *ᶜIqbotav shel Gabirol ba-qabbala*, in *Meʾassef Sofrē Ereẓ Yisraʾel* (1940), p. 174, where an anonymous Spanish Kabbalist is quoted who sought to reconcile Maimonides with the Kabbala and, to this end, identified the separate intellects with the *sefirot*.

107. Lines 96–109 and 135–156 in our text.

108. See Notes 63 and 74 on the Translation, where we have identified these passages. Narboni gives no reference.

found in the statement that in thinking Himself God thinks the existents in their noblest mode of existence. In other words, God's self-intellectualization, far from implying ignorance of the other existents, is a thinking of the very same forms which are found at the various levels of existence below Him; but He thinks them in a way in which no other being can think them: in their noblest mode and order. The various levels at which forms exist are, starting from the bottom, forms-in-matter, or material forms; forms as conceived by the human intellect; forms existing in the agent intellect and, in a rising scale of excellence, the forms in the other separate intellects, and, finally, the forms existing in the First Cause or God. Again, Averroes stresses the corollary of this view: "So it has become evident . . . that there is one single order and act in which all existents participate in common." Narboni takes this to mean that God is in fact "identical with His conceiving the existents in their most perfect and most glorious mode."[109] Quoting Averroes' saying that God was in some respect all existents,[110] he feels justified to apply to God Ibn Ezra's term "Image" in the sense of His being the imageless "universal aspect of all images."[111] In a subsequent passage he explains in the same way the verse (Numbers 11:8), "and the image of God doth he behold": "All existents are the image of God, seeing that they are in Him in the most noble [way of] existence."[112] The Averroean formula describing God as the most noble existence of the forms—as the existence of the forms "in perfect and simple unity"[113]—is linked by Narboni with Maimonides' concept of God as the "principle" (*al-mabdaʾ*) of all existent things (*Guide*, I, 16). It means, according to Narboni, that "He thinks the forms in the most glorious existence possible."[114] It is, then, clear that for him the essence of God consists in the simplicity and unity in which the forms exist in God, or, to put it differently, the most glorious level of existence of forms is tantamount to God's essence or existence, both being the same. In this view, which is reminiscent of Leibniz' concept of God as the central Monad,[115] God, while distinct from all other

109. Lines 210–211 in our text.
110. Lines 162–163.
111. Lines 161–162.
112. Lines 237–238.
113. Lines 120–121.
114. Lines 123–127.
115. See Leibniz, *The Monadology And Other Philosophical Writings*, trans. by Robert Latta (1898), p. 243, n. 75. The relevant paragraphs in the Monadology are nos. 57, 60, 62–63.

beings and transcending them, is yet intimately linked with them. He is their existence in its most superb mode, and there is, in Averroes' words, "one single order and act in which all existents participate in common."

It is this notion which struck Narboni as offering a key to the understanding of the allegorical meaning of *shiᶜur qomā*. Immediately after the quotation of the second Averroes passage, which, toward the end, contains the sentence just referred to, he comments: "It should be clear from all this that the sensible existents are abstract forms in the First Cause, and that it thinks them in the most noble way. This being the case, we may call the [confining] measure of the existents *shiᶜur qomā* ['measure of the body'] in accordance with the dictum of theirs (*Ḥagiga* 12a): 'The world went on expanding until the Holy One, blessed be He, rebuked it.' "[116] As he immediately explains, the totality of existents (which we take to mean all beings except God) is designated by the term *qomā*. He might have added that God is symbolically called its "measure" (*shiᶜur*). Yet the meaning is plain from the previous sentence as such, since it differentiates between the measure and the body, and by quoting the passage *Ḥagiga* 12a, identifies God with the measure.[117] God, then is the "measure" (*shiᶜur*) of the existents (*qomā*). The term "measure" is taken here in analogy to Aristotle's use of it, as has already been noted in Charles Touati's excellent study on Narboni.[118] According to Aristotle, the measure (*metron*) or principle (*archē*) is some invisible unit (*Metaphysics*, X, i, 1052b, 32), and it is always akin to the things measured. Thus, the measure of magnitude is magnitude; of sounds, a sound; and so on (1053a, 25ff.). Narboni is able to apply the term "measure" to God in relation to the world because he has adopted Averroes' notion of God as the existents in their most glorious mode of being, a notion which implies a certain kinship between God and the existents. It is this kinship which justifies the use of the term "measure," in the sense of "principle," with regard to God. In the commentary on *Ḥayy ibn Yaqẓān* he says distinctly that God is the measure of everything in a manner comparable to the one and

116. Lines 157–160.

117. In the same Talmudic passage Resh Laqish interprets the Divine name *Shadday* as denoting the measure: *ani she-ʾamarti la-ᶜolam day*. On the possibly Platonic background of the rabbinic concept see Manuel Joel, *Blicke in die Religionsgeschichte*, I (Breslau–Leipzig, 1880), 147, n. 1; for the motif of the "limit" (*horos*) in Gnosticism see Jean Doresse, *The Secret Books of the Egyptian Gnostics* (New York, 1960), 28.

118. "Dieu et le monde selon Moïse Narboni" (see Note 91), 195ff.

indivisible unit which is the principle and measure of the beings entering into that particular category.[119] Reflecting Aristotle's remark (*Metaphysics*, X, ii, 1053b, 29ff.) about white as the unity of color, he says in the commentary on the *Guide*: "Even as the white which is the measure of colors neutralizes vision, so that glorious substance [namely, God] which is the measure of all substances neutralizes the faculty of the intellect so as to make it incapable of comprehending Him on account of the power of His manifestation."[120] He bases this analogy on the fact that God is the principle of all substances in the way in which there is a principle in every genus such as sound, color, et cetera.

The reference to God as the "measure of all existents" is paralleled, in the Commentary on the *Guide*,[121] by the interpretation of the rabbinic designation of God as the "Place of the world." This term, Narboni explains, simply means that God is the "Form of the world" in the sense in which the form perfects and, at the same time, limits a thing. As in the *Epistle*, he quotes in this connection the rabbinic dictum describing God as having called a halt to the expanding universe by His "rebuke." He sees in it an allegorical reference to the limitation of the world by virtue of its formal principle (namely, God). "The Mover has a relation to the moved, or the Form to the formed," and in this sense limitation is a necessary corollary of the concept of God as the form-giving principle. It may, however, be noted that Narboni does not revert here to his interpretation of *shiᶜur qomā* in the dual sense of God (measure)–world (body) but takes it as a single term denoting the limited universe: " 'The heaven for height, and the earth for depth' (Proverbs 25:3)—this is the *shiᶜur qomā*." In his *Epistle* on Ibn Ezra's allegorical interpretation of the "garden" (see above, Page 242) he similarly speaks of the *shiᶜur* of what is between earth and heaven, and of the *shiᶜur* of Jacob's ladder.[122] The dual-term theory seems to be confined to the *Epistle on Shiᶜur Qomā*. It is reminiscent of the division of the term which we found in the *Tiqqunē Zohar*[123] where, however, the order is reversed in that *shiᶜur* denotes the lower, and *qomā* the higher principle.

119. Quoted by Touati, *op. cit.*, 195–196 from a manuscript of the Bibliothèque Nationale, Paris. Narboni distinctly refers to the discussion in book 10 of the *Metaphysics*.
120. CG, 10a–b (on I, 59).
121. CG, 14b (on I, 70).
122. CG, 41a.
123. See above, Page 236.

In our *Epistle*, *qomā* stands definitely for the total order of the existents, excluding God, who is the "measure." Unlike the kabbalistic view, which sees in the *shiᶜur qomā* a reference to the *Sefirot*, Narboni does not confine the *qomā* to the separate intellects (which, as we have seen, he equated with the *Sefirot*). In his interpretation the term covers all levels of existence: the three worlds of sublunar, celestial, and separate forms.[124] In this respect he follows Ibn Ezra, while the interpretation of *shiᶜur* as referring to God is entirely his own and based, as we have seen, on Averroes' concept of God as well as on Aristotle's notion of measure. There is, however, an echo of the Kabbalists' view in his identification of the *qomā* of the "perfect man," who is obviously a symbol of the macrocosm (see above, Page 230), with "what the adepts of the *Sefirot* call the 'Tree.' "[125] This equation is repeated later in the text when the macrocosm is said to be allegorized in Jacob's ladder and in the Kabbalists' tree.[126] Narboni obviously confused here the kabbalistic notion of the *shiᶜur qomā* as *Sefirot* with Ibn Ezra's view of it as the macrocosm or Meṭaṭron. His *lapsus* is an involuntary testimony to the challenge which the kabbalistic treatment of the theme had presented to him. In spite of his own involvement in Kabbala (see above, Pages 242–245), he did not, however, pursue this line but interpreted the *Shiᶜur Qomā* philosophically on an Averroean basis. The *shiᶜur qomā* is but the figurative expression of Averroes' notion of "one single order and act in which all existents participate in common."

The detailed exposition of this theme is modeled on Ibn Ezra's allegorical treatment of it. Significantly, Narboni introduces his philosophical disquisition (followed by the two quotations from Averroes) when a comment is called for on Ibn Ezra's reference to the "length" between the two extreme points: between the "Prince of the Presence" and the "end of the power."[127] It is this reference which serves as a cue prompting him to enter into the philosophical aspect of the matter. The upshot of his discussion is that the *qomā* as interpreted by him is what Ibn Ezra meant by the "length" from the highest but God to the lowest, and that God is the measure and principle of it. His detailed interpretation of the *shiᶜur qomā* begins

124. Cf. line 186 of our text: *we-hinē heẓib ha-qomā*; line 189: *we-ʾaḥar she-heᶜemid gobā ha-qomā*.
125. Line 207.
126. Lines 251–252.
127. See Notes 21 and 22 on the Translation.

by resuming the thread where he had left it off: "He [Ibn Ezra] established the *qomā*, saying: 'Length is [the extension] between two points'—is the *qomā*," and so on.[128] Ibn Ezra, he repeats a few lines below, has set up the "height of the Body" (*goba ha-qomā*).[129] It is visualized in the form of the human figure. It has a right side and a left, a front and a back. Narboni explains that right and left indicate high and low in the order of beings.[130] (The meaning of front and back will be discussed below.) Following Ezekiel's description of the division of the body into a part from the loins downward and a part from the loins upward (1:27), he allegorically interprets the soles of its feet, which are the very lowest part, as the accidents inherent in the sublunar bodies; the parts from the soles up to the knees as the sublunar bodies; the thighs as the celestial bodies; the upper part as the separate intellects, the head representing the first intellect;[131] and the face as God's essence.[132] The part from the loins upward is described by Ezekiel also in terms of "an appearance of splendor, as the color of electrum"; and the lower part as "the appearance of fire" (1:27; 8:2). Narboni sees here a symbolic reference to the separate intellects and the bodies (celestial and sublunar) respectively, and applies to the division thus indicated the terms "flame" (*shalhebet*) and "coal" (*gaḥelet*) in the sense in which they are used in the *Sefer Yeẓirā* (I, 7): as symbols of an indivisible unity.[133] In the commentary on the *Guide* the symbolism is slightly changed in that both the splendor and the fire (the flame and the coal) are applied to the realm of the separate intellects, higher and lower. They are all unified by virtue of the concept of God which they form (albeit from different aspects), and the denial of this unity is tantamount to what the mystics mean by "cutting the plants" (the term for heresy).[134] In the *Epistle*, where he is concerned with establishing the concept of the single and unified order of the *qomā* as the totality of existents, he applies the two divisions of the body to the entire universe.

Of special interest is the distinction between front and back. It

128. Line 186.

129. Line 189. The term *gobā ha-qomā* ("the height of the body") clearly shows that Narboni understood *qomā* in the sense of "body," and not of "height" or "stature," as Touati assumes (p. 198, n. 4).

130. Lines 190–196.

131. See Note 100 on the Translation.

132. Lines 220–223.

133. Lines 215–216.

134. CG, 48b.

stems from the famous Exodus passage (33:23) on which Ibn Ezra's treatment of the theme is based. The front or face of God is "His true essence which cannot be perceived."[135] This interpretation, which goes back to Philo,[136] is specified by the statement that God's Face stands for His way of conceiving the existents, while His Back stands for the manner in which the existents necessarily follow from Him. That the Face cannot be seen thus means that we are unable to know the quiddity of the concept which God has of the existents.[137] The Face of God is also said to stand for the existence of all things in Him:[138] namely, for the most glorious mode of the existence of forms. In other words, the Face is identical with the absolute and simple unity of intellect, intelligent, and intelligible which is God.[139] It is distinct from the "head" of the *qomā*—that is from the first intellect[140]—and having no image, it is the "universal aspect of all the images."[141] The term *Keter* which Narboni applies to God fits the concept of the Face as the supreme level of the existence of forms, since it has the connotation of that which "surrounds" and thereby limits *qua* form-giving principle.[142] Although in Narboni's outline of the *Sefirot* (see above, Page 244) *Keter* is not identical with *En-Sof* and hence is below God, he uses here this term probably to indicate the concept of God as the highest in the series of existencies. The symbol of the Face serves the same purpose. For although the Face is distinctly unknowable and transcendent, it is not separable from the figure designated as the Body (*qomā*). Being its measure and principle, it is akin to it. It is the eternally veiled Face of the Body. The Averroean notion of the single order and act in which all existents participate is thus maintained in the simile of the Face. In this sense Narboni can say toward the end of the *Epistle*[143] that all existents are the "image of God" since they are in Him in the most noble way.[144]

135. Line 223; see also 198–199, 239–240.
136. *De Specialibus Legibus*, I, 8, 43–46; *De Fuga et Inventione*, 166.
137. Lines 164–169.
138. Line 210.
139. Lines 120–127.
140. Line 223.
141. Lines 161–162.
142. In his outline of the *sefirot* in the commentary on *Ḥayy ibn Yaqẓān* the first *sefirā* is said to be called *keter* "because it surrounds everything" (see Vajda, *Recherches*, p. 400).
143. Lines 234–240.
144. The identification of the "Face" with the Self-thinking or essence of God, though based on the Exodus passage and its treatment in medieval Jewish philosophy, may also

Narboni was conscious of the fact that the concept of God as expressed in the *Epistle* meant a radical departure from the prevalent (Neoplatonic) theology which had stressed the total otherness of God. His epilogue clearly indicates the sense of reluctance he felt in committing his interpretation of *shiᶜur qomā* to writing. His decision to take that step, he tells us, was motivated by his awareness that the time in which he lived was ripe for a bolder disclosure of the truth that, until then, had been concealed in the form of allegory. Now "all Israelites" were to share in the "light" of truth and in the "true felicity" vouchsafed by its possession.[145] This is the authentic language of *Aufklärung*, and the truth propounded is tantamount to a radical reversion, under the influence of Averroes, to the Aristotelian concept of God as the Self-thinking supreme Intellect. Plotinus had rejected this concept as incompatible with the absolute unity of the One.[146] Maimonides, following Avicenna,[147] had admitted it (*Guide*, I, 68) but adhered, at the same time, to the negative theology of Neoplatonism. God's intellect, he insisted, has nothing in common with ours (*Guide*, III, 20). The ambivalence of this position did not escape severe criticism.[148] There were two alternative ways to avoid it: either to adopt the classical Neoplatonic view, which denied intellect to the One, or else to return to the Aristotelian concept of God, at the price of giving up negative theology. This alternative had been clearly formulated in an early Neoplatonic

---

owe something to the prominence which the concept of the "Face [*wajh*] of Allāh" acquired in the Koran (see *Shorter Encyclopaedia of Islam* [Leiden, 1953], p. 36) and the significance attached to it by al-Ghazālī. The phrase "Everything perishes, except His Face" (*Koran*, XXVIII:88) is explained by him to mean: "For everything other than Allāh is, when considered in and by itself, pure not-being; and if considered from the 'aspect' [*wajh*, lit. 'face'] of existence flowing from the First Being, it is viewed as existing, but not in itself; solely from the 'aspect' which belongs to Him who gives it existence . . . All existence is, exclusively, His Face" (see W. H. T. Gairdner, *Al-Ghazzali's Mishkāt Al-Anwār* [London, 1924], p. 104). The closeness of Narboni's interpretation of the "Face" to al-Ghazālī's is striking. Interestingly enough, the reproduction of God's answer to Moses' request (Ex. 34:21) in the Koran (VII:135) makes no mention of the "Face." It reads: "Said He, 'Thou shalt not see Me; but behold the mountain—if it stays fast in its place, then thou shalt see Me.' And when his Lord revealed Him to the mountain, He made it crumble to dust." An inexact rendering of this Koran passage is found in Narboni's CPC (MS. Michael, 126*r*), as noted already by Munk (*Mélanges*, p. 453, n. 1).

145. Lines 259–265. See also CG, 34a.

146. See *Enneads*, III.8.8; V.3.12–13; V.6.2.

147. Cf. S. Munk, *Le Guide des égarés . . . par Moïse ben Maimoun*, I (Paris, 1856), 301–302, n. 4; for Maimonides' indebtedness to al-Fārābī see my article "Maᵓamar be-yiḥud ha-Boreᵓ," *Tarbiz*, 27, nos. 2–3 (1958), p. 301, n. 2.

148. Such criticism is offered in the *Maᵓamar be-yiḥud ha-Boreᵓ* (anonymous) published by me (see preceding note).

work: Damascius' (fifth-century) *Dubitationes et solutiones de primis principiis in Platonis Parmenidem,*[149] where the first aporia reads: "Whether the so-called unique principle of all is beyond all things, or a certain one out of all; for example, the highest point of the class of things proceeding from it."[150] Averroes opted for the second alternative. He rejected the negative interpretation of the term "intellect" as applied to God: "for this is not true—on the contrary, it is the most special appellation for His essence according to the Peripatetics, in contrast to Plato's opinion that the intellect is not the First Principle and that intellect cannot be attributed to the First Principle."[151] Narboni sides with Averroes, as we have seen, and by describing God as the "measure" (*shiᶜur*) of the "body" (*qomā*)—that is, of the hierarchy of existents— affirms exactly what Damascius had pointed out as the Aristotelian alternative; he makes God into "a certain one out of all, for example, the highest point of the class of things proceeding from it." The corollary of this view is a doctrine of attributes which substitutes the principle of analogy (*per prius et posterius*) for that of homonymity. Narboni's fears lest Jewish susceptibilities be offended by his departure from negative theology were unfounded. His view had already been anticipated by Gersonides, and it was to be reiterated by even so staunchly an orthodox thinker as Abraham Bibago in his *Derek Emunā* (written toward the end of the fifteenth century). In formulations which echo Narboni's, Bibago says that God "comprehends Himself and thereby comprehends all beings; for they are Himself in an infinitely more glorious form of existence." God is said to be "the Form of the world in an infinitely glorious sense" (chapter ii, 12d–13a). "All things are, in a sense, the 'Face of the Most High' [*penē ᶜelyon*]" (13a), a statement which seems to elaborate Narboni's view of the "Face" of God. It should also be noted that Bibago lists the *Shiᶜur Qomā* among other mystical treatises (*Hekalot*, *Sefer Bahir*) which are said to contain metaphysics (*ḥokmā ᵓelohit*) of the highest order. This, again, appears to reflect Narboni's interpretation of the *Shiᶜur Qomā* in the *Epistle.*

149. Ed. C. A. Ruelle (Paris, 1889), vol. I, p. 1, 1–2. See Ronald F. Hathaway, "Hierarchy and the Definition of Order in the Letters of Pseudo-Dionysius" (unpubl. diss., Brandeis University, 1965), p. 30, n. 63.

150. Damascius, of course, adopted the Neoplatonic viewpoint. The Platonic phrase *epêkeina tōn pántōn* is frequently used by him. See Hathaway, *loc. cit.*

151. Averroes, *Tahāfut al-Tahāfut*, ed. Maurice Bouyges (Beirut, 1930), p. 310. We are quoting Simon van den Bergh's translation, I (London, 1954), 186.

The concept of God offered in the *Epistle* reappears in the *Treatise on Free Will* (*Ha-maʾamar ba-beḥirā*), written by Narboni at the very end of his life, and representing another valuable document of his personal faith.[152] What distinguishes the treatment of the theme in the *Epistle* is the wealth of symbolism employed in the service of explicating his notion of God and God's relation to the world. God is the *shiʿur* and the "Face," while the world is the *qomā*, the sanctuary (*mishkan*), the perfect Man or Man, Jacob's ladder, the image (*temunā*) of God, and, up to a point, the Kabbalists' tree. There is a superb concrescence of symbols and motifs in this unifying vision of his. The challenge presented by the kabbalistic interpretation of the *shiʿur qomā* is fully met on philosophical ground but not without some reverberations of kabbalistic influence.

The text of the *Epistle* was first published by Simḥa Pinsker in the periodical *Kokebe Yiẓḥaq* (ed. M. E. Stern), 30:25–33 (Vienna, 1864), on the basis of a single manuscript, which is described in *Catalog Pinsker*, pp. 18 and 54. The critical edition presented here is based on Pinsker's text (א), and on the following two manuscripts:

MS. Schwager (ב), described in *Catalog Schwager*, 20, 479, now in the possession of the Jewish Theological Seminary, New York, accession no. 35979, fols. 11*r*–14*v* (bound with Joseph Gikatila's *Sefer ha-meshalim*). It is written in an Italian hand of about the sixteenth century.

MS. Reggio 51 (ג) referred to by Steinschneider, *Cat. Bodl.*, col. 1974; *Idem, Hebr. Bibl.*, IX, no. 53 (1869), p. 139; XV, no. 87 (1875), pp. 49–50; now in the Bodleian Library, Oxford, and listed in *Catalog Neubauer*, no. 2250, 6, fols. 42*r*–46*v*.*

152. See *Cat. Bodl.*, col. 1977; The treatise is published in *Sefer Dibre Ḥakamim*, ed. Eliezer Ashkenazi (Metz, 1849), pp. 37–41. It is briefly analyzed in Yiẓḥaq Julius Guttmann, *Ha-Pilosofia shel ha-Yahadut* (Jerusalem, 1951), pp. 190–191.

* My sincere thanks are extended to The Keeper of Oriental Books, The Bodleian Library, Oxford, for permission to publish the text of the manuscript; and to Dr. Menahem Schmelczer, Associate Librarian, the Jewish Theological Seminary, New York, for permission to publish the text of the manuscript in the possession of the Seminary and for valuable bibliographical information.

2. The Text

כל הנקרא בשמי ולכבודי בראתיו יצרתיו אף עשיתיו.

למה שהיה הכל הוא השלם והשלם הוא אשר אין חוץ ממנו דבר היה הכל האמתי הוא אשר אין חוץ ממנו דבר כלל. וזהו הרצון במלת כל הנזכרת בזה הפסוק. ולמה שהיה הדעת והיודע והידוע אחד אמר כי הוא ר״ל כל הנמצאות נקראות בשמו, ירצה שהן עומדות בעצמו. אח״כ ביאר אופן התחייב היותם נמצאים בעצמם מלבד מציאותם בו ותכליתם האחרון ואמר ולכבודי בראתיו ר״ל הכבוד, יצרתיו ר״ל הגוף העליון, אף עשיתיו השפל. וירצה בכבודו עצמו אשר הוא רצונו וחכמתו כי הכל אחד שעצמו ג״כ נקרא כבודו כאמרו הראני נא את כבודך. הנה נראה מזה הפסוק כי הנמצאות כולן עומדות בשם הכבוד. ולפי שהן בעצמן במציאות אחרת נתחייב ממנו בארו הנביאים הסוד האלהי הזה וקראו הכל אדם וכנו חלקים מה בשם רגלים וחלקים אחרים מתנים וענין אחר אחורים והיותר מעולה שבהם הפנים. והם אמרו דמות אדם ואמרו ותחת רגליו. אח״כ לתוקף הגלות נתמעטו הלבבות ונצטרכו לבאור יותר ארוך וחברו על זה חכמי ישראל ספר שעור קומה. וכבר רמז עליו הר״מ בפרק ע׳ התחיל בו דע שהנמצא כלו כאיש אחד. והנה החכם ר׳ אברהם בן עזרא באר זה יותר בשלמות בפסוק ויאמר משה אל ה׳ ראה אתה אמר אלי כשאמר ז״ל:

וזה היום שראה משה מה שבקש היה לו כיום מתן תורה לישראל ולא הגיע אדם לפניו ואחריו אל מעלתו וחכמתו. ורבותינו ע״ה אמרו שהראה לו קשר של תפלין. ודברם נכון רק לא כאשר יפרשוהו חכמי הדורות שהוא כמשמעו כי סוד עמוק הוא עד מאוד. אמר אברהם המחבר כבר פירשתי כי השם הנכבד הנכתב ואינו נקרא ככה הוא שם העצם והעצם הוא הכבוד וכו׳ עד אמרו וכל חשבון שהוא מהאחדים. עוד אמר מתדבק לזה זה לשונו: הנה תמצא האחד שהוא הכל. על כן סוד התפלות והתהלות וטעם והתגדלתי והתקדשתי ועוד אשר בך אתפאר. והנה האחד האמתי אין לו תמונה והוא כדרך כלל לכל התמונות כי ממנו יצאו. והנה הגויות העליונות שהם המאורות והכוכבים אין להם פנים ואחור אף כי לנשמת אדם העליונה אף כי למשרתי עליון אף כי לעליון העליונים. והנה האורך בין שתי נקודות והנקודה הקרובה אל הפועל שר הפנים והנקודה האחרת סוף הכח. ותנועת האדם לפנים והגוף העליון

---

1 ב לכבודי | 2 אג אשר – דבר ב ליתא דבר אג ממנו היה ב ליתא ממנו אב האמתי
ג האמת | 3 בג הרצון א הרינון | 4 ב ליתא הידוע אג ליתא ר״ל | 6 א ואמר ב ואמרו
ג ויאמר | 8 אג נקרא ב יקרא | 9 אג הכבוד ב הנבחר אב בעצמן ג עצמן
בג במציאות א כמציאות א נתחייב בג נתחייבו | 10 ב הסוד האלהי הזה אג זה הסוד |
11 אג מעולה ב המעולה אג שבהם ב שבאדם אג והם אמרו ב והוא אמרו |
12 אג ואמרו ב ואמר | 13 אג ספר ב ליתא | 14 אג יותר בשלמות ב בשלמות יותר |
15 ב ליתא ויאמר משה אל ה׳ | 16 ב מה שבקש אג ובקש מה שבקש | 17 אג ורבותינו – אמרו
ב אמרו | 18 אג ודברם ב ודבריו | 19–18 אג סוד – מאוד ב סוד עמוק מאד |
19 ב ליתא כבר פירשתי ב ליתא הנכתב | 20 בג הוא א המה בג הוא הכבוד א היה
הכבוד ב וכל אג כל א מאחדים | 22 א ליתא והתהלות ב ליתא האמתי | 23 בג כדרך
כלל א כדרך כל א ממנו ב ממנה | 24 אג שהם (שהן) הכוכבים בג אף כי
א אף (שתי פעמים) | 25 א העליון אג קרובה |

אל הימין והצמח אל העליון. והנה משה יכול לדעת ולראות בעין לבו איך תדבקנה הבריות ביוצר בראשית ומדרך הכבוד אין כח בנברא לדעתו. וזהו לא יראני האדם וחי בעבור היות נשמת האדם עם הגוף. והנה אחרי מות המשכיל תגיע נשמתו למעלה גדולה שלא הגיע כן בחייו. והנה משה שב כללי. על כן אמר ידעתיך בשם כי הוא לבדו יודע הפרטים וחלקיהם בדרך כל. ובעבור כי הנכבד באדמה הוא האדם על כן צורת הכרובים. והנכבד באדם ישראל על כן דבר קשר של תפלין. על כן כתוב בס׳ שעור קומה כי השם בורא כל גוף וכל נכבד מהגוף והנבזה מהגוף הוא המקרה. ואמר ר׳ ישמעאל כל היודע שעורו של יוצר בראשית מובטח לו שהוא בן העולם הבא ואני ועקיבא ערבים בדבר זה. וזהו נעשה אדם בצלמנו כדמותנו. ואמר עוד וזה לשונו: והכף כדמות סתר כמסתיר עצם השמש בכפו שלא תפרד הנשמה מעל גויתו. והנה וראית את אחורי מפאת שהוא הכל וכבודו מלא הכל ומאתו הכל וכל תמונת כל. וזהו ותמונת ה׳ יביט.

עד הנה דברי החכם השלם ר׳ אברהם בן עזרא המחקה החכמה האלהית על אמתתה. אמנם שהם יצטרכו אל ביאור כדי שתובן כונתו בשלמות. על כן אני משה ב״ר יהושע בן מר דוד הנרבוני אמרתי בלבי לפרש זה הענין ולהרחיב בו המאמר ואומר: הנה אמרו שהראה לו קשר של תפלין והדברים נכונים ירצה שהראה לו קשר העלול בעלה שהוא העקר והכל תפל לו ונדבק בו והודיעו איך מתחייב ממנו שהוא סוד האלהות לא שהודיעו מהות המחוייב כי קצת נמנע לו וקצת אפשר לכל ועל כן אמר שהוא סוד עמוק עד מאד. אחרי כן באר אמתת השם כדי שילקח ממנו ביאור על השמות שבאו בשעור קומה אשר אין להם מובן כפי הנגלה ויודע בקבלה כאשר אמר אברהם אבינו ביצירה שקלן צרפן והתחיל ואמר כי השם הנכתב וכו׳ עד אמרו הנה תמצא האחד האמתי שהוא הכל על כן סוד התפלות והתהלות. ירצה כי הוא הברכה המלאה ומאתו ימלאו הצנורות כאמרו ומלא ברכת ה׳. והוא אמרו וטעם והתגדלתי והתקדשתי. ירצה שמציאותו משובחת בענין שממנו יצא מה שנמצא והוא לו פאר כאמרו אשר בך אתפאר, כי ישראל שם משותף. וכאשר באר זה רצה לבאר בו אחור ופנים איך יאמר בו ועשאו בתמונה כוללת במשל האחד ואמר והנה האחד האמתי אין לו תמונה והוא בדרך כלל לכל התמונות כי מאתו יצאו. ונשמר מן הגשמות ואמר והנה הגויות העליונות ואח״כ באר הנמשל ודמה צורה ליוצרה ואמר והנה האורך

---

27 אב אל הימין ג הימין אג אל העליון ב הוא העליון א משה ע״ה | 28 בג וזהו
א וזה בג האדם א אדם | 30 אג גדולה ב ליתא אב שב ג משב (?) אג אמר
ב אמר השם | 31 אג בדרך כל ב בדרך הכל | 33 אג כתוב ב כתיב אג בספר
שיעור קומה ב בשיעור קומה אג מגוף | 34–33 אג ליתא הוא המקרה | 35 א עולם הבא
בג ז״ל | 36 ג כדמות אב כדמותנו | 37 אג הנשמה ב נשמתו ב אחורי ופני לא יראו |
40 אג שתובן ב שתבין אג על כן ב וע״כ | 41 ב הנרבוני ז״ל | 42 אג ודבריהם
ב ודברים | 43–42 אג קשר העלול בעלה ב איך העלול – בעלה ב תפל אג טפל |
44 אג קצת ב קצתו | 46 אג השמות ב השלמות | 47 ב והתחיל בזה ג השם הנכבד
ב עד אמרו אג עוד אמר | 48 אג האחד האמתי ב האחד אב סוד ג סדור ג והתהלות
ב והתחנות א והתהוות | 49 אג ימלאו ב הכל ימלאו אג כאמרו ב באמרו | 50 ג שממנו
א שממנה ב ליתא | 51 אג כאמרו ועוד | 52–51 אג רצה לבאר בו ב רצה לבאר איך יאמרו
אחור ופנים בו | 53–52 אג והנה האחד האמתי ב וזה האחד | 53 ב כלל – יצאו אג כלל
וכו׳ | 54 אג והנה ב והנה מן ב ואח״כ אג ואחר ב באר אג בטל |

בין שתי נקודות. ואי אפשר לי מבלי שאביא בזה המקום מה שהתבאר באלהיות על דרך הקצור מזה הסוד ר״ל שעור קומה כי הוא פרי האלהיות והוא כח הכרחי בסבת זה המאמר ממנו ואומר:

נתישר מאת האל אל ההצלחה האמתית ויוצץ לנו הנכסף לחכמים באחרית הימים והוא סוד הש״י. בארו הפילוסופים כי אין בנמצא כי אם שנים האל ובריאותיו והנמצאות כולם זולת האל נמצאות מאתו והוא הנמצא האמתי היודע הכל ודעתו והוא הכל אחד והשכל והמשכיל והמושכל הכל אחד בו ית׳. וכבר הארכנו בבאור זה בבאורינו לספר כונות הפילוסופים ונודע לפי זה לשקועים בחכמה. ובארו שהנמצאות כלם יש להם מציאות מתחלף וחקו זה ואמרו שמציאותם הראשון הוא מציאותם ההיולאני בכסא הכבוד והשמים ושמי השמים והגופות השפלים בעצמם ומציאותם החמרי אשר להם במה שהוא חמרי הוא המציאות היותר פחות שישנו להם. אחר כן יתעלה מציאותם כפי אשר יראה מן החמר ותחלת התעלותם הוא פתוחם בספירות העין דרך משל כי יופשטו מן החמר באופן שהר גבוה אלף פרסא תכילהו בת עין. אחרי כן יופשט עוד מן החוש והוא שיראה אותם האדם אחר העלמם מן החוש וימצאם בנפש ר״ל בחוש המשותף. עוד תאמר הנפש למלאך ויתעלו ויתחקו בדמיון ויפריד קצתם מקצת וירכיב קצתם עם קצת כי זה פעל הדמיון רק הם עדיין חלקיים פרטיים. והנה ישובו למציאות יותר משובח בהפשיטם השכל ויפתחם צורות נכבדות נפרדות ותמונות כוללות בגדרים ובציורים. [אז] המגיע מהם בדעתו דרך משל מהמציאות המגיע לו בגדר האדם והוא שהוא חי מדבר. כי אין ספק שהמצוייר ההיולאני ישוב אז שכל ונמנה מהצורות השכליות. ועל זה רמז הר״מ כשאמר כי השכל כשישכיל צורת האילן והפשיט צורתו וכו׳. ואתה תוכל לדעת כי זה המציאות אשר לנמצאות ר״ל שכל בקנין ישיגהו הפחיתות במה שצורותיהם פותחו בשכל האדם באמצעות הגדרים וישיגם הרבוי מצד התיחסם לצורות והתרבותם בעצמם. וכאשר יוקשר עם אלו המושכלות כח הנקרא שכל היולאני פועל ויפעל בו השכל הפועל מה שנתנוהו שאר השכלים בתחלה והוא השיג עצמו יצייר הצורות הכוללות מופשטות בלתי מתיחסות לצורות הדמיוניות ולגדרים ועניניהם ידיעה כללית אחדית פשוטה כי השכל הפועל זה ענינו עם שהוא סבת הצורות האלו ר״ל שציורו סבת המצא הצורות השפלות לא הם סבת עצמו כמו שהם סבת שכל האדם הנקנה. ואלו הענינים הם הבדל בשכל הפועל מהשכל האנושי כל עוד שלא ישוב מלאך. הנה מציאות הנמצאות בשכל הפועל נבדל ממציאותם

---

55 בג בין   א בן   אג נקודות   ב הנקודות | 58 אג נתישר   ב ותיישר   א ויוצץ   ב ויצץ   ג ויוצא   אג לנו   ב אצלנו | 59–60 ב ליתא כי אם – הנמצא | 61 א ליתא הארכנו | 62 ב בבאורינו   אג בפרושנו   ב כונות הפילוסופים   אג הכונות | 63 אג וחקו זה   ב וחקירה | 65 אג אשר להם   ב אשר יש להם   ב שהוא   אג הוא   ב המציאות   אג מציאות | 66 ב התעלותם   אג העלותם   א פתוחם   ב פחותם | 67 אב עין   ג העין (?) | 69 אג תאמר   ב תארו   אג ויפריד   ב מפריד | 70 ב מקצת   אג בקצת   אג חלקיים חלקיים פרטיים | 71 ב ליתא נכבדות | 72 אז   אב או   ג אל   ב מהמציאות   אג ממציאות | 73 אג בגדר האדם   ב מהגדר באדם | 74 בג צורת   א צורות | 76 ב הפחיתות   אג הפתיחות   אג שצורותיהם   ב שצורותיה   אג פותחו   ב פיתחו | 79 אג יצייר   ב יסיר   אג הכוללות   ב כוללות | 80 ב הדמיוניות   אג הדמיונות   אג כללית   ב כוללת | 81 א לא הם צורות וסבת   ג לא הם צורת וסבת   אג כמו שהם סבת   ב ליתא סבת | 82 אג ליתא הפועל |

בשכל האדם בענין הכלליות והאחדות הפשוטה לצורה צורה וההפשט מהרבוי הקורה לה (אך בענין שיושפע ממנו אז תגיע ההישרה מה שאין כן בשאר הנפרדים) לסבת חמרם ובענין ששכל האדם עלול מהנמצאות על דרך הנזכרת ר״ל שנראו לו תחלה עד חקו בדמיון עד שנתלבש השכל מהן שהוא בתחלת ענינו כלוח המוכן לכתיבה. והנמצאות התחתונות עלולות מכנסת ישראל ר״ל שציורו להם הוא עלת היותם והוא מקבצם ולכן קראו התורניים השכל הפועל בשם הזה. עוד תדע כי כמו שנתעלו הנמצאות ממציאותם ההיולאני עד השכל הפועל כן לא יחדלו להתעלות מציאותם ר״ל מהותם בשכלים הנפרדים העשרה בפשיטותם ואחדותם בהם. וזה יתרון המלאך האחד על האחר ר״ל כפי יתרון פשיטות ואחדות הנמצאות בכל אחד ואחד. מצורף לזה צייר כל אחד מהם גלגל אחר. הציור ההוא הוא סבה בפנים מה להמצא הגלגל ובדרך הזאת היה השכל האחד סבה לגלגל האחד ר״ל במה שהוא מניעו אבל האל ית׳ סבת הכל. ואמר החכם זה לשונו:

ואמנם מה שנמשך בו מהמנהג מאנשי זמננו שיאמרו כשמניע כך הגיע ממנו מניע כך או הושפע ממנו או חויב והדומה לאלו המלות הוא דבר לא יתאמת מובנו על אלו ההתחלות הנבדלות כי אלו כלם מתארי הפועלים בתחלת המחשבה לא באמת. כי הפועל לא יגיע ממנו דבר כי אם הוצאת מה שבכח אל הפועל ואין בכאן כח ולזה אין בכאן פועל. ואולם שכל ומושכל משלים ונשלם בו ⟨שהמושכל הוא עלה למשכיל ולזה אין הנה פועל.⟩ ואמנם שם עלה ועלול על צד מה שנאמר שהמושכל הוא עלה למשכיל. וכאשר היה זה כן הנה אינו נמנע במה שהוא בעצמו שכל ומושכל שיהיה עלה למציאות חלקים מצד מה שיושכלו ממנו צדדים וזה כשהיו אלו השכלים יציירו ממנו צדדים מתחלפים מהציור היה מה שיצייר אם כן מהמניע הראשון המניע לגרם השמים והוא העלה בנפש השמים ⟨ר״ל בעצם (השמיני) [השמים]⟩ בלתי מה שיצייר ממנו מניע גלגל שבתי דרך משל. וכן הענין באחד אחד ר״ל שכל אחד מהם שלמותו הוא ציור עלתו אשר תיחדהו וציור העלה הראשונה ובזה היה תנועתם כלם ימשכו לדבר אחד והוא הסדר הנמצא לכל. ⟨והגרמים השמימיים אמנם יתנועעו להוציא מה שבכח באותן הצורות הנבדלות אל הפועל והם הצורות ההיולאניות.⟩ עכ״ל.

הנה גליתי לך אמתת מחשבתי ושהיא דעת הפילוסופים שיהיו לאלו הצורות שני מציאויות מציאות בפעל והוא מציאות ההיולאנית אשר להם ומציאות בכח והוא המציאות אשר להן באותן הצורות. ורצוני בכח הנה כמו שנאמר שהצורות המלאכותיות להן מציאות בפועל בהיולי ומציאות בכח בנפש עושן. ולזה מה שיראה שאלו הצורות

---

84 אג וההפשט ב והפשט | 85 אג אז ב או ב ליתא מה שאין כן | 86 אג חמרם ב חמרים ב ובענין אג וכענין ב שנראו תחלה לו | 87 אבג עוד חקו ב עד שהוא | 90 אג עד ב עם | 91 ב פשיטות א פשיטם ג פשיטת | 93 ב ליתא מהם אג הציור ב השר אב ליתא הוא אג סבה ב סבת | 94 אג האחד ב אחד (שתי פעמים) בג מניעו א מניני | 95 אג סבת הכל ב הוא עלת הכל | 96 ב מהמנהג אג המנהג ג שיאמרו א שיאמר ב כשאמרו בג כשמניע א בשמניע | 98 בג ההתחלות א התחלות | 100 אג ואולם ב ואמנם | 101 ג ליתא הוא | 102 אג ליתא הנה | 103 ב צדדים אג לצדדים | 103–104 אג ליתא וזה – צדדים | 104 ג שיצייר ב שיצוייר א שהוא צוייר בג ליתא מניע | 107 אג תיחדהו ב תיחדוה אג הראשונה ב ראשונה אג היה ב היו | 108 בג והגרמים א וגרמים | 109 ג עד כאן | 110 א מחשבתי ב מחשבתו | 111 אג ההיולאניות ב מציאות | 112 אג שנאמר ב ששני׳ ב המלאכיות |

להם שני מציאויות מציאות נבדל ומציאות בהיולי. והנבדל הוא סבה לאשר בהיולי. ואמנם יוחסה הפעלה להיולאניות אל השכל הפועל יותר משאר הנבדלים כי היה הוא היותר מתדמה למציאותם השפל. ולכן יוציא הצורות השפלות מן הכח אל הפועל בחמרים אחר הכנת הגרמים השמימיים לחמרים כמו שאמר כתפוח בעצי היער ר״ל שאין בהם עושה פרי כן דודי בין הכחות השמימיים כי אין מכלם נותן רק השכל הפועל. ולזה [דומות] הצורות אשר בשכל העושה אל הצורות השפלות יותר משאר הנפרדים כי הם בשאר השכלים בענין נפלא לא תצאנה הצורות מהם והם בעלה הראשונה בענין היותר משובח שיוכל שיהיה ובאחדות הגמורה הפשוטה. ולזה אמרו הפילוסופים שהש״י אחד ושהוא היותר משובח שבנמצאות ובזה הוא התחלתם. ולזה באר הר״מ ז״ל ונצבת על הצור. השען ועמוד על התבוננות היותו ית׳ התחלה שהוא המבוא אשר תגיע ממנו אליו ירצה בזה שתכלית ידיעתנו בשם ית׳ הוא שנדע איך הוא ית׳ התחלה כי בזה נדע באמתות כל מה שבטבענו לדעתו ר״ל כשנדע כי הוא התחלה בצד שהוא שכל ומשכיל ומושכל יושג בצדדים מתחלפים והוא משכיל הצורות במציאות היותר משובח שאפשר שיהיה ולהורות על היותו ית׳ התחלה בזה התואר תקנו מסדרי התפלות היום הרת עולם כי הוא ית׳ מחדשו חדוש אמתי תמידי. ולהורות על קשר הנמצאות בו ית׳ מצד ההשכלה אשר היא עצמו אמרו אם כבנים רחמינו כרחם אב על בנים ומצד הבדלם מאתו ית׳ במציאותם בעצמם אמרו אם כעבדים עינינו לך תלויות עד שתחוננו. ולהיות הוא המשכיל באופן היותר משובח שיהיה והקדוש שבקדושות ובעלוים השלים המאמר במלת קדוש ואמר עד שתחוננו ותוציא לאור משפטינו קדוש כי ממשפטנו ומכחנו להתדבק עם הנפרד ית׳ הקדוש אמן.

ובבאור אמר החכם ב״ר זה לשונו: ומחוייב אצל הפלוסופים שיהיה מה שישכילוהו השכלים הנפרדים הם צורות הנמצאות והסדור אשר בעולם כענין בשכל אנושי אחר שיהיה השכל אינו דבר זולת השגת צורות הנמצאות מצד שהם בזולת חמר. והנה לצורות הנמצאות המוחשות מדרגות במציאות. היותר פחות מהם מציאותם בחמרים. אח״כ מציאותם בשכל האנושי יותר [נכבד] ממציאותם בחמרים. אח״כ מציאותם בשכלים הנפרדים יותר נכבד ממציאותם בשכל האנושי. אח״כ להם באותם השכלים מדרגות מתעלות במציאות כפי התעלות אותם השכלים בעצמם. ואותן ההתחלות הנפרדות ישובו אל התחלה אחת נפרדת היא הסבה בכלם. הנה הראשון אצלם לא ישכיל אלא עצמותו והוא בהשכילו עצמותו משכיל כל הנמצאות ביותר

---

115 אג יוחסה ב ייוחסה ב להיולנית | 117 אג אחר ב אשר ב הגרמיים ב לחמריים | 118 אג השמימיות | 119 [דומות] ב ולזה לה אותות – העושה אג וזה להאותות הצורות אשר הוא עושה (לכאורה הנוסחאות נשתבשו) | 120 ב נפרדים אג תצאנה – מהם ב תצאנה ממנה הצורות להם ב ליתא והם | 122–121 אג ולזה אמנם אמרו | 123 אג ז״ל (=זה לשונו) בפר׳ י״ו פרק צור ב ליתא ז״ל – צור | 125 א כי בזה ב ובזה אג באמתת ב מאמתות | 126–125 בג שהוא א כי הוא | 126 בג ומושכל א ומושג | 129 אג הנמצאות ב המצאות בג הוא א היא אג אמרו ב אמר | 130 אג אמרו ב אמר | 131 אג הוא ב זה | 132 ג ובעלוים א והעלויים ב והעלוים | 133 ב ומכחנו אג וכחנו | 135 א וזה לשונו ב ז״ל | 137 בג בזולת א במלת | 138 אג והנה ב הנה אג במציאות ב מציאות | 139 אג האנושי ב ההיולני | 140 א הנפרדים בג הנבדלים | 141 אג ואותן ב ואותם | 142 אג אחת ב אותם |

מעולה שבמציאות ויותר מעולה שבמדרגה וסדור. ומה שתחתיו הנה עצמו אמנם הוא אשר ישכילהו מן הצורות וההדרגה והסדור אשר בשכל הראשון ושיתרונם אמנם הוא ביתרונם בזה הענין. הנה המאמר בשההתחלה הראשונה כאשר לא תשכיל אלא עצמותה הנה היא סכלה בכל מה שבראה הנה היה מחוייב זה לו היה מה שיושכל מעצמותה דבר הוא זולת הנמצאות בשלוח. ואמנם אשר יניחו שאשר ישכילהו הראשון מעצמותו הוא הנמצאות ביותר נכבד שבמציאות ושהוא השכל אשר הוא עלה לנמצאות לא שהוא ישכיל הנמצאות מצד שהם עלה לשכלו כענין בשכלנו. הנה ענין אמרנו שהוא לא ישכיל מה שתחתיו מן הנמצאות ר״ל שהוא לא ישכילם בצד אשר נשכילם אנחנו אבל בצד אשר לא ישכילם משכיל נמצא בזולתו ית׳ לפי שלו השכילם נמצא בצד מה שישכילם ישתפהו בידיעתו ית׳ האל מזה. וזהו התואר המיוחד בו יתעלה. הנה התבאר סדור אחד ופועל השתתפו בו כל הנמצאות שתוף אחד והעמידה על הסדור אשר השיגוהו המעיינים בנמצאות אצל העליה אל ידיעת הראשון קשה ואשר ישיגוהו השכלים האנושיים ממנו אמנם הוא כולל.

עד הנה דברי החכם. הנה נגלה מכל זה שהנמצאות המוחשות הן צורות נפרדות בעלה הראשונה והוא משכיל אותן באופן היותר משובח. ואחר שהוא כן הנה אפשר שנקרא שעור קומה מדת הנמצאות כאמרם היו נמתחים והולכים עד שגער בהם הקב״ה. רמז בזה על היחס שיש בין העלול לעלה ולזה חברו חכמי ישראל שעור קומה כי הנמצאות כלן הן קומה. ולכן נקרא כתר. הנה תבין מזה אמתת מאמרו כי הוא ית׳ אין לו תמונה והוא בדרך כלל לכל התמונות כי מאתו יצאו בציורו. ואחר שהוא כולל את כלם כמאמר החכם שהאל ית׳ בפנים מה הוא הנמצאות כלן הוא נקרא תמונה. הנה הקומה יש לו פנים ואחור והפנים הוא אמתת עצמו ר״ל ציורו לנמצאות על הצד אשר הוא מציירם. והאחור הוא איכות התחייב הנמצאות ממנו ואין ספק שהפנים הם בלתי נראים ר״ל שלא נוכל לדעת הציור אשר לאל ית׳ בנמצאות מה הוא ר״ל לדעת הנמצאות על הדרך ההיא והוא הפנים, אפילו מלאכי השרת אין מכירים אותה כמו שקדם כי היא עצם אמתת האלהות ולא ידע האל כי אם האל. אך משה ראה אחוריו ר״ל איכות התחייב הנמצאות מאתו כאשר ישיגהו השכל הפועל כי משה שב מלאך ה׳ והוא הנקרא קרון עור הפנים ר״ל התחדש ההכנה השנית עם הצורות אשר בקנין בהחרב הראשונה והוא ראותו לוקח מאתו אליהו כי הצורות המושכלות ההוות נפסדות כי כל הוה נפסד. והנצחות מצד הנצחי כי השכל

---

144 אג שבמציאות ב אשר במציאות אג שבמדרגה ב שבהדרגה | 145–146 אג ליתא
אשר ישכילהו – אמנם הוא [נשמט מחמת homoioteleuton] | 146 אג ליתא הראשונה |
147 אג מעצמותה ב בעצמותה | 148–150 ב ליתא ישכילהו הראשון – לא שהוא [נשמט
מחמת homoioteleuton] | 151 אג נשכילם ב נשכיל | 152 בג שלו א שלא |
153 אג בצד מה שישכיל ב בצד שישכילהו אג ליתא האל א המיוחר ב המאחר |
155 א ליתא ידיעת | 157 אג עד הנה ב ע״כ בג החכם השלם מתיר בשלמות כל דעת
בדוי צומח מהנוטים מדרך מתחיל החכמות ומשלימם כפלוסופיא. משוה דת האמת כאמת עצמו |
160 ב בזה א במדה א לעלה ב ליתא | 161 אג שעור קומה ב ליתא אג ולכן
ב ולזה | 163 אג כמאמר ב במאמר אג הוא נקרא ב הנה נקרא | 165 א אשר
הוא בג אשר הוא הוא | 166 ב הם אג ליתא | 167 אג ההיא ב ההוא אג מלאכי
ב למלאכי | 168 אג ידע ב ליתא | 170 בג עור הפנים א אור פנים | 172 ב נפסדות
אג הנפסדות אג הנצחי הנושע |

ההיולאני כמו שיאמר ארסטו נצחי ר״ל השכל הפועל הנקשר בנו. כי ידע את אשר שם ולא יזכור את אשר הנה. ואשר השיגוהו השכלים האנושיים הוא מה שאמרנוהו בשם הפילוסופים והוא שאיכות התחייב הנמצאות מאת האל הוא כי השכל הראשון ישכיל אלה הנמצאות באופן היותר משובח ושעצמותו יצוייר ממנו צדדים מתחלפים מהציור עד הגיע הנמצאות המוחשות העליונות והשפלות ובכלל כל הצורות מתדבקות כי התחתונות נשלמות בעליונות שלמות השגה הן משיגות מצד העליונות אם בהעתק לגמרי כענין בנפשיות ואם מצד שחשוקיהן העליונות כענין בנפרדות וכאלו הם נעתקות ושבות באמת יותר משכילות והבן זה. ודע כי עם כל זה שהתחתונות משיגות העליונות בנפרדות והן מצד זה מתדבקות התדבקות השגה הנה העליונות משיגות את התחתונות ונותנות להם מציאותם אשר הוא עצמותם אשר היא נפש ההשגה יותר משובח ומזה הצד גם כן הן משלימות את התחתונות ונותנות להן מציאותן והן מתדבקות בעליונות התדבקות מציאות והשגה וזהו המכונה באחורים ויספיק הרמז בזה אחר הצעת כל מה שקדם.

והנה הציב הקומה ואמר והנה האורך בין שתי נקודות והיא הקומה והנקודה הקרובה אל הפועל ר״ל הנמשל אל הפועל הגדול הוא הכבוד שר הפנים ר״ל והוא הנקודה העליונה ושם עצם הכח והיכולת והנקודה האחרת המקבלת לראשונה השפלה היא הנמשלת לסוף הכח. ואחר שהעמיד גובה הקומה נתן טעם למה נמשל האל לפנים ואמר ותנועת האדם לפנים. עוד נתן ימין ושמאל בקומה ואמר והגוף העליון אל הימין והצמח אל העליון. ירצה שהגופות העליונות יכונו בימין והשפלים בשמאל. ואמר שמן הגלגלים מה שיכונו בצד הימיני מן הגוף והם העליונים ומה שיכונו בצד השמאל והם הפחותים וכמו כן ברגלים יש מהם נקרא בשם ימין ומהם נקרא בשם שמאל ואם הם משל לגופות השפלים. ובאר זה ואמר והצמח אל העליון ירצה לומר שהצמח משפטו כעליון בערך השפלים וכאלו אמר שהצמח יכונה בשם ימין בשפלים וכל שכן הב״ח כי כבר אמר שהעליון אל הימין. ואחר הקמת המשכן באר הפנים והאחור על דרך שקדמה ואמר והנה משה יכול לראות בעין לבו איך תדבקנה ר״ל והוא האחור ומדרך הכבוד ר״ל מציאות האל אין כח בנברא לדעתו והוא הפנים כלומר עצמותו „לא יראני האדם וחי״. אח״כ נתן הסבה בהמשיל צורת האדם ליוצרה יותר משאר הצורות ואמר ובעבור כי הנכבד באדמה הוא האדם ע״כ צורת כרובים שהם

---

173 ב ר״ל שכל השכל הפועל | 174–173 אג את אשר שם ב אשר שם | 174 אג ולא יזכור
ב לא יזכר אג את אשר הנה ב אשר הנה אג השיגוהו ב השיגהו | 176 אג היותר משובח
ב היותר שלם משובח אג יצוייר ב יצויירו | 177 אג הגיע ב הגיעו | 179 בג בענין
א הענין א כענין בג בענין ב הנפרדות אג בנפרדים | 180 ב באמת א באחת אג כי עם
ב שעם | 181 אג מצד זה ב מזה הצד אג מתדבקות ב ליתא אג התדבקות השגה
ב התדבקות בדבקות השוה | 183 ב גם אג גם כן הם (הן) אג ונותנות – והן ב ליתא |
184 אג התדבקות ב המתדבקות אג וזהו ב וזה הוא | 186 אג נקודות ב הנקודות |
187 בג הפועל הגדול א הפעל הגדול אג והוא ב והי׳ | 188 אג ושם ב ועם בג עצם
א עוצם | 190 בג ותנועת א ותנועות | 191 אג שהגופות העליונות יכונו ב שהצורות נכבדים
יכוונו | 192 אג שמן ב שמין אג שיכונו ב שיכוונו ג בצד אב ליתא אג שיכונו
ב שיכינו | 193 אג יש מהם – ומהם ב ליתא | 194 אג לגופות ב גופות | 195 ב משפטו
כעליון אג אל עליון (העליון) משפטו | 196 ב הב״ח א בב״ח ג בבע״ה | 198 בג בנברא
א בנביא | 199 אג האדם ב אדם |

משכן קומה והכנפים לשלש סבות והשניות להוראת העלה והעלול. והנכבד באדם ישראל והם מניחי תפלין על כן היה האדם (המשלים) [השלם] מניח תפילין והוא אמרו ע״כ דבר קשר של תפלין. ולא הספיק במשל האחור לבד ואנחנו כבר נתננו הסבה הנרמזות בזה. ולפי שהוא השתדל בכל זה לבאר ספר שעור קומה כאשר הודעתיך הזכירו והביא ענינו על צד הבאור לא מלותיו ואמר ע״כ כתוב בשעור קומה כי השם בורא כל גוף וכל נכבד מגוף והנבזה מהגוף והוא המקרה ירצה שהנמצאות כלן הן קומת האדם השלם אשר יקראוהו בעלי הספירות ג״כ אילן. וחלקי הנמצאות הם הגוף ומקרי הגוף והוא הנקרא ממתניו ולמטה והנכבד מהגוף והוא השכל מהנבדלים והוא הנקרא ממתניו ולמעלה והוא הנקרא בספר שעור קומה „מירכותיו ולמעלה" והאחורים הם התחייבם ממנו והפנים הם אמתת מציאותם בו. ודע והבן כי למה שהיה האל ית׳ הוא ציירו הנמצאות ביותר שלם ומשובח שלהם והוא אשר לא ידעהו זולתו והיו הנמצאות קשורות בו על הדרך הזאת האלהית כמאמר שלמה המלך ע״ה בספר שיר השירים אחות לנו קטנה קרא ממתניו ולמעלה כמראה זוהר כעין החשמלה ואשר למטה כמראה אש כי החשמל הוא הבהיר שבשלהבת האש ובאש הזוהר הוא השכל הראשון ולכן נקרא אור שכל. והגופות הן האש הנקשר בשלהבת ולזה באר אברהם אבינו ע״ה בספרו וכלן קשורות זו בזו כשלהבת קשורה בגחלת. ואמר משה ע״ה בספר תורת י׳ ר״ל אשר אין בו דבר בטל בלי תועלת וירא אלהים את האור כי טוב ואמרו חכמי הקבלה כמדליק מנר לנר ומטיבם ולפי זה ההתאחדות היה יהוה שם העצם שהוא הכבוד והוא בעצמו שם תואר כולל כל הנבדלים והגויות עליונות ושפלות בעצמם והוא סוד גדול להורות כי הוא צורת העולם. ואחר שצייר קומת האדם ושם כפות רגליו מקרי הגוף ושם מן כפות עד הארכובות הגופים השפלים כאמרו והארץ הדום רגלי וקרא גופות הגלגלים ירכתו וקרא השכלים הנבדלים הגוף העליוני והעליון אל הימין וקרא ראשו השכל הראשון וקרא פניו אמתת מהותו אשר לא תושג כי יד על כס יה מלחמה לי׳ בעמלק מדור דור כי לא יושג בהשתתף עמו זולתו ולזה תהיה המלחמה נצחית כמו שבאר האלהי רבינו משה ע״ה. וקרא אחוריו מה שיושג והוא התיצבות על הצור.

גם את זו לעומת זו עשה האלהים. רצה להשלים הצורה ואמר: ודע כי כל הצמחים והחיים בארץ כעוף וכבהמה וכחיה וכו׳ עד סוף מאמרו כיון בזה כלו להשלים מדת הצורה ואמתתה בעינים וידים וזולתם. עוד נמשך אחר פשט הכתוב באמרו

---

201 ג העלה והעלול א העלה להעלול ב העלול והעלה | 202 אג מניחי ב מניחין אג היה ב היו | 203 בג האחור א האמור | 204 אג השתדל ב הסתכל אג ספר ב ליתא | 205 ב והביא ענינו אג ליתא | 206 אג והוא המקרה ב הוא המקרה | 207 אג יקראוהו ב קראוהו | 208 ג והוא אב הוא | 208–209 ב והנכבד – ולמעלה אג ליתא | 209 אג והוא הנקרא ב והוא אשר | 210 אג והאחורים ב והאחור | 211 אג שלם ב ליתא | 212 אג הזאת ב הזה ב המלך אג ליתא | 213 אג כעין ב ליתא | 219 ג יהוה א יהיה ב ליתא | 220 אג ושפלות ב ושפלים אג ואחר ב והוא | 221 א ג ושם ב ושב אג מקרי ב מחקי אג עד ב ליתא אג הגופים ב הגופות | 222 בג הנבדלים א הנפרדים | 224 אג יד ב ידו אג מדור דור ב ליתא | 225 א ג אחוריו ב אחותו | 227 בג האלהים א אלהים | 228 בג כיון א כמו | 229 אג ואמתתה ב ואמתתו בג באמרו א כאמרו |

ושכותי כפי עליך עד עברי. ולי נראה שרמז בו מה שבארוהו הפילוסופים כי העולם הרוחני והגשמי שני הפכים לא יקבלם נושא אחד ומי שזוכה להתענג באור הרוחני יסתר ממנו הגשמי, ידע את אשר שם ולא יזכור את אשר הנה, יתדבק עם הכל התדבקות השגה אחר התדבקות המציאות. לזה אמר ושכותי כפי עליך עד עברי כלומר שיסתרו ממנו הנמצאות הגשמיות עד הסתלק השגת התדבקות עם הנבדלים. אמנם אמרו וראית את אחורי מפאת שהוא הכל וכבודו מלא הכל ומאתו הכל. ירצה שהוא יראה אחוריו מצד השיגו הנמצאות אחר שהוא עצמותם המשובח וציורו כולל את כלם ובציור ההוא מתחדש הכל מאתו והוא אמרו וכל תמונת כל וזהו ותמונת ה׳ יביט. ירצה שכל הנמצאים הם תמונת הש״י אחר שהם בו במציאות היותר משובח והוא תארו אשר ייוחד בו ית׳ וזהו ותמונת ה׳ יביט כלומר עצמות הנמצאות אשר הם תמונתו לא פניו ית׳ כי זה נמנע אלא בעצמות האמת ית׳. ועל זה בנה שלמה המלך ע״ה ספר שיר השירים באמרו ראשו כתם פז, צוארו רגליו בטנו חכו שיניו קווצותיו. זה אינו כי אם חלקי העולם כלו והתעלות הנמצאות בו. אמנם עשו הנביאים המשל הנכבד והמשובח הזה שכשידעהו האדם מובטח לו שהוא בן עולם הבא. והש״י אינו גשם ולא כח קיים בגשם ולבלתי תכלית תהלתו אבל הוא נבדל למה שאין מציאותו בו. כי אינו צורה חלה באמצעות המרחקים. אבל האל בשמים למה שהוא נותן לו המציאות ועלוי המציאות. אל מי תדמיוני ואשוה יאמר קדוש. אמנם הביאם לזה לתת המושכל מוחש ולזה עשה משה את המשכן אשר הראהו הש״י בהר סיני ולזה ראו הנביאים על הרקיע דמות כסא וראו העם האש במעמד ההוא וראה אברהם תנור עשן ולפיד אש כמו שרמז עליו הר״מ ז״ל.

גם הפילוסופים הניחו עולם קטן דומה לעולם גדול והראשון במדרגת שכלנו הנבדל אשר הוא נפשנו האמתית. ויעקב המשיל הדבר לסולם והנה י׳ נצב עליו לא בו והתורניים המשילו זה לאילן. ומכללם התאר כי גבוה מעל גבוה שומר רמוז ג״כ בלולב ולזה אמרו נחלקה התיומת פסול כי אין בראשון שום רבוי. ובסוכה ג״כ רמזו על זה והסכך רמז על העליונים ולזה התנו בו שלא יהיה מדבר מקבל טומאה מה שלא התנו כן בדפנות ושאלו רחבה שבעה וגבוה עשרה כל זה להערה. ופחות משלשה כלבוד דמי כי שלשה חלקי הנמצאות מתאחדים כמו שבארנו. וכל אלו המשלים לחסרון כח השכל האנושי בטבעו והיותו נדבק בחמר והקשר הנצחי בהכנה ובהסתלק הענן מעל הכבוד יסור המשל וישוג הנמשל. ביום ההוא יהיה י׳ אחד ושמו אחד.

---

231 אג ולא ב לא | 233–232 אב יתדבק – עד עברי ג ליתא | 233 בג שיסתרו א שיסתר | 234 ג השגת א השגות ב השג אג הנבדלים ב הנפרדים | 236 בג כולל א כלל | 238 אג הנמצאים ב הנמצאות | 239 אג ייוחד ב ייחד | 240 אג אלא ב אליו בג בעצמות א בעצמותו ב המלך ע״ה אג ליתא | 241 ב באמרו אג כלומר בג בטנו א בנינו | 242 אג העולם כלו ב הנמצאות אג והתעלות – בו ב והתעלותם בו אג ואמנם ב אמנם | 243 אג שכשידעהו ב כשידעהו בג העולם א עולם אג אינו ב אין | 244 אג קיים בגשם ב ליתא | 247 אג את ב ליתא | 248 אג הנביאים ב כל הנביאים | 249 ב ליתא ז״ל | 252 אג התאר ב התמר בג רמוז א רומז | 253 אג רמזו ב רמוז | 254 ב בו שלא אג בשלא אג מדבר ב דבר | 256 אג המשלים ב הממשלים | 257 בג האנושי א האנוש | 258 ג הענן – הכבוד ב הכבוד מעל הענן (א העני) |

וזה סוף מה שכונתי לבארו בזאת האגרת והאל יכפר בעדנו כתבנו זה כי ידמה שסודות החכמות היו נמסרות מקדם פה אל פה כמו שהביא ההכרח לכתוב הענין בחדה כי הביא העת לעיין במשכיות התפוח ולהסתכל בהן. ועכ״פ אין מוסרין אותו אלא בראשי פרקים. והש״י יסיר ממנו כל מטריד וכל מעיק אשר מחוץ ומבפנים עד שנגיע אל ההצלחה האמתית אשר היא תכלית התכליות באורו המאיר כל מחשך כמאמר דוד המלך ע״ה כי עמך מקור חיים באורך נראה אור. אמן סלה. וכל ישראל בכלל הברכה.

תהלה לאל נורא עלילה. נשלמה ערב סוכות ממחברה לשנת מאה ושלש לאלף הששי לתחלת סבוב העולם ובריאתו בכלל מן ההעדר הגמור כי אין חוץ ממנו זולתו ית׳ וישתבח. אמן. סלה.

---

259 **אג** סוף מה שכונתי לבארו **ב** מה שכונתי לבאר | 260–259 **אג** כי ידמה שסודות החכמות היו נמסרות מקדם **ב** כי ירמוז בו סודות החכמה היו מקדם נמסרים | 260 **בג** הענין **א** הענת | 261 **אג** כן **ב** כי **אג** ולהסתכל בהן **ב** ולהשתכל בהם **ב** ועכ״פ **א** ועל כל פניין | 262 **בג** מעיק **א** מעים **אג** שנגיע **ב** נגיע | 264 **ב** המלך **אג** ליתא **ב** סלה **אג** ליתא | 266 **אג** תהלה – עלילה **ב** ליתא **א** ערב **ב** עת | 267–266 **א** לאלף הששי **ב** לשנת האלף הששי **אג** בכלל **ב** בכללו | 268–267 **אג** זולתו ית׳ **ב** זולת האל ית׳ | 268 **אג** ית׳ וישתבח **ב** יתעלה ויתברך סלה **ב** ליתא

3. Annotated Translation

"All that is called by My name and which I have created for My glory, I have formed it, yea I have made it" (Isaiah 43:7).

Since "all" is the whole, and the whole is that outside which there is nothing, [it follows that] what is truly "all" is that outside which there is nothing at all. This [latter] is meant by the word "all" which occurs in the verse quoted. And since knowledge, knower, and known are one,[1] it says that "all"—that is, all existents—[2]are called by His name: that is, subsist in His essence. It then explains the manner in which they necessarily exist in themselves, apart from their existence in Him, and their ultimate purpose by saying: "and which I have created for My glory," that is, [for] the *kabod*;[3] "I have formed it," that is, the supernal body;[4] "yea, I have made it," that is, the lower [body].[5] By His "glory" His essence is meant, which is His will and His wisdom, all denoting one and the same thing. For His essence is also called His "glory," as in [Moses'] saying: "Show me, I pray Thee, Thy glory" (Exodus 33:18).[6] From this verse it is apparent that all existents subsist in the glorious Name. Now because they are, in themselves, in another [kind of] existence which is necessitated by Him, the prophets elucidated this Divine mystery by calling the "All" a "Man" and by designating certain parts [of it] as "feet," other parts as "loins," some other aspect as the "back," and its most exalted [aspect] as the "face."[7] [In this sense] they spoke of "the likeness of a man" (Ezekiel 1:5) and [of what was] "beneath His feet" (Exodus 24:10). In later times, when under the impact of exile understanding diminished and the need for a fuller elucidation

1. According to the well-known doctrine of the Islamic Aristotelians, which gained currency among the Jewish philosophers through Maimonides (*Yesodē ha-Torā*, II, 10; *Guide*, I, 68).

2. While "all" is said here to denote "all existents" (i.e., all forms proceeding from God's Self-thinking or essence), "All" is also used as a designation of God's essence itself. See line 37 of the text and Note 15.

3. Viz., all that exists testifies to God's glory. Cf. lines 50–51.

4. Viz., the celestial spheres.

5. Viz., the sublunar world.

6. Cf. Maimonides, *Guide*, I, 54, 64; III, 13 (where reference is made to the verse from Isaiah with which we are dealing).

7. The "face" denotes the Self-thinking or essence of God, as will be explained in the text.

arose,[8] the sages of Israel composed the book *Shiᶜur Qomā* ("The Measure of the Body") concerning this matter.[9] Rabbi Moses [ben Maimon] alluded to the subject[10] in [The Guide to the Perplexed, Book I] chapter 70, which opens [with the words]: "Know that the totality of existents is like a single individual." The scholar Rabbi Abraham ben Ezra, however, explained it more fully in connection with the verse "And Moses said unto the Lord: 'See, Thou sayest unto me' " (Exodus 33:12) by stating as follows:[11]

"That day, when Moses saw what he desired [to see], was to him what the day of the Giving of the Torah was to Israel. No man before and after him ever attained to his rank and his wisdom. Our rabbis, peace be upon them, said that God showed him the 'knot of the *tefillin*.'[12] Their saying is correct, but not in its literal sense, as the sages in previous generations interpreted it; for this is an exceedingly deep mystery. Says Abraham the author: I have already explained[13] that the glorious Name which is written one way and pronounced another denotes the essence [of God], and the essence is the glory," etcetera, down to his [Ibn Ezra's] saying [of] "all number" that "it is the [number] One as multiplied."[14] Immediately following this [statement], he [Ibn Ezra] continues with these words: "Thus you will find that the 'One' is 'All.'[15] Hence the

8. The same phrase was used by Sherira Gaon in his famous *Epistle* for explaining the need for the elaboration of Halaka through the Talmudic discussions.

9. Narboni unequivocally attributes the authorship of the *Shiᶜur Qomā* to the "sages of Israel" (viz., Rabbi Yishmael and Rabbi ᶜAqiba). On this controversial issue see above, Pages 226ff.

10. Viz., of the *Shiᶜur Qomā*. In *CG* (I, 70, p. 14b) Narboni interprets Maimonides in accordance with this assumption. See above, Page 240. It is, however, chapter 72 which opens with the words quoted in the text.

11. The Ibn Ezra passage quoted is taken from the Long (Standard) Recension of the *Commentary on Exodus* (Schocken ed., fol. 148b), but omits parts and shows slight variations (noted by S. Pinsker in his edition of the text, *Kokbē Yiẓḥaq*, 30:26–27 [1864]).

12. *Berakot* 7a: " 'Thou shalt see My back'—this teaches that He showed him [Moses] the knot of the *tefillin*" (presupposing the haggadic image of God Himself putting on the phylacteries, see *Berakot* 6a). For an explanation see text, lines 27ff. Ibn Ezra identifies this vision granted to Moses with the vision of the "image" of God mentioned in Num. 12:8 (line 38 and in an earlier part of this passage not quoted by Narboni).

13. *Ad Exod.* 3:15, 6:3, and elsewhere, see David Rosin, "Die Religionsphilosophie Abraham Ibn Esra's," *Monatsschrift für Geschichte und Wissenschaft des Judentums*, 42 (N.F. 6): 154ff. (1898).

14. Lit., "is from ones." For Ibn Ezra's view of the number One as symbol of God, see the references given by Rosin, "Die Religionsphilosophie," pp. 60–61; and David Kaufmann, *Geschichte der Attributenlehre* . . . (1877), pp. 289, n. 110; 290, n. 113; 507.

15. For "All" as a designation of God in Ibn Ezra see Rosin, "Die Religionsphilosophie," p. 60. The same usage occurs in Eleazar of Worms' *Sodē Razaya* (see *Sefer Raziʾel* [Amsterdam, 1701], which contains on fols. 7b–24a the first part of the work, fol. 8b) and Juda

mystery of the prayers and the praises,[16] and the meaning of [the verse] 'Thus will I magnify Myself, and sanctify Myself' (Ezekiel 38:23); and, moreover, of [the verse] 'in whom I will be glorified' (Isaiah 49:3).[17] The truly One has no image. He is like the universal aspect of all the images,[18] for they proceed from Him. The supernal bodies—that is, the luminaries and stars—have no front and no behind, and this applies a fortiori to the supernal soul of man, and even more so to the [angelic] ministers of the Supreme, and even more so to the Most High Himself.[19] Length is [the extension] between two points, and the point nearest to the Agent[20] is the Prince of the Presence,[21] and the other point[22] marks the end of the power. The movement of man is forward;[23] the supernal body is toward the right;[24] and the plant is toward the supernal.[25] Moses was able to know and to see with his intellect's eye the way in which

---

ben Nissim ibn Malka (see G. Vajda, *Juda Ben Nissim Ibn Malka, philosophe juif marocain* [Paris, 1954], p. 79).

16. Cf. Ibn Ezra, *Yesod Mora'*, ed. M. Creizenach (Frankfurt a.M., 1840), chap. xii, p. 51 (Hebrew text): *ʿal ken yesod ha-tefilot.*

17. I.e., since God is All, all levels of existence indicate His glory. For Narboni's interpretation see below, lines 48–50.

18. Our translation is based on the reading *ke-derek kelal le-kol ha-temunot* found both in the printed (Schocken) edition and MSS. Vat. 38 (fol. 63v) and 451 (fol. 131r).

19. Similarly in Ibn Ezra's *Short Commentary on Exodus*, ed. S. J. Rapoport (Prague, 1840), p. 105.

20. Viz., God. Cf. Narboni's interpretation, line 187.

21. Viz., the Intellect (*Nous*) of the Neoplatonic system. Cf. Rosin, "Die Religionsphilosophie," p. 202. In *Yesod Mora'* (chap. xii, p. 50) Ibn Ezra identifies the Prince of the Presence with the angel Meṭaṭron.

22. Probably the center of the earth. Ibn Ezra's concept of the "Length" between the two extreme points seems to reflect the notion of the "straight line" (*khaṭṭ mustaqīm; qaw yashar*) between the all-encompassing sphere (the supernal limit) and the center of the earth (the lowest limit) found in al-Baṭalyawsī's (d. 1127) *Kitāb al-Ḥadā'iq* (ed. M. Asín Palacios, *Al-Andalus*, 5:71 [1940]). Narboni (lines 186, 189) refers to this Length as the Body (*ha-qomā*) and the height of the Body (*goba ha-qomā*). For Ibn Ezra's Neoplatonic cosmology see Rosin, "Die Religionsphilosophie," pp. 29–30; 206; 243–245.

23. *Le-panim*, "forward"; possibly alluding to the "Face" (*panim*)—that is, of God—in the sense of "toward the Face," as Narboni (line 190) suggests.

24. Cf. Aristotle, *De caelo*, B2, 285b 15, where it is said that both the sphere of the fixed stars and the spheres of the planets move toward the right. See also Averroes, *Tahāfut al-Tahāfut*, ed. Bouyges, p. 489. Notwithstanding the fact that the motions of the spheres are circular and midway, as it were, between the upward and downward motions of fire and earth respectively (see Ibn Ezra's *Commentary on the Psalms*, *ad* 68:5), a motion in the right direction is, therefore, also to be attributed to them. Narboni (lines 191ff.) offers a different interpretation of "right."

25. Shelomo Zalman Netter's supercommentary on Ibn Ezra (*ad locum*) explains: "It [sc. the plant] is connected with the supernal power, and its natural desire is toward it, [viz.] to grow by it . . ." Isaac Israeli, *Chapter on the Elements* (ed. A. Altmann, *Journal of Jewish Studies*, 7:49 [1956]) speaks of the plant's inclination toward the higher (sc., animal) soul, which results in its fragrance. Narboni (lines 194ff.) has a different interpretation.

the creatures are conjoined with the Creator, but it belongs to the way of the Glory that no created being is able to know it. This is meant by [the verse]: 'man shall not see Me and live' (Exodus 33:30); [that is, man shall not see Me] while the soul of man is still with the body, whereas after death the soul of the intelligent will attain to a level higher than is attainable during his lifetime. Moses turned into a universal. God, therefore, said: 'I know thee by name' (Exodus 33:17); for He alone knows the particulars and their parts in a universal way.[26] The noblest on earth is man, hence the form of the Cherubim.[27] The noblest among men are the Israelites; hence the reference to the 'knot of the *tefillin*.'[28] It is, therefore, written in the book *Shiʿur Qomā* that God creates all bodies and all that is nobler than body and [all] that is inferior to body: that is, the accidents.[29] Rabbi Yishmaʾel said: 'Everyone who knows the measure of the Creator may rest assured that he will share in the world-to-come; I and ʿAqiba vouch for this.'[30] This is meant by [the verse]: 'Let us make man in our image, after our likeness' (Genesis 1:26)."[31] He further said as follows: "And the hand was like a shelter, just as one shelters [the eye] with the palm of his hand against the sun, lest the soul detach itself from his body.[32] 'And thou shalt see My back'

26. Ibn Ezra reflects Avicenna's doctrine that God knows the individual or particular in a universal way. Cf. his *Commentary on Genesis ad* 18:21; *Short Commentary on Exodus ad* 33:12 (ed. Rapoport, p. 104). Moses, though an individual, was known to God not merely in a universal way but as a universal: i.e., free from matter, since he had achieved angelic rank. Cf. Rosin, "Die Religionsphilosophie," pp. 62–63; 505. For Avicenna's doctrine, see its presentation in al-Ghazālī's *Maqāṣid al-falāsifa* (Cairo, 1355/1936), pp. 79–81 [=*Algazel's Metaphysics*, ed. J. T. Muckle, pp. 71–73]; Avicenna, *Al-Shifāʾ*, Metaphysics VIII.6; *Al-Najāt*, 404ff. Averroes rejected this notion and attributed to God a knowledge above the distinction between the universal and particular. See *Tahāfut al-Tahāfut*, pp. 455ff. and G. Vajda, *Isaac Albalag* (Paris, 1960), pp. 66ff.

27. I.e., the cherubim bear human faces (see *Sukka* 5b) because man is a microcosm. Cf. Rosin, "Die Religionsphilosophie," p. 206.

28. For Narboni's interpretation see lines 201–203.

29. As Narboni (lines 204–207) points out, Ibn Ezra explains merely the subject matter, not the text, of the *Shiʿur Qomā*. According to Narboni (line 221), the "accidents" of the sublunar bodies are symbolized by the soles of the feet of the figure described in the *Shiʿur Qomā*.

30. See the text published in *Merkabā Shelemā*, ed. Shelomo Mussajov (Jerusalem, 1921), fol. 38b; in *Sefer Raziʾel*, fol. 38b. Ibn Ezra quotes an abbreviated formula both here and in *Yesod Moraʾ*, chap. xii, p. 50. For the notion of *Yoẓer Bereshit* see Scholem, *Jewish Gnosticism*, p. 28, n. 18; *idem*, *Ursprung und Anfänge der Kabbala* (Berlin, 1962), pp. 19, 184–188.

31. Ibn Ezra implies that man is created in the image of the supernal Man who is identical with the figure of the *Yoẓer Bereshit* depicted in the *Shiʿur Qomā*. Cf. Rosin, pp. 202, 446. For the notion that man is made in the image of the supernal Man see my article "The Delphic Maxim in Medieval Islam and Judaism," *Biblical and Other Studies*, ed. A. Altmann (Cambridge, Mass., 1963), pp. 208–210, 219–220.

32. Explaining the words (Exod. 33:22), "And I will cover thee with My hands until I have passed by" as a promise of protection. Ibn Ezra offers a different interpretation

(Exodus 33:23), considering that He is all, and His glory filleth all, and from Him is all, and all is the image of All.[33] And this is meant [by the verse]: 'And the image of God doth he behold' (Numbers 12:8)."

So far the words of the perfect scholar Rabbi Abraham ben Ezra, who faithfully reflects[34] the metaphysical science.[35] [His words] are, however, in need of elucidation if his intention is to be perfectly understood. I, Moses son of Rabbi Joshua son of Mar David of Narbonne, therefore decided to comment on this subject and enlarge on its presentation. I say: By stating that "God showed him the 'knot of the *tefillin*'" and that "their saying is correct" he meant to indicate that God showed him the connection of the caused with the [First] Cause[36] which is the root-principle from which all else is derived,[37] and with which [all else] is connected. God made known to him how it [all] necessarily follows from Him, this being the mystery of Divinity; He did, however, not make known to him the quiddity of the necessary, for some things are impossible for Him and some are possible.[38] For this reason he [Ibn Ezra] said that this is "an exceedingly deep mystery." He then explained the true mean-

---

in his *Short Com. Exodus ad locum:* "Like a cloud covering the light of the sun so that the eyes cannot see it. The meaning of the allegory is that one who enters into [mystical] union [with God] ceases to have sense perception, and in such a state the force of the soul departs from the body . . . and that day was to Moses what the day of the assembly at Mount Sinai was to Israel; moreover, his skin sent forth beams (Exod. 34:30)." Cf. Rosin, pp. 503–504.

33. See Note 15.

34. Lit., "imitates" (*meḥaqqē*). Cf. line 63: *we-ḥiqqu zeh; CG,* 3b: *demut luaḥ qaẓer me-ḥaqqē kelalē ha-nimzaᵓot; CG,* 39a: *me-ha-shemesh ha-meḥaqqē la-tenuᶜā ha-ᵓamitit.* The term as used by Narboni has the nuances of imitating, reflecting, illustrating. In the *puᶜal and hit-paᶜel* forms it means "being impressed" or "impressing itself." Cf. lines 69, 87.

35. Lit., "the Divine science" (theology).

36. Similarly Joseph Kaspi, *Perush ha-sodot le-ha-Rab Abraham ben Ezra,* ed. Isaac Last, *Zehn Schriften . . . ,* II (Pressburg, 1903), 160: *ha-kawwanā baᶜabur shalshelet ha-ᶜolam we-ḥibburo zeh ᶜim zeh ᶜim ha-shem ha-nikbad.*

37. Lit., is irrelevant, insignificant, of secondary rank (*tafel*). Narboni obviously links the word *tefillin* with the root *tafel*, a linguistic blunder which was pointed out by Jehuda Leon b. Solomon Mosconi in his supercommentary on Ibn Ezra, published by Abraham Berliner in *Magazin für die Wissenschaft des Judentums* (ed. A. Berliner and David Hoffmann), III, Berlin, 1876, Hebrew part, p. 25.

38. The text has "possible for all," which hardly makes sense. We suggest the reading *efshar lo* instead of *efshar la-kol.* On the unchangeable nature of the impossible see Maimonides, *Guide,* III, 15; cf. Simon van den Bergh, Averroes' *Tahāfut al-Tahāfut,* II (London, 1954), 40. According to Narboni's interpretation (*CG,* 36a), Maimonides accepted the validity of the statement that if God "wished to lengthen a fly's wing or to shorten a worm's foot, He would not be able to do it" (*Guide,* II, 22; borrowed from Avicenna) for the sublunar world.

ing of the [Divine] Name so as to facilitate thereby an explanation of the names which occur in the *Shiᶜur Qomā*, [names] which have no ostensible meaning[39] but [the significance of which] is known in the Kabbalah, as our Father Abraham[40] said in the [*Sefer*] *Yeẓirā* (II, 2): "He weighed them and combined them." He begins this [explanation] by saying that the [glorious] Name which is written [one way], etcetera, down to his saying: "Thus you will find that the truly 'One' is 'All.' Hence the mystery of the prayers and the praises." He means to say that God is the overflowing "Well" (*berekā*) from which all canals take their fill, as it says: "And full with the blessing of the Lord" (Deuteronomy 33:23).[41] This is also meant by his saying: "and the meaning of [the verse] 'Thus will I magnify Myself, and sanctify Myself' ": His existence is a glorious one by virtue of the fact that all that exists proceeds from Him and [thereby] adorns Him, as it says: "[Israel] in whom I will be glorified" (Isaiah 49:3), "Israel" being an equivocal term.[42] Having explained this, he wished to elucidate in what sense [the terms] "back" and "face" may be predicated of God, and he [therefore] presented Him as an all-comprising Image through the symbol of the [number] One, saying: "The truly One has no image. He is like the universal aspect of all the images, for they proceed from Him." In guarding against describing Him in corporeal terms, he said: "The supernal bodies [. . . have no front and no behind, and this

39. On the *nomina barbara* ("unverständliche Buchstabenkombinationen") of the *Shiᶜur Qomā* see Scholem, *Von der mystischen Gestalt der Gottheit* (Zurich, 1962), pp. 15–16. These names were indeed meant as representations of the Ineffable Name, as Narboni implies. See Scholem, *Jewish Gnosticism*, pp. 81–82, n. 20.

40. Who is traditionally considered the author of the *Sefer Yeẓirā*. For the most recent discussion of this work see Scholem, *Ursprung*, pp. 20–29.

41. Cf. *Sefer Bahir*, no. 4 (according to the numbering in Scholem's German translation; no. 5 in R. Margalioth's Hebrew text edition [Jerusalem, 1952]) where, following *Gen. Rabba* 39:11, the author identifies *berakā* (blessing) with *berekā* (well), and interprets the word *maleʾ* (full) in Deut. 33:23 in the Gnostic sense of *pleroma* as the highest aspect of Divinity. This exegesis yields the meaning: The Divine *pleroma* is the well from which "those in need" are watered. For a discussion of this Bahir passage see Scholem, *Ursprung*, pp. 61–62. Narboni slightly paraphrases the passage. The term "canals" (*ha-ẓinnorot*) which is substituted for "those in need" derives from Bahir, nos. 13 and 82 (Margalioth, nos. 20 and 113). Moreover, Narboni identifies Ibn Ezra's "One" who is "All" with the *pleroma* of the *Bahir*, and implies thereby that the term "blessing" in Deut. 33:23 denotes both the supernal well or *pleroma* and the benediction of God by His creatures in the form of the liturgical *berakā*.

42. Narboni possibly alludes to *Keneset Yisraʾel*, the tenth of the *Sefirot* of the Kabbalists, which he identifies with the agent intellect (line 89). Being the last of the separate intellects, it transmits the "flow" from the "well" to the lower world, and thereby "glorifies" God.

holds good . . . even more so of the Most High Himself]." He then explained the object of the allegory by "likening the form to Him Who formed it,"[43] saying: "Length is [the extension] between two points [. . .]." Here I cannot refrain from offering an epitome of what has been explained in metaphysics with regard to this mystery: that is, the *shiᶜur qomā*. For it[44] is the fruit of metaphysics, and it is[45] . . . for the reason of this treatise on it. I say:

May we be guided by God toward the true felicity in the hereafter, and may we experience the illumination[46] so ardently desired by the wise: [the knowledge of] the mystery of God, blessed be He. The philosophers have explained that there exists nothing but two things: God and His creatures;[47] and that all existents other than God exist through Him; [that] He is the truly existent Who knoweth all; [that] His knowledge and He are identical, and [that] in Him, blessed be He, intellect, intelligent, and intelligible are one and the same thing. We have already explained this at some length in our *Commentary* on the book *The Intentions of the Philosophers*,[48] and it will therefore be known to those conversant with science. Their explanation is that all existents have different [levels of] existence. The philosophers reflected[49] this [view in their] saying that the [existents'] first existence is their material existence [as found] in the throne of glory,[50] the heavens and the highest heavens, and the sublunar

43. Alluding to the phrase "Great is the power of the prophets who liken the form to its Former" (*Gen. Rabba*, 27:1; cf. 24:1), which is quoted by Maimonides, *Guide*, I, 46. Narboni (*CG*, 5a) explains that by "form" the imaginative form in the prophetic vision such as Ezekiel's (1:26) is meant. God is the "former" of the vision in the prophet's soul. In the present context the "form" stands for the totality of forms at all levels of existence or the *shiᶜur qomā*, as will be explained later.

44. Viz., the mystery of the *shiᶜur qomā*.

45. The text is difficult. The words *koaḥ hekraḥī* ("necessary force") yield no sense. Nor is it clear whether *we-huᵓ* refers to *shiᶜur qomā*. In spite of the unanimous reading of all three manuscripts, one has to assume that the sentence is corrupt.

46. Similarly in Narboni's *CPC* (MS. Michael 119, fol. 108*r*): *le-mā she-hayta ha-hazlahā ha-niẓhit hiᵓ ha-haẓlahā ha-ᵓamitit we-hiᵓ taklit aḥaron le-min ha-ᵓenushi . . . hinē mā she-yuẓaẓ eẓlenu min ha-ᶜolam ha-ruḥani raᵓuy she-yihyē yoter niksaf eẓlenu we-yoter nikbad . . .* This text confirms the reading *yuẓaẓ* in our passage.

47. Cf. Maimonides, *Guide*, I, 34, 71; Narboni, *CG*, 15b; 46b.

48. See Narboni, *CIP*, Vatican MS. 260, fols. 35*v*–37*r* (commenting on the passage III, 1, of al-Ghazālī's *Maqāṣid al-falāsifa = Algazel's Metaphysics*, ed. J. T. Muckle, p. 63, line 22—p. 64, line 20).

49. *Ḥiqqu*; see Note 34.

50. Maimonides interprets the "throne of glory" as denoting heaven (*Guide*, I, 9, 28; II, 26). Narboni (*CG*, 36b) equates it with the heaven called *ᶜarabot*, to which he also applies the figurative expression "the feet of God" (*ibid.* and 4a). In another place (*CG*, 47a) he identifies the "appearance of a throne" (Ezek. 1:26) with "a sphere called by some of the earlier philosophers 'heaven of beatitude' [*shemē ha-haẓlahā*]." The "heaven

bodies in themselves. The material existence they possess qua material represents their most inferior existence. Then their existence is elevated in as much as matter is made an object of vision, and the process of elevation starts when they are impressed as it were in the crystal lens of the eye.[51] For they are [then] abstracted from matter in a way that a mountain of an altitude of a thousand parasangs will be contained in the pupil of the eye. At the next level they will be abstracted from sense perception: they will be visualized by man and found by him [to exist] in his soul (in his *sensus communis*), even though they are no longer within range of the [visual] sense. At a still further stage "the soul speaks to the angel,"[52] and they will be elevated by being impressed in the imagination. [Imagination] will take them apart and combine some parts with others, this being its function, while they still remain particular and individual [existents]. They achieve, however, a still more noble [level of] existence when intellect abstracts them and through definitions and concepts takes hold of them[53] as separate forms and universal images. Then their [level of] existence attained by the mind will, for example, be the one attained by the definition of man: that he is a rational animal. For there can be no doubt that the imaginative form which is [still] material has now become intellect and is counted among the intelligible forms. Rabbi Moses [ben Maimon] alluded to this when he said that the intellect when thinking the form of a certain tree and abstracting it [from matter . . . is identical with the object of its thinking].[54] You will be able to understand that this [level of]

---

of beatitude" is above the heaven called *ᶜarabot* and represents the tenth sphere (see *CG*, 28a). Narboni also identifies the "firmament like the color of the terrible ice" (Ezek. 1:22) with that tenth sphere called "heaven of beatitude" (*CG*, 28b). We arrive at the number of ten spheres if we interpose, with Ibn Ezra, the sphere of the Zodiac between the all-encompassing sphere and the sphere of the fixed stars. Cf. Rosin, pp. 243–245.

51. Cf. David Kaufmann, *Die Sinne* (Leipzig, 1884), pp. 96, 116.

52. I.e., when common sense (=the soul) conveys its data to imagination (=the angel). The phrase is borrowed from a rabbinic dictum (*Kohelet Rabba* 10:20): "When a man sleeps, his soul speaks to the angel, and the angel speaks to the cherub." Maimonides (*Guide*, II, 6) interprets the angel as imagination and the cherub as intellect. According to Narboni, the soul denotes common sense (*CG*, 28a). Cf. H. A. Wolfson, "Maimonides on the Internal Senses," *Jewish Quarterly Review*, N.S. 25:445–447 (1934–35). Narboni uses the same interpretation in our text. See also *CPC* (fol. 112*r*), where the angel is said to signify the imaginative faculty. The *Kohelet Rabba* passage is quoted also by Joseph Gikatila in his *Shaᶜar Ha-Niqqud* (printed in *Arzē Lebanon* [Venice, 1601]; see fol. 34b) which discusses the nature of dreams. On this treatise cf. R. J. Z. Werblowsky's article in *Zeitschrift für Religions- und Geistesgeschichte*, 8:164ff. (1956).

53. Lit., "impresses them" (sc., in the intellect) (*wa-yepatḥem*). Cf. line 76; *putḥu ba-sekel*.

54. *Guide*, I, 68, and Narboni's *CG ad locum*.

existence—that is, the intellect *in habitu*—possessed by the existents is still characterized by [a measure of] inferiority in that the forms thereof are impressed in the intellect by way of definitions, and bear the marks of plurality on account of their relatedness to the [imaginative] forms and on account of being multiple in number themselves.[55] When, however, there connects with these intelligibles a force called "agent intellect"[56] . . . and thinks itself, if conceives the universal forms in [total] abstraction, unrelated to the imaginative forms and definitions and what appertains to them, in a knowledge which is universal, unified, and simple. For this is how the agent intellect acts, notwithstanding the fact that it is the cause of those forms; that is, its conceiving [them] is the cause of the lower forms' existence (the latter are, however, not the cause of its [i.e. the agent intellect's] thinking, while they are indeed the cause of man's acquired intellect). Herein lies the difference between the agent intellect and the human intellect so long as the latter has not yet become angelic. The existence of the existents in the agent intellect differs, therefore, from their existence in the intellect of man as regards the universality and simple unity of each form, and as regards its abstraction from the plurality which affects it[57] . . . on account of their matter, and as regards the fact that the intellect of man is caused by the existents

55. The above account reflects Avempace's view that the intelligibles obtained by the "natural method" (through abstraction) are still "material" and affected by plurality and multiplicity. See M. Asín Palacios, "Tratado de Avempace sobre la unión del intelecto con el hombre," *Al-Andalus*, 7:17 (37) (1942). Avempace insisted that abstraction from individuals, although constituting universality, did not wholly obliterate the relation to the individuals: viz., to matter. Cf. my article, "Ibn Bajja on Man's Ultimate Felicity," *Harry Austryn Wolfson Jubilee Volume*, English Section, I (Jerusalem, 1965), 55–60 *et passim*.

56. The omitted part of the sentence (lit., "and the agent intellect produces in it what the other intellects have given previously") is unintelligible. The text is obviously corrupt. The term *hayyulāni* (*hylic*) mentioned in the text as an attribute of the agent intellect has no place either in this context, although Averroes' doctrine of the material intellect might seem to justify it. On this doctrine see S. Munk, *Mélanges de philosophie juive et arabe* (Paris, 1857 [1927]), pp. 444–455. There is, however, no sense in using the term "agent hylic intellect" when dealing with the final stage of the intellectual process. Narboni, who follows Averroes' view (see *CG*, 13a–b; *CPC*, fols. 121*v*–127*r*), means to say: Having produced the intelligibles or the intellect *in habitu*, the agent intellect, in connecting with the latter anew, elevates and absorbs the previous intellect into itself, destroys it, and now thinks only itself.

57. The words placed within brackets in the Hebrew text and left untranslated do not fit into the context and probably represent a copyist's gloss partly corrupted. We suggest the reading: *af* (instead of *ak*) *be-ᶜinyan she-yushpaᶜ mimenu ᵓo tagiᶜa ha-haysharā mimenu mā she-ᵓeyn ken bi-sheᵓar ha-nifradim*," "also as regards the fact that it [the human intellect] receives its [the agent intellect's] emanation and guidance, which is not the case with the other separate intellects" (cf. lines 115–119). This gloss was inserted in a way that separates the words *le-sibbat ḥomram* from the words *ha-qorē lā*, to which they belong.

in the way mentioned: namely, that they are objects of vision first, then impressed in the imagination, and then invested in the intellect, which is at first but like a tablet ready to be inscribed.[58] The lower existents are caused by *Keneset Yisraʾel* [the agent intellect];[59] that is, the concept formed of them by the latter is the cause of their being, and comprises them, for which reason the followers of the Torah[60] called the agent intellect by that name. You should further know that just as the existents are raised up from their material [level of] existence to [that in] the agent intellect, so their existence—that is, their essence—continues to be elevated in the ten separate intelligences as regards [the degree of] their simplicity and unity. The superiority of one angel over another consists precisely in this: that is, in the varying degrees of the existents' simplicity and unity in the respective angels.[61] Each [angel] conceives, furthermore, a sphere, and this conception is, in some respect, the cause of the existence of the sphere.[62] In this way one particular intellect is the cause of one particular sphere—that is in so far as it moves it—but God, blessed be He, is the cause of all. The scholar [Ibn Rushd] said as follows:[63]

It has become customary for our contemporaries to assert that from such and such a mover there proceeds such and such a mover or that [such and such a mover] emanates from it, or necessarily follows from it,[64] or whichever similar expression one may use. Such statements, however, bear a meaning which does not fit those separate principles. For all those [separate principles] might be described as "agents" only at first blush, but not in truth, since

58. Aristotle, *De anima*, III.iv, 430a 1–2.

59. The tenth *Sefira* of the Kabbalists, which Narboni, following Joseph b. Abraham ibn Waqār and others (see Introduction, Page 245), identified with the agent intellect. The term *keneset* (lit., "assembly") is probably understood as an allusion to the agent intellect's function of assembling particulars under universal genera and species (*we-huʾ meqabbeẓam*, lines 88–89). Cf. *Ruaḥ Ḥen*, chap. 5, end: "for the meaning of 'species' is the 'assembling' [*qibbuẓ*] of its individuals to be 'assembled' [*ha-niqbaẓim*] by the intellect."

60. Viz., the Kabbalists.

61. Cf. Maimonides, *Yesodē Ha-Torā*, II, 8; Vajda, *Albalag*, pp. 83ff.

62. The well-known cosmological theory of al-Fārābī and Avicenna, which had been accepted by Maimonides (*Guide*, II, 11, 22) and by Averroes in his *Epitome of the Metaphysics* (see Simon van den Bergh, *Die Epitome der Metaphysik des Averroes* [Leiden, 1924], pp. 135–137) but rejected in his *Tahāfut al-Tahāfut* (van den Bergh, I, 107–108).

63. The text which follows is composed of two passages from Averroes' Long Commentary on Aristotle's *Metaphysics*. See *Tafsīr mā baʿd al-tabīʿat*, ed. Maurice Bouyges, III (Beirut, 1948), 1652, lines 5–11 (=lines 96–100 of our text) and 1649, lines 3–12 (=lines 101–109 of our text). Insertions into the Averroes text by Narboni are indicated by the sign ⟨ ⟩.

64. Narboni quotes this phrase (lines 96–97) and the complementary sentence (line 100) also in *CPC*, MS. Michael 119, fol. 139(ii)*r*, lines 13–14; he reproduces almost the entire Averroes text quoted here in *CIP*, Vat. MS. 260, fol. 55*r*, commenting on Tractate V (Muckle, p. 121).

from an agent nothing proceeds except the bringing forth of something potential into actuality. Here, however, there is no potentiality, and, hence, there is no agent but intellect and intelligible, something perfecting and something thereby perfected. ⟨For the intelligible is the cause of the intelligent, and for this reason there is here no agent.⟩ There is here, however, cause and caused in the sense in which we say of the intelligible that it is the cause of the intelligent.[65] This being so, it is not impossible for that which in its essence is intellect and intelligible to be the cause of [various levels of] existence[66] insofar as certain aspects are made the object of intellection. Hence the concept formed of the First Mover[67] by the mover of the celestial body[68]—as being the cause of the very soul ⟨and essence⟩[69] of the heaven—is other than the concept formed of it by the mover of the sphere of Saturn, for example. The same holds true of each one of them; that is to say that the perfection of each one of them consists in the concept it forms of its [immediate] cause which particularizes it, and the concept formed of the First Cause. In this way all their motions form one harmonious whole, which is the order that exists for all, ⟨and the heavenly bodies move so as to cause that which is potentially in those separate forms to pass into actuality, i.e., into material forms.⟩

I have thus shown you my true thought, and [have shown] it to be the view of the philosophers, that those forms have two existences: an actual one which is their material existence, and a potential one which they possess in those [separate] forms. By "potential" I mean here something similar to what is meant when we say that the forms of artifacts have actual existence in matter and potential existence in the soul of their maker. It, therefore, appears that those forms

65. The intelligible is the mover of the intellect or, in other words, the potential intellect is actualized by the intelligible. On the other hand, the intelligible is actualized by the intellect. For a discussion of this subject see O. Hamelin, *La Théorie de l'intellect d'après Aristote et ses commentateurs* (Paris, 1953), pp. 20ff.

66. Lit., "existence of parts" (*li-meẓiᵓut ḥalaqim*; the same expression also in the reproduction of the text in *CIP*, see Note 64). This seems an inadequate rendering of the Arabic *shayᵓ min*, "of a certain."

67. I.e., God, according to the theory proposed by Averroes, in his (now lost) *Treatise on the First Mover*, identifying the Necessary of Existence or First Cause (God) with the First Mover. For an exposition and critique of this view see Moses b. Joseph Ha-Levi's *Metaphysical Treatise* (French translation from the Arabic text by G. Vajda, *Revue Thomiste*, 3:480–508 [1948]). As Moses Ha-Levi noted, Averroes offered a different view in his *Epitome of the Metaphysics*, where he describes the Mover of the all-encompassing sphere as caused by God (see Vajda, *Revue Thomiste*, p. 503). Narboni follows Averroes' theory as stated in the *Treatise*. Cf. *CG*, 27b; *CPC*, MS. Michael 119, fol. 139(i)*v*.

68. I.e., the mover of the sphere of the fixed stars, which is adjacent to the all-encompassing sphere.

69. Lit., "of the soul of heaven ⟨viz., of the essence of heaven⟩" (reading *ha-shamayim* instead of *ha-shemini*, which makes no sense). The explanatory addition may be a gloss. For Averroes' use of *nafs* (soul) in the sense of "essence" see van den Bergh, *Epitome*, p. 135, where the two terms are interchangeably employed. See also Narboni, *CPC*, fol. 118*v*, where *nefesh* is used in the sense of essence.

have two existences, [namely,] one separate and one material, and that the former is the cause of the latter. Action [by the separate forms] upon the material ones is to be attributed to the agent intellect rather than to the rest of the separate [intellects], since the agent intellect bears the closest resemblance to the inferior existence they have. It is for this reason that it causes the lower forms to pass from potentiality to actuality in matter—their matter having been prepared by the [motions of the] heavenly bodies[70]—as it is said, "As an apple-tree among the trees of the wood" (Canticles 2:3)—that is, among [the trees] which do not produce fruit—"So is my beloved among [the sons]" (*ibid.*)—[that is, among] the heavenly powers—for among all of them it is only the agent intellect that produces.[71] For this reason the forms in the producing intellect bear a greater resemblance to the lower forms than the other [separate] forms, the latter [existing] in the other intellects in a wonderful way without [however] proceeding from them, and [they exist] in the First Cause in the most glorious manner possible in perfect and simple unity. For this reason the philosophers said that God, blessed be He, is one, and that He is the most glorious of existents, and that in this sense He is the latter's principle. Rabbi Moses [ben Maimon] of blessed memory therefore explained [the verse] "And thou shalt stand upon the rock" (Exodus 33:21): "Rely upon, and be firm in considering, God, may He be exalted, as the first principle. This is the entryway through which you shall come to Him" (*Guide*, I, 16). He means to say that the ultimate knowledge we may have concerning God, may He be exalted, consists in our knowing in which way He is the first principle. For thereby we know as much of the truth concerning Him as is in our nature to know: that is, [by knowing] that He is the first principle insofar as He is [the unity of] intellect, intelligent, and intelligible, which is perceived in a variety of ways, while He thinks the forms in the most glorious existence possible. In order to teach that He is the first principle after this fashion, those who arranged our prayers instituted [the prayer] "Today the world comes into being"[72]—for He, may He be exalted, creates it anew

70. Cf. Maimonides, *Guide*, I, 72, *et passim*.

71. Following an allegorical interpretation of Canticles prevalent among the Jewish Aristotelians, Narboni sees in the figure of the lover (*dod*) an allegory of the agent intellect. He quotes the same verse in the same sense also in *CIP*, Vat. MS. 260, fol. 56*r*, commenting on Tractate V (Muckle, 126, lines 5–10).

72. The prayer recited after the sounding of the *shofar* during the *mussaf* service on Rosh ha-Shanā. Although not found in Saᶜadya's *Siddur*, ed. I. Davidson, S. Assaf, B. I. Joel (Jerusalem, 1941; 2nd ed., 1963), it occurs in *Seder Rab ᶜAmram Gaon*, ed. Arye Leb

in an eternal creation which is the true meaning of creation.[73] And in order to point out the connection of the existents with Him, may He be exalted, in respect of the [self-] intellection which is [identical with] His essence, the prayer continues: "If we be like unto children, have mercy upon us, as a father has mercy upon his children." And in respect of their being separate from Him, may He be exalted, in an existence of their own, the prayer continues further: "If we be like unto servants, our eyes are fastened upon Thee to receive Thy graciousness." And seeing that He is intelligent in the most glorious way possible, and [that He is] the most Holy One to be sanctified and exalted, the prayer concludes with the word "Holy": "To receive Thy graciousness and Thy bringing forth to light of our judgment, Thou who art Holy"; for it belongs to our judgment and our power to achieve union with the separate [intellect], may the Holy One be exalted, Amen.

The scholar Ibn Rushd said expressly:[74] "In the view of the philosophers it necessarily follows that the objects of the intellection of the separate intellects are the forms of the existents, and the order which exists in the world, as is [also] the case with the human intellect, since intellect is nothing other than the perception of the forms of the existents insofar as they are without matter. [. . . This being so,] the forms of the sensible existents have different degrees of existence. The most inferior one is their existence in matters. Then [at a higher level,] their existence in the human intellect is superior to their existence in matters. Then their existence in the separate intellects is superior to their existence in the human intellect. Then they have in the separate intellects degrees of excellence of existence

---

Frumkin, II, 304; *Sefer Ha-Pardes le-Rashi*, ed. Ḥayyim Jehuda Ehrenreich (New York, 1959), 233a, in the Italian *Maḥzor* (Leghorn, 1856), and is, according to Ismar Elbogen, *Der jüdische Gottesdienst in seiner geschichtlichen Entwicklung*, 3rd ed. (Frankfurt a.M., 1931), p. 216, common to all rites.

73. According to the literal meaning of the prayer, "today" (viz., on New Year's Day) the world was created (cf. *Rosh Ha-Shanā* 27a). Narboni understands it to express the philosophers' view that the world, being eternal, is constantly ("today") recreated. Cf. Vajda, *Albalag*, p. 135. Ibn Waqār interprets the prayer kabbalistically (Vat. MS. 203, fol. 52*v*).

74. The text which follows (lines 135–156) is quoted from Averroes' *Tahāfut al-Tahāfut*, piecing together six separate passages of the Third Discussion, found on pp. 215, 216, 217, 226–227, and 233 in M. Bouyges' edition (*Bibliotheca Arabica Scholasticorum*, vol. III [Beirut, 1930]); pp. 128, 129, 130, 135, 139 in Simon van den Bergh's English edition of the text. Our translation is indebted to van den Bergh's but has sought to improve on it where greater precision seemed to be required. The omitted passages between the excerpts quoted by Narboni are indicated by three dots within square brackets.

according to the [different degrees of] excellence of those intellects in themselves. [. . . For this reason they believed that] these abstract principles derive from a single abstract principle which is the cause of all of them. [. . .] In their view, the First thinks only its own essence and, by thinking its essence, thinks at the same time all existents in the noblest mode of existence and in the noblest arrangement and order. The substance of everything below it is [according to] the intellection it has of the forms, the arrangement and the order which exist in the First Intellect; and their greater or lesser superiority consists only in this. [. . .] The statement that the First Principle, if it thinks only its own essence, must be ignorant of everything it has created would be a valid inference only if the object of its self-intellection were something absolutely other than the existents. They (the philosophers), however, assume that the object of the First's self-intellection is identical with the existents in their noblest mode of existence, and that it is the intellect which is the cause of the existents; and that it does not think the existents insofar as they are the cause of its intellect, as is the case with our intellect. The meaning of our saying that it does not think the existents which are below it is that it does not think them in the way we think them but that it thinks them in a way no other thinking existent can think them; for if another existent could think them in the way it thinks them, it would participate in the knowledge of God, and God is far too exalted for this. This is an attribute peculiar to Him. [. . .] So it has become evident [to the philosophers] that there is one single order and act in which all existents participate in common. To ascertain the order perceived by those contemplating the existents side by side with the ascent to the knowledge of the First is difficult, and what human intellects can perceive of it is only its general principle."

So far Ibn Rushd. It should be clear from all this that the sensible existents are abstract forms in the First Cause, and that It thinks them in the most noble way. This being the case, we may call the [confining] measure of the existents "measure of the body" [*shiᶜur qomā*], in accordance with the dictum of theirs (*Ḥagigah* 12a): "The world went on expanding until the Holy One, blessed be He, rebuked it."[75] Here an allusion may be found to the relation that

75. In *CG*, 14b, Narboni quotes this dictum in connection with his interpretation of "Place" as a term denoting God. He mentions there also the term *shiᶜur qomā*. See Introduction, Page 248.

obtains between the caused and the Cause. For this reason the Sages of Israel composed the [book] *Shi^cur Qomā*, the existents in their totality being [designated as] the "Body." For the same reason He [God] is called "Crown" [*Keter*].[76] This will help you to understand the truth of Ibn Ezra's statement that He, may He be exalted, has no image, and that He is like the universal aspect of all the images, for they proceed from Him by virtue of His conceiving them; and since He comprises them all—as was said by Ibn Rushd that God was in some respect all existents[77]—He may be called "Image." The "Body" has a "face" and a "back" and "Face" stands for God's true essence—that is, for His way of conceiving the existents—while "Back" stands for the manner in which the existents necessarily follow from Him. There can be no doubt that the "Face" cannot be seen, that is, that we are unable to know the quiddity of the concept which God has of the existents; I mean to say that to know the existents in that way (that is, [to see] the "Face") even the ministering angels are incapable of,[78] for, as already mentioned, this is the very essence of Divinity, and only God knows God.[79] Moses saw, however, His "Back"—that is, the manner in which the existents necessarily follow from Him—in the way this is perceived by the agent intellect; for Moses became an angel of the Lord.[80] This is [the rank] designated by the term "beaming of the skin of the face" (Exodus 34:35).[81] It means the coming into being of the second disposition when the first has been annihilated together with the forms [that exist] in the intellect *in habitu*.[82] This is [also] the meaning

76. Assuming the identity of the ten *Sefirot* of the Kabbalists with the philosophers' ten movers of the spheres, Narboni equates the first *Sefirā* (*Keter*) with the First Mover (God). In this he follows the precedent set by Ibn Waqār. Cf. Introduction, Page 244. He understood *Keter* in the sense in which some Kabbalists interpreted it as the "surrounding" (and thereby "confining") *Sefirā*. See Introduction, Page 251. For the Kabbalists' view see Joseph Gikatila, *Sha^carē Orā*, Riva di Trento, 83b, and the passages quoted in my article in *Kiryat Sefer*, 40:409 (1965).

77. Averroes says that "some of the best known philosophers affirm that God the Creator is Himself all existents" (*Tahāfut al-Tahāfut*, ed. Bouyges, p. 442).

78. *Sifra*ʾ 2.12; *Exodus Rabba* 23:15; *Pesiqta Rabbati* 20; Maimonides, *Yesodē Ha-Torā*, II, 8.

79. Al-Ghazālī, *Mishkat al-anwār* (Cairo, 1353/1934), p. 19: "For none knows Allāh with a real knowledge but He Himself." Medieval Jewish writers used the formula: "If I knew God, I would be He" (*ilu yeda^ctiv heyyitiv*). Both formulations are discussed by Vajda, *Juda ben Nissim ibn Malka*, p. 69, n. 1; see also *idem*, *Albalag*, p. 116. A reference to be added is Abraham Bibago, *Derek Emunā* (Constantinople, 1521), 84b.

80. Cf. lines 30–31 and 83 of the text and see Note 26.

81. Cf. Note 32.

82. According to Averroes' doctrine (see Note 56), the fully developed intellect *in habitu* vanishes when attracted to the agent intellect, and at this stage a "second disposi-

which attaches to Elisha's beholding Elijah being taken from him.[83] For the intelligible forms that have come to be perish, for all that comes to be perishes, and the eternal [intelligible forms] are imparted by what is eternal. For, as Aristotle said, the material intellect is eternal, that is, is the agent intellect which conjoins with us; for it knows what is yonder but does not remember what is here.[84] What human intellects can perceive has already been stated by us in the name of the philosophers: namely, that the manner in which the existents necessarily follow from God is [determined by the fact] that the First Intellect thinks these existents in the most noble way, and that of His essence conceptions are formed under varying aspects reaching down to the sensible existents, both high and low.[85] Altogether, all forms are conjoined. For the lower ones are perfected by the higher ones, the perfection being one of perception[86] in that they achieve [the more perfect perception] from the higher ones either by a complete transformation, as is the case with the psychic forms, or on account of the fact that the higher ones are the object of their desire, as is the case with the abstract forms, which are, as it were, transformed and become indeed more intelligent [thereby].[87] Try to understand this. Know also that while the lower ones among the abstract forms perceive the higher ones and in this respect conjoin with them perceptually, the latter both perceive the former and impart to them their existence which is their essence and the very soul of perception of a nobler kind. In this respect they also perfect the lower ones and give them their existence, and the latter conjoin with the higher ones in a conjunction of both existence

---

tion" comes into being: i.e., the material intellect is now denuded of all forms previously acquired and becomes again a *tabula rasa*, yet one ready this time to conceive the agent intellect.

83. As Narboni explains more fully in *CPC* (fol. 126*r*), Elijah and Elisha symbolize respectively the intellect *in habitu* and the material intellect. When Elijah is seen taken from Elisha (II Kings 2:10), the latter will achieve a "double portion" of the former's spirit (v. 9); i.e., when the intellect *in habitu* is destroyed, the material intellect will be capable of conjoining with the agent intellect. Narboni elaborates this allegorical interpretation as a Biblical parallel to the Koran passage quoted by Averroes. As Munk, *Mélanges*, p. 453, n. 1, has pointed out, Narboni misunderstood the Koran passage concerned.

84. Cf. *CG*, 13b.

85. I.e., the translunar and sublunar bodies.

86. Following Averroes, Narboni distinguishes between the "perfection of perception" (*shelemut hasagā*) from the "perfection of existence" (*shelemut meẓiʾut*). When, e.g., the imaginative forms are raised to the level of intelligibles, they achieve both kinds of perfection. When, on the other hand, the intellect *in habitu* operates on the imaginative forms, it is perfected by them in existence only. Cf. *CPC*, fols. 110*v*–112*v*.

87. Cf. Narboni's account of the hierarchy of forms, in lines 62–95 of the text.

and perception, and this is designated by the term "Back." The merest allusion will here suffice after all that has been placed [before the reader] in the previous discussion.

He [Ibn Ezra] established the "Body," saying: "Length is [the extension] between two points"—is the "Body"; "and the point nearest to the Agent" (that is, comparable to the Great Agent or Glory) "is the Prince of the Presence" (which is the highest point) "and there is" the essence of "the power" and the potency; "and the other point" (which, being the lowest, is the opposite of the first) is comparable to "the end of the power." Having [thus] set up the height of the "Body," he [Ibn Ezra] offers a reason why God is allegorically described as "the Face," saying: "The movement of man is forward [literally, "toward the Face"]."[88] Moreover, he attributes right and left to the "Body," saying: "the supernal [that is, celestial] body is toward the right, and the plant is toward the supernal"; that is, the supernal bodies are designated as "right" and the lower ones as "left."[89] He says [moreover] that among the spheres some are designated as being on the right side of the "Body"—namely, the higher spheres—and some are designated as being on the left side—that is, the inferior ones. The same applies to [the term] "Feet." Some are called by the term "left," although they [the "Feet"] are but allegories for the lower bodies. He [Ibn Ezra] explained [this latter point] by saying: "and the plant is toward the supernal." He meant to say that the status of the plant is one of superiority in relation to the lower [bodies],[90] as if to say that the plant is to be designated by the term "right" in respect of the lower [bodies], and this is a fortiori true of the animals, since he had already said that the higher was toward the right. Having thus set up the "Sanctuary,"[91] he explained [the meaning of] "Face" and "Back" in the manner we have mentioned previously, saying: "Moses was able to see with his intellect's eye the way in which they [the

88. I.e., aspiring toward a knowledge of the Divine essence, which, however, is denied to him.

89. Narboni interprets Ibn Ezra's use of the terms "right" and "left" as denoting positions not in space but in rank: viz., a relative superiority or inferiority.

90. I.e., the minerals.

91. Using Ibn Ezra's simile of the "Sanctuary" (*mishkan*) as symbol of the three worlds: of the separate intellects (=the Holy of Holies), of the spheres (=the holy precincts), and of the sublunar world (=the courtyard of the Sanctuary). Cf. Rosin, pp. 205–208. The "Body" (*qomā*) and the "Sanctuary" thus denote the same thing: viz., the totality of existents. Cf. line 201 of the text. The Sanctuary as a symbol of Man is discussed at length by Samuel ibn Tibbon. See Moritz Steinschneider, *Monatsschrift*, 32:91 (1883).

creatures] are conjoined [with the Creator]," which is [the vision of] the "Back"; "but it belongs to the way of the Glory"—that is, of God's existence—"that no created being is able to know it," namely, the "Face" by which His essence is meant: "man shall not see Me and live." He [Ibn Ezra] then gave the reason for comparing man's form rather than any other form with its Creator, saying: "The noblest on earth is man; hence the form of the Cherubim,"[92] viz., the Sanctuary, [which is] the Body, while the wings point to the three causes,[93] and the two figures indicate the Cause and the caused. "The noblest among men are the Israelites," and they put on the *tefillin*; hence the perfect man[94] puts on the *tefillin*, and this is the meaning of his saying: "hence the statement about the knot of the *tefillin*."[95] Thus, he did not content himself with the allegory of the "Back," and we have already given the reason here alluded to.[96] Since in all this he tried to explain the book *Shiᶜur Qomā*, as I have told you, he mentioned it [by name] and quoted its subject matter by way of interpretation, but not its [actual] words, saying: "It is, therefore, written in the *Shiᶜur Qomā* that God creates all bodies and all that is nobler than body and [all] that is inferior to the body: that is, the accidents." He meant to say that the totality of the existents is the "Body" of the Perfect Man whom the adepts of [the doctrine of] the *Sefirot* call also the "Tree."[97] The divisions of the existents form the "Body," and the accidents of the "Body" are what is called "from [the appearance of] his loins and downward" (Ezekiel 1:27), and that which is nobler than body is the intellect of the abstract [forms], and this is called "from [the appearance of] his loins and upward (Ezekiel 1:27). In the book *Shiᶜur Qomā* this latter is called "from his flanks and upward."[98] The "Back" stands for the [existents'] necessarily following from Him, and the "Face"

92. See Note 27.

93. Viz., God, who is the formal, efficient, and final cause of the universe. Cf. Maimonides, *Guide*, I, 69. By spreading their wings upward the cherubim point to God. For Maimonides' interpretation of the cherubim see *Guide*, III, 45; for his allegorical interpretation of "wing" see *Guide*, I, 43.

94. We have emended *ha-ʾadam ha-mashlim* to read, in conformity to the text in line 207, *ha-ʾadam ha-shalem*, viz., *Adam Qadmon*, which is yet another symbol for the *qomā or makroanthropos*.

95. See Note 12.

96. See lines 42–45 of the text.

97. For the kabbalistic symbol of the Sefirotic tree see Scholem, *Major Trends in Jewish Mysticism*, p. 214; *idem*, *Ursprung*, index, *s.v.* "Baumsymbolik."

98. The text in Mussajov's edition (*Merkabā Shelemā*, 36b) and in *Sefer Raziʾel* (37b) has *mi-yarkotav we-ᶜad ẓawwʾaro* ("from his flanks up to his neck").

for their existence in Him. Know and understand that inasmuch as God, may He be exalted, is identical with His conceiving of the existents in their most perfect and most glorious mode, and inasmuch as no one besides Him knows Him, and the existents are connected with Him in this Divine manner—as was said by King Solomon, peace be upon him, in the book *Canticles* (8:8): "We have a little sister"[99]—[the prophet Ezekiel] called that which is from the loins and upward "as the appearance of splendor, as the color of electrum" and that which is downward "as the appearance of fire" (Ezekiel 1:27; 8:2). For the electrum is the brightness in a flame of fire, and this splendor stands for the first intellect,[100] which is therefore called "the light of intellect." The bodies [,on the other hand,] stand for the fire that is connected with the flame,[101] and for this reason our Father Abraham, peace be upon him, explained in his book [*Sefer Yeẓirā*, I, 7] that all are connected with each other "as the flame is connected with the coal."[102] Moses, peace be upon him, said in the book of the Torah of God—that is to say [the book of the Torah] in which nothing is superfluous and without usefulness[103]—"And God saw the light, that it was good" (Genesis 1:4), which verse the Kabbalists interpret to mean: "Like one kindling light from light and trimming the lights."[104] According to this union, the proper name YHWH which denotes the Glory and is also an adjective,[105] comprises all the abstract [intellects] and the supernal and lower

99. A reference to the material intellect or the as-yet-not-fully-developed intellect *in habitu*, as suggested by the allegorical interpretation of Canticles. See Note 71 and Moses ibn Tibbon, *Perush ʿal Shir Ha-Shirim* (Lyck, 1874), 22b; Gersonides, *Perush ʿal Ḥamesh Megillot* (Königsberg, 1860), 21b.

100. Viz., the first of the separate intellects. Cf. *CG*, 49a, where the "first intellect" is clearly differentiated from the "First Cause" (God).

101. In *CG*, 48b, Narboni sees in the fire ("as the appearance of fire") an allusion to the last of the separate intellects, not, as here, to the celestial spheres.

102. In *CG*, 48b, Narboni quotes the same *Sefer Yeẓirā* passage in the sense that all separate intellects are unified in the first intellect, and all spheres in the first diurnal motion; moreover, that denying the essential unity of the intellects amounts to heresy ("cutting the plants"; on this metaphor see Scholem, *Jewish Gnosticism*, p. 16, n. 6).

103. Cf. Maimonides, *Guide*, III, 50, where the criticisms leveled against the alleged "uselessness" of the narrative part of the Tora are rebutted, and the "great principle" is laid down that "every narrative in the Tora serves a certain purpose in connection with religious teaching." See also Azriʾel of Gerona's *Perush Ha-ʾAggadot*, ed. I. Tishby (Jerusalem, 1945), pp. 37–38; Moses de Leon, *Sheʾelot U-Teshubot*, ed. I. Tishby, published in *Qobeẓ ʿAl Yad*, N.S., 5 (15):30 (Jerusalem, 1950); *Ẓohar*, I, 163a: *de-ʾinun milin pegimin de-let behu toʿalta.*

104. Cf. Azriʾel of Gerona's *Perush Ha-ʾAggadot*, 89.

105. Viz., denoting God's activity as the bestower of existence. Narboni adopted Ibn Ezra's doctrine according to which the Tetragrammaton is both a *nomen proprium* (*shem ʿeẓem*) and an adjective (*shem toʾar*). See Note 13 and Rosin, pp. 110, 156, 159.

bodies in their essences. It [the Divine Name] signifies a great mystery in that it indicates that He is the Form of the world. Then he [Ibn Ezra] conceived [the image of] the body of man (*qomat ha-ʾadam*), and figured the accidents of the body as the soles of his feet, and figured the lower bodies as [the parts] from the soles up to the knees—as is said, "And the earth is My footstool" (Isaiah 66:1)—and called the bodies of the spheres his thigh, and called the abstract intellects the upper [part of the] body—the supernal being to the right—and called his head the first intellect, and called his face His true essence which cannot be perceived, "For the hand upon the throne of the Lord: the Lord will have war with ʿAmalek from generation to generation" (Exodus 17:16); for [God's essence] cannot be perceived if any other being is associated with Him, and the war is therefore eternal, as our divine[106] teacher Moses [ben Maimon], peace be upon him, explained it.[107] And he called his back that which can be perceived, and this is meant by the "standing upon the rock."

"God hath made even the one as well as the other" (Ecclesiastes 7:14). He [Ibn Ezra] desired to complete the [account of the] Form and said:[108] "Know that all plants and animals on earth like fowl, cattle, beast, [and creeping things, and all men are connected with the supernal beings]," etcetera, down to the end of the passage. By all this he intended to complete [the account of] the true measure of the Form in respect of eyes, hands, and the other [organs]. He, again, followed the text when explaining [the verse (Exodus 33:22),] "and I will cover thee with My hand until I have passed by."[109] To me it seems that he alluded here to what the philosophers have explained: that the spiritual and the corporeal worlds are two contraries which cannot inhere in the same substratum; and that he to whom it was given to enjoy the spiritual light will be shut out from the corporeal; he will know what is yonder but fail to remember what is here;[110] he will conjoin with "All"[111] in a union of perception subsequent to a union of existence. Hence it is said: "and I will cover thee with My hand until I have passed by," which means to say

106. On the use of this epithet see Steinschneider, *Die hebräischen Übersetzungen*, p. 184.

107. Narboni expresses himself in similar terms in *CG*, 3a–b, with reference to Maimonides' terse remarks (*Guide*, I, 9) on the verse quoted. ʿAmalek stands here for the denier of the absolute unity of God whose essence does not admit of any composition or association.

108. In a section of his comments on Exod. 33:21 not included in Narboni's extracts.

109. See Note 32.

110. See lines 173–174 of the text and Note 84.

111. I.e., the forms of all existents as comprised in the agent intellect.

that the corporeal existents will be hidden from him as long as the perception arising from union with the abstract [intellects] has not departed.[112] When, however, he [Ibn Ezra] said: " 'Thou shalt see My back' inasmuch as it is 'all' and His Glory filleth 'all' and 'all' is from Him," he meant to say that Moses was to see His "Back" inasmuch as he was to perceive the existents, having regard to the fact that He is their noblest essence, and His act of conceiving [Himself] comprises them all, and through this act "all" is [continually] created by Him.[113] To this he [Ibn Ezra] referred when saying: "and 'all' is the image of 'All' and this is meant by [the verse] 'and the image of the Lord doth he behold' (Numbers 11:8)," the meaning of this [verse] being that all existents are the image of God, seeing that they are in Him in the most noble [way of] existence.[114] This is the attribute of God by which His unity is expressed, and this is meant by [the verse:] "and the image of God doth he behold": namely, [what he beholds is] the essence of the existents which are His image, not His face, for [to behold] this, [that is,] the true essence of God, is impossible except to the true essence [of God Himself], blessed be He. King Solomon, peace be upon him, wrote the book *Canticles* on the basis of this [concept],[115] as when he said: "His head is as the most fine gold" (Canticles 5:11) and [when he described] his neck, feet, belly, mouth, teeth, and locks,[116] all these signifying but the parts of the world[117] and the elevation of the existents in Him. The prophets used this glorious and noble allegory in order that man through knowing it may be assured of his portion in the

112. In *CPC*, fol. 112*r*, Narboni offers a different interpretation of the verse quoted: God had to cover Moses with His hand in order to prevent him from being distracted by sense perception. This was necessary in Moses' case of prophecy since his senses did not cease to operate during the prophetic act. While all other prophets received the influx from the agent intellect via imagination, Moses' imaginative faculty was not engaged in the act. Now the impinging of the influx upon imagination, which is a corporeal faculty, overwhelms the senses, both internal and external. Hence in Moses' prophecy the senses could remain intact. The difference is illustrated by the description of Balaam as "fallen down, yet with open eyes" (Num. 24:16), in contrast to Moses, who stood erect at the time of his union with the agent intellect. Cf. Maimonides, *Yesodē Ha-Torā*, VII, 6.

113. Narboni, *CG*, 15b, echoes Ibn Ezra's formula (see lines 37–38 of the text) when describing God in these terms: "He is all, and all is in Him; He is all-powerful, and from Him all proceeds; and all returns unto Him, who is exalted above all."

114. Cf. Narboni, *CG*, 52a: "For His image comprises all images."

115. Viz., of *shiʿur qomā*. Narboni departs here from the standard philosophical allegorization of Canticles (see Notes 71 and 99) in interpreting the limbs of the lover as symbols of the parts of the macrocosm (see also lines 250–251 of the text).

116. Narboni mixes the description of the lover and the beloved which occur in Canticles (5:15; 5:16; 5:11; 1:10 [4:5; 7:5]; 7:3; 4:2 [6:6].

117. On the microcosm motif, see my article "The Delphic Maxim," pp. 213–222.

world-to-come.[118] God, blessed be He, is, however, neither body nor a force resident in a body—His praise is infinite—but He is separate from that which does not have its existence in Him.[119] For He is not a form that inheres in what is [constituted] by means of the dimensions,[120] yet [it may be said that] God is in heaven because He gives it existence and elevation of existence.

"To whom will ye liken Me, that I should be equal?" (Isaiah 40:25). What led them to this [allegorical image] was [the intention] to present the intelligible as sensible. For this reason [also] Moses made the tabernacle which God had shown him on Mount Sinai;[121] and for this reason the prophets beheld upon the firmament the likeness of a throne;[122] and [for this reason] did the people see the fire at the Revelation on Sinai,[123] and did Abraham see the smoking furnace and the flaming torch,[124] as Rabbi Moses [ben Maimon], his memory be for a blessing, has indicated.[125]

The philosophers too assumed the microcosm to resemble the macrocosm,[126] and the First to occupy a position [in relation to the macrocosm analogous to that occupied by] our separate intellect, which is our true essence [in relation to the microcosm].[127] Jacob compared the matter[128] to a ladder: "And behold, the Lord stood above it" (Genesis 28:13), not upon it;[129] and the followers of the Torah[130] compared it to a tree.[131] To this category [of allegory] of theirs there belongs the description [of Him as the highest watchman, according to the verse:] "For one higher than the high watcheth" (Ecclesiastes 5:7);[132] also the allusion [to Him found]

118. See lines 34–35 of the text and Note 30.

119. But subsists in itself (cf. lines 5–6 of the text), although its existence is derived from God.

120. I.e., in bodies which are ultimately constituted by the dimensions or "form of corporeality" (see H. A. Wolfson, *Crescas' Critique of Aristotle* [Cambridge, Mass., 1929], pp. 579–590).

121. Exod. 25:9, 40, *et passim.*

122. Ezek. 1:26.

123. Exod. 19:18; Deut. 5:20, 22, 23.

124. Gen. 15:17.

125. *Guide*, I, 21.

126. See Note 117.

127. Cf. Maimonides, *Guide*, I, 72.

128. Viz., the various levels of existence.

129. Viz., God is not the highest on the ladder of being but above it. Narboni elaborates Maimonides' interpretation of Jacob's ladder (*Guide*, II, 10) in *CG*, 28b–29a. See also 41a.

130. I.e., the Kabbalists.

131. See Note 97.

132. Cf. Maimonides, *Yesodē Ha-Torā*, II, 5.

in the *lulab*, on account of which it was stated that "[a *lulab*] the twin leaves of which are divided is unfit for use,"[133] because in the First there is no plurality; there is also the allusion to this [found] in the *sukkā*, the ceiling [being said] to allude to the supernal beings, for which reason the stipulation was made that it must not consist of material susceptible to uncleanness[134] (a stipulation that was not laid down with regard to the walls). The question was posed: "[What about a *sukkā* which is] seven handbreadths in width and ten in height?"—all this [discussion] leading up to the remark that "what is separated by less than three handbreadths is considered as joined";[135] for the three parts [making up all] the existents form a unity, as we have explained. All these allegories are [necessary] on account of the deficiency inherent in the very nature of the human intellect's ability, and [on account of] its being attached to matter and [on account of] the eternal [intellect][136] being connected with the disposition.[137] When, however, the cloud lifts itself from the Glory, the allegory vanishes and that which it expressed by allegory is perceived. "In that day the Lord shall be one and His name one" (Zechariah 14:9).

This is the end of what I intended to explain in this letter. May God atone on our behalf for our having committed this [subject-matter] to writing, for it seems that matters of esoteric wisdom were previously transmitted from mouth to mouth [only];[138] but even as necessity had made it imperative to write about them in riddles, so the time is now ripe for looking through the [silver] filigree holding the [golden] apples and for contemplating them.[139] One does, nevertheless, transmit the matter only in terms of chapter-headings.[140] May God remove from us all that disturbs and hinders both from without and within until we attain to the true felicity, our ultimate purpose, through His light which illumines all darkness, according to the words of King David, peace be upon him: "For with Thee is

133. *Sukkā* 32a.
134. *Mishnā Sukkā* I, 4.
135. *Sukkā* 16b.
136. I.e., the agent intellect.
137. See Note 82.
138. Cf. Maimonides, *Guide*, introduction.
139. An allusion to Maimonides' interpretation of Prov. 25:11 (*Guide*, introduction). Narboni thought the time ripe for a closer look at the esoteric meaning of Scripture. He uses the same expression in *CG*, 34a.
140. I.e., of general principles. Cf. *Ḥagigā* 13a; Maimonides, *Yesodē Ha-Torā*, IV, 11.

the fountain of light; in Thy light do we see light" (Psalm 36:10). Amen. Selah. And all Israelites are included in the blessing.

Praise be unto God "Who is fearsome in His doing" (Psalm 66:5). [This letter] was completed by its author on the Eve of Sukkot in the year one hundred and three of the sixth millennium from the beginning of the circling of the world and the creation thereof altogether out of absolutely nothing, for there is nothing outside Him,[141] be He exalted and praised. Amen. Selah.

141. Cf. lines 2–3 of the text.

Greek into Hebrew:

Samuel ben Judah of Marseilles, Fourteenth-Century Philosopher and Translator

By LAWRENCE V. BERMAN

Dedicated to the Memory of
Professor Simon Rawidowicz

The title, *Greek into Hebrew*, may at first blush seem surprising. Was there a translator from Greek into Hebrew in fourteenth-century Provence? The answer, of course, on the linguistic level is "No." However, I refer to the transference of certain values contained in works originally composed in Greek and their translation into Hebrew by way of either previous Arabic translations, from the Greek original or from Syriac versions of the Greek, or independent Arabic works based on these translations. In this sense there did take place a translation into Hebrew of a portion of the Greek spiritual heritage.[1]

Provence in the thirteenth and fourteenth centuries was a place of great movement. Politically, there were a number of separate authorities vying with each other. In the spiritual realm one finds, notably, the Albigensian heresy and the crusades preached against it.[2] Inside the Jewish community, there were three main intellectual camps: the Rabbis, whose main interest was in questions of Halakhah and

1. Cf. R. Walzer, *Greek into Arabic* (London, 1962). For Greek into Hebrew, see M. Steinschneider, *Die hebräischen Übersetzungen des Mittelalters* (Berlin, 1893), (quoted hereafter as Steinschneider, *Heb. Üb.*) and the works of A. Altmann, S. Pines, S. Stern, G. Vajda, and H. A. Wolfson, the leading contemporaries in this field. For the Hellenistic period, see the recent article by S. Lieberman, "How Much Greek in Jewish Palestine?" in *Biblical and Other Studies*, ed. A. Altmann (Cambridge, Mass., 1963), pp. 123–141, and the literature quoted there.

2. For a survey of Provence in the twelfth century, see I. Twersky, *Rabad of Posquières* (Cambridge, Mass., 1962), pp. 19–29, and the literature quoted there. The term "Provence" as I use it and as it is used in Hebrew literature of the period includes Languedoc (see the *Jewish Encyclopedia* [New York, 1901–06], s.v. "Provence"). The geographical boundaries of Provence used in this sense correspond to the area in which Provençal was spoken. For a survey of Provence in the thirteenth and fourteenth centuries, see S. Baron, *A Social and Religious History of the Jews* (New York—London, 1965; Philadelphia, 1965), X, 82–92, nn. 32–44 (pp. 339–343).

Talmudic exegesis,[3] the Kabbalists, whose main concern was theosophical speculation,[4] and the philosophical group whose major intellectual interests were secular in nature.[5]

A representative member of the third group of intellectuals is the subject of this paper.

I

Samuel[6] of Marseilles, son of Judah son of Meshullam son of Isaac son of Solomon the Nadiv[7] son of Jacob the Nadiv Prophègue[8] son of David, a very rich man,[9] was born in 1294. He was also known as Miles of Marseilles, Miles Bongodas,[10] and as Barbevaire.[11]

Jacob[12] died around 1170 in Marseilles,[13] so we know that Samuel's

3. See I. Twersky, *Rabad of Posquières*, for the portrait of a representative of this type.

4. See G. Scholem, *Major Trends in Jewish Mysticism* (Jerusalem, 1941), pp. 202ff; *idem*, *Reshit ha-Qabbalah* (Jerusalem, 1948), pp. 99ff.; *idem*, *Ursprung und Anfänge der Kabbala* (Berlin, 1962), pp. 219ff. Cf. below at Note 27. For a later attempt, in some measure, to reconcile Kabbalistic thought with philosophy, see G. Vajda, *La Philosophie et la kabbale dans la pensée juive du moyen âge* (Paris and La Haye, 1962), pp. 115–297.

5. See Julius Guttmann, *Ha-Pilosophiyah shel ha-Yahadut* (Jerusalem, 1953), pp. 169ff. (English translation: *Philosophies of Judaism* [New York, 1964], pp. 183ff.). In general, see I. Zinberg, *Toledot Sifrut Yisra᾿el* (Tel Aviv, 1956), II, 11–123.

6. The article devoted to Samuel in E. Renan-[A. Neubauer], *Les Ecrivains juifs français du XIVe siècle* (Paris, 1893), vol. XXXI of *L'Histoire littéraire de la France*, pp. 553–567 (hereafter quoted as *Ecrivains*), is the basis of all subsequent accounts. See the *Jewish Encyclopedia*, s.v. Samuel ben Judah, as well as G. Sarton, *Introduction to the History of Science*, III (Baltimore, 1947), pp. 433–435. Sarton's statement (p. 61), "Ibn Rushd's commentary on the Organon, revised by Marsilli ben Judah," should read, "Ibn Rushd's *Epitome of Logic*, translated afresh by Samuel ben Judah." See below, Note 43. See also H. Gross, *Gallia Judaica* (Paris, 1897), pp. 379–381. The reference to Samuel in H. Graetz, *Divre Yeme Yisrael*, part 5 (Warsaw, 1897), p. 247 is almost completely erroneous. There is also a reference to Samuel in S. Munk, *Mélanges de philosophie juive et arabe* (Paris, 1859), p. 489.

7. A title given to wealthy men of a generous nature.

8. See *Ecrivains*, p. 553; Gross, *Gallia*, p. 380, who does not transcribe the Hebrew; E. Renan-[A. Neubauer], *Les Rabbins français du commencement du XIVe siècle* (Paris, 1877), vol. XXVII of *L'Histoire littéraire de la France*, p. 600 (quoted hereafter as *Rabbins*).

9. See Samuel's epilogue to his translation of Alexander's *De Anima* (*Ecrivains*, p. 566). There may be some significance in the fact that in the epilogue to the last work of his which we have, Samuel gives, after being buffeted by the winds of misfortune, his most complete genealogy.

10. For Miles, and for orthographic variations of Bongodas, see *Ecrivains*, p. 553; for the latter, see also Gross, *Gallia*, p. 379. *Ecrivains*, p. 553, states that "Bongodas" means "the son of Judah," but see Gross, *Gallia*, p. 382, where a certain Judah ben David is called Maestre Bongodas Bondavi. Cf. below, Note 46.

11. Graybeard. See Gross, *Gallia*, p. 379; *Ecrivains*, p. 553.

12. See Gross, *Gallia*, p. 371; Benjamin of Tudela, *Masa᾿ot* (Frankfurt a. M., 1904), p. 6; Joseph ibn Verga, *Shebeṭ Yehuda* (Jerusalem, 1947), p. 146, line 19, and p. 221; *Ecrivains*, p. 553 (read "Jacob ben David").

13. See Gross, *Gallia*, pp. 366–384, who mentions a number of distinguished personages who lived in Marseilles. It is especially noteworthy that the Ibn Tibbon family was closely connected with Marseilles. It is clear that Samuel was aware that in his translation and study of philosophy he was continuing the tradition of the Tibbonids.

family had been established in Provence for at least one hundred and fifty years by the time Samuel was born and that it had had money since the time of David. When Samuel signs his name he always mentions at least four of his ancestors, an act which certainly signifies that he takes a certain pride in his ancestry.[14]

In the year 1312, at the age of eighteen,[15] six years after the expulsion of the Jews from the realm of the French king and seven years after the ban pronounced against anyone who should undertake the study of the Greek natural sciences and metaphysics (with the exception of medicine) before his twenty-fifth year,[16] Samuel became a student of philosophy at Salon under the guidance of Sen (Don) Astruc de Noves,[17] a noted astronomer. He began his studies with the *Almagest* of Ptolemy,[18] which occupied an important place in the cycle of philosophic studies. That Samuel *did* study astronomy, which, unlike the study of medicine and the religious law,[19] was of no use for making money, is some indication that Samuel's immediate family was still of considerable wealth and could allow him the necessary leisure to indulge himself in the abstract sciences.

Some eight years pass without any definite knowledge of Samuel's activities, although it may be surmised that he studied medicine[20] and continued his studies in philosophy. On April 8, 1320 (the twenty-ninth of Nisan, 5080),[21] he finished his translation of the *Questions on Logic.*[22] As we shall see, logic was to remain one of his favorite subjects for investigation.

14. See F. Baer, *Toledot ha-Yehudim bi-Sefarad ha-Noẓerit* (Tel Aviv, 1959), p. 143, for the connection between the Jewish aristocracy and Averroism, and I. Zinberg, *Toledot Sifrut Yisra*ʾ*el*, II, pp. 62ff., for a somewhat different view.

15. Epilogue to his revision of Jābir ibn Aflaḥ's *Epitome of the Almagest;* see *Ecrivains*, p. 562; below, Appendix D. See also Note 51 below.

16. Cf. Baer, *Toledot ha-Yehudim bi-Sefarad ha-Noẓerit*, p. 172 (30 years), 177 (afterwards no mention of bans); I. Sarachek, *Faith and Reason* (Williamsport, 1935), pp. 230ff.; I. Zinberg, *Toledot Sifrut Yisra*ʾ*el*, II, 80 (text of R. Solomon ibn Adret).

17. See *Ecrivains*, pp. 548–552; E. Levy, *Provenzalisches Supplement-Wörterbuch* (Leipzig, 1915), s.v. Sen (vol. VII, p. 557); E. L. Adams, *Word Formation in Provençal* (New York, 1913), p. 279. Qalonymos ben Qalonymos, the most prolific translator of our period, also studied under Sen Astruc at Salon a few years before Samuel (*Ecrivains*, p. 73).

18. See Steinschneider, *Heb. Üb.*, pp. 519ff. (especially 523ff.) and below, Notes 47, 51.

19. *Rabbins*, p. 616 (from Jacob ben Makhir's Introduction to his astronomical tables).

20. *Ecrivains*, p. 554.

21. *Ecrivains*, p. 554, has "May." In checking these dates, I have used the tables in E. Mahler, *Handbuch der jüdischen Chronologie* (Leipzig, 1916).

22. See *Ecrivains*, p. 554; M. Steinschneider, *Die hebräischen Handschriften der K. Hof- und Staatsbibliotek in München* (Munich, 1895), pp. 22, 199; *Heb. Üb.*, pp. 96–108; for a Latin version, see Aristotle, *Opera* (ed. Juntas, Venice, 1574), vol. I, part II (after pagination

In the same year, he began his pioneering effort to put the study of political philosophy on a more solid basis than heretofore by undertaking to translate into Hebrew from Arabic Aristotle's *Nicomachean Ethics*, in the form of a *Middle Commentary*[23] by Ibn Rushd, and Plato's *Republic*, in the form of an *Epitome*[24] by the same savant. It seems likely that Samuel's interest in political philosophy stemmed from his general enthusiasm for philosophy. Moreover, judging from the writings which he translated and from his independent works, he was more interested in logic, physical science, and astronomy than he was in metaphysics, which is to say that he was more interested in subjects linked to matter than in those that were not. Further, he identified himself with the "school of the philosophers, seekers after the correspondence of knowledge to existing things,"[25]

---

of *De Demonstratione*), leaves 75G–218D (the order of questions in this edition is the same as that enumerated by Steinschneider, *Heb. Üb.*, *loc. cit.*, according to the edition of 1550). The statement in *Ecrivains*, p. 554, beginning "La traduction de Samuel . . . ," is erroneous.

23. In Arabic, *Talkhīṣ Kitāb al-Akhlāq*. See E. Renan, *Averroès et l'averroisme* (Paris, 1861), 2nd ed., pp. 454, line 4; 458, line 11; 462, line 15, and N. Morata, "Un Catálogo de los fondos árabes primitivos del Escorial," *Al-Andalus*, 2 (1934), nos. 71 and 74 (see E. I. J. Rosenthal, ed., *Averroes' Commentary on Plato's 'Republic'* [Cambridge, 1956], p. 9, n. 2). It is clear from the list published by Morata, no. 71, that Ibn Rushd used the text of the *Nicomachean Ethics* in eleven books which is extant in the unique Qarawīyīn MSS. 2508 and 3043. Since Ibn Rushd does not include the added Seventh Book, I presume that he was aware from some indication in the text that the Seventh Book was added. In any case, it seems clear that the Hebrew and Latin translations of Ibn Rushd's *Middle Commentary* should be used in an edition of the Qarawīyīn manuscripts, since the original Arabic of the *Middle Commentary* is lost except for certain excerpts quoted in the margins of the Fez manuscripts. I have dealt with this question in more detail in a note to an article entitled "The Revised Hebrew Translation of *Averroes' Middle Commentary on the Nicomachean Ethics*," to be published in the Seventy-fifth Anniversary Volume of the *Jewish Quarterly Review*. It was in the course of preparing an edition of Samuel's translation of the *Middle Commentary* that I became interested in Samuel himself.

24. Rosenthal, *Averroes' Commentary on Plato's Republic*, cited in previous Note. I share the opinion of J. L. Teicher in his review of Rosenthal's edition (*Journal of Semitic Studies*, 5:17 [1960]) that Ibn Rushd's work should more properly be called a "Compendium" or "Epitome" (see below). See further Steinschneider, *Heb. Üb.*, p. 221; P. Kraus and R. Walzer, *Galeni Compendium Timaei Platonis* (London, 1951), p. 1; Liddell and Scott, *A Greek–English Lexicon* (Oxford, 1961), p. 1724, col. 1; E. W. Lane, *An Arabic–English Lexicon* (London and Edinburgh, 1863), p. 458, col. 2; R. Dozy, *Supplément aux dictionnaires arabes*, 2nd ed. (Leiden and Paris, 1927), I, 216, col. 2. In general, see Steinschneider, *Heb. Üb.*, pp. 52–53, for a discussion of terms for Ibn Rushd's various works of philosophical commentary. In this essay, I have followed the usage of H. Wolfson, "Plan for the Publication of a CORPUS COMMENTARIORUM AVERROIS IN ARISTOTELEM," *Speculum*, 6:412–427 (1931).

25. סיעת הפילוסופים דורשי אמתות הידיעה בנמצאים (*Ecrivains*, p. 558, last line; p. 562, line 3 [Hebrew text]; Appendices B at n. 35 and D at n. 1, below). For the term *siʿah*, see J. Klatzkin, *Thesaurus Philosophicus Linguae Hebraicae et Veteris et Recentioris* (Leipzig, 1928), 4 vols., s.v. For the translation "correspondence of knowledge to," see Samuel ben Judah ibn Tibbon, *Perush me-ha-milot zaʾorot* (*sic*), at the end of Maimonides, *Moreh Nebukhim*

and "the thinkers interested in speculative reasoning, the congregation of true believers."[26] But, in addition, I think that his "aristocratic" background may have been a contributing factor. The Jewish community constituted an autonomous minority coming under the authority of only the secular prince. Most probably, Samuel's family played a great part in communal affairs because of its wealth and social position, and perhaps Samuel's interest in political philosophy and the governing state stems from this background.

There is also a more general consideration to be taken into account as a part of the background of Samuel's interest in political philosophy. In the century preceding Samuel's birth and continuing into his own time, there was a deep conflict over what were the true limits to intellectual inquiry. On the one hand, the Rabbis and their supporters claimed that true spirituality existed only within their own narrowly conceived system and that "Greek wisdom" was dangerous. Aligned with them on this point were the Kabbalists, whose theosophic system was "essentially an attempt to preserve the substance of naïve popular faith, now challenged by the rational theology of the philosophers."[27] On the other hand, there were those of a philosophic temperament who claimed that they had a corner on true spirituality and that their investigations were as worthy of attention as those of the Law. The most extreme example of this point of view was that of Isaac Albalag, who claimed complete spiritual autonomy for his philosophical investigations.[28] Samuel also (whose position vis-à-vis Albalag cannot be determined with certainty) and men like him recognized the importance of their undertakings and their spiritual value independent of any religious conception taken in a narrow sense.[29]

(Warsaw, 1872), s.v. *emet*. Cf. further Klatzkin, *Thesaurus*, s.v. *amitah*, *amitut*, *emet*, *me᾿emet*. In this interpretation, *amitut* is the equivalent of *imut*, used as the equivalent of the Arabic *taṣdīq*. See the beginning of Samuel's corrected translation of Ibn Rushd's *Epitome of Logic*; Klatzkin, *Thesaurus*, s.v. *ẓiduq*, *haẓdaqah*, and *ha᾿amatah*; Maimonides, *Guide*, I, 50.

26. המעיינים, קהל המאמינים *Ecrivains*, pp. 558, line 18; 559, line 6 [Hebrew text], and my Appendices B, at Note 26, and C, Note 1, below.

27. G. Scholem, *Major Trends in Jewish Mysticism* (New York, 1961), 3rd rev. ed., pp. 205ff. See also Scholem's remarks concerning Abraham Abulafia (pp. 126ff., 143, and 295).

28. See G. Vajda, *Isaac Albalag* (Paris, 1960), pp. 251–274 (especially pp. 251–252).

29. See Samuel's use of the phrase "the congregation of true believers" to designate the philosophers (see above, Note 26). See further the comments of G. Vajda, *Isaac Albalag*, p. 263. One might almost say that his religion was philosophy, its prophets being Aristotle, Ptolemy, al-Fārābī, and Jābir ibn Aflaḥ. (See below, Notes 73, 74, and Guttmann, *Philosophies of Judaism*, pp. 51–56, esp. p. 53). Maimonides also identified philosophy with

In the sphere of the political art, as conceived by Aristotle, a direct challenge to the claims of religion in the realm of action was posed. The political art, according to Aristotle, comprises at least two divisions, ethics and (in the narrow sense) politics.[30] The first part of political science, which is ethics, challenges most clearly one of the major claims of religion to existence: namely, the control of men in the sphere of action. If there is an ethic which may be founded on reason alone or on assumptions which must be reasonable, then religion must take care.

It is in the light of the foregoing, it seems to me, that Samuel's pioneering effort should be evaluated. Whether he was completely aware of the consequences of his endeavor is not of capital importance. The point is, I think, that he opened up yet another sphere of secular speculation which directly challenged the claims of religion to absolute authority in the sphere of action. In so far as he was successful, he showed himself truly to be what he considered himself to be: a member of the "sect of the philosophers."[31]

On November 24, 1320 (the twenty-second of Kislev, 5081) at Uzès,[32] Samuel finished his translation of Ibn Rushd's *Epitome* of *Plato's Republic*. Since the *Politics* of Aristotle was not available,

---

religion, identifying *maᶜase merkavah* with metaphysics and *maᶜase bereshit* with physics whereas the prescriptions of the law supply the requirements of the ideal state. Maimonides' statement at the end of his *Treatise on Logic* that "the learned men of past religious communities (*milal*) used to formulate, each of them according to his perfection, regimens and rules through which their princes governed the subjects; they called them nomoi; and the nations used to be governed by those nomoi . . . In these times, all this—I mean the regimens and the nomoi—has been dispensed with, and men are being governed by divine commands . . ." (M. Mahdi and R. Lerner, eds., *Medieval Political Philosophy, A Sourcebook* [Glencoe, Ill., 1963], p. 190, and see pp. 188–189) does not mean that he did not read the works of philosophers on ethics and politics in order to understand the law.

30. According to Aspasius, the political art has three divisions: ethics, household managements, and (in the restricted sense) politics. (See Aspasius, *In Ethica Nicomachea commentaria*, ed. G. Heylbut, *Commentaria in Aristotelem Graeca*, XIX, part 1 (Berlin, 1889), p. 6, lines 26–31. See Maimonides, *Treatise on Logic*, chap. xiv (Mahdi and Lerner, *Medieval Political Philosophy*, p. 189) and al-Fārābī, *al-Siyasāt al-madaniyyah* (Hyderabad, 1346 A.H.), p. 39 (English translation in Mahdi and Lerner, *Medieval Political Philosophy*, p. 32). The statement in Sarton, *Introduction to the History of Science*, III, 434 (partially following *Ecrivains*, p. 554) that "Jewish commentators considered the *Nicomachean Ethics* to be first part of the Politics, the second part being Plato's Republic" errs in ascribing this division to the Jewish commentators, who merely followed Ibn Rushd in this matter, and secondly in using the expression "the Politics" instead of "Political Science."

31. It would be interesting to compare the importance of the recovery of the Aristotelian political philosophy on the birth of the "lay" spirit in medieval Latin society (see G. de Lagarde, *La Naissance de l'esprit laïque au déclin du moyen âge* [Louvain–Paris, 1958], vol. II (Secteur social de la scolastique).

32. See Gross, *Gallia*, pp. 23, 380.

Ibn Rushd had taken Plato's *Republic* as a substitute for the second part of political philosophy. Samuel did have a copy of the Arabic text of the *Nicomachean Ethics*, the first part of political philosophy, but it was too difficult for him to translate. Finally, he acquired a copy of Ibn Rushd's *Middle Commentary on the Ethics*, which he finished translating at Beaucaire on the ninth of February, 1321 (the tenth of Adar, 5081). He left many blank spaces because of the unfamiliarity of the language of the *Ethics*, for he was used to the language of the more technical treatises concerned with logic and the physical sciences. On the twenty-first of September, 1321 (the twenty-seventh of Elul, 5081),[33] he finished his first revision of the translations of the two works, in prison at Beaucaire in the fort of Rodorta.[34] He states that he intends to get the help of Christian scholars who have the commentary of al-Fārābī[35] on the *Ethics*. Between June 17 and July 16, 1322 (Tammuz, 5082) he made the second and final revision of his translation.[36] He had not been able to make contact with the Christian savants, he said, because of the "magnitude of the annoyances and persecutions which have overtaken us on the part of this nation which exiles us."[37] This lack of contact must have been especially galling to a man of the idealistic temperament of Samuel, who believed in the primary value of philosophy and its study, which transcended accidental confessional differences.[38]

33. *Ecrivains*, p. 556, has 3 *septembre*. Rosenthal (*Averroes' Commentary on Plato's Republic*, p. 106) reads כ"ו.

34. *Ecrivains*, p. 556; not in Gross, *Gallia*, pp. 119–121, 379–381; Steinschneider, *Heb. Üb.*, p. 222, n. 828.

35. The commentary of al-Fārābī is not extant and this is the latest reference to its existence that I know. Al-Fārābī's commentary is commonly quoted as the source of his denial of immortality. See Averroes, *Epistle Concerning the Possibility of Continuation*, quoted by Munk, *Mēlanges*, p. 348, n. 3; Ibn Ṭufail, *Ḥayy b. Yaqẓān*, ed. L. Gauthier (Beirut, 1936), p. 14 (English translation in Mahdi and Lerner, *Medieval Political Philosophy*, p. 140); L. Massignon, *Recueil de textes inédits concernant l'histoire de la mystique en pays d'Islam* (Paris, 1929), pp. 129ff. (French translation in *Mémorial Henri Basset* [Paris, 1928], II, 125–126) for the opinion of Ibn Sabʿīn (committed suicide at Mecca, 1270) that in his old age al-Fārābī retracted his view of immortality; Averroes (*Vater und Sohn*), *Drei Abhandlungen über die Conjunction*, ed. J. Hercz (Berlin, 1869), pp. 9, 13, 14, 24; L. Strauss, *Persecution and the Art of Writing* (Glencoe, Ill., 1952), p. 13; S. Pines in Moses Maimonides, *The Guide of the Perplexed* (Chicago, 1963), pp. lxxxff. See further A. Altmann, "Ibn Bājja on Man's Ultimate Felicity," *Harry Austryn Wolfson Jubilee Volume* (Jerusalem, 1965), p. 49 and n. 4 (reprint).

36. *Ecrivains*, p. 556, speaks of a third revision, but is incorrect.

37. For the preceding, see Samuel's epilogue to his translation of the *Ethics* and the *Republic* (*Ecrivains*, p. 558, and below, Page 309, Appendix B); cf. also Steinschneider, *Heb. Üb.*, pp. 222–224.

38. Cf. his references to Aristotle, Alexander, Ptolemy, Jābir ibn Aflaḥ, and Ibn Rushd and Note 29 above.

Samuel keeps exceedingly close to the Arabic, making his translation very difficult to understand. For this reason he was severely criticized,[39] and an as yet anonymous individual made a somewhat free paraphrase of Samuel's translation in order to make it more easily comprehensible and to refine the barbaric character of the Hebrew.[40] In any event, to Samuel redounds the credit for introducing Aristotle's *Ethics* and Plato's *Republic* into the world of Hebrew letters, and this act of his stimulated a great deal of activity over the next two centuries in the form of paraphrases, retranslations, and commentaries, the history of which has yet to be written.

We next find Samuel at Murcia in southern Spain, where, at the age of thirty, he completed a preliminary translation of the *De Anima* of Alexander of Aphrodisias in December 1324 (Tebeth, 5084). He eventually revised the translation, and sixteen years later, he published it.[41]

On December 13, 1329 (the twentieth of Tebeth, 5090) we find him back in Provence at Tarascon,[42] where he retranslated Ibn Rushd's *Epitome of Logic*,[43] in order to replace the translation of Jacob ben Makhir, which he found deficient.

Some five years[44] earlier after returning to Tarascon from Murcia, he had wished to study the *Almagest*[45] once again with his learned young brother, En Bondavi[46] of Marseilles. They were able to study all of it except the last chapter. They were prevented from completing their studies because of certain disturbing factors, the nature of which is not detailed. Samuel was able to undertake the first in-

39. See remarks of Meir Alguadez in his introduction to his Hebrew translation of the *Ethics* from the Latin (Steinschneider, *Heb. Üb.*, p. 210) and see Moses Rieti in Rosenthal, *Averroes' Commentary on Plato's Republic*, p. 107 (English translation below, Appendix B, Note 36).

40. In line with Samuel's original intention (see *Ecrivains*, p. 557, line 2, bottom, and below, Appendix B, Page 309) and Moses Rieti's remarks (see reference in previous note). I have discussed the relationship of this paraphrase to Samuel's translation, in an article entitled "The Revised Hebrew Translation of Averroes' *Middle Commentary on the Nicomachean Ethics*," to appear in the Seventy-fifth Anniversary Volume of the *Jewish Quarterly Review*.

41. See below at Note 56.

42. See Gross, *Gallia*, p. 248.

43. See Steinschneider, *Heb. Üb.*, pp. 54–56; M. Bouyges, "Notes sur les philosophes connus des latins au moyen âge," *Mélanges de l'Université Saint-Joseph*, 8:9 (1922 [offprint]).

44. If we are to take literally his statement ועברו שלשים משנותי (*Ecrivains*, p. 562, Appendix D below, Page 314).

45. See above, Note 18.

46. See above, Note 10, and Levy, *Provenzalisches Supplement–Wörterbuch* (Leipzig, 1898), II, 407, s.v. En.

dependent work of which we hear, a commentary on the first three chapters of Ptolemy's *Almagest*, but he was prevented from completing his commentary because of other troubles which overtook him. He completed his work on the first treatise in September or October 1330 (Tishre, 5091)[47] and he completed his commentary on the third treatise on the twenty-seventh of March, 1331 (the eighteenth of Nisan, 5091)[48] at Tarascon. It seems probable that there in Tarascon he was in contact with Joseph ibn Caspi, who summarized Samuel's translation of the *Ethics* and the *Republic*.[49]

After Samuel had read Ibn Rushd's *Epitome of the Almagest*[50] and had realized that the only thing good about it was derived in turn from Jābir ibn Aflaḥ's *Epitome of the Almagest*,[51] and that much that was useful had been left out, Samuel and his brother humbled themselves for the sake of wisdom and went to Trinquetaille, a suburb of Arles on the right bank of the Rhone, in order to search for the book of Ibn Aflaḥ. After some effort, they found a very good copy of the Arabic text. They had the use of the text for only some two days, during which time they subsisted on bread and water in the house of one of the local philosophers. Then, after they had been able to copy only about an eighth of the book, consisting of the most difficult passages, they had to return to Tarascon on urgent business.

47. *Ecrivains*, p. 560, has October–November. See Steinschneider, *Heb. Üb.*, p. 524, and Note 18, above.

48. *Ecrivains*, p. 560, has May 26.

49. See *Ecrivains*, pp. 477–547, for the life and works of Joseph; Gross, *Gallia*, p. 250, *contra Ecrivains*, p. 486; Steinschneider, *Heb. Üb.*, pp. 225–227, with n. 860 end.

50. See Steinschneider, *Heb. Üb.*, pp. 546ff. (description). A reference to Samuel b. Judah should be added to Steinschneider, *Heb. Üb.*, pp. 548ff.

51. In Hebrew *Qiẓẓur sefer ha-magisti*. This is the title as given in Hebrew in MSS. 1014, 1024, 1025, and 1036 of the Bibliothèque Nationale in Paris, which are the only known manuscripts of Samuel's correction of Jacob b. Makhir's Hebrew translation of Jābir b. Aflaḥ's work, which is famous as a critique of the *Almagest*. In the remaining Arabic fragments of the work it is known as *Kitāb al-Haiʾah* (Book of Astronomy) and *Islāḥ al-Majisṭi* (Correction of the *Almagest*). See Steinschneider, *Heb. Üb.*, pp. 543ff.; Sarton, *Introduction*, II, 206; A. Mieli, *La Science arabe* (Leiden, 1938), p. 192; *Encyclopedia of Islam*, 2nd ed., s.v. Djābir b. Aflaḥ. It is interesting to note that Caleb Afendopolo ben Elia, a versatile Karaite scholar of Constantinople (died around 1499), is the scribe of the Paris MS. 1024. He states that he copied the manuscript from the autograph of Samuel b. Judah, so we know that an autograph of Samuel was extant in 1482 when Caleb wrote the manuscript (see Steinschneider, *Heb. Üb.*, index, s.v. Kaleb Afendopolo). A curious fact not noted by Steinschneider, in so far as I know, is that on leaf 117a of this manuscript there are three oaths, in the handwriting of three students of Caleb, not to teach anyone, without his permission, the information learned from Caleb. The last oath is dated Wednesday, the second of Tammuz, 5265 (June 4, 1505), a date that would extend the present known *terminus post quem* of Caleb's life. See further Z. Ankori, *Karaites in Byzantium* (New York and Jerusalem, 1959), pp. 200–201, n. 111.

Samuel was then forced to move to Aix-en-Provence,[52] where he discovered a copy of Jacob ben Makhir's translation[53] of Ibn Aflaḥ's *Epitome.* He humbled himself again until the owner of the manuscript agreed to allow him to copy it. Although it was the autograph of Jacob, Samuel discovered on copying it that it was full of mistakes; he was of course greatly disappointed. Finally, after great effort, Samuel was able to acquire the Arabic text of the Jābir opus, in fact the same one he had seen for a short time in Trinquetaille. Samuel compared Jacob's translation with the Arabic text, corrected Jacob's mistakes, and supplied whatever was deficient. He finished his revision of Jacob's translation of the *Epitome of the Almagest* on December 17, 1335 (the first of Tebeth, 5096) at the age of forty-one at Aix.[54] It was most probably at Aix also that we find him translating the text to accompany figures 30 and 31 of Euclid's treatise on *The Five Bodies.*[55] Samuel completed his translation on August 23, 1335 (the third of Elul, 5095).

The last date that we have for Samuel's activity is July 4, 1340 (the eighth of Tammuz, 5100), when he was forty-six years old. On this date he finished copying out his corrected translation of the *De Anima* of Alexander of Aphrodisias,[56] which he had first translated some sixteen years ago at the age of thirty at Murcia. He also introduced into the text divisions according to subject matter in order to aid the reader in understanding the book. He had once more changed his residence and was now at Montélimar.[57]

His appreciation of Alexander of Aphrodisias, whom he rates higher than Aristotle himself, is of some interest. His implied ac-

52. Gross, *Gallia*, pp. 45ff.

53. See Note 51, above.

54. Epilogue to Samuel's revision (*Ecrivains*, pp. 562–563, and below, Appendix D). Samuel's epilogue constitutes an interesting compact addition to Hebrew autobiographical literature.

55. I.e., the thirteenth book of the *Elements*. The reason why *Ecrivains*, p. 560, adds Hypsikles in parentheses is not clear to me.

56. See Alexander Aphrodisiensis, *De Anima Liber*, ed. I. Bruns, in *Supplementum Aristotelicum ii pars i* (Berlin, 1887), in which Samuel's translation is used by way of a German version by M. Steinschneider. The portion of Alexander's *De Anima* in Samuel's translation dealing with the intellect was published by A. Gunsz, *Die Abhandlung Alexanders von Aphrodisias über den Intellekt* (Berlin, 1886), Hebrew part, pp. 3ff. (Bruns, pp. 80, 19–92, 12), Gunsz, *op. cit.*, is not to be confused with J. Finnegan, "Texte arabe du ΠΕΡΙ ΝΟΥ d'Alexandre d'Aphrodise," *Mélanges de l'Université Saint Joseph*, 33:159–202 (1956), which corresponds to Bruns, pp. 106–113. See further M. Steinschneider, "Zu Alexander von Aphrodisia," *Magazin für die Wissenschaft des Judenthums*, 14:191–195 (1887).

57. See Gross, *Gallia*, p. 319, and *Ecrivains*, pp. 565ff. (See Appendix E, below, for an English translation.)

ceptance of Alexander's theory of the intellect, in particular, entails his acceptance of "an interpretation of Aristotle the most opposed . . . to every religious sentiment."[58]

We have mentioned all the works connected with his name which have come down to us, except for some translations of minor astronomical treatises.[59] His only independent work was the commentary on the *Almagest*.[60] However, Judah Cohen quotes Samuel quite extensively in a voluminous Commentary[61] on Ibn Rushd's *Middle Commentary on the Isagoge and the Categories*.[62]

Judah,[63] son of Isaac son of Moses son of Judah son of Morenu

58. See G. Théry, *Autour du décret de 1210: II–Alexandre d'Aphrodise* (Le Saulchoir Kain, 1926), p. 33. Théry deals with the doctrine of the ΠΕΡΙ ΝΟΥ only (pp. 27–33), but his analysis is equally valuable for the *De Anima*. Samuel's implied acceptance of "Alexandrism" also entails his disavowal of the position of Ibn Rushd in his commentaries on the *De Anima*. See Théry, pp. 41–67.

59. See *Ecrivains*, p. 566; Sarton, *Introduction*, III, 434. With respect to Samuel's translation of a treatise by al-Zarqālī on the "trepidation of the equinoxes," see B. R. Goldstein, "The Medieval Hebrew Tradition in Astronomy," *Journal of the American Oriental Society*, 85:147 and n. 7 (1965), and the references quoted there.

60. See Note 18, above.

61. Christ Church Hebrew MS. 201. See description in *Catalogue of the Hebrew Manuscripts in the Bodleian and College Libraries of Oxford*, compiled by A. Neubauer (Oxford, 1886), vol. I, no. 2452 and additions (col. 868 and 1163a).

62. At this time, it was common to comment on the text of Aristotle as understood by Ibn Rushd and not on the text itself. (See Steinschneider, *Heb. Üb.*, p. 51 and n. 44). The translation used is that of Jacob Anatolio. (See Steinschneider, *Heb. Üb.*, pp. 57ff. [Jakob Anatoli].) This is clear from a comparison of Judah's quotation with Paris, Bibliothèque Nationale MS. Hebrew 977 (written by Samuel's son); see also below, Note 69. Judah quotes corrections to Jacob's translation made by Samuel (Christ Church Hebrew MS. 201, leaf 4a), although a systematic revision of Jacob's translation of the *Middle Commentary* has not come down to us, if there ever was one. Bouyges doubts that Steinschneider is right in considering the *Isagoge* as the first book of the *Middle Commentary* of Ibn Rushd on the *Organon*, for in any case, Bouyges did not find a trace of an Arabic text of a *Middle Commentary* in the Arabic manuscripts of Ibn Rushd's *Organon* (M. Bouyges, "Notes sur les philosophes arabes connus des Latins au moyen âge. V. Inventaire des textes arabes d'Averroès," *Mélanges de l'Université Saint Joseph*, 8:13, par. 12). However, there can be no doubt that Ibn Rushd did compose a middle commentary on the *Isagoge*. The reason why the *Commentary on the Isagoge* is not included in the Arabic manuscripts of Ibn Rushd's commentaries on the *Organon* seems clear from the epilogue to above-mentioned commentary which I translate as follows: "The ideas which the Introduction [of Porphyry] includes are finished. What caused us to explain them was [the request] of some [or "one"] of our friends who are sharp and serious speculative thinkers from the group at Murcia, may God have mercy on them. Were it not for this, I would have left off for two reasons. The first is that I do not think that this *Introduction* is a necessary introduction to this art, for it is impossible that subject matter of [Porphyry's Introduction] belongs to what is common to the [whole] art [of logic] as some people think . . . The second reason is that the words of the man are, as it were, obvious in this *Introduction*. However, the desire to help the aforementioned students . . . made me explain it . . ." (Paris, Bibliothèque Nationale Hebrew MS. 977, leaf 58b, line 3 bottom and ff.).

63. See the "Notice" devoted to him in *Ecrivains*, pp. 653–655, and cf. Steinschneider, *Heb. Üb.*, p. 74.

Samuel Cohen, states in his short introduction to his voluminous and somewhat rhetorical commentary that he has written it at the request of Shelemyah of Lunel, whose time is limited on account of certain political duties.[64]

Judah's attitude to Samuel, whom he calls Barbevaire,[65] is one of great respect. "This is the true explanation of this statement [which I owe to] Barbevaire, who taught me this book when I was a youth . . . We give thanks . . . to Barbevaire who has taught us the perfect way and the straight method . . . This is a quotation from the teacher par excellence, Barbevaire, against the lion, the philosopher Maestre Leon of Bagnols [that is, Levi ben Gershom]."[66] Judah always mentions Levi with all due regard, however, explaining his mistakes as being the result of the undue influence of Ibn Rushd, who is Judah's bête noire.[67] Toward Porphyry and al-Fārābī he shows great respect because they belong to the authentic peripatetic tradition.

Samuel also upholds Porphyry and al-Fārābī against the criticism of Ibn Rushd and Levi. Samuel obviously feels great respect for Levi, as witness his careful reading of Levi's text and detailed questioning of Levi's position. By ascribing Levi's error to his being led astray by Ibn Rushd, Samuel tries to alleviate the heaviness of his challenge to an acknowledged intellectual luminary.

In general, Judah and Samuel represent a direct continuation of the Andalusian tradition, in the line of the School of Baghdad, in logical studies.[68] A detailed treatment of Judah's *Commentary* (which

64. *Derushim mediniyim.*

65. See Note 11, above. For the following quotations see Christ Church Hebrew MS. 221, leaves 5a, 6a, and 8b:

וזהו הפי' האמתי לזה המאמר לא מה שביארו בו זולתנו האלהים לולא הברבא ויירי נ"ע אשר הורנו הספר הזה בימי העלמות;

וניתן תודה לאל החונן לאדם דעת ולברבא ויירי נ"ע אשר הורנו הנתיב התמים והדרך הישרה;

אמר יהודה המבאר. הנה הבאתי דברי המורה מורה המורים הוא הברבא ויירי נגד הארי. הוא החכם מאישטרי ליאון דבש (?) יולש.

66. 1288–1344. See *Jewish Encyclopedia*, s.v. Levi ben Gershom and *Encyclopaedia Judaica*, s.v. Gersonides.

67. Following Samuel, whose disillusionment with Ibn Rushd appears in his epilogue to his translation of Ibn Aflaḥ's *Epitome of the Almagest* (*Ecrivains*, p. 563; my Appendix D, Page 315, below). It is of some interest to note that Ibn Sabᶜīn, the author of the answers to the "Sicilian Questions" posed by Frederick II von Hohenstaufen, characterized Ibn Rushd as being of limited intellectual ability but of high moral character (Massignon, *Recueil de textes inédits*, p. 128 [Arabic text]; *idem* in *Mémorial Henri Basset* [Paris, 1928], II, 125).

68. See N. Rescher, *The Development of Arabic Logic* (Pittsburgh, 1964), pp. 55–57; *idem, Studies in the History of Logic* (Pittsburgh, 1963), pp. 16–17. The preceding remarks are based on a close reading of leaves 1–10 of the Christ Church MS.

is still in manuscript), one of the many *desiderata* of the history of medieval philosophy in Hebrew, must be left for another time and place.

It is interesting to note, incidentally, that Samuel's son Asher copied out the *Middle Commentaries* of Ibn Rushd on Aristotle's *Organon* for a certain Yom Tov ben Menaḥem Lerma.[69]

II

Samuel shows a great deal of idealism in his pursuit of philosophy which makes his character attractive. His frequent journeys from place to place and the persecution which he had to undergo did not make him give up his devotion to the life of speculation. The epilogues to the works which he completed are trailmarks for the various places in which he stayed during his agitated life. He resembles a number of his colleagues,[70] whose desire for learning was not flagged by incessant travel or other external "hindrances."[71] Travel was a means to attain knowledge.

He was a man of independent judgement, as witness his evaluation of Alexander of Aphrodisias vis-à-vis Aristotle, and his criticism of Ibn Rushd and Levi ben Gershom. He undertook the translation and correction of philosophic works which he felt were important both for his own edification and that of those who shared his devotion

69. Hebrew MS. 977 of the *Bibliothèque Nationale*. On leaf 114b the colophon reads:

על יד ימין הצעיר אשר בכמ"ר שמואל דמרשייליאה נ"ע וכתבתיו אל המעולה החכם ר' יום טוב ב"ר מנחם נ"ע לירמא ספרדי.

and on leaf 178b the colophon reads:

העתקתי זה אני הקטן אשר ב"ר שמואל אל המעולה החכם הה"ר ר' יום טוב לירמא השם יזכהו להגות בו הוא וזרעו וזרע זרעו ובספרים אחרים עיקרי הדת עד סוף כל הדורות ויראה בנים לבניו ושלום רב עד בלי ירח (ע' תהלים ע"ב, ז).

The Paris catalogue (p. 173), which, I imagine, is the source of Steinschneider, *Heb. Üb.*, p. 56, mistakenly states the scribe to be Samuel of Marseilles. I see no compelling reason to suppose that this Asher is not the son of our Samuel of Marseilles. It is interesting, however, to note that the text copied by Asher does not contain the corrections of Samuel quoted by Yehuda Cohen in Samuel's name. Yom Tov ben Menaḥem Lerma is known to me only from this reference. I read לורמא in the manuscript. One could just as easily read לירמא. See J. N. Epstein, *Mabo le-Nusaḥ ha-Mishnah* (Jerusalem, 1948), II, 1286, who mentions a Samuel לירמא (or לירמה) quoted by S. M. Stern, *Tarbiz*, 23:76 (1952), and see also S. D. Sassoon in his Introduction to *Maimonidis Commentarius in Mischnam* (Copenhagen, 1956), I, 38 (English); p. 23 (Hebrew).

70. Such as Joseph ibn Kaspi (*Ecrivains*, pp. 477–547); Moses Narboni (*Ecrivains*, pp. 666–682); Qalonymos ben Qalonymos (*Ecrivains*, pp. 417–460).

71. *Meʿiqim*. Cf. Klatzkin, *Thesaurus*, s.v. *meʿiq* (from the Arabic *ʿāʾiq*).

to the cause of philosophy. Especially important are his pioneering translations into Hebrew of fundamental works of political philosophy. Through his enterprise, he introduced into the curriculum of Hebrew philosophical studies a new discipline which had a fruitful continuation for about a century and a half after his death.

He was a man of great diligence. He spared no effort to procure the best possible texts for translation and for the revision of these translations. He thus continued in a fitting manner the tradition of Ḥunain ibn Isḥāq,[72] the leading translator of Greek into Syriac and of Greek and Syriac texts into Arabic some four and a half centuries prior to Samuel.

Personal circumstances were favorable for developing his interest in philosophy. Marseilles had been the home of the Tibbonid family of translators and philosophers and had a long tradition of savants interested in philosophical studies. In addition, Samuel's "aristocratic," wealthy family afforded him the means necessary for leisure to pursue his philosophical studies from an early age. His younger brother, En Bondavi, had similar intellectual interests, although we do not hear of his translating or of his composing independent philosophical works. It is a rather nice tribute to Samuel that his son Asher was copying philosophic manuscripts at an early age.

Samuel, it seems to me, represents *l'homme moyen philosophe* of the Jewish community of fourteenth-century Provence. His family background and his complete identification with the "sect of the philosophers, the seekers after the correspondence of knowledge to existing things . . . the congregation of true believers," even his continual moving from place to place, make him representative of the philosophic group. He found his intellectual tastes gratified in the secular sphere, and more especially in logic, the physical sciences and political sciences. He looked on philosophy as a way of life and its "chiefs"[73] as "true prophets."[74]

In sum, Samuel had the necessary leisure and inclination to widen

72. See G. Bergsträsser, *Hunain ibn Ishāq über die syrischen und arabischen Galen–Übersetzungen* (Leipzig, 1925).

73. See below, Appendix D, Note 14, and Appendix E, Note 6. The term "first chief" is derived from al-Fārābī, *The Political Regime* (see Appendix B, n. 29), Hyderabad, p. 53; Mahdi and Lerner, *Medieval Political Philosophy* (translated as "supreme ruler"). The "first chief," in the terminology of al-Fārābī, is both a philosopher and prophet, founder and ruler of the virtuous state (cf. below, Appendix D, Note 34; next note; and M. Mahdi, "Alfarabi," in L. Strauss and J. Cropsie, eds., *History of Political Philosophy* (Chicago, 1963), pp. 160–180, for the relevant references.

74. See below, Appendix D, Note 35, and Appendix E, Note 5.

his intellectual horizon beyond the limits of halakhic investigation or theosophical speculation. He utilized his bent for philosophic investigation and made valuable contributions to the philosophic literature of his time. His particular outlook is in large measure due to the pervasive influence of Maimonides and those who followed him. However, I think that Samuel's interests were also a sign of the new spirit awakening in Europe generally. By his activities, Samuel won for himself, despite the overweening claims of the representatives of religiosity to complete competence in dealing with all the spiritual needs of man,[75] an autonomous domain which was both spiritual and secular.

Appendix A

The epilogue of Samuel's translation of Ibn Rushd's *Middle Commentary on the Nicomachean Ethics*. The first paragraph of the Hebrew text was published in *Ecrivains*, page 555, on the basis of Turin Hebrew MS. 169 (B. Peyron, *Codices Hebraici manu exarati Regiae Bibliothecae quae in Taurinensi athenaeo asservatur* [Turin, 1880], page 173), which was destroyed by fire in 1904, and Bodleian Library, Neubauer 1350, 3, which is now the only extant manuscript containing Samuel's epilogue to the *Ethics*. In the footnotes, I designate the *Ecrivains* text as E and the Bodleian manuscript text as O.

I. *Hebrew Text*

נשלם באור בן רשד לספר המדות לאריסטו הנקרא בלשון יון ניקומאכיה והוא החלק הראשון משני חלקי החכמה[1] המדינית הנקרא חלק החכמה[1] ויחסו אל החלק השני ממנה הנקרא חלק המלאכה הוא יחס מה שבספר הבריאות והחולי אל מה שבספר שמירת הבריאות והסרת החולי במלאכת הרפואה. והחלק השני הוא[2] בספר אשר ידוע בספר ההנהגה לפלוסוף אך לא נפל אל החכם בן רשד הספר ההוא וכבר התנצל בזה על כי לא בארו ובאר תמורתו מה שמצא מן החלק ההוא השני בספר הנהגת המדינה לאפלאטון ממאמריו המדעיים ולזאת הכונה המשכתי אני המעתיק אל החלק הראשון אעפ״י שלא חברם מחבר אחד אחר שהם חלקים מחכמה אחת ובאדם מבאר אחד. והעתקתי הספר הזה אשר הוא החלק הראשון מחכמה הזאת רצוני החכמה המדינית אני שמואל בן יהודה

75. See Lagarde, *La Naissance de l'esprit laïque au déclin du moyen âge*, vol. II.

1–1. Version O omits this passage.

2. Version O omits.

י״צ בן משלם בן יצחק בן שלמה נ״ע ממרשלייא בשנת שבע ועשרים משנותי וזה במגדל בלקיירי ונשלמה העתקתו יום ב י אדר ראשון משנת השמנים ואחד לפרט האלף הששי ליצירה[3] ישתבח העוזר ויתברך לנצח אמן אמן סלה.[3]

וכבר הנחתי בעת העתיקי אותו בהרבה מקומות ממנו חלק פנוי[4] מתיבה ותיבות ושורות למיעוט חכמתי ולקוצר השגתי בלשון הערב מצורף עם זה לזרות נושאיו רצוני מלותיו הנהוגות בו אשר לא ירוצו בשום חכמה מהחכמות האחרות. אחר כן עברתי עליו להשלים החסרונות ולהשלים השגיאות כפי כחי והפלגתי העיון בו עם עזר קצת משכילי אומתינו היתה עלינו ידם בזה תהי משכורתם שלמה מעם י״י אלהי ישראל והנה אמת כי עוד נשארו בהעתקת זה הספר שגיאות קצתן אולי היו מספר הערבי אשר העתקתי זה ממנו וקצתן מפני חסרוני ומיעוט הבנתי אבל אני בוטח אם יאריך השם חיי ויוציאני ממסגר אסיר ויכין לי הפנאי המועט כי עוד אוסף להפליא העיון בו אשלים ואתקן החסרונות כלם או רובם עד שלא תשאר בספר מבוכה מצדי ראוי לשים לב עליה ומי שיגיע לידו זה הספר טרם זה התקון הנה ינצלני.

והמעיין בהעתקתי זאת אין ראוי שייחסה[5] לסכלות ועזות והתפארותי במה שאין בי אבל חי י״י אשר עשה לי את הנפש ראוי ומחויב שישבחני בפעולתי זאת ויודה לשם כי העיר את רוחי ואמץ את לבבי וכי חלק[6] לי בחסדו הפנאי המועט עד שהמצאתי אל לשוננו המציאה הזאת המופלאה ברוממות מעלה והתנשאות מדרגה לגודל שאר תועלתיה וטובה אחר שלא קדם לנו שום מעתיק מבני תבון השרידים ז״ל וזולתם אל זה הספר או לא נפלה אלינו העתקתו והבוחנים האמת ומכיריו ידעו ויבינו בעיינם בו כי לא שבחתיו על צד מליצת השיר והפלגה וגוזמא כי אין זה מחקי והאל יודע אך על דרך האמת המעיד לעצמו ומסכים מכל[7] צד ולאהבתנו אותו וחריצותנו בו החזקתי במלאכה אחר שאלי מאלהי יורנו דרך זו אלך ולולא זה כבר משכתי ידי ממנה ואחשוך את נפשי מלדבר במה שלא הורשתי עם הסבה אחרת דחתה ידי והניעה קולמוסי עד תום המלאכה והיא תיקון ודיוק הספר הערבי אשר העתקתי זה ממנו ויפי כתיבתו ונוי נוקיו[8] ועל הכל יתגדל בעל העזר[9] העוזר לכל נעזר אשר תמך בידי כרצונו ובקדושתו אמן.

II. *English Translation*

The commentary of Ibn Rushd on the Ethics of Aristotle called in Greek *Nicomachean* is finished. It is the first part of the two parts of political science and it is called the theoretical part. Its relationship

3–3. Version E omits this passage.
4. Version E: ופנאי.
5. Version O: שיחסה.
6. Version O: חלקי.
7. Version O: על. See Hebrew text corresponding to Appendix C, Note 5.
8. Version O *sic*.
9. Version O has this word written above.

to the second part, which is called the practical, is the same as the relationship of the contents of the *Book of Health and Sickness*[1] to the contents of the *Book on the Preservation of Health and the Removal of Sickness*[2] in the medical art. The second part is contained in the book which is known as the *Politics* by the Philosopher, but that book did not fall into the hands of the philosopher Ibn Rushd. He has already apologized for not commenting on it. Instead, he explained the demonstrable statements of that second part, which he found in the *Republic* of Plato. For this reason, I, the translator, have continued to the first part, even though one author did not compose them, since they are parts of one science and one commentator has explained them. I, Samuel the son of Judah the son of Meshullam the son of Isaac the son of Solomon of Marseilles, translated this book, which is the first part of this science—that is, political science—in the twenty-seventh year of my life in the citadel of Beaucaire. Its translation was completed on Monday the tenth of Adar I in the year 5081 from the Creation. May the Helper be praised and blessed forever, Amen. Amen. Selah.

In translating it, I have left many places blank and free of one or more words and lines because of my limited knowledge and insufficient grasp of the Arabic language in addition to its uncommon subject matter; that is, the words used in it are not used in any of the other sciences. Afterwards, I revised it in order to complete what was missing and corrected its mistakes in so far as possible. I studied it intently with the help of some of the enlightened of our nation, who aided me in this project.[3] May their recompense be complete from the Lord God of Israel. It is true that there are still some mistakes in the translation. Some of them perhaps spring from the Arabic book from which I translated, and some of them from my inadequacy and limited understanding. However, if God lengthen my life, take me out of prison, and allow me a little time, I trust to study it intensively again. I will correct all or most of its defects so that no confusion caused by me, worthy of attention, will remain

1. A book of this title is not known to me. Cf. Steinschneider, *Heb. Üb.*, p. 655; *idem, Die arabischen Übersetzungen aus dem Griechischen* (Graz, 1960), p. 334; Ibn Bājjah, *Tadbīr al-Mutawaḥḥid* (Madrid-Granada, 1946), p. 11, last line; and the next note.

2. In Arabic: *Fī ḥifẓ al-siḥḥa wa-izālat al-maraḍ*. Cf. C. Brockelmann, *Geschichte der arabischen Litteratur* (Leiden, 1937–1949) SI 366; Ḥunain ibn Isḥāq, *Über die syrischen und araibschen Galen–Übersetzungen*, ed. and tr. G. Bergsträsser (Leipzig, 1925), no. 84; and previous note.

3. See Ezra 8:31.

in this book. May whoever comes across this book before its correction accept my apologies.

It would not be proper for whoever studies this translation of mine to attribute it to foolishness, arrogance, and claiming for myself qualities which I do not possess but, by the life of God who made me this soul, he ought and is duty bound to praise me for my activity; he should thank the Lord who roused my spirit, encouraged me, and apportioned to me in his kindness a little time so that I might bring into our language this find which is extraordinary in its exaltedness and magnificence because of the greatness of all its advantages and its goodness. He ought to thank me, I say, since no translator of the Ibn Tibbon family, the remnants,[4] nor anyone else besides them, has translated this book before—at least, no translation has reached me. Those who are able to discern the truth and recognize it will know and understand when they examine this book that my praise of it partakes neither of the rhetoric of the poet, nor excess, nor hyperbole because this does not suit my character—and God knows it—but I have praised it in truth which is its own witness and which is completely consistent.[5] Out of love of it and our diligence in it, I undertook this project after asking God to guide me in the path which I chose to follow. Were it not for this, I would have desisted from it and I would have saved myself from speaking about something I was not permitted to deal with.[6] In addition, another reason pushed my hand and moved my pen to the end of the task, namely, the correctness and accuracy of the Arabic book from which I translated, the beauty of its writing and the loveliness of its clarity.[7] Above all, let the Lord of help who helps everyone seeking help[8] be magnified, Who supported me in accordance with His will and in His Sanctity. Amen.

4. See Joel 3:5; Qimḥi *ad locum;* BT *Sanhedrin* 92a, and *Ḥullin* 133a.

5. See H. A. Wolfson, *Crescas' Critique of Aristotle* (Cambridge, Mass., 1929), pp. 198–199 and n. 79 (p. 456), for the source of this phrase, to which may be added A. Badawi, *Manṭiq Arisṭū* (Cairo, 1948), part 1, p. 203; S. Pines, "A Tenth-Century Philosophical Correspondence," *Proceedings of the American Academy for Jewish Research*, 24:108, n. 26 (1955); Appendix C, Note 5, below.

6. See Ecclesiasticus 3:22 and references in M. S. Segal, *Sefer Ben Sira ha-Shalem* (Jerusalem, 1953), *ad locum*.

7. The form *n w q y w* is not known to me.

8. See M. H. Gottstein, *Medieval Hebrew Syntax and Vocabulary as Influenced by Arabic* (Jerusalem, 1951), s.v. *ʿzr* (p. 219).

Appendix B

The epilogue of Samuel's translation of Ibn Rushd's *Epitome of Plato's Republic*, printed in *Ecrivains* (E), pp. 557–559 on the basis of MS. Milan, Biblioteca Ambrosiana R. 33 sup., and Turin XIV A 14 (destroyed by fire in 1904) and reprinted independently in E. I. J. Rosenthal, ed., *Averroes' Commentary on Plato's Republic* (Cambridge, 1956) (R), pp. 106–107. I have also compared the two printed versions with Florence, Medicea-Laurenziana Plut. 88.25 (F). There is a partial French translation in *Ecrivains*, p. 557, and Steinschneider, *Heb. Üb.*, p. 222, gives a detailed summary.

The *Commentary* of Ibn Rushd on the scientific statements[1] found in the *Republic* of Plato is complete. It[2] is the second part of political science.[2] Its translation was completed, in the city of Uzès,[3] on the twenty-second of Kislev in the year 5081 from the Creation. I, Samuel son of Judah son of Meshullam son of Isaac son of Solomon, Barbevaire of Marseilles,[4] referred to and called in Provençal and commonly, Miles Bongodas of Marseilles,[4] translated it. When I translated it,[5] I still did not have the commentary of Ibn Rushd on the *Ethics*[6] of the philosopher Aristotle which is the first part of[7] this science dealing with matters dependent on the will.[7] I had only the separate treatises on the *Ethics* by the philosopher, and I was unable to translate them on account of their profundity and difficulty. Therefore I put myself to much effort in order to procure a copy of the commentary of Ibn Rushd on that part, written in a pure and clear style, as is his habit in all of his commentaries,[8] and I roused myself to translate it. God, who is honored, in His kindness was partial to me so that I completed the translation of the commentaries on the whole of political science. In addition, I revised the whole translation of this science and corrected its mistakes in so far as I was able. The work of revision and correction was completed on the twenty-seventh[9] of Elul of that year in the citadel of Beaucaire, shut up and abandoned with the rest of my brethren, imprisoned in

1. E omits.
2–2. E omits and R adds *teḥilat* after *we-hu*.
3. See Note 32 to the body of the paper, above.
4–4. Omitted in F/R. Cf. R, p. 7, note.
5. E omits.
6. E omits.
7–7. E omits.
8. Note Samuel's high opinion of Ibn Rushd here. For a different, more mature opinion, see Appendix D.
9. R. כ"ו. Cf. Note 33 to the body of the paper.

one of its fortresses called Rodorta.[10] It is not impossible—rather it is possible, nay, it is unavoidable—that whoever examines my translation of the two parts of this science will be perplexed about some passages on account of the badness of the translation which is a result of my limited grasp of the Arabic language. But, by God's worship,[11] I hope and trust that those mistakes will be overlooked because they are few in comparison to the whole work. In addition, they are not too far removed from the customary[12] translations of other books by some of the translators who lived before me. And perhaps, by the decree of God, afterwards one of the unique and exceptional[13] individuals who are familiar with both languages will be roused with an understanding heart and a new spirit to cross out and destroy my errors[14] and mistakes, so that the translation of this science will become perfect. Because[15] of my liking and diligent attention to this science,[16] I thought and conceived the desire to correct this translation again together with the Christian philosophers, especially the first part of[17] it[17] because they have[18] the separate treatises of the philosopher on that part together with their explanation by Abū Naṣr al-Fārābī. By the Law and the Testimony,[19] as I had desired so would it have come about, if the above-mentioned long and arduous imprisonment which has us in its grasp at this time had not prevented me from performing this task. But if God gives me longer life, takes me out of confinement and prison, and will give me a little time, I will make an effort with regard to this first part of the Political Science, and I will study and investigate it exceedingly closely from the beginning of the science till its end systematically so that the translation will be as correct as possible.[20]

10. See above, Note 34 to the body of the paper.

11. See J. Levy, *Neuhebräisches und chaldäisches Wörterbuch über die Talmudim und Midrashim* (Leipzig, 1883), volume IV, s.v. *ʿabodah* (p. 607, col. 1, lines 1ff.); M. Jastrow, *A Dictionary of the Targumim, the Talmud Babli and Yerushalmi, and the Midrashic Literature* (New York, Berlin, and London, 1926), s.v. (p. 1036, bot.).

12. Reading הנוהג with R. E has הנודע.

13. Reading סגולות with F/R against E תכלית which is the *lectio facilior*. For סגולות, cf. J. Klatzkin, *Thesaurus*, part 3, s.v. (pp. 92–93).

14. F/R תעיותי E תעותי.

15. F/R ואני E וגם.

16. F/R אותה E זאת החכמה.

17–17. F/R ממנה E מזאת החכמה.

18. F/R נמצאים E הנמצאים. For the commentary of al-Fārābī on the *Ethics* mentioned presently, see above, Note 35 to the body of the paper.

19. See Isaiah 8:20 and Qimḥi *ad locum*.

20. F/R ביותר שלם E בו ותשלם. For the translation, cf. M. H. Gottstein, *Medieval Hebrew Syntax and Vocabulary*, chap. viii, pp. 26–29.

Therefore, let not the serious student of this science reproach me before I accomplish this task when he reaches the places of errors and mistakes, for "there is no one who does not miss the mark,"[21] and there is no craftsman who does not, at times, err in his work or craft. Especially is this true of the translator's art, which is burdensome and difficult. For the one who would be an accomplished craftsman in it must be familiar with the two languages—the one he translates from and the one he translates into—and secondly, he must be well educated, not only in the science or[22] art which he is translating but also in all sciences conventionally recognized as such, or most of them, because of the interconnectedness of all of the sciences and arts one with the other, since one always uses[23] analogies taken from other sciences.[23] The first translators who came before us have already testified to this or its like in apologizing for their translations. Despite the greatness of the calamities, confusion, and damage which overtook the members of our people, they continued coming one after the other, consecutively,[24] closely, and continually for a long time, and my contemporaries[25] have honored what we happened to translate at this time very highly. We praise God and give Him much thanks, because He has helped us with this. And in general,[26] I say, O you who are interested in rational speculation, the Congregation of Believers, the truth blazes its own path, so be grateful to whoever is worthy of it. For, until this day, no part of this science was translated or came into our possession,[27] neither from the pen of the Philosopher nor from anyone else, except what is to be found in the *Book of the Principles of Existing Things*[28] of Abū

21. See I Kings 8:46; II Chronicles 6:36.

22. F/R או E זו.

23–23. F תמשיל באחרות R תמשל באחרות E תמשיל בהאחרת. For the translation of תמשיל, see M. H. Gottstein, *Medieval Hebrew Syntax and Vocabulary*, s.v. (p. 198).

24. See J. Klatzkin, *Thesaurus*, II, 291, s.v. *mishshush* II.

25. Reading אחרונים for אחרונות. The translation from here to the end of the sentence is only probable.

26. F/R ובכלל E ובכן.

27. F/R אלינו E עליו.

28. Also known under the title of *The Political Regime(s)*. The second part of this treatise is concerned with political science, properly speaking. For a partial English translation and bibliographical information, see M. Mahdi and R. Lerner, eds., *Medieval Political Philosophy*, pp. 31ff.; a Hebrew translation by Moses ibn Tibbon was published by H. Filipowski in *Sefer he-Asif* (Leipzig, 1849), pp. 1–64 (cf. Steinschneider, *Heb. Üb.*, pp. 290ff.). This translation should be taken into account in any critical edition of the Arabic text, especially since it corresponds to MS. Feyzullah 1279, which is unique (cf. Mahdi and Lerner, pp. 32, 57, and L. Strauss, "Farabi's Plato," *Louis Ginzberg Jubilee Volume* [New York, 1945], English section, p. 358, n. 2).

Naṣr al-Fārābī, which many of our nation have. It contains a little[29] of the second part of this science, but nothing of the first part. I am the one who put on strength and was the first to begin to show the preciousness[30] of the splendor of the greatness[30] of this science and to give it existence in our language. Although because of my imperfection the good which exists in it is small, nevertheless the statement[31] is a beginning[31] and, although it is meager, yet is it great potentially. In any case, awake, O you sleepers, from the deep sleep of laziness and ignorance without having something truly your own which causes you to descend into the deep which is transitory and destroys absolute happiness. Awake, O you drunk with calamities,[32] rejoice, take hold of this fair portion which God has distributed to you. O deaf, hear what these two divine kings have said. O blind, look and see! Light is in them which is heavenly. Ask who created these wonders which are more exalted and excellent than can be praised. Contemplate this vision. Your wages are with you and your work is before you.

The translator stated: I promised to correct the translation of this science with the help of Christian philosophers but was unable [to do so] on account of the magnitude of the annoyances and persecutions which have overtaken us on the part of this nation which exiles us. We have become among them as a parable and proverb. They have made us as dust to tread upon. Nevertheless, I was diligent in examining it. With respect to all passages of [the meaning of which] I was not sure, I always referred to the book of the Philosopher and I corrected whatever was wrong insofar as I was able. I proceeded[33] in this manner with the *Ethics*, but with respect to the *Republic*, I had no other book. Despite all this, I am sure that there are few mistakes[34] in it. Let whoever studies it after me excuse me and judge me favorably as is proper for the sect of philosophers, seekers after the agreement of knowledge to existing things.[35] This correction was completed in the month of Tammuz in the year

29. F/R קצת מ E מעט מזער מן.
30–30. F/R יקר תפארת גדולת E גודל תפארת.
31. המאמר בהתחלה. The exact meaning of this phrase is unclear to me.
32. For the phrase beginning with "Awake . . . ," cf. Steinschneider, *Heb. Üb.*, p. 223, n. 836, and Maimonides, *Mishneh Torah*, *Sefer ha-Madda*ʾ, ed. S. Rawidowicz (Jerusalem, 1947), *Hilkhot Teshuvah*, chap. 3, Halakhah 4.
33. F/R התנהגתי E הנהגתי.
34. F/R שגיאותי E שגיאות.
35. See above, Note 25 to the body of the paper.

5082. May the Creator be praised who helped me and may He be exalted forever. Amen. Blessed be He who gives strength to the weary, and to those without power, He gives courage.[36]

Appendix C

Epilogue of Samuel's new translation of Ibn Rushd's *Epitome of Logic*. The Hebrew text was published in *Ecrivains*, page 559, on the basis of Paris, Bibliothèque Nationale Hebrew MS. 956 (P), which I have rechecked.

The *Epitome of Logic* is complete—thank God—which Ibn Rushd the Andalusian, the great philosopher and chief of the commentators, composed, and its translation is also complete. I, Samuel Marsilius son of Judah son of Meshullam son of Isaac son of Solomon, translated it from Arabic into Hebrew. It had already been translated before, but many mistakes fell into that translation so that the text became totally corrupt. Afterwards, outstanding contemporaries, familiar with Arabic, came and tried to correct that translation but they did not complete what they attempted to do. I might almost say that their correction was not worth consideration, so that the book

36. Florence, Medicea-Laurenziana, Conv. Suppr. 12, which was copied by Moses Rieti, the celebrated author of a Hebrew imitation of Dante's *Inferno*, omits Samuel's epilogue to the *Ethics* and the *Republic*. Rieti himself composed a short epilogue which Rosenthal has printed (p. 107). I think it not without interest to translate it here: "The name of the intellectual, translator of this book—i.e., the *Ethics* of Aristotle and the *Republic* of Plato—is Samuel son of Judah son of Meshullam son of Isaac son of Solomon of Marseilles. He is the one who translated it into Hebrew. He has apologized very much in various ways for the incorrectness of his translation of most of the *Ethics* and of many parts of the *Republic*. It seems that the young man was well acquainted with the Hebrew language but was less versed in the method of translation and the knowledge of the language he translated from, despite his high personal value. In any case, we ought to praise him and thank him for his sprightliness and his efforts to make available the translation of this art whether because of the obvious (l. מובן) value of the book itself or because it will arouse someone to correct its deficiencies and to bring it to perfection and the understanding of all of it, although this would entail much work. However, since we, on account of our sins, are scattered among the Gentiles, we should use their tools when we are able to cooperate with them till a purifier and refiner of silver will come (cf. Malachi 3:3) who will raise a poor and destitute people from the dust in his mercy. And I, Moses son of Isaac Rieti, have written this book despite the lack of perfection in its translation, when I was seventy years old in the year 5217. This book also should not be lacking to my son among the rest of the books which I wrote, caused to be written, and bought when I was young, in addition to what my father wrote. And let them find favor and good grace in the eyes of God and man (cf. Proverbs 3:4). Selah."

remained full of mistakes, confused, and unintelligible to us, the Congregation of Thinkers.[1] When I realized this state of affairs and at the same time realized[2] the great benefit which would accrue from this text, I inconvenienced myself, although time pressed on me and I had much difficulty[3] in translating it once again from the beginning.

My reason was that [although][4] this text was short, small in quantity, [it was] of exceedingly great quality, because it contained the choice and excellent material selected from Abū Naṣr's book on logic, which is of very high degree and excellence. For Ibn Rushd in this book collected those essential principles upon which Abū Naṣr founded his book on logic—that is, what seemed to [Ibn Rushd] to be necessary and indispensable in accordance with his intention—and Ibn Rushd followed in his footsteps, deviating neither to the right nor left. And God is my witness if my intention was to catch up and criticize the first translator and his correctors in order to make a name for myself in this art. Not at all, by God's life, my only motive was the search for truth which is its own witness and entirely consistent.[5] From God the rewarder, I ask only a spiritual reward for my trouble. I completed this work on the twentieth of Tebeth in the year 5090 of Creation in the citadel of Tarascon. May the Helper be praised and exalted. Amen.

Appendix D

Epilogue of Samuel's correction of Jacob ben Makhir's translation of Jābir ibn Aflaḥ's *Epitome of the Almagest.* The Hebrew text was published in *Ecrivains*, pages 562–563. I have compared it again with Paris, Bibliothèque Nationale Hebrew MSS. 1024 and 1025, the only two manuscripts which have Samuel's epilogue.

Samuel, son of Judah son of Meshullam son of Isaac son of Solomon, known commonly as Miles of Marseilles, said: Give ear, O heavens! Give ear, O earth! Listen, O philosophers! I bind you, seekers after

1. See above, Note 26 to the body of the paper.
2. For the translation of M. H. Gottstein, *Medieval Hebrew Syntax and Vocabulary*, s.v. *shʿr* (p. 261).
3. See Exodus 14:25.
4. P להיותו.
5. See Appendix A, English translation, Note 5, above

the correspondence of knowledge to existing things,[1] by the hosts of Heaven, there where He has placed in the highest heights a dwelling place and sanctified residence,[2] not to look at my treatise in hatred, competition, jealousy, and pettiness. Do not arouse and stir yourselves up to read it in foolishness and arrogance, in the manner of Yehu.[3]

My vocation was the Lord's since, at the age of eighteen, I came under the canopy of precious philosophizing and understood, from that time till now, the kindnesses of the Creator. I have had the privilege of peering and gazing into the clear glass of philosophy, the first of the arts, which lords, reigns, and rules over them. I thought that it was a time to translate and compose many books for the Lord's sake which would be tools helping me to gather and digest philosophy's fruits, for many books are indispensable for this task. But far be it from me to do my work shoddily. A small sister do we have,[4] slight is she in quantity, high in quality[5] in seeking the answers to many bothersome calculations,[6] unique is she, superior to all the crafts. Therefore, I thought to dress her with scarlet, with ornaments, and to deck her out with golden decorations of books. Therefore, in so far as possible, I made efforts from that day on to acquire them, and for the rarest of them, I put myself out considerably and expended much energy. This took place when I studied this honored science—that is, astronomy—with the venerable sage, the perfect philosopher, our teacher Rabbi Abba Mari, may God watch over him and give him life, who is known commonly as Sen Astruc de Noves, may he live for many years,[7] in the citadel of Salon. My ear heard and understood the exalted character of this book on the subject of astronomy which was composed by an individual who was a prince of God, an Ishmaelite philosopher known and called commonly Jābir ibn Aflaḥ of Seville. And while still a student,[8] the philosopher Ibn Rushd, who was a disciple of Ibn Aflaḥ, also wrote on the

1. See Note 25 to the body of the paper.
2. Cf. Deuteronomy 32:1; Isaiah 1:2; Song of Songs 2:7; Psalms 68:6; II Chronicles 30:27.
3. See II Kings 9:20.
4. See Song of Songs 8:8.
5. Supplying מעטה ⟨הכמות גדולת האכות⟩ בבקשת.
6. I.e., involved in astronomy.
7. See Psalms 61:7.
8. ומכותלי בית הספר. The exact meaning of the phrase and its connection with the rest of the sentence is unclear to me. See Steinschneider, *Heb. Üb.*, p. 548, for the deduction that Ibn Rushd wrote his *Epitome of the Almagest* in the first period of his literary activity.

subject of this science. I therefore knew that [Ibn Aflaḥ] had high authority.[9] And at that time, I was unable to acquire the treatise of Ibn Aflaḥ because it was to be found only in a translation by the philosopher Nathan ha-Meʾati,[10] I believe, and his translation was very corrupt, according to what was said. In addition, it was only to be found in the hands of a few people. Therefore, I quenched the fire of my great burning desire and I exchanged a cow for an ass,[11] that is, the *Almagest* of Ibn Rushd, which I mentioned, for I thought that since he was most recent and famous for his knowledge his book would be sufficient without [my] having recourse to another composition. For these reasons, I did not pursue this precious book [of Ibn Aflaḥ] with ardor. I comforted myself with its replacement, and since my judgment was not mature because I was being educated in the sciences and at the beginning of my scholarly career, at that time the statements of Ibn Rushd in his aforementioned book were very delectable to me. I thought that there was no one like him in excellence and the degree of his quality.[12]

However, after a number of years, when I reached the age of thirty, I ardently desired to return to this lofty science. Therefore, I turned to the first book, the great ass,[13] which the first chief,[14] Ptolemy Claudius,[15] composed, which is known as the *Almagest.* It is the book which I first studied in my youth. And although I knew that the book was profound, I longed, nevertheless, to read it again from the beginning. I read it at that time with the philosopher, my brother En Bondavi of Marseilles, who is perfect in every science, younger than I in years. We were able to read all of it except, because of certain hindrances[16] which overtook us,[17] for the last treatise. I also was able to complete at that time a commentary on the first three treatises, but I was unable to comment on the rest of the treatises of the book to the end as I wanted to, because of the greatness of the continuous[18] calamities which came upon me. This

9. See Ezekiel 28:2.

10. See Steinschneider, *Heb. Üb.*, pp. 670, 679, and index. Nathan's supposed translation is not mentioned by Steinschneider, pp. 543–544.

11. See *Baba Meẓiʿa*, Mishnah VIII, 4.

12. Contrast below with his mature judgment.

13. Perhaps a pun is intended here with *ḥamor* (ass) and *ḥamur* (weighty).

14. See above, Note 73 to the body of the paper.

15. הפלודי from the Arabic *al-Falūdī* < *al-Qalūdī*. See Steinschneider, *Heb. Üb.*, p. 519. For the *Almagest*, see Steinschneider, pp. 520ff.

16. *Meʿiqim.* Cf. Klatzkin, *Thesaurus*, s.v.

17. See Jastrow, *Dictionary*, s.v. (p. 1669, col. 1).

18. Reading *tekufot*. Cf. Klatzkin, *Thesaurus*, s.v. *tekufut*, part IV, p. 196.

period of study took place in the citadel of Tarascon because our house was there at that time. I was about thirty-five years old.

And when I achieved a good understanding at that time of this honored science and all or nearly all of the other sciences, I realized[19] from the words of Ibn Rushd in his book on this science that the good found in them was gleaned from the book of Ibn Aflaḥ, which is more precious than the most refined gold.[20] I also realized that most of the wonderful excellent statements found in the book of Ibn Aflaḥ were left out of that book by Ibn Rushd. There is almost nothing good in Ibn Rushd's whole book except that which he gleaned from this one. Therefore, my brother, the aforementioned philosopher, and I girded up strength and courage and stripped off our arrogance and grandeur in order to acquire wisdom. Therefore, we turned and journeyed from our city to Trinquetailles.[21] We exerted ourselves until we acquired a copy of the original Arabic of this book there, which had been revised very carefully in the usual manner. We copied it at that time very quickly, shut up two days in one of the houses of the seekers of wisdom[22] who lived there, nourished on a minimum of bread and water. Then we were forced to return the Arabic original to its owner and to return to our home because[23] of mundane affairs. Therefore, we had to glean from the book, not in a systematic manner, the passages which were most doubtful to us. The excerpted material did not amount to an eighth of the book. I said too hastily that this would comfort us.

Then came the day, and a mighty and strong wind splitting up my strength and breaking my bones, slung me around, exiled me, and carried me from the nests of my place of rest. Here,[24] I exerted myself and found this book translated by the philosopher Jacob ben Makhir.[25] My heart did not rest. I used cunning and I laid low my former arrogance for the sake of[26] this precious book until I came to an agreement[27] with its owner and he permitted me to copy it. I wrote it down, and the writing of the book from which I copied

19. שערתי. See Appendix C, Note 2.
20. See Psalms 119:127.
21. Understanding "Trinquetailles" as the object of *la-lekhet*.
22. Compare Ibn Khaldun, *The Muqaddimah*, tr. F. Rosenthal (New York, 1958), v. 3, p. 247, n. 1011.
23. *Be-galgal*. This form is not known to me. See Note 26, below.
24. In Aix.
25. Steinschneider, *Heb. Üb.*, p. 544.
26. See Note 23 above.
27. השותי עם. I have translated according to context.

was that of the aforementioned philosopher, the translator, but I felt[28] continually at the time of writing it down that its mistakes were many. Then I said: I have busied myself for nothing and I have come into the possession of falsity. Finally, I did not keep quiet until I was given divine aid, and there came to me today here the first Arabic text which I excerpted before. I have accurately compared this book with the Arabic text twice.[29] I also found in the Arabic text many readings which were not in the translation of the aforementioned sage. In addition, from the translation, the words of the author concerning the Milky Way,[30] the solid sphere,[31] and the figures appropriate for the fixed stars were missing. All that was lacking I completed and that which was incorrect I corrected in so far as I was able. As I live, I expended more effort in this matter and I had more expense of spirit because of the many[32] mistakes which I found in the translation of Jacob ben Makhir than if I had translated it from the Arabic afresh. I have heard that the philosopher, Moses ibn Tibbon, also translated it, but his translation[33] has not reached me nor have I seen it.

These recovered objects are wonderful and exalted. Who is so wise as to understand them? Who is so understanding as to know them? O House of Jacob, come let us walk in this great and fearful light of God, for there was never anyone like this author before him, a king of this science and a true prophet.[34] After him, who can find another like him? He has criticized the high priest of this science, Ptolemy Claudius. He mentioned[35] great criticisms and explained his treatises, revealed his secrets and shortened his lengthy passages. Everything is strong and established, as you will see in the book if you study it. Who is like him, teaching, ruling, giving close attention to a true matter?[36]

To this point God, let His name be blest, has helped us. This took place in the forty-second year of my life, the first of Tebeth, 5096 from the Creation, in the city of Aix.[37] Great praise and much

28. Cf. above, Note 19.

29. This seems to be the most probable translation. Otherwise, Samuel would have added *rabot*, as he does in Appendix E, Page 319, below.

30. From the Arabic: *al-majarrah*. Cf. Klatzkin, *Thesaurus*, s.v. *megorah*.

31. Klatzkin, *Thesaurus*, s.v. *kadur*, *mogsham*, and *megusham*.

32. Reading עוצם.

33. See Steinschneider, *Heb. Üb.*, p. 544.

34. See above, Note 74 to the body of the paper.

35. The text has *nizkar*.

36. Cf. Proverbs 29:12 and 17:4.

37. See above, Note 52 to the body of the paper.

thanks belong to the One who allots His glory and endows some of His splendor to those who fear Him, may His kingdom be exalted, amen. I say: I pray to the Lord my God who has deemed me worthy and has conferred upon me this precious find that he may deem me worthy again to study it completely before I am taken away. In Him has my heart trusted because there is no God beside Him. May His name be exalted. Amen.

Appendix E

Epilogue of Samuel's translation of Alexander of Aphrodisias' *De Anima* from the Arabic of Isḥāq ibn Ḥunain. It was first published partially in A. Günsz, *Die Abhandlung Alexanders von Aphrodisias über den Intellekt* (Berlin, 1886), page 39. The first complete printing was by M. Steinschneider in *Magazin für die Wissenschaft des Judenthums*, 14:8–10 (1887, Hebrew part). It was reprinted in *Ecrivains*, pages 565–566. I have rechecked it against Paris, Bibliothèque Nationale, Hebrew MSS. 893 and 894.

The treatise of Alexander of Aphrodisias entitled *De Anima* is complete and its translation is complete, praise God. It[1] was composed in Greek, and Isḥāq ibn Ḥunain translated it from that language into Arabic, as you may see at the beginning of the treatise. Afterwards, I translated it from Arabic to Hebrew. It is profound and difficult to understand because this is the manner of the author in general, and how much more so in treating this science which is the difficult and naturally profound science of the soul. Since it has been translated twice from language to language, as we have related, this increases the difficulty and obscurity. But although it is difficult and obscure for these two reasons, the one in itself and the other on account of its translation, as we have explained, whoever was correctly schooled in science will be able to understand it completely. Happy will be the one who is patient enough to finally understand his statements, for this treatise is[2] as perfect as possible, honored and precious, too great for praise. There[3] are two reasons for this: first, its author is the most perfect of the philosophers, no

1. Paris 894 omits מדעתי.
2. Paris 894 has שלם.
3. Paris 893 omits וזה.

one is like him, a sage[4] and true prophet[5] in the band of philosophers, as it were. Even Aristotle, the son of Nicomachus, the most famous among the Greeks in science who invented the sciences according to what has been related and was the first chief,[6] did not attain to the stature of this man in wisdom. His statements in this treatise and elsewhere bear witness to the truth of my words.[7] In any event it is clearly obvious that truly not one of all the philosophers after Aristotle to this day, of those whose words have reached us, has attained his degree and stature in philosophy.[8] The second reason is that this treatise has as its subject a precious science higher than all the sciences,[9] namely, physical science, and the treatise is concerned with the most honored part of all of its parts, namely, the psychological part, for it does not pertain to physical science alone, but it has a great connection with Metaphysics. Even the other branches of physical science share mightily with Metaphysics, but this part—that is, the psychological part—is superior to all of them in the community and closeness which exist between it and Metaphysics. For these[10] two reasons, this treatise is the most honored of treatises. Examine it carefully with the method of complete investigation and perfect speculative study; its meaning will come out like pure gold.[11]

I translated it when I was thirty years old, in the city of Murcia and finished it in the month of Tebeth in the year 5084 after the Creation. I found the Arabic from which I translated to have many marginal notations. At the end, there was a statement to the effect that it was accurately checked and compared with a true copy. But I did not follow, at the time [when] I translated it, all the marginal notations of variant readings, for at times I would depart from the marginal annotation and I would have more confidence in what I saw in the text of the book. In all respects, I acted in accord with what I thought to be close to the overwhelming truth.[12] After I translated this treatise, it remained shut up with me and

4. See E. Ben Yehuda, *Dictionary*, s.v. *ga'on*, p. 662, cols. 1ff.
5. See above, Note 74 to the body of the paper.
6. See Note 73 to the body of the paper.
7. Reading דברי with Paris 894.
8. Paris 894 adds הנה זאת היא הסבה האחת.
9. All of the sciences except for Metaphysics.
10. Paris 893 אלו; Paris 894 האלו; *Ecrivains*, לא.
11. See Job 23:10.
12. See Isaiah 42:13.

sealed among my personal belongings. It did not spread out among the contemporary speculative thinkers of our nation until this very day on account of the tremendous distractions which prevented me from understanding the profundity of the treatise and on account of its difficulty in itself. In addition, these distractions prevented me from accurately revising my translation in the most perfect manner according to the method of rational speculation and investigation.

When much time passed and I reached my forty-fourth year, Heaven deemed me worthy. I read this treatise intently and I investigated it completely from beginning to end systematically many times. I exerted myself greatly in accurately checking it and correcting it. Many of the corrections to be found in it originated as my conjecture and opinion and what seemed to me to be correct after extraordinary study. Since the first copy of my translation is not clearly legible now on account of its age and its marginal annotations, I wrote it out again in the clearest and most explicit manner I could, so that the reader may run through it and its advantage may spread widely among the mass of philosophers and those of our nation who ardently desire enlightenment so that they easily make it their own.

This second writing was completed in the month of Tammuz in my forty-sixth year. This took place in the citadel of Montélimar where my house is at this time. The name of the speaker and translator of this treatise from the Arabic language to the Hebrew language is Samuel son of Judah son of Meshullam son of Isaac son of the Nadiv Solomon son of the Nadiv Jacob Prophègue son of David, who was a very wealthy man in Marseilles. In the merit of this honored, divine author and master,[13] who was one of the great sages of the Gentile nations and one of their pious ones,[14] and in the merits of my holy forefathers, have I trusted and I was helped by Him who helps those who call out for help, may His name be blessed. May he be exalted and lifted up forever. Amen.

I have introduced some innovations in this translation of mine—namely, the separation between the various[15] subjects and different inquiries—because the text of the Arabic book from which I translated was entirely continuous without any separation. In order to

13. הרב המחבר.
14. Paris 894 omits from "who" to "ones."
15. Paris 894 omits.

make the understanding of the treatise[16] easier, I separated it into chapters as seemed most correct and proper to me. I separated those parts which were together improperly so that anyone interested in rational speculation might understand more easily which were the primary parts of the treatise and which the subordinate parts.[17] Let him examine the treatise and find it to be true. Let the Master of truth be praised who leads His servant in the path of truth.

16. Paris 894 adds הבנת.
17. Paris 894 adds ומה הם חלקי חלקיו.

The Rise of Art Music in the Italian Ghetto*

The Influence of Segregation on Jewish Musical Praxis

By ISRAEL ADLER

I. Introduction

The starting point of this study was the difficulty of understanding a chapter to be found in all Jewish music histories: the chapter dealing with synagogal art music in Italy during the first decades of the seventeenth century. Jewish music historians generally present this period according to the following scheme: during the first half of the seventeenth century a "reform" movement was formed in Northern Italy, with the intention of introducing art music into the synagogue; this movement was created by the activities of its two protagonists, the Mantuan musician Solomon Rossi and the famous and versatile Rabbi Leon Modena. This experiment, which did not outlast the first half of the seventeenth century, was condemned to disappear, together with its promoters, because of rabbinical opposition, and was not revived before the Emancipation, at the beginning of the nineteenth century, or a few decades earlier.

Should we not be intrigued by this sudden appearance of art music praxis in the seventeenth-century Italian synagogue? True, we know of many instances of Jews participating in the general musical life in Italy during the two preceding centuries and we could be inclined to follow the widely accepted view that considers this seventeenth-century evidence of art music in Jewish community life as a prolongation, a belated illustration, of one of the well-known

* This paper is based mainly on three chapters of my book (in French) on art music praxis in European Jewish communities during the seventeenth and eighteenth centuries, referred to below in Note 1. My main purpose in that book was to establish the fact that this musical praxis was a normal part of Jewish life in some European centers during this period. My purpose here is to single out one specific result of this research: the astonishing chronological coincidence between the rise of art music in Jewish community life and the enforcement of the ghetto system in Italy. I have tried to provide for this an explanation, which I am eager to submit to the opinion of scholars engaged in Jewish historical research.

features of Italian Jewry during the Renaissance: the assimilation of general cultural values from the surrounding civilization.

Nevertheless, the Rossi-Modena experiment coincides with the beginning of the period of decadence in general culture among Italian Jewry, due to the reinforcement of segregation which was already well under way in the first half of the seventeenth century. How, then, could this musical experiment be considered as a kind of swan song of the preceding period when no similar evidence of synagogal art music has come down to us from the heyday of the Renaissance?

The historians' attempt to link this seventeenth-century art music praxis to the preceding period thus seems to be unwarranted because of the lack of evidence for the existence of earlier synagogal art music. Furthermore, their incorrect description of the manifestations of art music in the Jewish life of the early ghetto period as a limited "episode" soon doomed to disappear "without leaving any trace," and their failure to grasp the link between these musical manifestations and those of the subsequent period, are due to the fact that they have not paid sufficient attention to the wealth of documentation available. In my study of Jewish art music praxis in European communities prior to the Emancipation I have presented the bulk of such evidence known to me before July 1963.[1] Although historians of Hebrew literature, especially Professor Ḥ. Schirmann,[2] had already drawn attention to such evidence, very little documentation bridging the gap between the time of Solomon Rossi and the period of Emancipation has hitherto come to the knowledge of Jewish music historians. It will suffice to quote at random some of the most reputable histories of Jewish music, or recent specialized studies, to demonstrate this point.

Thus, A. Z. Idelsohn writes, in 1925, apropos of Rossi's "reform": "It is well known that the episode had no enduring results. A strong conservative opposition destroyed that reform without leaving any trace . . ."[3] The same author stresses, in 1929, in a chapter entitled "The Introduction of Harmony and Polyphony into the Synagogue

1. I. Adler, *La Pratique musicale savante dans quelques communautés juives en Europe aux XVIIe et XVIIIe siècles* (Paris-Hague, 1966).

2. *EJ*, VI, cols. 1–17 (1930); *Maḥbarôt le-sifrût*, II, no. 4: 73–96 (Tel Aviv, 1943); *Beḥînôt be-viqqôret has-sifrût*, 6:44–52 (Jerusalem, 1954); *Zion*, 29:61–111 (1964).

3. Song and Singers of the Synagogue in the Eighteenth Century," *Hebrew Union College Jubilee Volume* (Cincinnati, 1925), p. ; *Zion*, 29:61–111 (1964).

in Italy by Salomon Rossi," the absence of Jewish art music praxis in Italy after Rossi:

> ... All desire for the *ars nova* was killed in the Jew. He abandoned his ambition to become a co-worker in the Renaissance and the few attempts made toward the introduction of European achievements in music were deserted. Soon Rossi's music was forgotten, and the Italian synagogue went back to the old traditional song with more zeal than ever ...[4]

Later on, in the same chapter, Idelsohn points out the effect which Rossi was supposed to have had on Jewish music in Central Europe:

> Thus we see that Rossi's songs vanished entirely from the Italian synagogue. But they did exert an influence, by arousing interest in elaborate music in another country, Germany. Indirectly, Rossi's efforts influenced the communities in Central Europe through the introduction of the Italian style, choral singing in parts or in octaves, and even instrumental music in the synagogue in the seventeenth and eighteenth centuries.[5]

Here, except for a reference to the instrumental reception of the Sabbath in some Central European synagogues, especially in Prague, Idelsohn does not allude to a true art music but to the *mešorerîm* praxis.[6]

In the same sense E. Werner writes in 1954:

> ... Two Italian Jewish composers, Salomone Rossi and his protector Rabbi Leon Juda da Modena, imitated the contemporary Venetian performance of antiphonal choruses in their synagogal music. This stirred up a good deal of orthodox reaction, which succeeded, after Rossi's and Modena's death, in reestablishing, for about a century, the old order ...[7]

and the same author follows Idelsohn also in his opinion of the influence Rossi was supposed to have exerted in Central Europe:

> Nach dem Tode Rossis und Modenas erwachte die orthodoxe Traditionsgläubigkeit zu neuem Leben, und diese starrköpfige Opposition verurteilte Rossis Musik zum Dornröschenschlaf in den Bibliotheken, aus dem sie erst in unseren Tagen wieder entdeckt worden ist. Vergessen wurde dieses grosse Experiment aber nicht mehr; und allerorten begannen nun die Kantoren,

4. *Jewish Music in its Historical Development* (New York, 1929), p. 201.
5. *Ibid.*, p. 203.
6. See Adler, *La Pratique musicale*, vol. I, chap. i, par. 4.
7. *Grove's Dictionary of Music and Musicians*, 5th ed., ed. Eric Blom (London, 1954), IV, 633.

gar unbelehrt, mit polyphonen Sätzen zu experimentieren ohne auch nur die elementaren Stufen kontrapunktischer Technik erreicht zu haben.[8]

Ḥ. Avenary also accepts his predecessors' views when he writes in 1958:

> Das hektische Hervorbrechen der jüd. Komp.—Tätigkeit in den knapp hundert Jahren der Mantuaner Zeit bezeugt den Druck der schöpferischen Kräfte unter der Oberfläche ständiger Abgeschlossenheit. Die mächtig einsetzende Gegenreformation stellte bald den alten Zustand wieder her.[9]

Here and there, there came to light some scraps of evidence, other than the documents related to Rossi and Modena, of art music praxis in Jewish community life before the Emancipation. Yet this documentation was too fragmentary, and the belief in the myth that Italian Jewish art music disappeared together with Solomon Rossi and Leon Modena was too deeply anchored: thus E. Werner, revealing the existence of an anonymous Italian manuscript of the seventeenth century, containing the upper vocal part for the second choir of a collection of music for double choirs, is inevitably led to attribute these compositions—after having eliminated Rossi—to Leon Modena.[10]

J. Newman, in his monograph on Rossi's madrigals, mentions Werner's discovery of "the only analogue to Rossi's liturgical music extant," and he continues: ". . . the experiment remained an isolated one. Not for a long time, in fact not until the Napoleonic Wars threw down the ghetto walls, did European Jewry have enough security to think about contriving figural music for the service and to indulge in this ancient controversy."[11] Ḥ. Avenary, alluding to the cantata *Le-el elîm* by A. Casseres[12] and the cantata *Kol han-nešamah* by C. G.

8. *Hebräische Musik* (Cologne, 1961) (vol. 20 of *Das Musikwerk*), pp. 18–19.

9. In F. Blume, ed., *Die Musik in Geschichte und Gegenwart*, vol. VII, col. 248 (Kassel, 1958).

10. In his first study of this document, "Manuscripts . . . in the Birnbaum Collection," *Hebrew Union College Annual*, 18:397–428 (1948), E. Werner advances in a very prudent manner the possibility of attributing these compositions to Modena. In a later article, "The Music of Post-Biblical Judaism," in *New Oxford History of Music*, I (London, 1957), 313–335, the prudent hypothesis has become certainty.

11. "The Madrigals of Salamon de' Rossi" (Ann Arbor, Michigan, University microfilms, 63–6121), p. 22. This unpublished Ph.D. dissertation (Columbia University, 1962), in spite of the shortcomings of its Jewish documentation, is a major contribution to the knowledge of Rossi's secular works. Jewish as well as general musicological institutions should be equally interested in hastening its publication.

12. Published by A. Krieg, *L'Keel Keelim* (Amsterdam, 1951), this cantata has been well known to scholars since the end of the nineteenth century. See E. Birnbaum, "Unsere erste Musikbeilage," *Israelitischer Lehrer und Cantor* . . . (supplement to *Die jüdische Presse*, Berlin, March 15, 1899), pp. 17–18; Idelsohn, "Song and Singers . . . ," pp. 418–419;

Lidarti,[13] the only specimens known to him from the rich and brilliant eighteenth-century repertoire of the Amsterdam Portuguese Jewish community, describes them as "... tastende Schritte zur echten Mehrstimmigkeit ... Diese ... religiöse Gelegenheitskompos. sind hauptsächlich als Talentproben zu werten; sie blieben einflusslos."[14]

To conclude these quotations we may recall that P. Gradenwitz, in the fourth version of his Jewish music history,[15] also transcribes, quasi-verbatim, the passage quoted above from Idelsohn's *Jewish Music* (see Note 4), and that L. Algazi writes in 1957:

> Abstraction faite des chœurs religieux de Salomon Rossi, on ne connait point avant l'époque contemporaine d'œuvres savantes inspirées par la tradition musicale juive si ce n'est celles qui ont été écrites par des compositeurs européens ou américains depuis l'introduction du chant choral et de l'orgue dans certaines synagogues voilà un peu plus d'un siècle.[16]

This attitude of Jewish music historians is quite comprehensible. On the one hand, musical praxis seems to have been proscribed by rabbinic authorities since the Talmudic period and, on the other hand, the apparent rarity of documents has contributed to hide this aspect of Jewish cultural life from the eyes of the historian.

In the introductory part of my above-mentioned study, I have dealt with some of the most significant testimonials to the rabbinical attitude toward music.[17] It will suffice here to summarize this point—which is of no immediate relevance to the main argument of this paper—very roughly, as follows: the basic rabbinic doctrine is mainly concerned with the functional character of music. Music serving a religious function is generally admitted or encouraged; the performance of profane music is generally prohibited. According to the regions, the periods, and the conditions of life prevailing in various Jewish centers, a more or less broad interpretation was

---

J. d'Ancona in *Geschiedenis der Joden in Nederland* ..., eds. H. Brugmans and A. Frank, I (Amsterdam, 1940; only one volume published), 299–300 and the facsimile in front of p. 305; J. Meyer, *The Stay of ... Luzzatto at Amsterdam* ... (Amsterdam, 1947), p. 27, n. 19. A fragment of this cantata has been recorded by E. Werner: side 6 of the album *Israel Sings* (New York, Union of American Hebrew Congregations, ca. 1945).

13. Published by E. Birnbaum, "Musikbeilage" to *Israelitischer Lehrer und Cantor* ..., no. 3 (1899).

14. "Jüdische Musik," *Musik in Geschichte und Gegenwart*, VII, 251.

15. *Die Musikgeschichte Israels* (Kassel, 1961), p. 105.

16. "Juive (musique)," *Larousse de la musique*, ed. N. Dufourcq, *et al.* (Paris, 1957).

17. Adler, *La Pratique musicale*, vol. I, chap. i, par. 1.

given to the concepts of "religious music" and "profane music." It may be observed that this religious musical praxis, admitted by the rabbis, was never confined to the liturgical service proper. Since every cultural manifestation in Jewish life must necessarily—in order to be acceptable—bear a religious character, the absence of a strict rabbinic regulation gave music lovers of the different Jewish communities the opportunity for a musical praxis according to their tastes and their musical means. Protagonists of art music stood on a sound halakhic ground whenever they had to oppose their detractors who demanded a complete prohibition of musical praxis in Jewish life, using such arguments as the mourning for the destruction of the Temple (*zeker la-ḥûrban*) or the desire to refrain from the "custom of the Gentile" (*ḥuqqat hag-gôy*).

The scarcity of documents concerning art music in Jewish life during the seventeenth and eighteenth centuries is only apparent, as I have already pointed out. The bulk of such documentation is hidden in "literary" testimonies of this period. Thus, the vast collections of rabbinical responsa, this faithful mirror of Jewish cultural and social life of the period, reveal much precious evidence, particularly apropos of polemics from both supporters and adversaries of music in the synagogue. Parallel testimonies are to be found in books of liturgy and customs, in itineraries, in archival documents, and especially in the imposing corpus of occasional poetry of this period, composed for such occasions as the festive ceremony of a fraternity, the dedication of a synagogue or a Torah scroll, for festive days, in particular Purim and *Simḥat Torah* but also for Pentecost and the seventh day of Passover, for a marriage or a circumcision. The music composed for some of these occasions has come down to us.[18]

The purpose of this article is to stress one of the results of my above-mentioned study:[19] the necessity of re-examining the historical significance of the early manifestations of art music praxis in Jewish community life in Italy, in the light of the new documentation which has enabled us to establish the fact of the continuity of such praxis, in Italy as well as other European Jewish centers, throughout the seventeenth and eighteenth centuries. Although we shall be mainly concerned with the rise of art music in Italian Jewish community life—that is to say, with the period stretching approximately from

18. See my *La Pratique musicale*, vol. I, for the literary evidence and vol. II for the editing of the main musical scores.

19. *La Pratique musicale*, of which I am using here mainly chapters iii–v of vol. I.

the middle of the sixteenth to the middle of the seventeenth century—we must also, so as to understand the background which enabled the introduction of western art music into the synagogue, summarize briefly the main data concerning Jewish musicianship in Italy during the preceding period.

II. Jews and Western Art Music During the Italian Renaissance

The period of the Renaissance in Italy is marked by the active participation of Jews in general cultural life, by the Jews' assimilation of means of expression from the surrounding civilization in such domains as art, the theater, music, and the dance.[20]

20. Apart from the reference to the numerous monographs on different localities, periods, and subjects of Italian Jewish history given in A. Milano's bibliography, *Bibliotheca historico italo-judaica* (Florence, 1954), we shall mention among modern works giving a comprehensive view of this period, C. Roth, *The History of the Jews of Italy*, chaps. v–viii (Philadelphia, 1946; without references); *idem*, *The Jews in the Renaissance* (Philadelphia, 1959) (on music see mainly pp. 274–304); M. A. Shulvass, *Jewish Life in Renaissance Italy* (in Hebrew; New York, 1955); and the fifth part of I. Zinberg's monumental history of Jewish literature, *Di Gešichte fun der literatur bay yidn*, vol. IV (Vilno, 1933; photographic reproduction, New York, 1943), pp. 1–241. Important studies have been done on Jewish musical history of this period in Italy. Yet no comprehensive work has as yet been undertaken embracing the bulk of available documentation such as archival documents, literary sources, and musical documents. Among the more important studies mention should be made of E. Birnbaum, *Jüdische Musiker am Hofe von Mantua von 1542–1628* (Vienna, 1893), who leans mainly on the works of A. Bertolotti and P. Canal on Mantuan musicians, also used by A. d'Ancona, who devotes the beginning of the chapter "Gli ebrei di Mantova e il teatro" in his *Origini del teatro italiano*, 2nd ed., II (Turin, 1891), 398–429, to the Jewish musicians from Mantua. Special subjects are studied by C. Roth, "L'accademia musicale del ghetto veneziano," *Rassegna mensile d'Israel*, 3:152–162 (1927–28); P. Nettl, "Musicisti ebrei del Rinascimento italiano," *Rassegna mensile d'Israel*, 2:59–71 (1926–27) as well as in his *Alte jüdische Spielleute und Musiker* (Prague, 1923); O. Kinkeldey, "A Jewish Dancing Master of the Renaissance, Guglielmo Ebreo," *A. S. Freidus Memorial Volume* (New York, 1929), pp. 329–372; E. Werner, "Manuscripts of Jewish Music in the E. Birnbaum Collection," *Hebrew Union College Annual*, 18:397–428 (1944); A. Einstein, "Salomone Rossi as Composer of Madrigals," *Hebrew Union College Annual*, 23: part 2, 383–396 (1950–51); Newman, "The Madrigals of Salamon de' Rossi" (see Note 11). For attempts at a comprehensive view see Idelsohn, *Jewish Music . . .*, chap. x; P. Gradenwitz, *Ham-mûsîqah be-Yiśra'el*, 2nd ed. (Tel Aviv, 1955–56, with adaptations in English, Spanish, and German which do not correct the errors to be found in the original version), pp. 94–121; the passages devoted to Italy in J. Stutschewsky, *Klezmôrîm* (Jerusalem, 1959), pp. 26–34. Among studies of a general character which are aware of evidence related to musical praxis, there are—apart from the works by C. Roth and M. A. Shulvass already mentioned—C. Roth, *Venice* (Philadelphia, 1930), pp. 200–202; H. Vogelstein and P. Rieger, *Geschichte der Juden in Rom*, II (Berlin, 1896), pp. 35, 119–122, 302–303, 310, 433–435; U. Cassuto, *Gli ebrei a Firenze . . .* (Florence, 1918), pp. 192–193, 228, 303, 326; S. Simonsohn, *History of the Jews in the Duchy of Mantua* (in Hebrew), vol. I (Jerusalem, 1962–63), but mainly vol. II (1964–65), chap. vii. Of particular importance are the studies of J. H. Schirmann,

Throughout the Renaissance, and after this period, Jews can be found engaged in the fields of music and the dance, which seem to have been then a normal part of the curriculum of studies of a young Italian Jew.[21] We have, on the one hand, testimonies concerning the theoretical and practical knowledge of music in cultivated Jewish circles, as well as evidence of the place occupied by music in Jewish education and social life. On the other hand, we know of professional Jewish musicians who were active mainly in Gentile society.

As early as the first half of the fifteenth century we hear of the existence of Jewish schools of music and the dance in Venice.[22] Well-known Jewish scholars, such as Yoḥanan ben Isaac Alemanno and Abraham Farissol of the second half of the fifteenth century and the beginning of the sixteenth century, have left some evidence of their interest in music. Alemanno, wishing to emphasize the importance of music in social life and education, has recourse not only to ancient Greek writings on music but also to his own personal experience. During the visit of the celebrated blind German organist Konrad Paumann to Mantua, circa 1470, Alemanno had the opportunity of listening to his performance, which he describes as an overwhelming experience.[23] The many-sided Abraham Farissol—apologist, geographer, commentator, and scribe—who was cantor at

---

who is always alert to indications concerning music: see his articles on the Hebrew theater in *EJ* 6:1–17 (1930) and in *Monatsschrift für die Geschichte und Wissenschaft des Judentums* 75:105 (1931); his study on the libretto of a cantata by Ephraim Luzzatto, *Qanṭaṭah ᶜivrît* in *Maḥbarôt lesifrût* 2, no. 4:73–96 (Tel Aviv, 1943), and of an anonymous cantata, for the seventh day of Passover, in *Tatzlil* 4:10–13 (Haifa, 1964); see also Schirmann's annual bibliography of studies on Hebrew poetry, published since 1950 in *Kirjath Sepher*, which includes valuable references to Jewish music and his extensive study, "Theater and Music in the Italian Ghetti between the Sixteenth and Eighteenth Centuries" (Hebrew), *Zion*, 29:61–111 (1964).

21. Shulvass, *Jewish Life*, pp. 157–158, 163–164, 168–169, 182, 226–231, 322; Roth, *Renaissance*, pp. 275ff.; L. Blau, *Leo Modenas Briefe . . .* (Budapest–Strasbourg, 1905–07), pp. 59–60, stresses that a program of studies of this kind was reserved for youngsters from the richer classes.

22. Roth, *History*, p. 196, and *Renaissance*, pp. 275–276.

23. See his philosophical commentary on the Song of Songs: *Ḥešeq Šelomoh*, ff. 115a, 120b, and mainly 126b–127a of the Berlin manuscript (no. 143 in Steinschneider's catalog). This text has not yet been published *in extenso*. Quotations of some of the passages related to music are given by the editor of the printed extracts, published under the title *Šaᶜar ha-ḥešeq* (Leghorn, 1790; Halberstadt, n.d.), in his preface, fol. 6b of the Leghorn edition and fol. 4b of the Halberstadt edition. In Alemanno's main work, *Ḥey ᶜolamîm* (MS. no. 21 in the municipal library of Mantua), music is also dealt with in a chapter devoted to the education of youth (fols. 49b–50b).

Cf. Cassuto, *Gli ebrei a Firenze*, p. 303; Roth, *Renaissance*, p. 118; Ḥ. Avenary in *Die Musikforschung* 16:156–157 (1963).

Ferrara for about fifty years,[24] is called "menaggen" (musician, instrumentalist?)[25] and signs his name on the title page of a Hebrew illuminated manuscript using the three notes *fa - re - sol*,[26] a device rather popular among musicians of his period.[27]

In the first half of the sixteenth century an Italian Jewish schoolmaster, having to leave for a voyage, prescribes the daily exercise of instrumental music[28] to his pupils.[29] At the same time the Florentine poet Moses ben Joab lets us perceive the echoes of music and dance in Florentine social life,[30] and we hear of musical sessions in the house of a Jewish banker from Pisa, Yeḥîʾel Nissim da Pisa, whose wife, Diamante, herself plays the lute.[31] As further evidence of the theoretical and practical interest in the art of music among Italian Jews of this period, we should mention the sixteenth-century *Manuscrit hébreu* 1037 of the Paris Bibliothèque Nationale, a collection of musical treatises in Hebrew which served most probably as a manual for the education of Jewish musicians in Northern Italy.[32] We should mention, furthermore, the presence, at the end of the six-

24. See the edition of his commentary on Qohelet by S. Bamberger in *Ḳobeẓ ʿal Yad* 2(12):34 (1937).

25. This name is also to be found as an Italian surname (*menaggen = sonatore*); see M. Mortara, *Indice alfabetico dei Rabbini . . . in Italia* (Padua, 1886), s.v.; M. S. Nepi and H. Ghirondi, *Tôledôt gedôlê yiśraʾel . . .* (Trieste, 1853), p. 169.

26. See M. Gaster, *The Ketubah* (Berlin–London, 1923), p. 50 and "Faresol nicht Peritsol," *Monatsschrift für die Geschichte und Wissenschaft des Judentums* 80:489–490 (1936), quoted by S. Bamberger in *Ḳobeẓ ʿal Yad* 2(12):3 (1937). Gaster, who saw this manuscript at Turin, has not given the reference. The manuscript seems to have been part of the manuscript holdings of the National and University Library of Turin, unfortunately destroyed by fire in 1904.

27. For Dufay's use of this device see the facsimile of a Bodleian manuscript given by W. Apel, *Notation of Polyphonic Music . . .* 4th ed. (Cambridge, Mass., 1953), p. 103. For similar praxis by fifteenth- and sixteenth-century composers (Lafage, La Rue, Pipelare, Valla, Misonne), see H. Riemann, *Handbuch der Musikgeschichte*, vol. II, part 1 (Leipzig, 1907), p. 507.

28. The Hebrew names of instruments mentioned in this source are *kinnor* and *nevel*, which should be understood as equivalents for "lute" and "viol"; see the sixteenth century Hebrew–Italian glossary by David ben Ṣiyyon ben Abraham of Modena, *Davar ṭôv* (Venice, 1587–88). This rare edition, which is not listed in the current bibliographies and catalogs of the Bodleian library, the British Museum, and the Jewish National and University Library, is preserved at the Bibliothèque Nationale under the signature A. 6011(4).

29. S. Assaf, *Meqôrôt le-tôledôt ha-ḥinnûk be-Yiśraʾel*, IV (2nd ed., Tel Aviv, 1947–48), 26; other sources on the place of music in the education of Italian Jews are given by Assaf in II (Tel Aviv, 1930–31), 124.

30. Cassuto, *Gli ebrei a Firenze*, p. 228.

31. See the story of David ha-Reʾûvenî, ed. A. Z. Aescoly (Jerusalem, 1939–40), p. 53, quoted by Shulvass, *Jewish Life*, pp. 163, 168.

32. I. Adler, "Juive (musique)," in *Encyclopédie de la musique*, ed. F. Michel *et al.*, vol. II (Paris, 1959), col. 649, and *La Pratique musicale*, vol. I, n. 193.

teenth century, of musical items in a list, which has recently been brought to light,[33] of books belonging to a Mantuan Jew.

From the end of the sixteenth and the beginning of the seventeenth centuries there have come down to us the writings of several Italian rabbis and scholars, mainly from Mantua, which prove their interest in the art of music and their knowledge of the musical theory and praxis of their period. The Mantuan rabbi Judah Moscato devotes the first item, "Higgayôn be-Kinnôr," in his collection of sermons, *Nefûṣôt yehûdah*,[34] to music.[35] Abraham Portaleone, the Mantuan physician, devotes chapters four to thirteen of his *Šilṭê hag-gibbôrîm*[36] to music, speculating mainly on the nature of music and musical instruments in Biblical times but showing also a keen knowledge of the musical theory and praxis of his time.[37] Some interesting references to music are also included in Samuel Archevolti's treatise on Hebrew grammar and prosody, *ᶜArûgat hab-bośem* (Venice, 1602).[38] A fourth Hebrew writer on music of this period may be added to our list. Judah ben Moses Saltaro da Fano was one of the Venetian rabbis who gave their approval to Leon Modena's responsum in favor of the choral chant at Ferrara in 1605.[39] In his approbation Judah Saltaro mentions the fact that chapter five of his work *Šîr Ṣiyyon* was devoted to the defense of music:

כתבתי בספר שי"ר צ"יון... במאמר חמישי הכרחתי מרבוי מאמרי חז"ל עליו בגמרא במדרשים ובספר הזהר וכמה ספרי חכמת האמת ומדעות כל הפוסקים כלם כי המוסי"קה טובה בעיני אלקים ואדם...

Unfortunately this work, which I have been unable to trace either in print or in manuscript, seems to have been lost.

Finally, mention should be made of the *ḥazzan* of the Ashkenazic community of Casale Monferrato, Jacob ben Isaac Finzi hal-Lewî (circa 1581–before 1670).[40] Finzi wrote down the music of a collec-

33. See S. Simonsohn in *Kirjath Sepher* 37:112 (1961).

34. First ed., Venice, 1589.

35. See the modern edition and translation of this text by H. Schmueli, *Higgajon bechinnor . . . des Jehudah . . . Moscato* (Tel Aviv, 1953) (originally Ph.D. diss., Zürich).

36. First ed. (Mantua, 1611–12), ff. 3a–10a.

37. Adler, *La Pratique musicale*, vol. I, chap. iii, par. 2.

38. *Ibid.*

39. This responsum has been printed several times since the first edition in Rossi's *Haš-šîrîm ašer li-Šelomoh* (Venice, 1622–23), fol. 4b, etc. It constitutes no. 6 of *Ziqnê yehudah*, Modena's responsa collection, ed. S. Simonsohn (Jerusalem, 1955–56).

40. His birth date is given in his grammatical work, *Divrê agûr* (Venice, 1604–05), fol. 1a. The manuscript, 479 of the Montefiore collection, Jews' College, contains, *inter alia*,

tion of liturgical chants, which has unfortunately not survived. Only a short fragment, comprising the notation of *ṭeʿamim* for the Psalms, has been preserved, thanks to a copy probably made by Abraham Joseph Solomon Graziano.[41]

Many studies have been devoted to the phenomenon of Jewish professional musicians active mainly in Gentile society during the Italian Renaissance,[42] and it will suffice here to recapitulate the main facts. In the first half of the fifteenth century we find the name of a dancing master, the Jew Musetto, active at Pesaro about 1429, and C. Roth also reports the existence of Jewish music and dancing masters at Parma at about 1466.[43]

Guiseppo Ebreo (second half of the fifteenth century) is the author of a basse danse included in the famous *Trattato dell'arte del ballo*, written by his coreligionist Guglielmo Ebreo, who was, like his predecessor Musetto, a native of Pesaro.[44] At the end of the fifteenth and the beginning of the sixteenth century, a converted Jew of German origin, Giovanni Maria, instrumentalist and composer, exercised his talents in Florence, Venice, and (mainly) in Rome at the court of Pope Leo X.[45] From the end of the sixteenth and the first decades of the seventeenth century there have come down to us the compositions of Solomon Rossi and of his nephew Anselmo Rossi, musicians at the court of Mantua, and the works of Davit (David) Civita, Allegro Porto, and David Sacerdote, who also seem to have been somehow linked with the Gonzagas.[46] The Gonzaga

---

grammatical glosses on the Pentateuch by Finzi. A. J. S. Graziano, the well-known bibliophile and rabbi of Modena, who is also the scribe of this part of the manuscript, when mentioning the name of Finzi in his introductory note, dated 1669–70, uses the usual formula indicating a deceased person.

41. MS. Montefiore, Jews' College, 479, fol. 147b; see Adler, *La Pratique musicale*, vol. I, chap. iii, par. 2.

42. See the literature referred to above, Note 20.

43. For Musetto see A. A. Bernardy, "Les Juifs dans la République de San Marin . . . ," *Revue des Etudes Juives* 48:242 (1904); C. Roth, who knows this reference (see *Renaissance*, p. 359), does not reveal his source concerning Parma.

44. See the references given by G. Reese, *Music in the Renaissance*, 2nd ed. (New York, 1959), p. 176, and M. Bukofzer, "A Polyphonic Basse Dance," in his *Studies in Medieval and Renaissance Music* (New York, 1950), pp. 190–216. Guglielmo is perhaps identical with Ambrogio da Pesaro (Christian name given to him after his conversion), see Reese; see also Roth, *Renaissance*, pp. 276–281.

45. See E. Birnbaum, *Jüdische Musiker*, pp. 8–16; Nettl, *Alte jüdische Spielleute*, pp. 4–5, and mainly Vogelstein and Rieger, *Geschichte der Juden in Rom*, II, 35, 119–120, 433–435, repeated by Roth, *Renaissance*, pp. 281–283, who corrects the common error attributing a Jewish origin to Giacomo di Sansecondo, contemporary of Giovanni Maria.

46. Birnbaum, *Jüdische Musiker*, pp. 8–16; Simonsohn, *Mantua*, vol. II, chap. vii; the name of Sacerdote, which is recorded by Eitner, *Quellenlexikon*, VIII, 382, has been

archives also reveal details of the activities of a certain number of other professional Jewish musicians, known as performers: Abramo dall' Arpa, his nephew Abramino dall' Arpa, and Jacchino (or Isacchino) Massarano flourished between 1542 and 1599; Solomon Rossi's sister, the mother of the above-mentioned Anselmo Rossi, was a singer known under the name of "Madama Europa."[47] Two other singers, Venetian Jewesses, are known from this period: "Bellina hebraea," who was described as a "colonna de la musica" in the middle of the sixteenth century,[48] was followed at the beginning of the seventeenth century by a certain Rachel, whose singing also achieved fame in Venetian society.[49] Some members of the Rossi family also served as musicians to the House of Savoy: one of the sons of Madama Europa, Angelo de Rossi, his two sons Giuseppe and Bonaiuto, as well as another Jewish musician, Benedetto Sessigli, are mentioned at Turin between 1608 and 1657.[50] At the beginning of the seventeenth century there is to be found, in the territory belonging to the House of Este, a Jewish dancing master, Leone Ebreo, at Reggio, and an instrumentalist, David Finzi of Modena.[51]

But by this time, the tolerance—inherent in the humanistic spirit of the Renaissance—which allowed Jews to exercise their talents in a Christian milieu could only be an exception. One of the consequences of the Counter Reformation was gradually to reinforce the segregation of Jews, first in the Papal States, and then in the rest of Italy. It seems the more astonishing that the first manifestations of art music in Italy within the Jewish community, in or around the synagogue, should coincide with this very same period.

---

brought to my attention, thanks to J. Newman, who included in his dissertation (see Note 11) a posthumous paper on Sacerdote by A. Einstein.

47. Birnbaum, *Jüdische Musiker*, pp. 11–13; Simonsohn, *Mantua*, vol. II, chap. vii.

48. Nettl, *Alte jüdische Spielleute*, p. 6; Roth, *Renaissance*, p. 300.

49. Blau, *Leo Modenas Briefe*, p. 153, no. 6; Roth, *Renaissance*, p. 301.

50. S. Foa, "Banchi e banchieri ebrei nel Piemonte," *Rassegna mensile d'Israel*, 31:63 (1955); Roth, *Renaissance*, pp. 286–287; Simonsohn, *Mantua*, vol. II, chap. vii, in particular n. 352.

51. Roth, *Renaissance*, pp. 299–300.

III. Art Music in Italian-Jewish Community Life in the Second Half of the Sixteenth Century and the First Half of the Seventeenth Century

The material in this section will be presented chronologically, so that we shall be able to grasp the connection between the enforcement of segregation and the rise of art music in Jewish life; we shall perceive the gradual growth of this art music praxis from a starting point, probably occurring in the second half of the sixteenth century, expanding through the first decades of the seventeenth century and becoming later a normal part of Italian-Jewish cultural life. Since this later evolution lies beyond the scope of our present study we had to fix, rather arbitrarily, a chronological limit to our investigation: the middle of the seventeenth century, which coincides with the death of Leon Modena (1648), whose name will be found connected with most of the early manifestations of art music in the Italian ghetto.

We shall be concerned with evidence of art music only: that is to say, compositions necessitating recourse to notation for their conception and performance. With the exception of two notated documents, we shall have only literary sources at our disposal. It will thus be necessary to examine each testimony very closely to determine its relevance, and we shall have to exclude from our investigation the many Hebrew sources concerning our period where manifestations of "popular" music are referred to.[52]

Our argument will be based exclusively on sources dealing with synagogal and cognate religious musical manifestations. Art music written or performed by Jews for a non-Jewish audience will not be considered here. Such musical performances certainly played a not-negligible part in the repertoire of Jewish theatrical troupes which can be traced in Italy from the end of the fifteenth century.[53] The only instances known to us before the seventeenth century, of

52. For an outline of these sources see Adler, *La Pratique musicale*, vol. I, in particular chap. i. It will suffice here to point out the widespread usage of adapting well-known melodies, religious or profane, to liturgical or other religious texts. The melody to be employed is often indicated, without recourse to music notation, by giving the name or the opening words of the song at the beginning of the literary text. See Adler, *La Pratique musicale*, vol. I, chap. i, n. 47.

53. See the studies by A. d'Ancona, C. Roth, M. A. Shulvass, J. Ḥ. Schirmann, and especially the paragraph devoted to the theater in S. Simonsohn's monograph on Mantuan Jews, vol. II, chap. vii, all referred to above, Note 20.

such musical events taking place in the framework of the Jewish community, were linked with the carnivalesque feast of Purim.[54] But Purim rejoicings, which probably always included music, dance, and plays, should really be considered as a separate category and should not be taken into account in our examination.

1. *Padua (1555–1565)*

The only source known to us concerned with Italian synagogal art music praxis prior to the seventeenth century is by the Venetian rabbi Ben Ṣiyyôn Ṣarfatî (died 1610).[55] He informs us about vocal art music performed in the synagogue of Padua. His text, dated the twenty-second of the month of Av 5365 (August 5, 1605), figures among the approbations which Leon Modena joined to his responsum in favor of synagogal choral music at Ferrara.[56] Ṣarfatî, in order to support his approval of synagogal song according to the art of music ("mûsîqah"), recalls his own experience while he was a youngster studying at Padua under the famous Meʾîr Katzenellenbogen, called "Maharam Padua" (1482–1565):

> He [Leon Modena] has well judged . . . [to authorize] the singing of prayers according to the order and rhythm of music [*middah we-mišqal ham-mûsîqah*]. I remember that in my youth, while I was assiduous at the doors of the Torah, in the holy community of Padua . . . headed . . . by our master . . . MHR"RM [Meʾîr Padua] . . . we were singing in the synagogue the whole order of the *qeduššah*, and many times, according to his request. For this is certainly preferable to those who strike up vulgar songs which are sung in the streets . . .[57]

Our first question, whether this testimony is related to an art music praxis, seems to deserve an affirmative answer on the following grounds: Modena's responsum, which Ṣarfatî wishes to support, is evidently—as we shall see later—concerned with art music. Ṣarfatî's

54. *Ibid.*; see also Adler, *La Pratique musicale*, vol. I, chap. i, nn. 134–136. The second version of the sixteenth-century Purim comedy by Leone Somme—the oldest extant Hebrew play—explicitly calls for the participation of musicians in its final act; see J. Ḥ. Schirmann, *Ham-maḥazeh ha-ʿivrî ha-riʾšôn* (Jerusalem, 1945–46), pp. 124–125.

55. Nepi–Ghirondi, *Tôledôt gedôlê Yiśraʾel* . . . , p. 55, no. 9; Blau, *Leo Modenas Briefe*, pp. 100–101.

56. See above, Note 39.

57. . . . יפה דן ויפה הורה הלכה למעשה לרנן על הרנה ועל התפלה במדה ומשקל המוסי"קה. זוכרני בימי חרפי בהיותי שוקד על דלתי התורה בק"ק פאדוואה עיר שכלה סופרים . . . בראשם הגאון א"מו כמהר"רם זצ"ל שוררנו בבית הכנסת כל סדר הקדושה ופעמים רבות לבקשתו דודאי לא גרע ועדיף מהני שנתנו עלינו בקולם משירי הדיוטות המרננים בחוצות וברחובות. בכן שירו לה' . . . נאם בן ציון צרפתי ב"ך יברך ישראל למנחם הש'ס"ה.

(*Haš-šîrîm ašer li-Šelomoh*, fol. 6a.)

wording of the preamble which preceded his report of the Paduan episode[58] leaves no place for misunderstanding, on his part, as to the issue at stake. We should also note that our testimony is limited to the singing of the *Qeduššah*, one of the liturgical items most frequently chosen, together with the *Qaddîš*, for synagogal art music settings. In the seventeenth century we shall again find the *Qeduššah* as number seven in Rossi's collection (Venice, 1622–23) and in the manuscript 4 F 71 of the Birnbaum Collection at the Hebrew Union College library at Cincinnati, where this item appears twice. The musical setting of the *Qeduššah* also occupies, as we shall see later, a prominent place in the heated disputes, about 1642–1645, about choral singing in the community of Senigallia.

Yet, our investigation as to whether this testimony may be definitely considered as evidence of art music praxis is linked somewhat to the question of dating this episode, which we shall now have to elucidate. We know that the episode occurred during the youth of Ṣarfatî. Although we do not know the date of his birth, it might be fixed approximately at about 1540–1550. He is known to have acceded to the superior position as first of the rabbinate of Venice in 1601 and he was only fourth of this rabbinate in 1589. If we suppose that at the time of this rather subordinate position he had not passed the age of fifty, the lower limit for his birth date would be the year 1539. The upper limit of his birth date, about 1550, is given by the fact that he was a disciple of Meʾîr Padua, one of the greatest rabbinic authorities of his time, who died at the age of eighty-three in 1565. It is most improbable that Meʾîr Padua was engaged in elementary schooling for children in his late sixties and seventies. It thus seems that we may situate the episode reported by Ṣarfatî in approximately 1555–1565. Considering that Ṣarfatî wrote down what he recalled from his Paduan experience only forty to fifty years later in 1605, we should exercise caution and conclude with a query in our investigation, as to whether this music praxis at the Paduan synagogue in 1555–1565 could be unequivocally characterized as art music.

2. *Ferrara (about 1605)*

The two known sources related to art music in the Jewish community of Ferrara about 1605 are both from the pen of Leon Modena

58. יפה . . . הורה . . . לרנן על הרנה ועל התפלה במדה ומשקל המוסיק"ה . . .

(1571–1648).[59] This prolific and many-sided author, who will be found associated with most of the Italian Jewish manifestations of art music of his time, was a musician himself.[60] During the years 1604 to about 1606–07 Leon Modena resided at Ferrara,[61] where he was active as a preacher and, in particular, as a tutor in the house of a distinguished Ferrarese Jew, Joseph Zalman Diena.[62] Modena's responsum on choral chant at the synagogue of Ferrara dates from this period. It will here suffice to dwell only on those elements of this well-known responsum which are of immediate relevance to our argument.[63] Thus we shall be mainly interested in the account of the background to the quarrel stirred up by the introduction of art music in the synagogue of Ferrara. Details of this event have come down to us from two sources: (A) the "question" part of Leon Modena's responsum; (B) a letter, recently discovered by S. Simonsohn,[64] by Leon Modena to Judah Saltaro da Fano.[65]

A

שאלה. יש אתנו יודע עד מה בחכמת השיר ר"ל המוסי"קה ששה או שמנה בני דעת מבני קהלנו י"צו אשר בחגים ובמועדים ישאו קולם וירונו בבית הכנסת שיר ושבחה הלל וזמרה אין כאלהינו עלינו לשבח יגדל ואדון עולם וכיוצא לכבוד ה' בסדר ויחס ערך הקולות בחכמה הנזכרת. ויקם אדם לגרשם . . . ואומר כי לא נכון לעשות כן כי אם לשוש אסור והמזמור אסור והלולים כאשר המה בחכמת הזמר האמור אסורים משחרב בית המקדש משום אל תשמח ישראל אל גיל כעמים . . .[66]

B

. . . אחרי בואי פה פיראר‍ה נתגלגלו הדברים להציב מעט חכמת המוסיקא על מכונה. כי נתעוררו הישנים ונתאוו חדשים. ועשינו לנו בית ועד ושכרנו לנו מלמד אשר בכל יום

59. See his autobiography, *Sepher Chaje Jehuda . . . edidit . . . A. Kahana* (Kiev, 1911); Blau, *Leo Modenas Briefe . . .*; the collection of his poems, *The Divan of Leo de Modena*, ed. S. Bernstein (Philadelphia, 1932), and the studies referred to by A. Milano, *Bibliotheca historica italo-judaica* (Florence, 1954), pp. 77, 133–134, 143, 146–148, 158, to which should be added N. S. Libowitz, *Leon Modena . . .*, 2nd ed. (New York, 1901).

60. For an outline of the principal facts concerning Leon Modena's relationship to music, see Adler, *La Pratique musicale*, vol. I, chap. iv, paragraph 2.

61. Blau, *Leo Modenas Briefe*, p. 67, no. 1; p. 77.

62. *Ibid.* and Bernstein, *Divan*, nos. 89 (p. 132), 212–213 (pp. 218–220).

63. For the bibliographical references see above, Note 39; for a more detailed analysis of this source see Adler, *La Pratique musicale*, vol. I, chap. iv.

64. See his edition of Leon Modena's responsa, *Ziqnê yehûdah* (Jerusalem, 1955–56), p. xxvi of the introduction.

65. The Venetian rabbi, author of the lost *Šir Ṣiyyôn* mentioned above (see the paragraph referred to in Note 39).

66. *Haš-šîrîm ašer li-Šelomoh*, fol. 4b.

בא ללמד ונמצא למד . . . ואף היה מכוין דעתו עמי וזולתי להדריך מעשינו לש"ש להודות לה' בשיר בשבתות וי"ט. ותהי רשות למלאכתנו ליל שבת נחמו זה מקרוב עבר אשר בב"ה הגדולה בקהל רבה נזמרה. אמרנו יגדל ואדון עולם והמון חוגג וכל הקהל שמחו מזה. ולא ידעתי למה קם נגדנו החכם ר' משה קואימבראן, ובחוצות וברחובות יתן קולו, לומר כי חטאנו לה' אלהנו, ואיך אפשר כי בעלי התורה אשר עליהם המשא להדריך אחרי' ולמיגדר מלתא ליעבדו איסורא כי האי בפרסום וגלוי? כי איך נשיר את שיר ה' על אדמת נכר, מקרא לא הוא? ובדברי רז"ל כתוב איסור דבר זה אחר החרבן. ואלה הדברים הולך ואומר עד כי . . . כמה מן ההדיוטות הדוברים עלינו עתק, ומאמינים כי עברנו תורות, חלפנו חוק. להוציא מדברי השומעים כלנו בהשואה יחד הסכמנו להביא דעת החכמים משם . . .[67]

The "question" in Text A is anonymous and there is no hint in its formulation that Leon Modena was personally involved in the quarrel:

> We have among us some connoisseurs of the science of chant, that is to say of music, six or eight persons of knowledge from our community . . . who raise their voice at the time of feasts and they sing at the synagogue songs of praise . . . *ên keʾlohenû*, *ᶜalênû le-šabbeaḥ*, *yigdal* and *adôn ᶜôlam* and similar [songs] in honor of God, according to the order and the proportion of the voices[68] of the mentioned art. And a man stood up to chase them away . . . saying that it is not right to do so, because it is forbidden to rejoice and . . . the hymns and praises . . . according to the mentioned science of chant are forbidden since the Temple was destroyed . . .

In spite of its anonymous presentation this question is probablv from Leon Modena's own quill. He really had no better means of defending the praxis he approved than by adopting this responsorial device of which the Italian rabbinic world of his time was particularly fond. The current usage of submitting a responsum to other authorities in the hope of approval (*haskamôt*) provided the author with the opportunity of availing himself of a solid halakhic backing. Leon Modena's authorship of the "question" becomes more evident in the light of Text B (Leon Modena's letter to Judah Saltaro da Fano), which tells us the same story as Text A, with some interesting complementary details, and which reveals to what degree Leon Modena, one of those valiant Ferrarese choristers, was personally involved in the quarrel.

67. Quoted after Simonsohn, *Ziqnê yehûdah*, p. xxvi of the introduction.

68. The Hebrew term *seder* (translation of the Latin *ordo*) is used by Leon Modena and in the Florence Hebrew manuscript Magl. III, 70, fol. 1a (a musical treatise copied in the sixteenth-century), in the sense of the *disposition* of parts, sung according to the rules of musical art; for the Hebrew terms *yaḥas* and *ᶜerek* in musical theory see Ḥ. Avenary, "Mun neḥê ham-mûsîqah . . . ," *Lešonenû* 13:144 (1944–45).

The preamble of Text B includes the important information that after Leon Modena settled in Ferrara (in 1604) a Jewish musical association was founded there, probably on his initiative. The old and new amateurs of this art came together with the purpose of cultivating the "science of music": "and we provided for ourselves a place of meeting and we engaged a master who came every day to teach . . . and to [practice] . . ."[69]

Of particular relevance for our study, as we shall see, is the following passage of this text. Leon Modena indicates that he himself, the music master, and the other members of the group intended "to guide our praxis towards a sacred objective [*le-šem šamayim*]." Thus on the occasion of *šabbat naḥamû* they gave a musical performance of the *piyyuṭîm* "Yigdal" and "Adon ᶜôlam" to the satisfaction of the whole community. Text B also reveals the name of the adversary of synagogal art music, Moses Coïmbran, who is unnamed in Text A ("and a man stood up . . .").

From the "answer" part of Modena's responsum it will here suffice to give a brief résumé disregarding the elaborate casuistic sections which are usually *de rigueur* in this kind of literature. Leon Modena states his main point—the admissibility of all music linked to a religious function—with vigor: "And I cannot see who could doubt . . . that praising God with chant at the days of special Sabbaths[70] and the feasts would be a good action as well as rejoicing the bridegroom and the bride, since every holy Sabbath is a bride for us which we have to embellish . . ."[71]

Most of the different categories and shades of appreciation discussed by the author are already well known from the Talmudic and rabbinic literature.[72] Only one of these categories—the admissibility of musical praxis for the purposes of study—is an original supplement by Modena: ". . . for if [music] is legitimate for a religious prescription how shall they exercise without studying it first? And even after having learned it . . . they have to perfect themselves more and fix in their memory what they know already, since [otherwise] all will be forgotten in the following days . . ."[73] Another

69. This is probably what Leon Modena meant by *baʾ le-lammed we-nimṣaʾ lamed.* It should be noted here that a quarter of a century later we shall find Leon Modena heading a similar musical association, the Venetian Accademia di Musica, where he will assume the position of *maestro di capella* (see paragraph 4 of this chapter).

70. *Šabbatôt rešûmîm*: e.g., the four Sabbaths preceding Passover or *Šabbat naḥamû.*

71. *Haš-šîrîm ašer li-Šelomoh*, fols. 5a–b.

72. See Adler, *La Pratique musicale*, vol. I, chap. i, par. 1 and chap. iv, par. 2.

73. *Haš-šîrîm ašer li-Šelomoh*, fol. 5b.

interesting point in this responsum is the description of the Ashkenazic *mešorerîm*[74] praxis which Modena uses as a supplementary argument in defense of synagogal art music: "... and beside him [the cantor] stand assistants[75] ... [who join his singing] without order,[76] *a aria* [monodic chant],[77] according to the usual custom of the Ashkenazic communities, and sometimes there would result encounters in [harmonic] proportion ..."[78] And Modena logically concludes that art music should be at least as permissible as this *mešorerîm* praxis.

The responsum is followed by the endorsements of five rabbis: Ben-Ṣiyyôn Ṣarfatî, dated August 5, 1605,[79] [Judah] Lêb Saraval,[80] Baruch Ben Samuel,[81] ᶜEzrā da Fano,[82] and Judah ben Moses [Saltaro] da Fano.[83]

Both from the "question" and "answer" of the responsum, and in particular from Modena's letter to Judah Saltaro da Fano (Text B) we may conclude, then, that art music, although practiced before by Ferrarese Jews outside the synagogue, was introduced about 1605 as a new praxis without precedent in the synagogue of Ferrara. This is made particularly clear by the wording of Text B, in which Leon Modena tells us that after his coming to Ferrara he found some old and new amateurs who were anxious to cultivate music (נתעוררו הישנים ונתאוו חדשים). They provided a place of meeting, they engaged a master, and then they had the idea of guiding their praxis toward a sacred objective (ואף היה מכוין דעתו עמי וזולתי להדריך מעשינו לש״ש). The novelty obviously consisted in the transfer of their art music praxis to the synagogue, for if there had been a precedent in the Ferrarese synagogue, the pro-music party to the dispute would

74. See above, the passage referred to in Note 6.
75. Leon Modena uses the Talmudic term *mesayᶜîm*.
76. See above, Note 68.
77. Modena uses the Italian term, in Hebrew characters.
78. ... יעמדו אצלו מסייעים אשר חננם ה׳ קול ערב ובלי סדר רק א״ה ארי״אה כנהוג כל היום בין קהלות האשכנזים יזמרו עמו ויקרה שיתיחסו ויערכו לו ... (*Haš-šîrîm ašer li-Šelomoh*, fol. 5b).
79. Nepi–Ghirondi, *Tôledôt gedôlê Yiśraʾel ...*, p. 55, no. 9; Blau, *Leo Modenas Briefe*, pp. 100–101.
80. Venetian rabbi, d. 1617, see Nepi–Ghirondi, *Tôledôt gedôlê Yiśraʾel*, pp. 218–220, no. 2; Blau, *Leo Modenas Briefe*, pp. 114–116.
81. Venetian rabbi, see Nepi–Ghirondi, *Tôledôt gedôlê Yiśraʾel*, p. 57, no. 11; Blau, *Leo Modenas Briefe*, p. 132.
82. Mantuan rabbi who seems to have resided at this period in Venice; see Nepi–Ghirondi, *Tôledôt gedôlê Yiśraʾel*, p. 289, no. 5; Blau, *Leo Modenas Briefe*, pp. 132, 134.
83. Venetian rabbi, *ca.* 1550–1629, whose text has been analyzed above; see the passage referred to in Note 39. He was the addressee of Leon Modena's letter quoted at the beginning of this paragraph.

surely not have failed to use the classic argument in rabbinic legislation of the established "custom."

We may now stress the significance of the date (about 1605) on which this introduction of art music in the Ferrarese synagogue took place: it was only a few years after the annexation of Ferrara to the Papal States (1597), which caused an immediate deterioration in the situation of its Jewish residents.

Furthermore, we may point out that this musical occurrence at Ferrara was not only without relation to Solomon Rossi but that it no doubt preceded the introduction of art music in the Mantuan synagogue. Leon Modena, who recalls the *mešôrerîm* praxis in order to support his argument in favor of synagogal art music, would certainly have mentioned a Mantuan precedent if he had known about it. It is, of course, quite improbable that Leon Modena, a cantor and musician himself, could have been ignorant of the nature of musical praxis in the Mantuan community, situated at a distance of less than a hundred kilometers from his Ferrarese residence. But even on this most improbable supposition, the Mantuan rabbi ᶜEzrā da Fano would surely have mentioned this fact in his approval.

3. *Mantua (after 1605–circa 1628)*

Nowhere else has the transfer of Jewish musicianship from the outer world to the service of the synagogue left a more remarkable imprint than in Mantua. In the preceding chapter we referred briefly to the well-known phenomenon of Jewish musicianship at the court of the Gonzagas. The most remarkable of these musicians, Solomon Rossi,[84] has left an outstanding contribution to synagogal art music in his *Haš-šîrîm ašer li-Šelomoh*, printed in Venice, 1622–23.[85] Like

84. For the outline of the available biographical data concerning Rossi, see Adler, *La Pratique musicale*, chap. iv; to the literature referred to there (see in particular notes 221–224) should be added Simonsohn, *Mantua*, vol. II, chap. vii, and Newman, "The Madrigals of Salamon de' Rossi," chap. ii. In spite of the many important studies devoted to Rossi, very little is known about his life. His first publication is dated 1589 and his last, 1628, which has generally been considered as the year of his disappearance. Nevertheless, in a Hebrew source of the winter of 1645, which we shall analyze later on in this chapter, Rossi still seems to be presumed alive. The *terminus ad quem* for his death is 1648, the year in which Leon Modena died: in his collection of poems, Modena mentions Rossi and employs the customary formula designating a deceased person; see Bernstein, *Divan*, p. 82, no. 37.

85. For a detailed bibliographic description of the only complete copy kept at the Music Department of the Bibliothèque Nationale, see I. Adler, *Les Incunables hébraïques de la Bibliothèque Nationale* (Paris, 1962), Appendix B, pp. 47–49. The attribution to this pub-

his older fellow citizen of Mantua, Leone de Sommi, who directed a dramatic troupe whose Jewish members most probably also participated in plays performed before a Jewish public, Rossi seems to have headed a group of Jewish musicians who provided the music on certain religious occasions. The fact that Rossi directed a company of musicians in the service of the court of Mantua appears from a letter written by the prince of Mirandola, Alessandro I, on September 19, 1612, to Annibale Chieppio, counselor of the duke of Mantua: he asks him to send "the Jew Solomon and his company" to Mirandola for a concert in honor of his father-in-law, the duke of Modena. E. Birnbaum,[86] followed by C. Roth,[87] puts forward the hypothesis that this company was composed of Rossi's coreligionists, or at least that it included some Jews. We may add a second source confirming this hypothesis. Netanʾel Trabotto, in a responsum of the year 1645, testifies to have listened to the performance of liturgical chants by "De Rossi and his company" (החכם מן האדומים וסיעתו).[88] But our knowledge of synagogal art music in Mantua at this period is almost entirely based on the *Haš-šîrîm ašer li-Šelomoh*, and mainly its prefatory texts. Reprinted several times, these texts[89] have been studied by numerous scholars,[90] and we shall thus be justified in limiting ourselves here chiefly to one question of particular importance for our study: at what date were Rossi's compositions introduced to the Mantuan synagogue?

Two passages, in the prefatory parts of *Haš-šîrîm ašer li-Šelomoh*, testify that the date of publication (1622–23; rabbinical privilege, fol. 6b, dated Ḥešwan 5583 [September–October 1622]) does not represent a starting point of art music praxis in the synagogue of Mantua. On the contrary, it appears that this publication has to

---

lication, by S. Naumberg (followed by Riemann, P. Nettl, A. Sendrey, and others) of the erroneous date 1620, instead of 1622–23, has been discussed in my *Pratique musicale*, vol. I, chap. iv, where I have also given a brief analysis of Rossi's synagogal compositions.

86. *Jüdische Musiker*, pp. 26–27.

87. *Renaissance*, p. 289.

88. MS. 151, no. 147, of the Kaufmann collection at Budapest, ed. D. Kaufmann in "Nathanael Trabot über die Behandlung der Gebete in der Composition . . . ," *MGWJ*, N.S., 3:350–357 (1895). See below, the section dealing with Senigallia.

89. Fol. 2a: Rossi's dedicatory epistle to Moses Sullam; fol. 2b: two anonymous poems (I. Davidson, *Thesaurus*, כ 396 and ש 2220); fols. 3a–b: preface by Leon Modena; fol. 4a: anonymous poem (attributed to Leon Modena by Davidson, *Thesaurus*, ש 1352); fols. 4b–6b: Leon Modena's responsum, followed by five rabbinic approvals, which we have analyzed above in the section devoted to Ferrara; fol. 6b: rabbinical privilege.

90. See Adler, *La Pratique musicale*, vol. I, chap. ii, n. 166; chap. iv, n. 243.

be considered as a result of an evolution of this praxis, introduced gradually over a certain period of time which we shall try to determine. In his dedicatory epistle to his benefactor Moses Sullam, Rossi says:

...מאז פתח לי אזן ה'... ויחנני להבין ולהורו' בחכמת המוסי"קה...
השתעשעה נפשי... להודות לרוכב בערבות בקול רנה ותודה... ויהי ה' למשען
לי ויתן בפי זמירות חדשות אשר עשיתי בסד"ר... לזמני ששון ולמועדים טובים...
תמיד... הוספתי השתדלות להגדיל מזמורי דוד מלך ישראל ולהאדירם עד אשר
שמתי חק גבול להרבה מהם בדרכי המוסיקה... (*fol. 2a*)

Since God opened my ear . . . and has given me the grace to understand and to teach the science of music[91] . . . my soul rejoiced . . . to thank [God] . . . with song and praise . . . and God was a support to me and he put into my mouth new songs which I have done according to the order[92] . . . for the times of joy and the feasts . . . and always . . . I have multiplied my efforts to make sublime the Psalms of David . . . until I had set . . . many of them to music . . .

The second text indicating that Rossi's compositions had already gradually been introduced to the synagogue is found in Leon Modena's preface. After having spoken of Rossi's secular compositions, he adds:

...פעל ועשה להוסיף מחול על הקדש... ויום יום לעומת מחברתו היה מביא
איזה מזמור לדוד או ממכשירי תפלה או שבחה הלל וזמרת יה עד כי משכיל לאסף קבץ
כמה מהם והיו לאחדים בידו וכאשר שוררו אנשי' אותם והתענגו על רוב טובם...
חזקו עליו דברי שרידי עם ובראשם הנדיב... כמ"ה משה סלם... יואל לתתם אל
הדפוס... גם אנכי מאז נמניתי במספר אוהביו הפצרתי בו עד מאד...
והסכים לשלם נדרו להדפיס...[93]

. . . and he took from the secular to add it to the sacred . . . and day by day he entered into his collection some psalm of David or . . . prayers or . . . [songs of praise] until he had gathered together several of them . . . and when people sang them and took pleasure in these delights he let himself [be persuaded] by the notables . . . and he agreed to let them be printed . . . I also, since I count myself among the number of his friends, I have much pressed him . . . and he has consented to acquit himself of his promise to print . . .

It is therefore certain that the musical performance of certain prayers or religious chants in Mantua was already a well established custom in 1622. Nevertheless, it does not seem that the beginning of Rossi's text quoted above can be taken literally. According to this it

91. No other source testifying to Rossi's activity as a teacher is known to us.
92. That is to say: according to the rules of the art of music; see above, Note 68.
93. *Haš-šîrîm ašer li-Šelomoh*, fols. 3a–b.

would appear that his first religious compositions were written at about the time of his debut as a composer, in about 1589. But in our discussion above of Modena's responsum concerning the choral chant in the synagogue of Ferrara about 1605, it became clear that art music had not yet made its appearance in the Mantuan synagogue at this date. Let us attempt to reach a conclusion from these data: introduced after 1605 but already well established in 1622, art music praxis in the Mantuan synagogue may have begun about 1613–1614; that it is to say, only a short time after the ghetto of Mantua had been instituted (1610–1612).[94] To what extent such a chronological coincidence might be considered as an illustration of cause and effect will be discussed in our conclusions. This praxis does not seem to have lasted much beyond 1622–23. With the extinction of the Italian branch of the Gonzaga family in 1627 a bitter struggle for the succession began, which resulted in the seizure of Mantua by the Austrians in 1630. Although the expulsion of the Jews of Mantua, as a result of this conquest, was only temporary, it cut short the leading role played by the Jewish community of Mantua in the field of music.

Among the other points of interest supplied by this source we should mention that Solomon Rossi seems to have been the only important Jewish composer known to Leon Modena,[95] who, by the way, stresses once more the importance of the teaching of music: "And you shall teach the art of music to your sons . . . and I am confident that from the day this work sees the light, students [of this art] will multiply in Israel . . ."[96] Furthermore, it is obvious from Leon Modena's preface that opposition to synagogal art music was to be feared: Modena explains his care to add to the publication of *Haš-šîrîm ašer li-Šelomoh* his Ferrarese responsum, in the event that "there would be found . . . any whatsoever among the bigots who repulse whatever is new and intelligent . . ."[97]

94. Decree of 1610, enforced in 1612. See V. Colorni, *Gli ebrei nel sistema del diritto comune fino alla prima emanzipazione* (Milan, 1956), p. 58, n. 363; Simonsohn, *Mantua*, I, 29–33.

95. . . . נשגב שלמה לבדו בימינו בחכמה זו ויחכם מכל האדם לא לבד מאומתנו . . . . .
(*Haš-šîrîm ašer li-Šelomoh*, fol. 3a).

96. . . . ולמדתם אותם את בניכם להבין בחכמ' הנגון . . . כי כן בטחתי מיום צאת חבור זה לאורה ירבו לומדיה בישראל . . . .
(*Haš-šîrîm ašer li-Šelomoh*, fol. 3b).

97. . . . אם . . . ימצא . . . איזה אחד מן המתחסדי' המרחיקי' כל חדש וכל בינה אשר אין להם חלק בה יחפוץ לאסור אסר דבר זה מדגרים ולא דייק, ראיתי להעלות פה על ספר אשר כתבתי בתשובת שאלה זה י"ח שני' בהיותי מרביץ תורה בק"ק פירא"רה . . . בנדון זה . . .
(*Haš-šîrîm ašer li-Šelomoh*, fol. 3b).

We should also note the information concerning the circumstances which gave rise to an art music praxis. We have already noticed in the passages quoted above from Leon Modena's responsum of 1605, that those musical performances took place only on special occasions, such as feasts and "special Sabbaths." Thus there was no question of regular musical performance during the service on every Saturday, or, a fortiori, during the daily services. We can come to the same conclusion as regards Mantua. Solomon Rossi, in the citation from his dedicatory epistle, mentions "the times of rejoicing and the festivals" (*li-zemanê śaśôn û-le-môᶜadîm*). By "times of rejoicing" one should understand the rejoicings connected with a religious ceremony such as a wedding. Besides, this is what Leon Modena points out in his preface, where he expressly speaks of this type of rejoicing.[98] These statements in the prefatory texts of *Haš-širîm ašer li-Šelomoh* are the more valuable because most of the liturgical texts of this collection do not in themselves disclose the ceremonies for which they are intended: most of the texts (twenty out of thirty-three) are, as Rossi emphasizes, psalms, of which some belong to the common body of the daily, Sabbath, and festival liturgies, and could have been sung on other occasions as well. Prayers such as *Yigdal*, *Adôn ᶜôlam*, *Ên keʾlohenû*, *Barekû*, *Haškivenû* and the *Qaddîš* are likewise common to the daily liturgy and to that of Sabbaths and feasts. It is therefore thanks only to the information given in the prefatory texts that we can know that the musical performance of these texts was reserved for special occasions. It is important to stress this point because certain historians speak of the institution of a "regular choir" at the synagogue in the time of Rossi, having in mind a musical organization similar to that introduced in the nineteenth century by the Reform movement, where the choirs regularly took part in all the Sabbath services.

4. *Venice (circa 1628–circa 1639)*

We have seen above (section II) that art music activity of Venetian Jews is attested to from the first half of the fifteenth century. It is also probable that the theatrical performances—mainly linked to

98. And later on:
וישראלים ירונו במועדים ובחדושים של מצוה . . . תנו כבוד לה' לפאר מקום מקדש מעט ושמחות מצוה בהם בזמנים זמניהם . . .
(*Haš-širîm ašer li-Šelomoh*, fols. 3a–b.) This type is represented in Rossi's collection by no. [33]: למי אחפוץ לעשות יקר.

the feast of Purim—in Venetian Jewish circles from the first half of the sixteenth century[99] presented an occasion for the use of art music. But from the second quarter of the seventeenth century we also have testimonies to performances of art music in the synagogue, other than those linked to the feast of Purim. These manifestations are connected with the well known Venetian Jewish musical "academy," about the activities of which we have information from two sources.

The first is an account by Leon Modena's disciple, Samuel Naḥmias (1612–1683), a native of Salonica, who converted to Christianity in 1649, taking the name of Giulio Morosini.[100] In the second part of his דרך אמונה—*Via della fede* . . . (Rome, 1683), chapter forty-six is devoted to a description of the feast of Śimḥat Tôrah. Morosini mentions there, *inter alia*, his recollection of a particularly brilliant celebration of this feast, "about 1628," in Venice:

Io mi ricordo bene di quello, che a' tempi miei successe in Venetia del 1628 in circa, se non erro, quando da Mantova per causa della guerra fuggiti gli Ebrei, se ne vennero in Venetia. E coll'occasione che fioriva la città di Mantova in molti sorti di studii, anche gli Ebrei havevano applicato alla musica e agl'istromenti. Arrivati questi in Venetia si formo nel Ghetto, che ivi stà, un'Accademia di musica, nella quale per ordinario si cantova due volte per settimana di sera e vi si congregavano solamente alcuni principali e ricchi di quel Ghetto che la sostentavano, tra i quali io pure mi trovavo: e'l mio maestro Rabbi Leon da Modena era maestro di capella. In quell'-anno essendo stati eletti per sposi . . . [*ḥatan tôrah*, *ḥatan berešît*] due persone ricche e splendide, delli quali uno era della medesima Accademia, fecero nella Scuola Spagnuola (ricchissimamente apparata . . .) fare due cori ad usanza nostra per li musici, e le due sere cioè nell'ottava della festa [*šemînî ᶜaṣeret*] . . . e [Śimḥat Tôrah] . . . si canto in musica figurata in lingua ebraica parte della [*ᶜarvît*] . . . e diversi salmi, e la [*minḥah*] . . . dell'ultimo giorno con musica solenne che duro alcune hore della notte, dove vi concorse molta nobiltà di signori, e di Dame con grand'applauso . . . Tra gl'istromenti fù portato in Sinagoga anche l'Organo, il qual pero non fù permesso da i Rabbini, che si sonasse per essere instromento che per ordinario si suona nelle nostre chiese. Ma' che? Tutto questo fù un fuoco di paglia, duro poco l'Accademia . . . (page 793).

99. See Roth, *Venice*, pp. 198–202, and his "L'accademia musicale del ghetto veneziano," pp. 152–162, esp. pp. 155–156. The particular inclination of seventeenth-century Venetian Jewry for the theater, going as far as the establishing of a regular Jewish theater, is well known through the vigorous opposition of the Venetian rabbi Samuel Aboab (1610–1694) to this praxis, see no. 4 of his responsa collection *Devar Šemû᾽el*, Venice, 1701–1702, fol. 2a.

100. See on G. Morosini and his דרך אמונה—*Via della fede*, D. Simonsen, *Giulio Morosinis Mitteilungen über seinen Lehrer Leon da Modena und seine jüdischen Zeitgenossen*, in *Festschrift . . . A. Berliner* . . . (Frankfurt am Main, 1903), pp. 337–344, and the passage concerning Leon Modena and music, pp. 342–343.

It is in this source that we find the first mention of the existence of an "accademia di musica" in the ghetto of Venice. Let us briefly summarize the facts given in this testimony, which has already often been studied.[101] Morosini connects the foundation of this "accademia" with the influx into Venice of Jewish musicians from Mantua, as war fugitives. The information given by Morosini on the brief duration of this experiment, which was only a "flash in the pan," is repeated in our second source. From among the interesting statements made by Morosini we may point out that the "accademia" held two musical sessions or rehearsals each week, that Leon Modena figured as "maestro di capella," and above all, that the "accademia" had at its disposal an extensive Hebrew musical repertoire of "musica figurata," including compositions for double choirs and calling for instrumental accompaniment, capable of lasting "several hours." For a detailed analysis of Morosini's text we refer the reader to the study by E. Werner (see Note 101), who discovered in the Birnbaum collection of the Hebrew Union College of Cincinnati a manuscript (MS. 4 F. 71) which contains the upper part for the second choir from a collection of music for double choirs, which could have served, according to Werner's hypothesis, for the *Śimḥaṭ Tôrah* festivities described by Morosini. We have already mentioned above the conjectural conclusion reached by Professor Werner concerning the author of the manuscript. In his first article, published in 1944,[102] he disposes of the possibility that Solomon Rossi was the author: "It is very improbable that Salamone Rossi was the composer; certainly we would have heard about it." Then he considers, very prudently, the possibility of attributing the authorship to Leon Modena. But in another article, published in 1957,[103] this prudent attribution has become a certitude: "The practice of having double choirs, then popular in Venice, was introduced to the ghetto by Rabbi da Modena, and he himself composed a series of such choral pieces in the style of the Gabrielis." The footnote relating to this passage refers us to the 1944 article. We do not know whether or not Professor Werner has at his disposal other information relevant to this question. In the absence of any source proving the contrary,

101. Especially by D. Simonsen, in 1903 (see the preceding note), Roth, "L'accademia musicale . . . ," and Werner, "Manuscripts . . . in the Birnbaum collection," pp. 397–428, who gives an English translation of this passage.

102. In *Hebrew Union College Annual* 18:397–428 (1948).

103. In *New Oxford History of Music*, I, 313–335.

we find this attribution to Leon Modena doubtful. Among the sources relating to Leon Modena's musical activity, we have found nothing to suggest that he had ever attempted musical composition, and yet no other Jewish personality of the seventeenth century in Italy has left us so many biographical details as has Leon Modena.[104] Thus, to take up the argument put forward by Professor Werner to dipose of the attribution to Solomon Rossi, if Leon Modena had been the author of a musical work of such importance, "we would have heard about it."

The second source, which contains complementary details on the "accademia di musica" of which Morosini speaks, was disclosed by Cecil Roth, in 1927–28, in the article quoted above, Note 99. This is a letter by Leon Modena, preserved in MS. Or. 5395 of the British Museum, one of the two collections of letters and various writings by Leon Modena in the possession of that library, of which most of the Hebrew texts were published by L. Blau in 1905. In this letter, dated the second of August 1639, Leon Modena answers a correspondent who suggests to him a cooperation between the latter's musical association, of recent date, and the older one of Leon Modena. A detailed analysis of this letter is found in Roth's article, where among other matters he emphasizes the importance of this document in transmitting the name of this association, but it seems to us that he has not interpreted the passage relating to this question with sufficient precision:

> Hebbe una volta il nostro Congresso musicale nome giustam. te d'accademia perche v'erano alcuni non indegni d'esser connumerati tra musici e di voci e di mano. Era impresa che con molti d'istrumenti da suono appel.i col motto *Dum recordaremur Sion* [. . .] et il nome era de gli impediti tutto per alluder all'infelice stato della captività nostra che n'impedisce ogni atto virtuoso la compitezza. Ma agguintasi lo sciagura che l'anno della peste perdemmo i migliori suggetti che v'erano, nostra compagnia rimase si sola, riservando il nome infatti, piochè non piu accademia, allhora per communi impedimenti rade volte siamo insieme e imperfettamento vien esercitata [. . .]

Then at the foot of the letter, the date: "2 Ag.to 39" and the signature "La Compag.a dei Musici del Ghetto de Ven.a."[105] According to Roth the quotation from Psalm 137, "Dum recordaremur Sion,"

104. See Adler, *La Pratique musicale*, vol. I, chap. iv, paragraph 2.

105. Quoted from Roth, "L'accademia musicale," pp. 160–161. Roth's reading of the name of the company, "impediti," as "imperiti" is erroneous.

which the editor of this text transcribes into Hebrew, *be-zokrenû et Ṣiyyôn*, represents the Hebrew name of this association, which he compares to the Hebrew names of Jewish confraternities of this period, such as the *ḥevrat ḥesed we-emet* or the *šômrîm lab-boqer*. In fact, we have here the *motto* of this association, which was called at an earlier stage Accademia degli Impediti and whose Hebrew name, if it had one at all, has not come down to us. It was in fact the custom of these "academies"—the type of association known as "academy" was widespread in Italy at that period—[106] to have a motto and an emblem. Thus, for example, one finds at Ancona, in 1669, an Accademia degli Anelanti, having as its emblem a figure representing a galloping horse, and as motto "Sine calcaribus metam."[107] In Florence one finds a Jewish academy of the same name in 1670, with a tortoise climbing a mountain as its device, and as motto "Im îgaᶜ aggîaᶜ" ("If I strive, I shall arrive"). The Hebrew name of this association has reached us: *Ḥavûrat haš-šoᵓafîm.*[108] Also it is necessary to state—C. Roth is not very clear on this subject—that the two names, *Accademia degli Impediti* and *Compagnia dei musici del Ghetto di Venezia*, were not names that existed simultaneously, but that they corresponded to two different stages in the life of this association, as appears clear from the text. The first applies to the stage before the plague (1630), when the association was still fully active and worthy of carrying the appellation of "Accademia."[109] The second applies to the period after the plague, when the association, having lost its best members, came together only on rare occasions and "exercised imperfectly"; it then abandoned the name of Accademia for that, less ambitious, of Compagnia.

Leon Modena, after having taken into account the difficulties suffered by the members of his "company" which caused them to meet only rarely, nevertheless accepted the suggestion of collaboration. This was to consist chiefly, it seems, in the exchange of musical works. While rejoicing in the prospect of this collaboration—"This would give a fullness of harmony to our lukewarmness; we would thus willingly benefit from the effects of your courtesy; we would reveal the ripe fruits produced in your new academy . . ."—he gives his

106. See M. Maylender's five-volume account, *Storia delle accademie d'Italia* . . . (Bologna, 1926–1930).

107. *Ibid.*, I, 178.

108. See Mortara, *Ḳobeẓ ᶜal Yad*, I, 129.

109. Modest appellations such as "degli impediti" were then current and should not surprise us. Similar names can be found in Maylender, *Storia* . . . , III, 167–177.

correspondent honest warning: "... we cannot offer you so much ourselves, for we have no efflorescence of composers ..."

C. Roth concludes from this letter, rightly, it seems, that it presents the final stage of this enterprise. This is no doubt true as far as the active part that Leon Modena could take in this kind of activity is concerned. In 1639 he had already reached the age of sixty-eight. Besides, he was in a precarious financial position during the years 1639–1640, and it is undoubtedly also to this that he alludes when speaking of the "difficulties" reducing the activity of his "company."[110] In a Hebrew letter of the same year he complains of the expensiveness of living: "Everything costs twice as much as before the plague." In the same letter, speaking of his sixty-eight years, he describes himself as "saturated with sorrow and with despair, and my tongue no longer [pronounces] words of poetry and song."[111] During the few years that remained to him, even if he did still happen to write some poems and another responsum relating to music, his true participation in Jewish musical life in Italy seems to have reached its end. But this last testimony of the Venetian musical association, in 1639, is not the swan song of art music praxis in a Jewish context in Italy. We have to wait twenty-two years for evidence of the next manifestation of it in Venice,[112] yet only three years later, we can perceive the lively traces of a young and impulsive generation of musicians of the synagogue, who, without being able to pretend to the distinction of their illustrious forebears, nevertheless assured its continuity.

5. *Senigallia* (*circa 1642–1652* [*?*])

A group of sources has come down to us from the middle of the seventeenth century relating to the art music praxis of the Jewish community of Senigallia, near Ancona. These sources, unknown, it would appear, to historians of Jewish music—[113] although one of these sources was published and analyzed as early as 1895—[114]

110. See Blau, *Leo Modenas Briefe*, p. 77, and the letters 171–204, belonging to the period 1639–1640.
111. *Ibid.*, letter 173.
112. See Adler, *La Pratique musicale*, vol. I, chap. vi.
113. Including A. Sendrey, *Bibliography of Jewish Music* (New York, 1951).
114. Kaufmann, "Nathanael Trabot über die Behandlung der Gebete in der Composition ...," pp. 350–357.

represent an important link in the chain of evidence of musical activity in a Jewish context in Italy after Solomon Rossi. Perhaps beyond the actual facts that are recorded—the youthful ardor of the votaries of art music in the synagogue, the existence of two choral societies in this minor community—one should point out that the promoters of this praxis were in no way out-of-the-ordinary people. Thus the picture which emerges of the religious musical life of this community does not represent an exception, but the norm. If we hear of it at all this is because the disputes concerning the liturgical choral chant have, fortunately, left their trace in rabbinical correspondence of the period. Neither of the parties discusses—at least not openly—the actual admissibility of art music in the synagogue. The point at issue concerns the excessive repetition of the sacred words of the prayer, and especially of the sacred name of God, or of an allusion to this name.

The complex development of these polemics, the special rabbinic language of the period—not always easy to understand—and, above all, the fact that we have been able to see only part of the listed sources relating to this question, have prevented us from elucidating it in full detail. Recourse to the above-mentioned study by D. Kaufmann—almost all the texts relating to this affair are manuscripts in his private collection—has been all the more valuable because this scholar, who has published only one text, certainly saw other parts of the record of which he gives an account in the analysis preceding the published text.

I have found mention of at least seventeen texts relating to these polemics, but I have been able to trace only six of these. Five of these texts are preserved in two manuscript collections of responsa and various rabbinical writings in the Kaufmann collection,[115] compiled by the rabbi of Modena, A. J. S. Graziano, zealous collector of Hebrew manuscripts and printed books. I have given lengthy extracts and a detailed analysis of these texts in my *La Pratique musicale*,[116] where I have also established the relationship of the sixth text—a responsum by Leon Modena—[117] to these disputes between the partisans and

115. Numbers 151, 147; 151, 155, 31; 158, 19; 158, 20; 158, 23 in the catalogue of M. Weisz, *Néhai . . . Kauffmann Dávid Tanár . . .* (Budapest, 1906). A further text, number 151, 132, concerning the dispute between two choral associations of Senigallia, will be discussed later.

116. Vol. I, chap. v; vol. II, Appendix A, 22–26.

117. See below, Note 130.

adversaries of choral chant in the synagogue of Senigallia. It will suffice to limit ourselves here to a description of the background to these disputes and to quote only such passages from our texts as are essential for the purposes of this paper.

Senigallia belonged to the Dukes of Urbino until 1631. The transfer of the duchy, at that date, to the authority of the Pope had as an immediate consequence the deterioration of the position of the Jews of Senigallia and their segregation in a ghetto. Senigallia seems to have been at that period one of the very small communities of Italy. According to U. Cassuto, there were thirty-nine Jewish families there in 1626.[118] The reduced size of this community some time after the annexation of Senigallia to the Papal States is also reflected in a responsum by Leon Modena,[119] relating to the conflict aroused by the establishment of a second "lending shop" in this community. In order to support the owner of the older "shop," who feared competition from the new enterprise, Leon Modena stresses that there is no place for two "lending shops" in such a small community.

Nevertheless, the life of the community seems to have had a firm basis. The rabbinical court of Senigallia had a good reputation in 1640.[120] In the middle of the seventeenth century the community made a gift of forty ducats for the relief of persecuted coreligionists in Eastern Europe. In 1641, ten years after its transfer to the ghetto, the synagogue was restored. It is also at about this date that we hear for the first time of an art music praxis in the synagogue of this community.

Among the principal persons involved in the disputes three are residents of Senigallia: Mordekay ben Moses della Rocca was the young and impetuous leader of the local choristers, and probably their "maestro di capella"; Samuel Isaac Norci (or Norsa), della Rocca's teacher, was the principal advocate of the promusic party of Senigallia; Samuel ben Abraham Corcos,[121] the principal adversary of della Rocca and Norci, was the rabbi of Senigallia. Two personalities from outside were intimately associated with this affair: Netanʾel ben Benjamin ben ʿAzrîʾel Trabotto (1568/69–1653),[122]

118. See Cassuto's article "Sinigaglia," *Evreĭskaĭa entsiklopediĭa*, XIV, 302.

119. *Ziqnê yehudah*, ed. Simonsohn, responsum no. 88, pp. 138–140.

120. See Blau, *Leo Modenas Briefe*, letter no. 201, pp. 184–185 of the Hebrew part.

121. See Mortara, *Indice*, p. 17; *Jewish Encyclopedia*, IV, 265.

122. See Nepi–Ghirondi, *Tôledôt gedôlê Yiśraʾel*, p. 271, no. 1; Mortara, *Indice*, p. 65; S. Jona, "A. J. S. Graziani . . . ," *Revue des Etudes Juives* 4:114 (1882); D. Kaufmann in his article referred to above, Note 114, and "Quatre élégies . . . ," *Revue des Etudes Juives*

the rabbi of Modena, one of the important rabbinical authorities of his time, became the central figure and the arbiter; Abraham Joseph Solomon ben Mordekay Graziano (died 1683),[123] disciple of Trabotto and later his successor as rabbi at Modena, to whose zeal in collecting the writings of his master we owe the fact that some of the documents concerning the Senigallia disputes have come down to us, also took part personally in the polemics. Although Trabotto finishes by supporting the party of the local rabbi, Samuel Corcos, he was in principle favorable to the praxis of art music in the synagogue, as was Graziano. Although Graziano's rabbinic "decision" concerning Senigallia, referred to in his introductory notes to Trabotto's texts, has not reached us, his favorable attitude to art music is well known from other sources.[124]

For convenience our texts will be listed, and referred to hereafter, under the following sigla:

1. *Trabotto A.*[125] "Decision" (*pesaq*) by Netanʾel Trabotto, dated Modena, November 9, 1645, addressed to Samuel Isaac Norci, Senigallia, concerning repetitions of the name of God, or of allusions to this name, such as the word *Keter*, in synagogal choral chant at Senigallia.
2. *Corcos.*[126] Letter by Samuel ben Abraham Corcos, dated Senigallia, November 15, 1645, addressed to Netanʾel Trabotto, Modena, concerning the same subject.
3. *Norci.*[127] Letter by Samuel Isaac Norci (in answer to *Trabotto A*), dated Senigallia, November 17, 1645, addressed to Netanʾel Trabotto, Modena, concerning the same subject.
4. *Trabotto B.*[128] "Decision" by Netanʾel Trabotto, dated Modena,

---

35:256–263 (1897); *Jewish Encyclopedia*, XII, 214–215; Blau, *Leo Modenas Briefe*, p. 178 of the Hebrew part, note 1; Simonsohn, ed., *Ẓiqnê yehudah*, p. 42 of the introduction.

123. See Nepi–Ghirondi, *Tôledôt gedôlê Yiśraʾel*, pp. 3–5, no. 4; p. 34, no. 81; Mortara, *Indice*, p. 28; Jona, "A. J. S. Graziani . . . ," pp. 113–126; D. Kaufmann, "Nathanael Trabot . . ."; U. Cassuto in *EJ*, VII, cols. 1654–1655; S. Baron, *Tešuvah be-śafah îṭalqît* in *Studies . . . in Memory of A. S. Freidus . . .* (New York, 1929), pp. 122–137 of the Hebrew part.

124. See Adler, *La Pratique musicale*, vol. I, chap. iii (the passage related to n. 199), chap. v (the passage related to n. 275), chap. vi (the paragraph devoted to Modena), and vol. II, Appendix A, 27.

125. Ed. D. Kaufmann, "Nathanael Trabot . . . ," pp. 350–357. See Adler, *La Pratique musicale*, vol. II, Appendix A, 22.

126. Adler, *La Pratique musicale*, vol. II, Appendix A, 23.

127. *Ibid.*, Appendix A, 24.

128. *Ibid.*, Appendix A, 25.

November 20, 1645, addressed to the "chiefs and administrators" (*roʾšê û-farnesê qq"y*) of the Senigallia community, concerning the same subject.

5. *Consultation.*[129] Consultation from the community of Senigallia concerning the same subject.
6. *Modena.*[130] Responsum by Leon Modena, in reply to a consultation from an unnamed community concerning the same subject.

Obviously, the four dated texts—*Trabotto A*, *Corcos*, *Norci*, *Trabotto B*—belong to a moment when this dispute, which had been brewing for about three years, seemed to have reached a crisis: these four communications were exchanged between Senigallia and Modena—a distance of two hundred and ten kilometers as the crow flies—in only eleven days, from the ninth to the twentieth of November 1645. The first of these texts, *Trabotto A*, in answer to a preceding letter from Norci, represents at least the second intervention by Trabotto in the quarrel. Many of the details are only referred to in it by allusions, which one must attempt to elucidate on the basis of the other texts or of the introductory notes by Graziano, who was, as we have pointed out, closely enough involved in the dispute. Our two undated texts—*Consultation* and *Modena*—are without doubt prior to the four dated texts. From *Norci* we know that consultations on this subject had already been sent to various Italian rabbis[131] in order to obtain their approval of the choral praxis at Senigallia. *Consultation* seems to be one of these. *Modena* is undoubtedly a reply by Leon Modena to the copy of the consultation which had been addressed to him. *Modena* is in any case prior to *Norci* (November 17, 1645), which quotes verbatim some of the arguments in *Modena*, without, however, naming the source.

The fact that the subject of litigation does actually concern a choral chant of art music character emerges clearly from *Trabotto A*, from *Modena*, from *Norci*, and from *Trabotto B*, as well as from the

129. MS. Kaufmann, numbers 151, 155, 131 in the catalogue of M. Weisz. This text, which I have not yet been able to see, is known to me only from the description by M. Weisz.

130. Responsum no. 131 of Leon Modena's *Ziqnê yehudah*, ed. Simonsohn, pp. 176–178. See Adler, *La Pratique musicale*, vol. II, Appendix A, p. 26.

131. ... וכמו שכתבו כל רבני ויניציאה, וירונא, מאנטובה, פיראררה, לוגו ורומא שכלם מתנבאים בסגנון אחד ... שמותר לכפול מלת כתר ...

and later on:

... ואם נזרקה שאלה לפני ... בית דינו ... מכת המתנגדים ... כל זה עשו מפני שאני כתבתי שאלה אל הרבה ב"ד ...

introductory notes of Graziano,[132] all in favor, in principle, of the admissibility of art music in the synagogue. The only one who does not allude to the fact that this is the issue is *Corcos*, the fierce opponent of the choristers. His opposition is ostensibly solely concerned with the abuse of the repetition of the sacred words practiced by the choristers of Senigallia. But *Norci*, zealous defender of the choral chant, sees only a pretext in this: according to him, the underlying cause of Corcos' opposition was the latter's aversion to music. *Trabotto A*, who had learnt from *Norci* that at first Corcos accepted choral praxis, also asks himself: "... and as far as concerns ... Corcos ... who according to you has changed his mind, I wonder why he at first accepted [the choral chant] and then he reprimanded the singers; I do not know what was his first reasoning, and what was his final reasoning, except to say that his object was to obstruct music [considered as the practice of] buffoonery [*leṣanût*] ..."[133]

According to *Norci* such singing had been practiced for three years (since 1642, therefore), and he observes in passing that before this the same praxis had already been current at Pesaro.[134] The account of the situation given by *Corcos* also indicates a certain passage of time: "On the eve of the feast [of the Tabernacles (?)] they repeated the name of God several times,[135] [and] I kept silent ... and although the chief of the singers [Mordekay della Rocca] had already been warned the year before, I appealed to him gently and in friendship the next day ... that they should not begin again ... but this was of no use ..."[136]

The name of Mordekay della Rocca, whom *Corcos* refers to without naming in the passage quoted above, is given in Graziano's introductory note to *Trabotto A*: "Second [rabbinical] decision ... concerning the repetition of many words in the chant according to the music

132. It will suffice to quote at random one of the many relevant passages:
פסק שני . . . ע"ד כפילת הרבה מלות בחכמת השיר והמוסיקא כאשר נוהגים הבחורים ההם מסינגאליא לשורר ובפרט הח"ר מרדכי בכ"ר משה מלרוקה . . .
(From Graziano's introductory note to *Trabotto A*.)

133. . . . ועל דבר מעשה האלוף קורקוס נר"ו שלפי דבריך חזר בו אתמהא, שמעיקרא הרשה ואח"כ נער במזמרים לא ידענא טעמא מעיקרא מאי סבר, ולבסוף מאי סבר אם לא שנאמר שיטתו היה למנוע המוסיקה בעבור לצנות . . .

134. . . . שזה ג' שנים נאמרה בע[יר] הזאת, כמו שאמרוה בעיר פיסארו כמה שנים . . .

135. He is probably alluding here to the prayer *Eleh môᶜadê h*ᵓ, which will be dealt with later.

136. . . . ומ[עיד ?] אני כי ליל מועד שכפלו שם הויה כמה פעמ' שתקתי . . . והגם שראש המשוררים מותרה ועומד הוא מהשנה שעברה למחרתו קראתי אותו בקריאה של אהבה וחבה . . . שלא ישובו עוד לכסלה . . . ולא הועיל כלום אצלו . . .

as these young men of Senigallia and in particular Mordekay . . . della Rocca are accustomed to sing it . . ."[137] The text of *Trabotto A* is also partly devoted to della Rocca. It seems this young music enthusiast did not hesitate to show his disagreement with the local rabbi in an irreverent manner. A complaint against his conduct was addressed to Trabotto, as well as a defense of the young man by his patron Norci. *Trabotto A*, which is older than those two texts, which have not come down to us, speaks indulgently of this young man (*ᶜubbar zeh*), whom Trabotto certainly knew personally and who was besides related to him.[138]

No other chorister's name, no other information concerning the size of the choir, has reached us. There were at least four members, as appears from an important passage of *Norci*, which we shall analyze later. In this same passage, the composer of the choral piece *Eleh moᶜadê h'* is mentioned, anonymously, and it is possible that this composer is none other than della Rocca, although Norci takes care not to refer to his pupil by name in his long text.

The question of the propriety of the repetition by the choristers of certain words is examined in great detail, with elaborate recourse to quotations from the Talmudic, rabbinic, and cabbalistic literature. It concerns us here only to the extent that these debates reveal incidentally a certain amount of valuable information relating to Jewish musical praxis of the period. It will suffice to remark that the opposition to the repetition of the holy words emanated above all from an anxiety to avoid everything that could infringe on the dogma of the unity of God. It is the fear of evoking two deities, or, to use the rabbinical term, "two authorities" (*šetê rešûyôt*), that forbids, with possible exceptions, the duplication in prayers of the name of God or of an allusion to this name. Thus, extremely lively and prolonged discussions were provoked by the repetition of the word *Keter* ("crown") which introduces the Sephardic preamble to the *qeduššah* in the *mûsaf* prayer. To the cabbalistic mentality, very widespread in Italiam Judaism of the period, the "crown"—first of the ten cabbalistic *sefîrôt*—inevitably evoked the Divinity. The defenders of the choral chant, who, with the exception of Leon Modena, were probably no less cabbalistic than their adversaries, went to a great

137. See the Hebrew text in Note 132.
138. Della Rocca was Graziano's cousin (*aḥ šenî*) and thus related to Trabotto, who was a cousin of Graziano's father.

deal of trouble to prove that in the case of the *qeduššah* the word "crown" had no mystic significance, but meant "praise."

Apart from the word *Keter* the discussions dealt mainly with the repetitions of the name of God in the verse *Eleh moᶜadê hʾ*, from the evening prayer for feasts, according to the Sephardic ritual. Here our sources disclose some interesting information relating to the music of the choristers of Senigallia. *Norci* explains that in fact each of the choristers pronounced the name of God only once:

... ובפסוק אלה מועדי שהחכם המסדר הזמרה תיקן וכתב השם לכל אחד מהארבעה משוררים פעם אחד, שכל אחד מזכיר לעצמו, לא ידעתי איסורו מהיכי תיתי...

"And in the verse *Eleh moᶜadê* which the learned orderer of the chant [the composer] arranged so that the name of God [appears] once in each of the four choristers [parts], each [singer] pronouncing it for himself, I do not know why this should be forbidden . . ." This same description of a polyphonic treatment for this item appears in *Modena*, and constitutes an additional proof of the fact that *Modena* actually deals with the dispute of Senigallia:

שאלה. בק"ק פלוני בימי המועד שוררו בבה"כ כת משוררי'... במוסיקה וכפלו מלת כתר וגם ה' באלה מועדי ה' היינו הזכרת השם כל א' היה מזכיר בחלק פעם א' ולא ישנה לו כמשפט המחברים במוסיקה שכופלים לפעמים המלה להמתיק הנגון...

This information about the polyphonic setting allows us to dispose of the hypothesis that the music was by Rossi, because Rossi's *Eleh moᶜadê hʾ*, number [6] of his collection, is a short homophonic piece for three voices. It is probable that the singers of Senigallia could have known and performed the music of Rossi. Indeed it is not one of the least merits of our sources that they reveal, among other information, not only that the remembrance of Rossi was very much alive, but also—and this is of prime importance for our purpose—that synagogal art music was by 1645 a widespread custom in Italian communities. The fact that this evidence is given by such an authority as Netanʾel Trabotto confers additional importance on our source. *Trabotto A* wishes to make quite clear that his reservations do not in any way concern the principle of art music praxis in the synagogue:

... והאלקים כי לא היה דעתי לדבר תועה נגד המזמרים בנגוני המוסיקה באשר בכל הגלילות שעברתי נוהגים לשורר ולזמר לכבוד אלקינו, בחגים ובמועדים...

"By God! It is not my intention to condemn those who sing according to the music, for in all the regions through which I have passed, there is the custom of singing [thus] in honor of our God on the days of the feasts . . ." After having made a distinction between the reprehensible repetition of words evoking the Divinity, and the (permissible) repetition of other words or of entire verses, he cites Rossi's collection, where in fact one never finds repetitions of the objectionable type. Then Trabotto recalls his personal experience: "And I have never heard the learned Rossi and his company, nor my honored spouse, the late Madame Judith, who was very erudite and instructed in [the praxis] of the lute and the viol, and she sang with music the *qeduššah* of *keter*, and they never pronounced the word [*keter*] more than once. But in the verses of the Psalms they did as seemed good to them."

. . . אין לך מקום להרבות דברים . . . כאלו עיני סמוייות ולא ראיתי ספרי הר׳ שלמה מהאדומים שנדפסו . . . כי גם אני מודה ובא שיכולים לכפול המלות פעמים ושלש כל היכא שאינם מלות כתר הרומז לכתר עליון ומלת שמע והזכרת ה׳ כמה פעמים ללא צורך דנראה לעם דאיכא כמה רשויות חלילה ואם במזמור הבו לה׳ בני אלים שמזכירים פסוק אחד פעמים שלש אין כאן שום חשש מאחר שמזמרים כל הפסוק ההוא ב׳ או ג׳ פעמים הוא לתקון הנגון בדרכי המוסיקה אבל להזכיר תיבה דאפשר דנפיק מינה חורבא אחוינא ומחוינא לאסור. ולא שמעתי מעולם לא החכם מן האדומים וסיעתו וגם הכבודה אשתי תנצ״בה מרת יודיטה שהיתה חכמה גדולה ומשכלת בכינור ועוגב ומזמרת במוסיקא קדושת כתר ומעולם לא שנו התיבה רק פעם א׳. אבל בפסוקי המזמורים עשו כנראה בעיניהם . . .

The other points in these polemics contain little of interest as far as we are concerned. Let us only remark that *Trabotto B*—which is separated in time from *Trabotto A* by only eleven days—seems to include the complete prohibition of the choral praxis in Senigallia, at least whenever this praxis gave rise to disputes. Trabotto states quite precisely the reason for his change of attitude, which does not concern the principle of art music praxis in the synagogue, nor even so much the repetitions of the sacred words: "In conclusion: all these things, even if it were possible to admit them, we cannot authorize them, for they are cause for dispute . . . and it is also necessary that all the members of the community respect the honor of their rabbi . . ."[139] In the interval Trabotto had certainly received Corcos' letter dated November fifteenth, demanding with insistence that he should support the local rabbinic authority. It is also possible that *Trabotto B*, dated November twentieth, is already a reaction to

139. סוף דבר כל הדברים הללו, אף אם אפשר היה לצדד בהם שום היתר אין אנו להרשותם מפני המחלוקת . . . וראוי ג״כ לכל בני הקק״י שיזהרו בכבוד המורה שלהם . . .

Norci of the seventeenth of November. Norci, in fact, sets out in detail the serious latest developments of the quarrel, which had then reached its culmination, going so far as to provoke the intervention of the non-Jewish judicial authorities, that is to say, of ecclesiastics, since this was a Papal State. This was surely too much for the old rabbi of Modena, who would rather see the suspension of a music praxis that had all his sympathies than the perpetuation of internal quarrels, which he detested.

We cannot ascertain from *Trabotto B* whether, after this latest intervention by Trabotto of November 20, 1645, the Senigallia choristers were hampered only to the extent that they had to exclude the reprehensible items from their repertoire, or whether Corcos' opposition brought art music in the Senigallia synagogue to a complete standstill. But even assuming this extreme case, this could have been only a brief temporary cessation, as we may learn from the following source which has come down to us from this period.

This source, also a responsum by Trabotto, provides information on the activities of the two choral associations in Senigallia. D. Kaufmann has already briefly referred to this source in his study of *Trabotto A*:[140]

"In this community of music lovers, there were even two associations who had set themselves the task of illustrating the services by their choral chant on the days of feasts and on solemn occasions such as marriages and similar celebrations. A dispute between these two associations, which had peacefully coexisted for a long time, was appeased by the authority of Nathanael Trabot." Kaufmann also mentions the date reference which he has found in the manuscript, and which he interprets, with some reserve, as giving the date of 1652.

The responsum referred to by Kaufmann is certainly the manuscript listed as number 151,132 in the catalogue by M. Weisz. Trabotto describes the background of the quarrel as follows:

בעיר סיניגאליא לימים עברו נמצאו שם שתי חבורות לשורר ולזמר בחגים ובמועדים מזמורי דוד וכמו כן במזמוטי חתן וכלה או המילה כבוד אלקינו וא' מהחבורות הנ"ל היתה קדומה לאחרת בלי ערעור והשנית היתה נשמעת אל הראשונה להקדימה לכל דבר שבקדושה והאמת והשלו' יאהבו וככה היו נוהגים בשלו' ובמישור ומ[ס]תברא דביש נדא גוה [=גבה] טורא ביניהו ומבקשים בני חבורה ראשונה לקעקע ביצת החבורה

140. See p. 352 of his "Nathanael Trabot."

השנית ולפתות במילי וכתבי ובכל טצדקי דאפשר שיניחו חברתם ויבאו להתחבר עמהם . . .
באופן שבני הכת והחבורה הראשונה מתוך ריסי עיניהם ניכר שהם מבקשים להרוס אותה
והם לבדם יעשו השררה הזאת על הקהל . . .

In the city of Senigallia, in past times, there were two choral associations for singing the Psalms of David on feasts as well as at rejoicings of the bridegroom and bride and circumcision[s] [in] honor of our Lord. And one of the above-mentioned associations was unquestionably anterior to the other and the second eagerly collaborated with the first on all sacred occasions. And they loved truth and peace, and thus they dwelt in peace and righteousness. And it seems that, unfortunately, 'a mountain grew between them,'[141] and the members of the older association, desirous of eradicating the younger association, persuaded [them], by word of mouth and in writing [using] all possible argument, to abandon their association and to come and join them . . . in such a way that it was obvious that the members of the older association wanted to destroy [the younger association] so that they alone would assume this office in the community . . .

The quarrel was brought before Trabotto, who once again assumed his role as an arbitrator, bearing chiefly in mind the desire to see peace reign among the Children of Israel. It will suffice for our purpose to summarize Trabotto's lengthy responsum as follows. His first point is to establish the admissibility of art music praxis in Jewish life. After having quoted the Talmudic distinction between instrumental and vocal music, he emphasizes the well-known rabbinic doctrine that all music serving a religious function is admitted: . . . **אבל לכבוד אלקינו לכבדו בשירות ותשבחות לרומם הדרו כל אפיא שוין דמשרא שרי** . . . Then, to support his opinion that such an art music praxis should not only be admitted but encouraged "with all force," he recalls once more—as he already had in *Trabotto A*—the synagogal art music praxis in other Italian communities, namely "in Mantua and Lombardy":

. . . וכן נהגו במנטובא ובלומברדיאה לשורר במוסי' מזמורים ופזמ[ונ]ים בחגי'
ובמועדי' ובמעמד אנשים גד[ו]לי' וח"ו לא מיחו בידם דכל לשם שמים מצוה עלינו לסייע
להחזיק ידי עושי מצוה בכל עוז . . .

The following parts of the responsum are devoted to establishing—with the usual recourse to quotations from Talmudic and rabbinic literature—the unequivocal right of the younger choral association to continue its existence side by side with the older association. Trabotto's arbitration is of course accompanied by an appeal for

141. After *BT Ḥullîn*, 7b.

peaceful collaboration, which he embroiders with one of those untranslatable wordplays, currently to be found in this kind of literature:

...והחבורות תהיינה חוברות ולא חבורות פצע ח"ו כי בזה יתוקן המעוות ויתן שלו' בארץ וישירו המשוררים שירותם בקדושה ובטהרה...

"... And the associations should collaborate and ... peace should be given on earth and the singers shall sing their songs in sanctity and pureness ..."

The responsum is signed and dated as follows:

נתנאל בכמ"ר בנימין טרבוט זצ"ל כותב וחותם פה מודינא ס' חיים כולכם היום כתפארת אדם לשבת בית לפ"ק.

There is no doubt that the indication of the year is given by the word *BaYiT*, although the letters are not provided with any of the usual diacritical signs. We therefore have the date: sabbatical section *wa-etḥannan*, (5) 412; that is to say the week of July 14–20, 1652.

Thus, thanks to this latest responsum by Trabotto—which he wrote in the year preceding his death at the age of eighty-four—we learn that seven years after Corcos' opposition had obstructed art music activity in the Senigallia synagogue, the youthful ardor of our Senigallia musicians had swiftly regained the upper hand, and applied itself to new musical activities and, also, to new disputes.

IV. Conclusion

By the middle of the seventeenth century, the performance of art music had become a widespread custom in Italian Jewish cultural life. The musical evidence which has come down to us from this period is indeed limited to Rossi's *Haš-širîm ašer li-Šelomoh* and to the Birnbaum Manuscript 4 F 71; nevertheless, our literary sources testify that such musical manifestations should not be considered as limited episodes. This point has been sufficiently demonstrated by the more important of our sources, listed and analyzed above—concerning Padua, Ferrara, Mantua, Venice and Senigallia—which may be complemented by some minor sources.[142] Testimony to what

142. Evidence of at least two other manifestations of art music prior to 1648 may be traced in Leon Modena's *Divan*: one took place on the occasion of the inauguration of a Torah scroll in the community of Modena; the other occurred during the celebration of

extent art music manifestations spread in the Jewish life of these communities during the first half of the seventeenth century appears with particular clarity in Netanʾel Trabotto's statement of November 9, 1645, referred to above: "By God! It is not my intention to condemn those who sing according to the music, for in all the regions through which I have passed, there is the custom of singing [thus] in honor of our God on the days of the feasts . . ." We should also bear in mind that the evidences known to us today of art music during this period should not be considered exhaustive. They represent only that part of a documentation that the accidents of research have already uncovered, and most certainly our knowledge may be augmented by future research.

The documentation concerning the following period, from the middle of the seventeenth to the end of the eighteenth centuries, clearly establishes the fact that art music was then a normal part of Italian Jewish cultural life.[143]

In the light of these firmly established facts it becomes obvious that the hitherto current view (expounded in detail in our introduction) concerning the art music manifestations in the Italian synagogue during the first decades of the seventeenth century becomes unacceptable. This art music praxis can no longer be considered as an afterglow of the splendor of Renaissance days, as a solitary remnant from the period of the efflorescence among Italian Jews of general culture, soon doomed to disappear as a result of the enforcement of segregation. In other words, the musical performances which we observed in the synagogues of Padua, Ferrara, Mantua, et cetera, should not be considered as the final point of the preceding period, but as the starting point of a new chapter in the history of Jewish musical praxis in Italy, as first manifestations of the rise of art music in the Italian ghetto.

We may now attempt to provide an answer to our question concerning the causes which brought about, at this particular moment in Italian Jewish history, the rise of art music in Jewish cultural life. As long as our knowledge of art music manifestations in an Italian Jewish context was limited to the documentation concerning the activities of Solomon Rossi and Leon Modena, as long as we were

---

a *siyyûm* in an unidentified community; see Adler, *La Pratique musicale*, vol. I, chap. vi, paragraphs 1 and 4.

143. See Adler, *La Pratique musicale*, vol. I, chaps. vi–ix.

unaware of the continuity of this praxis throughout the seventeenth and eighteenth centuries, we might have been inclined to consider the phenomenon of synagogal art music in Ferrara, Mantua, or Venice as the prolongation of the phenomenon of Jewish musicianship in Italy during the Renaissance. We have seen above that the many fifteenth- and sixteenth-century professional Jewish musicians who were active mainly in Gentile society, later disappeared from the Italian scene. This disappearance was rightly considered by historians of Jewish music to be a consequence of the forced segregation that followed the Counter Reformation. The error of these historians consisted in the analogy which they drew between the fate of Jewish professional musicians active in Gentile society during the Renaissance, on the one hand, and, on the other hand, the art music praxis in the Italian synagogue of the early seventeenth century, which they also considered to have come to a standstill because of segregation.

It seems now that both these phenomena were actually linked by a relation of cause and effect to the anti-Jewish reaction of the Counter Reformation. Yet these effects were of a rigorously contradictory nature: during the fifteenth and sixteenth centuries, we observe, on the one hand, the flourishing activity, which was to disappear with the enforcement of segregation on Italian Jewry, of Jewish musicians outside Jewish society. At the same time our documentation does not reveal any evidence of an art music praxis within a Jewish context for this period, and the first signs of it appear only after the enforcement of segregation.

We are thus tempted to consider segregation as a direct cause of the rise of art music in the Italian ghetto. The line of thought ascribing to the effects of outside persecution the tendency to develop cultural and social activities in the interior of Jewish society seems plausible enough. It is superfluous to call on farfetched analogies with recent events such as those, for instance, that brought into being the activities of the German "Kulturbund." The history of Jewish social life in Italy after the Catholic reaction—and mainly during the seventeenth century, as compared with the preceding period—has sufficiently illustrated the general observation that "as the social gap between Jews and the outside world widened, so the social activity of Jews among themselves increased."[144] Yet like

144. Simonsohn, *Mantua*, vol. II, chap. vi.

every general idea, this one also should be applied with caution to concrete historic events. In order to avoid misunderstanding of our attempt to establish a relationship of cause and effect between the establishment of the ghetto and the consequent introduction of art music to the synagogue, we have to bear in mind that the seclusion of the Jews in Italy during this time was a long, continuous process. The execution of a decree establishing a ghetto in a given community—representing in fact the culminating point of the process of segregation—did not necessarily imply a drastic and sudden change in legislation or in the social attitude of Christians to Jews on the particular date of the decree or of its implementation. Furthermore, in many cases the Jewish population tended to accept segregation voluntarily—in spite of the sacrifices and sufferings involved—since they considered their isolation within the ghetto boundaries as a means of protection from the surrounding hostile society.[145] Nevertheless, there can be no doubt that the physical transfer into the ghetto confines, the heavy financial sacrifices involved, the moving into crowded and promiscuous dwelling conditions, the very fact of being surrounded by the ghetto "wall," the closing of the ghetto gates: all these factors had deep psychological effects capable of provoking a reaction that would give rise to an intensification of internal cultural activities and social relationships.

In the case of Padua the musical praxis which we have observed in its synagogue dates back to some time between 1555 and 1565. Although the ghetto was officially instituted in this city at a much later date (1601), the process of segregation had already been going on during a long period, beginning in the forties of the sixteenth century.[146]

In Ferrara we have observed the introduction of art music into the synagogue in 1605. We have pointed out, in our study of Source "B" concerning Ferrara, the significance of this source, which indicates clearly that synagogal art music was introduced at this date as a new praxis without precedent in the synagogue of Ferrara. Our Ferrarese musicians, in transferring their art music praxis to the synagogue, expressly proclaim the intention "to guide our praxis

145. See, for instance, C. Roth, "La Fête de l'institution du ghetto: une célébration particulière a Vérone," *REJ* 79:163–169 (1924), S. Simonsohn, "The Italian Ghetto and its Administration," reprint from *I. F. Baer Jubilee Volume* (Jerusalem, 1960), pp. 270–286, and his *Mantua*, I, 30.

146. Simonsohn, "The Italian Ghetto," p. 273, n. 11.

towards a sacred objective." This transfer of art music to the synagogue occurred, as we have pointed out above, only a few years after the political change consisting of the annexation of Ferrara to the Papal States in 1597, which brought with it a considerable deterioration in the situation of the Ferrarese Jews.

In the case of Mantua we have been able to observe a similar connection between the enforcement of segregation and the rise of art music in the Jewish life of this community. We have seen that the introduction of art music into the Mantuan synagogue occurred after 1605: that is to say, at a period when the process of segregation of this community was already well advanced.[147] On the other hand, our sources show that this musical praxis was already a well established custom in 1622. We would thus not be surprised if future research established that the introduction of art music to the Mantuan synagogue occurred toward the intermediary date of 1613 or 1614, that is to say, a short time after the institution of the Mantuan ghetto between 1610 and 1612.

Finally, in Senigallia we have seen that the first echoes of art music in the synagogue date back to 1642, some ten years after the annexation of the Duchy of Urbino by the Papal States, and of the transfer of the synagogue to the ghetto.

Our documentation thus seems to suggest a pattern, as if the Jewish musician, whose flourishing activity of the Renaissance period came to a standstill because of segregation, being prevented from exercising his art in gentile society, from that time on turned toward the synagogue.

147. The first effects of the Catholic reaction imposing segregationary measures on the Jewish population of Mantua date back to the seventies of the sixteenth-century. Although the ghetto was not to be instituted until between 1610 and 1612, the plan for its establishment had already been announced in 1602; Simonsohn, "The Italian Ghetto," p. 274, and *Mantua*, I, pp. 29–30, 83–86.

INDEXES

Index of Scriptural Quotations

Genesis
1:1, pp. 189n, 215, 216; 1:4, p. 283; 1:6, p. 185n; 1:26, p. 268
2:8, p. 179
3:21, p. 209n
10:4, p. 23
11:2, p. 236; 11:3, p. 237; 11:4, p. 236
12:3, p. 34n
15:9, p. 46n; 15:17, p. 286n
18:21, p. 268n
24:1, p. 271n
25:23, pp. 33, 34, 36, 37, 38n, 45n
27:1, p. 271n; 27:22, p. 22; 27:39–40, p. 21n; 27:40, p. 47n
28:13, p. 286
32:25–33, p. 170n; 32:33, p. 171
36:6, p. 44
49:10, p. 37n
50:9, p. 41n

Exodus
3:5, p. 178n; 3:10, p. 208n; 3:15, pp. 204n, 208n
13:9, p. 179
14:25, p. 312n
17:16, p. 284
19-18, p. 286n
20:2, p. 130n; 20:17, p. 233
23:13, p. 232; 23:15, p. 279n
24:10, pp. 232, 265
33:11, p. 99; 33:12, p. 266; 33:17, p. 268; 33:18, p. 265; 33:20, p. 268; 33:21, pp. 230, 240, 242, 276; 33:22, pp. 268n, 284; 33:23, pp. 251, 269
34:21, p. 252; 34:30, p. 269; 34:35, p. 279

Leviticus
26:27–28, p. 103

Numbers
11:8, pp. 246, 285
12:8, pp. 232, 269
19:14, p. 99
22:7, p. 169n
24:14, p. 22; 24:16, p. 285n; 24:17–19, p. 22

Deuteronomy
5:20, p. 286n; 5:22, p. 286n; 5:23, p. 286n
6:4, pp. 19, 72, 131
24:8, p. 44; 24:20, p. 44
32:1, p. 313n
33:23, p. 270

Joshua
5:15, p. 178n
10:12–14, p. 177n

I Samuel
28:24, p. 177n

I Kings
8:45, p. 309n

II Kings
2:10, p. 280n
9:20, p. 313n

Isaiah
1:2, p. 313n
21:11, pp. 22, 23n
25:1, p. 105
34:7, p. 22; 34:9, p. 26
40:18, p. 227; 40:25, p. 286
42:13, p. 318n
43:7, p. 265
44:6, p. 19
49:3, pp. 267, 270
55:12, p. 176
60:21, p. 121
66:1, p. 284

Jeremiah
2:16, p. 1
5:12, p. 125
32:19, p. 105
42:5–7, p. 6

Ezekiel
1:5, p. 265; 1:26, pp. 230, 271n, 286; 1:27, pp. 230, 250, 282
8:2, pp. 250, 283
27:20, pp. 217, 218n
28:2, p. 314n
38:23, p. 267

Hosea
11:4, p. 101n

Joel
3:5, p. 306n

Obadiah
1:3–4, p. 24; 1:21, p. 19

Zechariah
4:2–12, p. 217
11:15, p. 47n
14:4, p. 176; 14:9, pp. 19, 287

Malachi
3:3, p. 311n

Psalms
9:12, p. 38n
36:10, p. 288
61:7, p. 313n
66:5, p. 288
68:6, p. 313n
119:105, p. 105; 119:127, p. 315n
137:1, pp. 347n–348n; 137:7, p. 20n

Proverbs
3:4, p. 311n; 3:22, p. 106
4:2, p. 26
17:4, p. 316n
22:20, p. 105n
25:3, p. 248; 25:11, p. 287
29:12, p. 316

Job
23:3, p. 208n; 23:10, p. 318n

Canticles
1:10, p. 285n
2:3, p. 276; 2:5, p. 103; 2:7, p. 313n
4:2, p. 285n; 4:5, p. 285n
5:10–16, p. 226n; 5:11, p. 285; 5:15, p. 285n; 5:16, p. 285n
6:6, p. 285n
7:3, p. 285n; 7:5, p. 285n; 7:8, pp. 226, 236
8:8, pp. 283, 313n

Lamentations
1:4, p. 24; 1:5, p. 24; 1:10, p. 24
2:1, p. 24n
4:21–22, p. 24
5:17–18, p. 24n

Ecclesiastes
3:22, p. 306n
5:7, p. 286
7:14, p. 284
10:20, p. 272n
12:10, p. 212

Daniel
2:39, p. 46n
5:28, p. 234
7:14, p. 47n
10:21, p. 208n

Ezra
8:31, p. 305n

II Chronicles
6:36, p. 309n
30:27, p. 313n

IV Ezra
3:13–16, p. 21n
6:7–10, p. 21

Romans
2:25, p. 35n
9:6–13, pp. 21, 31

Galatians
3:7, p. 32n
4:24–25, p. 32
6:16, p. 32n

I Peter
5:13, p. 23n

Revelation
14:8, p. 23n

Index of Authors

Aaron ben Elijah, 73n
Aaron ha-Levi, 113n
Abba Mari ben Moses, 167n, 169n, 178, 291, 313
Abba Saul, 122n, 181
Abbaye, 112
Abo'ab, Isaac, 206
Abo'ab, Samuel, 345n
Abraham bar Ḥiyya, 172, 200, 206, 218
Abraham ben David of Posquières. *See* Rabad
Abraham ben Isaac of Gerona, 211, 213
Abraham of Cologne, 245n
Abrahams, I., 159n
Abravanel, I., 30n, 31, 43, 114n, 116n, 120n, 121n, 127n, 136n, 138n, 141n, 177n, 185, 192n, 193
Abū Kathir, 229n
Abū 'l-Barakāt Solomon, 161n
Abū l-Hudhayl, 57n
Abū Naṣr, 312
Abū Qurra, T., 56n–57n, 67n, 70
Abū Rā'iṭa, 57n, 67, 68, 70
Abū Rīdah, 66n
Abulafia, Abraham, 222, 245n, 293n
Abulafia, Ṭodros ben Joseph, 210, 211n, 217, 218n, 221
Adams, E. L., 291n
Adler, I., 322n, 323n, 325n, 326n, 329n, 330n, 331n, 333n, 334n, 336n, 338n, 340n, 341n, 347n, 349n, 352n, 353n, 361n
Aescoly, A. Z., 329n
Aetius, 75n
Agobard, Bishop, 229
Aḥad Ha-ʿAm, 98n
Alʿami, Shelomo, 184n
Albalag, Isaac, 185, 206, 293
Albeck, C., 44n, 121n. *See also* Theodor, J.
Albinus, 207
Albo, J., 30n, 121n, 123n, 178n, 184n, 200n
Alemanno, Joḥanan, 190, 328
Alexander of Aphrodisias, 290n, 295n, 296, 298, 299, 301, 317
Alfasi, 106n
Algazi, L., 325
Alguadez, Meir, 296n
Allony, N., 28n
Altmann, A., 49n, 66n, 101n, 103n, 124n, 139n, 190, 191n, 198n, 199n, 206n, 208n, 210n, 213n, 216n, 227n, 232n, 233n, 237n, 252n, 267n, 268n, 273n, 285n, 289n, 295n
Ambrose, 37
Anan, 78, 84, 85, 87
Anatoli, J., 100n, 113, 173, 176n, 180n, 217, 299n
Anawati, M.-M., 178n
Anaxagoras, 79, 81
d'Ancona, A., 333n
d'Ancona, J., 325n, 327n
Ankori, Z., 30n, 47n, 297n
Apel, W., 329n
Aptowitzer, V., 216n
ʿAqiba, 22, 25, 26, 122n, 226, 228, 230, 268
ʿArama, Isaac, 179, 184n, 192n, 193
Archevolti, Samuel, 330
Aristotle, 66, 75, 77n, 79, 83, 84n, 85n, 87n, 89, 183, 184, 185, 188, 190, 191, 192, 193, 194, 197, 201, 205, 214, 247, 248, 252, 253, 267n, 274n, 291n, 292, 293n, 294, 295n, 296, 298, 299, 301, 304, 307, 310, 311n, 318
Aronius, J., 36n
Aronson, I. M., 30n
Asclepiades, 79, 81, 92n
al-Ashʿarī, 57n
Asher ben Samuel of Marseilles, 299n, 301, 302
Asher ben Yeḥiel, 145, 183
Ashi, 102n, 117
Ashkenazi, Eliezer, 254n
Asín Palacios, M., 190n, 228n, 267n, 273n
Askari, E., 105n
Aspasius, 294n
Assaf, S., 99n, 104n, 108n, 110n, 157, 276n, 329n
Astruc, Sen. *See* Abba Mari
Augustine, 30n, 37, 38n
Avempace. *See* Ibn Bājja
Avenary, H., 324, 328n, 337n
Averroes. *See* Ibn Rushd
Avicenna, 126n, 195n, 252, 268n, 269n
ʿAzariah de Rossi, 97n
Azri'el of Gerona, 199n, 213, 215, 216, 217, 221, 234n, 283n

Bacha, C., 57n, 70n
Bacher, W., 22n, 23n, 26n, 109n, 179, 180n, 181n, 209n
Badawi, A., 77n, 79n, 306n

Baeck, Leo, 176
Baer, F. Y., 23n, 27n, 32n, 34n, 40n, 42n, 100n, 189n, 291n
Bahlūl, B., 68n
Baḥya ben Asher, 113n, 208n, 219
Baḥya ibn Paqūda, 59n, 70
Bailey, C., 82n, 91n
Bamberger, S., 329n
Baneth, D., 89n, 90n, 95n, 96, 111n, 113n
Barbevaire. *See* Samuel ben Judah of Marseilles
Barnabas, 32, 33
Baron, S. W., 23n, 32n, 36n, 37n, 40n, 96n, 98n, 99n, 136n, 289n, 352n
Baruch ben Samuel, 339
Barzilai, Juda ben, 49n, 59n, 71
al-Baṭalyawsī, 190, 191, 195n, 198, 199, 206, 207, 208, 209, 267n
Bede, 35n
Bedershi, Abraham, 175n
Bedershi, Samuel ben Reuben, 169n, 175, 176
Bedershi, Y., 116n, 165–184
Bell, H. Idris, 4n
Benedikt, B., 116n
Ben Horin, M., 30n
Benjamin of Tudela, 4, 290n
Ben Sina. *See* Avicenna (Ibn Sīnā)
Ben Yehudah, E., 318
Bergh, Simon van den, 253n, 269n, 274n, 275n, 277n
Bergsträsser, G., 302n, 305n
Berlin, M., 102n
Berliner, A., 186n, 241n, 269n
Berman, A., 199n
Berman, L., 137, 292n
Bermann, S. H., 208n
Bernardy, A. A., 331n
Bernstein, S., 336n, 340n
Bertinoro, Obadyah, 122n
Bertolotti, A., 327n
Bibago, Abraham, 253, 279n
Bickerman, E. J., 36n
Billerbeck, P. *See* Strack, H. L.
Birnbaum, E., 324n, 325n, 327n, 331n, 332n, 341
Blau, J. L., 47n
Blau, L., 328n, 332n, 334n, 336n, 339n, 347, 349n, 351n, 352n
Bloch, S., 166n
Blume, F., 324n
Blumenkranz, B., 30n, 32n, 33n, 34n, 35n, 36n, 37n, 38n, 39n
Bondavi, En, 296, 302, 314
Bongodas, Miles. *See* Samuel ben Judah of Marseilles
Bonwetsch, N., 32n, 34n
Boṭarel, Moses, 186n
Bouriout, U., 229n
Bouyges, M., 66n, 192n, 253n, 267n, 274n, 277n, 279n, 296n, 299n
Breithaupt, J. F., 40n, 41n, 44n
Brill, N., 201n
Brockelmann, C., 68n, 146n, 305n
Brody, H., 96n
Brüll, N., 23n
Bruns, I., 68n, 298n
Bryce, J., 39n
Buber, S., 22n, 23n, 189n
Bukofzer, M., 331n
Burckhardt, 184n
Burke, Edmund, 225
Burnet, J., 75n, 80n, 89n

Caleb Afendopolo ben Elia, 297n
Canal, P., 327n
Cantor, N., 38n
Casanova, P. *See* Bouriout
Cassiodorus, 35n
Cassuto, U., 327n, 328n, 329n, 351, 352n
Chajes, Ẓ. H., 113n
Chavel, C. B., 48n
Chwolson, D., 4n
Cicero, 33n
Cochrane, C. N., 25n
Cohen, B., 115n
Cohen, G. D., 20n, 41n
Cohen, Judah, 299–300
Cohen, Y., 301n
Colorni, U., 343n
Commodian, 34
Comparetti, D., 39n
Corcos, Samuel ben Abraham, 351, 352, 354, 357, 358, 360
Cordovero, 203n, 208n, 222
Cornford, F. M., 35n
Costa ben Luca, 76n
Cowley, A. E., 4n
Crescas, Ḥasdai, 121n, 173n, 177n, 184n, 192, 193, 194
Critas, 83n
Cropsie, J., 302n
Cusanus, Nicholas, 208n

Damascius, 253
Danby, H., 105n
Daniel, N., 46n
Daniélou, J., 34n
Dante, 311n
David ben Abraham ha-Laban, 220n, 222
David ben Ṣiyyon ben Abraham of Modena, 329n
David ha-Reʾûvenî, 329n

Davidson, I., 19n, 121n, 174n, 228, 276n, 341n
Davies, W. D., 35n
Deane, H. A., 38n
Delitzsch, F., 73n
Delmedigo, J. S., 189n, 239n, 241
Democritus, 79, 80, 81, 82, 88, 89, 90n, 91, 92
Dicaearchus, 79
Dick, I., 67n
Diels, H., 75n, 78n
Dieterici, F., 78n, 84n, 85n, 86, 199n, 209n
Dodd, C. H., 32n
Doresse, Jean, 247n
Dozy, R., 93n, 292n
Dukes, L., 195n
Dunash ben Labrat, 27, 28n
Duran, Profiat, 113n, 117n
Duran, Shimᶜon ben Yosef, 166n, 169
Duran, Simon ben Ẓemaḥ, 104, 110n, 113n, 114n, 178n, 184n, 190
Duran, Ẓemaḥ ben Solomon, 185n
Duval, R., 38n, 68n

Ebreo, Guglielmo, 331
Efros, I., 201n
Ehrenreich, Ḥayyim Jehuda, 277n
Einstein, Alfred, 332n
Eisler, R., 216n
Eitner, 331n
Elbogen, I., 19n, 277n
Eleazar of Worms, 98n, 233, 234, 235, 238, 266n
Eliezer ben Hyrcanus (Eliezer the Great), 214, 216, 217
Elijah Gaon, 104n, 109, 118n
Emden, J., 97n
Empedocles, 83, 84, 89n, 92–93
Epicurus, 79, 80, 81, 82, 88n, 90n, 91, 92, 125
Eppenstein, S., 145n
Epstein, A., 21n
Epstein, J. N., 301n
Erhardt, A., 36n
Euclid, 298
Eugarius, 37n
Eusebius, 36
Ezra of Gerona, 199n, 201n, 211, 216, 217, 221

Falaḳera, Shemtov. *See* Ibn Falaḳera
da Fano, ᶜEzrā, 339, 340
da Fano, Judah Saltaro. *See* Saltaro
al-Fārābī, 85n, 137n, 138n, 190, 195, 196, 197, 198, 199n, 200, 252n, 274n, 293n, 294n, 295, 300, 302n, 308, 309–310
Farissol, Abraham, 328
al-Fāsi, David ben Abraham, 6
Festugière, A. J., 69n
Filipowski, Z., 85n, 309n
Finkel, J., 99n
Finkelstein, L., 19n, 24n, 122n
Finnegan, J., 298n
Finzi hal-Lewî, Jacob ben Isaac, 330, 331n
Fishman, J. L., 102n
Flusser, D., 40n, 41n
Foa, S., 332n
Folz, R., 29n
Frederick II von Hohenstaufen, 217n, 300n
Freeman, K., 83n
Freimann, A., 27n, 95n, 99n, 101n, 110n, 111n, 145n, 146n, 147n, 149n, 183n
Fried, S., 191n
Friedländer, I., 71n, 120n, 127n, 167n
Friedländer, M., 209n
Frumkin, Arye Leb, 276n–277n
Fuks, A., 2n, 3n, 4n

Gairdner, W. H. T., 252n
Gandz, S., 170n
Gardet, L., 178n, 181n
Gaster, Moses, 225n
Gaster, T., 229
Gauthier, L., 295n
Geiger, A., 176n, 228, 239n
Gerondi, S., 186n
Gershom, R., 112
Gersonides. *See* Levi ben Gershom
al-Ghazālī, 192n, 195n, 239, 243, 252n, 268n, 271n, 279n
Ghirondi, H., 334n, 339n, 351n, 352n, 392n
Gikatila, Joseph, 204n, 215n, 219, 254, 272n, 279n
Ginsberg, H. L., 23n, 25n, 47n
Ginzberg, L., 23n, 41n, 42n, 44n, 98n, 99n, 114n, 117n
Ginzburg, I. O., 49n, 59n
Glatzer, N. N., 23n, 27n
Goitein, S. D., 10n, 94n, 117n, 151n, 152n, 154, 157n, 159n, 163n
Golb, N., 5n, 8n, 10n, 137n
Goldberg, A., 114n
Goldenthal, Jacob, 242n
Goldin, J., 26n
Goldschmidt, L., 44n
Goldstein, B. R., 299n
Goldziher, I., 43, 94n, 98n, 171n, 228n, 229n
Gottheil, R., 163n
Gottlieb, M., 120n, 122n, 128n, 129n, 141n, 231n
Gottstein, M. H., 306n, 308n, 309n, 312n
Gradenwitz, P., 325, 327n
Graetz, H., 187, 225n, 229, 290n

Graf, G., 57n, 67n, 70n
Grayzel, S., 37n
Graziano, Abraham Joseph Solomon, 331, 350, 352, 353, 354, 355n
Gregory the Great, 37
Grintz, Y. M., 27n
Griveau, 3n
Gross, Heinrich, 174n, 176n, 290n, 294n, 295n, 296n, 297n, 298n
Grünbaum, M., 23n, 26n, 42n
Grunebaum, G. E. von, 93n, 94n
Güdemann, Moritz, 170n
Guillaumont, A., 68n
Günsz, A., 298n, 317
Guthrie, W. K. C., 192n
Guttmann, Jakob, 75, 76, 78n, 83n, 87n, 190, 201n, 204n, 206n, 209n, 210n
Guttmann, Julius, 58n, 76, 83n, 85n, 86, 87, 88, 98n, 138, 178n, 209n, 222, 254n, 290n, 293n

Hadassi, J., 30n, 47n, 73n
Hai Gaon, 108n, 177, 226, 227
ha-Kohen, Isaac (of Castile), 207, 217, 221
Halberstam, S. J., 112
Ha-Levi, J. *See* Judah Ha-Levi
Halkin, A. S., 20n, 30n, 46n, 47n, 49n, 62n, 95n, 96n, 103n, 106n, 111n, 168n, 171n
al-Hamdāni, Ḥ., 69n
ha-Meʾati, Nathan. *See* Nathan ha-Meʾati
Hamelin, O., 275n
Ḥananel, 112
Ḥanina, 124
ha-Reʾûvenî, D. *See* David ha-Reʾûvenî
al-Ḥarizi, Judah, 120n, 191n, 201
Hathaway, R. F., 253n
Hayward, 182n
Ḥayyat, Judah, 186, 234n, 235, 236, 237, 288
Hegel, Georg Wilhelm Friedrich, 222, 223
Heinemann, I., 20n, 21n, 23n, 104n, 135n, 173n, 176, 180, 206n
Heller, C., 130n
Heraclitus, 80, 85n, 88, 89, 90
Hercz, J., 295n
Hershler, M., 113n
Heschel, A. J., 23n, 203n, 204n
Higger, M., 46n
Hillel ben Samuel, 232n
Hippolytus of Rome, 33
Hirschfeld, H., 190n
Hoffmann, D., 241n, 269n
Holzer, J., 120n, 122n, 126n, 128n
Honorius of Canterbury, 38n
Horovitz, S., 27n, 75, 76, 77n, 78n, 83n, 85n, 86n, 200n, 206n
Hourani, G. F., 137n, 138n
Husik, I., 30n, 58n, 123n
Hyamson, M., 131n, 132n, 136n
Hyman, A., 105n, 139, 142n

Ibn Abbas, Judah ben Samuel, 170n
Ibn Adret, Solomon, 104, 116n, 181, 291n
Ibn Aflaḥ, 174, 291n, 293n, 295n, 297, 298, 300n, 312, 313, 314, 315
Ibn Allah, 174n
Ibn ᶜAqnin, Joseph, 96
Ibn ᶜAqnin, Joseph ben Judah, 47, 96, 103n, 110n, 111n, 113, 115, 168n, 170, 171
Ibn Bājja, 196, 197n, 273n, 305n
Ibn Daud, Abraham, 27n, 30n, 48n, 193n
Ibn Ezra, Abraham, 45, 46n, 47, 48, 108n, 169, 170n, 174n, 179n, 186n, 200, 204, 208, 209, 210, 211, 212n, 213, 222, 225–288 *passim*
Ibn Ezra, Moses, 190, 194, 195n, 200, 205n, 208
Ibn Falaḳera, Shemtov, 138n, 168n, 170, 173n, 202n
Ibn Farḥi (Isaac), 237n
Ibn Gabirol, Solomon, 199n, 200, 201, 202, 203, 204, 205, 207, 209, 210, 212, 215, 217, 219
Ibn Ḥabib, Moses, 206
Ibn Ḥazm, 77n, 228
Ibn Ḥunain, Isḥāq, 317
Ibn Isḥāq, H., 302, 305n
Ibn Jacob, Solomon ben Joseph, 120n
Ibn Kaspi, Joseph, 138n, 168n, 169n, 172, 173, 174n, 178n, 185, 242, 269n, 297, 301n
Ibn Khaldun, 41n, 315n
Ibn Laṭif, Isaac, 110n, 115n, 185–223
Ibn Malka, Juda ben Nissim, 266n–267n
Ibn Pakudah, Baḥya, 208
Ibn Rushd, 66n, 67, 137n, 141, 173n, 174, 196, 197n, 239, 240, 241, 244n, 245, 246, 247, 249, 251, 252, 253, 267n, 268n, 269n, 274, 275n, 277n, 278, 279, 280n, 289–320 *passim*
Ibn Sabᶜīn, 295n, 300n
Ibn Ṣaddiḳ, Joseph, 59n, 191, 200, 203n, 206, 208, 210
Ibn Saqawaihi, 228
Ibn Sīnā. *See* Avicenna
Ibn Tayyib al-Baghdādi, 174
Ibn Tibbon family, 290n, 302, 306
Ibn Tibbon, Judah, 77n
Ibn Tibbon, Moses, 190n, 283n, 309n, 316
Ibn Tibbon, Samuel, 120n, 171, 174n, 180n, 185, 188n, 191n, 201, 281n, 292n
Ibn Ṭufayl, 197, 242, 244, 295n

Ibn Verga, Joseph, 290n
Ibn Waḳār, J., 222n, 241, 242, 243, 244, 245, 274n, 277n, 279n
Idelsohn, A. Z., 322, 323, 324n, 325, 327n
Ikhwān al-Ṣafāʾ, 78n, 83n, 85n, 86, 190, 199n, 209
Innocent III, 37n
Irenaeus, 33
Isaac of Acco, 236
Isaac ben Sheshet, 185, 215
Isaac the Blind, 213, 216, 221
Ishmael. *See* Yishmaʾel
Isidore of Seville, 37
Israeli, Isaac, 190, 191, 198n, 200, 206, 208n, 210n, 216n, 267n
Isserles, Moses, 118

Jacob ben Asher, 45n, 145
Jacob ben Makir, 172n, 291n, 296, 297n, 298, 312, 315, 316
Jacob ben Meir Tam, 145
Jacob ben Reuben, 30n
Jacob ben Sheshet, 201n, 207, 217, 220, 221, 245n
Jacob ha-Kohen, 221, 245n
Jaeger, Werner, 192n
Jaffe, Mordecai, 237n
Jastrow, M., 308n, 314n
Jellinek, A., 173n, 186n, 200n, 209n, 210n, 233n, 234n
Jerome, 23, 30n, 33, 34n, 36, 38n
Joel, I., 119n, 247n, 276n
Joḥanan ben Zakkai, 112, 175n
John Philoponus, 85n
Jona, S., 351n, 352n
Jonathan ha-Kohen of Lunel, 106n, 110n
Joseph ibn Ṣadīq. *See* Ibn Ṣaddiḳ
Joseph Rosh ha-Seder, 117
Josephus, 1, 21n, 40
Joshua ben Levi, 124
Josippon, 40, 41, 42, 43, 44, 46
Juda ben Nissim ibn Malka. *See* Ibn Malka, Juda ben Nissim
Judah ben Barzillai, 112, 117, 227n
Judah ha-Levi, 96n, 112, 114, 161, 191n, 192n, 200, 232, 233
Judah ha-Nasi, 107
Judah Ḥayyat. *See* Ḥayyat, Judah
Juster, J., 2n, 36n, 37n
Justin Martyr, 32, 33

Kadushin, M., 20n
Kāfih, J., 46n
Kahana, A., 336n
Kahana, K., 113n
Ḳalonymus ben Ḳalonymus. *See* Qalonymos ben Qalonymos
Kapaḥ, 102n, 108n
Karo, Joseph, 99, 113, 118
Kasher, M. M., 41n
Kaspi. *See* Ibn Kaspi
Katz, J., 29n
Katz, S., 37n
Katzenellenbogen, Meʾîr. *See* Padua
Kaufmann, D., 49, 57n, 58n, 59n, 180, 181n, 190n, 199n, 201n, 206n, 208n, 209n, 227n, 266n, 272n, 341n, 349n, 350, 351n, 352n, 358
al-Khayyāṭ, 57n
Kimḥi, David, 44n, 113n, 177n, 306n, 308n
al-Kindī, 66, 69n, 190
Kinkeldey, O., 327n
Kisch, G., 37n
Kister, M. J., 148n
Klatzkin, 292n, 293n, 301n, 308n, 309n, 314n, 316n
Koebner, R., 25n
Kook, S. H., 111n
Kraus, P., 76n, 123n, 292n
Krauss, S., 23n, 27n, 42n, 124n
Krieg, A., 324n
Krochmal, N., 218n, 222

Lagarde, P. A. de, 294n, 303n
Landauer, S., 52n, 77n
Lane, E. W., 89n, 292n
Laqish, Resh. *See* Resh Laqish
Last, Isaac, 242n, 269n
Lattes, Isaac ben Judah de, 72n
Lauterbach, J. Z., 23n, 25n, 27n
Leibniz, Gottfried Wilhelm von, 246
Leon of Bagnols, Maestre. *See* Levi ben Gershom
Lerner, R. *See* Mahdi, M.
Levi ben Abraham ben Ḥayyim, 115n, 169, 170
Levi ben Gershom, 193n, 253, 283n, 300, 301
Levi della Vida, G., 41n, 43n
Levinger, J., 116n
Levy, E., 291n, 296n
Levy, J., 308n
Lew, M. S., 20n
Lewin, B. M., 30n, 112, 117n
Lewy, J. H., 33n
Libowitz, N. S., 336n
Lieberman, Saul, 19n, 20n, 22n, 27n, 99n, 108n, 114n, 120n, 124n, 225n, 231n, 232n, 240n, 289n
Livy, 25, 40
Loewe, Raphael, 226n
Lord, L. E., 33n
Luzzato, S. D., 186n

Mahdi, M., 294n, 295n, 302n, 309n
al-Mahdī, 57n
Mahler, E., 165n, 291n
Maimonides, Abraham ben Moses, 30n, 45, 46n, 51, 106n, 109, 111n, 145–164
Maimonides, Moses, 30n, 46n, 59n, 71, 95–118 *passim*, 119–144, 162, 163, 164, 165, 168, 171, 173, 174n, 178, 179, 180, 181, 182, 185, 187, 188, 189, 191n, 193n, 194, 195, 198, 200, 201, 204, 205, 211, 212, 214, 216, 219n, 220, 221n, 231, 232, 239, 240, 242, 243, 245n, 252, 265n, 266, 269n, 271n, 272, 274n, 276, 279n, 282n, 283n, 284n, 285n, 286, 287n, 293n, 294, 295n, 303, 310n
Maimuni. *See* Maimonides
Malter, H., 75n, 77n, 93n, 228n, 229n, 241n
Mandelbaum, 22n
Mann, J., 10n, 11n, 12n, 96n, 117n, 152, 162n
al-Maqrīzī, 5, 229
Margalioth, R., 169n, 270n
Margulies, 46n
Marmorstein, A., 20n, 191n
Marmura, M. E., 66n
Marx, A., 23n, 102n, 110n, 121n, 188n, 241n
Masnuth, Samuel ben Nissim, 44n
Massignon, L., 295n
Masᶜūdī, 93n, 94n
Mathews, H. J., 46n
Maximian the Arian, 36n
Maylender, M., 348n
Medigo, J. del. *See* Delmedigo
Meir, R., 22, 31
ha-Meᵓiri, Menaḥem ben Solomon, 101n, 113n, 118, 166n, 169
Melamed, E. Z., 23n
Melito of Sardis, 32n
Menaḥem ben Zeraḥ, 99n, 195n
Menasce, P. J. de, 52n
Meyer, J., 325n
Meyerhof, M., 94n
Michael the Interpreter, 68n
Mieli, A., 297n
Migne, J.-P., 23n, 34n, 36n, 37n, 38n
Milano, A., 327n, 336n
Miles of Marseilles. *See* Samuel ben Judah of Marseilles
Mingana, A., 57n
Modena, L., 46n, 321, 322, 323, 324, 330, 333, 334, 335, 336, 337, 338, 340n, 343, 344, 345, 346, 347, 348, 349, 350, 351, 352n, 353n, 356, 360n, 361
Mommsen, T. H., 28n
Moore, G. F., 22n, 121n, 191n
Morata, N., 292n
Morosini, Giulio, 345, 346
Mortara, M., 329n, 348n, 351n, 352n
Moscato, Leon Judah, 193n, 241, 330
Mosconi, Jehuda Leon ben Solomon, 269n
Moses ben Joab, 329
Moses ben Solomon of Salerno, 204n, 217
Moses de Leon, 173n, 207, 219, 283n
Moses of Burgos, 217, 221
Moses Taku, 177, 232
Muckle, J. T., 271n, 276n
Mundhirī, ᶜAbd al-ᶜAẓimal, 146
Munk, S., 51n, 119n, 197n, 202n, 209n, 239n, 252n, 273n, 280n, 290n, 295n
Musetto, 331
Mussajov, Shelomo, 268n, 282n

Nachmanides, Moses, 30n, 44n, 48n, 169n, 178n, 207, 213, 216, 218, 221, 234n, 236
Nader, A., 57n
Naḥmias, Samuel. *See* Morosini
al-Nairizi, 207
Narboni, Moses, 168n, 185, 225–288
Nathan ha-Meᵓati, 314
Naumberg, S., 341n
al-Naẓẓām, 85n
Nemesius of Emesa, 76, 86
Nemoy, L., 71n, 72, 73n
Nepi, M. S., 329n, 334n, 339n, 351n, 352n
Netter, Shelomo Zalman, 267n
Nettl, P., 327n, 331n, 332n, 341n
Neubauer, A., 48, 239n, 290n
Neuburger, C., 104n
Neumark, D., 120n, 128n, 129n, 135n, 136, 140n, 187, 188, 217n
Neusner, J., 20n
Neustadt-Ayalon, D., 9n
Newman, J., 324, 327n, 332n, 340n
Nissim, 108n
Noeldeke, T., 48
Nonnos, 67, 68
Norci, Samuel Isaac, 351–356, 358
Nyberg, S., 57n

Origen, 30n, 34

Padua, Meᵓîr (Maharam), 334n, 335
Parkes, J., 35n, 36n, 37n
Paul of Burgos, 31
Pauly, A., 76n
Payne-Smith, R., 38n, 39n, 68n
Pelagius, 36n
Pellat, Charles, 184n
Perles, F., 176n, 234n
Perlmann, M., 94n

Petrus Alfonsi, 46n
Peyron, B., 303
Philo, 32n, 35n, 38, 100n, 181n, 190, 202, 251
Phinehas, 109, 110n
Pines, S., 51n, 76n, 98n, 119n, 137n, 188n, 194, 195n, 197n, 198n, 199n, 289n, 295n, 306n
Pinsker, Simḥa, 254, 266n
Pinto, O., 93n
Plato, 79, 80, 82, 85n, 86, 88n, 91, 92, 188, 189, 190, 191, 197, 201, 216, 247n, 253, 292, 294, 295, 296, 305, 307, 310, 311n
Plotinus, 205, 207, 209, 252
Plutarch (attr.), 75–94 *passim*
Porphyry, 299n, 300
Portaleone, Abraham, 330
Poznánski, S. A., 30n, 181n
Pseudo-Augustine, 37n
Pseudo-Cyprian, 32n, 33
Pseudo-Gikaṭila, 219
Pseudo-Jonathan, 22n
Pseudo-Orosius, 41n
Ptolemy, 291, 293n, 295n, 296, 297, 299, 314, 316
Puech, H.-C., 52n
Pythagoras, 79, 80, 82, 88n, 90n, 91, 92

Qalonymos ben Qalonymos, 173n, 174, 291n, 301n
al-Qirqisānī, Abu Yusuf Yaʿqūb, 6, 67, 71, 72, 73
Quasten, J., 33n

Rab, 124, 126
Rabad, 238
Rabba, 112
Rabbinowitz, J., 20n
Rabinowitz, M.D., 120n
Radbaz, 101n
Rahman, F., 126n, 197n, 198n
Rahmer, M., 38n
Rankin, O. L., 30n
Rapoport, S. J. L., 23n, 267n, 268n
Rashba. *See* Solomon ben Adret
Rashbam (Rabbi Samuel ben Meir), 145, 179
Rashi, 44n, 99, 112, 122n, 145, 175n
Rawidowicz, S., 168n
al-Rāzī, Abū Ḥātim, 69
Recanati, Menaḥem, 234, 235, 236, 237n
Reese, G., 331n
Reith, G., 33n
Remigius, 37n
Renan, E., 166n, 174n, 175n, 176n, 239n, 290n, 291n, 292n, 295n, 297n, 298n, 303, 307, 317
Rescher, N., 300n
Resh Laqish, 247n
Rice, E. F., Jr., 28n
Rieger, P., 327n
Rieger, R., 42n, 331n
Riemann, H., 329n, 341n
Rieti, Moses, 296n, 311n
Rist, J. M., 66n
Riṭba, 113n
Ritter, H., 57n, 181n
Rosenblatt, S., 52n, 145n, 147
Rosenthal, E. I. J., 292n, 295n, 296n, 307
Rosenthal, F., 164, 190n
Rosenthal, J., 30n, 45n, 46n
Rosin, D., 95n, 179n, 266n, 267n, 268n, 269n, 272n, 281n, 283n
Rossi, Solomon, 321, 322, 323, 324, 325, 327n, 330n, 331, 332, 335, 340, 342, 343, 344, 346, 347, 350, 356, 357, 360, 361
Roth, Cecil, 327n, 328n, 331, 332n, 333n, 341, 345n, 346n, 347, 348, 349, 363n

Saʿadya Gaon, 30n, 46n, 47, 49n, 52n, 59n, 75–94 *passim*, 104n, 176, 177, 178, 192n, 194, 227, 228, 229n, 230, 233, 276n
Sachs, M., 23n
Sachs, Senior, 185n, 187n, 200n, 201n, 210n, 211
Sacks, J. L., 111n
Sacy, S. de, 229
Salmon ben Yeruḥim, 228
Saltaro, Judah ben Moses, 330, 336, 337, 339
Samuel ben Ḥofni Gaon, 177
Samuel ben Judah of Marseilles, 289–320
Samuel ben Meir, 179
Samuel ben Reuben of Beziers. *See* Bedershi, Samuel ben Reuben
Samuel ha-Nagid, 108n, 228n
Sarachek, J., 181n, 182n, 291n
Saraval, [Judah] Lêb, 339
Ṣarfatî, ben Ṣiyyôn, 334, 335, 339
Sarton, G., 290n, 294n, 299n
Sassoon, S., 30n, 106n, 109n, 145n, 231n, 301n
Schachter, J., 105n
Schechter, S., 120n, 121n, 136, 191n
Scheiber, A., 95n, 158n
Schelling, Friedrich von, 222
Scheyer, S. B., 126n
Schirmann, J. H., 322, 327n–328n, 333n, 334n
Schlatter, A., 21n, 32n

Schmueli, H., 330n
Schneider, F., 28n
Schoenblum, S., 186n, 210n
Schoeps, H. J., 20n, 34n, 35n
Scholem, G., 98n, 173n, 183n, 187n, 195n, 202n, 203n, 204n, 207n, 209, 211–221 *passim*, 225n, 231n, 233n, 237n, 242n, 245n, 268n, 270n, 282n, 283n, 290n, 293n
Schorr, J. H., 185n, 186n
Schramm, P. E., 25n, 28n, 39n, 40n, 46n
Schreiner, M., 77n, 85n
Schwarzfuchs, S., 99n
Scotus, Michael, 180n
Segal, M. S., 306n
Sendrey, A., 341n, 349n
Shabazi, Salam, 222
al-Shahrastānī, 228, 229
Shaked, S., 10n
Shalom, Abraham, 206
Shelemyah of Lunel, 300
Shem Tob, ben Joseph ben Shem Tob, 97n
Sherira Gaon, 112, 226, 227, 266n
Sheshet, R., 110n
Shoḥet, A., 97n
Shulvass, M. A., 327n, 328n, 329n, 333n
Silver, A. H., 30n
Simeon ben Laqish. *See* Resh Laqish
Simeon ben Yoḥai, 23, 26
Simeon the Just, 113
Simon, M., 35n, 36n
Simonsen, D., 345n, 346n
Simonsohn, S., 327n, 330n, 331n, 332n, 333n, 336, 337n, 340n, 343, 352n, 353n, 362n, 363n, 364n
Simplicius, 207
Sirat, C., 169n
Smalley, 171n, 180n, 181n
Solomon ben Adret, 165–184 *passim*
Somme, Leono, 334n
Sonne, Isaiah, 11n
Souter, A., 36n
Southern, R. W., 35n, 46n
Sperber, A., 26n
Stein, L., 45n
Steinschneider, Moritz, 4, 27n, 46n, 76n, 197n, 201n, 209n, 239, 241, 242n, 254, 281n, 284n, 289n, 291n, 292n, 295n, 296n, 297n, 298n, 299n, 301n, 305n, 307, 309n, 310n, 313n, 314n, 315n, 316n, 317, 328n
Stenning, J. F., 26n
Stern, M., 2n, 3n, 254
Stern, S. M., 49n, 190n, 191n, 198n, 208n, 210n, 289n, 301n
Stern, Z., 186n, 189n, 192n, 202n, 203n, 204n, 210n, 214n, 220n
Stobaeus, 75, 86
Strack, H. L., 23n, 31n
Strauss, A., 182n
Strauss, L., 51n, 98n, 131n, 142n, 195n, 295n, 302n, 309n
Stutschewsky, J., 327n
Sulami, 148

Tauhīdī, 93n, 94n
Taylor, H. O., 38n
Tcherikover, V. A., 2n, 3n, 4n
Teicher, J. L., 292n
Tertullian, 34, 37
Thales, 79
Theodor, J., 22, 27n, 189n, 216n
Theophrastus, 75
Théry, G., 299n
Timothy, 57n
Tineius Rufus, 26
Tobias ben Moses, 47n
Ṭodros of Beaucaire, 175
Ṭoledano, J., 96n
Touati, Charles, 243n, 247, 248n, 250n
Trabotto, Netanʾel, 341, 351, 352, 353, 354, 355, 356, 357, 358, 361
Trismegistus, Hermes, 69n
Twersky, I., 98n, 101n, 102n, 111n, 289n, 290n

Ullmann, W., 29n, 30n
Urbach, E. E., 34n, 117n, 177n, 183n

Vajda, G., 49n, 58n, 64n, 67n, 69n, 99n, 201n, 217n, 220n, 222n, 241n, 242n, 243n, 244n, 251n, 267n, 268n, 275n, 277n, 279n, 289n, 290n, 293n
Van Roey, A., 57n, 67n
Ventura, M., 52n, 77n
Vidal, Don Crescas, 174, 175
Virgil, 25, 40
Vogelstein, H., 327n, 331n

Wallenstein, M., 8n
Walzer, R., 197n, 198n, 289n, 292n
Weisz, M., 350n, 353n, 359, 360
Wensinck, A. J., 68n, 69n
Werblowsky, R. J. Z., 97n, 103n, 272n
Werner, E., 323, 324, 327n, 346, 347
Wertheimer, A. J., 44n
Wertheimer, S. A., 44n, 45n
Wieder, N., 145n, 148n, 150n
Wiesenberg, E., 106n, 109n, 145n
Wilensky, S. O. Heller, 185n, 192n, 193n, 200n, 203n, 211n, 213n, 216n, 217n, 222n
Williams, A. Lukyn, 31, 33n

Wissowa, G. *See* Pauly, A.
Wolfson, H. A., 20, 32n, 35n, 57n, 58n, 66n, 95n, 104n, 114n, 120n, 142n, 184n, 189n, 190n, 191n, 192n, 193n, 194n, 202n, 207, 272n, 286n, 289n, 292n, 306n
Wüstenfeld, F., 3n

Yabeẓ, Yosef, 184n
Yadin, Y., 23n
Yahuda, A. S., 70n
Yishmaʾel, 26n, 226, 227, 228, 230, 234, 266n, 268
Yoḥanan. *See* Joḥanan
Yose ben Yose, 19n
Young, K., 38n

Zaehner, R. C., 216n
Ẓaraẓa, Samuel, 206
al-Zarqali, 299n
Zeraḥya Gracian, 232n
Zimmels, H. J., 40n
Zimra, David ben Solomon ibn Avi. *See* Radbaz
Zinberg, I., 180n, 290n, 291n, 327n
Zullay, M., 27n
Zunz, L., 21n, 27n, 44n, 45n

Index of Subjects

Aaron, 60
Abel, 34, 38
Abraham, 31, 34n, 105, 150, 166, 270, 283
Abrasax formula, 12
academies, music, 345, 346, 347, 348
accident, 53, 54, 56, 57n, 62n, 64, 68, 77, 78, 83, 84, 86, 87, 90n, 92, 103, 268n, 282, 284. *See also* adventitiousness
action, 53, 54, 78n, 294
Active Intellect. *See* Agent Intellect
Adam, 38n
"Adôn ᶜôlam," 337, 338
ᵓadshānāyā, 67–68
adventitiousness, 50, 51, 53, 55n, 56, 57, 64, 68n. *See also* accident
Aeneas, 41
agency, 50, 55, 274, 275, 276
Agent Intellect, 129, 197n, 209, 220, 221, 244, 245n, 246, 270n, 273, 274, 276, 279n, 280, 285n, 287n. See also *Keneset, Yisraᵓel*
aggadot, 112, 168n, 173, 176, 216n, 219, 266n
Agnios. *See* Aeneas
"ᶜAlênû le-šabbeaḥ," 337
Alexander the Great, 195
Alexandria, 3, 7, 11, 109, 153, 161
ᶜamal, 206
ᶜAmalek, 284
Ambrogio de Pesaro, 331
ᶜAmmānī family, 161
Amoraim, 19, 107, 112
Amsterdam, 325
anagrams, 215, 216, 219
ᶜAnaniyya, 229
Ancona, 348, 349
angels, 13, 60, 112, 204, 210, 214, 225, 231, 267, 268n, 272, 274, 279
"ᵓAni maᵓamīn," 121, 129
Anṣinā, 8, 9
anthropomorphism, 57n, 168n, 225, 226, 227, 228, 229, 231, 232
Antichrist, 39
Antinoë, 1, 7, 15
ᵓapiḳoros, 122, 123, 124, 125, 128. See also *Epiḳoros*
Apocalypse of John, 23
apocalyptic. *See* prophecy
apocrypha, 44
Apollinopolis Magna, 1, 7
apologetics, 28, 29, 35, 38, 39
apostasy, 31
Aramaic, 12, 26
archeology, 1–3
dall' Arpa, Abramino, 332
dall' Arpa, Abramo, 332
Arsinoë, 1, 7
ars nova, 323
asceticism, 150, 151, 153, 164
al-Ashᶜarī, 69n
Ashᶜariyya, 173n
Ashkenazim, 157, 339
Ashmaᶜath, 229
assimilation, 3
associations, musical. *See* musical associations
astrology, 103, 167, 241, 243, 245
astronomy, 243, 291, 292, 299, 313
Aswān, 7, 9
Asyūt, 8, 9
atheism, 94n, 167
Athribis, 1, 7
atoms, 86, 88, 193
Ayyalon, 177
aẓilut, 238

Babli. *See* Talmud
Babylon, 7, 23, 24, 29, 36
Babylonians, 2, 10, 11, 17, 229
Balaam, 285n
ban, 165, 166, 170, 172n, 174, 180, 181, 291, 357. See also *ḥerem*
Baraita, 107
Barcelona, 165, 177
"Barekû," 344
Bar Koseba, Simeon, 22, 33
Batiniyya, 171
Ben Koseba. *See* Bar Koseba
Ben Sira, 195n
Bethar, 24n
Bethel, 42
Bilbeis, 7, 8, 9, 158
Binā, 236, 244
binyan, 238

Cain, 33, 38
Cairo, 158, 163
calendar, 112, 169n

cantatas, 324, 328n
Canticles, 25, 103, 170, 201n, 226, 236, 276n, 285
cantors, 323, 328, 330, 339
Casseres, A., 324
catechism, 107, 136
chance, 125
chant, 342; choral chant, 325, 331, 336, 337, 338, 341, 343, 352–355, 358; monodic chant, 339
Chariot of Ezekiel, 217, 218n
Chariot of Isaiah, 217
cherubim, 233, 268, 272n, 282
Chieppio, Annibale, 341
choirs, 325, 344, 351, 355, 356, 358; double choirs, 324, 346
choruses, antiphonal, 323
Christ, 32, 33, 34, 35, 36. *See also* Christianity, Jesus
Christianity, 3, 6, 12, 23, 26, 27, 28, 29, 30–39, 43–48, 50, 56, 57n, 61–63, 66–68, 70, 85n, 114, 136, 171, 180, 181, 182, 229, 310, 332. *See also* Manicheanism, trinitarianism
city of refuge, 101
Civita, David, 331
codices, of Torah, 5, 8
Coïmbran, Moses, 338
Constantine, 35, 36, 46
Constantinople, 29n
contracts, engagement, 11
conversion, 3, 100, 345
Coptic Church, 5, 15; Coptic language, 16
cosmogony, 49–58, 69, 78n, 79, 85n, 125, 135n, 188, 189, 191, 194, 201–203, 207, 212, 213, 216, 218, 222, 274, 277, 288
cosmology, 61, 183, 192, 193, 214, 244, 245, 267n, 274, 275
Counter Reformation, 324, 332, 362
covenant, 25, 32, 34
Crusades, 2, 9
Cynopolis, 1, 8

Dalās, 7, 8
Damascus, 162
Dammūh, 4–8
Dan, 42
dance, 327–329, 331, 334
Daniel, 27, 46, 48
David, House of, 29, 30, 37n, 153, 162
David, King, 34, 41–43
dayyānīm, 150, 154, 159, 162
demiurge, 188
demonology, 220. *See also* jinn
derāsh, 148, 219
determination, 194
Diaspora, 2, 3, 10
Dido, 41n
Diena, Joseph Zalman, 336
diwan, 115
Djālūtiyya, 229
doxographies, 75–76, 86
drama, 327, 333–334, 341, 344–345
dualism, 50–54, 57, 58, 62n

Ebreo, Giuseppo, 331
Ebreo, Leone, 332
Ecclesiastes, 186n, 201n, 206n, 212n
Eden, 242
Edfu, 7, 9
Edom, 20–31, 36, 38, 39n, 40, 42–48
Egypt, 1–18, 31, 35n, 157–159, 162–163
eïdos, 67–68
election, doctrine of, 20, 25–26, 31
"Eleh moᶜadê hᵓ," 355–356
elements, four, 60, 61, 78, 79, 89, 165, 167, 209; three, 215
Elephantine-Syne, 1–2
Eli, 34
Elijah, 161
Elohim, 215
emanation, 129, 189, 202, 203, 208, 209, 213–215, 217, 235, 238
"En keᵓlohenû," 337, 344
En-Sof, 215, 251
entelechy, 77–79, 87n, 89
Ephraim, 33, 34
Epicureanism, 123, 124n, 125
Epiḳoros, 167, 170. See also ᵓ*apiḳoros*
epithets, 35
ᶜ*Erūv*, 160
Esau, 19–48
eschatology, 19–21, 24, 25, 27, 30, 39, 47, 48
essence, 52–55, 61, 70, 72, 203, 274, 275, 278, 281, 282, 284, 286; Divine, 222, 243, 246, 250, 253, 265, 279, 280; of soul, 84n, 85–87
Este, House of, 332
Europa, Madama, 332
exhalation, 80, 89, 90
Exilarch, 93, 94n, 153
existence, 271, 272, 274–276, 278, 280, 283, 286
existents, 265, 271, 273, 274, 276–279, 281n, 282, 283, 285
experience, 221
extreme points, 228
Ezekiel, 29, 226, 283

Fāᶜil, 53
al-Faramā, 7, 9
Farissol, Abraham, 328

Ferrara, 329, 334, 335–340, 343, 360, 362, 363
Finzi, David, 332
First Cause, 238, 244–247, 269, 275, 276, 278, 279, 283n
First Mover, 208, 244, 275, 279n
Flood, 34n
Florence, 329, 348
form, 228, 249, 253, 278, 280n, 282, 284, 286
free will, 168, 194
fumigations, 14, 16
Fusṭāṭ, 11, 15, 158, 159, 163
Fusṭāṭ-Miṣr, 5–7, 9, 10

Gabriel, Archangel, 42, 60
Gabrieli, Andrea, 346
Gabrieli, Giovanni, 346
gaonate, 10, 93
Gaza, 1, 2, 9
Gemara, 107, 108, 111, 112, 124
gemara, 110, 115–117, 124
gematriot, 112
Genesis, 40
Genizah, 2, 4, 6, 8, 10–17, 146, 149, 151–155, 157–159, 161, 164
Gentiles, 20, 31, 32, 136n, 180n, 319n, 326, 327, 331, 362. *See also* Christianity
Germany, 183, 233, 323
Gerona, 209, 211, 212, 213, 218, 219, 221
Ghaifah, 1, 7–9
Gibeon, 177
gilgul, 220n
Gizeh, 5–7
Gnosticism, 214, 220, 221, 270n
goba ha-qomā, 250, 267n
Gonzaga family, 331, 340, 343

hafṭarot, 217
Hagar, 34
ḥākhamīn, 155, 231n
halakah, 44, 96, 99, 101, 107, 108, 112, 114–118, 131, 132, 145, 163, 179, 180, 266n, 289, 303, 326, 337
harmony, 322, 339
ḥasīdīm, 149, 150, 152, 155, 185, 233
ḥasīdūt. *See* pietism
haskamôt, 337
"Haškivenû," 344
Hasmoneans, 29, 30
hāvēr, 160
ḥazzan. *See* cantor
heaven, 271, 275n, 286
hegemony, 1–3, 9, 10
Hekalot, 225, 253
Hellenism, 35, 151, 166, 168, 170, 173n, 175, 188–200, 289–320 *passim*
heqdesh, 5
Heracleopolis Magna, 1, 7, 8
heresy, 35, 36n, 124, 150, 167, 171, 173, 174, 178, 182, 227n, 250; Albigensian, 289
ḥerem, 165n
Hermopolis Magna, 1, 8
Herod, 21n
Ḥesed, 244
ḥibbur, 109
Hod, 244
ḥokmah, 95, 99, 100, 102, 103, 113, 114, 115, 117, 215, 217, 244
homophony, 356
ḥudūth, 50
humanism, 151, 332
humours, four, 89

ᶜibbur, 220n
idolatry, 20, 28, 46, 128, 129, 131, 132
Ikhmīm, 17
ᶜilm, 206
imagination, 197, 198, 209, 271n, 272, 274, 280n, 285n. *See also* irrational faculty
imago Dei, 270, 279, 285
imitatio Dei, 191
immortality of the soul, 197, 200, 210, 295n
incantation, 12–15
incomparability, Divine, 57n, 61, 62, 68, 71, 72, 205, 228, 267, 279
incorporeality, Divine, 50–51, 54, 60, 64n, 128, 129, 132, 134, 135, 137, 139n, 141, 168, 228; of the soul, 79
India, 157
infinity, Divine, 50–51, 56, 64n, 69n, 73, 102, 128, 130n, 132, 134, 135, 139n, 194, 202n, 205, 234
innate qualities, 198
instrumental music, 323, 329, 330, 331, 345, 346, 357
insubstantiality, Divine, 50, 51, 54, 55, 64
intellect, 60n, 78, 82, 85n, 98, 119, 126, 127, 129, 134, 170, 188, 192, 197, 199, 204, 214, 220, 221, 242, 244–246, 249, 250–253, 267, 271–277, 279n, 280, 281, 283–286, 299; *See also* Agent Intellect, rational faculty
intellectualism, 105
intelligence, 271, 276, 277
intuition, 199
ᶜIr, 22
irrational faculty, 80, 82, 88, 198
Isaac, 30, 31, 32, 34, 39
Isaiah, 29
Ishmael, 32, 34, 35, 41, 46, 47, 48
Islam, 3, 12, 15, 45, 46, 47, 57n, 68, 69, 93, 94n, 114, 136, 146, 148, 151, 157,

159, 163, 164, 171, 178, 180n, 182, 184, 190, 206, 225, 228, 229, 265n
Isma^cilians, 69
Israelite, defined, 123
Israelites, 127, 138n, 141, 142n, 252, 268, 288. See also *Kol Yisra[>]el*
Italy, 40, 41, 43, 45, 184, 321–364

Jacob, 20–22, 26, 31, 33–35, 37, 38, 43, 44, 167, 169, 170, 249, 254, 286
Jacobites, 62, 67
Janus-Saturnus, 41
Japheth, 23, 39
Jeremiah, 1
Jeroboam, 42
Jesus, 46
jinn, 13–15
Job, 186n
Joḥanan b. Kareaḥ, 6
Joseph, 35, 41
Joshua, 178
Jove. *See* Jupiter
Jubilee, 218
Jupiter, 25, 244

Kabbala, 173, 183, 185–187, 189n, 204n, 207, 209–223, 226, 234–238, 240–243, 245, 249, 254, 270, 274n, 277n, 279n, 282n, 286, 290, 293, 355
kabod, 227, 233, 265
Kaddish. See *Qaddîš*
Kalam theory, 86, 173n, 181n, 194
Ḳaraites, 6, 11, 12, 17, 71, 73n, 78, 84, 85, 95n, 156, 178, 227–229
kashrūt, 157, 171
Keneset Yisra>el, 244, 270n, 274. *See also* Agent Intellect
Ḳesamim, 169n
Keter, 244, 245n, 251, 279, 352, 355–357 *passim*
ketubba, 158, 159
khilāf, 54, 57n
Kittim, 23, 39, 41, 42, 45, 47, 48
Kol Yisra>el, 123. *See also* Israelites
Kurds, 163

Laban, 35, 44
Lamentations, 239
Languedoc, 289n
Lateran Council, fourth, 182
Latinus, 42
law, 95, 97, 98, 100, 104, 109, 110n, 115, 121, 122, 124n, 147, 150, 156, 157, 158, 200, 291; canon law, 98. *See also* legislation
Leah, 33, 34
legislation, 36, 37, 45
Lerma, Yom Tov b. Menaḥem, 301
Levi b. Abraham b. Ḥayyim of Villefranche, 174–176
libraries, public, 93
Lidarti, C. G., 324–325
limits, 228
literalism, 95
litigation, 155. *See also* law
liturgy, 324, 326, 331, 333, 334, 341, 344, 355, 356. *See also* Rosh ha-Shanah
Logos, 202
Lombardy, 359
Lot, 34n
Lot's wife, 34n
lulab, 287
Luxor, 8
Luzzatto, Ephraim, 328n

ma>amarot, 214, 215
ma^caseh, 112; *ma^casē merkabā*, 232, 294n
macrocosm, 230, 240, 249, 285n, 286
magical practices, 12–16, 17n, 103–104, 106
magnetic attraction, 193
malkut, 237, 244, 245n
Manasseh, 33, 34
Manicheanism, 52
Mantua, 321, 324, 328, 330, 339, 340, 346, 359, 360, 362, 364
maqālāt, 49
Maria, Giovanni, 331
Mars, 21n, 244
Masoretes, 2
Massarano, Jacchino, 332
matter, 189, 203, 204, 222
Memphis, 1, 2, 5–8
menaggen, 329
Menorah of Zekhariah, 217
Me^con Ẓedeq, 244
Mercury, 244
Merkabah, 112, 187, 225, 230, 243, 268n
mēsīt umaddīaḥ, 150
mešorerîm, 323, 339, 340
Messiah, 20, 25, 56, 128, 129, 133, 135, 136, 144, 218
Messianic age, 20, 25, 29, 30, 46, 98, 129, 169n, 194, 218. *See also* World-to-Come
Meṭaṭron, 225, 230, 249, 267n, 281
Micah, 29
Michael, Archangel, 42, 60
microcosm, 56, 230, 240, 242, 268n, 285n, 286
midrash, 1, 2, 20, 21–22, 23, 25, 26, 32, 34, 35, 37, 43, 95, 99n, 171n, 189n, 216, 226, 232
miracles, 168, 169n, 177, 220n
mishkan, 254, 281n
Mishnah, 31, 107–112, 173n, 226, 227

mishnah, 116, 117, 121–124, 127, 128, 131, 138, 139
mizvah, mizvot, 105, 108, 109, 117, 148, 172, 232
Moabites, 169n
Modena, 331n, 332, 350, 352, 353, 358
Monad, 246
Monophysites. *See* Jacobites
monotheism, 49–73; universal monotheism, 19–20
Moses, 5, 35, 46n, 60, 108, 124n, 128, 129, 133, 134, 135, 136, 142, 143, 168, 178, 231, 266, 267, 268, 269n, 285, 286
al-Muhadhdhab, Sheikh, 160
Muhammad, 46n
muqaddam, 160
musāwāt, 66
music, 321–364
musical associations, 338, 339, 341, 347, 348, 350n, 358, 359
Mutakallimūn, 51, 56n. *See also* Kalam theory
Muᶜtazilites, 57n, 173n
mythology, Jewish, 41, 42, 112, 187, 212, 220; Roman mythology, 40, 42

Nadiv, title, 290
Nagid, title, 151n
Nasi, 153, 162
Nathaniel ha-Levi ha-Shishshi, 162
Nebat, 42
Nebuchadnezzar, 26
Neoplatonism, 190, 191, 201, 205, 207, 208, 210, 214, 221, 241, 252, 253, 267
Nero, 31n
Nezaḥ, 244
ha-nibrāʾ ha-rishon, 219
Nicomachus, 318
Nissim, Yeḥiʾel (da Pisa), 329
Noah, 34n, 40
nomina barbara, 225, 232, 270n
nomoi, 294n
nonexistence, 191
notation, musical, 333
Nous, 267

Obadiah, 24
Old Cairo. *See* Fusṭaṭ
orthodoxy, 57n, 69n, 151, 168n, 176, 181, 182, 184, 239, 323
orthography, 23, 290n
Oxyrhynchus, 1, 4, 8

Padua, 334–335, 360, 363
Palestinians, 2, 3, 4, 10, 11, 14, 17, 162
Pamalya, 189
pantheism, 203
papacy, 36n, 38n, 39, 332, 340, 351, 358, 364
papyri, 1–4, 8, 10, 13–17
paradise, 242. *See also* heaven
parasangs, 234, 236, 272
pardes, 106, 111, 113, 116–118
parnāsīm, 159
Passover, 326, 328n
Paul of Tarsus, 21, 32, 33
Paumann, Konrad, 328
penē ᶜelyon, 253
Pentecost, 326
perfection, 200; intellectual, 196–198; moral, 191
peri nou, 299n
Peripatetics, 66, 253, 300
perush, 109
Pesaro, 331, 354
peshāṭ, 148, 219
Pharaoh, 5, 35, 42
philosopher-kings, 197
pietism, 6, 145–164
pilgrimages, 4–6, 10
Pinon, 28
Pisa, 329
piyyūtīm, 4, 337, 338
pleroma, 270n
pluralism, 49–73 *passim*
pneuma, 79, 81, 82, 88, 90
poetry, 2, 4, 27, 28, 45, 96n, 102, 121n, 326, 328n, 341n
polyphony, 322, 323, 324, 356
point, primordial, 188
Porto, Allegro, 331
Potiphar's wife, 35
Prague, 323
prayer, 147, 220, 221. *See also* names of individual prayers
prime matter, 209
Prime Mover. *See* First Mover
Prince of the Presence. *See* Meṭaṭron
prophecy, 19–23, 29, 30, 35, 114, 115, 124n, 125, 128, 129, 131, 133–136, 142, 143, 168, 195–200, 201n, 271n, 285n
Provence, 45, 165, 166, 168n, 169, 170, 171, 173, 181, 183, 239, 289, 291, 296, 298, 302, 307
Proverbs, 164
Providence, 125, 136, 201n, 220, 221
Psalms, as sung, 342, 357, 359
Ptolemy, 296, 299
punishment, 127, 128, 132, 133, 134, 139n, 143, 144; capital punishment, 122
punning, 22, 27, 314n
Purim, 326, 334, 345

Qaddiš, 335, 344
Qaṣr al-Muqawqaz, 15–16
qeduššah, 334, 335, 355, 356, 357
Qetura, 41
qomā, 226, 232, 237, 247–251, 253, 254, 281n
Quran, 46n, 57n, 171n, 173n, 280n

Rabbanites, 11, 17, 228, 229
Rabbinic literature, 19, 20, 21n, 22, 23, 24, 26, 27, 28n, 31, 43, 45, 47, 105n, 107, 112, 121n, 123, 124n, 171, 178n, 189, 325, 355
Rachel, 33, 34
rational faculty, 80, 82, 88, 91, 126n, 198, 209
rationalism, 95–98, 104, 179, 181, 182n, 183, 187
Rayyis al-Yahūd, 151, 155, 162
Reading of the Law, cycles, 11
reality, 203
Reconquista, 48
Remus, 42
Renovatio, 40
resh galuta, 229n
resurrection of the dead, 122, 128, 129, 133, 135, 136, 144
reward, 127, 128, 132, 133, 134, 139n, 143, 144
ritual, 100, 104, 147, 148, 150, 153, 156, 356
della Rocca, Mordekay b. Moses, 351, 354, 355
Rome, 20–23, 26, 28, 29, 34, 36, 39, 40, 42–48
Romulus, 20, 41, 42, 43
Rosh ha-Shanah, 19, 276n
Rossi, Angelo de, 332
Rossi, Anselmo, 331, 332
Rossi, Bonaiuto, 332
Rossi, Giuseppe, 332
ruaḥ ha-qodesh, 227

Saᶜadya Gaon, 8, 10
Sabaeans, 62
Sabbath, 6
Sacerdote, David, 331, 332n
sacrifice, 14, 211
Saladin, 162
Samaᵓel, 244n
Samuel, 34, 177
Sansecondo, Giacomo di, 331n
Saracens, 35
Sarah, 34, 165–167 *passim*
Sar Shalom, 162
Sassanids, 48
Satan, 14, 172n
Saturn, 244, 275
Saul, 34, 177
Savoy, House of, 332
scapegoat, 244n
Sefer Bahir, 253
Sefer Yeẓirah, 210, 214, 215, 270, 283
sefirot, 211–215, 217, 218, 234, 237, 238, 242–245, 249, 251, 270n, 279n, 282, 355
segregation, 321–364 *passim*
Seᶜir, 22, 27
Senigallia, 335, 349–360, 364
Sennacherib, 45
senses, 79–81, 89, 90, 165, 167, 269n, 285n
Sephardim, 355, 356
Sessigli, Benedetto, 332
shape. *See* form
shekinah, 126, 164, 227, 233, 238, 243
"Shemaᶜ," 72, 130–131
shemiṭṭot, 218
shibh, shabah, 57n
shiᶜur, 242, 247, 253, 254
Shiᶜur Qomā, 225–288
shoresh yesh, 204
Sifra, 107
Sifre, 107
siḳlut, 95
Simḥat Torah, 326, 345, 346
simplicity, Divine, 59–61, 68, 71, 72
Sinai, 25, 32n, 33, 108, 140, 165, 269n, 286
slavery, 35, 36, 37, 156, 157
Solomon, King, 42, 283, 285
Sommi, Leone de, 341
Song of Songs. *See* Canticles
Spain, 27, 40, 45, 46, 47, 157, 161, 165, 179, 183–188, 190, 211, 219, 221, 222, 239, 296
spirit, 85n, 112
Stoics, 79, 80, 81, 92
sublunar world, 61, 204–205, 209, 215, 242, 249, 250, 265n, 269n, 271–272, 280n, 281n, 283–284
substance, 51, 55n, 56, 57, 61, 62, 64, 67, 68n, 70, 77, 79, 83n, 84–87, 92, 205, 206
Sufism, 146, 148, 149, 164
sukkā, 287, 288
Sulami, Samuel, 174, 175
Sullam, Moses, 342
Sumatra, 157
superstition, 103, 104, 106
syllogisms, 96
Syriac, 38n–39n, 63n, 67, 68, 289, 302

Tabernacles, 10
Talmud, 31, 42, 45, 46, 99, 100, 101, 102, 105, 107, 108, 110, 112, 114, 115, 116, 121, 122n, 129n, 145, 148, 156, 163, 164n, 189n, 197n, 218, 227, 228, 235, 247, 266n, 290, 325, 339, 355

Talmudists, 229
Ṭammūḥ, 5, 6. *See also* Dammūḥ
Tannaim. *See* Rabbinic literature
taqqāna, 162
tashbih. *See* anthropomorphism
teaching, 96, 100–102
tefillin, 266, 268, 269, 282
Tell el-Yahūd, 1, 7, 9
Tell el-Yahūdiyeh, 1, 9
Temple, Second, 29, 30, 40; Destruction, 5, 20, 21, 24n, 25, 47, 326, 337
temunā, 254
Tetragrammaton, 283n
theater. *See* drama
theophany, 226
theosophy, 214, 293, 303
Tiber, 26, 41
Tifʾeret, 244
tikkun, 105
Tiqqunē Zohar, 236, 248
Toledo, 183, 211, 242
Tosefta, 108
Tower of Babel, 171, 236
trance, 15
translation, 289–320
translunar world, 194, 280n
transmigration of the soul, 220
treasure, hidden, 15, 16
trinitarianism, 50, 52, 58, 61–64, 66n, 67n, 68, 70, 73
Tubal, 39
tummin, 165, 167, 169
Turin, 332
Turnus, 44
typology, 19–48 *passim*

unity, Divine, 128–131, 132, 133, 135, 139n, 168, 203, 205, 207, 276, 284n
Urbino, Duchy of, 351, 364
urim, 165, 167, 169
Uz, 24

Vannes, Council of, 36
Venice, 328, 335, 338n, 339, 344, 360, 362
Venus, 244
Vidal, Bonafus, 174n
"Virtuous City," 195, 196

wāḥid, 62, 67, 69, 71, 72, 73n
waqf, 5
will, Divine, 200–205, 212, 213, 215, 218
wisdom, 34n, 95, 99, 100, 102, 103, 114, 115, 127n, 195, 197, 221, 287. See also *ḥokmah*
Wisdom of Solomon, 34n, 35n
Witch of Endor, 177
World-to-Come, 101, 121, 123, 125–127, 131, 133, 138n, 139, 141, 142, 143, 144, 226, 230, 234, 268, 286. *See also* Messianic age
wuṣūl, 149

Yerushalmi, 2, 108. *See also* Talmud
Yesod, 244
"Yigdal," 121, 337, 338, 344
Yom Kippur, 111n
Yozer Bereshit, 268

zaddiq, 236
Zealots, 21n
Zechariah, 29
Zepho, 41–44
Zerubbabel, 29, 30
Zion, 33
zodiac, 50, 165, 167, 169
Zohar, 179, 188, 207, 215, 219, 222